Professional Review Guide for the CCS Examination
2015 Edition

Patricia J. Schnering, RHIA, CCS
Crystal A. Clack, MS, RHIA, CCS
Lisa M. Delhomme, MHA, RHIA
Lauralyn Kavanaugh-Burke, DrPH, RHIA, CHES, CHTS-IM
Leslie Moore, RHIT, CCS

CENGAGE
Learning

Australia • Brazil • Japan • Korea • Mexico • Singapore • Spain • United Kingdom • United States

Professional Review Guide for the CCS Examination, 2015 Edition
Patricia J. Schnering, RHIA, CCS

SVP, GM Skills & Global Product Management: Dawn Gerrain

Senior Production Director: Wendy Troeger

Production Director: Andrew Crouth

Product Manager: Jadin B. Kavanaugh

Senior Director, Development: Marah Bellegarde

Senior Product Development Manager: Juliet Steiner

Content Developer: Amy Wetsel

Product Assistant: Mark Turner

Vice President, Marketing Services: Jennifer Ann Baker

Marketing Manager: Erica Glisson

CL Mfg Planner: Beverly Breslin

Art and Cover Direction, Production Management, and Composition: S4Carlisle Publishing Services

Cover image: Frank Krahmer/Getty Images

For product information and technology assistance, contact us at
Cengage Learning Customer & Sales Support,

1-800-354-9706

For permission to use material from this text or product, submit all requests online at **www.cengage.com/permissions**

Further permissions questions can be emailed to
permissionrequest@cengage.com

Library of Congress Control Number: 2014954388

Book Only ISBN: 9781285863405
Package ISBN: 9781285863368

Cengage Learning
20 Channel Center Street
Boston, MA 02210
USA

Cengage Learning is a leading provider of customized learning solutions with office locations around the globe, including Singapore, the United Kingdom, Australia, Mexico, Brazil, and Japan. Locate your local office at: **www.cengage.com/global**

Cengage Learning products are represented in Canada by Nelson Education, Ltd.

To learn more about Cengage Learning, visit **www.cengage.com**
Purchase any of our products at your local college store or at our preferred online store **www.cengagebrain.com**

Notice to the Reader

Printed in United States of America
Print Number: 01   Print Year: 2015

ABOUT THE AUTHORS

Patricia J. Schnering, RHIA, CCS

Patricia J. Schnering was the founder of PRG Publishing, Inc. and Professional Review Guides, Inc. Mrs. Schnering is a 1995 graduate of the Health Information Management program at St. Petersburg College in St. Petersburg, Florida. In 1998, she was certified as a CCS and, in 1999, she received her RHIA certification. She also has a Bachelor degree from the University of South Florida in Tampa, Florida, with a major in Business Administration. Her HIM experiences include working in Health Information Services supervisory positions, as an HIM consultant, and as an adjunct HIM instructor at St. Petersburg College. She has been active in her local and state HIM associations. Mrs. Schnering was awarded the Florida Health Information Management Association (FHIMA) Literary Award in 2000 and 2005.

Lisa M. Delhomme, MHA, RHIA

Lisa M. Delhomme is an Instructor in the Health Information Management Department at the University of Louisiana at Lafayette, located in Lafayette, Louisiana. She has a Bachelor's degree in Health Information Management and a Master's degree in Health Services Administration. She teaches several courses, including CPT coding, legal aspects for health care, and computers in health care organizations. Prior to teaching, she held a management position at a physician practice and ambulatory surgery center. Mrs. Delhomme has been an active member of the American Health Information Management Association for 11 years. In addition, she has been involved with committees and projects for the Louisiana Health Information Management Association and the Louisiana Medical Group Management Association.

Lauralyn Kavanaugh-Burke, DrPH, RHIA, CHES, CHTS, IM

After receiving a BS degree in Medical Record Administration with a minor in biology from York College of Pennsylvania, Dr. Burke worked in several hospitals in Virginia and Maryland in various management positions, including DRG Analyst, Assistant Director, and Director of Medical Record/Health Information departments. During this time, her interest in pathophysiology intensified after working with several physicians in their research endeavors. She started teaching at an associate's degree Health Information Technology (HIT) program at Fairmont State College in West Virginia where she was able to strengthen her anatomy and pathophysiology skills, not only instructing HIT students, but also working with the medical laboratory and veterinary technology programs there. This position gave her the chance to complete her MS degree in Community Health Education from West Virginia University, which perfectly blended health information management and education. She achieved her Certified Health Education Specialist (CHES) credential shortly afterward. She then moved back to Pennsylvania and returned to the hospital arena as a DRG and coding consultant. Dr. Burke had the opportunity to teach at her alma mater and lay the foundation for an associate's degree program in HIT at a local community college.

Subsequent to relocating to Florida, she became a faculty member at Florida A&M University's BS degree program in Health Informatics & Information Management Division. She continued her pursuit of more training in pathophysiology, and soon after received her Doctor of Public Health (DrPH) with a concentration in epidemiology from Florida A&M University. Dr. Burke's main areas of interest are in disaster preparedness for hospitals, and bioterrorism and infectious diseases. She recently achieved certification as a Health Information Technology Implementation Manager (HITPRO-IM) after completing her HITECH training through Santa Fe College.

Crystal Clack, MS, RHIA, CCS

Crystal A. Clack is a dual-master's of science degree graduate of the College of St. Scholastica, Duluth, Minnesota, where she earned her degrees in Health Information Informatics Management and I.T. Leadership. Clack has worked in a variety of jobs and settings including HIM department management, Coding and Charge Capture department management, privacy officer, and release of information and coding. Clack's real passion, however, resides in education and she is currently an adjunct professor at Lane Community College, Eugene, Oregon. Recently, Clack was elected Director of Education for the Oregon Health Information Management Association and is heavily involved with planning relevant HIM events for Oregon members, as well as advocating for the profession.

Leslie A. Moore, RHIT, CCS

Leslie A. Moore has been Director of Operations for Charts In Time, Inc. since 2007. Ms. Moore oversees and manages the performance, productivity, and quality of the coding staff at Charts In Time. She is an AHIMA-certified ICD-10 trainer and has developed all the education service lines for CIT. Leslie's experience spans 25+ years as Corporate Coding Director, adjunct coding faculty, and as Independent Coding Consultant in both inpatient and outpatient settings, with extensive experience in physician coding and documentation.

ACKNOWLEDGMENTS

First and foremost, I wish to express my gratitude to the authors who collaborated on the book. They are educators and clinical coding experts who worked diligently to provide comprehensive coverage of coding procedures. I am very grateful to have such seasoned professionals working with me on the book.

I would like to express my gratitude to all of the authors who have worked on the educational materials PRG Publishing has produced. They are seasoned professionals and excellent educators. They inspire me to work harder to produce better products. Each one of these educators presents a facet of HIM practice necessary to view the HIM arena as a whole. It is a pleasure to be able to call them friends and professional peers.

There are very special people in my family who always knew I could do it when I was not sure I could. My late husband, Bob, always kept me grounded when I tended to spin off in space as I became engrossed in working on the books. He graciously listened to me go on and on about the work's progress throughout the process. And, I could never forget the encouragement my mother provided. Mom, you were always there for me! Throughout the years, my mother has been my role model for perseverance leading to success. She embodied grace, courage, strength, and endurance. I have been blessed to have had both of them in my life.

I appreciate all the help from my Cengage Learning family. They have all the answers and have been extremely patient and helpful in guiding me through the publishing system. Thank you all very much!

My thanks would not be complete without acknowledging all the HIM/HIT educators and students who support our efforts by purchasing PRG Publishing products.

My special reward is knowing that the materials you study here may assist you in preparing for the challenge of the CCS Examination. Thank you for the letters and words of encouragement.

I wish you the very best now and throughout your career.

Until we meet....

Patricia J. Schnering, RHIA, CCS

PJSPRG@AOL.COM

TABLE OF CONTENTS

Introduction

Patricia J. Schnering, RHIA, CCS

INTRODUCTION TO THE PROFESSIONAL REVIEW GUIDE FOR THE CCS EXAMINATION

This examination review guide represents a renewed effort to provide materials for HIM students and professionals. In reviewing the results of past examinations, we found that it would be beneficial for examination candidates to have additional practice in answering multiple-choice questions. We have selected questions and cases to cover the broad topic categories necessary in sitting for the CCS Certification Examination. Researching the questions and cases as you study should increase your knowledge such that, when you encounter similar questions and cases, you can arrive at the correct answer. We believe that this review material will jog your memory and build on information you have already gained through your education and professional experiences. This book provides you with a mix of coding questions and case exercises to both increase your coding skills and provide you with testing that mimics the exam format.

The beginning of this book offers suggestions for studying and test-taking strategies. The book is then divided into two additional parts. The first part is a coding review section containing multiple-choice questions and coding case studies. The second part of the book is a mock examination that contains three sections.

You will have two different sets of exam questions for practice for Section 1 and Section 2. Each Mock Exam for Section 1 and Section 2 has one set of eighty-one (81) multiple-choice questions and one set of eight multiple-selection questions. Section 3 has mock medical record cases to code in which you will fill in the number of blank boxes provided.

The back matter of the book contains appendices with information on pharmacology, laboratory testing, and the ICD-9-CM Coding Guidelines.

The questions and cases in this examination review guide are based on the broad competencies listed in the AHIMA Candidate Handbook for the CCS Examination. Review the latest Candidate Handbook when preparing for the exam.

Table I-1 displays the major content areas of this book by sections.

Table I-1 Chapter Contents for the Professional Review Guide for the CCS Examination

Professional Review Guide for the CCS Examination Chapters	Questions /Cases
Introduction	
Examination Study Strategies and Resources	
Coding Review	
Part 1 of the book includes the following chapters:	Questions /Cases
Health Data Content and Standards	75
Medical Sciences	146
Classification Systems and Secondary Data Sources	110
Medical Billing and Reimbursement Systems	114
ICD-9-CM Coding	2010
CPT Coding	217
CCS Case Study Coding Review	32 Cases
Part 2 of the book includes the following mock exams	
Mock Examination Multiple-Choice Questions Test 1	81
Mock Examination Multiple-Select Questions Test 1	8
Mock Examination Multiple-Choice Questions Test 2	81
Mock Examination Multiple-Select Questions Test 2	8
Mock Examination Cases	12 Cases
Appendices	
Appendix A Pharmacology	
Appendix B Laboratory Testing	
Appendix C ICD-9-CM Coding Guidelines Effective October 1, 2012	

ABOUT THE COMPETENCIES FOR THE CCS EXAMINATION

We suggest that you start by examining the competencies for the Certified Coding Specialist. They are listed as domains and task statement. The competencies were created to reflect the necessary skill level for professional practice. A detailed list of the competencies will be provided in the AHIMA Candidate Handbook for the CCS Examination.

It is the responsibility of American Health Information Management Association's (AHIMA) Commission on Certification for Health Informatics and Information Management (CCHIIM) to assess what job tasks are frequently executed by newly certified practitioners. Additionally, the CCHIIM determines the job tasks that are critical to the practice—in other words, the job tasks that, if done incorrectly, could create a negative impact. The task statements are also referred to as the test specifications.

The process of identifying those critical job functions was accomplished by conducting a job analysis. The objective was to determine how the practice is evolving and to develop the test specifications and a certification examination to correspond with changes that are occurring in the field. The data that were collected as a result of this research provided the essential elements that were necessary to establish the test specifications for the certifying exam. The CCHIIM is responsible for developing and administering the certification examination and determining the eligibility of applicants to write the exam. The task statements for the Certified Coding Specialist are grouped into nine domains. Weights for each domain are assigned. Each weight correlates to the degree of emphasis, or importance, given to each domain as it relates to the health information practice. Table I-2 displays the domains you will be responsible for on the examination.

Crosswalks between the competencies for the CCS Certification Examination and the questions in the chapters are provided in Table I-3. In addition to the competencies, the questions are written in three cognitive levels of testing, which are explained after Table I-3.

Table I-2 CCS Section 1 and Section 2 Examination Content

CCS Section 1 and Section 2 Examination Content with Percentage Questions by Domain	
Domains	Percentage of Exam
Domain 1: Health Information Documentation	8–10%
Domain 2: Diagnosis and Procedure Coding	64–68%
Domain 3: Regulatory Guidelines and Reporting Requirements for Acute Care (Inpatient) Service	6–8%
Domain 4: Regulatory Guidelines and Reporting Requirements for Outpatient Services	6–8%
Domain 5: Data Quality and Management	6–8%
Domain 6: Information and Communication Technologies	1–3%
Domain 7: Privacy, Confidentiality, Legal, and Ethical Issues	2–4%
Domain 8: Compliance	2–4%
TOTAL	100 %

Resource: AHIMA Certified Coding Specialist (CCS) Examination Content Outline
http://www.ahima.org/~/media/AHIMA/Files/Certification/CCS_Content_Outline.ashx (retrieved 9/29/2014)
Reminder: Monitor AHIMA's Web site for updates on the testing information.

Table I-3 Crosswalk of the CCS Examination Competencies and the Questions in the Chapters

Crosswalk of the CCS Examination Competencies and the Questions in the Chapters									
	1	2	3	4	5	6	7	8	Total
Health Data Content and Standards	34	0	1	1	16	9	1	13	75
Medical Science	145	0	0	0	0	0	0	0	145
Classification Systems and Secondary Data Sources	50	22	0	0	3	10	0	2	87
Medical Billing and Reimbursement Systems	114	0	0	0	0	0	0	0	114
ICD-9-CM Coding	0	210	0	0	0	0	0	0	210
CPT Coding	0	203	0	0	0	0	0	0	203
CCS Mock Examination 1	0	0	0	0	0	0	0	0	0
Section 1	9	55	7	1	3	2	4	0	81
Section 2	0	8	0	0	0	0	0	0	8
CCS Mock Examination 2	0	0	0	0	0	0	0	0	0
Section 1	36	31	7	4	0	1	0	2	81
Section 2	0	8	0	0	0	0	0	0	8
Total Questions	388	537	15	6	22	22	5	17	1012

ABOUT THE COGNITIVE LEVELS OF TESTING FOR THE CCS EXAMINATION

The examination questions test your knowledge on three cognitive levels:

- Recall (RE)
- Application (AP)
- Analysis (AN)

The recall level tests your memory of basic facts such as being able to identify terms, methods, and procedures. The application level tests your ability to interpret data and information, to apply concepts and principles, to recognize relationships among data, and to calculate mathematical problems. The analysis level measures your ability to solve specific problems by evaluating, comparing, and selecting appropriate solutions for action; and to evaluate information and perform multiple calculations to assemble various elements into a total picture.

The general format of the exam is primarily designed to engage your problem-solving and critical thinking skills. These types of questions require you to translate what you have learned and apply it to a situation.

There are sample questions provided on the AHIMA Web site (http://www.AHIMA.org) so that you can experience the testing situation.

CCS EXAMINATION TESTING TIME, ITEM TYPES, AND CONTENT

The CCS examination is in a computer-based format. Carefully read the latest Candidate Handbook for the CCS Examination and continue to monitor AHIMA's Web site to look for updated information on the examination format. The handbook is available for downloading in PDF format on the AHIMA Web site (http://www.AHIMA.org).

Testing Time for the Examination

The total testing time for the examination is 4 hours.

The examination is one continuous exam without breaks.

The examination will be given in sections with instructions on how to answer the questions. (See Examination Contents information below and visit the AHIMA Web site for additional information.)

Each section must be completed before continuing on to the next section.

You will be in charge of monitoring your own time throughout the examination.

CCS Item Types

1. <u>Multiple-Choice Questions</u> — You must select the single best option from four possible choices.

2. Multiple-Select — You will be required to select more than one correct answer as prompted within the question (Example: select two correct answers out of four presented).

3. <u>Quantity Fill in the Blank</u> — More than one answer will be required. The appropriate number of blank boxes will be provided for you to enter diagnosis and procedure codes.

Examination Contents

Section 1: The test begins with 81 multiple-choice questions (63 of the questions are scored and 18 of the questions are not scored).

Section 2: This section consists of 8 multiple-select questions (6 of the questions are scored and 2 of the questions are not scored.)

Section 3: This section consists of medical record coding of 12 medical cases.
- For inpatient diagnoses and procedures, use your ICD-9-CM volumes 1–3.
- Outpatient care diagnoses are to be coded with ICD-9-CM volumes 1 and 2; and procedures are to be coded with CPT.
- You must fill in every code box required for a case before you will be allowed to move to the next medical record case.

Table I-4 provides a summary of the CCS exam content.

Table I-4 CCS Examination Content

Section 1: Multiple-Choice Questions	
Number of multiple-choice questions	81
Section 2: Multiple-Select Questions	
Number of multiple-select questions	8
Section 3: Fill in the Blank (Medical Record Cases)	
Number of fill in the blank medical record cases	12
Total time for examination	4 hours

Reminder: Monitor AHIMA's Web site for the latest updates on the testing information.

CCS EXAMINATION SCORING, PASSING SCORES, AND PASS RATES

Scoring for Examination Questions

Section 1: Multiple-Choice Questions

Correct answer = 1 point   Incorrect answer = 0 points

Section 2: Multiple-Select Questions

Correct answers = 1 point   Incorrect answer = 0 points

You must select all right answers to get the entire question correct.

Section 3: Fill in the Blank

Each code that is correctly assigned is worth 1 point.

Correct codes = 1 point   Incorrect code = 0 points

(Example: getting 6 of 8 required codes will give you a total of 6 points for that medical record case.)

Current Passing Scores and Pass Rates

Content experts estimate the passing probability of each item on the examination. The examination Construction Committee follows strict guidelines in selecting the questions for each of the examination forms to ensure that all versions of the exam are parallel in difficulty. Check for the current passing scores and pass rates that are published on the AHIMA Web site. Table I-5 shows the pass rates for 2011, 2012, and 2013. The passing scores may vary annually from one testing period to the next to adjust for fluctuations in examination difficulty over time.

Table I-5 CCS Examination Pass Rates for the CCS Exam for First-Time Test Takers

Year	Number of exam takers	Pass rate	Total credentials awarded
2013	3,411	68.4%	2,212
2012	2,592	47.9%	1,242
2011	2,675	47.8%	1,287

Examination pass rates are based on the calendar year (January 1 through December 31).

Source: http://www.ahima.org/downloads/pdfs/certification/

The key to success on the exam is a thorough knowledge of coding, which can be achieved only through extensive use of and familiarity with the code books. Having to use the code books to answer questions will help increase your speed in the use of both coding books.

This book is only one of many tools available to you to prepare. Use a variety of review methodologies (multiple-choice questions, case studies, review of theory, mock exams, etc.) as an effective means of reviewing. These tools can help prepare you for the challenge of the CCS coding exam. In the following chapters there are a myriad of suggested resources.

ADDITIONAL INSIGHTS ABOUT THE CCS EXAMINATION

1. **Computerized testing:** You will be able to review questions on the computer screen to check your answers before you close the exam file on the computer.

2. **On-Screen information:** Any additional information needed to complete the multiple-choice questions in Section 1 of the examination will be available on the screen in the testing software.

3. **Medical sciences:** These questions tend to be interspersed throughout other topic categories. Medical terminology, pathophysiology, and anatomy and physiology are a part of the general knowledge base for Health Information Management, coding, and reimbursement.

4. **National exam:** Keep in mind that this is a national examination. Concentrate on federal legislation, statutes, and legal issues that would be appropriate nationally in all 50 states.

5. **Be prepared to shift gears quickly throughout the exam.** Questions on the examination are scrambled and change topics from question to question. Therefore, you may have a CPT coding question, followed by a reimbursement question, followed by an ICD-9-CM question, etc.

6 **You will need to bring your ICD-9-CM and AMA CPT-4 coding books to the test.** In addition, you may bring a medical dictionary for reference. Practicing coding using your coding books will help increase your speed in finding the codes by the book. Remember, the test is timed. The faster you code, the more time you have to choose your answers. It may make the difference in being able to successfully complete the examination in the time allotted. You will be allowed to use the coding books throughout the examination.

7. **The focus is on critical concepts.** Our major focus is on covering the concepts and competencies in the body of knowledge for the Certified Coding Specialist (CCS). The questions and cases on the examination may combine several concepts into one question that may increase the level of difficulty in the question or case.

8. **Review the latest candidate handbook.** The AHIMA Candidate Handbook for the Certification Examinations contains information on the exam, how to apply for the examination, what to bring, and other pertinent information you need.

9. **Make sure that you have the necessary items for admission for testing.** Again, review your handbook for specific information on what you will need to bring with you to the examination center. You will need to bring your Authorization to Test (ATT) and two forms of identification (review the accept forms of identification listed in your handbook). You will need code books for the exam. Bring the following:
   - The ICD-9-CM code book volumes 1–3 (for inpatient diagnoses and procedures); ambulatory care diagnoses are to be coded with ICD-9-CM volumes 1 and 2.
   - AMA CPT (ambulatory procedures are to be coded with CPT).
   - You may also bring a medical dictionary.

AFTER THE EXAM

Our advice is to reclaim your life and focus on your career. One good way to start is to plan a special reward for yourself at some point immediately following or shortly after the exam. Schedule a family vacation or a relaxing weekend get-away. Just find some way of being good to yourself. You certainly deserve it! You have worked hard, so relish your success.

Fully Revised Professional Review Guide Series Online Quizzing Software

Follow the instructions on the Printed Access Card bound into this text to access the online quizzing software for this title.

Features include:
- All of the quizzes and mock exams available in the text, customizable by subject area
- Immediate feedback options by subject area and competency for better self-assessment
- New to this edition: Case studies found in the text are now also available as part of the interactive online quizzing experience

For Instructors:
- The ability to track student and class progress by domain or subject area in real-time for better classroom focus
- Excel™ exporting feature for gradebooks

Go to www.cengagebrain.com to create a unique instructor user login. Contact your sales representative for more information.

I. Examination Study Strategies and Resources

Patricia J. Schnering, RHIA, CCS

FORMAT OF THE EXAMINATION

The examination questions and cases developed for the examinations are based on specifications currently referred to as domains and task statements. A complete copy of these entry-level specifications is provided in the AHIMA Candidate Handbook. The handbook and additional information on the examination are available for downloading in PDF format on the AHIMA Web site (http://www.AHIMA.org).

The CCS examination consists of three sections. Although the exam is one continuous test with a time limit of 4 hours for completion, each section must be completed before moving to the next section.

Section 1 of the Examination consists of 81 multiple-choice coding questions. These require that only one answer per question is accepted. Of the 81 multiple-choice questions, 60 are scored and 21 are unscored.

Section 2 of the Examination consists of 8 multiple-response items (6 scored and 2 unscored). These multiple-response questions require more than one answer per question. There will be directions giving the number of answers needed for each question. (Example: Choose 3 of the 5 responses.)

Section 3 of the Examination consists of 12 coding cases covering inpatient and outpatient services. As explained in the introduction, the cases will contain the exact number of boxes needed to provide codes for entering on the computer screen.

The general format of the exam is primarily designed to engage your problem-solving and critical thinking skills. These types of questions require you to translate what you have learned and apply it to a situation. There are sample questions and cases provided on the AHIMA Web site (http://www.AHIMA.org), so that you can experience the testing situation.

How to Use This Book

We suggest you answer the multiple-choice questions and code the case studies in the review section of the book before taking the mock examination. It will give you a baseline to begin your CCS examination preparation. Your strengths and weaknesses will become more apparent, allowing you to plan your study time more effectively and focus on your problem areas.

After working through the review questions and case studies in the book, take the mock examination. It will provide you an opportunity to assess your speed in answering multiple-choice questions and in coding cases.

STUDY STRATEGIES

Theoretically, material learned thoroughly after one study session will fade predictably with time. After one day, the average person retains only 80% of what was learned. Ultimately, he or she will remember about 30% of the material originally learned. That is why you are relearning information that you acquired over a period of years. Your aim is to achieve maximum recall through effective review.

BEGIN BY BUILDING YOUR STUDY STRATEGIES

First, you must get organized

You must be deliberate about making sure that you develop and stick to a regular study routine. Find a place where you can study, either at home or at the library. How you schedule your study time during the week is an individual decision. However, we recommend that you avoid all-nighters and other unreasonably long study sessions. The last thing you want to do is burn yourself out by working too long and too hard at one time. Try to do a little bit at a time, and maintain a steady pace that is manageable for you.

Second, develop your individual study program

Write the exam topics and subjects in a list. Outline the chapters in your coding textbooks, and review the sections in your code books. Pinpoint your weakest subjects. Pause at each chapter outline and recall basic points. Do you draw a blank, recall them more or less, or do you feel comfortable with your recall? By using this approach, you can see where you stand.

Then, weigh the importance of each subject

How are the topics emphasized in the examination competencies, textbooks, professional journal articles, coding guidelines, and coding books? Take a look at the top MS-DRGs and APCs. Try to pick out concepts that would make good examination questions.

Personalize your list of the topics in the order that you plan to study them

Avoid trying to make a head-on attack by giving equal time and attention to all topics. Reorganize your list of the topics in the order that you plan to study them. Use the outline you have made to identify your weakest topics. Determine which topics you believe will require a significant amount of study time and which will only require a brief review. Your list will give you a clear mental picture of what you need to do and will keep you on track. Some experts suggest that you begin your plan with your strongest topics and concentrate on your weaknesses as you get closer to your exam date. That way they will be fresh in your mind.

Use your list: Your list will give you a clear mental picture of what you need to learn and will keep you on track. There are three additional advantages to a list.
1. It builds your morale as you steadily cross off items that you have completed as you monitor your progress.
2. Glancing back at the list from time to time serves to reassure you that you are on target.
3. You can readily see that you are applying your time and effort where they are most needed.

Keep the list conspicuously in view. Carefully plan your pre-exam study time and stick to your plan. Go to the exam like a trained and disciplined runner going to a marathon event!

Design a 10-week study program: Make your study process a systematic review of all topic categories, followed by achieving mastery of strategically selected subjects within the topic categories. To facilitate this effort, we recommend that you design a 10-week study program. You should plan on spending an average of 10 to 12 hours per week studying. The idea is to study smart, not to bulldoze through tons of material in a haphazard way.

Consider a study group: Everyone has his or her own particular study style. Some people prefer to study alone; others work best in a group. Regardless of your preference, we strongly recommend that you take advantage of group study at least some of the time. Studying with others can prove very helpful when working through your weakest areas. Each member of the study team will bring strengths and weaknesses to the table, and all can benefit from the collaboration. So, even if you are a solitary learner, you may occasionally want to work with a group for those topics you find more challenging. If you do not have easy access to a study group for the examination, you may want to study with other HIM professionals over the Internet. The AHIMA Communities of Practice (CoPs) on the Internet is an excellent avenue to find others who are in the same position.

Increase your endurance: Preparing for a major exam is similar to preparing for a marathon athletic event. Know the time allotted for your certification examination. Then, use your study process to slowly build up your concentration time until you can focus your energy for the appropriate period of time. This is like the runner who begins jogging for 30 minutes and builds up to 1 hour, then 1½ hours, and so on, and gradually increases the endurance time to meet the demands of the race. Try this strategy; it could work for you!

Go to the exam like a trained and disciplined runner going to a marathon event!

Sample Study Schedule

Week 1   Use your references to review for the concepts listed in the domains and tasks relating to:
- Health Information Documentation
- Data Quality and Management
- Information and Communication Technologies
- Privacy, Confidentiality, Legal and Ethical Issues

Answer the questions in the Health Data Content and Structure chapter in this book.

Week 2   Use your references for medical sciences and answer the questions in the Medical Science chapter:
- Clinical vocabularies and terminologies
- Anatomy and physiology
- Pathophysiology (disease process and pharmacology)
- Review Appendix A and Appendix B at the back of this book.

Week 3   Review your resources for the domains and tasks relating to:
- Diagnosis Coding and Procedure Coding
- Regulatory Guidelines and Reporting Requirements for Acute Care (Inpatient) Services
- Regulatory Guidelines and Reporting Requirements for Outpatient Services
- Compliance

Study the Coding Review section on ICD-9-CM and CPT coding concepts in this book.
Answer the questions in the Billing and Reimbursement chapter.
Answer the questions in the Classification and Secondary Data Sources chapter.

Week 3   Gather and review references for competencies in domains and tasks with the focus on ICD-9-CM.
Reference examples include:
- ICD-9-CM Coding Books
- Coding conventions (These can be found in the front of the code book.)
- ICD9-CM Official Guidelines for Coding and Reporting

Study the Coding Review section on ICD-9-CM coding in this book.
Answer the questions in the ICD-9-CM Coding chapter.

Week 4   Use references for domains and tasks with the focus on CPT.
- Review the references on the CPT Coding rules.
- Review the references on the CPT Evaluation and Management Guidelines. Review "Documentation Guidelines for Evaluation and Management Services," *CPT Assistant* (May 1997), as well as information in other *CPT Assistant* issues.
- Review the references on the CPT Surgery section and remaining CPT sections, including using modifiers.

Use this review guide by studying the Coding Review section (outpatient coding concepts). Answer the questions in the CPT Coding chapter of this review guide.

Week 5 & 6 Work the case studies provided in the book.
Continue working on the case studies.

Week 7 & 8 Continue your review of ICD-9-CM and CPT materials.
Answer the questions in the Mock Examinations for Section 1 and Section 2 of the CCS examination. Work the Mock Examination Cases for Section 3 of the CCS examination.

Week 9 & 10   Use your references to continue your review of ICD-9-CM and CPT materials.
Do an overall coding review and look over areas of weakness for a final review.

STUDY RESOURCES

Don't spend time trying to memorize something you do not understand. The main issue is to understand the materials so that you can use the knowledge in a practical way. Search for additional information that will help make the subject clearer to you. There are four basic sources of information: books, people, educational programs/colleges, and Internet resources.

Books and Other Written Resources

➤ A different textbook may use another style of presentation that you are more receptive to and may be all you need to gain a better insight into the subject. It can offer a fresh point of view, provide relief from boredom, and encourage critical thinking in the process of comparing the texts. There are a variety of books and workbooks available to use in studying for your coding certification.

➤ Periodical literature in the field provides well-written articles that may open up the subject to you and turn your study into an adventure in learning. AHIMA publishes authoritative and insightful information on every aspect of coding. In addition to the ongoing coding articles in the *Journal of AHIMA, ADVANCE for Health Information Professionals* has a special series of articles called "CCS Prep!" The magazine, *For the Record*, has articles on coding in each issue. Sometimes an article can help put the subject material into practical perspective and pull it together so that you gain a deeper understanding. Don't forget to use the *Coding Clinics* and *CPT Assistant* to refresh your memory and learn more about specific coding guidelines. All of these publications will help you keep updated on new information on coding issues that may be incorporated into the exams.

➤ Take advantage of the local college library by using reserved materials specifically set aside for HIM student study purposes.

Your HIM Community

➤ Interaction with others can be truly beneficial in keeping you motivated and on track.

➤ Professional contacts can also be helpful in your study effort. Most people in our field are eager to share their knowledge and are flattered by appeals for information. Schedule a conference with the director of the HIM/Coding program at your local college or university. These educators may have current information and resources you are not aware of. Talking to those who have recently taken the examination can also be of great assistance.

➤ Collaboration with other test applicants can reveal fresh viewpoints, stimulate thought by disagreement, or at least let you see that you are not alone in your quest. Organize study groups, and set aside specific times to work together. This interaction can be truly beneficial in keeping you motivated and on task.

Classes, Workshops, and Seminars and Coding Teleconferences

Classes, workshops, seminars, and coding teleconferences can present opportunities to learn and review the subject matter in a new light and keep you updated on changes. Take advantage of any coding review sessions available in your area.

Internet Resources

➤ In this dynamic, changing environment, the most up-to-date materials may not be available in a book. Do not overlook the power of AHIMA's Web site. The AHIMA resources online are extensive and quite easy to access at www.ahima.org. In addition, the Communities of Practice (CoPs) are a phenomenal source of contact with HIM professionals and other students preparing for the examination on myriad subjects. AHIMA is available online for members. You may find other examination applicants to work with by using e-mail.

➤ There are innumerable resources for coding and reimbursement on the Internet. **Just be aware that you may want to verify the information, because it is only as good as the source.**

Some Suggested Study Resources

1. **MANDATORY**: AHIMA *Candidate Handbook for the CCS Examination*
2. **MANDATORY**: ICD-9-CM Code Books (refer to instructions from AHIMA for the appropriate version)
3. **MANDATORY**: "ICD-9-CM Official Guidelines for Coding and Reporting" is available online at http://www.cdc.gov/nchs/icd/icd9cm or http://www.ahacentraloffice.org
4. **MANDATORY**: *AMA CPT Code Book* (refer to instructions from AHIMA for the appropriate version)
5. *Coding Clinic* (fourth quarter 1996), as well as past issues of *Coding Clinic* for ICD-9-CM (for the last 3–4 years)
6. HCPCS Level II Code Book (refer to instructions from AHIMA for the appropriate version)
7. "Documentation Guidelines for Evaluation and Management Services," *CPT Assistant* (May 1997) as well as information in other *CPT Assistant* issues
8. Professional journal articles on coding
   Journal of AHIMA
   ADVANCE for Health Information Professionals
   For the Record
9. Medical dictionaries (Check for latest edition.)
10. Coding class, seminar, and workshop notes and tests
11. Study groups/partners
12. On-the-job experience
13. Examination review sessions
14. Review books written for the CCS examinations
15. Various online resources. For online coding practice sites, as well as those for information and Internet interaction with others, visit the following examples:
    MANDATORY: http://www.AHIMA.org
    MANDATORY: http://www.cms.hhs.gov
    http://www.hospitalconnect.com
    http://go.cms.gov/MLNGenInfo
    http://www.cdc.gov/nchs/icd/icd9cm
16. HIM textbooks and Class textbooks: There is a large variety of textbooks for HIM and coding available on the market. Both Cengage Delmar Learning (www.cengage.com) and AHIMA (www.ahima.org) have a variety of HIM products.

Those resources marked **MANDATORY** are essential for you to have in order to prepare for the examination.

Contact Information for Resources for CCS Examination Review Studies

AMA CPT Code Book 2015
> American Medical Association (AMA): Phone: (800) 621-8335
> Website: http://www.ama-assn.org/ama
> https://www.amacatalog@ama-assn.org.

HCPCS II, Code Book 2015 Edition
> American Medical Association: Phone: (800) 621-8335

AMA CPT Assistant
> American Medical Association: Phone: (800) 621-8335 Fax: (312) 464-5600
> *Documentation Guidelines for E & M Coding*
> Published May 1995 and revised November 1997
> American Medical Association (AMA) and HCFA
> Printed in the *CPT Assistant* May 1997 and November 1997
> Online at Centers for Medicare and Medicaid Services:
>> http://www.cms.hhs.gov/
>> http://go.cms.gov/MLNGenInfo

ICD-9-CM Code Books with October 2012 updates
> OptumInsight, Web site https://www.optumcoding.com/

ICD-9-CM Official Guidelines for Coding and Reporting
> Central Office on ICD-10-CM of the American Hospital Association (AHA)
> Phone: (312) 422-3000 or it can be accessed online at the
> Web site for National Center for Health Statistics (NCHS) http://www.cdc.gov/nchs

AHIMA has developed a series of HIM and coding resources.
> To place an order, call (800) 335-5535.
> For additional resources and information about the coding certification examinations, visit the AHIMA Web site at http://www.ahima.org

OptumInsight has an array of coding, reimbursement, and compliance products.
> Contact them at 1-800-464-3649, choose Option 1 for speedier service.
> Visit their Web site at https://www.optumcoding.com/

Cengage Learning has a multitude of HIM products. In addition, they have partnered with OptumInsight so that you can order your resources through Delmar Cengage Learning also.

For a complete list, contact:
> Cengage Learning, Inc.
> Email: esales@cengage.com
> Web site: http://www.cengagebrain.com/
> Phone: 866-994-2427

For additional information on these Health Information resources, visit Delmar Cengage Learning at **www.cengage.com\delmar**.

A SUMMARY OF TIPS FOR ORGANIZING YOUR TIME AND MATERIALS

1. **Make a list of exam topics.**
   Review the major topic categories and determine what your areas of strength are and what areas are in need of improvement.

2. **Focus on your weaknesses.**
   Using the list, identify your weaknesses. It is natural to spend time on the areas where you feel confident. However, it is important to spend more time and energy studying your areas of weakness. Remember, every question counts toward that passing score!

3. **Set up a realistic study schedule.**
   Refer to the sample schedule provided in this book and customize it to meet your needs. Consider having a study group that meets regularly.

4. **Organize and review all of the following items.**
   a. The latest AHIMA Candidate Handbook for the Examination
   b. Official Coding Guidelines for Inpatient and Outpatient Services
   c. Coding textbooks and any coding course syllabi, outlines, class notes, and tests
   d. Coding books
   e. *Coding Clinic* from the past 3–4 years
   f. *CPT Assistant* from the past 3–4 years
   g. Professional journal articles on documentation, reimbursement, and coding issues
   h. List of pertinent Web sites for research and review

5. **Organize and enter valuable coding information directly into your code books.**
   You will not be allowed to have loose materials in your books. However, information that is permanently attached or written into the code book is acceptable.

6. **Practice taking timed tests.**
   One of the best ways to study for an examination is to take tests. Practice answering questions and working coding cases as much as possible. Time yourself so that you become accustomed to taking, on average, less than 1 minute per each multiple-choice question. Work the cases striving for completing a case in less than 14 minutes. Work with your watch in front of you.

7. **MANDATORY! Read the certification guide.**
   Carefully read the latest AHIMA Candidate Handbook for the certification exam you are taking. If anything in the Certification Guide is unclear, seek assistance from AHIMA. You are held accountable for the important information, deadlines, and instructions addressed in this material.

THE DAY BEFORE, AND THE MORNING OF, THE EXAM

1. **Know the exam location.**

   If there are several testing sites, make sure you have the correct directions to the correct center. Going to the wrong address for a test and then having to hustle to get to the right testing center is very stressful.

2. **Avoid studying the night before the exam.**

   Last-minute studying tends to increase your anxiety level. However, you may want to allocate a small amount of time to review any information that you feel you must look at one more time.

3. **Organize in advance all the materials you need to take with you to the exam.**

   Review the candidate handbook carefully, and be sure to have all the items that are required, especially the admission card, proof of identity, and your code books.

4. **Get a good night's sleep.**

   Taking a 4-hour test with little rest the night before may prevent you from having the energy and stamina you need to complete the exam.

5. **Have a healthy meal before your exam.**

   Four hours is a long time to go on an empty stomach. Try to eat a nutritious meal—for instance, cereal and fruit, bagel and fruit or juice, or a meal with protein such as cheese and crackers or eggs and toast. You need something to give you energy to keep going. Take a healthy snack bar to munch on if you get hungry and need to take a short break at the testing center.

6. **Dress comfortably.**

   Plan for possible variations in room temperature. Dressing in layers may prove helpful if the room is too cold or too hot for you.

7. **Arrive early.**

   Allow yourself plenty of time so that you arrive at the test site early. Take a practice drive. If the exam test site is a great distance from your home, spend the night before the examination in a nearby hotel or motel.

TAKING THE EXAMINATION

You have stuck to your study schedule and have conditioned yourself to be in the best physical and mental shape possible. Now comes the "moment of truth": the examination pops up on the screen before your eyes. Every paratrooper knows that, in addition to having a parachute, one must know how to open it. You have mastered the major topics and you have the parachute. Now you need to utilize good test-taking techniques to apply the knowledge you have gained. Open the parachute!

Section 1 (81 multiple-choice questions) and Section 2 (8 multiple-select questions) of the Examination

1. **Taking the practice test.** Prior to starting the exam, you will be given a chance to practice taking an examination on the computer. Time will be allotted for this practice test; however, you may quit the practice test and begin the actual exam when you are comfortable with the computerized testing process.

2. **Read all directions and questions carefully.** Try to avoid reading too much into the questions. Be sensible and practical in your interpretation. Read ALL of the possible answers because the first one that looks good may not be the best one. Some test takers read the question only, then try to formulate an answer before he/she reads the choices, and then look for a choice that matches his/her first mental response.

3. **Scan the screen quickly for the general question format.** Like the marathon runner, pace yourself for the distance. A good rule of thumb is about 1 minute per each multiple-choice question. You will be responsible for checking your time throughout the exam. For example, at question 30, about one-half hour will have elapsed, etc.

4. **Coming back to questions.** Some people answer all questions in the section that they are certain of first. Then they go back through that section of the exam a second time to answer any questions they were uncertain about. Others prefer not to skip questions, but make their best choice on encountering each question and go on. Both can be good approaches; choose the one that works best for you. You can "mark" questions that you have left unanswered and/or those questions you may want to review. Before you sign off on that section of the exam or run out of time, you have the ability to go back to those questions for a final review.

5. **Answer all the questions.** For both sections 1 and 2 of the exam, there is no penalty for guessing, but you must enter an answer for every response required before moving on to the next section of the exam.

6. **Process of elimination.** Use deductive reasoning and the process of elimination to arrive at the most correct answer. Some questions may have more than one correct answer. You will be asked to select the "best" possible answer based on the information presented.

7. **Determine what is being asked.** If the question is written in a scenario format, first identify the question being asked and then review the entire question for the information needed to determine the correct answer or answers.

8. **Use all the time available to recheck your answers.** However, avoid changing your answers unless you are absolutely certain it is necessary. Second-guessing yourself often results in a wrong answer. All of that practice in taking multiple-choice exams will pay off here.

9. **You MUST complete Section 1 of the examination before moving on to Section 2. Section 1 and Section 2 must be completed before moving on to Section 3 of the examination.**

Section 3 of the Examination: Medical Record Coding Cases

1. **Taking the practice test.** Prior to starting the exam, you will be given a chance to practice taking an examination on the computer. Time will be allotted for this practice test; however, you may quit the practice test and begin the actual exam when you are comfortable with the computerized testing process.

2. **Follow the procedures given in the Candidate Handbook for coding the test cases.** Do not use hospital, regional, or insurance standards that may differ from those used in the national examination directions. The test will be scored using the coding procedures given.

3. **Read all abstracts completely.** Identify the qualifying words and statements.

4. **Try to avoid reading too much into the information given.** Be sensible and practical in your interpretation. Do not make any assumptions. Points are deducted for inappropriate codes.

5. **Carefully review ancillary reports.** Ancillary reports may or may not contain information that is pertinent to the coding of the case. Do not assign codes for abnormal findings listed on ancillary reports unless the physician documents clinical significance.

6. **Only the codes themselves are considered in scoring.** Carefully check the computer screen to verify that you have entered the codes for a given case abstract into the spaces provided for that case.

7. **Use all the time available** to recheck your codes and make sure your answer form has been filled in correctly. However, avoid changing your answers unless you are absolutely certain that it is necessary. Second-guessing yourself often results in a wrong answer.

8. **The first code for inpatient cases should be the "principal" diagnosis.** Then, list any additional diagnoses that are appropriate. The additional diagnoses do not need to be sequenced in any special order, unless coding rules stipulate otherwise.

9. **The first diagnosis code for outpatient cases should be the "first listed" diagnosis.** Then, list any additional diagnoses that are appropriate. The additional diagnoses do not need to be sequenced in any special order, unless coding rules stipulate otherwise.

AFTER THE EXAMINATION

After taking the examination, it is time to reclaim your life and focus on your career. Plan a special reward for yourself at some point after the exam. Schedule a family vacation or a relaxing weekend getaway. Just find some way of being good to yourself. You certainly deserve it! You have worked hard, so relish your success.

Now Available – All New Professional Review Guide Series Online Quizzing Software

For 2015, we are providing you with new dynamic quizzing software for more effective study results. Follow the instructions on the Printed Access Card bound into this text to access the online quizzing software for this title.

Features include:
- All of the quizzes and mock exams available in the text, customizable by subject area
- Immediate feedback options by subject area and competency for better self-assessment
- Flashcards for self-review
- Case Studies available as Adobe PDF documents in the quizzing software for independent review

For Instructors:
- The ability to track student and class progress by domain or subject area in real time for better classroom focus
- An Excel™ exporting feature for gradebooks

Go to www.cengagebrain.com to create a unique instructor user login. Contact your sales representative for more information.

PAT'S EXAM EXPERIENCE

The CCS examination was a moment of truth for me. Some people asked me what I was going to do if I failed the examination. Now there is something to give you nightmares—to co-author an exam review book and then FLUNK the exam! That was when I decided to borrow a line from the movie *True Lies*, "fear is not an option," and adapted it for my own motto—"failure is not an option."

There were many days and nights when I doubted that I had what it takes. When I felt really fearful and uncomfortable, I made myself look back over the years of going to classes and all of the coding practice. I had completed all the courses required. I had studied hard and long in each one of them. I had made good grades. In fact, I graduated with honors. I was studying virtually every day to prepare for the exam. What more could I do? ABSOLUTELY NOTHING! Therefore, if I had done the best I could and I was doing the best I could, then the worry was just taking up space in my head.

I told myself there was no way I could fail the exam. This was a routine that I had to repeat, sometimes several times a day when the doubt would creep in. Positive attitudes can and will make the pretest jitters disappear. If you feel you can't do this, tell yourself that you have done it and that *this is just one more test!* I had prepared myself. I had taken many, many, many tests successfully before. This one is JUST ONE MORE!

The night before the test, I tried to study just a little, but I just could not concentrate. I gave up trying to cram more information into my head and went to bed.

The next morning at the testing center, I had coffee while we waited for the room to be prepared. One of the students milling around commented that she had failed the CCS examination twice before and hoped to pass it this time. I was really nervous then because this person had over 10 years of experience of coding in a hospital setting next to my measly experience. There were a lot of very nervous people there.

I had to remind myself to keep thinking: "I think I can. I think I can." I tried my best not to panic. After waiting what seemed like forever to start the exam, we were finally told to open the booklet for Part I and begin. I panicked at the first question. I could not understand what it asked. I had to stop, take a deep breath, and relax. I went to the next question, and was able to answer it quickly. I went back to the first question and it looked simple! I found myself going down the page breezing along and answering the questions. Then, I gasped as I thought, "What if I am not going fast enough?" I stopped, looked at the question number, checked the time and figured that I was answering them in about 1 minute each. Right on schedule. So, I calmed myself down and got back to business. Before I knew it, I had answered all the questions. I even had enough time to go back and review the ones I was not sure about.

One of the most difficult parts of the exam is the length of time sitting. I did take one break in the middle of the exam to use the restroom and walk around for a minute to clear my head.

Part I was the easy part. I was very adept at taking multiple-choice question exams. The section with the coding cases was my hardest section. I found that I wasn't completing the cases in 13 to 14 minutes, so I needed to speed up to finish the exam. It was really hard for me not to mull over each case.

When the exam was over, I was relieved, to say the least. For months it had been hanging over my head, and now IT WAS OVER! I left not knowing if I had passed the examination or not. But, no matter what the results were, I had done the best I could, and I was still a winner! Do the best you can and you will pass the exam, too. YOU CAN DO IT!

Affirmation: "I can handle anything on the exam—one question at a time." ~ Kathy DeAngelo, 1995

II. Coding Review

Leslie Moore, RHIT, CCS

Lisa Delhomme, MHA, RHIA

HEALTH RECORD CODING REVIEW
CODING PROCESS

Fine-tune your coding skills by seeking complete documentation and selecting the most detailed codes.

1. Assess the case by performing a quick review of the record's demographic information and the first few lines of the History and Physical.

2. Get an overview of key reports because they contain valuable detailed information.
   A. The <u>discharge summary</u> sums up the patient's hospital course and confirms conditions or complications. In ambulatory records, look at the final progress note and/or discharge instructions.
   B. Review the <u>physician orders</u> for treatment protocols. The orders may indicate chronic or acute conditions for which the patient is receiving treatment.
   C. Review the <u>history and physical</u> to complete the clinical picture. Social and family history, as well as past and present illnesses, may have clinical implications.
   D. Read the <u>progress notes</u> to track the course of hospitalization or outpatient treatment. These provide information concerning daily status, reactions, or postoperative complications.
   E. Study the <u>operative reports</u>. Additional procedures may be identified in the body of the operative report.

3. Check all data from clinical reports.
   A. <u>Laboratory</u> reports may show evidence of conditions such as anemia, renal failure, infections, and metabolic imbalances.
   B. <u>Radiology</u> reports may confirm diagnosis of pneumonia, COPD, CHF, degenerative joint diseases, and traumatic injuries.
   C. <u>Medication Administration Reports (MARs)</u> indicate all drugs that were administered to the patient. Look for documentation of diagnoses elsewhere in the medical record to correlate with each drug. If uncertain why a medication was administered, query the physician.
   D. <u>Respiratory therapy notes</u> document the use of mechanical ventilation and describe severity of respiratory disorders.
   E. <u>Physical therapy</u> reports detail useful information for coding musculoskeletal dysfunctions.
   F. <u>Dietary</u> reports describe nutritional deficiencies (e.g., malnutrition).
   G. <u>Speech pathology</u> reports give information on dysphasia, aphasia, and other speech-related conditions.
   H. <u>Pathology</u> reports are essential for accurate coding of conditions where excised tissue has been submitted for interpretation.

4. Perform a coding evaluation.
   A. Establish the principal diagnosis and formulate secondary diagnoses codes.
   B. Exclude all conditions not relevant to the case. Abnormal lab and x-ray findings and previous conditions having no effect on current management of the patient are not coded.

5. Take time to review and refine your coding.
   A. Review all diagnoses and procedures to confirm the selections of appropriate principal and secondary diagnoses and all procedure codes.
   B. For inpatient records, determine if each diagnosis was present on admission (POA) to adequately identify the POA indicator.
   C. Refine code assignments, where necessary, to make changes to more accurately classify the diagnoses and procedure codes selected.

Some Additional Tips for Coding

1. When a patient is admitted with or develops a condition during his or her stay, look to see if there is documentation to differentiate if the complication is acute, chronic, or both acute and chronic.

2. When a patient presents with or develops infectious conditions, seek documentation of any positive cultures (urine, wound, sputum, blood) pertaining to that condition. If the positive cultures are available for that condition (e.g., sepsis due to Pseudomonas), it will help in being more specific in coding the diagnoses and may increase reimbursement in some cases. For example, in a case of pneumonia due to Pseudomonas, the MS-DRG may increase considerably. According to coding guidelines, if the culture is not documented, even though present in laboratory reports, the condition is to be coded as unspecified, which can affect reimbursement. Examples: sepsis, cellulitis, UTI, pneumonia, etc.

3. If a condition is due to surgery, ask the physician to verify and document that it is due to the procedure. If the patient has been discharged, and you are not sure but believe it was due to the procedure, seek verification that it is possibly due to the procedure by querying the physician.

4. If the patient had outpatient surgery for removal of a lesion, look for documentation of the size of the lesion that may have been removed. It should be documented in the operative report.
   The American Medical Association's publication, *CPT Assistant* (issues from Fall 1995 and August 2000) states, "Since the physician can make an accurate measurement of the lesion(s) at the time of the excision, the size of the lesion should be documented in the OP (operative) report. A pathology report is likely to contain a less accurate measurement due to the shrinking of the specimen or the fact that the specimen may be fragmented."
   Reimbursement is based on the diameter of the lesion(s). Even 1 millimeter (mm) off in the diameter calculation can mean fewer dollars for the hospital and the physician. The documentation in the record ensures appropriate reimbursement.

5. Look for documentation in the final diagnoses in the discharge summary for clarification or to differentiate whether specific conditions are currently present, or if the patient only has a history of the condition.

   Examples: 1. Acute CVA versus history of CVA
   2. Current drug or alcohol abuse versus history of drug or alcohol abuse
   3. Current neoplasm being treated versus history of malignancy

6. Verify if a condition is a manifestation of an existing condition.
   Example: CRF secondary to DM or CRF due to HTN

7. Look for documentation of conditions that are secondary to previous conditions.
   Examples: 1. Quadriplegia due to fall
   2. Dysphagia due to previous CVA

8. When coding charts of discharged patients:
   A. <u>Rule out</u> conditions are coded as confirmed for inpatients. The condition is still considered to be a possibility if stated as possible, probable, likely, questionable, or suspected. According to coding guidelines, rule out diagnoses are coded as established, based on the fact that the diagnostic workup and initial therapeutic approach would have addressed this condition even though a final determination was not made. (Note: For outpatients, do not code rule out, possible, probable, questionable, or suspected conditions as confirmed. Rather, code the condition to the highest degree of certainty, such as symptoms, signs, and abnormal test results, or other reason for the visit.)
   B. <u>Ruled out</u> conditions are <u>not</u> coded as confirmed for inpatients. The condition originally considered is no longer a possibility. Documentation should clarify if the condition was ruled out/not found. Symptoms may be coded instead. If no symptoms are documented, it may be appropriate to code "Observation for suspected condition, not found."

Commonly Missed Complications and Comorbidities (CCs)

Depending on the patient's principal diagnosis, this list of commonly missed complications and comorbidities (CCs) and major complications and comorbidities (MCCs) may or may not help the MS-DRG when documented and coded. If any of these conditions are being managed while the patient is being hospitalized, it may change the MS-DRG to a higher paying one. Some MS-DRGs will not change even if these are present. The MS-DRG may or may not change if the patient has a major procedure performed. Some of these conditions may be considered CCs, while others may be considered Major CCs.

- Acidosis
- Alcoholism acute/chronic
- Alkalosis
- Anemia due to blood loss, acute/chronic (e.g., from GI bleed, or surgery)
- Angina pectoris (stable or unstable angina)
- Atrial fibrillation/flutter
- Atelectasis
- Cachexia
- Cardiogenic shock
- Cardiomyopathy
- Cellulitis
- CHF
- Combination of both acidosis/alkalosis
- COPD
- Decubitus ulcer
- Dehydration (volume depletion)
- Diabetes: If DM is uncontrolled (type 1 or 2)
- Electrolyte imbalance
- Hematuria
- Hematemesis
- Hypertension (HTN) accelerated or malignant HTN only qualifies (not uncontrolled, hypertensive urgency or hypertensive crisis)
- Hypertensive heart disease with CHF
- Hyponatremia ($\downarrow$ Na)
- Hypernatremia ($\uparrow$ Na)
- Hypochloremia ($\downarrow$ Cl)
- Hyperchloremia ($\uparrow$ Cl)
- Hyperpotassemia ($\uparrow$ K)
- Malnutrition
- Melena
- Pleural effusion (especially if it has to be treated by a procedure, e.g., thoracentesis)
- Pneumonia
- Pneumothorax
- Postoperative complications
- Renal failure, acute or chronic (not renal insufficiency)
- Respiratory failure
- Septicemia
- Urinary retention
- UTI (e.g., urosepsis): If urosepsis is documented, it will be coded as a UTI unless otherwise specified.

Note: This is not an all-inclusive listing of possible complications and comorbidities.

International Classification of Diseases, Ninth Revision, Clinical Modification Coding Guidelines and Updates Effective October 1, 2012

Information regarding ICD-9-CM Coding Guidelines and updates effective October 1, 2012, may be found at   http://www.cdc.gov/nchs/icd/icd9cm_addenda_guidelines.htm

ICD-9-CM Guidelines. (PDF)

These official guidelines for coding have been approved by the Cooperating Parties and the Editorial Advisory Board for Coding Clinic for the ICD-9-CM.
Note: These guidelines are effective as of 10/01/2012.

ICD-9-CM Code Conversion Table. (10/01/2012) (PDF)

A conversion table for diagnostic and procedural code changes between 1986 and 2012 is provided to assist users in data retrieval. The table shows the date the new code became effective and its previously assigned code equivalent. Any new codes effective October 1, 2012, are shown in bold.

ICD-9-CM Addenda and Addenda Errata

The annual update to ICD-9-CM is provided as addenda changes to the index and tabular list of ICD-9-CM, effective October 1, 2012. In the index, additions are marked with bold and underlining, revisions are marked with bold, underlining, and italic, while deletions are marked with bold and strikeout.

ICD-9-CM CODE BOOK CONTENTS

Three Volumes of ICD-9-CM are:

Vol. 1:   Tabular List (Diseases)
Vol. 2:   Alphabetic Index (Diseases)
Vol. 3:   Tabular List and Alphabetic Index (Procedures)

Special Alphanumeric Codes

V-codes   Used for patient encounters that influence health status other than for disease or injury
E-codes   Describe external causes of injury, poisoning, or other adverse reactions
M-codes   Used to report the morphology of the neoplasms

CONVENTIONS USED IN TABULAR LIST (DISEASES) (PROCEDURES)

Abbreviations

NEC—Not Elsewhere Classified (other specified)
1. Ill-defined terms. Terms for which a more specific code does not exist.
2. Used only when the coder lacks the information necessary to code the term to a more specific category code.
3. Information in the medical record provides detail for which a specific code does not exist.
4. "Other" or "Other Specified" codes are those usually with a fifth digit of "8" or a fifth digit of "9" for diagnosis codes.

NOS—Not Otherwise Specified (unspecified)
1. Used when the information in the medical record is insufficient to assign a more specific code.
2. "Unspecified" codes are those usually with a fourth digit of "9" or a fifth digit of "0" for diagnosis codes.

Punctuation

[Brackets] Brackets enclose synonyms, alternative wordings, or explanatory phrases.
{Braces} Braces enclose a series of terms, each of which is modified by the statement appearing at the right of the brace.
(Parentheses) Parentheses enclose supplementary words that may be present or absent in the statement of a disease or procedure without affecting the code assigned (nonessential modifiers).
Colon: Colons are used in the Tabular List after an incomplete term that needs one or more of the modifiers following the colon in order to make it assignable to a given category.

Symbols

[]   Lozenge symbol in the left margin preceding the disease code indicates that contents of a fourth digit category have been moved or modified, so that it is not the same as in ICD-9.
§   Section mark symbol preceding a code denotes the placement of a note at the top of the page that is applicable to all subdivisions in that category.

Other Conventions

Bold typeface is used for all codes and titles in the Tabular List.

Italicized typeface is used

1.   For all exclusion notes
2.   To identify those subcategories that are not to be used for primary tabulation of diseases (Italicized codes must always follow the code for the underlying cause of the disease.)

Format—indented format for ease in reference.

And—the word "and" is interpreted to mean either "and" or "or" when it appears in a title.

With—the word "with" is interpreted to mean "associated with" or "due to" when it appears as an instructional note in the Tabular List.

Instructional Notations

Includes further defines, or gives example of, the contents of the category. It appears immediately under a two- or three-digit code title.

Excludes are to be coded elsewhere as indicated in each case.

Use additional code—placed in those categories where the user may wish to add further information to give a more complete picture of the diagnosis.

Code first underlying disease—used in those codes not intended to be used as a principal diagnosis. Requires that the underlying disease etiology be recorded first and the particular manifestation recorded second.

Code also—used only in the Tabular List of Procedures as an instruction to code

1.   Each component of a procedure accomplished at the same time
2.   The use of special adjunctive (accompanying) procedures or equipment

Code if applicable, any causal condition first—a code with this note may be the principal diagnosis if no casual condition is applicable or known.

CONVENTIONS USED IN ALPHABETIC INDEX (DISEASES) (PROCEDURES)

Main Terms

The Alphabetic Index of Diseases is organized by "main terms" printed in boldface type.

1.   Diseases (e.g., influenza, bronchitis)
2.   Conditions (e.g., fatigue, fracture, injury)
3.   Nouns (e.g., disease, disorder, and syndrome)
4.   Adjectives (e.g., double, large, kink)
5.   Anatomical sites are not used for main terms. Look under the condition or disease term.

The Alphabetic Index of Procedures is also organized by "main terms" printed in boldface type.

1.   Procedure performed (e.g., excision of lesion).
2.   Anatomical sites are not used for main terms. Look under the name of the procedure performed.

Conditions may be found in more than one place in the Alphabetic Index of Diseases.

1.   Obstetrical conditions may be found under the name of the condition and under entries for delivery, pregnancy, and puerperal.
2.   Complications of medical and surgical care are indexed under the name of the condition and/or under Complications.
3.   Late effects (e.g., of infections, injury) will be found under late effects.

4. V-codes can be found under main terms, such as admission, examination, history of, observation, problem with, status, vaccination, and screening.
5. Main terms that are general adjectives, such as acute, chronic, or lymphoid, and references to anatomical site, such as leg or limb, may appear as main terms, but they have only a "see condition" reference.
6. A main term followed by a list of subterms are essential modifiers and do have an effect on the selection of the appropriate code for a given diagnosis.

Abbreviations

NEC—Not elsewhere classified (other specified)
1. Ill-defined terms.
2. Use only if more precise information is not available.
3. Use when terms for a more specific code are not provided and no amount of additional information will alter the code.

Punctuation

(Parentheses)—A main term may be followed by a series of supplementary terms within parentheses. The presence or absence of these terms has no effect on the selection of the code. These are called nonessential modifiers.
[Brackets]—Brackets identify manifestation codes in the Alphabetic Index of Diseases.

Other Conventions

Cross-references show possible modifiers for a term or its synonyms.
1. **See**—explicit directions to look somewhere else.
2. **See also**—go elsewhere only if all the information the user is searching for cannot be located.
3. **See category**—directs the user to the Tabular List for important information about the use of a specific code.
Notes—used to define terms or give coding instructions.
And—the word "and" is interpreted to mean either "and" or "or" when it appears in a title.
With—the word "with" is interpreted to mean "associated with" or "due to" when it appears in a code title or Alphabetic Index.

Instructional Notations

Omit code—used in the Alphabetic Index of Procedures as an instruction to omit coding of incisions made only for the purpose of performing further surgery.

Eponyms

In the Alphabetic Index of Diseases, diseases or syndromes named for persons are listed both as main terms in their appropriate alphabetic sequence and under the main terms "Disease" or "Syndrome." A description of the disease or syndrome is usually included in parentheses following the eponym.

Joined Main Terms

Two main terms may be joined together by combination terms listed in the Alphabetic Index of Diseases as subterms (e.g., associated with, complicated [by], due to, following, in, secondary to, with, without). These terms advise the coder to use one or two codes depending on the condition. The terms are also often indented under subterms in the Alphabetic Index. Combination codes may identify all of the components of a diagnosis. These codes are provided for terms that occur together frequently (e.g., hypertensive heart and renal disease) and must be used whenever a patient has both conditions rather than assigning codes from both categories.

Etiology and Manifestation of Diseases—For certain conditions it is important to record both the etiology (cause) and the manifestation (demonstration of sign, symptom, or alteration) of the disease.
1. Accomplished with a single five-digit code (e.g., syphilitic myocarditis 093.82).
2. The two facets of the disease are coded individually and the Alphabetic Index lists both codes. The codes must be recorded in the same sequence used in the Alphabetic Index.
   Example: Diabetic retinopathy 250.5 x [362.01]. The first code represents the etiology, and the code in brackets represents the manifestation.

General Coding Guidelines

1. Use both Alphabetic Index and Tabular List to assign a specific code.
2. Read and be guided by all instructional notations.
3. Assign the code at the highest number of digits available. A code is invalid if it has not been coded to the full number of digits required for that code.
4. Coding the sign or symptom rather than the diagnosis is acceptable when a related diagnosis has <u>not</u> been established.
5. Signs and symptoms that are routinely associated with a diagnosis should not be coded, unless instructed to do so.
6. If the same condition is described as both acute (or subacute) and chronic and separate entries exist in the Alphabetic Index at the same indentation level, code both and sequence the acute (subacute) code first.
7. Assign only the combination code when that code fully describes all the elements documented in the diagnosis. When the combination code lacks necessary specificity, an additional code should be added.
8. If at the time of discharge, a condition is documented as "impending" or "threatened," and it did occur, code it. If it did not occur, but there is a main term or subterm in the Alphabetic Index for "impending" or "threatened," use that specified code. If there is no main term or subterm code, code the existing underlying condition and not the condition described as "impending" or "threatened."
9. If a condition is stated as bilateral, code it only once. If two different conditions are classified to the same ICD-9-CM diagnosis code, code it only once.
10. Not all conditions that occur during or after medical care or surgery should be coded as complications. There must be a documented cause-and-effect relationship. If in doubt, query the physician.

SOME AREAS OF SPECIAL INTEREST

Abortions

- The primary axis for coding abortion is the type of abortion: spontaneous, legally induced, illegally induced, or failed attempted abortion.
- Fourth digits are used with categories 634–638 to indicate whether a complication is present and the general type of complication.
- The fifth-digit subclassification is used to indicate whether the abortion was unspecified (0), incomplete (1), or complete (2).
- When a patient is readmitted because of a complication subsequent to an abortion, a code from category 639 is assigned.
- If the readmission is for the purpose of dealing with retained products of conception, following a spontaneous or legally induced abortion, a code from category 634 or 635 with a fifth digit of "1" (incomplete) is assigned rather than 639.
- Codes from categories 640–649 and 651–659 can be assigned as additional codes with an abortion code to indicate the complication that necessitated the abortion.
- When an abortion results in a live birth, the code for early onset of delivery (644.21) is used rather than the abortion code with an appropriate code from category V27.

Adhesions

- When minor adhesions are present, but do not cause symptoms or increase the difficulty of an operative procedure, coding a diagnosis of adhesions and a lysis procedure is inappropriate.
- When adhesions are dense or strong or create problems during a surgical procedure, it is appropriate to code both the diagnosis of adhesions and the operative procedure to lyse the adhesions.

Adverse Effects/Poisonings/Toxic Effects

Adverse effects: Caused when medication is correctly prescribed and properly administered.
- First, code the manifestation or effect of the adverse reaction. (e.g., vomiting, tachycardia, respiratory failure).
- Next, assign the E-code for the drug from the "Therapeutic Use" column (E930–E949 series) in the Table of Drugs and Chemicals. (Do not use an E-code from the "Therapeutic Use" column for a poisoning.) It is mandatory to report E-codes for all conditions identified as adverse effects. If two or more drugs are reported, code each individually.

Poisoning: Caused when substance is not used according to a physician's instructions (e.g., overdose, wrong dose, and interaction with alcohol).
- First, code the drug or agent in the Table of Drugs and Chemicals from the poisoning column (960–979 series).
- Then, code the specified effect or manifestation of the poisoning (e.g., vomiting, tachycardia, respiratory failure) as a secondary code.
- Finally, assign the E-code from the Table of Drugs and Chemicals. (Use the Accident, Suicide Attempt, Assault, or Undetermined column.)

Toxic effects: when a harmful substance is ingested or comes in contact with a person.
- First, Code the toxic effect (980–989 series) by selecting the substance (e.g., Drano, gasoline, bleach) under the Poisoning column in the Table of Drugs and Chemicals.
- Next, code the result of the toxic effect (e.g., vomiting, tachycardia, respiratory failure).
- Finally, assign the E-code from the Table of Drugs and Chemicals. (Use the Accident, Suicide Attempt, Assault, or Undetermined column.)

Late effects: Caused by a previous adverse effect or a code poisoning.

- When the condition being coded is a late effect of an adverse effect of a drug, medicinal, or biological substance, a code is assigned for the residual condition first with code 909.5 assigned as an additional code. An E-code is used to identify the drug.
- When the condition being coded is a late effect of a poisoning or a late effect of toxic effects, the residual is coded first with code 909.0 or 909.1 used as an additional code. A late effect E-code should be used.

Anemia

- The coder must distinguish between chronic blood loss anemia and acute blood loss anemia because the two conditions are assigned to different category codes.
- Acute blood loss anemia occurring after surgery may or may not be a complication of surgery. The physician must clearly identify postoperative anemia as a complication of the surgery in order to use the complication code.
- Depending on the primary reason for admission, anemia of chronic disease can be used as the principal diagnosis (if the reason for admit is to treat the anemia) or as the secondary diagnosis.
- When assigning code 285.21 (anemia in chronic kidney disease), also assign a code from category 585 (chronic kidney disease) to identify the stage of chronic kidney disease.

Asthma

- Asthma is classified to category 493 with a fourth digit indicating the type of asthma. A fifth digit is used with codes 493.0–493.2 and 493.9 indicating whether status asthmaticus is present (1), unspecified (0), or with acute exacerbation (2).
- Acute exacerbation of asthma is increased severity of asthma symptoms, such as wheezing and shortness of breath.
- Terms suggesting status asthmaticus include intractable asthma, refractory asthma, severe intractable wheezing, and airway obstruction not relieved by medication. It is a life-threatening complication that requires emergency care.
- The coder must not assume status asthmaticus is present. The physician must document the condition in order to code it.
- It is inappropriate to assign an asthma code with the fifth digit 2 with acute exacerbation, together with an asthma code with fifth digit 1, with status asthmaticus. Only the fifth digit 1 should be assigned.

Body Mass Index (BMI)

- The code(s) for body mass index should only be reported as secondary diagnoses and must meet the definition of a reportable additional diagnosis.
- Documentation from clinicians (such as dieticians) may be used for code assignment as long as the physician has documented the diagnosis of obesity.
- If there is conflicting documentation, query the attending physician.

Burns

- When coding multiple burns, assign separate codes for each site and sequence the burn with the highest degree first.
- When coding burns of the same site with varying degrees, code only the highest degree.
- Necrosis of burned skin is coded as a nonhealing burn. Nonhealing burns are coded as acute burns.
- Posttraumatic wound infection (958.3) should be reported as an additional diagnosis for documented infected burn site.
- Category 946 (burns of multiple, specified sites) should only be used if the location of the burns is not documented.

- Category 948 (extent of body surface) codes are used when
  - The site of the burn is not specified;
  - There is a need for more data (for burn units to evaluate burn mortality); or
  - There is mention of a third degree burn involving 20% or more of the body surface.
- In category 948:
  - The fourth digit identifies the percentage of total body surface involved (all degrees).
  - The fifth digit identifies the percentage of body surface that is third degree.
  - The fifth digit of "0" is assigned when "0 to less than 10%" of total body surface is third degree.
- Category 948 is based on the classic "rule of nines" in estimating body surface involved, as indicated below:

  9% = head and neck
  9% = left arm
  9% = right arm
  18% = left leg
  18% = right leg
  18% = anterior trunk
  18% = posterior trunk
  1% = genitalia
  100% = total body surface

Note: Hospitals can adjust percentages to accommodate for infants, children, or obese patients.

Cellulitis

- Coders must not assume that documentation of redness at the edges of a wound represents cellulitis. Rely on physician documentation of cellulitis.
- Coding of cellulitis with an injury or burn requires one code for the injury and one for the cellulitis. Sequencing will depend on the circumstances of admission.
- When the patient is seen primarily for treating the original injury, sequence that code first. When the patient is seen primarily for treatment of the cellulitis, the code for cellulitis is the principal diagnosis.

Cerebral Infarction/CVA

- Stroke, CVA, and cerebral infarction, NOS is coded to 434.91 (cerebral artery occlusion, unspecified).
- Code also any neurologic deficits associated with the acute CVA regardless of whether or not the neurologic deficit resolves prior to discharge.
- If the CVA is documented as a result of medical intervention, use code 997.02 (iatrogenic CVA or hemorrhage). An additional code from 430–432, 433, or 434 should be added to identify the type of infarct or hemorrhage.

Chronic Kidney Disease (CKD)

- Chronic Kidney Disease (CKD) is the correct terminology, rather than chronic renal failure.
- CKD is coded based upon severity. The fourth digit identifies the stage:
  - 585.1: Stage I
  - 585.2: Stage II (mild)
  - 585.3: Stage III (moderate)
  - 585.4: Stage IV (severe)
  - 585.5: Stage V
  - 585.6: End-Stage Renal Disease
- End-stage renal disease (ESRD) is assigned when documented. If both stages of CKD and ESRD are documented, assign the code for ESRD only.

Chronic Obstructive Pulmonary Disease (COPD)

- A general term used to describe a variety of conditions that result in obstruction of the airway.
- It can appear as chronic obstructive asthma (493.2x), obstructive chronic bronchitis (491.2x), emphysema (492.8), or obstructive chronic bronchitis without exacerbation (with emphysema) (491.20).
- When the diagnosis is stated only as COPD, the coder should review the record to see if a more definite diagnosis can be made.
- Acute bronchitis with COPD is coded to 491.22.
- Acute bronchitis with COPD with acute exacerbation is coded to 491.22.
- COPD with acute exacerbation without mention of acute bronchitis is coded to 491.21.

Complications

- When coding complications of surgical and medical care (996–999), if the code fully describes the condition, no additional code is necessary. If it does not fully describe the condition, an additional code should be assigned.

Congenital Anomalies

- A congenital anomaly (categories 740–759) may be a principal or secondary diagnosis.
- When there is a code that identifies the congenital anomaly, do not assign additional codes for the inherent manifestations. Do assign additional codes for manifestations that are not an inherent component.
- For the birth admission, V30 is still the principal diagnosis followed by any congenital anomaly code (740–759).
- Codes from Chapter 14, Congenital Anomalies, can be reported for patients of any age. Many congenital anomalies do not manifest any symptoms until much later in life.

Coronary Artery Bypass Graft (CABG)

- A coronary artery bypass is a surgery that is performed to bypass blood around the clogged arteries in the heart.
- The axis for coding coronary artery bypass grafts is the number of arteries involved.
- An internal mammary bypass graft is done by loosening the mammary artery from the normal position and using it to bring blood to the heart.
- The axis for coding internal mammary bypass grafts is whether one or both internal mammary arteries are used.

Debridement

- Excisional debridement (86.22) is the surgical removal or cutting away of tissue. It may be performed by a physician or other health care practitioner.
- Nonexcisional debridement (86.28) is the mechanical nonsurgical brushing, irrigating, scrubbing, or washing of tissue.

Diabetes Mellitus

- When the type of diabetes mellitus is not documented, code it as type 2.
- Uncontrolled or Out of Control: The physician must specifically document this in order to use the fifth digits of 2 (type 2 or unspecified type, uncontrolled) or 3 (type 1—juvenile type—uncontrolled).
- Diabetes with a manifestation or complication requires documentation of a causal relationship to be coded. Assign as many codes from category 250 as needed to identify all associated conditions.
- Even if the patient is using insulin, it does not necessarily mean that the patient is type 1.
- Most patients with type 1 diabetes develop the condition before reaching puberty. That is why type 1 diabetes mellitus is also referred to as juvenile diabetes.
- For type 2 patients who routinely use insulin, code V58.67 (long-term, current use of insulin) should also be assigned. Do not use this code if the patient receives insulin to temporarily bring a type 2 patient's blood sugar under control.
- An underdose of insulin due to an insulin pump failure should be assigned 996.57 (mechanical complications due to insulin pump) as the principal diagnosis code, followed by a code from category 250.
- When the patient has an insulin pump malfunction resulting in an overdose of insulin, assign 996.57 as the principal diagnosis code with an additional code of 962.3 (poisoning by insulin and antidiabetic agents). Also code the appropriate diabetes mellitus code from 250.
- Use codes from category 249 (secondary diabetes mellitus) to identify diabetes caused by another condition or event. Category code 249 is listed first followed by the code for the associated condition.

  The patient may be admitted for treatment of the secondary diabetes or one of its associated conditions OR for treatment of the condition causing the secondary diabetes. Code the primary reason for the encounter as the principal diagnosis, which will be a code from category 249 followed by the code for the associated condition or a code for the cause of the secondary diabetes.
- Assign code 251.3 for post-pancreatectomy diabetes mellitus. Assign a category code from 249 for secondary diabetes mellitus. Also assign V88.1 for acquired absence of the pancreas. Also code any diabetes manifestations, if any.

Dysplasia of the Vulva and Cervix

- A diagnosis of cervical intraepithelial neoplasia (CIN) III or vulvar intraepithelial neoplasia (VIN) III is classified as carcinoma in situ of the site.
- A diagnosis of CIN III or VIN III is made only on the basis of pathological evaluation of tissue.

E-Codes

- Never used as a principal diagnosis.
- If two or more events caused separate injuries, an E-code is assigned for each. The first listed E-code should correspond to the cause of the most serious diagnosis, following this order of hierarchy:
  1. E-codes for adult and child abuse
  2. E-code for terrorism events
  3. E-codes for cataclysmic events
  4. E-codes for transport accidents
  5. E-codes for activity (describes the activity of a person seeking care for injuries)
  6. E-codes for external cause status (describes the status of the person at the time of the event: civilian, military, volunteer, other, or unspecified)
  7. E-codes for place of occurrence (describes where the event occurred)
- When the condition code for the diagnosis is a late effect, a late effect E-code must be used.

- Activity E-codes describe the activity of a person seeking care for injuries.
- External cause status codes are assigned to record the status of the person at the time of the event (civilian, military, volunteer, other, or unspecified).

Elevated Blood Pressure vs. Hypertension

- A diagnosis of high or elevated blood pressure without a firm diagnosis of hypertension is reported using code 796.2.
- This code is never assigned on the basis of a review of blood pressure readings; the physician must document elevated blood pressure/hypertension.

Fracture

- Traumatic fractures (800–829) are coded as long as the patient is receiving active treatment.
- Use aftercare codes (V54.0, V54.1, V54.8, or V54.9) when the patient is receiving routine care during the healing phase (examples of aftercare include cast change, removal of device, and medication adjustment).
- An open fracture is one in which there is communication with the bone. The following terms indicate open fracture: compound, infected, missile, puncture, and with foreign body.
- A closed fracture does not produce an open wound. Some types of closed fractures are impacted, comminuted, depressed, elevated, greenstick, spiral, and simple.
- When a fracture is not identified as open or closed, the code for a closed fracture is used.
- The most common fracture treatment is "reduction." The first axis for coding reductions is whether the reduction is open or closed. The second axis identifies the use of internal fixation.
- Internal fixation devices include screws, pins, rods, staples, and plates.
- External fixation devices include casts, splints, and traction device (Kirschner wire) (Steinman pin).

Gastrointestinal Hemorrhage

- Patients may be admitted for an endoscopy after a history of GI bleeding. It is acceptable to use a code for GI hemorrhage even if there is no hemorrhage noted on the current encounter.

Glaucoma

- Codes from 365.7 (Glaucoma stage) can only be used as additional codes to identify the glaucoma stage.
- If a patient has bilateral glaucoma with both being the same stage, assign one code for the type of glaucoma and one code for the stage.
- If a patient has bilateral glaucoma with each eye being different stages, assign one code for the type of glaucoma and one code for the highest glaucoma stage.
- If a patient has bilateral glaucoma with each eye being different types of glaucoma and each eye being different stages, assign one code for the type of glaucoma and one code for the highest glaucoma stage.
- If a patient is admitted in one glaucoma stage and it progresses to another stage, assign one code for the highest stage.
- Code 365.74 is for glaucoma whose stage cannot be clinically determined.
- Code 365.70 is for glaucoma stage, unspecified (indicates there is no documentation regarding the stage).

Heart Failure

- Fifth digits specify whether the heart failure is acute (1), chronic (2), acute on chronic (3), or unspecified (0).
- Right-sided failure secondary to left-sided failure is classified as congestive heart failure (428.0).

Hematuria
- Many conditions in the genitourinary system have hematuria as an integral associated symptom and, therefore, the hematuria is not coded separately unless it is excessive and has been documented as such by the physician.
- Blood in the urine discovered on a urinalysis is not coded as hematuria but is coded to 791.2, Hemoglobinuria.
- Hematuria following a urinary procedure is not considered a postoperative complication.

Human Immunodeficiency Virus (HIV)
- Documentation of HIV infection as "suspected," "possible," "likely," or "questionable": physician must be queried for clarification. Code only confirmed cases of HIV infection. Confirmation does not require documentation of positive test results for HIV. A physician's documentation is sufficient.
- 042: Patients with symptomatic HIV disease or AIDS. If HIV test results are positive and the patient has symptoms. Patients with known diagnosis of HIV-related illness should be coded to 042 on every subsequent admission.
- V08: Patients with physician-documented asymptomatic HIV infection who have never had an HIV-related illness. If HIV results are positive and the patient is without symptoms. Do not use this code if the term "AIDS" is used or if the patient is being treated for HIV-related conditions. In these cases use code 042.
- 795.71: Patients with inconclusive HIV test results but no definite diagnosis.
- Patients previously diagnoses with HIV-related illness (042) should never be assigned 795.91 or V08.
- V73.89: Patient seen to determine his or her HIV status (screening).
- V69.8: Use as a secondary code if an asymptomatic patient is in a known high-risk group.
- V65.44: This can be used as the principal diagnosis if the HIV test results are negative (counseling). Use as a secondary code if the HIV test results are positive (counseling).
- Patients admitted with an HIV-related condition are assigned code 042 as the principal diagnosis followed by additional diagnosis codes for all reported HIV-related conditions.
- Patients admitted for a condition unrelated to the HIV (such as traumatic injury) are assigned the code for the unrelated condition as the principal diagnosis, then code 042.
- When an obstetric patient has the HIV infection, a code from subcategory 647.6x is sequenced first with either code 042 (symptomatic) or V08 (asymptomatic) used as an additional code.

Hypertension
- The Hypertension Table is found under the main term "Hypertension" and contains a complete listing of all conditions due to or associated with hypertension. These conditions are classified as malignant, benign, and unspecified (401.x). If the physician does not specify the hypertension as malignant or benign, it is classified as unspecified.
- 402.xx: Hypertensive heart disease. Physician must document causal relationship between hypertension and heart disease that is stated as "due to hypertension" or implied by documenting "hypertensive" (425.8, 429.0–429.3, 429.8, and 429.9). Use an additional code from category 428 to identify the type of heart failure, if present. If the heart disease is stated as occurring "with hypertension," do not assume a cause-and-effect relationship and code it separately.
- 403.xx: Hypertensive chronic kidney disease. ICD-9-CM assumes a causal relationship between hypertension and chronic kidney disease (CKD) (585 or renal stenosis (587)). There is no causal relationship with acute renal failure. Use an additional code from category 585 to identify the stage of CKD.

- 404.xx: Hypertensive heart and chronic kidney disease. Physician must document causal relationship with the heart disease, but you may assume a causal relationship with chronic kidney disease. Assign an additional code for category 428 to identify the type of heart failure, if present. More than one code for category 428 may be assigned if the patient has systolic or diastolic failure and congestive heart failure. Use an additional code from category 585 to identify the stage of CKD.

Influenza

- Code only documented "confirmed" cases of avia, 2009 H1N1, or novel influenza virus. This is an exception to the hospital inpatient guidelines regarding the coding of uncertain diagnosis (possible, probable, suspected, etc.). If the physician documents "possible" avian, 2009 H1N1, or novel influenza, select a code from category 487 (influenza). Do not select a code from category 488 (influenza due to certain identified influenza viruses). Confirmation does not require the documentation of positive laboratory testing.

Injuries

- Superficial injuries (e.g, abrasions, contusions) are not coded when there are more severe injuries of the same site.

Ischemic Heart Disease (Chronic)

- Category 414 includes forms of chronic heart diseases such as atherosclerosis.
- Code 414.0x includes arteriosclerotic heart disease, coronary arteriosclerosis, coronary stricture, and coronary atheroma. Fifth digits provide information about the type of coronary artery involved such as native, vein bypass, or artery bypass.

Late Effects

- A late effect is a residual condition that remains after the acute phase of the illness or injury has passed.
- There is no set time period before a condition is considered a late effect.
- Coding of late effects generally requires two codes. Sequence first the residual condition or nature of the late effect, then sequence the late effect code next.
- There are times when the late effect code is expanded (fourth and fifth digits) to also incorporate the manifestation.
- The code for the acute phase of the illness or injury that caused the late effect is never coded with a code for the late effect.

Example: "Burn" is the acute phase, "contracture" is the residual; therefore, code "contracture" first, then "late effect of burn." Do not code "burn."

Late Effects of Cerebrovascular Disease

- Codes in category 438, late effect of cerebrovascular disease, are combination codes that indicate the residual as well as the "late effect" of the CVA.
- Codes from 438 are used for remaining deficits when the patient is admitted at a later date following a cerebrovascular injury. These codes are used only for late effects of cerebrovascular disease, not for neurological deficits associated with an acute CVA.
- Use code V12.54 (transient ischemic attack and cerebral infarction without residual deficits) for a history of cerebrovascular disease when no neurologic deficits are present.

Mechanical Ventilation

- Codes for mechanical ventilation indicate whether the patient was on the ventilator for less than 96 consecutive hours or more than 96 consecutive hours.
- Codes for intubation or tracheostomy should also be assigned.
- It is possible for a patient to be placed back on mechanical ventilation, thus necessitating two codes for mechanical ventilation on the same admission.

Methicillin-Resistant Staphylococcus aureus (MRSA)

- Do not assign 041.12 (MRSA) as an additional code with 038.12 (MRSA Septicemia) or 482.42 (MR pneumonia due to SA) because 038.12 and 482.42 already includes the MRSA and the type of infection.
- To code a current infection due to MRSA when that infection does not have a combination code that includes MRSA, code the infection first, then add code 041.12 (MRSA).
- Use code V02.53 for MSSA (Methicillin-Susceptible *Staphylococcus aureus*) colonization.
- Use code V02.54 for MRSA (Methicillin-Resistant *Staphylococcus aureus*) colonization.
- Use code V02.59 for other types of *Staphylococcus* colonization.

Myocardial Infarction (MI)

- An MI that is documented as acute or with a duration of 8 weeks or less is coded to category 410, Acute MI.
- Fourth digits indicate the area or wall involved.
- Fifth digits indicate whether the encounter is for the initial episode of care (1), for a subsequent episode of care (2), or unspecified (0).
- Fifth digit 1 is used for the initial or first encounter for care after an infarction. It can be used by more than one facility when the patient is transferred from one hospital or another.
- Fifth digit 2 is used when the patient is seen for further care of a previously treated MI (within 8 weeks) or for an unrelated condition.
- When a patient has a second infarction at the time of the encounter for the original infarction, both should be coded.
- Subcategory codes 410.0–410.6 and 410.8 are used for "ST elevation MI" (STEMI).
- Subcategory 410.7 (subendocardial infarction) is used for "non-ST elevation MI" (NSTEMI) and nontransmural MI.
- If only STEMI or transmural MI without the documentation of the site, query the physician.
- If an AMI is documented as transmural or subendocardial, but the site is provided, it is still coded as subendocardial AMI.
- If STEMI converts to an NSTEMI due to thrombolytic therapy, it is still coded as STEMI.

Neoplasms

- Neoplasms are listed in the Alphabetic Index in two ways:
    - The Table of Neoplasms provides code numbers for neoplasms by anatomic site. For each site, there are six possible code numbers according to whether the behavior of the neoplasm is malignant primary, malignant secondary, malignant in situ, benign, of uncertain behavior, or of unspecified nature.
    - Histological terms for neoplasms (e.g., adenoma, adenocarcinoma, and sarcoma) are listed as main terms in the appropriate alphabetic sequence and are usually followed by a cross reference to the neoplasm table.
- Morphology codes (M-codes) identify the histological type of tumor and its behavior (benign, malignant, etc.). M-codes are optional.
- In sequencing neoplasms, when the treatment is directed toward the malignancy, then the malignancy of that site is designated as the principal diagnosis, unless the patient is admitted for one of the reasons listed below.
- When the patient has a primary neoplasm with metastasis and the treatment is directed toward the secondary site only, the secondary site is sequenced as the principal diagnosis.
- When a patient is admitted solely for chemotherapy, immunotherapy, or radiation therapy, a code from category V58 (V58.11, V58.12, or V58.0) is assigned as the principal diagnosis with the malignant neoplasm coded as an additional diagnosis.

- Codes from category V10 are used when the primary neoplasm is totally eradicated and the patient is no longer having treatment and there is no evidence of any existing primary malignancy. Code V10 can only be listed as an additional code, not as a principal diagnosis. If extension, invasion, or metastasis is mentioned, code secondary malignant neoplasm to that site as the principal diagnosis.
- When a patient is admitted for pain management associated with the malignancy, code 338.3 as the principal diagnosis followed by the appropriate code for the malignancy. When a patient is admitted for management of the malignancy, code the malignancy as the principal diagnosis with code 338.3 as an additional code.
- When a patient is admitted for management of an anemia associated with the malignancy, and the treatment is only for anemia, code the anemia code (such as code 285.22) as the principal diagnosis followed by the appropriate code for the malignancy. Code 285.22 can be used as a secondary code if the patient has anemia and is being treated for the malignancy.
- When a patient is admitted for management of dehydration associated with the malignancy or the therapy, or both, and only the dehydration is being treated (intravenous rehydration), the dehydration is sequenced first, followed by the code(s) for the malignancy.
- If the patient is admitted for surgical removal of a neoplasm followed by chemotherapy or radiation therapy, code the neoplasm (primary or secondary) as the principal diagnosis.
- If the patient has anemia associated with chemotherapy, immunotherapy, or radiotherapy and the only treatment is for the anemia, code anemia due to antineoplastic chemotherapy, then code the neoplasm as an additional code.
- If the patient is admitted for chemotherapy, immunotherapy, or radiation therapy and then complications occur (such as uncontrolled nausea and vomiting or dehydration), code V58.11 and V58.12, or V58.0 as the principal diagnosis followed by any codes for the complications.
- If the primary reason for admission is to determine the context of the malignancy or for a procedure, even though chemotherapy or radiotherapy is administered, code the malignancy (primary and secondary site) as the principal diagnosis.
- When a malignant neoplasm is associated with a transplanted organ, code 996.8 (complications of transplanted organ), followed by code 199.2 (malignant neoplasm associated with transplanted organ) followed by a code for the specific malignancy.

Newborn
- Newborn (perinatal) codes (760–779) are never used on the maternal record.
- The perinatal period is defined as before birth through the 28th day following birth.
- A code from categories V30 to V39 is assigned as the principal diagnosis for any live birth.
- The fourth digit indicates whether the birth occurred in the hospital (0) or born before admission to hospital (1) or born outside hospital and not hospitalized (2).
- For live births in the hospital, a fifth digit indicates whether the delivery was with or without mention of c-section.
- Other diagnoses may be coded for significant conditions noted after birth as secondary diagnoses.
- Insignificant or transient conditions that resolve without treatment are not coded.
- Codes are provided to indicate immaturity or prematurity. Fifth digits indicate birth weight. There is no time limit for using these codes. Immaturity and prematurity may continue to be coded, as long as the physician indicates that the birth weight is an issue.
- A code from V29, observation and evaluation of newborns and infants for suspected condition not found, is used when a healthy baby is evaluated for a suspected condition that proves to not exist. These codes are used when the baby exhibits no signs or symptoms.

Obstetrics

- Chapter 11 codes take sequencing precedence over other chapter codes, which may be assigned to provide further specificity as needed.
- The postpartum period begins immediately after delivery and continues for 6 weeks after delivery.
- The peripartum period is defined as the last month of pregnancy to 5 months.
- Codes from Chapter 11 can continue to be used after the 6-week period if the doctor documents that it is pregnancy related.
- When the mother delivers outside the hospital prior to admission and no complications are documented, code V24.0 (postpartum care and examination immediately after delivery) as the principal diagnosis. If there are complications, the complications would be coded instead. Do not code a delivery diagnosis code because she delivered prior to admission.
- Principal diagnosis is determined by the circumstances of the encounter or admission.
- Complications: Any condition that occurs during pregnancy, childbirth, or the puerperium is considered to be a complication unless the physician specifically documents otherwise.
- A code from category V27 is assigned as an additional code to indicate the outcome of delivery on the maternal chart. V27 codes are not to be used on subsequent records or on the newborn record.
- Code 650, normal delivery, is used only when a delivery is perfectly normal and results in a single live birth. No abnormalities of labor or delivery or postpartum conditions can be present; therefore, there can be no additional code from Chapter 11. V27.0, single liveborn, is the only outcome of delivery code appropriate for use with 650.
- V-code categories V22, V23, and V24 are used when no obstetric complications are present and should not be used with any codes from Chapter 11.
- Code 677 is assigned when an initial complication of a pregnancy or delivery develops a residual or sequela at a late date. As with other late-effect codes, the residual is sequenced first followed by code 677.
- When the fetal condition is responsible for modifying the management of the mother (requires diagnostic studies or additional observation, special care, or termination of pregnancy), use codes from categories 655 and 656. The mere fact that the condition exists does not justify assigning a code from categories 655 and 656.
- When in utero surgery is performed on the fetus, assign codes from category 655. No code from Chapter 15 (the perinatal codes) should be used on the mother's record to identify fetal conditions.
- Patients with HIV-related illness during pregnancy, childbirth, or the puerperium should have codes 647.6x and 042.
- Patients with asymptomatic HIV infection status during pregnancy, childbirth, or the puerperium should have codes 647.6x and V08.
- Patients with diabetes during pregnancy, childbirth, or puerperium should have codes 648.0x and category 250 or 249. Also code V58.67 (long-term, current use of insulin), if the diabetes is being treated with insulin.

Open Wounds

- Open wounds are considered complicated when the following conditions are present: delayed healing, delayed treatment, foreign body in wound, or infection.

Pain
- Use a code from category 338 in addition to other codes to provide more detail about whether the pain is acute, chronic, or neoplasm-related pain.
- If pain is not specified as acute or chronic, do not assign a code from category 338 except for postthoracotomy pain, postoperative pain, neoplasm-related pain, or central pain syndrome.
- A code from subcategories 338.1 and 338.2 should not be used if the underlying diagnosis is known unless the primary reason for admission is pain control.
- A code from category 338 can be the principal or first-listed diagnosis code when pain control or management is the reason for the admission or encounter. Code the underlying cause of the pain as an additional diagnosis.
- When a patient is admitted for a procedure for purposes of treating the underlying condition (e.g., spinal fusion), code the underlying condition (e.g., spinal stenosis) as the principal diagnosis. Do not code the pain from category 338.
- When a patient is admitted for the insertion of a neurostimulator for pain control, assign the code for pain as the principal diagnosis.
- If the patient is admitted primarily for a procedure to treat the underlying condition and a neurostimulator is inserted for pain, code the underlying condition as the principal diagnosis, followed by a code for the pain.
- If a code describes the site of the pain, but does not indicate whether the type of pain is acute or chronic (category 338), use two codes (one for the site and one for the type). If the admission is for pain control, assign category code 338 (acute or chronic) as the principal diagnosis. If the admission is not for pain control and a related definitive diagnosis is not documented, assign the code for the specific site of the pain as the principal diagnosis.
- Routine or expected postoperative pain immediately after surgery should not be coded.
- Pain due to devices, implants, or grafts left in a surgical site is coded using a code in Chapter 17 followed by a code from category 338.
- Postoperative pain not associated with a specific postoperative complication is coded using the appropriate code in category 338.
- Postoperative pain associated with a specific postoperative complication is coded using a code in Chapter 17 followed by a code from category 338.
- Postoperative pain can be listed as the principal diagnosis when the reason for admission is pain control.

Pathological Fractures
- Pathological fractures are fractures caused by disease rather than trauma. These may be described as "spontaneous."
- When the term "compression" fracture is used, the coder should review the record for evidence of disease or trauma. If in doubt, query the physician.
- Pathological fractures are coded as 733.1x (with the fifth digit indicating the bone involved) when the fracture is newly diagnosed and the patient is receiving active treatment.
- When the patient is receiving routine care during the healing phase, use aftercare codes (subcategories V54.0, V54.2, V54.8, or V54.9).
Examples of aftercare: cast change, removal of devices, or medication adjustment.

Pleural Effusion
- Pleural effusion is almost always integral to the underlying condition and therefore is usually not coded.
- When the effusion is addressed and treated separately, it can be coded.
- Pleural effusion noted only on an x-ray is not coded.

Pneumonia
- There are many combination codes that describe the pneumonia and the infecting organism.
- In some situations, the pneumonia is a manifestation of an underlying condition. In this situation, two codes are needed—one for the underlying condition and the other for the pneumonia.
- Lobar pneumonia does not refer to the lobe of the lung that is affected. It is a particular type of pneumonia.
- Gram-negative pneumonias are much more difficult to treat than gram-positive pneumonias. If the findings suggest a gram-negative pneumonia, and it is not documented as such, query the physician.
- Signs of gram-negative pneumonia include: worsening of cough, dyspnea, fever, purulent sputum, elevated leukocyte count, and patchy infiltrate on chest x-ray.
- When the physician has documented Ventilator Associated Pneumonia (VAP), use code 997.31. Add an additional code to identify the organism. Do not assign an additional code from categories 480–484 to identify the type of pneumonia. Do not use code 997.31 just because the patient is on a ventilator and has pneumonia. The physician must document that the pneumonia is attributed to the ventilator.

Postoperative Complications
- Physician must document that a condition is a complication of the procedure before assigning a code from 996 to 999.
- "Expected" conditions occur in the immediate post-op period. These are not reported unless they exceed the usual post-op period and meets criteria for reporting as an additional diagnosis.

Pressure Ulcers
- Two codes are required to code pressure ulcers: a code from subcategory 707.0 (pressure ulcer) to identify the site of the pressure ulcer and a code from subcategory 707.2 to identify the stage of the pressure ulcer.
- The code(s) for pressure ulcer stages (707.2) should only be reported as secondary diagnosis and must meet the definition of a reportable additional diagnosis.
- Documentation from clinicians (such as nurses) may be used for code assignment as long as the physician has documented the diagnosis of pressure ulcer.
- If there is any conflicting documentation, query the attending physician.
- Do not use codes from subcategory 707.2 with other types of ulcers (i.e., stasis ulcer).
- Use code 707.25 (pressure ulcer, unstageable) when the stage cannot be clinically documented because:
  - The ulcer is covered by eschar;
  - The ulcer has been treated with a skin or muscle graft;
  - The ulcer is documented as deep tissue injury but not documented as due to trauma.
- Use code 707.20 (pressure ulcer, stage unspecified) when there is no documentation regarding the stages of the pressure ulcer.
- When the patient has bilateral pressure ulcers at the same site (e.g., both buttocks) and both are at the same stage, code one for the site and the other for the stage.
- When the patient has bilateral pressure ulcers at the same site (e.g., both buttocks) and each is at a different stage, code the site and the appropriate codes for the pressure ulcer stages.
- When the patient has multiple pressure ulcers at different sites and each is at different stages, code each of the sites and each of the different stages.
- When the patient has pressure ulcers documented as "healed," no code is assigned.
- When the patient has pressure ulcers documented as "healing," code the site(s) and the stage(s).
- When the patient has a pressure ulcer at one stage at the time of admission, but then it progresses to a higher stage, assign the code for the highest stage.

Procedures
- The UHDDS requires that all significant inpatient procedures be coded.
- A significant procedure is one that is surgical in nature, carries an anesthetic or surgical risk, or requires specialized training.
- The principal procedure is described as the one performed for definitive treatment.
- The operative approach is not coded separately when a definitive procedure has been performed.
- When only a diagnostic procedure is performed such as a biopsy, the operative approach is coded.
- When a laparoscopic, thoracoscopic, or arthroscopic procedure is converted to an open one, only the open procedure is coded. A code from V64.4x is used to describe this situation.
- Closed biopsies are those performed percutaneously by needle, brush, aspiration, or endoscopy.
- An open biopsy generally involves an incision into the body part.
- When a procedure is cancelled after admission, a code from category V64, persons encountering health services for specific procedures not carried out, should be used as an additional code. The principal diagnosis code is still the reason for admission. If the cancellation is due to a complication, the complication should be coded.
- When a planned procedure is begun, but cannot be completed, it is coded to the extent that it was performed. If only an incision is made, code to incision of the site. If an endoscopic approach is used, but the physician is unable to reach the site, code the endoscopy only. If the cavity or space was entered, code to exploration of site.

Pulmonary Edema
- Pulmonary edema can be cardiogenic or noncardiogenic.
- Pulmonary edema is a manifestation of heart failure and, as such, is included in heart failure, hypertension, or rheumatic heart disease. Therefore, it is not coded separately.
- Noncardiogenic acute pulmonary edema occurs in the absence of heart failure or other heart disease.

Rehabilitation
- When a patient is admitted for rehabilitation, code first the V code from category V57 (care involving use of rehabilitation procedures), then code the condition for which the service is being performed.
- Only one code from category V57 is required. If more than one type of rehabilitation occurs, use code V57.89.

Respiratory Failure (Acute)
- Careful review of the medical record is required for the coding and sequencing of acute respiratory failure. If it meets the definition of principal diagnosis, it is coded as such. If it does not, it is coded as a secondary diagnosis.
- When a patient is admitted with acute respiratory failure and another acute condition, the principal diagnosis will depend on the individual patient's condition and the chief (main) reason that caused the admission of the patient to the hospital.

Septicemia
- A diagnosis of bacteremia (790.7) refers to the presence of bacteria in the bloodstream following relatively minor injury or infection.
- Septicemia and sepsis are often used to mean the same thing, but they have two distinct and separate meanings.

- <u>Septicemia</u> is a systemic condition associated with pathogenic microorganisms or toxins in the blood (such as bacteria, viruses, fungi, or other organisms). Most septicemias are classified to category 038. Fourth and fifth digits identify the infecting organism. Additional codes are assigned for any manifestations, if present.
- Negative blood cultures do not preclude a diagnosis of septicemia or sepsis. Query the physician. A code for septicemia is used only when the physician documents a diagnosis of septicemia.
- Urosepsis is assigned to 599.0. The coder should verify with the physician that this is the appropriate code instead of the more serious septicemia. Add a secondary code for the causal organism, if known.
- Systemic Inflammatory Response Syndrome (SIRS) refers to the systemic response to infection, trauma, burns, or other insult (such as cancer) with symptoms (such as fever, tachycardia, tachypnea, and leukocytosis).
- When a patient has SIRS with no subsequent infection, and is a result of a noninfectious disease (such as trauma, cancer, or pancreatitis), code the noninfectious disease first, then code 995.93 or 995.94. If an acute organ dysfunction is documented, code that also.
- Sepsis generally refers to SIRS due to infection.
- Severe sepsis generally refers to sepsis with associated acute organ dysfunction.
- If sepsis or severe sepsis is present on admission and meets the definition of principal diagnosis, the systemic infection code (such as 038.xx or 112.5) should be coded first, followed by code 995.91 sepsis, or 995.92 severe sepsis. Codes from subcategory 995.9 can never be assigned as a principal diagnosis. An additional code should be added for any localized infection, if present.
- If sepsis or severe sepsis develops during admission, the systemic infection code and code 995.91 or 995.92 should be assigned as a secondary diagnosis. If the sepsis or severe sepsis was not confirmed until after admission, but it appears that it may have been present on admission, query the physician.
- Septic shock is defined as sepsis with hypotension, which is a failure of the cardiovascular system. Septic shock is used as an additional code when the underlying infection is present.
- For all cases of septic shock, code the systemic infection first (such as 038.xx or 112.5) followed by codes 995.95 and 785.52. Any additional codes for other acute organ dysfunction should also be assigned.

Substance Abuse
- Substance abuse and dependence are classified as mental disorders in ICD-9-CM.
- Alcohol dependence is classified to category 303, and nondependent alcohol use is coded to category 305.
- Drug dependence is classified to category 304, and nondependent drug use is classified to category 305.
- Both abuse and dependence codes have fifth digits that represent the pattern of abuse as
  - Unspecified (0)
  - Continuous (1)
  - Episodic (2)
  - In remission (3)

  The physician documentation must indicate the pattern of use.
- There are codes for alcohol withdrawal and drug withdrawal symptoms. These codes are used in conjunction with the dependence codes.
- When a patient is admitted in withdrawal or when withdrawal develops after admission, the withdrawal code is principal.
- There are procedure codes for rehabilitation, detoxification, and combination rehabilitation and detoxification for both alcohol and drug dependence.

V-codes

- V-codes are not procedure codes.
- There are V-codes to indicate contact with an exposure to communicable diseases (V01), asbestos, body fluids, and lead (V15.84–V15.86) and metals, chemicals, or compounds (V87.0–V87.3).
- There are V-codes for encounters for inoculations and vaccinations (V03–V06).
- There are "status" V-codes to reflect that this status may affect the patient's course of treatment or outcome. This is different from a "history" code that indicates that the patient no longer has the condition.
- Some V-codes can only be principal diagnosis/first-listed codes, some may only be additional codes, and others may be principal/first-listed or additional.
- Aftercare V-codes (V51–V58) are used when the initial treatment of the disease or injury has ended, but the patient requires continued care.
- A code from V67 is used as the reason for encounter when a patient is admitted for follow-up or surveillance purposes after treatment for a disease or injury.
- There are V-codes to indicate a personal or family history of various conditions.
- When a condition is still present or still under treatment, the personal history code should not be reported.
- Category V09 is used to identify infections that are resistant to the various medications. It is always coded in addition to the code for the infection.
- A code from category V71, observation and evaluation for suspected conditions not found, is assigned when a patient is admitted or has an encounter for workup for a suspected condition when there are no signs or symptoms present.
- Special main terms for V-codes in the Alphabetic Index of Diseases include:

Abnormal	Foreign Body
Admission	Healthy
Aftercare	History (family)
Anomaly	History (personal)
Attention to	Maintenance
Boarder	Maladjustment
Care of	Observation
Carrier	Problem with
Checking	Procedure (surgical)
Complication	Prophylactic
Contraception	Replacement
Counseling	Screening
Delivery	Status
Dialysis	Supervision (of)
Donor	Test
Examination	Transplant
Exposure to	Unavailability of medical facilities
Fitting of	Vaccination
Follow-up	

Sample 10-Step Inpatient ICD-9-CM Coding Process

1. **Locate Patient's Gender, Age, and Discharge Date.**

2. **Locate Discharge Status (Disposition). Some examples include:**
   - **01:** Home
   - **02:** Short-term hospital
   - **03:** Skilled nursing facility
   - **04:** Facility providing custodial or supportive care
   - **05:** Cancer or child hospital
   - **06:** Home health services
   - **07:** Against medical advice
   - **20:** Expired
   - **30:** Still a patient
   - **61:** Swing bed
   - **62:** Inpatient rehab facility or distinct rehab unit
   - **63:** Long-term care hospital
   - **65:** Psychiatric hospital or distinct psych unit
   - **66:** Critical access hospital

3. **List consultants** as you go through the consults.
   Write down pertinent diagnoses (histories and present illnesses).

4. **Locate and list all procedures.**
   Review description of each procedure performed.

5. **Go through the physician orders and medication administration orders.**
   This is where you will find drugs ordered and administered. Make sure that you look for the diagnosis that corresponds with each medication. If not, query the physician.

6. **Read the H&P, ER record, and progress notes.**
   Write down all diagnoses that meet criteria for principal and secondary diagnosis:
   If a diagnosis is ruled out, just cross it off the list.

7. **Select the Principal Diagnosis.**
   UHDDS Definition: The condition established *after study* to be chiefly responsible for occasioning the admission of the patient to the hospital for care.

Sample 10-Step Inpatient ICD-9-CM Coding Process (continued)

8. **Select Other Diagnoses and indicate whether each was present on admission (POA) or not. Up to 17 secondary diagnoses may be included on the UB-04.**

   UHDDS Definition: All conditions that coexist at the time of admission, develop subsequently, or affect the treatment received and/or the length of stay. Diagnoses that relate to an earlier episode of care that have no bearing on the current hospital stay are to be excluded.
   Complication UHDDS Definition: A condition arising during hospitalization, which increases the patient's length of stay by 1 day in 75% of cases.
   Comorbidity UHDDS Definition: Condition present at admission, in addition to the principal diagnosis, which increases the patient's length of stay by 1 day in 75% of cases.

   For reporting purposes the definition of "other diagnoses" is interpreted as additional conditions that affect patient care in terms of requiring
   - clinical evaluation
   - therapeutic treatment
   - diagnostic procedures
   - extended length of hospital stay
   - increased nursing care and/or monitoring

9. **Principal Procedure.**

   UHDDS Definition: One performed for definitive treatment (rather than performed for diagnostic or exploratory purposes) or one that was necessary to care for a complication. If two or more procedures appear to meet the definition, then the one most closely related to the principal diagnosis should be selected as the principal procedure.

10. **Other Procedures—up to five may be included on the UB-04.**

    UHDDS Definition for significant procedures: One that meets any of the following conditions: is surgical in nature, carries an anesthetic risk, carries a procedural risk, or requires specialized training.

ICD-9-CM Coding for Outpatient Diagnostic Tests

The following are instructions to determine the use of ICD-9-CM codes for coding diagnostic test results. Note that physicians are responsible for the accuracy of the information submitted on a bill.

A. Determining the Appropriate first listed ICD-9-CM Diagnosis Code for Diagnostic Tests Ordered Due to Signs and/or Symptoms

1. If the physician has confirmed a diagnosis based on the results of the diagnostic test, the physician interpreting the test should code that diagnosis. The signs and/or symptoms that prompted the order for the test may be reported as additional diagnoses if they are not fully explained or related to the confirmed diagnosis.

2. If the diagnostic test did not provide a diagnosis or was normal, the interpreting physician should code the sign(s) or symptom(s) that prompted the treating physician to order the study.

3. If the results of the diagnostic test are normal or nondiagnostic, and the referring physician records a diagnosis preceded by words that indicate the uncertainty (e.g., probable, suspected, questionable, rule out, or working), then the interpreting physician should not code the referring diagnosis. Rather, the interpreting physician should report the sign(s) or symptom(s) that prompted the study. Diagnoses labeled as uncertain are considered by the ICD-9-CM Coding Guidelines as unconfirmed and should not be reported. This is consistent with the requirement to code the diagnosis to the highest degree of certainty.

B. Instructions to Determine the Reason for the Test: The referring physicians are required to provide diagnostic information to the testing entity at the time the test is ordered. All diagnostic tests "must be ordered by the physician who is treating the beneficiary." An order by the physician may include the following forms of communication:

1. A written document signed by the treating physician/practitioner, which is hand delivered, mailed, or faxed to the testing facility.

2. A telephone call by the treating physician/practitioner or his or her office to the testing facility.

3. An electronic mail by the treating physician or practitioner or his or her office to the testing facility.

Note: Telephone orders must be documented by both the treating physician or practitioner office and the testing facility.

If the interpreting physician does not have diagnostic information as to the reason for the test, and the referring physician is unavailable, it is appropriate to obtain the information directly from the patient or patient's medical record. Attempt to confirm any information obtained from the patient by contacting the referring physician.

C. Incidental Findings: Incidental findings should never be listed as first listed diagnoses. They may be reported as secondary diagnoses by the physician interpreting the diagnostic test.

D. Unrelated/Coexisting Conditions/Diagnoses: Unrelated and coexisting conditions/diagnoses may be reported as additional diagnoses by the physician interpreting the diagnostic test.

E. Diagnostic Tests Ordered in the Absence of Signs and/or Symptoms (e.g., screening tests): When a diagnostic test is ordered in the absence of signs/symptoms or other evidence of illness or injury, the physician interpreting the diagnostic test should report the reason for the test (e.g., screening) as the first listed ICD-9-CM diagnosis code. The results of the test, if reported, may be recorded as additional diagnoses.

F. Use of ICD-9-CM to the Greatest Degree of Accuracy and Completeness: Code the ICD-9-CM code that provides the highest degree of accuracy and completeness for the diagnosis resulting from the test or for the sign(s)/symptom(s) that prompted the ordering of the test.

Resource: CMS Publication 60AB, Transmittal AB-01-144. Date: September 26, 2001.

Tips for Outpatient ICD-9-CM Coding.

ICD-9-CM Outpatient/Ambulatory Coding Guidelines

Note: This is a brief overview. ICD-9-CM codes are used for diagnoses. CPT codes are used for procedures for billing purposes.

1. Documentation should include specific diagnoses as well as symptoms, problems, and reasons for visits.

2. Codes from 001.0 to V89 must be provided to identify the reason for encounter/visit.

3. Codes from 001.0 to 999.9 identify diseases and injuries and are most frequently used.

4. Signs and symptoms may be coded if no diagnosis is made.

5. Codes from V01.0 to V89 are used for reasons for encounters other than for a disease or injury.

6. Fourth and fifth digits must be assigned where available. If not, the code is considered invalid.

7. First-listed diagnosis is listed first with other codes following.

8. Qualified diagnoses should not be coded (such as "suspected"). Instead code the signs and symptoms.

9. Chronic diseases may be coded as long as the patient receives treatment.

10. Code all documented conditions that coexist at the time of the visit and are treated or affect treatment. History codes may be used if they impact treatment.

11. Diagnosis coding for Diagnostic Services: Code the diagnosis chiefly responsible for the service. Secondary codes may follow.

12. Diagnosis coding for Therapeutic Services: Code the diagnosis chiefly responsible for the service. Secondary codes may follow.

13. Exception to 12: For chemotherapy, radiation therapy, and rehabilitation, the V-code for the service is listed first and the diagnosis chiefly responsible for the service is listed second.

14. Diagnosis coding for Preoperative Evaluations: Sequence first a code from V72.8x. Then assign a code for the condition that is the reason for surgery. Code also any resulting findings.

15. Diagnosis coding for Ambulatory Surgery: Code the diagnosis for which surgery was done. Use the postoperative diagnosis if it is available and more specific.

Sample 10-Step Outpatient ICD-9-CM Coding Process:

Never code only from the index. Always consult the Tabular List.

Coding must accurately reflect provider's diagnostic statement as well as coding rules.

General Conventions are summarized earlier in this chapter.

Indentations are used for all subterms below the term to which they apply.

Caution is advised in following the several levels of indentations of subterms.

---

1. **Main Terms** (conditions) are boldface type and are followed by the code number.

   Qualified Diagnosis is a working diagnosis that is not yet proven or established. Do not code diagnoses with terms such as *suspected, rule out, ruled out, possible, probably, questionable*, etc. Code the sign(s) and/or symptom(s) that are documented.

   Special Main Terms should be reviewed and considered. See list in text.
   See Condition indicates a descriptive term was looked up rather than the condition.
   See directs the coder to a more specific term.
   See Also refers to an index entry that may provide additional information.

---

2. **(Nonessential Modifiers) do not have to be included in the diagnostic statement.** These subterms clarify or qualify the main term and are enclosed in parentheses.

---

3. **Essential Modifiers/Subterms that MUST BE included in the diagnostic statement** are indented below the main term in alphabetic order (except "with" and "without"). They clarify the main term listing alternative sites, etiology, or clinical status.

---

4. **Select Preliminary Code** before turning to the Tabular List.

---

5. **Locate Preliminary Code** number and review the code descriptions.
   See Category refers to the Tabular List category (three-digit code).

---

6. **Includes Notes** appears with three-digit categories and further defines or adds clarification.
   Excludes Notes directs the coder to another location for proper code assignment.
   Return to the Index of Diseases for other possible code selections if the code description in the Tabular List does not appear to fit the condition or reason for visit.
   NEC or "not elsewhere classified" identifies codes to be assigned when information needed to assign a more specific code cannot be located in the code book.
   NOS or "not otherwise specified" indicates that the code lacks specificity and the provider should be asked for a more specific diagnosis before assigning a code.

---

7. **Assign Fourth or Fifth Digit** if one is available. Instructional notes about additional digits are found below the category or subcategory description.

---

8. **Use Additional Code** indicates a second code is required to add necessary detail.

---

9. **First-Listed Diagnosis** is the most significant condition for which services and/or procedures were provided and is sequenced first.
   Secondary Diagnosis coexists with the first-listed diagnosis, has the potential to affect treatment of the primary condition, and is a condition being actively managed.
   Code First Underlying Condition indicates the code is to be sequenced as a secondary code. The code, title, and instructions are italicized.

---

10. **Record Final Code(s).**

OUTPATIENT PROCEDURE CODING REVIEW

CMS (Centers for Medicare and Medicaid Services, formerly HCFA, Health Care Financing Administration) administers Medicare and Medicaid.

HCPCS (Healthcare Common Procedure Coding System)
- A coding system describing the physician and nonphysician patient services covered by the government's Medicare and Medicaid programs.
- Designed by CMS and used primarily to report reimbursable services rendered to the patient.
- Consists of two levels of HCPCS codes for ambulatory (outpatient) patients.

LEVEL I—CPT (Current Procedural Terminology) is a coding system developed by the American Medical Association (AMA) to convert descriptions of medical, surgical, and diagnostic services rendered by health care providers into five-digit numerical codes. The codes are updated annually by AMA.

The CPT coding system:
- provides uniform language to accurately designate medical, surgical, and diagnostic services.
- provides effective means of reliable, nationwide communication between physicians, patients, and third-party payers.
- allows for ability to compare reimbursements for procedures.

Justification for listing of a procedure:
- The procedure is commonly performed by physicians nationally.
- The procedure must be consistent with modern medical practice.

LEVEL II—National Codes
- Updated annually by CMS
- Five-digit alphanumeric codes

Rules for Coding CPT

1. Determine the service provided by analyzing the statement provided by the physician.
2. Identify the main term(s) in the Alphabetic Index.

   To locate a code in the index, the coder should first look up the procedure or service provided. If the procedure is not listed, look under the anatomic site involved, the condition, the synonym, or the eponym. Follow the guidance of the index in locating the code most accurately describing the service.
3. Write down or note the code number(s) found for the term.
   - If a single code number is given, locate the code in the body of the CPT book. Verify the code and its description against the statement, ensuring they match.
   - If two or more codes separated by a comma are given, locate each code in the body of the CPT book. Read the description of each and select the appropriate code matching the statement.
   - If a range of codes is given, locate the range of codes in the body of the CPT book. Review the description of each entry prior to selecting a code.
4. NEVER code from the Alphabetic Index; look up the codes to verify accuracy.
5. Read all notes that apply to the code selected.

   Notes may appear at the beginning of a section, subsection, before or after a code, or within the code description. Notes are utilized throughout the CPT, requiring special attention and review by the coder. Some of these notes define terms, such as *simple, intermediate,* and *complex wound repair.* Other notes provide specific coding instruction applicable to specific codes.
6. Select the appropriate modifier, if applicable, to complete the code description.
7. Code multiple procedures from highest resource intensive to lowest (most complicated to least complicated).

Common Errors That Prevent Payment to Physicians

1. No documentation or incomplete documentation for services billed
2. Missing signatures
3. Consistently assigning the same level of services
4. Billing of a consult instead of an office visit
5. Using invalid codes in the bill due to use of old coding resources or forms
6. Unbundling procedure codes
7. Not listing the chief complaint
8. Abbreviations that are misinterpreted
9. Billing of services included in global fee as a separate professional fee
10. Not using a modifier or use of an inappropriate modifier for accurate payment of a claim

CPT Code Book Format Information

Guidelines provide specific instructions about coding for each section. The guidelines contain definitions of terms, explanations of notes, subsection information, unlisted services, and special reports information.

Sections: There are eight major areas into which all CPT codes and descriptions are categorized. The majority of CPT codes are arranged in numerical order in each section. The first six sections are comprised of five-digit numerical codes. The codes in the last two sections, Category II and Category III Codes, are comprised of five-digit codes—four numbers and a letter.

> Evaluation and Management
> Anesthesia
> Surgery
> Radiology
> Pathology/Laboratory
> Medicine
> Category II Codes
> Category III Codes

Category II Codes are optional tracking codes used to measure performance.

Category III Codes are temporary codes for emerging technology, services, and procedures. These codes can be used for data collection purposes or possibly in the FDA approval process. If a Category III code is available, this code must be reported instead of a Category I unlisted code.

Subsections, subcategories, and headings divide the sections into smaller units, based on anatomy, procedure, condition, description, or approach.

Symbols used in CPT coding: The following symbols are special guides that help the coder compare codes and descriptors with the previous year's CPT edition, or that provide additional coding guidance.

- Bullet is used to indicate a new procedure or service code added since the previous edition of the CPT manual.

▲ Triangle indicates that the code has been changed or modified since the last CPT manual edition.

+ A plus sign is used to indicate an add-on code.

⊘ Null symbol is used to identify a modifier -51 exempt code.

►◄ A right and left triangle indicates the beginning and end of the text changes.

⊙ A circled bullet indicates the code includes moderate sedation.

↻ Reference to CPT Assistant, Clinical Examples in Radiology, and CPT Changes

\# The number sign is used to identify codes that have been resequenced and are not placed numerically.

○ Indicates a reinstated/recycled code.

Modifiers: Two-character codes added to CPT codes to supply more specific information about the services provided.

Special reports: Detailed reports that include adequate definitions or descriptions of the nature, extent, and need for the procedure, and the time, effort, and equipment necessary to provide the service.

Unlisted procedures: Procedures that are considered unusual, experimental, or new and do not have a specific code number assigned. Unlisted procedure codes are located at the end of the subcategories, or headings, and may be used to identify any procedure that lacks a specific code and require a "special report" submitted at the time of billing.

CPT Index: Located at the back of the CPT manual and arranged alphabetically. To locate terms in the alphabetic index, look under the

Service/procedure

Anatomic site/body organ

Condition/disease/problem

Synonym

Eponym (procedure named after someone)

Abbreviation or acronym (e.g., CBC)

Notations:

"see" sends you to a more appropriate section.

"see also" cross-reference to refer to another main term.

CPT Appendices in back section of the CPT manual:

Appendix A: Lists all modifiers with complete explanations for use

Appendix B: Contains a complete list of additions to, deletions from, and revisions of the previous year's edition

Appendix C: Provides clinical examples of Evaluation and Management (E&M) codes

Appendix D: Contains a listing of the CPT add-on codes

Appendix E: Contains a list of modifier-51 exempt codes

Appendix F: Contains a list of modifier-63 exempt codes

Appendix G: Summary of CPT codes that include moderate (conscious) sedation

Appendix I: Genetic testing code modifiers

Appendix J: Electrodiagnostic medicine listing of sensory, motor, and mixed nerves

Appendix K: Product pending FDA approval

Appendix L: Vascular families

Appendix M: Crosswalk to deleted CPT codes

Appendix N: Summary of resequenced CPT codes

Appendix O: Multianalyte Assays with Algorithmic Analyses

General E&M Coding Guidelines

1. Determine place of service: office, emergency room, or nursing home.

2. Determine type of service: consult, admission, newborn.

3. Determine patient status: new unless seen in last 3 years by the physician or another physician of the same specialty in the same group.

4. Determine the level of each of the three key components:
   A. **History:** problem focused, expanded problem focused, detailed, comprehensive
   B. **Physical examination:** problem focused, expanded problem focused, detailed, comprehensive
   C. **Medical decision making:** straightforward, low, moderate, high
      - New patients, consultations, emergency department services, and initial care: generally require all three key components.
      - Established patients and subsequent care: usually require two of the three key components.
      - Some codes are based on time: critical care, prolonged services.

5. Read Critical Care guidelines carefully. Watch for the procedures that are included in the codes.

6. Read Inpatient Neonatal and Pediatric Critical Care Services and intensive (noncritical) low birth weight services guidelines carefully. Watch for procedures that are inclusive in this area.

7. Be sure to read the coding guidelines for E&M coding carefully.

8. Review definition for "consultations" and determine when consult codes are more appropriate than office visit codes.

9. There are specific codes used for hospital observation services (initial care, subsequent care, and discharge services) and codes for same-day admissions and discharges.

10. When a patient is admitted as an inpatient on the same day that services are provided at another site (office, ER, observation, etc.), only the inpatient services are reported. The E&M services provided in these outpatient settings can be used to determine the level of inpatient services provided.

11. Preventive Care codes are based on the patient's age.

Some Additional Areas of Interest When Coding with CPT

Abortion

"**Incomplete Abortions**" **and** "**Miscarriages**" are alternate terms for missed and spontaneous abortions.

Spontaneous abortion that occurs during any trimester and is completed surgically, assign 59812.

Missed abortion that occurs during the first trimester, assign 59820.

Induced abortion, which combines curettage and evacuation, assign 59851.

Induced abortion by dilation and evacuation, code 59841.

Induced abortion by dilation and curettage, code 59840. Code 58120 is used for a nonobstetrical D&C.

Angioplasty

Determination of the site and whether it is open or percutaneous.

Open transluminal angioplasty of renal or other visceral arteries, aortic, brachiocephalic, or venous sites code from 35450 to 35460.

Percutaneous transluminal angioplasty of renal or other visceral arteries, aortic, brachiocephalic, or venous sites code from 35471 to 35476.

Endovascular revascularization (open or percutaneous, transcatheter) of lower extremities code from 37220 to 37235.

PTCA: Percutaneous transluminal coronary angioplasty: assign code appropriately from 92920 and 92921.

Codes 92928 and 92929 for stent placement include the PTCA and thus the PTCA is not coded separately.

Appendectomy

There are several codes that are used to describe appendectomies: open surgical appendectomy (including incidental), laparoscopic appendectomy, appendectomy done for a ruptured appendix, and appendectomy done for a specified purpose at the time of other major surgery.

Auditory

Simple mastoidectomy also called a transmastoid antrotomy (69501).

Apicetomy is the excision of the tip of the petrous bone. This is often performed with a radical mastoidectomy (69530). It would be inappropriate to code 69511 in addition.

Tympanostomy (requiring insertion of ventilating tube). Code 69436, Tympanostomy (requiring insertion of ventilating tube) general anesthesia, and 69433, Tympanostomy (requiring insertion of ventilating tube), local or topic anesthesia, are used for "insertion of tubes."

Removal of impacted cerumen from one or both ears, use code 69210.

Some Additional Areas of Interest When Coding with CPT (continued)

Bronchoscopy and Biopsy

Surgical bronchoscopy includes a diagnostic bronchoscopy.

Code appropriate endoscopy for each anatomic site examined.

Endobronchial biopsy, code 31625.

Review for types of specimen collection:

- **Biopsy** forceps used to remove tissue
- **Bronchial brush** used to obtain surface cells
- **Bronchial alveolar lavage (BAL)** used to collect cells from peripheral lung tissue
- **Cell washings** used to exfoliate cells from crevices

   Note: Cell washings or brushings are NOT biopsies.

Transbronchial biopsy is performed by positioning the scope in the bronchus nearest to the lesion. A hole is punctured through the bronchus into the lung tissue where the lesion is located. The lesion is then biopsied. Transbronchial lung biopsy is reported with code 31628.

Transbronchial needle aspiration biopsy (31629).

Catheter aspiration of tracheobronchial tree at bedside (31725).

CABG

To report combined arterial-venous grafts, it is necessary to report two codes:

1. The appropriate combined arterial-venous graft code (33517–33523)
2. The appropriate arterial graft code (33533–33536)

Procurement of the saphenous vein graft is included in the description of the work for 33517–33523 and is not reported separately.

Procurement of an upper extremity artery is reported separately.

Casting and Strapping

Services in the musculoskeletal system include the application or removal of the first cast or traction device only. Subsequent replacement of casts, traction devices, or removals is reported using codes from the 29000–29750 series of codes.

The codes in the 29000–29750 series of codes have very specific guidelines directing the use of the codes.

Endoscopy

Codes specify the purpose and site of application.

Dx endoscopy is coded only if a surgical procedure was not done. Surgical endoscopy always includes a diagnostic endoscopy.

Code as far as the scope is passed.

Stomach endoscopy is included with UGI endoscopy, not separately.

Multiple codes may be necessary to cover one endoscopic episode.

Removal of gastrostomy tube by endoscopy, code 43247.

Colonoscopy: first determine the route the procedure follows (via colostomy, colotomy, or rectum).

Colonoscopy with dilation of rectum or anorectum, code 45999.

Biliary endoscopy (47550) is only used with 47420 or 47610.

EGDs are coded to 43235–43259.

Some Additional Areas of Interest When Coding with CPT (continued)

Eye and Ocular

Preliminary iridectomy is not coded separately if performed as part of a cataract extraction or prior to lens extraction. It is included in the code for the lens extraction.

Two types of cataract extraction:

- ICCE: Intracapsular cataract extraction
- ECCE: Extracapsular cataract extraction

Do not code medication injections used in conjunction with cataract surgery. Injections are considered part of the procedure.

Cataract removal includes the following in codes 66830–66984.

DO NOT CODE THE FOLLOWING PROCEDURES SEPARATELY: anterior capsulotomy, enzymatic zonulysis, iridectomy, iridotomy, lateral canthotomy, pharmacological agents, posterior capsulotomy, viscoelastic agents, subconjunctival, and subtendon injections.

Female Genital System

Codes 57452–57461 are used to report various cervical colposcopic procedures.

Code 57455 describes colposcopy with single or multiple biopsies of the cervix.

Code 58150 describes total abdominal hysterectomy with or without removal of tube(s) or ovary(s).

Code 58611 is an add-on code that describes tubal ligation or transection when done at the time of cesarean delivery or intra-abdominal surgery.

Fractures/Dislocations

- Treatment of fractures/dislocations can be open or closed.
- Closed treatment means that the fracture or dislocation site is not surgically opened. It is used to describe procedures that treat fractures by three methods: without manipulation, with manipulation, and with or without traction.
- Open treatment implies that the fracture is surgically opened and the fracture is visualized to allow treatment.
- Skeletal fixation is neither open nor closed treatment. Usually pins are placed across the fracture using x-ray guidance.
- Manipulation is used to indicate the attempted reduction or restoration of a fracture or dislocation.

Genitourinary

Many of the procedures in the urinary system are performed endoscopically—cystoscopy, urethroscopy, cystourethroscopy, ureteroscopy, pyeloscopy, and renal endoscopy.

Most cystourethroscopy codes are unilateral. When a cysto is performed bilaterally modifier –50 should be appended.

Codes in the 52320–52355 series include the insertion and removal of a temporary stent during diagnostic or therapeutic cystourethroscopic intervention(s).

Cystourethroscopy with removal of a self-retaining/indwelling ureteral stent, planned or staged during the associated normal postoperative follow-up period of the original procedure, is reported by means of code 52310 or 52315 with the modifier –58 appended as appropriate.

Be careful to differentiate between codes for ureteral and urethral procedures.

Some Additional Areas of Interest When Coding with CPT (continued)

GI Biopsy

Code only the biopsy if a single lesion is biopsied but not excised.

Code only the biopsy and list only one time if multiple biopsies are done (from the same or different lesions) and none of the lesions are excised.

Code only the excision if a biopsy of a lesion is taken and the balance of the same lesion is then excised.

Code both the biopsy and the excision if both are performed and if the biopsy is taken from a lesion different from that which is excised, and the code for the excision does not include the phrase "with or without biopsy." If such a phrase is in the code narration, then a separate biopsy code should not be used.

Surgical endoscopy always includes a diagnostic endoscopy.

Modifier -59 may be used to explain unusual circumstances when coding both biopsy and removal of a different lesion.

Hernia Repair

- Hernia repair codes are categorized by type (inguinal, femoral, etc.).
- Hernias are further categorized as "initial" or "recurrent" based on whether or not the hernia has required previous repair.
- Age and clinical presentation (reducible versus strangulated).
- Code 49568 is used only with nonlaparscopic incisional or ventral hernia repairs.

Immunizations

Codes 90460–90474 are used to report the administration of vaccines/toxoids.

Codes 90476–90749 identify the vaccine PRODUCT alone.

If a combination vaccine code is provided (MMR) it is not appropriate to report each component of the combination vaccine separately.

When the physician provides face-to-face counseling of the patient and family during the administration of a vaccine, report codes 90460–90461.

Do not append modifier -51 to the vaccine/toxoid product codes 90476–90749.

Integumentary

Three types of repairs: Add lengths of repairs together and use one code for repairs of the same location and same type.

- **Simple:** Superficial wound involving skin and/or subcutaneous tissues and requiring simple suturing.
- **Intermediate:** Involving skin, subcutaneous tissues, and fascia and requiring layer closure. May also be used when a single closure requires intensive cleaning.
- **Complex** repairs requiring reconstructive surgery or time-consuming or complicated closures.

Debridement is coded separately: When gross contamination requires cleaning, when appreciable amounts of devitalized or contaminated tissue are removed, and when debridement is carried out separately without primary closure.

Lesion size is best found on the operative report.

Benign or malignant lesion(s): Code each lesion excised separately; simple closure after excision of lesion(s) is included in the code.

Adjacent tissue transfers include excision of tissues, including lesions.

Some Additional Areas of Interest When Coding with CPT (continued)

Integumentary (continued)

Free skin grafts: Identify by size and location of the defect (recipient area) and the type of graft; includes simple debridement of granulations or recent avulsion.

There are three code ranges:

- Use 15002–15005 for initial wound preparation.
- Use 15040–15261 for autografts and tissue-cultured autografts.
- Use 15271–15278 for skin substitute grafts (homografts, allografts, and xenografts).

Repair of donor site requiring skin graft or local flaps is to be added on as an additional procedure.

Report excision of lesion(s) separately.

Excisional biopsy is used when the entire lesion, whether benign or malignant, is removed.

Breast lesion excisions performed after being identified by pre-op radiological marker (localization wires), use codes 19125 and 19126.

Placement of needle localization wires prior to biopsies, excisions, and other breast procedures, use additional codes 19290 and 19291.

Laryngoscopy

Many of the codes used to report laryngoscopies include the use of an operating microscope. Therefore, code 69990, microsurgical techniques, requiring the use of operating microscope (list separately in addition to code primary procedure), would not be used with any codes that include the use of the microscope.

Maternity Care and Delivery

Antepartum care or services provided above the normally expected care (as defined in the CPT book) should be coded separately.

Medical problems complicating labor and delivery management may require additional resources and should be identified by using E&M codes in addition to the codes for maternity care.

For surgical complications of pregnancy, see services in the surgery section.

If a physician provides all or part of the antepartum and/or postpartum patient care, but does not perform delivery due to termination of pregnancy by abortion or referral to another physician for delivery, see the antepartum and postpartum care codes 59425–59426 and 59430.

Patients who have had previous cesarean delivery and now present with the expectation of a vaginal delivery are coded using codes 59610–59622. If the patient has a successful vaginal delivery after a previous cesarean delivery (VBAC), use codes 59610–59614. If the attempt is unsuccessful and another cesarean delivery is carried out, use codes 59618–59622.

Nasal Hemorrhage

Was it anterior or posterior?

- If anterior, was the hemorrhage simple or complex?
- If posterior, was the control of hemorrhage an initial or subsequent procedure?

Anterior nasal hemorrhage has likely occurred if the physician inserts gauze packing or anterior packing or performs cauterization.

Posterior nasal hemorrhage has likely occurred if the physician inserts nasal stents, tampons, balloon catheters, or posterior packing, or if the patient is taken to the OR for ligation of arteries to control bleeding.

Nosebleed subsequent to initial one (30906).

Some Additional Areas of Interest When Coding with CPT (continued)

Neurology/Spine Surgery

The spinal and spinal cord injection codes reflect the specific spinal anatomy, such as subarachnoid or epidural; the level of the injection (cervical, thoracic, lumbar, or sacral); and the types of substances injected, such as anesthetic steroids, antispasmodics, phenol, etc.

Injection of contrast material during fluoroscopic guidance is included in codes 62263–62264, 62267, 62270–62273, 62280–62282, and 62310–62319. The fluoroscopic guidance itself is reported by code 77003. Code 62263 describes treatment involving injections of various substances over a multiple-day period. Code 62263 is not reported for each individual injection but is reported once to describe the entire series of injections or infusions.

Code 62264 describes multiple treatments performed on the same day.

Other codes in this section refer to laminectomies, excisions, repairs, and shunts. A basic distinction among the codes is the condition, such as herniated disk, as well as the approach used, such as anterior or posterior or costovertebral.

Lumbar punctures (62270) are also called spinal taps and are used to obtain cerebrospinal fluid by inserting a needle into the subarachnoid space in the lumbar area.

When coding surgery on the spine, there are many sets of guidelines for the coder to review, including those at the beginning of the subsection as well as throughout the subsection.

Co-surgery is common in spinal surgeries. When two surgeons work together, both as primary surgeons, each surgeon should report his or her distinct operative work by adding modifier -62 to the procedure code and any associated add-on codes for that procedure as long as both surgeons continue to work together as primary surgeons.

Spinal instrumentation is used to stabilize the spinal column during repair procedures. There are two types: segmental and nonsegmental.

- Segmental instrumentation involves attachment at each end of the spinal area and at least one intermittent fixation.
- Nonsegmental instrumentation involves attachment at each end and may span several vertebral segments without intermittent fixation.

Pacemakers

1. Is it permanent or temporary?
2. What was the approach (transvenous or epicardial)?
3. What type of device (electrodes and/or pulse generator)?
4. Where were the electrodes placed (atrial, ventricle, or both)?
5. Is this an insertion of a new or replacement permanent pacemaker? Insertion or replacement of a temporary pacemaker? Repair of electrodes? Removal of a pacemaker? Repositioning?
6. Was revision of the skin pocket done?

Sentinel Nodes

Sentinel node procedures utilize injection of a radiotracer or blue dye. After absorption of dye, the physician can visualize the node(s). Code 38792 is used for identification of sentinel nodes. For excision of sentinel nodes, see 38500–38542.

Use appropriate lymph node excision codes to report the excision.

A second sentinel node from a different lymphatic chain excised from a separate incision, report the excision and add modifier -59.

Lymphoscintigraphy, code 78195.

Injection for gamma probe node detection with imaging code 38790.

Some Additional Areas of Interest When Coding with CPT (continued)

Thyroid

Recall that **the thyroid has two lobes**, one on each side of the trachea. The procedure may only be unilateral (60220), but it is still considered to be a total lobectomy.

Thyroidectomy may be

- Total or complete (60240), removing both the lobes and the isthmus. It is not necessary to list the code twice.
- Partial lobectomy (60210), unilateral, with or without isthmusectomy.

Thyroidectomy with neck dissection (60252 and 60254). Do not assign these codes if an isolated lymph node is excised or biopsied.

Tonsillectomy and Adenoidectomy

Separate codes describe tonsillectomy and adenoidectomy; tonsillectomy alone, whether primary or secondary; adenoidectomy alone, primary; adenoidectomy alone, secondary.

Separate codes are reported for procedures performed on patients under age 12, and age 12 or older.

A primary procedure is one in which no prior tonsillectomy or adenoidectomy has been performed. A secondary procedure is one that is performed to remove residual or regrowth of tonsil or adenoid tissue.

Wound Exploration

Wound exploration codes (20100–20103) are used when repair of a penetrating wound requires enlargement of the existing defect for exploration, cleaning, and repair.

If the wound does not need to be enlarged, then only repair codes from the integumentary section are used.

III. Health Data Content and Standards

Debra W. Cook, MAEd., RHIA

1. In preparation for an EHR, you are working with a team conducting a total facility inventory of all forms currently used. You must name each form for bar coding and indexing into a document management system. The unnamed document in front of you includes a microscopic description of tissue excised during surgery. The document type you are most likely to give to this form is
    A. recovery room record.
    B. pathology report.
    C. operative report.
    D. discharge summary.

REFERENCE: Abdelhak, p 114
               Green and Bowie, pp 167
               LaTour, Eichenwald-Maki, and Oachs, pp A32–A33
               Sayles, p 88

2. Patient data collection requirements vary according to health care setting. A data element you would expect to be collected in the MDS but NOT in the UHDDS would be
    A. personal identification.
    B. cognitive patterns.
    C. procedures and dates.
    D. principal diagnosis.

REFERENCE: Abdelhak, pp 137–138, 141
               LaTour, Eichenwald-Maki, and Oachs, p 30
               Sayles, pp 147, 152

3. In the past, Joint Commission standards have focused on promoting the use of a facility-approved abbreviation list to be used by hospital care providers. With the advent of the Commission's national patient safety goals, the focus has shifted to the
    A. prohibited use of any abbreviations.
    B. flagrant use of specialty-specific abbreviations.
    C. use of prohibited or "dangerous" abbreviations.
    D. use of abbreviations used in the final diagnosis.

REFERENCE: Abdelhak, p 117
               LaTour, Eichenwald-Maki, and Oachs, pp 251, 264, 672

4. A risk manager needs to locate a full report of a patient's fall from his bed, including witness reports and probable reasons for the fall. She would most likely find this information in the
    A. doctors' progress notes.
    B. integrated progress notes.
    C. incident report.
    D. nurses' notes.

REFERENCE: Abdelhak, pp 460–461, 544–545
               Green and Bowie, p 88
               LaTour and Eichenwald-Maki, p 861
               McWay, p 132
               Sayles, p 613

5. For continuity of care, ambulatory care providers are more likely than providers of acute care services to rely on the documentation found in the
    A. interdisciplinary patient care plan.
    B. discharge summary.
    C. transfer record.
    D. problem list.

REFERENCE: Abdelhak, p 136
               Green and Bowie, p 91
               Sayles, p 108

6. Joint Commission does not approve of auto authentication of entries in a health record. The primary objection to this practice is that
   A. it is too easy to delegate use of computer passwords.
   B. evidence cannot be provided that the physician actually reviewed and approved each report.
   C. electronic signatures are not acceptable in every state.
   D. tampering too often occurs with this method of authentication.

REFERENCE: Green and Bowie, p 78
              LaTour, Eichenwald-Maki, and Oachs, pp 174, 897

7. As part of a quality improvement study you have been asked to provide information on the menstrual history, number of pregnancies, and number of living children on each OB patient from a stack of old obstetrical records. The best place in the record to locate this information is the
   A. prenatal record.   C. postpartum record.
   B. labor and delivery record.   D. discharge summary.

REFERENCE: Abdelhak, pp 114–115
              Green and Bowie, p 182

8. As a concurrent record reviewer for an acute care facility, you have asked Dr. Crossman to provide an updated history and physical for one of her recent admissions. Dr. Crossman pages through the medical record to a copy of an H&P performed in her office a week before admission. You tell Dr. Crossman
   A. a new H&P is required for every inpatient admission.
   B. that you apologize for not noticing the H&P she provided.
   C. the H&P copy is acceptable as long as she documents any interval changes.
   D. Joint Commission standards do not allow copies of any kind in the original record.

REFERENCE: Abdelhak, p 109
              Green and Bowie, p 145

9. You have been asked to identify every reportable case of cancer from the previous year. A key resource will be the facility's
   A. disease index.   C. physicians' index.
   B. number control index.   D. patient index.

REFERENCE: Abdelhak, pp 486–487
              LaTour, Eichenwald-Maki, and Oachs, pp 245, 250–251
              McWay, p 140
              Sayles, p 437

10. Discharge summary documentation must include
    A. a detailed history of the patient.
    B. a note from social services or discharge planning.
    C. significant findings during hospitalization.
    D. correct codes for significant procedures.

REFERENCE: Abdelhak, pp 111, 113
              Green and Bowie, p 144
              LaTour and Eichenwald-Maki, pp 200–201
              Sayles, p 93

11. The performance of qualitative analysis is an important tool in ensuring data quality. These reviews evaluate
    A. quality of care through the use of preestablished criteria.
    B. adverse effects and contraindications of drugs utilized during hospitalization.
    C. potentially compensable events.
    D. the overall quality of documentation.

REFERENCE: Abdelhak, pp 130–131
               LaTour, Eichenwald-Maki, and Oachs, pp 250–251

12. Ultimate responsibility for the quality and completion of entries in patient health records belongs to the
    A. chief of staff.   C. HIM director.
    B. attending physician.   D. risk manager.

REFERENCE: LaTour, Eichenwald-Maki, and Oachs, p 242

13. The foundation for communicating all patient care goals in long-term care settings is the
    A. legal assessment.   C. interdisciplinary plan of care.
    B. medical history.   D. Uniform Hospital Discharge Data Set.

REFERENCE: Abdelhak, p 109
               LaTour, Eichenwald-Maki, and Oachs, pp 31, 254
               Sayles, p 83

14. As part of Joint Commission's National Patient Safety Goal initiative, acute care hospitals are now required to use a preoperative verification process to confirm the patient's true identity and to confirm that necessary documents such as x-rays or medical records are available. They must also develop and use a process for
    A. including the primary caregiver in surgery consults.
    B. including the surgeon in the preanesthesia assessment.
    C. marking the surgical site.
    D. apprising the patient of all complications that might occur.

REFERENCE: Abdelhak, p 459
               LaTour, Eichenwald-Maki, and Oachs, p 672

15. In quality review activities, departments are directed to focus on clinical processes that are
    A. high volume.
    B. high risk.
    C. problem prone.
    D. all of the above

REFERENCE: LaTour, Eichenwald-Maki, and Oachs, p 652

16. Using the SOAP method of recording progress notes, which entry would most likely include a differential diagnosis?
    A. assessment
    B. plan
    C. subjective
    D. objective

REFERENCE: Abdelhak, pp 118–119
               Green, pp 91, 343
               LaTour, Eichenwald-Maki, and Oachs, pp 249, 256–257
               Sayles, p 126

17. You have been asked by a peer review committee to print a list of the medical record numbers of all patients who had CABGs performed in the past year at your acute care hospital. Which secondary data source could be used to quickly gather this information?
    A. disease index
    B. physician index
    C. master patient index
    D. operation index

REFERENCE: LaTour, Eichenwald-Maki, and Oachs, p 369
               Sayles, p 437

18. The best example of point-of-care service and documentation is
    A. using an automated tracking system to locate a record.
    B. using occurrence screens to identify adverse events.
    C. doctors using voice recognition systems to dictate radiology reports.
    D. nurses using bedside terminals to record vital signs.

REFERENCE: Abdelhak, p 38
               LaTour, Eichenwald-Maki, and Oachs, p 96

19. Which of the following is a form or view that is typically seen in the health record of a long-term care patient but is rarely seen in records of acute care patients?
    A. pharmacy consultation
    B. medical consultation
    C. physical exam
    D. emergency record

REFERENCE: Abdelhak, p 141

20. In determining your acute care facility's degree of compliance with prospective payment requirements for Medicare, the best resource to reference for recent certification standards is the
    A. CARF manual.
    B. hospital bylaws.
    C. Joint Commission accreditation manual.
    D. Federal Register.

REFERENCE: Abdelhak, p 441
               Green and Bowie, p 29
               LaTour, Eichenwald-Maki, and Oachs, pp 301–302, 453, 466, 915

21. In an acute care hospital, a complete history and physical may not be required for a new admission when
    A. the patient is readmitted for a similar problem within 1 year.
    B. the patient's stay is less than 24 hours.
    C. the patient has an uneventful course in the hospital.
    D. a legible copy of a recent H&P performed in the attending physician's office is available.

REFERENCE: Abdelhak, p 109
               Green and Bowie, p 145
               LaTour, Eichenwald-Maki, and Oachs, pp 245, 252, 925

22. When developing a data collection system, the most effective approach first considers
    A. the end user's needs.
    B. applicable accreditation standards.
    C. hardware requirements.
    D. facility preference.

REFERENCE: Odom-Wesley, p 230

23. A key data item you would expect to find recorded on an ER record but would probably NOT see in an acute care record is the
    A. physical findings.
    B. lab and diagnostic test results.
    C. time and means of arrival.
    D. instructions for follow-up care.

REFERENCE: Abdelhak, pp 138–139
               LaTour, Eichenwald-Maki, and Oachs, p 255
               Sayles, p 107

24. Under which of the following conditions can an original paper-based patient health record be physically removed from the hospital?
    A. when the patient is brought to the hospital emergency department following a motor vehicle accident and, after assessment, is transferred with his health record to a trauma designated emergency department at another hospital
    B. when the director of health records is acting in response to a subpoena duces tecum and takes the health record to court
    C. when the patient is discharged by the physician and at the time of discharge is transported to a long-term care facility with his health record
    D. when the record is taken to a physician's private office for a follow-up patient visit postdischarge

REFERENCE: Abdelhak, pp 531–534

25. Using the SOAP style of documenting progress notes, choose the "subjective" statement from the following.
    A. sciatica unimproved with hot pack therapy
    B. patient moving about very cautiously, appears to be in pain
    C. adjust pain medication; begin physical therapy tomorrow
    D. patient states low back pain is as severe as it was on admission

REFERENCE: Abdelhak, pp 111–112
               Green and Bowie, p 91
               LaTour and Eichenwald-Maki, p 91

26. In 1987, OBRA helped shift the focus in long-term care to patient outcomes. As a result, core assessment data elements are collected on each SNF resident as defined in the
    A. UHDDS.
    B. MDS.
    C. Uniform Clinical Data Set.
    D. Uniform Ambulatory Core Data.

REFERENCE: Abdelhak, pp 141–143
               Green and Bowie, p 253
               LaTour, Eichenwald-Maki, and Oachs, pp 199, 435, 931
               Sayles, pp 150–152

27. Before you submit a new form to the Forms Review Committee, you need to track the field name of a particular data field and the security levels applicable to that field. Your best source for this information would be the
    A. facility's data dictionary.
    B. MDS.
    C. Glossary of Health Care Terms.
    D. UHDDS.

REFERENCE: Abdelhak, pp 502–503
               LaTour, Eichenwald-Maki, and Oachs, pp 202, 907, C7
               Sayles, pp 882–883

28. You notice on the admission H&P that Mr. McKahan, a Medicare patient, was admitted for disc surgery, but the progress notes indicate that due to some heart irregularities, he may not be a good surgical risk. Because of your knowledge of COP regulations, you expect that a(n) _____ will be added to his health record.
    - A. interval summary
    - B. consultation report
    - C. advance directive
    - D. interdisciplinary care plan

REFERENCE: Abdelhak, pp 111–112
               Green and Bowie, p 148
               LaTour, Eichenwald-Maki, and Oachs, pp 249, 905

29. An example of objective entry in the health record supplied by a health care practitioner is the
    - A. past medical history.
    - B. physical assessment.
    - C. chief complaint.
    - D. review of systems.

REFERENCE: Abdelhak, pp 118–119
               Green and Bowie, p 148
               LaTour, Eichenwald-Maki, and Oachs, p 245
               Sayles, p 78

30. You have been asked to recommend time-limited documentation standards for inclusion in the Medical Staff Bylaws, Rules, and Regulations. The committee documentation standards must meet the standards of both the Joint Commission and the Medicare Conditions of Participation. The standards for the history and physical exam documentation are discussed first. You advise them that the time period for completion of this report should be set at
    - A. 12 hours after admission.
    - B. 24 hours after admission.
    - C. 12 hours after admission or prior to surgery.
    - D. 24 hours after admission or prior to surgery.

REFERENCE: Abdelhak, p 109
               Green and Bowie, p 145
               LaTour, Eichenwald-Maki, and Oachs, p 245

31. Based on the following documentation in an acute care record, where would you expect this excerpt to appear?

    "With the patient in the supine position, the right side of the neck was appropriately prepped with betadine solution and draped. I was able to pass the central line which was taped to skin and used for administration of drugs during resuscitation."

    - A. physician progress notes
    - B. operative record
    - C. nursing progress notes
    - D. physical examination

REFERENCE: Abdelhak, pp 113–114
               LaTour, Eichenwald-Maki, and Oachs, p 250
               Sayles, p 88

32. One essential item to be captured on the physical exam is the
    A. general appearance as assessed by the physician.
    B. chief complaint.
    C. family history as related by the patient.
    D. subjective review of systems.

REFERENCE: Abdelhak, p 109
                Green and Bowie, p 149
                LaTour, Eichenwald-Maki, and Oachs, p 245
                Sayles, p 80

33. An example of a primary data source for health care statistics is the
    A. disease index.   C. MPI.
    B. accession register.   D. hospital census.

REFERENCE: Abdelhak, pp 480–481
                LaTour, Eichenwald-Maki, and Oachs, pp 289, 368

34. During a retrospective review of Rose Hunter's inpatient health record, the health information
    clerk notes that on day 4 of hospitalization there was one missed dose of insulin. What type of
    review is this clerk performing?
    A. utilization review   C. legal review
    B. quantitative review   D. qualitative review

REFERENCE: Abdelhak, pp 130–131
                Green and Bowie, p 99
                LaTour, Eichenwald-Maki, and Oachs, p 943
                McWay, p 126

35. Which of the following is least likely to be identified by a deficiency analysis technician?
    A. missing discharge summary
    B. need for physician authentication of two verbal orders
    C. discrepancy between post-op diagnosis by the surgeon and pathology diagnosis by the
        pathologist
    D. x-ray report charted on the wrong record

REFERENCE: Abdelhak, pp 130–131
                Green and Bowie, p 99
                McWay, p 126
                Sayles, p 351

36. Which of the following reports would normally be considered a consultation?
    A. tissue examination done by the pathologist
    B. impressions of a cardiologist asked to determine whether patient is at good surgical risk
    C. interpretation of a radiologic study
    D. technical interpretation of electrocardiogram

REFERENCE: Abdelhak, pp 111–112
                Green and Bowie, p 148
                LaTour, Eichenwald-Maki, and Oachs, p 115

37. The health care providers at your hospital do a very thorough job of periodic open record review to ensure the completeness of record documentation. A qualitative review of surgical records would likely include checking for documentation regarding
    A. the presence or absence of such items as preoperative and postoperative diagnosis, description of findings, and specimens removed.
    B. whether a postoperative infection occurred and how it was treated.
    C. the quality of follow-up care.
    D. whether the severity of illness and/or intensity of service warranted acute level care.

REFERENCE: Abdelhak, pp 113–114
               Green and Bowie, p 99
               LaTour, Eichenwald-Maki, and Oachs, pp 35, 655

38. In your facility, the health care providers from every discipline document progress notes sequentially on the same form. Your facility is utilizing
    A. integrated progress notes.   C. source-oriented records.
    B. interdisciplinary treatment plans.   D. SOAP notes.

REFERENCE: Abdelhak, pp 118–119
               Green and Bowie, p 153
               LaTour, Eichenwald-Maki, and Oachs, p 248

39. Which of the following services is LEAST likely to be provided by a facility accredited by CARF?
    A. chronic pain management   C. brain injury management
    B. palliative care   D. vocational evaluation

REFERENCE: Abdelhak, pp 26–29
               Green and Bowie, p 30
               LaTour, Eichenwald-Maki, and Oachs, p 254
               Sayles, p 679

40. Reviewing a medical record to ensure that all diagnoses are justified by documentation throughout the chart is an example of
    A. peer review.   C. qualitative review.
    B. quantitative review.   D. legal analysis.

REFERENCE: Abdelhak, pp 130–131
               Green and Bowie, p 99
               LaTour, Eichenwald-Maki, and Oachs, pp 34–35
               McWay, p 126

41. Accreditation by Joint Commission is a voluntary activity for a facility and it is
    A. considered unnecessary by most health care facilities.
    B. required for state licensure in all states.
    C. conducted in each facility annually.
    D. required for reimbursement of certain patient groups.

REFERENCE: Abdelhak, pp 113–114
               LaTour, Eichenwald-Maki, and Oachs, pp 37–38

42. Which of the following indices might be protected from unauthorized access through the use of unique identifier codes assigned to members of the medical staff?
   - A. disease index
   - B. procedure index
   - C. master patient index
   - D. physician index

REFERENCE: Green and Bowie, p 240
               LaTour, Eichenwald-Maki, and Oachs, pp 369–370
               Sayles, p 398

43. Which of the four distinct components of the problem-oriented record serves to help index documentation throughout the record?
   - A. database
   - B. problem list
   - C. initial plan
   - D. progress notes

REFERENCE: Abdelhak, pp 118–119
               Green and Bowie, p 91
               LaTour, Eichenwald-Maki, and Oachs, pp 255–256
               Sayles, p 126

44. You have been asked to report the registry's annual caseload to administration. The most efficient way to retrieve this information would be to use
   - A. patient abstracts.
   - B. patient index.
   - C. accession register.
   - D. follow-up files.

REFERENCE: LaTour, Eichenwald-Maki, and Oachs, p 371
               Sayles, p 349

45. Based on the following documentation in an acute care record, where would you expect this excerpt to appear?

"Initially the patient was admitted to the medical unit to evaluate the x-ray findings and the rub. He was started on Levaquin 500 mg initially and then 250 mg daily. The patient was hydrated with IV fluids and remained afebrile. Serial cardiac enzymes were done. The rub, chest pain, and shortness of breath resolved. EKGs remained unchanged. Patient will be discharged and followed as an outpatient."

   - A. discharge summary
   - B. physical exam
   - C. admission note
   - D. clinical laboratory report

REFERENCE: Abdelhak, p 113
               LaTour, Eichenwald-Maki, and Oachs, p 251
               Sayles, p 93

46. The best resource for checking out specific voluntary accreditation standards and guidelines for a rehabilitation facility is the
   - A. Conditions of Participation for Rehabilitation Facilities.
   - B. Medical Staff Bylaws, Rules, and Regulations.
   - C. Joint Commission manual.
   - D. CARF manual.

REFERENCE: LaTour, Eichenwald-Maki, and Oachs, p 903
               Sayles, p 74

47. Stage I of meaningful use focuses on data capture and sharing. Which of the following is included in the menu set of objectives for eligible hospitals in this stage?
    A. use CPOE for medication orders
    B. smoking cessation counseling for MI patients
    C. appropriate use of HL-7 standards
    D. establish critical pathways for complex, high-dollar cases

REFERENCE: HealthIT.hhs.gov

                https://www.cms.gov/Regulations-and-Guidance/Legislation/EHRIncentivePrograms/Downloads/EP_MU_TableOf Contents.pdf

                http://www.cms.gov/Regulations-and-Guidance/Legislation/EHRIncentivePrograms/Downloads/Stage1ChangesTip sheet.pdf

48. Which of the following is a secondary data source that would be used to quickly gather the health records of all juvenile patients treated for diabetes within the past 6 months?
    A. disease index
    B. patient register
    C. pediatric census sheet
    D. procedure index

REFERENCE: Green and Bowie, pp 240–243
                LaTour, Eichenwald-Maki, and Oachs, p 369
                Sayles, p 436

49. Your job description includes working with agents who have been charged with detecting and correcting overpayments made to your hospital in the Medicare Fee for Service program. You will need to develop a professional relationship with
    A. the OIG.
    B. MEDPAR representatives.
    C. QIO physicians.
    D. recovery audit contractors.

REFERENCE: Green and Bowie, pp 325–326
                LaTour, Eichenwald-Maki, and Oachs, pp 851, 944
                Sayles, p 309

50. A primary focus of screen format design in a health record computer application should be to ensure that
    A. programmers develop standard screen formats for all hospitals.
    B. the user is capturing essential data elements.
    C. paper forms are easily converted to computer forms.
    D. data fields can be randomly accessed.

REFERENCE: Abdelhak, pp 119–120, 124
                LaTour, Eichenwald-Maki, and Oachs, p 51
                McWay, pp 131–132
                Sayles, pp 384–385

51. Before making recommendations to the Executive Committee regarding new physicians who have applied for active membership, the Credentials Committee must query the
    A. peer review organization.
    B. National Practitioner Data Bank.
    C. risk manager.
    D. Health Plan Employer Data and Information Set.

REFERENCE: Abdelhak, pp 471–472
               Green and Bowie, pp 251, 255
               LaTour, Eichenwald-Maki, and Oachs, p 16

52. The lack of a discharge order may indicate that the patient left against medical advice. If this situation occurs, you would expect to see the circumstances of the leave
    A. documented in an incident report and filed in the patient's health record.
    B. reported as a potentially compensable event.
    C. reported to the Executive Committee.
    D. documented in both the progress notes and the discharge summary.

REFERENCE: LaTour, Eichenwald-Maki, and Oachs, pp 251, 910

53. You recommend that the staff routinely check to verify that a summary on each patient is provided to the attending physician so that he or she can review, update, and recertify the patient as appropriate. The time frame for requiring this summary is at least every
    A. week.   C. 60 days.
    B. month.   D. 90 days.

REFERENCE: Abdelhak, p 143

54. You want to review the one document in your facility that will spell out the documentation requirements for patient records; designate the time frame for completion by the active medical staff; and indicate the penalties for failure to comply with these record standards. Your best resource will be
    A. medical staff bylaws.
    B. quality management plan.
    C. Joint Commission accreditation manual.
    D. medical staff rules and regulations.

REFERENCE: Green and Bowie, p 16
               LaTour, Eichenwald-Maki, and Oachs, p 26
               Odom-Wesley, p 367

55. For inpatients, the first data item collected of a clinical nature is usually
    A. principal diagnosis.   C. admitting diagnosis.
    B. expected payer.   D. review of systems.

REFERENCE: Davis and LaCour, p 94
               Green and Bowie, p 140

56. In addition to diagnostic and therapeutic orders from the attending physician, you would expect every completed inpatient health record to contain
    A. standing orders.   C. stop orders.
    B. telephone orders.   D. discharge order.

REFERENCE: Abdelhak, p 108
               Green and Bowie, p 154
               LaTour, Eichenwald-Maki, and Oachs, p 248

57. When asked to explain how "review of systems" differs from "physical exam," you explain that the review of systems is used to document
    A. objective symptoms observed by the physician.
    B. past and current activities, such as smoking and drinking habits.
    C. a chronological description of patient's present condition from time of onset to present.
    D. subjective symptoms that the patient may have forgotten to mention or that may have seemed unimportant.

REFERENCE: Green and Bowie, p 147

58. Based on the following documentation, where would you expect this excerpt to appear?

    "The patient is alert and in no acute distress. Initial vital signs: T98, P 102 and regular, R 20 and BP 120/69…"

    A. physical exam
    B. past medical history
    C. social history
    D. chief complaint

REFERENCE: Abdelhak, p 107
                LaTour, Eichenwald-Maki, and Oachs, p 245

59. The federally mandated resident assessment instrument used in long-term care facilities consists of three basic components, including the new care area assessment, utilization guidelines, and the
    A. UHDDS.   C. OASIS.
    B. MDS.   D. DEEDS.

REFERENCE: Sayles, p 111

60. Skilled nursing facilities may choose to submit MDS data using RAVEN software, or software purchased commercially through a vendor, provided that the software meets
    A. Joint Commission standards.   C. HL-7 standards.
    B. NHIN standards.   D. CMS standards.

REFERENCE: Green and Bowie, p 253

61. To enter the results of a CBC into the computer system, you would use a(n)
    A. laboratory system.   C. pharmacy system.
    B. radiology system.   D. order entry/results reporting system.

REFERENCE: Green and Bowie, pp 156, 170–171

62. An example of a primary data source is the
    A. disease index.   C. MPI.
    B. accession register.   D. hospital census.

REFERENCE: Abdelhak, pp 480–481
                LaTour, Eichenwald-Maki, and Oachs, pp 289, 368

63. The Recovery Audit Contractor (RAC) program was developed to identify and reduce improper payments for
   A.   Medicaid claims.
   B.   Medicare claims.
   C.   both B and D
   D.   collection of overpayments.

REFERENCE: LaTour, Eichenwald-Maki, and Oachs, pp 855–856
               McWay, p 71
               Sayles, p 310

64. You have been asked to give an example of a clinical information system. Which one of the following would you cite?
   A.   laboratory information system   C.   billing system
   B.   financial information system   D.   admission-discharge-transfer

REFERENCE: McWay, pp 302–303

65. The PQRS is a reporting system established by the federal government for physician practices that participate in Medicare for

   A.   monetary incentives.
   B.   meaningful use incentives.
   C.   quality measure reporting.
   D.   all of the above

REFERENCE: LaTour, Eichenwald-Maki, and Oachs, p 129
               Sayles, p 968

66. Surgical case review includes all of the following EXCEPT
   A.   determination of surgical justification based on clinical indication(s) in cases where no tissue has been removed.
   B.   cases with elements missing in the preoperative anesthesia consultation.
   C.   cases where there is a significant discrepancy between preoperative, postoperative, and pathological diagnoses.
   D.   cases with serious surgical complications or surgical mortalities.

REFERENCE: LaTour, Eichenwald-Maki, and Oachs, p 665

67. While performing routine quantitative analysis of a record, a medical record employee finds an incident report in the record. The employee brings this to the attention of her supervisor. Which best practice should the supervisor follow to deal with this situation?

   A.   Remove the incident report and send it to the patient.
   B.   Tell the employee to leave the report in the record.
   C.   Remove the incident report and have nursing personnel transfer all documentation from the report to the medical record.
   D.   Refer this record to the Risk Manager for further review and removal of the incident report.

REFERENCE: Green and Bowie, p 88
               LaTour, Eichenwald-Maki, and Oachs, pp 860–863
               McWay (2008), p 110
               Sayles, pp 378–379

68. In compiling statistics to report the specific cause of death for all open-heart surgery cases, the quality coordinator assists in documenting

    A. patient care outcomes.
    B. utilization of hospital resources.
    C. delineation of physician privileges.
    D. compliance with OSHA standards.

REFERENCE: LaTour and Eichenwald-Maki, pp 21, 579
               McWay, p 153

69. Your hospital is required by the Joint Commission and CMS to participate in national benchmarking on specific disease entities for quality of care measurement. This required collection and reporting of disease-specific data is considered

    A. an environment of care.
    B. a group of sentinel events.
    C. a series of core measures.
    D. risk assessment.

REFERENCE: LaTour, Eichenwald-Maki, and Oachs, pp 201, 382, 670–671
               Sayles, pp 156, 968i, pp 538–539
               Shaw, pp 132, 359

70. Needlesticks, patient or employee falls, medication errors, or any event not consistent with routine patient care activities would require risk reporting documentation in the form of an

    A. operative report.   C. incident report.
    B. emergency room report.   D. insurance claim.

REFERENCE: Abdelhak, p 653
               LaTour and Eichenwald-Maki, pp 860–863
               McWay, p 189
               Sayles, pp 613–620

71. The Utilization Review Coordinator reviews inpatient records at regular intervals to justify necessity and appropriateness of care to warrant further hospitalization. Which of the following utilization review activities is being performed?

    A. admission review   C. retrospective review
    B. preadmission   D. continued stay review

REFERENCE: Abdelhak, p 463
               LaTour, Eichenwald-Maki, and Oachs, pp 28–29, 331, 430, 464
               McWay, p 227
               Sayles, pp 610–611

72. Which feature is a trademark of an effective PI program?

    A. a one-time cure—all for a facility's problems
    B. an unmanageable project that is too expensive
    C. a cost-containment effort
    D. a continuous cycle of improvement projects over time

REFERENCE: LaTour and Eichenwald-Maki, and Oachs, pp 650–653, 808
               McWay, pp 172, 187–189
               Sayles, p 595

73. Patient mortality, infection and complication rates, adherence to living will requirements, adequate pain control, and other documentation that describe end results of care or a measurable change in the patient's health are examples of

A. outcome measures.

B. threshold level.

C. sentinel events.

D. incident reports.

REFERENCE: Abdelhak, p 442

LaTour, Eichenwald-Maki, and Oachs, pp 628–631, 670

McWay, pp 124–128, 183

Sayles, pp 600, 604

74. Engaging patients and their families in health care decisions is one of the core objectives for

A. achieving meaningful use of EHRs.

B. Joint Commission's National Patient Safety goals.

C. HIPAA 5010 regulations.

D. establishing flexible clinical pathways.

REFERENCE: HealthIT.hhs.gov

LaTour, Eichenwald-Maki, and Oachs, p 286

75. Where in the health record would the following statement be located?
"Microscopic Diagnosis: Liver (needle biopsy), metastatic adenocarcinoma"

A. operative report

B. pathology report

C. anesthesia report

D. radiology report

REFERENCE: Abdelhak, p 114

Green and Bowie, p 167

LaTour and Eichenwald-Maki, p 200

76. In quality review activities, departments are directed to focus on clinical processes that are

A. high volume.

B. high risk.

C. problem prone.

D. all of the above

REFERENCE: LaTour, Eichenwald-Maki, and Oachs, p 652

Answer Key for Health Data Content and Standards

ANSWER   EXPLANATION

1.   B   (C and D) Although a gross description of tissue removed may be mentioned on the operative note or discharge summary, only the pathology report will contain a microscopic description.

2.   B   Answers A, C, and D represent items collected on Medicare inpatients according to UHDDS requirements. Only B represents a data item collected more typically in long-term care settings and required in the MDS.

3.   C   The Joint Commission requires hospitals to prohibit abbreviations that have caused confusion or problems in their handwritten form, such as "U" for unit, which can be mistaken for "O" or the number "4." Spelling out the unit is preferred.

4.   C   Factual summaries investigating unexpected facility events should not be treated as part of the patient's health information and therefore would not be recorded in the health record.

5.   D   (A, B, and C) Patient care plans, pharmacy consultations, and transfer summaries are likely to be found on the records of long-term care patients.

6.   B   Auto authentication is a policy adopted by some facilities that allows physicians to state in advance that transcribed reports should automatically be considered approved and signed (or authenticated) when the physician fails to make corrections within a preestablished time frame (e.g., "Consider it signed if I do not make changes within 7 days."). Another version of this practice is when physicians authorize the HIM department to send weekly lists of unsigned documents. The physician then signs the list in lieu of signing each individual report. Neither practice ensures that the physician has reviewed and approved each report individually.

7.   A   The antepartum record should include a comprehensive history and physical exam on each OB patient visit with particular attention to menstrual and reproductive history.

8.   C   Joint Commission and COP allow a legible copy of a recent H&P done in a doctor's office in lieu of an admission H&P as long as interval changes are documented in the record upon admission. In addition, when the patient is readmitted within 30 days for the same or a related problem, an interval history and physical exam may be completed if the original H&P is readily available.

9.   A   The major sources of case findings for cancer registry programs are the pathology department, the disease index, and the logs of patients treated in radiology and other outpatient departments. B. The number index identifies new health record numbers and the patients to whom they were assigned. C. The physicians' index identifies all patients treated by each doctor. D. The patient index links each patient treated in a facility with the health number under which the clinical information can be located.

10. C   A. Some reference to the patient's history may be found in the discharge summary but not a detailed history. B. The attending physician records the discharge summary. D. Codes are usually recorded on a different form in the record.

11. D   A and B deal with issues directly linked to quality of care reviews. C deals with risk management. Only D points to a review aimed at evaluating the quality of documentation in the health record.

12. B   Although the nursing staff, hospital administration, and the health information management professional play a role in ensuring an accurate and complete record, the major responsibility lies with the attending physician.

13. C   Unlike the acute care hospital, where most health care practitioners document separately, the patient care plan is the foundation around which patient care is organized in long-term care facilities because it contains the unique perspective of each discipline involved.

14. C   The Joint Commission requires hospitals to mark the correct surgical site and to involve the patient in the marking process to help eliminate wrong site surgeries.

15. D   Among those abbreviations considered confusing or likely to be misinterpreted are those containing a leading decimal.

Answer Key for Health Data Content and Standards

ANSWER   EXPLANATION

16. A The assessment statement combines the objective and subjective into a diagnostic conclusion, sometimes in the form of a differential diagnosis, such as "peritonitis versus appendicitis."

17. D A. The disease index is a listing in diagnostic code number order. B. The physician index is a listing of cases in order by physician name or number. C. The MPI cross-references the patient name and medical record number.

18. D A, B, and C all refer to a computer application of managing health information, but only answer D deals with the clinical application of data entry into the patient's record at the time and location of service.

19. A Pharmacy consults are required for elderly patients who typically take multiple medications. These consults review for potential drug interactions and/or discrepancies in medications given and those ordered.

20. D CMS publishes both proposed and final rules for the Conditions of Participation for hospitals in the daily *Federal Register*.

21. D A. An interval H&P can be used when a patient is readmitted for the same or related problem within 30 days. B and C. No matter how long the patient stays or how minor the condition, an H&P is required.

22. A The needs of the end user are always the primary concern when designing systems.

23. C Answers A, B, and D are required items in BOTH acute and ER records.

24. B A and C. In these situations a transfer summary or pertinent copies from the inpatient health record may accompany the patient, but the original record stays on the premises.

25. D A represents the assessment statement, B the objective, and C the plan.

26. B OBRA mandates comprehensive functional assessments of long-term care residents using the Minimum Data Set for Long-Term Care.

27. A Answers B and D are types of data sets for collecting data in long-term (MDS) and acute care (UHDDS) facilities. A data dictionary should include security levels for each field as well as definitions for all entities.

28. B COP requires a consultation report on patients who are not a good surgical risk as well as those with obscure diagnoses, patients whose physicians have doubts as to the best therapeutic measure to be taken, and patients for whom there is a question of criminal activity.

29. B The medical history, including a review of systems and chief complaint, is information supplied by the patient. A physical assessment adds objective data to the subjective data provided by the patient in the history.

30. D This meets both Joint Commission and COP standards.

31. B This entry is typical of a surgical procedure.

32. A The medical history (including chief complaint, history of present illness, past medical history, personal history, family history, and a review of systems) is provided by the patient or the most knowledgeable available source. The physical examination adds objective data to the subjective data provided by the patient. This exam begins with the physician's objective assessment of the patient's general condition.

33. D Answers A, B, and C are examples of secondary data sources.

34. D Quantitative analysis involves checking for the presence or absence of necessary reports and/or signatures, while qualitative analysis may involve checking documentation consistency, such as comparing a patient's pharmacy drug profile with the medication administration record.

35. C A, B, and D all represent common checks performed by a quantitative analysis clerk: missing reports, signatures, or patient identification. Answer C represents a more in-depth review dealing with the quality of the data documented.

Answer Key for Health Data Content and Standards

ANSWER   EXPLANATION

36. B A, C, and D represent routine interpretations that are not normally considered to be consultations.

37. A B represents an appropriate job for the infection control officer. Answer C represents the clinical care evaluation process, rather than the review of quality documentation. Answer D is a function of the utilization review program.

38. A Progress notes may be integrated or they may be separated, with nurses, physicians, and other health care providers writing on designated forms for each discipline.

39. B The Commission on Accreditation of Rehabilitation Facilities is an independent accrediting agency for rehabilitation facilities. Palliative care (answer B) is most likely to be provided at a hospice.

40. C A. Peer review typically involves quality of care issues rather than quality of documentation issues. D. Legal analysis ensures that the record entries would be acceptable in a court of law.

41. D A. Advantages of accreditation are numerous and include financial and legal incentives. B. State licensure is required for accreditation but not the reverse. C. Joint Commission conducts unannounced on-site surveys approximately every 3 years.

42. D Because information contained in the physicians' index is considered confidential, identification codes are often used rather than the physicians' names.

43. B In a POMR, the database contains the history and physical; the problem list includes titles, numbers, and dates of problems, and serves as a table of contents of the record; the initial plan describes diagnostic, therapeutic, and patient education plans; and the progress notes document the progress of the patient throughout the episode of care, summarized in a discharge summary or transfer note at the end of the stay.

44. C The accession register is a permanent log of all the cases entered into the database. Each number assigned is preceded by the accession year, making it easy to assess annual workloads.

45. A The excerpt clearly indicates an overall summary of the patient's course in the hospital, which is a common element of the discharge summary.

46. D The manual published by the Commission on Accreditation of Rehabilitation Facilities will have the most specific and comprehensive standards for a rehabilitation facility.

47. A See all objectives for Stage I of meaningful use on the HealthIT.hhs.gov website.

48. A The disease index is compiled as a result of abstracting patient code numbers into a computer database, allowing a variety of reports to be generated.

49. D The RAC program is mandated to find and correct improper Medicare payments paid to health care providers participating in the Medicare reimbursement program. (A) OIG (Office of Inspector General); (B) MEDPAR (Medicare Provider Analysis and Review); (C) QIO (Quality Improvement Organization).

50. B Both paper-based and computer-based records share similar forms and view design considerations. Among these are the selection and sequencing of essential data items.

51. B With the passage of the Health Care Quality Improvement Act of 1986, the NPDB was established. Hospitals are required to query the data bank before granting clinical privileges to physicians.

52. D A. Incident reports are written accounts of unusual events that have an adverse effect on a patient, employee, or facility visitor and should never be filed with the patient's record. B. PCEs are occurrences that could result in financial liability at some future time. A patient leaving AMA does not in itself suggest a PCE. C. It is not typical to report AMAs to the Executive Committee. D. Documenting the event is crucial in protecting the legal interests of the health care team and facility.

Answer Key for Health Data Content and Standards

ANSWER   EXPLANATION

53. C   This 60-day time frame is often referred to as the patient's certification period. Recertification can continue every 62 days until the patient is discharged from home health services.

54. D   Although the medical staff bylaws reflect general principles and policies of the medical staff, the rules and regulations outline the details for implementing these principles, including the process and time frames for completing records, and the penalties for failure to comply.

55. C   Clinical data include all health care information collected during a patient's episode of care. During the registration or intake process, the admitting diagnosis, provided by the attending physician, is entered on the face sheet. If the patient is admitted through the ED, the chief complaint listed on the ED record is usually the first clinical data collected. A. The principal diagnosis is often not known until after diagnostic tests are conducted. B. Demographic data are not clinical in nature. D. The review of systems is collected during the history and physical, which is typically done after admission to the hospital.

56. D   Although many patient health records may feasibly contain all of the orders listed, only the discharge order is required to document the formal release of a patient from the facility. Absence of a discharge order would indicate that the patient left against medical advice and this event should be thoroughly documented as well.

57. D   Answer A refers to the physical exam. Answer B refers to the social history. Answer C refers to the history of present illness.

58. A   Answers B, C, and D represent components of the medical history as supplied by the patient, while the physical exam is an entry obtained through objective observation and measurement made by the provider.

59. B   The Minimum Data Set is a basic component of the long-term care RAI. A. UHDDS is used in acute care; C. OASIS is used in home health; D. DEEDS is used in emergency departments.

60. D   MDS data are reported directly to the Centers for Medicare and Medicaid Services and must conform to agency standards.

61. A

62. B

63. D

64. A

65. C

66. D

67. A   Incident reports are written accounts of unusual events that have an adverse effect on a patient, employee, or facility visitor and should never be filed with the patient's record.

68. A

69. C

70. C

71. D

72. D

73. A

74. A   There are several core objectives for achieving meaningful use, and engaging patients and their families is one of these objectives.

75. B

REFERENCES

Abdelhak, M., Grostick, S., Hanken, M. A. & Jacobs, E. (Eds.). (2012). *Health information: Management of a strategic resource* (4th ed.). Philadelphia: W. B. Saunders.

CMS. Fiscal Year 2009 Quality Measure Reporting for 2010 Payment Update https://www.cms.gov/HospitalQualityInits/downloads/HospitalRHQDAPU200808.pdf

Davis, N. & LaCour, M. (2014). *Health information technology* (3rd ed.). Maryland, MO: Elsevier (Saunders).

Green, M. A. & Bowie, J. (2011). *Essentials of health information management: Principles and practices.* (2nd ed.)Clifton Park, NY: Delmar Cengage Learning.

LaTour, K., Eichenwald-Maki, S. & Oachs, P. (2013). *Health information management: Concepts, principles and practice* (4th ed.). Chicago: American Health Information Management Association (AHIMA).

McWay, D. C. (2014). *Today's health information management, an integrated approach* (2nd ed.). Clifton Park, NY: Delmar Cengage Learning.

Sayles, N. (2013). *Health information management technology: An applied approach* (4th ed.). Chicago: American Health Information Management Association (AHIMA).

CCS COMPETENCIES BY QUESTION FOR HEALTH DATA

Question	CCS Domains							
	1	2	3	4	5	6	7	8
1					X			
2			X					
3	X							
4								X
5	X							
6	X							
7					X			
8	X							
9				X				
10	X							
11					X			
12								X
13	X							
14	X							
15					X			
16	X							
17	X							
18						X		
19	X							
20								X
21	X							
22					X			
23	X							
24							X	
25	X							
26	X							
27						X		
28	X							
29	X							
30								X
31	X							
32	X							
33	X							
34					X			
35					X			
36	X							
37					X			
38	X							
39	X							
40					X			

Question	CCS Domains							
	1	2	3	4	5	6	7	8
41								X
42						X		
43	X							
44						X		
45	X							
46								X
47								X
48	X							
49					X			
50						X		
51								X
52	X							
53	X							
54								X
55	X							
56	X							
57	X							
58	X							
59								X
60						X		
61						X		
62						X		
63					X			
64						X		
65								X
66								
67					X			
68					X			
69								X
70	X							
71					X			
72					X			
73					X			
74	X							X
75	X							

IV. Medical Science

Lauralyn Kavanaugh-Burke, DrPH, RHIA, CHES
CHTS-IM

Infectious and Parasitic Diseases

1. The prevention of illness through vaccination occurs due to the formation of
   A. helper B cells.
   B. immunosurveillance.
   C. mast cells.
   D. memory cells.

   REFERENCE: Jones, pp 350–351
                  Scott and Fong, p 307

2. Many bacterial diseases are transmitted directly from person to person. Which of the diseases listed next is a bacterial disease transmitted by way of a tick vector?
   A. Legionnaires' disease
   B. Lyme disease
   C. tetanus
   D. tuberculosis

   REFERENCE: Jones, pp 228–229
                  Moisio, p 434
                  Neighbors and Tannehill-Jones, p 345
                  Scott and Fong, p 329

3. All of the following are examples of direct transmission of a disease EXCEPT
   A. contaminated foods.
   B. coughing or sneezing.
   C. droplet spread.
   D. physical contact.

   REFERENCE: Neighbors and Tannehill-Jones, pp 5–6
                  Scott and Fong, pp 328–329

4. The most common rickettsial disease in the United States is
   A. hantavirus.
   B. Lyme disease.
   C. Rocky Mountain spotted fever.
   D. syphilis.

   REFERENCE: Moisio, pp 434–435
                  Neighbors and Tannehill-Jones, p 57
                  Scott and Fung, p 326

5. The most common bloodborne infection in the United States is
   A. *Helicobacter pylori*.
   B. hepatitis A.
   C. hepatitis C.
   D. hemophilia.

   REFERENCE: Scott and Fong, p 389

6. The causative organism for severe acute respiratory syndrome (SARS) is a
   A. bacterium.
   B. coronavirus.
   C. fungus.
   D. retrovirus.

   REFERENCE: Mayo Clinic (3)
                  Moisio, p 241
                  NLM (5)
                  Scott and Fong, p 360

7. The childhood viral disease that unvaccinated pregnant women should be prevented from contracting because it may be passed to the fetus, thus causing congenital anomalies such as mental retardation, blindness, and deafness, is
   A. rickets.
   B. rubeola.
   C. rubella.
   D. tetanus.

   REFERENCE: Moisio, p 435
                  Neighbors and Tannehill-Jones, p 389

8. United States healthcare providers are concerned about a possible pandemic of avian flu because
   A. there is no vaccine currently available.
   B. it is caused by a group of viruses that mutate very easily.
   C. the causative virus is being spread around the world by migratory birds.
   D. of all of the above.

REFERENCE: CDC (2)

9. Ingrid Anderson presents with a skin infection that began as a raised, itchy bump, resembling an insect bite. Within 1 to 2 days, it developed into a vesicle. Now it is a painless ulcer, about 2 cm in diameter, with a black necrotic area in the center. During the history, her doctor learns that she has recently returned from an overseas vacation and becomes concerned that she may have become infected with anthrax. He will prescribe an
   A. antibiotic.   C. antiparasitic.
   B. antineoplastic.   D. antiviral.

REFERENCE: Scott and Fong, p 360

10. The organism transmitted by a mosquito bite that causes malaria is a
    A. bacteria.   C. protozoa.
    B. prion.   D. virus.

REFERENCE: Moisio, p 432
               Neighbors and Tannehill-Jones, pp 54–55, 57
               Rizzo, p 309
               Scott and Fong, p 326

11. A pharyngeal culture is taken from a 13-year-old male patient presenting to the ER with fever, painful cervical lymph nodes, purulent tonsillar exudate, and difficulty swallowing. A blood agar culture plate shows complete hemolysis around *Streptococcus pyogenes* bacterial colonies. The patient is given a prescription for erythromycin. The diagnosis in this case is
    A. a group A beta-hemolytic streptococcal throat infection.
    B. a methicillin-resistant *Staphylococcus aureus* skin infection.
    C. tuberculosis with drug-resistant *Mycobacterium tuberculosis*-positive sputum.
    D. meningitis due to *Neisseria meningitidis*-positive cerebrospinal fluid.

REFERENCE: Estridge and Reynolds, pp 739–742
               Labtestsonline (7)

12. A 19-year-old college student, who lives on campus in a dormitory, is brought to the ER by his roommates, complaining of a severe headache, nuchal rigidity, fever, and photophobia. The ER physician performs an LP and orders a CSF analysis with a bacterial culture and sensitivity. The young man is admitted to the ICU with a provisional diagnosis of
    A. a group A beta-hemolytic streptococcal throat infection.
    B. a methicillin-resistant *Staphylococcus aureus* skin infection.
    C. tuberculosis with drug-resistant *Mycobacterium tuberculosis*-positive sputum.
    D. meningitis due to *Neisseria meningitidis*-positive cerebrospinal fluid.

REFERENCE: CDC (12)
               Labtestsonline (10)

13. There has been a significant increase in the number of cases and deaths from pertusis. Health care professionals attribute this disease trend to which of the following?
    A. A decrease in the number of people immunized with TDaP
    B. An increase in the virulence of the bacteria
    C. Drug-resistant strains of the bacteria
    D. All of the above

REFERENCE: CDC (5)

14. A new strain of influenza, H1N1, is a highly virulent strain that spread all over the world. This type of epidemiological disease pattern is referred to as a(n)
   A. cluster.
   B. outbreak.
   C. epidemic.
   D. pandemic.

REFERENCE: CDC (7)

Neoplasia

15. Dr. Zambrano ordered a CEA test for Mr. Logan, a 67-year-old African American male patient. Dr. Zambrano may be considering a diagnosis of
   A. cancer.
   B. carpal tunnel syndrome.
   C. cardiomyopathy.
   D. congestive heart failure.

REFERENCE: NLM (4)

16. Which disease is a malignancy of the lymphatic system?
   A. cystic fibrosis
   B. Hodgkin's disease
   C. neutropenia
   D. Von Willebrand's disease

REFERENCE: Jones, p 355
              Moisio, p 216
              Neighbors and Tannehill-Jones, pp 114, 119, 121, 380
              Rizzo, p 354
              Scott and Fong, p 305

17. _____ is the most common type of skin cancer and _____ is the most deadly type of skin cancer.
   A. Malignant melanoma, basal cell carcinoma
   B. Basal cell carcinoma, malignant melanoma
   C. Oat cell carcinoma, squamous cell carcinoma
   D. Squamous cell carcinoma, oat cell carcinoma

REFERENCE: Jones, pp 117, 122–123, 934–935, 939–940
              Neighbors and Tannehill-Jones, p 351
              Rizzo, p 132
              Scott and Fong, p 75
              Sormunen, pp 114, 115

18. Cancer derived from epithelial tissue is classified as a(n)
   A. adenoma.
   B. carcinoma.
   C. lipoma.
   D. sarcoma.

REFERENCE: Jones, p 931
              Neighbors and Tannehill-Jones, p 26
              Rizzo, p 90
              Sormunen, p 302

19. The most fatal type of lung cancer is
   A. adenocarcinoma.
   B. large cell cancer.
   C. small cell cancer.
   D. squamous cell cancer.

REFERENCE: Scott and Fong, p 362

20. A pathological diagnosis of transitional cell carcinoma is made. The examined tissue was removed from the
    A. bladder.
    C. oral cavity.
    B. esophagus.
    D. pleura.

REFERENCE: Neighbors and Tannehill-Jones, p 235
                      Rizzo, pp 102–103

21. The patient's pathology report revealed the presence of Reed–Sternberg cells. This is indicative of
    A. Hodgkin's disease.
    C. non-Hodgkin's lymphoma.
    B. leukemia.
    D. sarcoma.

REFERENCE: Neighbors and Tannehill-Jones, p 119

22. Which of the following BEST summarizes the current treatment of cervical cancer?
    A. A new three-shot vaccination series protects against the types of HPV that cause most cervical cancer cases.
    B. All stages have extremely high cure rates.
    C. Early detection and treatment of cervical cancer does not improve patient survival rates.
    D. Over 99% of cases are linked to long-term HPV infections.

REFERENCE: CDC (1)

23. A 63-year-old patient with terminal pancreatic cancer has started palliative chemotherapy. Palliative means
    A. alleviating or eliminating distressing symptoms of the disease.
    B. increasing the immune response to fight infections.
    C. quick destruction of cancerous cells.
    D. the combining of several medications to cure the cancer.

REFERENCE: ACS (3)
                      Woodrow, p 229

24. Mary Smith, a 48-year-old patient, is receiving an IV mixture of four different medications to treat stage 2 invasive ductal breast carcinoma. Each of the medications acts upon a different aspect of the cancer cells. This mixture is typically termed a(n)
    A. amalgamation.
    B. cocktail.
    C. blend.
    D. mash-up.

REFERENCE: CDC (8)

Endocrine, Nutritional, and Metabolic Disorders

25. Mary Mulholland has diabetes. Her physician has told her about some factors that put her more at risk for infections. Which of the following factors would probably NOT be applicable?
    A. hypoxia
    C. increased blood supply
    B. increased glucose in body fluids
    D. both A and C

REFERENCE: Neighbors and Tannehill-Jones, pp 253–257

26. Which of the organs listed below has endocrine and exocrine functions?
    A. kidney
    B. liver
    C. lung
    D. pancreas

REFERENCE: Moisio, p 266
              Neighbors and Tannehill-Jones, p 252
              Rizzo, pp 282–283, 274
              Scott and Fong, p 212

27. Which of the following is an effect of insulin?
    A. decreases glycogen concentration in liver
    B. increases blood glucose
    C. increases the breakdown of fats
    D. increases glucose metabolism

REFERENCE: Moisio, pp 301–302, 304
              Neighbors and Tannehill-Jones, pp 244, 252–256
              Rizzo, pp 274–276, 282, 284–285
              Scott and Fong, pp 222–223
              Sormunen, p 554

28. Diabetic microvascular disease occurs
    A. as a direct result of elevated serum glucose.
    B. as a result of elevated fat in blood.
    C. due to damage to nerve cells.
    D. only in patients with type 1 diabetes.

REFERENCE: Neighbors and Tannehill-Jones, pp 254–255
              Rizzo, pp 284–285
              Scott and Fong, pp 227–229

29. Old age, obesity, and a family history of diabetes are all characteristics of
    A. type 1 diabetes.
    B. type 2 diabetes.
    C. juvenile diabetes.
    D. IDDM.

REFERENCE: Rizzo, pp 284–285
              Scott and Fong, p 228

30. Clinical manifestations of this disease include polydipsia, polyuria, polyphagia, weight loss, and hyperglycemia. Which of the following tests would be ordered to confirm the disease?
    A. fasting blood sugar
    B. glucagon
    C. glucose tolerance test
    D. postprandial blood sugar

REFERENCE: Neighbors and Tannehill-Jones, pp 253–254
              Rizzo, pp 84–85
              Scott and Fong, pp 229–230

31. Which of the following is characteristic of Graves' disease?
    A. It is an autoimmune disease.
    B. It most commonly affects males.
    C. It usually cannot be treated.
    D. It usually affects the elderly.

REFERENCE: Jones, p 560
              Neighbors and Tannehill-Jones, p 248
              Rizzo, pp 280, 285
              Scott and Fong, p 310

32. A toxic goiter has what distinguishing characteristic?
    A. iodine deficiency
    B. parathyroid involvement
    C. presence of muscle spasm
    D. thyroid hyperfunction

REFERENCE: Moisio, p 304
               Neighbors and Tannehill-Jones, pp 247–248
               Rizzo, p 280
               Sormunen, p 567

33. How can Graves' disease be treated?
    A. antithyroid drugs
    B. radioactive iodine therapy
    C. surgery
    D. all of the above

REFERENCE: Jones, pp 560–561
               Neighbors and Tannehill-Jones, pp 247–248
               Rizzo, p 285
               Sormunen, p 567

Blood and Blood-Forming Conditions

34. The etiology of aplastic anemia is
    A. acute blood loss.
    B. bone marrow failure.
    C. chronic blood loss.
    D. inadequate iron intake.

REFERENCE: Jones, pp 331, 337, 340
               Moisio, p 213
               Neighbors and Tannehill-Jones, p 117
               Scott and Fong, p 246

35. A 75-year-old patient has a sore tongue with tingling and numbness of the hands and feet. She has headaches and is fatigued. Following diagnostic workup, the doctor orders monthly injections of vitamin B_{12}. This patient most likely has which of the following conditions?
    A. aplastic anemia
    B. autoimmune hemolytic anemia
    C. pernicious anemia
    D. sickle cell anemia

REFERENCE: Jones, p 332
               Moisio, p 213
               Neighbors and Tannehill-Jones, p 116
               Scott and Fong, p 245

36. Which one of the following is NOT a pathophysiological factor in anemia?
    A. excessive RBC breakdown
    B. lack of RBC maturation
    C. loss of bone marrow function
    D. loss of spleen function

REFERENCE: Jones, pp 331–333, 338–341
               Neighbors and Tannehill-Jones, p 116
               Rizzo, p 308
               Scott and Fong, pp 245–246

37. In systemic circulation, which of the following vessels carries oxygenated blood?
  A. right vena cava
  B. renal arteries
  C. pulmonary veins
  D. left ventricle

REFERENCE: Jones, pp 380–382
                 Moisio, pp 176–178
                 Neighbors and Tannehill-Jones, p 128
                 Rizzo, pp 322, 335
                 Scott and Fong, pp 277-279
                 Sormunen, p 206

38. O_2 is carried in the blood
  A. bound to hemoglobin.   C. plasma.
  B. in the form of carbonic acid. D. serum.

REFERENCE: Moisio, p 208
                 Neighbors and Tannehill-Jones, p 112
                 Rizzo, pp 408, 413
                 Sormunen, p 247

39. In general, excessive RBC breakdown could result in
  A. Crohn's disease.   C. high bilirubin levels.
  B. elevated BUN.   D. peptic ulcers.

REFERENCE: Labtestsonline (1)
                 Neighbors and Tannehill-Jones, p 209
                 NLM (1)

40. In _____ anemia, the red blood cells become shaped like elongated crescents in the presence of low oxygen concentration.
  A. aplastic   C. sickle cell
  B. folic acid   D. vitamin B_{12}

REFERENCE: Jones, p 333
                 Moisio, p 213
                 Rizzo, p 308
                 Scott and Fong, p 246

41. A 72-year-old white male patient is on Coumadin therapy. Which of the following tests is commonly ordered to monitor the patient's Coumadin levels?
  A. bleeding time   C. partial thromboplastin time
  B. blood smear   D. prothrombin time

REFERENCE: Jones, p 339
                 Labtestsonline (3)
                 Moisio, p 219
                 Neighbors and Tannehill-Jones, p 235
                 NLM (2)

42. An African American couple are undergoing genetic counseling to determine the likelihood of producing children with a recessively genetic blood condition. The genetic tests reveal that the father carries the trait to produce abnormal hemoglobin, HbS, which causes crystallization in RBCs and deforms their shape when O_2 is low. This condition causes painful crises and multiple infarcts and is termed
    A. hemophilia.
    B. thalassemia.
    C. sickle cell anemia.
    D. iron-deficiency anemia.

REFERENCE: Estridge and Reynolds, pp 328–330
               Labtestsonline (4)

Mental Disorders

43. The most common etiology of dementia in the United States is
    A. autism.
    B. Alzheimer's disease.
    C. alcohol abuse.
    D. anxiety disorder.

REFERENCE: Jones, p 1084
               Neighbors and Tannehill-Jones, p 273

44. Contributing factors of mental disorders include
    A. heredity.
    B. stress.
    C. trauma.
    D. all of the above.

REFERENCE: Jones, pp 1008, 1010
               Neighbors and Tannehill-Jones, p 408

45. Why are there "black box warnings" on antidepressant medications regarding children and adolescents?
    A. Antidepressants increase the risk of suicidal thinking and behavior in some children and adolescents.
    B. Dosage requirements must be significantly higher in children and adolescents compared to adults.
    C. There is no established medical need for treatment of depression in children and adolescents.
    D. Antidepressants interfere with physiological growth patterns in children and adolescents.

REFERENCE: FDA (2)
               Woodrow, p 379

Nervous System/Sense Organ Disorders

46. The leading cause of blindness in the United States is a vision-related pathology caused by diabetes. It is called
    A. retinal detachment.
    B. retinoblastoma.
    C. retinopathy.
    D. rhabdomyosarcoma.

REFERENCE: Jones, pp 569, 606–607, 1075–1077
               Moisio, p 403
               Neighbors and Tannehill-Jones, pp 254–255, 289, 294–295, 300
               Scott and Fong, p 192

47. Which of the following is a hereditary disease of the cerebral cortex that includes progressive muscle spasticity and mental impairment leading to dementia?
    A. Huntington's disease
    B. Lou Gehrig's disease
    C. Bell's palsy
    D. Guillain–Barré syndrome

REFERENCE: Jones, pp 277–278
               Moisio, p 294
               Neighbors and Tannehill-Jones, p 280
               Scott and Fong, p 473

48. A disease of the inner ear with fluid disruption in the semicircular canal that causes vertigo is
    A. labyrinthitis.
    B. mastoiditis.
    C. Meniere's disease.
    D. both A and C.

REFERENCE: Moisio, pp 411–412
               Neighbors and Tannehill-Jones, pp 300–301
               Scott and Fong, pp 198-199

49. A treatment for sensorineural hearing loss is
    A. cochlear implants.
    B. myringotomy.
    C. removal of impacted cerumen.
    D. stapedectomy.

REFERENCE: Jones, p 628
               Scott and Fong, p 199

50. A condition that involves the fifth cranial nerve, also known as "tic douloureux," causes intense pain in the eye and forehead; lower lip, the section of the cheek closest to the ear and the outer segment of the tongue; or the upper lip, nose, and cheek.
    A. Bell's palsy
    B. thrush
    C. trigeminal neuralgia
    D. Tourette's disorder

REFERENCE: Jones, pp 283, 288
               Moisio, p 396
               Scott and Fong, p 178

51. The hypothalamus, thalamus, and pituitary gland are all parts of the
    A. brainstem.
    B. cerebellum.
    C. exocrine system.
    D. limbic system.

REFERENCE: Rizzo, pp 157–158

52. Photophobia or visual aura preceding a severe headache is characteristic of
    A. malnutrition.
    B. mastitis.
    C. migraines.
    D. myasthenia gravis.

REFERENCE: Jones, pp 275–276
               Neighbors and Tannehill-Jones, p 271
               Scott and Fong, p 160

53. A "pill-rolling" tremor of the hand is a characteristic symptom of
    A. epilepsy.
    B. Guillain–Barré syndrome.
    C. myasthenia gravis.
    D. Parkinson disease.

REFERENCE: Jones, pp 282–283, 1066–1067
               Neighbors and Tannehill-Jones, p 281
               Scott and Fong, p 159

54. Etiologies of dementia include
    A. brain tumors.
    B. ischemia.
    C. trauma.
    D. all of the above.

REFERENCE: Neighbors and Tannehill-Jones, p 414
              Rizzo, pp 937, 946
              Sormunen, p 597

55. Which of the following pieces of equipment records the electrical activity of the brain?
    A. EEG
    B. EMG
    C. ECG
    D. EKG

REFERENCE: Jones, p 290
              Moisio, p 397
              NLM (5)

Cardiac Disorders

56. Which of the following conditions is NOT a predisposing risk associated with essential hypertension?
    A. age
    B. cigarette smoking
    C. low dietary sodium intake
    D. obesity

REFERENCE: Jones, p 404
              Neighbors and Tannehill-Jones, p 134
              Scott and Fong, pp 289–290

57. Which of the following is a lethal arrhythmia?
    A. atrial fibrillation
    B. atrial tachycardia
    C. bradycardia
    D. ventricular fibrillation

REFERENCE: Jones, p 411
              Neighbors and Tannehill-Jones, p 144

58. Diastole occurs when
    A. cardiac insufficiency is present.
    B. the atria contracts.
    C. the ventricles contract.
    D. the ventricles fill.

REFERENCE: Jones, pp 384, 387
              Neighbors and Tannehill-Jones, p 130
              Rizzo, p 333
              Scott and Fong, pp 285–286
              Sormunen, p 207

59. Henry experienced sudden sharp chest pain that he described as heavy and crushing. His pain and past medical history caused Dr. James to suspect that Henry was having an acute myocardial infarction (AMI). Which of the following tests is a more specific marker for an AMI?
    A. AST
    B. CK-MB
    C. LDH1
    D. Troponin I

REFERENCE: Labtestsonline (2)

60. Margaret Vargas needs to have her mitral valve replaced. Her surgeon will discuss which of the following issues with her before the surgery?
    A. A mechanical valve will require that she take a "blood thinner" for the rest of her life.
    B. A biological valve (usually porcine) will last 10 to 15 years.
    C. A mechanical valve increases the risk of blood clots that can cause stroke.
    D. All of the above.

REFERENCE: NHLBI

61. A common cardiac glycoside medication that increases the force of the cardiac contraction without increasing the oxygen consumption, thereby increasing the cardiac output is typically given to patients with heart failure. However, a very narrow therapeutic window between effectiveness and toxicity and the patient must be monitored closely. This common cardiac medication is
    A. COX-2 inhibitor.   C. digoxin.
    B. nitroglycerin.   D. acetylsalicylic acid.

REFERENCE: NLM (9)
               Woodrow, pp 31, 503–504

Respiratory Disorders

62. Each of the following conditions fall under the category of COPD EXCEPT
    A. chronic bronchitis.   C. pneumonia.
    B. emphysema.   D. smoking.

REFERENCE: Moisio, pp 238, 240
               Neighbors and Tannehill-Jones, pp 160–161
               Rizzo, p 407
               Scott and Fong, pp 361–362

63. Which of the following sequences correctly depicts the flow of blood through the heart to the lungs in order for gas exchange to occur?
    A. right atrium, right ventricle, lungs, pulmonary artery
    B. right atrium, right ventricle, pulmonary artery, lungs
    C. right ventricle, right atrium, lungs, pulmonary artery
    D. right ventricle, right atrium, pulmonary artery, lungs

REFERENCE: Jones, pp 380–382
               Moisio, pp 176–177
               Neighbors and Tannehill-Jones, p 128
               Rizzo, pp 322, 325
               Scott and Fong, pp 277–279
               Sormunen, p 206

64. Gas exchange in the lungs takes place at the
    A. alveoli.   C. bronchioles.
    B. bronchi.   D. trachea.

REFERENCE: Neighbors and Tannehill-Jones, p 154
               Rizzo, pp 402–404
               Scott and Fong, p 277
               Sormunen, p 345

65. Most carbon dioxide is carried in the
    A. blood as CO_2 gas.
    B. blood bound to hemoglobin.
    C. blood plasma in the form of carbonic acid.
    D. red blood cells.

REFERENCE: Rizzo, pp 408, 413
               Scott and Fong, p 239
               Sormunen, p 247

66. The presence of fluid in the alveoli of the lungs is characteristic of
    A. COPD.
    B. Crohn's disease.
    C. pneumonia.
    D. tuberculosis.

REFERENCE: Neighbors and Tannehill-Jones, p 163
               Rizzo, p 407

67. Which of the following BEST describes tuberculosis?
    A. a chronic, systemic disease whose initial infection is in the lungs
    B. an acute bacterial infection of the lung
    C. an ordinary lung infection
    D. a viral infection of the lungs

REFERENCE: Neighbors and Tannehill-Jones, pp 49, 392–393
               Scott and Fong, pp 359–360
               Sormunen, p 272

68. A sweat test was done on a patient with the following symptoms: frequent respiratory infections, chronic cough, and foul-smelling bloody stools. Which of the following diseases is probably suspected?
    A. cystic breast disease
    B. cystic fibrosis
    C. cystic lung disease
    D. cystic pancreas

REFERENCE: Neighbors and Tannehill-Jones, p 380

69. *Mycobacterium tuberculosis* is the organism that causes tuberculosis (TB), typically a respiratory disorder. It is currently experiencing resurgence in the United States and many other countries. What is the average timeframe in which all patients with new, previously untreated TB must have daily antibiotic therapy?
    A. 4–7 days
    B. 6–9 months
    C. 6–9 weeks
    D. 4–7 years

REFERENCE: CDC (4)
               Labtestsonline (13)

70. Which of the following is a severe, chronic, two-phased, bacterial respiratory infection that has become increasingly difficult to treat because many antibiotics are no longer effective against it?
    A. SARS
    B. MDR-TB
    C. MRSA
    D. H1N1

REFERENCE: CDC (6)

Digestive System Disorders

71. Which of the following anatomical parts is involved in both the respiratory and digestive systems?
    A. larynx
    B. nasal cavity
    C. pharynx
    D. trachea

REFERENCE: Moisio, p 233
               Rizzo, p 371
               Scott and Fong, pp 348–349
               Sormunen, pp 344, 383

72. Most of the digestion of food and absorption of nutrients occur in the
    A. ascending colon.
    B. esophagus.
    C. small intestine.
    D. stomach.

REFERENCE: Neighbors and Tannehill-Jones, p 185
               Rizzo, pp 377–378
               Scott and Fong, pp 383–384
               Sormunen, p 374

73. A chronic inflammatory bowel disease where affected segments of the bowel may be separated by normal bowel tissue is characteristic of
    A. appendicitis.
    B. Crohn's disease.
    C. diverticulitis.
    D. Graves' disease.

REFERENCE: Moisio, p 270
               Neighbors and Tannehill-Jones, pp 193, 198
               Rizzo, p 381
               Sormunen, p 392

74. Early detection programs apply screening guidelines to detect cancers at an early stage, which provides the likelihood of increased survival and decreased morbidity. Which of the following would NOT be a diagnostic or screening test for colorectal cancer?
    A. double contrast barium enema
    B. sigmoidoscopy
    C. fecal occult blood test
    D. upper GI x-ray

REFERENCE: ACS (1)
               Neighbors and Tannehill-Jones, p 200
               Scott and Fong, p 392

75. Prevention programs identify risk factors and use strategies to modify attitudes and behaviors to reduce the chance of developing cancers. Which of the following would NOT be an identified risk factor for colorectal cancer?
    A. alcohol use
    B. physical inactivity
    C. a high-fiber diet
    D. obesity

REFERENCE: ACS (2)

76. The first stage of alcoholic liver disease is
    A. alcoholic hepatitis.
    B. cirrhosis.
    C. fatty liver.
    D. jaundice.

REFERENCE: Neighbors and Tannehill-Jones, p 211

77. Portal hypertension can contribute to all of the following EXCEPT
    A. ascites.
    B. dilation of the blood vessels lining the intestinal tract.
    C. esophageal varices.
    D. kidney failure.

REFERENCE: Mayo Clinic (1)
               Neighbors and Tannehill-Jones, pp 211–214

78. Which of the following is a risk factor involved in the etiology of gallstones?
    A. being overweight   C. low-fat diets
    B. being an adolescent   D. the presence of a peptic ulcer

REFERENCE: Rizzo, p 215

79. Increasing peristalsis of the intestines, increasing salivation, and a slowing heart rate are examples of
    A. automatic nervous system responses.
    B. higher brain functions.
    C. parasympathetic nervous system responses.
    D. sympathetic nervous system responses.

REFERENCE: Jones, p 263
               Rizzo, pp 227, 251
               Scott and Fong, pp 176–177
               Sormunen, p 585

80. One of the most common causes of peptic ulcer disease is the consumption of aspirin and NSAIDs. Another common cause is infection by *Helicobacter pylori,* and the usual treatment for this condition is use of
    A. antivirals.   C. antifungals.
    B. antibiotics.   D. antiemetics.

REFERENCE: NLM (10)
               Woodrow, p 300

Genitourinary Conditions

81. Genital warts are caused by
    A. HAV.
    B. HIV.
    C. HPV.
    D. VZV.

REFERENCE: Jones, p 716
               Moisio, p 436
               Scott and Fong, p 460

82. A physician prescribes a diuretic for his patient. He could be treating any of the following disorders EXCEPT
    A. congestive heart failure.   C. pneumonia.
    B. mitral stenosis.   D. pulmonary edema.

REFERENCE: Neighbors and Tannehill-Jones, p 162

83. Common kidney stone treatments that allow small particles to be flushed out of the body through the urinary system include all of the following EXCEPT
    A. extracorporeal shock wave lithotripsy.
    B. fluid hydration.
    C. ureteroscopy and stone basketing.
    D. using medication to dissolve the stone(s).

REFERENCE: Neighbors and Tannehill-Jones, p 229

84. Which of the following tubes conveys sperm from the seminal vesicle to the urethra?
    A. ejaculatory duct   C. oviduct
    B. epididymis   D. vas deferens

REFERENCE: Moisio, p 332
                Neighbors and Tannehill-Jones, p 481
                Rizzo, p 444

85. The most common type of vaginitis is
    A. yeast.   C. viral.
    B. protozoan.   D. both A and B.

REFERENCE: Neighbors and Tannehill-Jones, p 315

86. _____ is usually the first symptom of benign prostate hyperplasia.
    A. Abdominal pain   C. Difficulty in urinating
    B. Burning pain during urination   D. Pelvic pain

REFERENCE: Neighbors and Tannehill-Jones, pp 322–324
                Rizzo, p 444
                Scott and Fong, pp 457–458

87. A 37-year-old female goes to her family physician complaining of dysuria, urgency, fever, and malaise. A UA is performed and upon gross examination is found to be turbid and has an unusual odor. Microscopic examination reveals a rod-shaped microorganism. A 24-hour culture produces a colony count greater than 100,000/mL of *Escherichia coli*. This would indicate a diagnosis of
    A. UTI.   C. PID.
    B. FUO.   D. KUB.

REFERENCE: Estridge and Reynolds, pp 751–753
                Labtestsonline (5)

88. Microbiological lab culture and sensitivity tests were performed on the skin scrapings of a groin lesion on a 27-year-old male patient who presented to a local health department clinic. The results confirm infection with *Treponema pallidum*. He was given a prescription for penicillin and told to return for a follow-up visit in 2 weeks. His diagnosis is
    A. syphilis.   C. herpes.
    B. HIV.   D. HPV.

REFERENCE: CDC (13)
                Labtestsonline (11)

89. A common contraceptive that is implanted in the uterus induces slight endometrial inflammation, which attracts neutrophils to the uterus. These neutrophils are toxic to sperm and prevent the fertilization of the ovum. This contraception is termed
    A. oral contraceptives.   C. spermicides.
    B. progestin injections.   D. an IUD.

REFERENCE: Jones, pp 755–756

Pregnancy, Childbirth, Perperium Conditions

90. Cervical cerclage is a procedure used to help prevent
    A. breathing restrictions.
    B. miscarriage.
    C. torsion.
    D. torticollis.

REFERENCE: Jones, pp 802, 817

91. A 28-year-old female presents to her general practitioner with morning nausea and vomiting, weight gain, and two missed menstrual cycles. The physician orders a pregnancy test. What chemical in the urine does this lab test detect?
    A. alpha-fetoprotein
    B. creatine phosphokinase
    C. carcinoembryonic antigen
    D. human chorionic gonadotropin

REFERENCE: Estridge and Reynolds, pp 471–472
               Labtestsonline (9)

92. What common vitamin should be taken by pregnant women to substantially reduce the occurrence of neural tube defects, such as spina bifida, in a developing fetus?
    A. folic acid
    B. calcium
    C. B_{12}
    D. E

REFERENCE: CDC (10)

Skin/Subcutaneous Tissue Disorders

93. Impetigo can be
    A. spread through autoinoculation.
    B. caused by *Streptococcus pyogenes*.
    C. caused by *Staphylococcus aureus*.
    D. either A or B.

REFERENCE: Jones, pp 121, 855
               Neighbors and Tannehill-Jones, pp 344, 393
               Scott and Fong, pp 72

94. Pain is a symptom of which of the following conditions?
    A. first-degree burn (superficial)
    B. second-degree burn (partial thickness)
    C. third-degree burn (full thickness)
    D. both A and B

REFERENCE: Jones, pp 116–117
               Neighbors and Tannehill-Jones, p 356
               Scott and Fong, pp 76–77

95. Necrosis extending down to the underlying fascia is characteristic of a decubitus ulcer in stage
    A. one.
    B. two.
    C. three.
    D. four.

REFERENCE: Scott and Fong, pp 77, 79

96. Scabies, a highly contagious condition that produces intense pruritus and a rash, is caused by
    A. pediculosis capitis.
    B. itch mites.
    C. candidiasis.
    D. ringworm.

REFERENCE: Jones, pp 124–125
               Moisio, p 108
               Neighbors and Tannehill-Jones, p 347

97. When a decubitus ulcer has progressed to a stage in which osteomyelitis is present, the ulcer has extended to the
   A. bone.
   B. fascia.
   C. muscle.
   D. subcutaneous tissue.

REFERENCE: Neighbors and Tannehill-Jones, pp 92–93
               Scott and Fong, p 79

Musculoskeletal and Connective Tissue Disorders

98. Softening of the bone in children is termed _____.
   A. Raynaud's disease
   B. Reye's syndrome
   C. rickets
   D. rubella

REFERENCE: Neighbors and Tannehill-Jones, p 92
               Rizzo, p 147
               Scott and Fong, p 110

99. The Phalen's wrist flexor test is a noninvasive method for diagnosing
   A. carpal tunnel syndrome.
   B. Down syndrome.
   C. severe acute respiratory syndrome.
   D. Tourette's syndrome.

REFERENCE: NINDS

100. Rheumatoid arthritis typically affects the
   A. intervertebral disks.
   B. hips and shoulders.
   C. knees and small joints of the hands and feet.
   D. large, weight-bearing joints.

REFERENCE: Jones, p 230
               Moisio, p 149
               Neighbors and Tannehill-Jones, pp 71–72, 94–95
               Rizzo, p 183
               Scott and Fong, pp 106–107

101. Fractures occur in patients with osteoporosis due to
   A. falling from loss of balance.
   B. fibrous joint adhesions tearing apart small bones.
   C. loss of bone mass.
   D. a tendency to fall from a lack of joint mobility.

REFERENCE: Jones, pp 174–175
               Moisio, p 149
               Neighbors and Tannehill-Jones, pp 90–92
               Scott and Fong, p 109

102. Henrietta Dawson presents with a chief complaint of pain and weakness in her arms and neck. After an H and P and a review of diagnostic tests that include a myelogram, her doctor diagnoses a herniated nucleus pulposus at the _____ level of her spine.
    A. cervical
    B. lumbar
    C. sacral
    D. thoracic

REFERENCE: Jones, pp 160, 228, 277
                Moisio, p 147
                Neighbors and Tannehill-Jones, p 103
                Rizzo, pp 157, 170
                Sormunen, pp 158, 161

103. Carpal tunnel syndrome is caused by entrapment of the
    A. medial nerve.
    B. radial nerve.
    C. tibial nerve.
    D. ulnar nerve.

REFERENCE: Jones, p 270
                Moisio, p 142
                Neighbors and Tannehill-Jones, p 104
                NINDS
                Rizzo, p 182
                Sormunen, p 158

Congenital Disorders

104. Sex-linked genetic diseases
    A. are transmitted during sexual activity.
    B. involve a defect on a chromosome.
    C. occur equally between males and females.
    D. occur only in males.

REFERENCE: Neighbors and Tannehill-Jones, p 14
                Rizzo, p 457
                Scott and Fong, pp 470–471

105. Before leaving the hospital, all newborns are screened for an autosomal recessive genetic disorder of defective enzymatic conversion in protein metabolism. With early detection and a protein-restricted diet, brain damage is prevented. This disease is
    A. cystic fibrosis.
    B. hereditary hemochromatosis.
    C. phenylketonuria.
    D. Tay–Sachs disease.

REFERENCE: Neighbors and Tannehill-Jones, p 378
                Scott and Fong, p 472

106. Which of the following is a congenital condition that is the most severe neural tube defect?
    A. meningocele
    B. myelomeningocele
    C. severe combined immunodeficiency
    D. spina bifida occulta

REFERENCE: Neighbors and Tannehill-Jones, p 374

Perinatal Conditions

107. Children at higher risk for sudden infant death syndrome (SIDS) include those
    A. with sleep apnea.
    B. with respiratory problems.
    C. who are premature infants.
    D. all of the above.

REFERENCE: Jones, pp 455, 867–868
               Neighbors and Tannehill-Jones, p 395
               Scott and Fong, p 362

Injuries and Poisonings

108. Sam Spade has been severely injured in an MVA because he was not wearing a seat belt. The organ in his body, situated at the upper left of his abdominal cavity, under the ribs, that is part of his lymphatic system has been ruptured, and he is bleeding internally. Sam needs a surgical procedure known as
    A. sequestrectomy.
    B. sialoadenectomy.
    C. sigmoidoscopy.
    D. splenectomy.

REFERENCE: Jones, p 345
               Moisio, p 219
               Rizzo, p 346
               Sormunen, pp 275, 399

109. John Palmer was in a car accident and sustained severe chest trauma resulting in a tension pneumothorax. Manifestations of this disorder include all of the following EXCEPT
    A. severe chest pain.
    B. dyspnea.
    C. shock.
    D. clubbing.

REFERENCE: Jones, p 454
               Neighbors and Tannehill-Jones, p 166

Immune System Conditions

110. A bee stung little Bobby. He experiences itching, erythema, and respiratory distress caused by laryngeal edema and vascular collapse. In the emergency room where he is given an epinephrine injection, Bobby is diagnosed with
    A. allergic rhinitis.
    B. allergic sinusitis.
    C. anaphylactic shock.
    D. asthma.

REFERENCE: Jones, pp 965, 974
               Neighbors and Tannehill-Jones, p 69

111 Which of the following cells produce histamine in a type I hypersensitivity reaction?
    A. lymphocyte
    B. macrophages
    C. mast cells
    D. neutrophils

REFERENCE: Jones, p 106
               Neighbors and Tannehill-Jones, p 47
               Rizzo, p 104

112. Which one of the following cells produces antibodies?
     A. A cells
     B. cytotoxic T cells
     C. helper T cells
     D. plasma cells

REFERENCE: Neighbors and Tannehill-Jones, p 64
                  Rizzo, pp 349, 350, 352

113. A patient, who is HIV positive, has raised red or purple lesions that appear on his skin, in his mouth, and most anywhere on his body. What is the stage of his disease process in today's medical terminology?
     A. ARC
     B. AIDS
     C. AZT
     D. HIV positive

REFERENCE: Jones, pp 714–715
                  Neighbors and Tannehill-Jones, p 78

114. Which of the following autoimmune diseases affects tissues of the nervous system?
     A. Goodpasture's syndrome
     B. Hashimoto's disease
     C. myasthenia gravis
     D. rheumatoid arthritis

REFERENCE: Jones, pp 281–282, 356
                  Neighbors and Tannehill-Jones, pp 72, 107
                  Scott and Fong, pp 136, 310

115. Full-blown AIDS sets in as
     A. CD4 receptors increase.
     B. helper T-cell concentrations decrease.
     C. HIV virus concentrations decrease.
     D. immunity to HIV increases.

REFERENCE: Scott and Fong, pp 316–319
                  Sormunen, p 271

116. The HPV vaccine, Gardasil, is recommended for all children/young adults between the ages of 9 and 26 years. It is a quadrivalent vaccine. What is the definition of quadrivalent?
     A. It must be administered every 4 years to be effective.
     B. It is administered in a series of four shots over a 6-month period.
     C. It prevents infection from the four most prevalent types of HPV that cause cervical cancer.
     D. It reduces the risk of infection by four times.

REFERENCE: CDC (3)
                  FDA (1)
                  Labtestsonline (12)

117. Some immunizations, such as tetanus, require a second application, to strengthen or "remind" the immune system in response to antigens. The subsequent injections are termed
     A. alerting shots.
     B. warning shots.
     C. booster shots.
     D. unnecessary shots.

REFERENCE: CDC (9)

118. Why must influenza immunizations be developed and administered on an annual basis?
     A. The virus mutates significantly each year.
     B. People develop resistance to the vaccine.
     C. The immunization is only strong enough for one year.
     D. The pharmaceutical companies produce the lowest dosage possible.

REFERENCE: CDC (11)

Pharmacology

119. The drug commonly used to treat bipolar mood swings is
    A. Lanoxin.
    B. Lasix.
    C. lithium carbonate.
    D. lorazepam.

REFERENCE: Neighbors and Tannehill-Jones, p 417
              Woodrow, p 385

120. Penicillin is effective in the treatment of all of the following diseases EXCEPT
    A. influenza.
    B. Lyme disease.
    C. strep throat.
    D. syphilis.

REFERENCE: Jones, pp 453, 1070
              Neighbors and Tannehill-Jones, pp 89–90, 190, 345, 325
              Rizzo, p 459

121. The positive belief in a drug and its ability to cure a patient's illness, even if this drug is an inactive or inert substance, typically positively influences a patient's perception of their outcome. This effect is termed a
    A. synergistic effect.
    B. potentiation effect.
    C. placebo effect.
    D. antagonistic effect.

REFERENCE: Sormunen, pp 79, 92
              Woodrow, pp 32, 352

122. The interaction of two drugs working together to where each simultaneously helps the other achieve an effect that neither could produce alone is termed a
    A. placebo effect.
    B. synergistic effect.
    C. potentiation effect.
    D. antagonistic effect.

REFERENCE: Woodrow, p 33

123. The opposing interaction of two drugs in which one decreases or cancels out the effects of the other is termed a
    A. placebo effect.
    B. potentiation effect.
    C. synergistic effect.
    D. antagonistic effect.

REFERENCE: Woodrow, p 33

Surgical and Medical Procedures

124. A stapedectomy is a common treatment for
    A. atherosclerosis.
    B. multiple sclerosis.
    C. otosclerosis.
    D. scoliosis.

REFERENCE: Jones, p 630
              Moisio, pp 412–413
              Neighbors and Tannehill-Jones, p 298
              Scott and Fong, p 198

125. A procedure performed with an instrument that freezes and destroys abnormal tissues (including seborrheic keratoses, basal cell carcinomas, and squamous cell carcinomas) is
    A. cryosurgery.
    B. electrodesiccation.
    C. phacoemulsification.
    D. photocautery.

REFERENCE: Moisio, p 110
              Rizzo, pp 81, 469

126. Maria Giovanni is in the hospital recovering from colon resection surgery. Based on her symptoms, her doctors are concerned about the possibility that she has developed a pulmonary embolism. Which of the following procedures will provide the definitive diagnosis?
    A. chest x-ray
    B. lung scan
    C. pulmonary angiography
    D. none of the above

REFERENCE: Neighbors and Tannehill-Jones, p 168
               Scott and Fong, p 362

127. A surgical procedure that cuts into the skull to drain blood from a subdural hematoma in order to decrease the intracranial pressure is termed a(n)
    A. craniectomy.
    B. craniotomy.
    C. angioplasty.
    D. hemispherectomy.

REFERENCE: NLM (6)

128. A surgical procedure that is performed to realign and stabilize a fractured femur with a rod and screws is referred to as a(n)
    A. closed reduction with external fixation.
    B. closed reduction with internal fixation.
    C. osteotomy.
    D. open reduction with internal fixation.

REFERENCE: Jones, pp 180–181
               Moisio, p 152

129. Which of the following procedures is typically performed on children to facilitate the drainage of serous exudate behind the tympanic membrane in chronic otitis media?
    A. cochlear implants
    B. stapedectomy
    C. myringotomy with tympanostomy tubes
    D. cerumen evacuation

REFERENCE: Jones, p 624
               Moisio, p 413

130. Coronary arteries may become blocked, either partially or totally, due to athereosclerosis and lead to an AMI. Which of the following procedures would be used to improve the coronary blood flow by building an alternate route for the blood to bypass the blockage by inserting a portion of another blood vessel, typically the saphenous vein?
    A. PTCA
    B. CABG
    C. carotid endarterectomy
    D. cardiac catheterization

REFERENCE: Jones, p 1086
               Moisio, pp 185–186

131. A standard surgical procedure used for the treatment of early-stage breast cancer involves the removal of the cancerous tumor, skin, breast tissue, areola, nipple, and most of the axillary lymph nodes, but leaves the underlying chest muscles intact. This procedure is termed a(n)
    A. modified radical mastectomy.
    B. partial mastectomy.
    C. lumpectomy.
    D. incisional breast biopsy.

REFERENCE: Jones, pp 760, 936
               Moisio, p 361
               WebMD.com (1)

132. The least invasive restrictive gastric surgery used to reduce the size of the stomach to facilitate weight loss in obese patients is
   A. a gastric bypass.
   B. Roux-en-Y gastric surgery.
   C. laparoscopic gastric banding.
   D. a biliopancreatic diversion.

REFERENCE: WebMD.com (2)

133. Which of the following procedures would be performed for the removal of the gall bladder due to excessive gallstone formation?
   A. ERCP
   B. cholangiography
   C. hemicolectomy
   D. cholecystectomy

REFERENCE: WebMD.com (3)
                NLM (7)

Laboratory Tests

134. A patient's history includes the following documentation:
   • Small ulcers (chancres) appeared on the genitalia and resolved after four to six weeks
   • Elevated temperature, skin rash, and enlarged lymph nodes

   Which procedure will be used to initially diagnose the patient?
   A. bone marrow test   C. serology test
   B. chest x-ray   D. thyroid scan

REFERENCE: Jones, p 328
                Moisio, p 437
                Neighbors and Tannehill-Jones, p 329

135. Diagnostic testing for meningitis usually involves
   A. blood cultures.   C. stool C and S.
   B. cerebrospinal fluid analysis. D. testing urine.

REFERENCE: Jones, p 292
                Neighbors and Tannehill-Jones, p 266

136. Which of the following is a liver function test?
   A. AST (SGOT)   C. ECG
   B. BUN   D. TSH

REFERENCE: Neighbors and Tannehill-Jones, pp 211–214
                Sormunen, p 389

137. A serum potassium level of 2.8 would indicate
   A. Addison's disease.   C. diabetic ketoacidosis.
   B. anemia.   D. hypokalemia.

REFERENCE: Mayo Clinic (2)
                NLM (3)

138. An elevated serum amylase would be characteristic of
     A. acute pancreatitis.
     B. gallbladder disease.
     C. postrenal failure.
     D. prerenal failure.

REFERENCE: Neighbors and Tannehill-Jones, p 219

139. A 68-year-old female patient has no visible bleeding, but remains anemic. Her physician is concerned about possible gastrointestinal bleeding. Which of the following tests might be ordered?
     A. DEXA scan
     B. guaiac smear test
     C. Pap smear test
     D. prostatic-specific antigen test

REFERENCE: Estridge and Reynolds, pp 680–681
                  Sormunen, p 388

140. When a physician orders a liver panel, which of the following tests are NOT included?
     A. albumin
     B. alkaline phosphatase
     C. bilirubin
     D. creatinine

REFERENCE: Estridge and Reynolds, pp 608–609

141. A 13-year-old patient is brought to her pediatrician with a 2-week history of fatigue, an occasional low-grade fever, and malaise. The pediatrician indicates it is a possible infection but needs to know what type of infection. She orders a hematology laboratory test to determine the relative number and percentage of each type of leukocytes. This test is referred to as a
    A. hematocrit.
    B. CBC.
    C. WBC diff.
    D. hemoglobin determination.

REFERENCE: Estridge and Reynolds, p 198

142. A 62-year-old female presents to her family doctor complaining of fatigue; constantly feeling cold, especially in her hands and feet; weakness; and pallor. O_2 must be transported to the cells and exchanged with CO_2, which is then transported back to the lungs to be expelled. A hematology laboratory test that evaluates the oxygen-carrying capacity of blood is referred to as a
    A. hematocrit.
    B. CBC.
    C. WBC diff.
    D. hemoglobin determination.

REFERENCE: Estridge and Reynolds, pp 206–207
                  Labtestsonline (15)

143. A 57-year-old male patient is having his annual physical. Due to a family history of coronary artery disease and his sedentary lifestyle, his doctor orders a total blood cholesterol panel. What is the optimal level of total cholesterol in the blood for adults?
    A. < 200 mg/dL
    B. 200–239 mg/dL
    C. 300–339 mg/dL
    D. >500 mg/dL

REFERENCE: Estridge and Reynolds, pp 662–667
                  Labtestsonline (6)

144. An 81-year-old male with arteriosclerosis and a long-standing history of taking Coumadin presents to his physician's office for his biweekly prothrombin time (PT) test. The PT test is one of the most common hemostasis tests used as a presurgery screening and monitoring Coumadin (warfarin) therapy. This test evaluates
   A. coagulation of the blood.
   B. the iron-binding capacity of RBCs.
   C. the oxygen-carrying capacity of RBCs.
   D. the type and cross-match of blood.

REFERENCE: Estridge and Reynolds, p 394
                Labtestsonline (8)

Radiological Tests and Procedures

145. The key diagnostic finding for typical pneumonia is
   A. abnormal chemical electrolytes.   C. lung consolidation on CXR.
   B. elevated WBC.   D. a positive sputum culture.

REFERENCE: Neighbors and Tannehill-Jones, p 162

146. A radiological test for bone mineral density (BMD) is a useful diagnostic tool for diagnosing
   A. osteoarthritis.   C. osteoporosis.
   B. osteomyelitis.   D. rheumatoid arthritis.

REFERENCE: Jones, p 184
                Neighbors and Tannehill-Jones, pp 90–92

Answer Key for Medical Science

1.	D	50.	C	99.	A
2.	B	51.	D	100.	C
3.	A	52.	C	101.	C
4.	C	53.	D	102.	A
5.	C	54.	D	103.	A
6.	B	55.	A	104.	B
7.	C	56.	C	105.	C
8.	D	57.	D	106.	B
9.	A	58.	D	107.	D
10.	C	59.	B	108.	D
11.	A	60.	D	109.	D
12.	D	61.	C	110.	C
13.	A	62.	C	111.	C
14.	D	63.	B	112.	D
15.	A	64.	A	113.	B
16.	B	65.	D	114.	C
17.	B	66.	C	115.	B
18.	B	67.	A	116.	C
19.	C	68.	B	117.	C
20.	A	69.	B	118.	A
21.	A	70.	B	119.	C
22.	A	71.	C	120.	A
23.	A	72.	C	121.	C
24.	B	73.	B	122.	B
25.	C	74.	D	123.	D
26.	D	75.	C	124.	C
27.	D	76.	C	125.	A
28.	A	77.	D	126.	C
29.	B	78.	A	127.	B
30.	C	79.	C	128.	D
31.	A	80.	B	129.	C
32.	D	81.	C	130.	B
33.	D	82.	C	131.	A
34.	B	83.	C	132.	C
35.	C	84.	A	133.	D
36.	D	85.	D	134.	C
37.	D	86.	C	135.	B
38.	A	87.	A	136.	A
39.	C	88.	A	137.	C
40.	C	89.	D	138.	A
41.	D	90.	B	139.	B
42.	C	91.	D	140.	D
43.	B	92.	A	141.	C
44.	D	93.	D	142.	D
45.	A	94.	D	143.	A
46.	C	95.	C	144.	A
47.	A	96.	B	145.	C
48.	D	97.	A	146.	C
49.	A	98.	C		

REFERENCES

American Cancer Society (ACS). http://www.cancer.org
  ACS (1)

    http://www.cancer.org/healthy/findcancerearly/index

    http://www.cancer.org/healthy/findcancerearly/cancerscreeningguidelines/american-cancer-society-guidelines-for-the-early-detection-of-cancer

  ACS (2)

    http://www.cancer.org/acs/groups/cid/documents/webcontent/003096-pdf.pdf

    http://www.cancer.org/Cancer/ColonandRectumCancer/DetailedGuide/colorectal-cancer-detection

  ACS (3)

    http://www.cancer.org/Cancer/CancerofUnknownPrimary/DetailedGuide/cancer-unknown-primary-treating-palliative-care

Centers for Disease Control and Prevention (CDC). http://www.cdc.gov/index.htm
  CDC (1)

    http://www.cdc.gov/std/Hpv/STDFact-HPV-vaccine-young-women.htm#why
  CDC (2)

    http://www.cdc.gov/flu/avian/gen-info/pdf/avian_facts.pdf
  CDC (3)

    http://www.cdc.gov/Features/HPVvaccine/
  CDC (4)

    http://www.cdc.gov/tb/topic/treatment/default.htm
  CDC (5)

    http://www.cdc.gov/pertussis/outbreaks-faqs.html
  CDC (6)

    http://www.cdc.gov/tb/topic/treatment/default.htm
  CDC (7)

    http://www.cdc.gov/flu/spotlights/pandemic-global-estimates.htm
  CDC (8)

    http://www.cdc.gov/cancer/breast/basic_info/
  CDC (9)

    http://www.cdc.gov/vaccines/vac-gen/default.htm
  CDC (10)

    http://www.cdc.gov/NCBDDD/folicacid/about.html
  CDC (11)

    http://www.cdc.gov/vaccines/vac-gen/default.htm

Estridge, B. H., & Reynolds, A. P. (2012). *Basic clinical laboratory techniques* (6th ed.). Clifton Park, NY: Delmar Cengage Learning.

Food and Drug Administration (FDA). http://www.fda.gov/default.htm
    http://www.fda.gov/BiologicsBloodVaccines/Vaccines/ApprovedProducts/ucm094042.htm

Jones, B. D. (2011). *Comprehensive medical terminology* (4th ed.). Clifton Park, NY: Delmar Cengage Learning.

Labtestsonline. http://www.labtestsonline.org
  Labtestsonline (1)

    http://www.labtestsonline.org/understanding/analytes/bilirubin/glance.html
  Labtestsonline (2)

    http://www.labtestsonline.org/understanding/analytes/troponin/related.html
  Labtestsonline (3)

    http://www.labtestsonline.org/understanding/analytes/pt/test.html

REFERENCES (continued)

Labtestsonline (4)
   http://labtestsonline.org/understanding/conditions/sickle
Labtestsonline (5)
   http://labtestsonline.org/understanding/analytes/urinalysis/tab/test
Labtestsonline (6)
   http://labtestsonline.org/understanding/analytes/cholesterol/tab/test
Labtestsonline (7)
   http://labtestsonline.org/understanding/analytes/strep/tab/sample
Labtestsonline (8)
   http://labtestsonline.org/understanding/analytes/pt/tab/sample
Labtestsonline (9)
   http://labtestsonline.org/understanding/wellness/pregnancy/first-hcg
Labtestsonline (10)
   http://labtestsonline.org/understanding/conditions/meningitis?start=3
Labtestsonline (11)
   http://labtestsonline.org/understanding/analytes/syphilis/tab/glance
Labtestsonline (12)
   http://www.cdc.gov/vaccines/vpd-vac/hpv/default.htm
Labtestsonline (13)
   http://labtestsonline.org/understanding/conditions/tuberculosis/?start=4

Mayo Clinic. http://www.mayoclinic.com
   Mayo Clinic (1)
      http://www.mayoclinic.com/print/esophageal-varices/DS00820/
   Mayo Clinic (2)
      http://www.mayoclinic.com/health/diabetic-ketoacidosis/DS00674
   Mayo Clinic (3)
      http://www.mayoclinic.org/diseases-conditions/sars/basics/causes/con-20024278

Moisio, M. A. (2010). *Medical terminology for insurance and coding*. Clifton Park, NY: Delmar Cengage Learning.

National Library of Medicine. http://www.nlm.nih.gov/medlineplus/
   NLM (1)
      http://www.nhlbi.nih.gov/health/dci/Diseases/ha/ha_diagnosis.html
      http://www.nlm.nih.gov/medlineplus/ency/article/003479.htm
   NLM (2)
      http://www.nlm.nih.gov/medlineplus/ency/article/003652.htm
   NLM (3)
      http://www.nlm.nih.gov/medlineplus/ency/article/003498.htm
   NLM (4)
      http://www.nlm.nih.gov/medlineplus/ency/article/003574.htm
   NLM (5)
      http://www.nlm.nih.gov/medlineplus/ency/article/007192.htm

NHLBI—National Heart Lung and Blood Institute. http://www.nhlbi.nih.gov
      http://www.nhlbi.nih.gov/health/dci/Diseases/hvd/hvd_treatments.html

NINDS—National Institute of Neurological Disorders and Stroke.
      http://www.ninds.nih.gov/disorders/carpal_tunnel/detail_carpal_tunnel.htm

Neighbors, M., & Tannehill-Jones, R. (2009). *Human Diseases* (3rd ed.). Clifton Park, NY: Delmar Cengage Learning.

REFERENCES (continued)

Rizzo, D. C. (2006). *Fundamentals of Anatomy and Physiology* (2006). (2nd ed.) . Clifton Park, NY: Delmar Cengage Learning.

Scott, A. S., & Fong, P. E. (2014). *Body structures and functions* (12th ed.). Clifton Park, NY: Delmar Cengage Learning.

Sormunen, C. (2010). *Terminology for allied health professionals* (6th ed.). Clifton Park, NY: Delmar Cengage Learning.

Woodrow, R. (2015). *Essentials of pharmacology for health occupations* (7th ed.). Clifton Park, NY: Delmar Cengage Learning.

Medical Sciences Competencies

Questions	CCS Competencies
1-146	Domain 1

V. Classification Systems and Secondary Data Sources

Lisa M. Delhomme, MHA, RHIA

1. Which system is a classification of health and health-related domains that describe body functions and structures, domains of activities and participation, and environmental factors that interact with all of these components?
    A. International Classification of Primary Care (ICPC-2)
    B. International Classification on Functioning, Disability, and Health (ICF)
    C. National Drug Codes
    D. Clinical Care Classification (CCC)

REFERENCE: Latour, Eichenwald-Maki, and Oachs, p 393
                Sayles, pp 196–197

2. A physician performed an outpatient surgical procedure on the eye orbit of a patient with Medicare. Upon searching the CPT codes and consulting with the physician, the coder is unable to find a code for the procedure. The coder should assign
    A. an unlisted Evaluation and Management code from the E/M section.
    B. an unlisted procedure code located in the eye and ocular adnexa section.
    C. a HCPCS Level Two (alphanumeric) code.
    D. an ophthalmologic treatment service code.

REFERENCE: AMA (2014), p 63
                Green, p 384
                Smith, p 25

3. A system of preferred terminology for naming disease processes is known as a
    A. set of categories.   C. medical nomenclature.
    B. classification system.   D. diagnosis listing.

REFERENCE: Abdelhak, p 224
                Green, p 9
                Green and Bowie, p 304
                LaTour, Eichenwald-Maki, and Oachs, pp 207–208, 348, 388–389
                McWay, pp 149–150
                Sayles, p 180

4. Which of the following is NOT included as a part of the minimum data maintained in the MPI?
    A. principal diagnosis   C. full name (last, first, and middle)
    B. patient medical record number   D. date of birth

REFERENCE: Abdelhak, p 107
                Green and Bowie, pp 237–239
                LaTour, Eichenwald-Maki, and Oachs, pp 170, 271–272
                McWay, pp 139–140
                Sayles, pp 322–323

5. The Health Information Department receives research requests from various committees in the hospital. The Medicine Committee wishes to review all patients having a diagnosis of anterolateral myocardial infarction within the past 6 months. Which of the following would be the best source to identify the necessary charts?
    A. operation index   C. disease index
    B. consultation index   D. physician's index

REFERENCE: Green and Bowie, pp 240–243
                LaTour, Eichenwald-Maki, and Oachs, pp 369–370
                McWay, p 140
                Sayles, pp 436–437

6. One of the major functions of the cancer registry is to ensure that patients receive regular and continued observation and management. How long should patient follow-up be continued?
   A. until remission occurs
   B. 10 years
   C. for the life of the patient
   D. 1 year

REFERENCE: Abdelhak, p 485
LaTour, Eichenwald-Maki, and Oachs, pp 370–372
McWay, pp 142–143
Sayles, pp 438–440

7. In reviewing the medical record of a patient admitted for a left herniorrhaphy, the coder discovers an extremely low potassium level on the laboratory report. In examining the physician's orders, the coder notices that intravenous potassium was ordered. The physician has not listed any indication of an abnormal potassium level or any related condition on the discharge summary. The best course of action for the coder to take is to
   A. confer with the physician and ask him or her to list the condition as a final diagnosis if he or she considers the abnormal potassium level to be clinically significant.
   B. code the record as is.
   C. code the condition as abnormal blood chemistry.
   D. code the abnormal potassium level as a complication following surgery.

REFERENCE: Bowie and Shaffer (2012), p 69
Green, pp 15–16
Johnson and Linker, pp 5–36
LaTour, Eichenwald-Maki, and Oachs, pp 441–442

8. DSM-IV-TR is used most frequently in what type of healthcare setting?
   A. behavioral health centers
   B. ambulatory surgery centers
   C. home health agencies
   D. nursing homes

REFERENCE: Green, p 865
LaTour, Eichenwald-Maki, and Oachs, pp 394–395
McWay, p 152
Sayles, pp 208–210

9. A coder notes that a patient is taking prescription Pilocarpine. The final diagnoses on the discharge summary are congestive heart failure and diabetes mellitus. The coder should query the physician about adding a diagnosis of
   A. arthritis.
   B. glaucoma.
   C. bronchitis.
   D. laryngitis.

REFERENCE: Green, pp 15–16, 174–175
Nobles, p 689

10. The patient is diagnosed with congestive heart failure. A drug of choice is
    A. ibuprofen.
    B. oxytocin.
    C. haloperidol.
    D. digoxin.

REFERENCE: Nobles, p 329

11. ICD-10-CM utilizes a placeholder character. This is used as a 5th character placeholder at certain 6 character codes to allow for future expansion. The placeholder character is
    A. "Z."
    B. "O."
    C. "1."
    D. "x."

REFERENCE: Bowie, p 30
Green, p 52

12. The local safety council requests statistics on the number of head injuries occurring as a result of skateboarding accidents during the last year. To retrieve this data, you will need to have the correct
    A. CPT code.
    B. Standard Nomenclature of Injuries codes.
    C. ICD-10-CM codes.
    D. HCPCS Level II codes.

REFERENCE: Green, pp 209–220
              Johnson and Linker, pp 16, 66–69
              McWay, pp 154–155
              Schraffenberger (2013), pp 384–385

13. All children will be entered into which of the following registries at birth, and thus will continue to be monitored by the registry in their geographic area?
    A. Birth defects registry   C. Cancer registry
    B. Trauma registry   D. Immunization registry

REFERENCE: Latour, Eichenwald-Maki, and Oachs, p 375
              McWay, p 141
              Sayles, pp 447–449

14. In general, all three key components (history, physical examination, and medical decision making) for the E/M codes in CPT should be met or exceeded when
    A. the patient is established.
    B. a new patient is seen in the office.
    C. the patient is given subsequent care in the hospital.
    D. the patient is seen for a follow-up inpatient consultation.

REFERENCE: AMA (2014), p 10
              Bowie, p 63
              Green, p 414
              Johnson and Linker, p 144

15. This registry collects data on recipients of heart valves and pacemakers.
    A. Transplant registry
    B. Implant registry
    C. Cancer registry
    D. Hypertension registry

REFERENCE: LaTour, Eichenwald-Maki, and Oachs, p 374
              McWay, p 141
              Sayles, pp 445–446

16. Which classification system was developed to standardize terminology and codes for use in clinical laboratories?
    A. Systematized Nomenclature of Human and Veterinary Medicine International (SNOMED)
    B. Systematized Nomenclature of Pathology (SNOP)
    C. Read Codes
    D. Logical Observation Identifiers, Names and Codes (LOINC)

REFERENCE: Abdelhak, pp 237–239
              Latour, Eichenwald-Maki, and Oachs, pp 399–400
              McWay, p 151

17. Which classification system is used to classify neoplasms according to site, morphology, and behavior?
    A. International Classification of Diseases for Oncology (ICD-O)
    B. Systematized Nomenclature of Human and Veterinary Medicine International (SNOMED)
    C. Diagnostic and Statistical Manual of Mental Disorders (DSM)
    D. Current Procedural Terminology (CPT)

REFERENCE: Abdelhak, p 252
               Latour, Eichenwald-Maki, and Oachs, pp 392–393

18. According to the UHDDS, a procedure that is surgical in nature, carries a procedural or anesthetic risk, or requires special training is defined as a
    A. principal procedure.   C. operating room procedure.
    B. significant procedure.   D. therapeutic procedure.

REFERENCE: Green, p 263
               Latour, Eichenwald-Maki, and Oachs, p 197
               Schraffenberger (2013), p 53

19. You need to analyze data on the types of care provided to Medicare patients in your geographic area by DRG. Which of the following would be most helpful?
    A. National Practitioner Data Bank
    B. MEDPAR
    C. Vital Statistics
    D. RxNorm

REFERENCE: LaTour, Eichenwald-Maki, and Oachs, p 377
               McWay, p 187
               Sayles, pp 450–451

20. An encoder that prompts the coder to answer a series of questions and choices based on the documentation in the medical record is called a(n)
    A. logic-based encoder.   C. grouper.
    B. automated codebook.   D. automatic code assignment.

REFERENCE: LaTour, Eichenwald-Maki, and Oachs, p 444

21. Which of the following classification systems was designed with electronic systems in mind and is currently being used for problem lists, ICU unit monitoring, patient care assessments, data collection, medical research studies, clinical trials, disease surveillance, and images?
    A. SNOMED CT
    B. SNDO
    C. ICDPC-2
    D. GEM

REFERENCE: Abdelhak, pp 235–237
               LaTour, Eichenwald-Maki, and Oachs, pp 398–399
               McWay, pp 150–151

22. The Unified Medical Language System (UMLS) is a project sponsored by the
    A. National Library of Medicine.   C. World Health Organization.
    B. CMS.   D. Office of Inspector General.

REFERENCE: LaTour, Eichenwald-Maki, and Oachs, pp 405–406
               McWay, p 151
               Sayles, p 458

23. You have recently been hired as the Medical Staff Coordinator at your local hospital. Which database/registry will you utilize most often?
    A. Trauma Registry
    B. MEDPAR
    C. LOINC
    D. National Practitioner Data Bank (NPDB)

REFERENCE: LaTour, Eichenwald-Maki, and Oachs, p 377
               McWay, p 270
               Sayles, p 451

24. You need to retrieve information on a particular physician in your facility. Specifically, you need to know how many cases he saw during the month of May. What would be your best source of information?
    A. Healthcare Integrity and Protection Data Banks (HIPDB)
    B. Physician Index
    C. MEDLINE database
    D. National Practitioner Data Bank (NPDB)

REFERENCE: LaTour, Eichenwald-Maki, and Oachs, pp 369–370
               McWay, p 140
               Sayles, p 437

25. You just completed a process through which you reviewed a patient record and entered the required elements into a database. What is this process called?
    A. Case finding
    B. Staging
    C. Abstracting
    D. Nomenclature

REFERENCE: LaTour, Eichenwald-Maki, and Oachs, p 382
               McWay, p 140
               Sayles, p 394

26. Which system is used primarily to report services and supplies for reimbursement purposes?
    A. LOINC
    B. HCPCS
    C. NLM
    D. ASTM

REFERENCE: Green, pp 341–342
               LaTour, Eichenwald-Maki, and Oachs, p 394
               McWay, p 164
               Sayles, p 182

27. You are looking at statistics for your facility that include average length of stay (ALOS) and discharge data by DRG. What type of data are you reviewing?
    A. Aggregate data
    B. Patient-identifiable data
    C. MPI data
    D. Protocol data

REFERENCE: LaTour, Eichenwald-Maki, and Oachs, p 368
               McWay, p 208
               Sayles, p 41

28. In which registry would you expect to find an Injury Severity Score (ISS)?
    A. Cancer Registry
    B. Birth Defects Registry
    C. Trauma Registry
    D. Transplant Registry

REFERENCE: LaTour, Eichenwald-Maki, and Oachs, p 372
                Sayles, pp 441–442

29. A service provided by a physician whose opinion or advice regarding evaluation and/or management of a specific problem is requested by another physician is referred to as
    A. a referral.   C. risk factor intervention.
    B. a consultation.   D. concurrent care.

REFERENCE: AMA (2014), p 19
                Bowie, pp 61–63
                Green, pp 435–436
                Johnson and Linker, pp 153–154, 644
                Smith, pp 215–216

30. Which of the following groups maintain healthcare databases in the public and private sectors?
    A. Healthcare provider organizations
    B. Healthcare data organizations
    C. Healthcare payor organizations
    D. Healthcare supplier organizations

REFERENCE: LaTour, Eichenwald-Maki, and Oachs, p 59

31. The most widely discussed and debated unique patient identifier is the
    A. patient's date of birth.
    B. patient's first and last names.
    C. patient's social security number.
    D. Unique Physician Identification Number (UPIN).

REFERENCE: LaTour, Eichenwald-Maki, and Oachs, pp 243–244

32. A nomenclature of codes and medical terms that provides standard terminology for reporting physicians' services for third-party reimbursement is
    A. Current Medical Information and Terminology (CMIT).
    B. Current Procedural Terminology (CPT).
    C. Systematized Nomenclature of Pathology (SNOP).
    D. Diagnostic and Statistical Manual of Mental Disorders (DSM).

REFERENCE: Bowie, p 8
                Green, p 10
                Johnson and Linker, p 110
                Schraffenberger and Kuehn, p 10

33. A cancer program is surveyed for approval by the
    A. American Cancer Society.
    B. Commission on Cancer of the American College of Surgeons.
    C. State Department of Health.
    D. Joint Commission on Accreditation of Healthcare Organizations.

REFERENCE: Abdelhak, p 483
                LaTour, Eichenwald-Maki, and Oachs, pp 371–372
                Sayles, p 440

34. The nursing staff would most likely use which of the following to facilitate aggregation of data for comparison at local, regional, national, and international levels?
    A. READ codes
    B. ABC codes
    C. SPECIALIST Lexicon
    D. LOINC

REFERENCE: Green and Bowie, p 309
                McWay, p 164

35. The Level II (national) codes of the HCPCS coding system are maintained by the
    A. American Medical Association.
    B. CPT Editorial Panel.
    C. local fiscal intermediary.
    D. Centers for Medicare and Medicaid Services.

REFERENCE: Bowie, p 9
                Green and Bowie, p 24
                Johnson and Linker, pp 110–111

36. A patient is admitted with pneumonia. Cultures are requested to determine the infecting organism. Which of the following, if present, would alert the coder to ask the physician whether or not this should be coded as gram-negative pneumonia?
    A. pseudomonas
    B. clostridium
    C. staphylococcus
    D. listeria

REFERENCE: Green, pp 15–17

37. The Level I (CPT) codes of the HCPCS coding system are maintained by the
    A. American Medical Association.
    B. American Hospital Association.
    C. local fiscal intermediary.
    D. Centers for Medicare and Medicaid Services.

REFERENCE: Bowie, pp 2, 9
                Green, p 10
                Green and Bowie, pp 24, 307–308
                Johnson and Linker, pp 110–111
                McWay, p 416

38. A physician excises a 3.1 cm malignant lesion of the scalp that requires full-thickness graft from the thigh to the scalp. In CPT, which of the following procedures should be coded?
    A. full-thickness skin graft to scalp only
    B. excision of lesion; full-thickness skin graft to scalp
    C. excision of lesion; full-thickness skin graft to scalp; excision of skin from thigh
    D. code 15004 for surgical preparation of recipient site; full-thickness skin graft to scalp

REFERENCE: AMA, CPT Assistant, vol. 7, no. 9, Sept. 1997, pp 1–3
                Green, pp 517–520, 527–529
                Johnson and Linker, pp 222, 227–229
                Smith, pp 61–62, 72–75

39. A patient is seen by a surgeon who determines that an emergency procedure is necessary. Identify the modifier that may be reported to indicate that the decision to do surgery was made on this office visit.

    A. -25   B. -55   C.   -57   D. -58

    REFERENCE: AMA (2014), pp 679–684
                        Bowie, p 21
                        Green, pp 387–395
                        Smith, p 212

40. A patient develops difficulty during surgery and the physician discontinues the procedure. Identify the modifier that may be reported by the physician to indicate that the procedure was discontinued.

    A. -52   B. -53   C.   -73   D. -74

    REFERENCE: AMA (2015), pp 679–684
                        Bowie, pp 20, 23
                        Green, pp 387–395
                        Johnson and Linker, p 456
                        Smith, pp 46–50

41. A barrier to widespread use of automated code assignment is
    A. inadequate technology.   C.   resistance by physicians.
    B. poor quality of documentation.   D.   resistance by HIM professionals.

    REFERENCE: LaTour, Eichenwald-Maki, and Oachs, pp 444–445

42. In assigning E/M codes, three key components are used. These are
    A. history, examination, counseling.
    B. history, examination, time.
    C. history, nature of presenting problem, time.
    D. history, examination, medical decision making.

    REFERENCE: AMA (2014), pp 9–10
                        Bowie, pp 42–43
                        Green, p 414
                        Johnson and Linker, p 131
                        Smith, p 197

43. Mrs. Jones had an appendectomy on November 1. She was taken back to surgery on November 2 for evacuation of a hematoma of the wound site. Identify the modifier that may be reported for the November 2 visit.

    A. -58   B. -76   C.   -78   D. -79

    REFERENCE: AMA (2014), pp 679–684
                        Bowie, p 24
                        Green, pp 387–395
                        Johnson and Linker, p 461
                        Smith, pp 46–50

44. The primary goal of a hospital-based cancer registry is to
   A. improve patient care.
   B. allocate hospital resources appropriately.
   C. determine the need for professional and public education programs.
   D. monitor cancer incidence.

REFERENCE: Abdelhak, p 486
               McWay, pp 142–143

45. A secondary data source that houses and aggregates extensive data about patients with a certain diagnosis is a(n)
   A. disease index.
   B. master patient index.
   C. disease registry.
   D. admissions register.

REFERENCE: Green and Bowie, pp 240–243
               LaTour, Eichenwald-Maki, and Oachs, p 370

46. After reviewing the following excerpt from CPT, code 27646 would be interpreted as

27645	Radical resection of tumor; tibia
27646	Fibula
27647	Talus or calcaneus

   A. 27646   radical resection of tumor; tibia and fibula.
   B. 27646   radical resection of tumor; fibula.
   C. 27646   radical resection of tumor; fibula or tibia.
   D. 27646   radical resection of tumor; fibula, talus or calcaneus.

REFERENCE: Bowie, pp 5–6
               Green, p 374
               Smith, pp 19–20

47. A population-based cancer registry that is designed to determine rates and trends in a defined population is a(n)
   A. incidence-only population-based registry.
   B. cancer control population-based registry.
   C. research-oriented population-based registry.
   D. patient care population-based registry.

REFERENCE: Abdelhak, p 487
               LaTour, Eichenwald-Maki, and Oachs, p 370
               Sayles, pp 438–440

48. Given the diagnosis "carcinoma of axillary lymph nodes and lungs, metastatic from breast," what is the primary cancer site(s)?
   A. axillary lymph nodes
   B. lungs
   C. breast
   D. A and B

REFERENCE: Green, pp 156–157
               Johnson and Linker, p 63
               Schraffenberger (2013), pp 93–94

49. According to CPT, in which of the following cases would an established E/M code be used?
    A. A home visit with a 45-year-old male with a long history of drug abuse and alcoholism. The man is seen at the request of Adult Protective Services for an assessment of his mental capabilities.
    B. John and his family have just moved to town. John has asthma and requires medication to control the problem. He has an appointment with Dr. You and will bring his records from his previous physician.
    C. Tom is seen by Dr. X for a sore throat. Dr. X is on call for Tom's regular physician, Dr. Y. The last time that Tom saw Dr. Y was a couple of years ago.
    D. A 78-year-old female with weight loss and progressive agitation over the past 2 months is seen by her primary care physician for drug therapy. She has not seen her primary care physician in 4 years.

REFERENCE: AMA (2014), pp 4–5
               AMA, CPT Assistant, vol. 8, no. 10, Oct. 1998
               Bowie, pp 38–42
               Green, pp 411–412
               Smith, pp 195–196

50. In order to use the inpatient CPT consultation codes, the consulting physician must
    A. order diagnostic tests.
    B. document his findings in the patient's medical record.
    C. communicate orally his opinion to the attending physician.
    D. use the term "referral" in his report.

REFERENCE: AMA (2014), pp 19–21
               Bowie, pp 61–63
               Smith, pp 215–216

51. The attending physician requests a consultation from a cardiologist. The cardiologist takes a detailed history, performs a detailed examination, and utilizes moderate medical decision making. The cardiologist orders diagnostic tests and prescribes medication. He documents his findings in the patient's medical record and communicates in writing with the attending physician. The following day the consultant visits the patient to evaluate the patient's response to the medication, to review results from the diagnostic tests, and to discuss treatment options. What codes should the consultant report for the two visits?
    A. an initial inpatient consult and a follow-up consult
    B. an initial inpatient consult for both visits
    C. an initial inpatient consult and a subsequent hospital visit
    D. an initial inpatient consult and initial hospital care

REFERENCE: AMA (2014), pp 19–21
               Bowie, pp 61–63
               Green, pp 435–438
               Smith, pp 215–216

52. According to the American Medical Association, medical decision making is measured by all of the following except the
    A. number of diagnoses or management options.
    B. amount and complexity of data reviewed.
    C. risk of complications.
    D. specialty of the treating physician.

REFERENCE: AMA (2014), p 10
                       Bowie, pp 53–54
                       Green, pp 416–417
                       Johnson and Linker, pp 139–140
                       Smith, pp 205–208

53. CPT provides Level I modifiers to explain all of the following situations EXCEPT
    A. when a service or procedure is partially reduced or eliminated at the physician's discretion.
    B. when one surgeon provides only postoperative services.
    C. when a patient sees a surgeon for follow-up care after surgery.
    D. when the same laboratory test is repeated multiple times on the same day.

REFERENCE: AMA (2014), pp 679–684
                       Bowie, pp 16–26
                       Green, pp 387–395
                       Johnson and Linker, pp 449–464

54. The best place to ascertain the size of an excised lesion for accurate CPT coding is the
    A. discharge summary.   C. operative report.
    B. pathology report.   D. anesthesia record.

REFERENCE: Green, pp 517–520
                       Johnson and Linker, pp 220–221
                       Smith, pp 61–62

55. Which of the following is expected to enable hospitals to collect more specific information for use in patient care, benchmarking, quality assessment, research, public health reporting, strategic planning, and reimbursement?
    A. LOINC
    B. ICD-10-CM
    C. NDC
    D. NANDA

REFERENCE: Abdelhak, p 249
                       Johnson and Linker, pp 82–89

56. Case definition is important for all types of registries. Age will certainly be an important criterion for accessing a case in a(n) _____ registry.
    A. implant   C. HIV/AIDS
    B. trauma   D. birth defects

REFERENCE: LaTour, Eichenwald-Maki, and Oachs, p 373

57. To gather statistics for surgical services provided on an outpatient basis, which of the following codes are needed?
    A. ICD-10-CM codes
    B. evaluation and management codes
    C. HCPCS Level II Codes
    D. CPT codes

REFERENCE: Green and Bowie, pp 240–243
               McWay, p 164
               Schraffenberger and Kuehn, p 10

58. The Cancer Committee at your hospital requests a list of all patients entered into your cancer registry in the last year. This information would be obtained by checking the
    A. disease index.   C. suspense file.
    B. tickler file.   D. accession register.

REFERENCE: LaTour, Eichenwald-Maki, and Oachs, p 371
               Sayles, p 439

59. The reference date for a cancer registry is
    A. January 1 of the year in which the registry was established.
    B. the date when data collection began.
    C. the date that the Cancer Committee is established.
    D. the date that the cancer program applies for approval by the American College of Surgeons.

REFERENCE: Abdelhak, p 486

60. The abstract completed on the patients in your hospital contains the following items: patient demographics; prehospital interventions; vital signs on admission; procedures and treatment prior to hospitalization; transport modality; and injury severity score. The hospital uses these data for its
    A. AIDS registry.   C. implant registry.
    B. diabetes registry.   D. trauma registry.

REFERENCE: Abdelhak, p 496
               LaTour, Eichenwald-Maki, and Oachs, pp 372–373
               Sayles, pp 441–442

61. In relation to birth defects registries, active surveillance systems
    A. use trained staff to identify cases in all hospitals, clinics, and other facilities through review of patient records, indexes, vital records, and hospital logs.
    B. are commonly used in all 50 states.
    C. miss 10% to 30% of all cases.
    D. rely on reports submitted by hospitals, clinics, or other sources.

REFERENCE: Abdelhak, p 492

62. In regard to quality of coding, the degree to which the same results (same codes) are obtained by different coders or on multiple attempts by the same coder refers to
    A. reliability.   C. completeness.
    B. validity.   D. timeliness.

REFERENCE: LaTour, Eichenwald-Maki, and Oachs, pp 442–443

63. The Healthcare Cost and Utilization Project (HCUP) consists of a set of databases that include data on inpatients whose care is paid for by third-party payers. HCUP is an initiative of the
  A. Agency for Healthcare Research and Quality.
  B. Centers for Medicare and Medicaid Services.
  C. National Library of Medicine.
  D. World Health Organization.

REFERENCE:　　　LaTour, Eichenwald-Maki, and Oachs, pp 381, 631
　　　　　　　　　McWay, p 175

64. The coding supervisor notices that the coders are routinely failing to code all possible diagnoses and procedures for a patient encounter. This indicates to the supervisor that there is a problem with
  A. completeness.
  B. validity.
  C. reliability.
  D. timeliness.

REFERENCE:　　　LaTour, Eichenwald-Maki, and Oachs, pp 442–443

65. When coding free skin grafts, which of the following is NOT an essential item of data needed for accurate coding?
  A. recipient site
  B. donor site
  C. size of defect
  D. type of repair

REFERENCE:　　　Bowie, p 122
　　　　　　　　　Green, pp 527–530
　　　　　　　　　Smith, pp 72–76

66. In CPT, Category III codes include codes
  A. to describe emerging technologies.
  B. to measure performance.
  C. for use by nonphysician practitioners.
  D. for supplies, drugs, and durable medical equipment.

REFERENCE:　　　AMA (2014), p 659
　　　　　　　　　Bowie, p 9
　　　　　　　　　Johnson and Linker, pp 120, 130
　　　　　　　　　Smith, pp 3–4

67. The information collected for your registry includes patient demographic information, diagnosis codes, functional status, and histocompatibility information. This type of registry is a
  A. birth defects registry.
  B. diabetes registry.
  C. transplant registry.
  D. trauma registry.

REFERENCE:　　　LaTour, Eichenwald-Maki, and Oachs, pp 374–375

68. Patient Jamey Smith has been seen at Oceanside Hospital three times prior to this current encounter. Unfortunately, because of clerical errors, Jamey's information was entered into the MPI incorrectly on the three previous admissions and consequently has three different medical record numbers. The unit numbering system is used at Oceanside Hospital. Jamey's previous entries into the MPI are as follows:

09/03/12	Jamey Smith	MR# 10361
03/10/13	Jamey Smith Doe	MR# 33998
07/23/14	Jamie Smith Doe	MR# 36723

The next available number to be assigned at Oceanside Hospital is 41369. Duplicate entries in the MPI should be scrubbed and all of Jamey's medical records should be filed under medical record number

A. 10361.
B. 33998.
C. 36723.
D. 41369.

REFERENCE: Green and Bowie, pp 237–240
McWay, pp 139–140

69. The method of calculating errors in a coding audit that allows for benchmarking with other hospitals, and permits the reviewer to track errors by case type, is the

A. record-over-record method.
B. benchmarking method.
C. code method.
D. focused review method.

REFERENCE: Schraffenberger and Kuehn, p 319

70. The most common type of registry located in hospitals of all sizes and in every region of the country is the

A. trauma registry.
B. cancer registry.
C. AIDS registry.
D. birth defects registry.

REFERENCE: Green and Bowie, p 248
McWay, p 142

71. A radiologist is asked to review a patient's CT scan that was taken at another facility. The modifier – 26 attached to the code indicates that the physician is billing for what component of the procedure?

A. professional
B. technical
C. global
D. confirmatory

REFERENCE: Bowie, p 18
Green, pp 387–395
Johnson and Linker, pp 453–454

72. When coding neoplasms, topography means

A. cell structure and form.
B. site.
C. variation from normal tissue.
D. extent of the spread of the disease.

REFERENCE: Abdelhak, p 488

73. According to CPT, antepartum care includes all of the following EXCEPT
    A. initial and subsequent history.
    B. physical examination.
    C. monthly visits up to 36 weeks.
    D. routine chemical urinalysis.

REFERENCE: Bowie, pp 331–332
               Green, pp 687–688
               Johnson and Linker, pp 346–347
               Smith, p 146

74. The Cancer Committee at Wharton General Hospital wants to compare long-term survival rates for pancreatic cancer by evaluating medical versus surgical treatment of the cancer. The best source of these data is the
    A. disease index.
    B. operation index.
    C. master patient index.
    D. cancer registry abstracts.

REFERENCE: Abdelhak, pp 487–488
               LaTour, Eichenwald-Maki, and Oachs, pp 370–371
               McWay, pp 142–143

75. A list or collection of clinical words or phrases with their meanings is a
    A. data dictionary.
    B. language.
    C. medical nomenclature.
    D. clinical vocabulary.

REFERENCE: LaTour, Eichenwald-Maki, and Oachs, p 389

76. The main difference between concurrent and retrospective coding is
    A. when the coding is done.
    B. what classification system is used.
    C. the credentials of the coder.
    D. the involvement of the physician.

REFERENCE: Sayles, p 396
               Schraffenberger and Kuehn, p 30

77. A PEG procedure would most likely be done to facilitate
    A. breathing.
    B. eating.
    C. urination.
    D. none of the above.

REFERENCE: Johnson and Linker, p 89
               Schraffenberger (2013), p 253

78. CMS published a final rule indicating a compliance date to implement ICD-10-CM and ICD-10-PCS. The use of these two code sets will be effective on
    A. January 1, 2014.
    B. October 1, 2014.
    C. January 1, 2015.
    D. October 1, 2015.

REFERENCE: Bowie and Schaffer (2), p 3

79. Mappings between ICD-9-CM and ICD-10-CM were developed and released by the National Center for Health Statistics (NCHS) to facilitate the transition from one code set to another. They are called
    A. GEMS (General Equivalency Mappings).
    B. Medical Mappings.
    C. Code Maps.
    D. ICD Code Maps.

REFERENCE: Green, pp 79–80
               LaTour, Eichenwald-Maki, and Oachs, p 392

80. The code structure for ICD-10-CM differs from the code structure of ICD-9-CM. An ICD-10-CM code consists of
    A. five alphanumeric characters.
    B. 10 characters.
    C. three to seven characters.
    D. seven digits.

REFERENCE: Bowie, p 566
               Green, pp 48, 52

81. The first character for all of the codes assigned in ICD-10-CM is
    A. an alphabet.
    B. a number.
    C. an alphabet or a number.
    D. a digit.

REFERENCE: Green, pp 38–39

82. ICD-10-PCS will be implemented in the United States to code
    A. hospital inpatient procedures.
    B. physician office procedures.
    C. hospital inpatient diagnoses.
    D. hospital outpatient diagnoses.

REFERENCE: Green, p 40

83. ICD-10-PCS codes have a unique structure. An example of a valid code in the ICD-10-PCS system is
    A. L03.311.
    B. 013.2.
    C. B2151.
    D. 2W3FX1Z.

REFERENCE: Green, pp 38–39
               Schraffenberger, pp 33–34

84. ICD-10-PCS utilizes the third character in the Medical and Surgical section to identify the "root operation." The name of the root operation that describes "cutting out or off, without replacing a portion of a body part" is
    A. destruction.
    B. extirpation.
    C. excision.
    D. removal.

REFERENCE: Green, p 72
               Schraffenberger, p 132

85. In ICD-10-PCS, to code "removal of a thumbnail," the root operation would be
    A. removal.
    B. extraction.
    C. fragmentation.
    D. extirpation.

REFERENCE: Green, p 277
               Schraffenberger, p 120

86. In ICD-10-CM, the final character of the code indicates laterality. An unspecified side code is also provided should the site not be identified in the medical record. If no bilateral code is provided and the condition is bilateral, the ICD-10-CM Official Coding Guidelines direct the coder to
    A. assign the unspecified side code.
    B. assign separate codes for both the left and right side.
    C. not assign a code.
    D. query the physician.

REFERENCE: Green, p 138
               CMS.gov

87. An example of a valid code in ICD-10-CM is
    A. 576.212D.
    B. Z3A.34
    C. 329.6677.
    D. BJRT23x.

REFERENCE: CMS.gov

Answer Key for Classification Systems and Secondary Data Sources

NOTE: Explanations are provided for those questions that require mathematical calculations and questions that are not clearly explained in the references that are cited.

ANSWER   EXPLANATION

1.   B

2.   B

3.   C

4.   A

5.   C

6.   C

7.   A   A coder should never assign a code on the basis of laboratory results alone. If findings are clearly outside the normal range and the physician has ordered additional testing or treatment, it is appropriate to consult with the physician as to whether a diagnosis should be added or whether the abnormal finding should be listed.

8.   A

9.   B   Pilocarpine is used to treat open-angle and angle-closure glaucoma to reduce intraocular pressure.

10.   D   Digoxin is used for maintenance therapy in congestive heart failure, atrial fibrillation, atrial flutter, and paroxysmal atrial tachycardia. Ibuprofen is an anti-inflammatory drug. Oxytocin is used to initiate or improve uterine contractions at term, and haloperidol is used to manage psychotic disorders.

11.   D

12.   C   HCPCS codes (Levels I and II) would only give the code for any procedures that were performed and would not identify the diagnosis code or cause of the accident. The correct name of the nomenclature for athletic injuries is the Standard Nomenclature of Athletic Injuries and is used to identify sports injuries. It has not been revised since 1976.

13.   D

14.   B   All three key components (history, physical examination, and medical decision making) are required for new patients and initial visits. At least two of the three key components are required for established patients and subsequent visits.

15.   B

16.   D

17.   A

18.   B

19.   B

20.   A

21.   A

22.   A

23.   D

Answer Key for Classification Systems and Secondary Data Sources

	ANSWER	EXPLANATION
24.	B	
25.	C	
26.	B	
27.	A	
28.	C	
29.	B	
30.	B	
31.	C	
32.	B	
33.	B	
34.	B	
35.	D	
36.	A	
37.	A	
38.	B	
39.	C	
40.	B	
41.	B	
42.	D	
43.	C	
44.	A	
45.	C	
46.	B	
47.	A	
48.	C	
49.	C	
50.	B	
51.	C	
52.	D	
53.	C	
54.	C	
55.	B	
56.	D	
57.	D	
58.	D	
59.	B	
60.	D	
61.	A	
62.	A	
63.	A	
64.	A	
65.	B	
66	A	
67.	C	
68.	A	
69.	A	
70.	B	

Answer Key for Classification Systems and Secondary Data Sources

	ANSWER	EXPLANATION

71. A With CPT radiology codes, there are three components that have to be considered. These are the professional, technical, and global components. The professional component describes the services of a physician who supervises the taking of an x-ray film and the interpretation with report of the results. The technical component describes the services of the person who uses the equipment, the film, and other supplies. The global component describes the combination of both professional and technical components. If the billing radiologist's services include only the supervision and interpretation component, the radiologist bills the procedure code and adds the modifier –26 to indicate that he or she did only the professional component of the procedure.

72. B

73. C

74. D

75. D

76. A

77. B

78. D

79. A

80. C

81. A

82. A

83. D Immobilization of Left Hand Using Splint
2W3FX1Z is a billable ICD-10-PCS procedure code that can be used to specify a medical procedure.

84. C

85. B

86. B

87. B ICD-10-CM codes begin with an alphabetical letter. There is a decimal after the third character. Codes can consist of three to seven characters.

ICD-10-CM Official Guidelines for Coding and Reporting FY 2015
Section 15: Pregnancy, Childbirth, and the Puerperium
(15.b.1) Selection of OB Principal or First-listed Diagnosis
Routine outpatient prenatal visits
For routine outpatient prenatal visits when no complications are present, a code from category Z34, Encounter for supervision of normal pregnancy, should be used as the first-listed diagnosis. These codes should not be used in conjunction with chapter 15 codes.
Section 21: Factors influencing health status and contact with health services (Z00-Z99)
(21.c.11) Encounters for Obstetrical and Reproductive Services
See Section I.C.15. Pregnancy, Childbirth, and the Puerperium, for further instruction on the use of these codes.
Codes in category Z3A, Weeks of gestation, may be assigned to provide additional information about the pregnancy. The date of the admission should be used to determine weeks of gestation for inpatient admissions that encompass more than one gestational week.

REFERENCES

Abdelhak, M., Grostick, S., Hanken, M.A., & Jacobs, E. (Eds.). (2012). *Health information: Management of a strategic resource* (4th ed.). St. Louis, MO: Saunders Elsevier.

American Medical Association (AMA). *CPT assistant.* Chicago: AMA, CPT Assistant, vol. 7, no. 9, Sept. 1997, pp 1–3.

AMA, CPT Assistant, vol. 8, no. 10, Oct. 1998.

American Medical Association (AMA). (2014). *Physicians' current procedural terminology (CPT) 2015, Professional Edition.* Chicago:

Bowie, M. J. (2014). *Understanding ICD-10-CM and ICD-10-PCS: A worktext* (2nd ed.). Clifton Park, NY: Delmar Cengage Learning.

Bowie, M. J. (2015). *Understanding procedural coding: A worktext* (4th ed.). Clifton Park, NY: Cengage Learning.

CMS.gov
https://www.cms.gov/Medicare/Coding/ICD10/Downloads/icd10cm-guidelines-2015.pdf (accessed 12/1/2014)

DeVault, K., Barta, A., & Endicott, M. (2014). *ICD-10-CM Coder Training Manual.* Chicago: American Health Information Management Association (AHIMA).

Green, M. (2014). *3-2-1 Code it* (4th ed.). Clifton Park, NY: Delmar Cengage Learning.

Green, M. A., & Bowie, M. J. (2011). *Essentials of health information management: Principles and practices* (2nd ed.). Clifton Park, NY: Delmar Cengage Learning.

Johnson, S. L., & Linker, C. S. (2013). Understanding medical coding: A comprehensive guide (3rd ed.). Clifton Park, NY: Delmar Cengage Learning.

LaTour, K., Eichenwald-Maki, S., and Oachs, P. (2013). *Health information management: Concepts, principles and practice* (4th ed.). Chicago: American Health Information Management Association (AHIMA).

McWay, D. C. (2013). *Today's health information management: An integrated approach* (2nd ed.). Clifton Park, NY: Delmar Cengage Learning.

Nobles, S. (2002). *Delmar's drug reference for health care professionals.* Clifton Park, NY: Delmar Cengage Learning.

Sayles, N. (2013). *Health information management technology: An applied approach* (4th ed.). Chicago: American Health Information Management Association (AHIMA).

Schraffenberger, L. A. (2013). *Basic ICD-10-CM/PCS and ICD-9-CM coding.* Chicago: American Health Information Management Association (AHIMA).

Schraffenberger, L. A., & Kuehn, L. (2011). *Effective management of coding services* (4th ed.). Chicago: American Health Information Management Association (AHIMA).

Smith, G. (2014). *Basic current procedural terminology and HCPCS coding 2014.* Chicago: American Health Information Management Association (AHIMA).

CCS COMPETENCIES BY QUESTION FOR

Classification Systems and Secondary Date Sources

Question	CCS Domains							
	1	2	3	4	5	6	7	8
1	X							
2	X							
3	X							
4						X		
5	X					,		
6								X
7	X							
8	X							
9	X							
10	X							
11	X							
12	X							
13	X							
14				X				
15	X							
16	X							
17	X							
18	X							
19					X			
20					X			
21					X			
22					X			
23								X
24					X			
25					X			
26					X			
27					X			
28	X							
29				X				

Question	CCS Domains							
	1	2	3	4	5	6	7	8
30								X
31	X							
32	X							
33	X							
34					X			
35	X							
36	X							
37	X							
	1	2	3	4	5	6	7	8
38					X			
39				X				
40				X				
41						X		
42				X				
43				X				
44	X							
45						X		
46				X				
47						X		
48			X					
49				X				
50				X				
51				X				
52				X				
53				X				
54				X				
55								X
56	X							
57				X				
58						X		
59	X							
60	X							

Question	CCS Domains							
	1	2	3	4	5	6	7	8
61					X			
62					X			
63								X
64					X			
65				X				
66				X				
67						X		
68						X		
69					X			
70	X							
71				X				
72	X							
73				X				
74						X		
75	X							
76	X							
77	X							
78	X							
79	X							
80	X							
81			X					
82			X					
83			X					
84			X					
85			X					
86			X					
87			X					

VI. Medical Billing and Reimbursement Systems

Crystal A. Clack, MS, RHIA, CCS

1. The case-mix management system that utilizes information from the Minimum Data Set (MDS) in long-term care settings is called
   A. Medicare Severity Diagnosis Related Groups (MS-DRGs).
   B. Resource Based Relative Value System (RBRVS).
   C. Resource Utilization Groups (RUGs).
   D. Ambulatory Patient Classifications (APCs).

REFERENCE: Green, p 862

2. The prospective payment system used to reimburse home health agencies for patients with Medicare utilizes data from the:
   A. MDS (Minimum Data Set).
   B. OASIS (Outcome and Assessment Information Set).
   C. UHDDS (Uniform Hospital Discharge Data Set).
   D. UACDS (Uniform Ambulatory Core Data Set).

REFERENCE: Green, p 863
               Schraffenberger and Kuehn, p 140

3. Under APCs, the payment status indicator "N" means that the payment
   A. is for ancillary services.
   B. is for a clinic or an emergency visit.
   C. is discounted at 50%.
   D. is packaged into the payment for other services.

REFERENCE: Sayles, pp 275–276

4. All of the following items are "packaged" under the Medicare outpatient prospective payment system, EXCEPT for
   A. recovery room.   C. anesthesia.
   B. medical supplies.   D. medical visits.

REFERENCE: LaTour, Eichenwald-Maki, and Oachs, p 393
               Sayles, p 330

5. Under the RBRVS, each HCPCS/CPT code contains three components, each having assigned relative value units. These three components are
   A. geographic index, wage index, and cost of living index.
   B. fee-for-service, per diem payment, and capitation.
   C. conversion factor, CMS weight, and hospital-specific rate.
   D. physician work, practice expense, and malpractice insurance expense.

REFERENCE: Green, p 867

6. The prospective payment system used to reimburse hospitals for Medicare hospital outpatients is called
   A. APGs.
   B. RBRVS.
   C. APCs.
   D. MS-DRGs.

REFERENCE: Green, p 863
               Schraffenberger and Kuehn, p 196

7. A Medicare patient was seen by Dr. Zachary, who is a nonparticipating physician. The charge for the office visit was $125. The Medicare beneficiary had already met his deductible. The Medicare Fee Schedule amount is $100. Dr. Zachary does not accept assignment. The office manager will apply a practice termed as "balance billing," which means that the patient is
   A. financially liable for the Medicare Fee Schedule amount.
   B. financially liable for charges in excess of the Medicare Fee Schedule, up to a limit.
   C. not financially liable for any amount.
   D. financially liable for only the deductible.

REFERENCE: Sayles, pp 295–297

8. The prospective payment system based on resource utilization groups (RUGs) is used for reimbursement to _____ for patients with Medicare.
   A. freestanding ambulatory surgery centers
   B. hospital-based outpatients
   C. intermediate care facilities
   D. skilled nursing facilities

REFERENCE: Schraffenberger and Kuehn, p 212

9. The _____ is a statement sent to the provider to explain payments made by third-party payers.
   A. remittance advice
   B. advance beneficiary notice
   C. attestation statement
   D. acknowledgment notice

REFERENCE: Green, p 886
               Green and Rowell, p 89

10. How many major diagnostic categories are there in the MS-DRG system?
    A. 100
    B. 2,000
    C. 80
    D. 25

REFERENCE: Scott, p 37

11. The computer-to-computer transfer of data between providers and third-party payers in a data format agreed upon by both parties is called
    A. HIPAA (Health Insurance Portability and Accountability Act).
    B. electronic data interchange (EDI).
    C. health information exchange (HIE).
    D. health data exchange (HDE).

REFERENCE: Green and Rowell, p 721

12. A computer software program that assigns appropriate MS-DRGs according to the information provided for each episode of care is called a(n)
    A. encoder.
    B. case-mix analyzer.
    C. grouper.
    D. scrubber.

REFERENCE: Casto and Forrestal, p 134

13. The standard claim form used by hospitals to request reimbursement for inpatient and outpatient procedures performed or services provided is called the
    A. UB-04.
    B. CMS-1500.
    C. CMS-1491.
    D. CMS-1600.

REFERENCE: Brown and Tyler, p 37
              Green and Rowell, p 741
              Scott, p 76

14. Under ASCs, when multiple procedures are performed during the same surgical session, a payment reduction is applied. The procedure in the highest level group is reimbursed at _____ and all remaining procedures are reimbursed at _____.
    A. 50%, 25%
    B. 100%, 50%
    C. 100%, 25%
    D. 100%, 75%

REFERENCE: Casto and Forrestal, p 192

15. The _____ refers to a statement sent to the patient to show how much the provider billed, how much Medicare reimbursed the provider, and what the patient must pay the provider.
    A. Medicare summary notice
    B. remittance advice
    C. advance beneficiary notice
    D. coordination of benefits

REFERENCE: Green and Rowell, p 731
              LaTour, Eichenwald-Maki, and Oachs, p 445
              Sayles, pp 289–290

16. Currently, which prospective payment system is used to determine the payment to the "physician" for physician services covered under Medicare Part B, such as outpatient surgery performed on a Medicare patient?
    A. MS-DRGs
    B. APCs
    C. RBRVS
    D. ASCs

REFERENCE: Green, p 867
              Schraffenberger and Kuehn, p 210

17. Which of the following best describes the situation of a provider who agrees to accept assignment for Medicare Part B services?
    A. The provider is reimbursed at 15% above the allowed charge.
    B. The provider is paid according to the Medicare Physician Fee Schedule (MPFS) plus 10%.
    C. The provider cannot bill the patients for the balance between the MPFS amount and the total charges.
    D. The provider is a nonparticipating provider.

REFERENCE: Green and Rowell, p 731

18. When the MS-DRG payment received by the hospital is lower than the actual charges for providing the inpatient services for a patient with Medicare, then the hospital
    A. makes a profit.
    B. can bill the patient for the difference.
    C. absorbs the loss.
    D. can bill Medicare for the difference.

REFERENCE: LaTour, Eichenwald-Maki, and Oachs, p 432

19. Under ASCs, bilateral procedures are reimbursed at _____ of the payment rate for their group.
    A. 50%   C. 200%
    B. 100%   D. 150%

REFERENCE: Casto and Forrestal, p 192

Use the following table to answer questions 20 through 23.

Plantation Hospital's TOP 10 MS-DRGs

MS-DRG	Description	Number of Patients	CMS Relative Weight
470	Major joint replacement or reattachment of lower extremity w/o MCC	2,750	1.9871
392	Esophagitis, gastroent & misc. digestive disorders w/o MCC	2,200	0.7121
194	Simple pneumonia & pleurisy w CC	1,150	1.0235
247	Perc cardiovasc proc 2 drug-eluting stent w/o MCC	900	2.1255
293	Heart failure & shock w/o CC/MCC	850	0.8765
313	Chest pain	650	0.5489
292	Heart failure & shock w CC	550	1.0134
690	Kidney & urinary tract infections w/o MCC	400	0.8000
192	Chronic obstructive pulmonary disease w/o CC/MCC	300	0.8145
871	Septicemia w/o MV 96+ hours w MCC	250	1.7484

20. The case-mix index (CMI) for the top 10 MS-DRGs above is
    A. 1.164.   C. 0.782.
    B. 1.278.   D. 1.097.

REFERENCE: Abdelhak, Grostick, and Hanken, p 671
                 Casto and Forrestal, p 127
                 Sayles, p 269

21. Which individual MS-DRGs has the highest reimbursement?
    A. 247
    B. 470
    C. 871
    D. 293

REFERENCE: Casto and Forrestal, p 127
      Sayles, p 269

22. Based on this patient volume, during this time period, the MS-DRG that brings in the highest "total" reimbursement to the hospital is
    A. 470.
    B. 247.
    C. 392.
    D. 871.

REFERENCE: Casto and Forrestal, p 127
      Sayles, p 296

23. Based on this patient volume, the MS-DRG that brings in the highest total profit to the hospital is
    A. 470.
    B. 247.
    C. 392.
    D. It cannot be determined from this information.

REFERENCE: Casto and Forrestal, p 127
      Sayles, p 269

24. The Health Insurance Portability and Accountability Act (HIPAA) requires the retention of health insurance claims and accounting records for a minimum of _____ years, unless state law specifies a longer period.
    A. six
    B. five
    C. seven
    D. ten

REFERENCE: Green and Rowell, pp 188–119

25. _____ is knowingly making false statements or representation of material facts to obtain a benefit or payment for which no entitlement would otherwise exist.
    A. Fraud
    B. Whistle-blowing
    C. Abuse
    D. Assault

REFERENCE: Abdelhak, Gorstick, and Hanken, p 672

26. These are assigned to every HCPCS/CPT code under the Medicare hospital outpatient prospective payment system to identify how the service or procedure described by the code would be paid.
    A. geographic practice cost indices
    B. major diagnostic categories
    C. minimum data set
    D. payment status indicator

REFERENCE: Casto and Forrestal, p 177

27. The term used to indicate that the service or procedure is reasonable and necessary for the diagnosis or treatment of illness or injury consistent with generally accepted standards of care is
    A. appropriateness.
    B. evidence-based medicine.
    C. benchmarking.
    D. medical necessity.

REFERENCE: Green and Rowell, p 370

28. This law prohibits a physician from referring Medicare patients to clinical laboratory services where the doctor or a member of his family has a financial interest.
    A. the False Claims Act
    B. the Civil Monetary Penalties Act
    C. the Federal Antikickback Statute
    D. the Stark I Law

REFERENCE: Green, p 884
                 Green and Bowie, p 325

29. ____ are errors in medical care that are clearly identifiable, preventable, and serious in their consequences for patients.
    A. Sentinel events
    B. Adverse preventable events
    C. Never events
    D. Potential compensable events

REFERENCE: Green and Bowie, p 326

30. When a provider, knowingly or unknowingly, uses practices that are inconsistent with accepted medical practice and that directly or indirectly result in unnecessary costs to the Medicare program, this is called
    A. fraud.
    B. abuse.
    C. unbundling.
    D. hypercoding.

REFERENCE: Abdelhak, Gostick, and Hanken, p 672

31. What prospective payment system reimburses the provider according to prospectively determined rates for a 60-day episode of care?
    A. home health resource groups
    B. inpatient rehabilitation facility
    C. long-term care Medicare severity diagnosis-related groups
    D. the skilled nursing facility prospective payment system

REFERENCE: Green and Bowie, p 313

32. If the Medicare non-PAR approved payment amount is $128.00 for a proctoscopy, what is the total Medicare approved payment amount for a doctor who does not accept assignment, applying the limiting charge for this procedure?
    A. $140.80   C. $192.00
    B. $143.00   D. $147.20

REFERENCE: Green and Rowell, p 66

33. Under the inpatient prospective payment system (IPPS), there is a 3-day payment window (formerly referred to as the 72-hour rule). This rule requires that outpatient preadmission services that are provided by a hospital up to three calendar days prior to a patient's inpatient admission be covered by the IPPS MS-DRG payment for
   A. diagnostic services.
   B. therapeutic (or nondiagnostic) services whereby the inpatient principal diagnosis code (ICD-9-CM) exactly matches the code used for preadmission services.
   C. therapeutic (or nondiagnostic) services whereby the inpatient principal diagnosis code (ICD-9-CM) does not match the code used for preadmission services.
   D. both A and B.

REFERENCE: Green, pp 858–859
               Green and Bowie, p 313
               Green and Rowell, p 325

34. This initiative was instituted by the government to eliminate fraud and abuse and recover overpayments, and involves the use of _____. Charts are audited to identify Medicare overpayments and underpayments. These entities are paid based on a percentage of money they identify and collect on behalf of the government.
   A. Clinical Data Abstraction Centers (CDAC)
   B. Quality Improvement Organizations (QIO)
   C. Medicare Code Editors (MCE)
   D. Recovery Audit Contractors (RAC)

REFERENCE: Green, p 850
               Scott, p 119

35. When a patient is discharged from the inpatient rehabilitation facility and returns within three calendar days (prior to midnight on the third day) this is called a(n)
   A. interrupted stay.   C. per diem.
   B. transfer.   D. qualified discharge.

REFERENCE: Casto and Forrestal, pp 233–234
               Scott, pp 68–69

36. In a global payment methodology, which is sometimes applied to radiological and similar types of procedures that involve professional and technical components, all of the following are part of the "technical" components EXCEPT
   A. radiological equipment.   C. radiological supplies.
   B. physician services.   D. radiologic technicians

REFERENCE: Green and Rowell, pp 275–276
               LaTour, Eichenwald-Maki, and Oachs, p 430
               Sayles, pp 263–264

37. Changes in case-mix index (CMI) may be attributed to all of the following factors EXCEPT
   A. changes in medical staff composition.
   B. changes in coding rules.
   C. changes in services offered.
   D. changes in coding productivity.

REFERENCE: Schraffenberger and Kuehn, pp 484–485

38. This prospective payment system replaced the Medicare physician payment system of "customary, prevailing, and reasonable (CPR)" charges whereby physicians were reimbursed according to their historical record of the charge for the provision of each service.
    A. Medicare Physician Fee Schedule (MPFS)
    B. Medicare Severity-Diagnosis Related Groups (MS-DRGs)
    C. Global payment
    D. Capitation

REFERENCE: Green, p 867
                Green and Rowell, pp 379–380

39. CMS-identified "Hospital-Acquired Conditions" mean that when a particular diagnosis is not "present on admission," CMS determines it to be
    A. medically necessary.
    B. reasonably preventable.
    C. a valid comorbidity.
    D. the principal diagnosis.

REFERENCE: LaTour, Eichenwald-Maki, and Oachs, pp 433–434

40. This process involves the gathering of charge documents from all departments within the facility that have provided services to patients. The purpose is to make certain that all charges are coded and entered into the billing system.
    A. precertification
    B. insurance verification
    C. charge capturing
    D. revenue cycle

REFERENCE: Diamond, p 9

41. The Correct Coding Initiative (CCI) edits contain a listing of codes under two columns titled "comprehensive codes" and "component codes." According to the CCI edits, when a provider bills Medicare for a procedure that appears in both columns for the same beneficiary on the same date of service
    A. code only the component code.
    B. do not code either one.
    C. code only the comprehensive code.
    D. code both the comprehensive code and the component code.

REFERENCE: Green, pp 395–398
                Green and Rowell, pp 283–288

42. The following type of hospital is considered excluded when it applies for and receives a waiver from CMS. This means that the hospital does not participate in the inpatient prospective payment system (IPPS)
    A. rehabilitation hospital
    B. long-term care hospital
    C. psychiatric hospital
    D. cancer hospital

REFERENCE: Green, p 858

43. These are financial protections to ensure that certain types of facilities (e.g., children's hospitals) recoup all of their losses due to the differences in their APC payments and the pre-APC payments.
    A. limiting charge
    B. indemnity insurance
    C. hold harmless
    D. pass through

REFERENCE: Casto and Forrestal, p 176

44. LCDs and NCDs are review policies that describe the circumstances of coverage for various types of medical treatment. They advise physicians which services Medicare considers reasonable and necessary and may indicate the need for an advance beneficiary notice. They are developed by the Centers for Medicare and Medicaid Services (CMS) and Medicare Administrative Contractors. LCD and NCD are acronyms that stand for
    A. local covered determinations and noncovered determinations.
    B. local coverage determinations and national coverage determinations.
    C. list of covered decisions and noncovered decisions.
    D. local contractor's decisions and national contractor's decisions.

REFERENCE: Green, p 775
               Green and Rowell, pp 305–307

Use the following table to answer questions 45 through 50.

EXAMPLE OF A CHARGE DESCRIPTION MASTER (CDM) FILE LAYOUT

Charge Service Code	Item Service Description	General Ledger Key	HCPCS Code		Charge	Revenue Code	Activity Date
			Medicare	Medicaid			
49683105	CT scan; head; w/out contrast	3	70450	70450	500.00	0351	1/1/2013
49683106	CT scan; head; with contrast	3	70460	70460	675.00	0351	1/1/2013

45. This information is printed on the UB-04 claim form to represent the cost center (e.g., lab, radiology, cardiology, respiratory, etc.) for the department in which the item is provided. It is used for Medicare billing.
    A. HCPCS
    B. revenue code
    C. charge/service code
    D. general ledger key

REFERENCE: Green, pp 870–871
               Green and Rowell, p 342
               Schraffenberger and Kuehn, pp 225–226

46. This information is used because it provides a uniform system of identifying procedures, services, or supplies. Multiple columns can be available for various financial classes.
    A. HCPCS code
    B. revenue code
    C. general ledger key
    D. charge/service code

REFERENCE: Green, p 880
               Green and Rowell, p 295
               Schraffenberger and Kuehn, pp 226–227

47. This information provides a narrative name of the services provided. This information should be presented in a clear and concise manner. When possible, the narratives from the HCPCS/CPT book should be utilized.
    A. general ledger key
    B. HCPCS
    C. item/service description
    D. revenue code

REFERENCE: Green, p 872
               Green and Rowell, pp 340–342
               Schraffenberger and Kuehn, p 225

48. This information is the numerical identification of the service or supply. Each item has a unique number with a prefix that indicates the department number (the number assigned to a specific ancillary department) and an item number (the number assigned by the accounting department or the business office) for a specific procedure or service represented on the chargemaster.
    A. charge/service code
    B. HCPCS code
    C. revenue code
    D. general ledger key

REFERENCE: Green, pp 870–871
               Green and Rowell, pp 340–342
               Schraffenberger and Kuehn, p 225

49. This information is used to assign each item to a particular section of the general ledger in a particular facility's accounting section. Reports can be generated from this information to include statistics related to volume in terms of numbers, dollars, and payer types.
    A. general ledger key
    B. charge/service code
    C. revenue code
    D. HCPCS code

REFERENCE: Green, p 872
               Schraffenberger and Kuehn, p 225

50. Under APCs, the patient is responsible for paying the coinsurance amount based upon ____ of the national median charge for the services rendered.
    A. 50%
    B. 15%
    C. 20%
    D. 80%

REFERENCE: Green and Bowie, p 314

51. ____ is a joint federal and state program that provides health care coverage to low-income populations and certain aged and disabled individuals.
    A. TRICARE
    B. Medicare Part A
    C. Medicaid
    D. Medicare Part B

REFERENCE: Green, p 851

52. The DNFB report includes all patients who have been discharged from the facility but for whom, for one reason or another, the billing process is not complete. DNFB is an acronym for

    _____.
    A. diagnosis not finally balanced
    B. days not fiscally balanced
    C. dollars not fully billed
    D. discharged not final billed

REFERENCE: Schraffenberger and Kuehn, p 461

53. The limiting charge is a percentage limit on fees specified by legislation that the nonparticipating physician may bill Medicare beneficiaries above the non-PAR fee schedule amount. The limiting charge is
    A. 10%.
    B. 15%.
    C. 20%.
    D. 50%.

REFERENCE: Green and Rowell, p 498

Use the following case scenario to answer questions 54 through 58.

> A patient with Medicare is seen in the physician's office.
> The total charge for this office visit is $250.00.
> The patient has previously paid his deductible under Medicare Part B.
> The PAR Medicare Fee Schedule amount for this service is $200.00.
> The non-PAR Medicare Fee Schedule amount for this service is $190.00.

54. The patient is financially liable for the coinsurance amount, which is
    A. 80%.
    B. 100%.
    C. 20%.
    D. 15%.

REFERENCE: Green and Rowell, p 498

55. If this physician is a participating physician who accepts assignment for this claim, the total amount the physician will receive is
    A. $200.00.
    B. $250.00.
    C. $218.50.
    D. $190.00.

REFERENCE: Green and Rowell, p 498

56. If this physician is a nonparticipating physician who does NOT accept assignment for this claim, the total amount the physician will receive is
    A. $250.00.
    B. $200.00.
    C. $218.50.
    D. $190.00.

REFERENCE: Green and Rowell, p 498

57. If this physician is a participating physician who accepts assignment for this claim, the total amount of the patient's financial liability (out-of-pocket expense) is
    A. $200.00.
    B. $40.00.
    C. $160.00.
    D. $30.00.

REFERENCE: Green and Rowell, p 498

58. If this physician is a nonparticipating physician who does NOT accept assignment for this claim, the total amount of the patient's financial liability (out-of-pocket expense) is
    A. $66.50.
    B. $38.00.
    C. $190.00.
    D. $152.00.

REFERENCE: Green and Rowell, p 498

59. A fiscal year is a yearly accounting period. It is the 12-month period on which a budget is planned. The federal fiscal year is
    A. October 1st through September 30 of the next year.
    B. January 1st through December 31.
    C. July 1st through the June 30 of the next year.
    D. April 1st through March 31 of the next year.

REFERENCE: Casto and Forrestal, p 309

60. There are times when documentation is incomplete or insufficient to support the diagnoses found in the chart. The most common way of communicating with the physician for answers is by
    A. e-mailing physicians.
    B. using physician query forms.
    C. calling the physician's office.
    D. leaving notes in the chart.

REFERENCE:　　Green, pp 15–17
　　　　　　　Scott, pp 189–199

61. Under APCs, payment status indicator "X" means
    A. ancillary services.
    B. clinic or emergency department visit (medical visits).
    C. significant procedure, multiple procedure reduction applies.
    D. significant procedure, not discounted when multiple.

REFERENCE:　　Casto and Forrestal, p 177
　　　　　　　Diamond, p 337
　　　　　　　LaTour, Eichenwald-Maki, and Oachs, p 436

62. Under APCs, payment status indicator "V" means
    A. ancillary services.
    B. clinic or emergency department visit (medical visits).
    C. inpatient procedure.
    D. significant procedure, not discounted when multiple.

REFERENCE:　　Casto and Forrestal, p 177
　　　　　　　Diamond, p 337
　　　　　　　LaTour, Eichenwald-Maki, and Oachs, p 436

63. Under APCs, payment status indicator "S" means
    A. ancillary services.
    B. clinic or emergency department visit (medical visits).
    C. significant procedure, multiple procedure reduction applies.
    D. significant procedure, multiple procedure reduction does not apply.

REFERENCE:　　Casto and Forrestal, p 177
　　　　　　　Diamond, p 337
　　　　　　　Green and Rowell, p 328
　　　　　　　LaTour, Eichenwald-Maki, and Oachs, p 436

64. Under APCs, payment status indicator "T" means
    A. ancillary services.
    B. clinic or emergency department visit (medical visits).
    C. significant procedure, multiple procedure reduction applies.
    D. significant procedure, not discounted when multiple.

REFERENCE:　　Casto and Forrestal, p 177
　　　　　　　Diamond, p 337
　　　　　　　Green, pp 863–864
　　　　　　　LaTour, Eichenwald-Maki, and Oachs, p 436

65. Under APCs, payment status indicator "C" means
    A. ancillary services.
    B. inpatient procedures/services.
    C. significant procedure, multiple procedure reduction applies.
    D. significant procedure, not discounted when multiple.

REFERENCE: Casto and Forrestal, p 177
              Diamond, p 337
              LaTour, Eichenwald-Maki, and Oachs, p 436

66. This is a 10-digit, intelligence-free, numeric identifier designed to replace all previous provider legacy numbers. This number identifies the physician universally to all payers. This number is issued to all HIPAA-covered entities. It is mandatory on the CMS-1500 and UB-04 claim forms.
    A. National Practitioner Databank (NPD)
    B. Universal Physician Number (UPN)
    C. Master Patient Index (MPI)
    D. National Provider Identifier (NPI)

REFERENCE: Green and Rowell, p 886

67. In the managed care industry, there are specific reimbursement concepts, such as "capitation." All of the following statements are true in regard to the concept of "capitation," EXCEPT
    A. each service is paid based on the actual charges.
    B. the volume of services and their expense do not affect reimbursement.
    C. capitation means paying a fixed amount per member per month.
    D. capitation involves a group of physicians or an individual physician.

REFERENCE: Green and Rowell, p 45

68. Which of the following statements is FALSE regarding the use of modifiers with the CPT codes?
    A. All modifiers will alter (increase or decrease) the reimbursement of the procedure.
    B. Some procedures may require more than one modifier.
    C. Modifiers are appended to the end of the CPT code.
    D. Not all procedures need a modifier.

REFERENCE: Richards, p 147

69. This document is published by the Office of Inspector General (OIG) every year. It details the OIG's focus for Medicare fraud and abuse for that year. It gives health care providers an indication of general and specific areas that are targeted for review. It can be found on the Internet on CMS' Web site.
    A. the OIG's Evaluation and Management Documentation Guidelines
    B. the OIG's Model Compliance Plan
    C. the Federal Register
    D. the OIG's Workplan

REFERENCE: Sayles, p 305

70. Accounts Receivable (A/R) refers to
    A. cases that have not yet been paid.
    B. the amount the hospital was paid.
    C. cases that have been paid.
    D. denials that have been returned to the hospital.

REFERENCE: Schraffenberger and Kuehn, p 458

71. The following coding system(s) is/are utilized in the MS-DRG prospective payment methodology for assignment and proper reimbursement.
    A. HCPCS/CPT codes
    B. ICD-9-CM codes
    C. both HCPCS/CPT codes and ICD-9-CM codes
    D. none of the above

REFERENCE: Green, p 885
              Sayles, p 267

72. The following coding system(s) is/are utilized in the Inpatient Psychiatric Facilities (IPFs) prospective payment methodology for assignment and proper reimbursement.
    A. HCPCS/CPT codes
    B. ICD-9-CM codes
    C. both HCPCS/CPT codes and ICD-9-CM codes
    D. none of the above

REFERENCE: Green, p 865
              Sayles, p 285

73. An Advance Beneficiary Notice (ABN) is a document signed by the
    A. utilization review coordinator indicating that the patient stay is not medically necessary.
    B. physician advisor indicating that the patient's stay is denied.
    C. patient indicating whether he/she wants to receive services that Medicare probably will not pay for.
    D. provider indicating that Medicare will not pay for certain services.

REFERENCE: Green, p 358
              LaTour, Eichenwald-Maki, and Oachs, pp 449–450

74. CMS identified Hospital-Acquired Conditions (HACs). Some of these HACs include foreign objects retained after surgery, blood incompatibility, and catheter-associated urinary tract infection. The importance of the HAC payment provision is that the hospital
    A. will receive additional payment for these conditions when they are not present on admission.
    B. will not receive additional payment for these conditions when they are not present on admission.
    C. will receive additional payment for these conditions whether they are present on admission or not.
    D. will not receive additional payment for these conditions when they are present on admission.

REFERENCE: LaTour, Eichenwald-Maki, and Oachs, pp 433–434

75. Under Medicare Part B, all of the following statements are true and are applicable to nonparticipating physician providers, EXCEPT
    A. providers must file all Medicare claims.
    B. nonparticipating providers have a higher fee schedule than that for participating providers.
    C. fees are restricted to charging no more than the "limiting charge" on nonassigned claims.
    D. collections are restricted to only the deductible and coinsurance due at the time of service on an assigned claim.

REFERENCE: Green and Rowell, pp 380–383

76. Under Medicare, a beneficiary has lifetime reserve days. All of the following statements are true, EXCEPT
    A. the patient has a total of 60 lifetime reserve days.
    B. lifetime reserve days are usually reserved for use during the patient's final (terminal) hospital stay.
    C. lifetime reserve days are paid under Medicare Part B.
    D. lifetime reserve days are not renewable, meaning once a patient uses all of their lifetime reserve days, the patient is responsible for the total charges.

REFERENCE: Green and Rowell, pp 528–529

77. When a provider bills separately for procedures that are a part of the major procedure, this is called
    A. fraud.   C. unbundling.
    B. packaging.   D. discounting.

REFERENCE: Brown and Tyler, p 192

78. Once all data are posted to a patient's account, the claim can be reviewed for accuracy and completeness. Many facilities have internal auditing systems. The auditing systems run each claim through a set of edits specifically designed for the various third-party payers. The auditing system identifies data that have failed edits and flags the claim for correction. These "internal" auditing systems are called
    A. scrubbers.   C. groupers.
    B. pricers.   D. encoders.

REFERENCE: Casto and Forrestal, p 262

79. To compute the reimbursement to a particular hospital for a particular MS-DRG, multiply the hospital's base payment rate by the
    A. conversion factor.   C. geographic practice cost index.
    B. case-mix index.   D. relative weight for the MS-DRG.

REFERENCE: Casto and Forrestal, p 134

80. Under the APC methodology, discounted payments occur when
    A. there are two or more (multiple) procedures that are assigned to status indicator "T."
    B. there are two or more (multiple) procedures that are assigned to status indicator "S."
    C. modifier-73 is used to indicate a procedure is terminated after the patient is prepared but before anesthesia is started.
    D. both A and C.

REFERENCE: Green and Rowell, pp 373–374
                 Schraffenberger and Kuehn, pp 207–209

81. This prospective payment system is for _____ and utilizes a Patient Assessment Instrument (PAI) to classify patients into case-mix groups (CMGs).
    A. skilled nursing facilities
    B. inpatient rehabilitation facilities
    C. home health agencies
    D. long-term acute care hospitals

REFERENCE: Green and Rowell, p 331
               Schraffenberger and Kuehn, p 213

82. Home Health Agencies (HHAs) utilize a data entry software system developed by the Centers for Medicare and Medicaid Services (CMS). This software is available to HHAs at no cost through the CMS Web site or on a CD-ROM.
    A. PACE (Patient Assessment and Comprehensive Evaluation)
    B. HAVEN (Home Assessment Validation and Entry)
    C. HHASS (Home Health Agency Software System)
    D. PEPP (Payment Error Prevention Program)

REFERENCE: Green and Rowell, p 321
               LaTour, Eichenwald-Maki, and Oachs, p 438
               Sayles, p 278

83. This information is published by the Medicare Administrative Contractors (MACs) to describe when and under what circumstances Medicare will cover a service. The ICD-9-CM and CPT/HCPCS codes are listed in the memoranda.
    A. LCD (Local Coverage Determinations)
    B. SI/IS (Severity of llness/Intensity of Service Criteria)
    C. OSHA (Occupational Safety and Health Administration)
    D. PEPP (Payment Error Prevention Program)

REFERENCE: Green and Rowell, p 377

84. The term "hard coding" refers to
    A. HCPCS/CPT codes that are coded by the coders.
    B. HCPCS/CPT codes that appear in the hospital's chargemaster and will be included automatically on the patient's bill.
    C. ICD-9-CM codes that are coded by the coders.
    D. ICD-9-CM codes that appear in the hospital's chargemaster and that are automatically included on the patient's bill.

REFERENCE: Schraffenberger and Kuehn, pp 228–229

85. This is the amount collected by the facility for the services it bills.
    A. costs
    B. charges
    C. reimbursement
    D. contractual allowance

REFERENCE: Schraffenberger and Kuehn, pp 433–434

86. Assume the patient has already met his or her deductible and that the physician is a Medicare participating (PAR) provider. The physician's standard fee for the services provided is $120.00. Medicare's PAR fee is $60.00. How much reimbursement will the physician receive from Medicare?
   A. $120.00
   B. $ 60.00
   C. $ 48.00
   D. $ 96.00

REFERENCE: Green and Rowell, p 498

87. This accounting method attributes a dollar figure to every input required to provide a service.
   A. cost accounting
   B. charge accounting
   C. reimbursement
   D. contractual allowance

REFERENCE: Schraffenberger and Kuehn, p 433

88. This is the amount the facility actually bills for the services it provides.
   A. costs
   B. charges
   C. reimbursement
   D. contractual allowance

REFERENCE: Schraffenberger and Kuehn, p 433

89. This is the difference between what is charged and what is paid.
   A. costs
   B. customary
   C. reimbursement
   D. contractual allowance

REFERENCE: Schraffenberger and Kuehn, p 433

90. When appropriate, under the outpatient PPS, a hospital can use this CPT code in place of, but not in addition to, a code for a medical visit or emergency department service.
   A. CPT Code 99291 (critical care)
   B. CPT Code 99358 (prolonged evaluation and management service)
   C. CPT Code 35001 (direct repair of aneurysm)
   D. CPT Code 50300 (donor nephrectomy)

REFERENCE: Kirchoff, p 42

91. To monitor timely claims processing in a hospital, a summary report of "patient receivables" is generated frequently. Aged receivables can negatively affect a facility's cash flow; therefore, to maintain the facility's fiscal integrity, the HIM manager must routinely analyze this report. Though this report has no standard title, it is often called the
   A. remittance advice.
   B. periodic interim payments.
   C. DNFB (discharged, no final bill).
   D. chargemaster.

REFERENCE: LaTour, Eichenwald-Maki, and Oachs, p 470

92. Assume the patient has already met his or her deductible and that the physician is a nonparticipating Medicare provider but does accept assignment. The standard fee for the services provided is $120.00. Medicare's PAR fee is $60.00 and Medicare's non-PAR fee is $57.00. How much reimbursement will the physician receive from Medicare?
   A. $120.00
   B. $60.00
   C. $57.00
   D. $45.60

REFERENCE: Green and Rowell, p 498

93. CMS assigns one _____ to each APC and each _____ code.
    A. payment status indicator, HCPCS
    B. CPT code, HCPCS
    C. MS-DRG, CPT
    D. payment status indicator, ICD-9-CM

REFERENCE: Kirchoff, p 11

94. All of the following statements are true of MS-DRGs, EXCEPT
    A. a patient claim may have multiple MS-DRGs.
    B. the MS-DRG payment received by the hospital may be lower than the actual cost of providing the services.
    C. special circumstances can result in a cost outlier payment to the hospital.
    D. there are several types of hospitals that are excluded from the Medicare inpatient PPS.

REFERENCE: Green and Rowell, pp 367–370
               Johns, pp 321–324
               LaTour, Eichenwald-Maki, and Oachs, pp 431–433
               Sayles, pp 266–270

95. This program, formerly called CHAMPUS (Civilian Health and Medical Program—Uniformed Services), is a health care program for active members of the military and other qualified family members.
    A. TRICARE   C. Indian Health Service
    B. CHAMPVA   D. workers' compensation

REFERENCE: Green and Rowell, p 573
               Richards, pp 116–118, 300
               Sayles, p 251

96. When health care providers are found guilty under any of the civil false claims statutes, the Office of Inspector General is responsible for negotiating these settlements and the provider is placed under a
    A. Fraud Prevention Memorandum of Understanding.
    B. Noncompliance Agreement.
    C. Corporate Integrity Agreement.
    D. Recovery Audit Contract.

REFERENCE: Brown and Tyler, p 267

97. Regarding hospital emergency department and hospital outpatient evaluation and management CPT code assignment, which statement is true?
    A. Each facility is accountable for developing and implementing its own methodology.
    B. The level of service codes reported by the facility must match those reported by the physician.
    C. Each facility must use the same methodology used by physician coders based on the history, examination, and medical decision-making components.
    D. Each facility must use acuity sheets with acuity levels and assign points for each service performed.

REFERENCE: Diamond, pp 285–287

98. CMS adjusts the Medicare Severity DRGs and the reimbursement rates every
    A. calendar year beginning January 1.
    B. quarter.
    C. month.
    D. fiscal year beginning October 1.

REFERENCE: Sayles, p 268

99. In calculating the fee for a physician's reimbursement, the three relative value units are each multiplied by the
    A. geographic practice cost indices.
    B. national conversion factor.
    C. usual and customary fees for the service.
    D. cost of living index for the particular region.

REFERENCE: Green, p 867
Green and Rowell, pp 333–334

100. If a participating provider's usual fee for a service is $700.00 and Medicare's allowed amount is $450.00, what amount is written off by the physician?
    A. none of it is written off
    B. $250.00
    C. $340.00
    D. $391.00

REFERENCE: Green and Rowell, pp 380–383

101. Health plans that use _____ reimbursement methods issue lump-sum payments to providers to compensate them for all the health care services delivered to a patient for a specific illness and/or over a specific period of time.
    A. episode-of-care (EOC)
    B. capitation
    C. fee-for-service
    D. bundled

REFERENCE: Sayles, p 262

102. _____ offers voluntary, supplemental medical insurance to help pay for physician's services, outpatient hospital services, medical services, and medical-surgical supplies not covered by the hospitalization plan.
    A. Medicare Part A
    B. Medicare Part B
    C. Medicare Part C
    D. Medicare Part D

REFERENCE: Kirchoff, p 296

103. Commercial insurance plans usually reimburse health care providers under some type of _____ payment system, whereas the federal Medicare program uses some type of _____ payment system.
    A. prospective, retrospective
    B. retrospective, concurrent
    C. retrospective, prospective
    D. prospective, concurrent

REFERENCE: Green and Rowell, p 51
Sayles, pp 260–261

104. When the third-party payer refuses to grant payment to the provider, this is called a
    A. denied claim.
    B. clean claim.
    C. rejected claim.
    D. unprocessed claim.

REFERENCE: Green, p 29

105. Some services are performed by a nonphysician practitioner (such as a Physician Assistant). These services are an integral yet incidental component of a physician's treatment. A physician must have personally performed an initial visit and must remain actively involved in the continuing care. Medicare requires direct supervision for these services to be billed. This is called
    A. "Technical component" billing.
    B. "Assignment" billing.
    C. "Incident to" billing.
    D. "Assistant" billing.

REFERENCE: Green and Rowell, pp 339, 417

106. When payments can be made to the provider by EFT, this means that the reimbursement is
    A. sent to the provider by check.
    B. sent to the patient, who then pays the provider.
    C. combined with all other payments from the third party payer.
    D. directly deposited into the provider's bank account.

REFERENCE: Richards, p 175

107. The following services are excluded under the Hospital Outpatient Prospective Payment System (OPPS) Ambulatory Payment Classification (APC) methodology.
    A. surgical procedures
    B. clinical lab services
    C. clinic/emergency visits
    D. radiology/radiation therapy

REFERENCE: Diamond, p 333

108. A HIPPS (Health Insurance Prospective Payment System) code is a five-character alphanumeric code. A HIPPS code is used by
    A. ambulatory surgery centers (ASC).
    B. home health agencies (HHA).
    C. inpatient rehabilitation facilities (IRF).
    D. B and C.

REFERENCE: Casto and Forrestal, p 310

109. The Centers for Medicare and Medicaid Services (CMS) will make an adjustment to the MS-DRG payment for certain conditions that the patient was not admitted with, but were acquired during the hospital stay. Therefore, hospitals are required to report an indicator for each diagnosis. This indicator is referred to as
    A. a sentinel event.
    B. a payment status indicator.
    C. a hospital acquired condition.
    D. present on admission.

REFERENCE: Casto and Forrestal, pp 293–294

110. A patient is admitted for a diagnostic workup for cachexia. The final diagnosis is malignant neoplasm of lung with metastasis. The present on admission (POA) indicator is
   A. Y = Present at the time of inpatient admission.
   B. N = Not present at the time of inpatient admission.
   C. U = Documentation is insufficient to determine if condition was present at the time of admission.
   D. W = Provider is unable to clinically determine if condition was present at the time of admission.

REFERENCE: Green, p 861
              LaTour, Eichenwald-Maki, and Oachs, pp 433–434

111. A patient undergoes outpatient surgery. During the recovery period, the patient develops atrial fibrillation and is subsequently admitted to the hospital as an inpatient. The present on admission (POA) indicator is
   A. Y = Present at the time of inpatient admission.
   B. N = Not present at the time of inpatient admission.
   C. U = Documentation is insufficient to determine if condition was present at the time of admission.
   D. W = Provider is unable to clinically determine if condition was present at the time of admission.

REFERENCE: Green, p 861
              LaTour, Eichenwald-Maki, and Oachs, pp 433–434

112. A patient is admitted to the hospital for a coronary artery bypass surgery. Postoperatively, he develops a pulmonary embolism. The present on admission (POA) indicator is
   A. Y = Present at the time of inpatient admission.
   B. N = Not present at the time of inpatient admission.
   C. U = Documentation is insufficient to determine if condition was present at the time of admission.
   D. W = Provider is unable to clinically determine if condition was present at the time of admission.

REFERENCE: Green, p 861
              LaTour, Eichenwald-Maki, and Oachs, pp 433–434

113. The nursing initial assessment upon admission documents the presence of a decubitus ulcer. There is no mention of the decubitus ulcer in the physician documentation until several days after admission. The present on admission (POA) indicator is
   A. Y = Present at the time of inpatient admission.
   B. N = Not present at the time of inpatient admission.
   C. U = Documentation is insufficient to determine if condition was present at the time of admission.
   D. W = Provider is unable to clinically determine if condition was present at the time of admission.

REFERENCE: Green, p 861
              LaTour, Eichenwald-Maki, and Oachs, pp 433–434

114. The present on admission (POA) indicator is required to be assigned to the _____ diagnosis(es) for _____ claims on _____ admissions.
    A. principal and secondary, Medicare, inpatient
    B. principal, all, inpatient
    C. principal and secondary, all, inpatient and outpatient
    D. principal, Medicare, inpatient and outpatient

REFERENCE: Green, p 861
             LaTour, Eichenwald-Maki, and Oachs, pp 433–434

Answer Key for Medical Billing and Reimbursement Systems

ANSWER   EXPLANATION

1. C
2. B
3. A
4. D
5. D
6. C
7. B
8. D
9. A
10. D
11. B
12. C
13. A The UB-04 is used by hospitals. The CMS-1500 is used by physicians and other noninstitutional providers and suppliers. The CMS-1491 is used by ambulance services.
14. B
15. A
16. C The prospective payment system used to reimburse the "hospital" for outpatient surgery is APCs. The prospective payment used to reimburse a "free-standing surgery center" for outpatient surgery is ASCs. The prospective payment system used to reimburse the "physician" for outpatient surgery is RBRVS.
17. C Since the provider accepts assignment, he will accept the Medicare Physician Fee Schedule (MPFS) payment as payment in full.
18. C
19. D
20. B 12781.730/10,000 = 1.278

MS-DRG	Description	Number of Patients	CMS Relative Weight	Total CMS Relative Weight
470	Major joint replacement or reattachment of lower extremity w/o MCC	2,750	1.9871	5464.525
392	Esophagitis, gastroent & misc. digestive disorders w/o MCC	2,200	0.7121	1566.620
194	Simple pneumonia & pleurisy w CC	1,150	1.0235	1177.025
247	Perc cardiovasc proc 2 drug-eluting stent w/o MCC	900	2.1255	1912.950
293	Heart failure & shock w/o CC/MCC	850	0.8765	745.025
313	Chest pain	650	0.5489	356.785
292	Heart failure & shock w CC	550	1.0134	557.350
690	Kidney & urinary tract infections w/o MCC	400	0.8000	320.000
192	Chronic obstructive pulmonary disease w/o CC/MCC	300	0.8145	244.350
871	Septicemia w/o MV 96+ hours w MCC	250	1.7484	437.100
	Total	10,000		12781.730
	Case-Mix Index Total CMS Relative Weights (12781.730) divided by (10,000) patients			1.278

Answer Key for Medical Billing and Reimbursement Systems

	ANSWER	EXPLANATION
21.	A	(See table on answer key under question 20.)
22.	A	(See table on answer key under question 20.)
23.	D	Total profit cannot be determined from this information alone. A comparison of the total charges on the bills and the PPS amount (reimbursement amount) that the hospital would receive for each MS-DRG could identify the total profit.
24.	A	
25.	A	
26.	D	
27.	D	
28.	D	
29.	C	
30.	B	
31.	A	
32.	D	The limiting charge is 15% above Medicare's approved payment amount for doctors who do NOT accept assignment ($128.00 × 1.15 = $147.20).
33.	D	
34.	D	
35.	A	
36.	B	
37.	D	Coding productivity will not directly affect CMI. Inaccuracy or poor coding quality can affect CMI.
38.	A	The Medicare Physician Fee Schedule (MPFS) reimburses providers according to predetermined rates assigned to services.
39.	B	
40.	C	
41.	C	
42.	D	Cancer hospitals can apply for and receive waivers from the Centers for Medicare and Medicaid Services (CMS) and are therefore excluded from the inpatient prospective payment system (MS-DRGs). Rehabilitation hospitals are reimbursed under the Inpatient Rehabilitation Prospective Payment System (IRF PPS). Long-term care hospitals are reimbursed under the Long-Term Care Hospital Prospective Payment System (LTCH PPS). Skilled nursing facilities are reimbursed under the Skilled Nursing Facility Prospective Payment System (SNF PPS).
43.	C	
44.	B	
45.	B	
46.	A	
47.	C	
48.	A	
49.	A	
50.	C	
51.	C	
52.	D	
53.	B	
54.	C	

Answer Key for Medical Billing and Reimbursement Systems

ANSWER   EXPLANATION

55.   A   If a physician is a participating physician who accepts assignment, he will receive the lesser of "the total charges" or "the PAR Medicare Fee Schedule amount." In this case, the Medicare Fee Schedule amount is less; therefore, the total received by the physician is $200.00.

56.   C   If a physician is a nonparticipating physician who does not accept assignment, he can collect a maximum of 15% (the limiting charge) over the non-PAR Medicare Fee Schedule amount. In this case, the non-PAR Medicare Fee Schedule amount is $190.00 and 15% over this amount is $28.50; therefore, the total that he can collect is $218.50.

57.   B   The PAR Medicare Fee Schedule amount is $200.00. The patient has already met the deductible. Of the $200.00, the patient is responsible for 20% ($40.00). Medicare will pay 80% ($160.00). Therefore, the total financial liability for the patient is $40.00.

58.   A   If a physician is a nonparticipating physician who does not accept assignment, he may collect a maximum of 15% (the limiting charge) over the non-PAR Medicare Fee Schedule amount.

$190.00 = non-PAR Medicare Fee Schedule amount

$190.00 × 0.20 = $38.00 = patient liable for 20% coinsurance (patient previously met the deductible)

$190.00 × 0.80 = $152.00 = Medicare pays 80%

$190.00 × 0.15 = $28.50 = 15% (limiting charge) over non-PAR Medicare Fee Schedule amount

Physician can balance bill and collect from the patient the difference between the non-PAR Medicare Fee Schedule amount and the total charge amount. Therefore, the patient's financial liability is $38.00 (coinsurance) + 28.50 (limiting charge) = $66.50.

59.   A

60.   B

61.   A   Under the APC system, there exists a list of status indicators (also called service indicators, payment status indicators, or payment indicators). This indicator is provided for every HCPCS/CPT code and identifies how the service or procedure would be paid (if covered) by Medicare for hospital outpatient visits.

62.   B   Under the APC system, there exists a list of status indicators (also called service indicators, payment status indicators, or payment indicators). This indicator is provided for every HCPCS/CPT code and identifies how the service or procedure would be paid (if covered) by Medicare for hospital outpatient visits.

63.   D   Under the APC system, there exists a list of status indicators (also called service indicators, payment status indicators, or payment indicators). This indicator is provided for every HCPCS/CPT code and identifies how the service or procedure would be paid (if covered) by Medicare for hospital outpatient visits. Payment Status Indicator (PSI) "S" means that if a patient has more than one CPT code with this PSI, none of the procedures will be discounted or reduced. They will all be paid at 100%.

64.   C   Under the APC system, there exists a list of status indicators (also called service indicators, payment status indicators, or payment indicators). This indicator is provided for every HCPCS/CPT code and identifies how the service or procedure would be paid (if covered) by Medicare for hospital outpatient visits. Payment Status Indicator (PSI) "T" means that if a patient has more than one CPT code with this PSI, the procedure with the highest weight will be paid at 100% and all others will be reduced or discounted and paid at 50%.

Answer Key for Medical Billing and Reimbursement Systems

ANSWER   EXPLANATION

65.   B   Under the APC system, there exists a list of status indicators (also called service indicators, payment status indicators, or payment indicators). This indicator is provided for every HCPCS/CPT code and identifies how the service or procedure would be paid (if covered) by Medicare for hospital outpatient visits.

66.   D

67.   A

68.   A

69.   D

70.   A

71.   B

72.   B

73.   C

74.   B   When these conditions are not present on admission, it is assumed that it was hospital acquired and therefore, the hospital may not receive additional payment.

75.   B   Under Medicare Part B, Congress has mandated special incentives to increase the number of health care providers signing PAR (participating) agreements with Medicare. One of those incentives includes a 5% higher fee schedule for PAR providers than for non-PAR (nonparticipating) providers.

76.   C   Lifetime reserve days are applicable for hospital inpatient stays that are payable under Medicare Part A, not Medicare Part B.

77.   C

78.   A

79.   D   The relative weight is a number assigned to each MS-DRG published in the Federal Register, and it is used as a multiplier to determine reimbursement. Each hospital's prospective payment system (PPS) rate is a dollar amount based on that hospital's costs of operating as determined by several blended factors. This base payment rate is multiplied by the MS-DRG's (relative) weight to calculate that hospital's reimbursement for a given MS-DRG. Additional payments are made if applicable (such as disproportionate share, teaching hospital, cost outlier, etc.). The prospective payment system used to reimburse the "hospital" for outpatient surgery is APCs. The prospective payment used to reimburse a "free-standing surgery center" for outpatient surgery is ASCs. The prospective payment system used to reimburse the "physician" for outpatient surgery is RBRVS.

80.   D   Discounts are applied to those multiple procedures identified by CPT codes with status indicator "T" and also those CPT codes assigned with the modifier-73.

81.   B

82.   B

83.   A   Local Coverage Determinations (LCDs) were formerly called local medical review policies (LMRPs).

84.   B

85.   C

86.   C   If the physician is a participating physician (PAR) who accepts the assignment, he will receive the lesser of the "total charges" or the "PAR amount" (on the Medicare Physician Fee Schedule). Since the PAR amount is lower, the physician collects 80% of the PAR amount ($60.00) x .80 =$48.00, from Medicare. The remaining 20% ($60.00 x .20 = $12.00) of the PAR amount is paid by the patient to the physician. Therefore, the physician will receive $48.00 directly from Medicare.

Answer Key for Medical Billing and Reimbursement Systems

ANSWER EXPLANATION

87. A

88. B

89. D

90. A When a patient meets the definition of critical care, the hospital must use CPT Code 99291 to bill for outpatient encounters in which critical care services are furnished. This code is used instead of another E&M code.

91. C DNFB stands for "Discharged, Not Final Billed"

92. D Since the physician is a nonparticipating physician, he will receive the non-PAR fee.
The Medicare non-PAR fee is $57.00.
Medicare will pay 80% of the non-PAR fee ($57.00 x 0.80 = $45.60).
The patient will pay 20% of the non-PAR fee ($57.00 x 0.20 = $11.40).
Since the physician is accepting assignment on this claim, he cannot charge the patient any more than the 20% copayment. Therefore, the physician will receive $45.60 directly from Medicare.

93. A

94. A Only one MS-DRG is assigned per inpatient hospitalization.

95. A

96. C

97. A

98. D

99. A The three relative value units are physician work, practice expense, and malpractice expense. These are adjusted by multiplying them by the geographical practice cost indices. Then, this total is multiplied by the national conversion factor.

100. B The participating physician agrees to accept Medicare's fee as payment in full; therefore, the physician would write off the difference between $700.00 and $450.00, which is 250.00.

101. A

102. B

103. C

104. A

105. C

106. A

107. B

108. D Inpatient Rehabilitation Facilities (IRF) reports the HIPPS (Health Insurance Prospective Payment System) code on the claim. The HIPPS code is a five-digit CMG (Case Mix Group). Therefore, the HIPPS code for a patient with tier 1 comorbidity and a CMG of 0109 is B0109. Home Health Agencies (HHA) report the HIPPS code on the claim. The HIPPS code is a five-character alphanumeric code. The first character is the letter "H." The second, third, and fourth characters represent the HHRG (Home Health Resource Group). The fifth character represents what elements are computed or derived. Therefore, the HIPPS code for the HHRG C0F0S0 would be HAEJ1.

109. D

110. A The malignant neoplasm was clearly present on admission, although it was not diagnosed until after the admission occurred.

111. A The atrial fibrillation developed prior to a written order for inpatient admission; therefore, it was present at the time of inpatient admission.

Answer Key for Medical Billing and Reimbursement Systems

ANSWER   EXPLANATION

112.   B   The pulmonary embolism is an acute condition that was not present on admission because it developed after the patient was admitted and after the patient had surgery.

113.   C   Query the physician as to whether the decubitus ulcer was present on admission or developed after admission.

114.   A

REFERENCES

Abdelhak, M., Grostick, S., and Hanken, M. (2012). *Health information management: management of a strategic resource* (4th ed.). St. Louis, MO: Elsevier Saunders.

Brown, S. and Tyler, L. (2014). *Guide to advanced medical billing: a reimbursement approach* (3rd ed.). Upper Saddle River, NJ: Pearson Education, Inc.

Casto, A. B., & Forrestal, E. (2013). *Principles of healthcare reimbursement* (4th ed.). Chicago: American Health Information Management Association (AHIMA).

CMS Web site: http://www.cms.hhs.gov/home/Medicare.asp (This Web site provides links to pages containing official informational materials on all of the Medicare Fee-For-Service Payment Systems.)

Diamond, M. S. (2012). *Understanding hospital coding and billing: A worktext* (2nd ed.).Clifton Park, NY: Delmar Cengage Learning.

Green, M. A. (2014). *3-2-1-Code It!* (4th ed.). Clifton Park, NY: Delmar Cengage Learning.

Green, M. A., & Rowell, J. C. (2015). *Understanding health insurance: A guide to billing and reimbursement* (12th ed.). Clifton Park, NY: Delmar Cengage Learning.

Green, M. A., & Bowie, M. J. (2011). *Essentials of health information management: Principles and practices* (2nd ed.). Clifton Park, NY: Delmar Cengage Learning.

Kirchoff, S. (2009). *Coding and reimbursement for hospital outpatient services.* Chicago: American Health Information Management Association (AHIMA).

LaTour, K., Eichenwald-Maki, S. and Oachs, P. (2013). *Health information management: Concepts, principles, and practice* (4th ed.). Chicago: American Health Information Management Association (AHIMA).

Richards, C. (2010). *Medical billing and reimbursement fundamentals.* Clifton Park, NY: Delmar Cengage Learning.

Sayles, N. (2013). *Health information management technology: An applied approach* (4th ed.). Chicago: American Health Information Management Association (AHIMA).

Schraffenberger, L. A., & Kuehn, L. (2011). *Effective management of coding services* (4th ed.). Chicago: American Health Information Management Association (AHIMA).

Scott, K. (2011). *Coding and reimbursement for hospital inpatient services* (3rd ed.). Chicago: American Health Information Management Association (AHIMA).

Medical Billing and Reimbursement Systems
Competencies

Questions	CCS Competencies
1-114	Domain 1

VII. ICD-9-CM Coding

Leslie Moore, RHIT, CCS

Infectious and Parasitic Diseases

1. A patient is admitted with a left ankle fracture. The patient also has AIDS with Kaposi's sarcoma of the skin. He had a closed reduction with internal fixation of the ankle fracture.
    A. 042, 176.0, 824.8, 79.16
    B. 824.8, 176.0, V08, 79.16
    C. 176.1, 824.8, V08, 79.16
    D. 824.8, 042, 176.0, 79.16

    REFERENCE: Brown, pp 115–116, 413–408, 416–417
                   Schraffenberger, pp 82–84
                   Ingenix, pp 617–618

2. A patient was admitted with septicemia due to methicillin-resistant *Staphylococcus aureus*. The patient also was admitted with septic shock and decubitus ulcer of the sacrum. She had a central line inserted and infusion of drotrecogin alfa.
    A. 038.19, 785.59, 707.02, 38.91
    B. 038.12, 707.03, 995.92, 785.52, 707.20, 38.93, 00.11
    C. 707.00, 038.11, 785.59, 38.93, 00.11
    D. 038.11, 785.59, 995.92, 38.93

    REFERENCE: Bowie and Shaffer, pp 92–93
                   Brown, pp 109–113, 241–242
                   Schraffenberger, pp 80–82
                   Ingenix, pp 47, 348

3. A patient was diagnosed with nephropathy due to tuberculosis (confirmed histologically) of the kidney. He had a right nephrectomy performed.
    A. 016.05, 583.81, 55.51
    B. 583.81, 016.06, 55.52
    C. 016.02, 583.81, 55.51
    D. 016.02, 583.81, 55.52

    REFERENCE: Brown, pp 108–109, 220–222
                   Schraffenberger, p 78
                   Ingenix, pp 466–467

4. A patient is admitted with fever and severe headache. The diagnostic workup revealed viral meningitis. She also has asthma with acute exacerbation and hypertension, both of which are treated.
    A. 047.9, 780.60, 784.0, 493.90, 401.9
    B. 047.8, 493.92, 401.1
    C. 047.9, 493.92, 401.9
    D. 780.60, 784.0, 047.9, 493.90, 401.9

    REFERENCE: Brown, pp 107, 161–162, 186–187, 347–349
                   Schraffenberger, pp 78, 181–182, 184–186

5. Nurse Jones suffers a needlestick and presents for HIV testing. She sees her physician for the test results and counseling.
    A. V72.60, 795.71
    B. 795.71, V65.8
    C. V08, V72.60, V65.44
    D. V73.89, V65.44, V01.79

    REFERENCE: Brown, pp 115–116
                   Schraffenberger, p 84

6. A patient presents with right arm paralysis due to poliomyelitis that the patient suffered from as a child.
   A. 045.11, 342.81
   B. 138, 344.41
   C. 344.40, 138
   D. 138, 344.41

REFERENCE: Brown, pp 108–109

Neoplasms

7. A patient is admitted for chemotherapy for treatment of breast cancer with liver metastasis. She had a mastectomy 4 months ago. Chemotherapy is given today.
   A. 197.7, V10.3, 99.25
   B. 174.9, 197.7, 99.25
   C. V58.11, V10.3, 197.7, 99.25
   D. V58.11, 174.9, V45.71, 197.7, 99.25

REFERENCE: Bowie and Schaffer, pp 119–120
Brown, pp 380–381, 383–385, 391–395
Schraffenberger, pp 94–98
Ingenix, pp 807–808

8. A patient with a history of malignant neoplasm of the lung is admitted with seizures. The workup revealed metastasis of the lung cancer to the brain.
   A. 780.39, V10.11, 198.3
   B. 162.9, V10.11, 198.3, 780.39
   C. 198.3, 780.39, V10.11
   D. 198.3, 780.39, 162.9

REFERENCE: Bowie and Schaffer, p 116
Brown, pp 380–381, 383–385
Schraffenberger, pp 107–109

9. A patient is admitted to the hospital for treatment of dehydration following chemotherapy as treatment for ovarian cancer.
   A. 276.51, 183.0
   B. 183.0, 276.51, 99.25
   C. 276.50, 183.0, 99.25
   D. 183.0, 276.51

REFERENCE: Bowie and Schaffer, p 118
Brown, pp 391–395

10. A patient has malignant melanoma of the skin of the back. She undergoes a radical excision of the melanoma with full-thickness skin graft.
    A. 173.59, 86.4, 86.63
    B. 172.5, 86.4, 86.63
    C. 173.59, 86.3, 86.63
    D. 172.5, 86.3, 86.63

REFERENCE: Brown, p 377
Schraffenberger, p 94
Ingenix, p 718

11. A patient is admitted with abdominal pain. The needle biopsy of the liver reveals secondary malignancy of the liver. The patient has an exploratory laparotomy to determine the primary site. The primary site is unknown at the time of discharge.
    A. 197.7, 199.1, 54.11, 50.12
    B. 197.7, 789.00, 54.11, 50.11
    C. 197.7, 199.1, 54.11, 50.11
    D. 197.7, 199.1, 789.00, 54.11, 50.12

REFERENCE: Brown, pp 383–385
Ingenix, pp 431, 452

12. A patient with a history of cancer of the colon and status postcolostomy is admitted for closure of the colostomy. The patient is also being treated for chronic obstructive pulmonary disease and diastolic heart failure. He has a takedown of the colostomy.
   A. 153.2, 496, 428.30, 46.52
   B. V55.3, 496, V10.05, 428.30, 46.52
   C. V55.3, 496, V10.05, 428.0, 46.52, 45.79
   D. V10.05, 492.8, 428.30, 46.52

REFERENCE: Brown, pp 187, 339–340, 391
                Schraffenberger, pp 436, 447–448
                Ingenix, pp 409–410, 414

Endocrine, Nutritional, and Metabolic Diseases and Immunity Disorders

13. A female, 68 years old, was admitted with type 2 diabetes mellitus with a diabetic ulcer of the left heel. The patient was taken to the operating room for excisional debridement of the ulcer.
   A. 250.80, 707.14, 86.22   C. 250.81, 707.13, 86.22
   B. 707.14, 250.80, 86.22   D. 250.82, 707.14, 86.28

REFERENCE: Brown, pp 119–126, 242–243
                Schraffenberger, pp 122–124, 294
                Ingenix, pp 715–716

14. A 67-year-old man is admitted with acute dehydration secondary to nausea and vomiting that is due to acute gastroenteritis. He is treated for dehydration. An esophagogastroduodenoscopy is performed.
   A. 558.9, 787.01, 276.51, 45.13   C. 276.51, 787.01, 558.9, 45.13
   B. 558.9, 787.01, 276.51, 45.16   D. 276.51, 558.9, 45.13

REFERENCE: Schraffenberger, pp 126, 236
                Ingenix, pp 404–405

15. A patient was found at home in a hypoglycemic coma. This patient had never been diagnosed as being diabetic.
   A. 250.30   C. 251.1
   B. 251.0   D. 251.2

REFERENCE: Brown, p 128

16. A patient is admitted with aplastic anemia secondary to chemotherapy administered for multiple myeloma.
   A. 284.89, 203.00, E933.1   C. 284.9, 203.00, E933.1
   B. 203.00, 284.81, E933.1   D. 203.01, 284.89, E933.1

REFERENCE: Bowie and Schaffer, p 145
                Brown, pp 153–154, 445–446

17. A male patient is admitted with gastrointestinal hemorrhage resulting in acute blood-loss anemia. A colonoscopy and esophagogastroduodenoscopy fail to reveal the source of the bleed.
   A. 285.9, 578.1, 45.13, 45.23   C. 578.9, 285.1, 45.13, 45.23
   B. 578.1, 285.1, 45.13, 45.23   D. 578.9, 280.0, 45.13, 45.23

REFERENCE: Brown, pp 152–153, 199–200
                Ingenix, pp 404–407

18. A patient is admitted with severe malnutrition. The physician performs a percutaneous endoscopic gastrostomy.
    A. 263.9, 43.11
    B. 261, 43.11
    C. 261, 43.19
    D. 263.8, 43.11

REFERENCE: Brown, p 129
                Ingenix, pp 392–393

Diseases of the Blood and Blood-Forming Organs

19. A patient is admitted with thrombocytopenia and purpura. A splenectomy is performed.
    A. 287.49, 41.5
    B. 287.8, 41.5
    C. 287.9, 41.42
    D. 287.30, 41.5

REFERENCE: Schraffenberger, p 136
                Ingenix, pp 379–380

20. A patient is admitted with sickle cell anemia with crisis.
    A. 282.61
    B. 282.62
    C. 282.63
    D. 282.69

REFERENCE: Brown, p 154
                Schraffenberger, p 134

21. A patient is admitted with sickle cell pain crisis.
    A. 282.62
    B. 282.60
    C. 282.5
    D. 282.42

REFERENCE: Bowie and Schaffer, p 145
                Brown, p 154
                Schraffenberger, p, 134

22. A patient is admitted with Cooley's anemia.
    A. 282.41
    B. 282.0
    C. 282.49
    D. 282.44

REFERENCE: Brown, p 151
                Schraffenberger, p 134

23. A patient is admitted with anemia due to end-stage renal disease. The patient is treated for anemia.
    A. 285.8
    B. 285.21, 585.6
    C. 285.22, 585.6
    D. 285.9

REFERENCE: Brown, p 151
                Schraffenberger, p 135

24. A patient is admitted with pernicious anemia.
    A. 280.9
    B. 280.8
    C. 281.1
    D. 281.0

REFERENCE: Brown, p 151
                Schraffenberger, pp 133–134

Mental Disorders

25. A patient is admitted with mild mental retardation due to an old viral encephalitis.
    A. 319, 049.8
    B. 317, 326
    C. 317, 047.8
    D. 317, 139.0

REFERENCE: Brown, p 108

26. A patient is admitted with anxiety with depression.
    A. 300.11, 311
    B. 300.4
    C. 309.28
    D. 300.00, 311

REFERENCE: Brown, p 139

27. A patient is admitted with delirium tremens with alcohol dependence.
    A. 291.0, 303.90
    B. 303.91, 291.0
    C. 291.3, 303.90
    D. 291.0, 303.00

REFERENCE: Brown, pp 141–142
               Schraffenberger, pp 143, 146–149

28. A patient is admitted with latent schizophrenia, chronic with acute exacerbation.
    A. 295.52
    B. 295.55
    C. 295.54
    D. 295.53

REFERENCE: Bowie and Schaffer, pp 157–158
               Brown, p 137

29. A patient with chronic paranoia due to continuous cocaine dependence is admitted. Drug rehabilitation is provided.
    A. 301.0, 305.61, 94.63
    B. 297.1, 304.21, 94.64
    C. 297.1, 305.61, 94.64
    D. 297.1, 304.21, 94.63

REFERENCE: Brown, p 143
               Schraffenberger, pp 143, 146–149
               Ingenix, pp 784-786

30. A patient is diagnosed with psychogenic paroxysmal tachycardia.
    A. 427.2, 316
    B. 306.2, 427.1
    C. 427.1, 306.2
    D. 316, 427.2

REFERENCE: Brown, p 139

Diseases of the Nervous System and Sense Organs

31. A 5-year-old female is admitted to ambulatory surgery with chronic otitis media. She has bilateral myringotomy with insertion of tubes.
    A. 381.20, 20.01
    B. 381.3, 20.01
    C. 382.9, 20.01, 20.01
    D. 381.89, 20.01

REFERENCE: Schraffenberger, p 165
               Ingenix, pp 208–209

32. A patient is a type 2 diabetic with a diabetic cataract. He has phacoemulsification of the cataract with synchronous insertion of the lens.
    A. 250.51, 366.42, 13.59, 13.71
    B. 250.50, 366.41, 13.41, 13.71
    C. 250.52, 366.41, 13.41, 13.71
    D. 366.41, 250.50, 13.41, 13.71

REFERENCE: Brown, pp 125, 172
               Schraffenberger, pp 122–124, 164
               Ingenix, pp 171–174

33. A patient has epilepsy and paraplegia as residuals of a head injury he suffered 5 years ago.
    A. 345.90, 344.1, 907.0
    B. 345.91, 344.1, 907.0
    C. 959.01, 345.90, 344.1
    D. 345.81, 344.2, 907.0

REFERENCE: Brown, pp 164–165
               Schraffenberger, pp 161–162

34. A patient is diagnosed with Alzheimer's disease with dementia.
    A. 331.0, 294.8
    B. 294.8
    C. 331.0, 294.10
    D. 331.0

REFERENCE: Brown, p 136

35. A patient is admitted with meningitis sarcoidosis.
    A. 321.2, 136.1
    B. 135, 321.4
    C. 136.1, 321.2
    D. 321.4, 135

REFERENCE: Brown, p 162

36. A patient with carpal tunnel syndrome is admitted for arthroscopic release of the carpal tunnel.
    A. 354.0, 04.43
    B. 354.1, 80.23
    C. 354.1, 04.43, 80.23
    D. 354.0, 04.43, 80.23

REFERENCE: Brown, p 167
               Ingenix, pp 110–111, 623

Diseases of the Circulatory System

37. A patient is admitted with acute cerebral infarction with left hemiparesis. The hemiparesis resolved by discharge.
    A. 342.90
    B. 434.91
    C. 436, 342.90
    D. 434.91, 342.90

REFERENCE: Brown, pp 343–344

38. A patient is admitted with multiple problems. He has hypertensive kidney disease, congestive heart failure, and acute systolic heart failure.
    A. 593.9, 401.9, 482.0, 428.21
    B. 404.11, 428.0, 428.21
    C. 403.90, 428.0, 428.21
    D. 404.91

REFERENCE: Brown, pp 348–349
               Schraffenberger, pp 182, 192–193

39. A patient is admitted with acute inferior wall myocardial infarction with unstable angina. He also has coronary artery disease and atrial fibrillation.
   A. 410.41, 411.1, 414.01, 427.31
   B. 410.41, 414.00, 411.1, 427.31
   C. 410.40, 414.00, 427.31
   D. 410.41, 414.00, 427.31

REFERENCE: Bowie and Schaffer, pp 197–199
              Brown, pp 333–339
              Schraffenberger, pp 186–191, 194

40. A patient with a diagnosis of aortic valve stenosis and mitral valve regurgitation is admitted for aortic valve replacement. The patient is also under treatment for congestive heart failure. He undergoes the placement of aortic valve prosthesis with cardiopulmonary bypass.
   A. 396.2, 398.91, 35.22, 39.61
   B. 424.1, 424.0, 428.0, 35.22
   C. 396.2, 428.0, 35.22, 39.61
   D. 424.1, 424.0, 428.0, 35.21, 39.61

REFERENCE: Brown, pp 329–332
              Schraffenberger, p 179
              Ingenix, pp 303–304, 357–358

41. A patient with atherosclerotic peripheral vascular disease of the lower leg with claudication is admitted for angioplasty of the lower leg artery.
   A. 440.20, 39.50
   B. 440.21, 39.50
   C. 444.22, 38.08
   D. 443.9, 39.50

REFERENCE: Brown, pp 351–352
              Ingenix, pp 340–342, 355

Diseases of the Respiratory System

42. A patient presents to the outpatient department for a chest x-ray. The physician's order lists the following reasons for the chest x-ray: fever and cough, rule out pneumonia. The radiologist reports that the chest x-ray is positive for pneumonia.
   A. 486
   B. 486, 780.61, 786.2, V72.5
   C. 780.61, 786.2
   D. V72.5, 780.60, 786.2

REFERENCE: Brown, pp 179–184
              Schraffenberger, p 219

43. A patient has aspiration pneumonia with pneumonia due to *Staphylococcus aureus*. The patient also has emphysema.
   A. 507.0, 482.9, 496
   B. 507.0, 482.41, 496
   C. 507.0, 491.21
   D. 507.0, 482.41, 492.8

REFERENCE: Brown, pp 179–183
              Schraffenberger, pp 218–219

44. A patient is admitted with acute respiratory failure due to congestive heart failure. The patient is placed on the ventilator for 3 days following insertion of the endotracheal tube.
   A. 518.81, 428.0, 96.71, 96.04
   B. 518.81, 428.0, 96.72, 96.04
   C. 428.0, 518.81, 96.71, 96.04
   D. 428.0, 518.83, 96.72, 96.04

REFERENCE: Brown, pp 157–159, 189–191, 339–340
              Schraffenberger, pp 192–194, 223–226
              Ingenix, pp 793, 798

45. A child has hypertrophic tonsillitis and is admitted for bilateral tonsillectomy and adenoidectomy.
    - A. 463, 28.3, 28.3
    - B. 474.00, 28.3
    - C. 474.02, 28.3, 28.3
    - D. 463, 28.3

    REFERENCE: Schraffenberger, p 218
                               Ingenix, p 257

46. A patient is admitted with chronic obstructive pulmonary disease with an exacerbation of acute bronchitis.
    - A. 491.22
    - B. 496, 466.0
    - C. 466.0, 496
    - D. 491.22, 466.0

    REFERENCE: Brown, pp 186–187
                               Schraffenberger, p 218

47. A patient is admitted with extrinsic asthma with status asthmaticus.
    - A. 493.11
    - B. 493.90
    - C. 493.01
    - D. 493.81

    REFERENCE: Brown, pp 186–188
                               Schraffenberger, pp 222–223

48. A patient is experiencing exacerbation of myasthenia gravis resulting in acute respiratory failure. The patient required mechanical ventilation for 10 hours, following endotracheal intubation.
    - A. 358.00, 518.81, 96.71, 96.04
    - B. 518.81, 358.01, 96.71, 96.04
    - C. 358.00, 581.89, 96.71, 96.05
    - D. 518.82, 358.00, 96.72, 96.04

    REFERENCE: Brown, pp 189–191, 194–195
                               Schraffenberger, pp 223–226
                               Ingenix, pp 793–794, 798

Diseases of the Digestive System

49. A patient is admitted to the hospital for repair of a ventral hernia. The surgery is canceled after the chest x-ray revealed lower lobe pneumonia. The patient is placed on antibiotics to treat the pneumonia.
    - A. 553.20, 486, V64.1
    - B. 486, 553.20, V64.3
    - C. 486, 553.20
    - D. 553.20, 486

    REFERENCE: Brown, pp 72–73, 181–182, 208–210
                               Schraffenberger, pp 45–46, 220, 235

50. A patient is admitted with gastric ulcer with hemorrhage resulting in acute blood-loss anemia. An esophagogastroduodenoscopy is performed.
    - A. 531.20, 285.1, 45.13
    - B. 285.1, 531.20, 45.13
    - C. 531.40, 280.0, 45.14
    - D. 531.40, 285.1, 45.13

    REFERENCE: Bowie and Schaffer, pp 218–219
                               Brown, pp 116–117, 203
                               Schraffenberger, pp 135, 234
                               Ingenix, pp 404–405

51. A patient has diverticulitis of the large bowel with abscess. The physician performs a right hemicolectomy with colostomy.
   A. 562.10, 45.74, 46.03
   B. 562.11, 45.73, 46.10
   C. 562.11, 569.5, 45.73, 46.10
   D. 562.11, 569.5, 45.74, 46.11

REFERENCE: Brown, p 205
                 Ingenix, pp 109, 411

52. A patient is admitted with acute and chronic cholecystitis with cholelithiasis. A laparoscopic cholecystectomy was attempted, and then it was converted to an open procedure.
   A. 574.00, 574.10, V64.41, 51.22
   B. 574.00, 574.10, 51.22, 51.23
   C. 574.00, 51.22, 51.23
   D. 574.00, V64.41, 51.22

REFERENCE: Brown, pp 206–207
                 Schraffenberger, p 224
                 Ingenix, p 437

53. A patient is admitted with bleeding esophageal varices with alcoholic liver cirrhosis and portal hypertension. The patient is alcohol dependent. An esophagogastroduodenoscopy is performed for control of the hemorrhage.
   A. 456.20, 571.2, 303.90, 42.33
   B. 571.2, 456.20, 303.90, 280.0, 42.33
   C. 572.3, 571.2, 303.90, 456.20, 42.33
   D. 303.90, 456.20, 303.90, 42.33

REFERENCE: Brown, pp 141–145, 203
                 Ingenix, pp 385–386

54. A patient is admitted for workup for melena. The laboratory results reveal chronic blood-loss anemia. The colonoscopy with biopsy reveals Crohn's disease of the descending colon.
   A. 578.1, 555.1, 45.25, 45.43
   B. 555.1, 45.25
   C. 555.1, 578.1, 45.25
   D. 555.1, 578.1, 45.25, 45.23

REFERENCE: Brown, p 151
                 Schraffenberger, p 236
                 Ingenix, pp 405–408

Diseases of the Genitourinary System

55. A patient is admitted with acute urinary tract infection due to *E. coli*.
   A. 599.0, 041.49
   B. 599.0
   C. 041.49, 599.0
   D. 590.2, 041.49

REFERENCE: Brown, p 112
                 Schraffenberger, pp 250–251

56. A patient presents with complaints of gross hematuria. The diagnosis is benign prostatic hypertrophy and the patient undergoes a transurethral prostatectomy.
   A. 600.01, 60.21
   B. 600.00, 60.29
   C. 600.00, 599.71, 60.29
   D. 600.00, 599.71, 60.21

REFERENCE: Brown, pp 225–226
                 Ingenix, p 507

57. A male patient presents to the ED with acute renal failure. He is also being treated for hypertension.
    A. 410.00, 586
    B. 401.9, 584.9
    C. 585.9, 401.1
    D. 584.9, 401.9

REFERENCE: Brown, pp 219–221

58. A patient is admitted with hemorrhagic cystitis. A cystoscopy with biopsy of the bladder is performed.
    A. 595.9, 57.33
    B. 595.9, 041.49, 57.32
    C. 595.82, 57.33
    D. 596.7, 57.33

REFERENCE: Brown, p 217
              Schraffenberger, p 251
              Ingenix, p 484

59. A patient is admitted with chronic kidney disease due to hypertension and type 1 diabetes mellitus.
    A. 250.41, 403.90, 585.9
    B. 250.40, 403.10, 585.1
    C. 403.90, 250.41, 585.9, V58.67
    D. 403.10, 250.41, 585.2

REFERENCE: Brown, p 220

60. A patient has end-stage kidney disease, which resulted from malignant hypertension.
    A. 403.01, 585.6
    B. 585.9, 401.0
    C. 403.00
    D. 401.0, 585.9

REFERENCE: Brown, pp 219–220
              Schraffenberger, pp 182, 250

Complications of Pregnancy, Childbirth, and the Puerperium

61. A woman has a vaginal delivery of a full-term liveborn infant. She undergoes an episiotomy with repair and post-delivery elective tubal ligation.
    A. 650, V25.2, V27.0, 73.6, 66.32
    B. 648.91, V27.0, 73.6, 66.32
    C. 650, V27.0, 66.32
    D. 650, V27.0

REFERENCE: Bowie and Schaffer, p 260
              Brown, pp 269–271, 282–283
              Schraffenberger, pp 272–274
              Ingenix, pp 540–541, 585–586

62. A woman has an incomplete spontaneous abortion complicated by excessive hemorrhage. The physician performs a dilation and curettage.
    A. 634.12, 69.09
    B. 634.12, 285.1, 69.09
    C. 634.11, 69.02
    D. 634.91, 69.02

REFERENCE: Brown, pp 293–295
              Schraffenberger, pp 264–265
              Ingenix, p 562

63. A patient has obstructed labor due to breech presentation. A single liveborn infant was delivered via cesarean section.
   A. 660.81, 74.1
   B. 660.01, 652.21, V27.0, 74.99
   C. 660.01, V27.0, 74.1
   D. 660.81, 652.21, 74.99

REFERENCE: Brown, pp 269–271, 283
               Ingenix, pp 587–588

64. A woman was admitted for delivery of a single newborn at 43 weeks gestation. It was a manually assisted delivery.
   A. 650, V27.0, 73.59
   B. 645.20, V27.0, 73.59
   C. 644.21, V27.0, 73.59
   D. 645.21, V27.0, 73.59

REFERENCE: Brown, pp 280–283
               Schraffenberger, pp 274–275
               Ingenix, p 585

65. A female who is 26 weeks pregnant is treated for a fractured distal radius and ulna. A closed reduction of the fracture is performed.
   A. 813.44, 79.02
   B. 648.93, 813.44, 79.02
   C. 813.44, V22.2, 79.02
   D. V22.2, 813.44, 79.02

REFERENCE: Brown, pp 269–270
               Schraffenberger, pp 275–277, 353
               Ingenix, p 617

66. A patient is diagnosed with a tubal pregnancy. She undergoes a unilateral salpingectomy for removal of the tubal pregnancy.
   A. 633.20, 66.63
   B. 633.11, 66.62
   C. 633.00, 66.61
   D. 633.10, 66.62

REFERENCE: Brown, pp 298–299
               Schraffenberger, pp 270–273
               Ingenix, p 542

Diseases of the Skin and Subcutaneous Tissue

67. A patient is admitted with an abscess with cellulitis of the abdominal wall. The culture is positive for *Staphylococcus aureus*.
   A. 682.8, 041.11
   B. 682.2, 041.11
   C. 682.2, 707.8
   D. 682.2

REFERENCE: Brown, p 292
               Schraffenberger, p 244

68. A patient had a cholecystectomy 6 days ago and is now coming back with evidence of staphylococcal cellulitis at the site of operative incision.
   A. 958.3, 682.2, 041.19
   B. 998.51, 682.8, 041.11
   C. 958.3, 682.8, 041.11
   D. 998.59, 682.2, 041.10

REFERENCE: Brown, pp 242–243

69. A patient has chronic ulcers of the calf and the back. Both ulcers are excisionally debrided and the ulcer on the back has a split-thickness skin graft.
    A. 707.12, 707.8, 86.22, 86.22, 86.69
    B. 707.12, 707.8, 86.22
    C. 707.8, 86.22, 86.69
    D. 707.8, 86.22, 86.22, 86.69

REFERENCE: Brown, pp 242–244
                    Schraffenberger, pp 294, 296–297
                    Ingenix, pp 717, 719

70. A patient presents with dermatitis due to prescription topical antibiotic cream used as directed by physician.
    A. 692.4
    B. 692.3, E930.9
    C. 692.3
    D. 692.3, E930.1

REFERENCE: Brown, pp 239–240
                    Schraffenberger, p 292

71. A patient developed a boil on the left side of the face. An incision and drainage was performed.
    A. 680.0, 86.04
    B. 680.0, 86.09
    C. 680.8, 86.11
    D. 680.0, 86.04, 86.11

REFERENCE: Brown, p 239
                    Ingenix, p 712–715

72. A patient has an abscessed pilonidal cyst. An excision of the cyst was performed.
    A. 685.1, 86.04
    B. 686.09, 86.04
    C. 685.0, 86.21
    D. 686.01, 86.22

REFERENCE: Brown, p 239
                    Ingenix, pp 712–713, 715

Diseases of the Musculoskeletal System and Connective Tissue

73. A patient has a pathological fracture of the femur due to metastatic bone cancer. He has a history of lung cancer.
    A. 198.5, 733.14, V10.11
    B. 733.14, 198.5, V10.11
    C. 733.19, 198.5, V10.11
    D. 821.00, 162.9

REFERENCE: Brown, p 255
                    Schraffenberger, pp 108, 305–306

74. A 69-year-old man has a herniated lumbar intervertebral disc with paresthesia. A lumbar laminectomy with diskectomy is performed.
    A. 722.11, 80.51, 03.09
    B. 839.20, 80.51
    C. 722.10, 80.59, 03.09
    D. 722.10, 80.51

REFERENCE: Brown, pp 251–252
                    Schraffenberger, pp 304–305
                    Ingenix, pp 99–100, 624–626

75. A patient developed pyogenic arthritis of the hip due to Group A *Streptococcus*. An arthrocentesis was done.
   A. 716.95, 041.01, 81.91
   B. 715.95, 041.01, 81.92
   C. 711.05, 041.01, 81.91
   D. 711.05, 81.91

REFERENCE: Brown, p 253
Schraffenberger, pp 79–80, 304–305
Ingenix, p 655

76. A patient is admitted with a bunion of the left foot and a hammertoe of the right foot. Keller procedure and hammer toe repair were performed.
   A. 727.1, 735.4, 77.59, 77.56
   B. 727.1, 735.8, 77.52, 77.59
   C. 727.2, 735.4, 77.52, 77.58
   D. 727.1, 735.3, 77.56, 77.59

REFERENCE: Schraffenberger, pp 304–305
Ingenix, pp 608–610

77. A patient developed a malunion of the humeral fracture. The original injury occurred 1 year ago. Open reduction with internal fixation was performed.
   A. 812.20, 79.39
   B. 733.82, 905.2, 79.31
   C. 733.81, 905.2, 79.31
   D. 733.94, 905.2, 79.32

REFERENCE: Schraffenberger, p 306
Ingenix, pp 618–619

78. A patient has recurrent internal derangement of the left knee. A diagnostic arthroscopy of the knee is performed.
   A. 715.96, 80.26
   B. 718.36, 80.26
   C. 836.2, 80.26
   D. 718.36, 80.6

REFERENCE: Brown, p 254
Ingenix, pp 623, 626

Congenital Anomalies

79. A liveborn infant is born in hospital with a cleft palate and cleft lip.
   A. 749.00, 749.10
   B. 749.20
   C. V30.00, 749.20
   D. V30.00, 749.00, 749.10

REFERENCE: Bowie and Schaffer, pp 290–291
Brown, pp 307, 314
Schraffenberger, pp 320, 442–443

80. A newborn is born in the hospital with tetralogy of Fallot.
   A. 745.8
   B. V30.01, 746.09
   C. 745.2
   D. V30.00, 745.2

REFERENCE: Brown, pp 307, 314

81. A newborn infant is transferred to Manasota Hospital for treatment of an esophageal atresia. What is the code for Manasota Hospital?
   A. V30.00
   B. 750.3
   C. V30.00, 750.3
   D. 750.3, V30.00

REFERENCE: Brown, p 307

82. A patient presents with cervical spina bifida with hydrocephalus.
    A. 741.02
    B. 741.93
    C. 741.01
    D. 741.91

REFERENCE: Brown, p 307
               Schraffenberger, pp 316–317

83. An infant is seen with clubfoot, which is corrected by the Evans operation.
    A. 754.70, 83.84
    B. 754.71, 83.84
    C. 736.71, 83.84
    D. 736.79, 83.84

REFERENCE: Brown, p 307
               Schraffenberger, p 322
               Ingenix, p 667

84. A full-term infant born in hospital is diagnosed with polycystic kidneys.
    A. 753.12
    B. V30.00, 753.12
    C. V30.00
    D. 753.12, V30.00

REFERENCE: Brown, pp 307, 314
               Schraffenberger, pp 317, 321, 442–443

Certain Conditions Originating in the Perinatal Period

85. A full-term newborn is born in hospital to a mother who is addicted to cocaine; however, the infant tested negative.
    A. V30.00, 760.75
    B. 779.5 V29.8
    C. V30.00, 779.5
    D. V30.00, V29.8

REFERENCE: Brown, pp 314, 318–319
               Schraffenberger, pp 317, 442–443

86. A preterm infant is born via cesarean section and has severe birth asphyxia.
    A. V30.01, 765.10, 768.5
    B. 765.10, 768.5, V30.01
    C. 768.5, 765.10
    D. 768.5

REFERENCE: Brown, pp 315–316

87. A preterm infant born in the hospital has neonatal jaundice. Phototherapy is done to treat the jaundice.
    A. V30.00, 774.2, 99.83
    B. 774.2, 99.83
    C. V30.00, 99.83
    D. V30.00, 774.2

REFERENCE: Brown, p 314
               Ingenix, p 811

88. A 1-week-old infant is admitted to the hospital with a diagnosis of urinary tract infection contracted prior to birth. The urine culture is positive for *E. coli*.
    A. V30.00, 599.0
    B. 599.0, 041.49
    C. V30.00, 599.0, 041.49
    D. 771.82, 041.49

REFERENCE: Brown, pp 107, 319

89. An infant has hypoglycemia with a mother with diabetes.
    A. 251.2
    B. 775.1
    C. 775.0
    D. 251.1

REFERENCE: Brown, p 313, 320–321

90. A full-term infant is born in the hospital. The birth is complicated by cord compression, which affected the newborn.
   A. V30.00, 762.5
   B. V30.00
   C. 762.5
   D. 762.6, V30.00

REFERENCE: Bowie and Schaffer, pp 300–301
              Brown, pp 314, 319
              Schraffenberger, pp 317, 442–443

Symptoms, Signs, and Ill-Defined Conditions

91. A patient is admitted with abdominal pain. The discharge diagnosis is listed as abdominal pain due to gastroenteritis or diverticulosis.
   A. 789.00
   B. 562.10, 558.9
   C. 789.00, 558.9, 562.10
   D. 558.9, 562.10, 789.00

REFERENCE: Bowie and Schaffer, pp 317–318
              Brown, pp 97–99
              Schraffenberger, pp 236, 338–340

92. A patient has a lung mass. A diagnostic bronchoscopy is performed.
   A. 518.89, 33.23
   B. 786.6, 33.23
   C. 793.19, 33.27
   D. 786.6, 33.27

REFERENCE: Brown, pp 97–99
              Ingenix, pp 278–280

93. A woman has a Pap smear that detected cervical high-risk human papillomavirus (HPV). The DNA test was positive.
   A. 795.05
   B. 795.09
   C. 795.04
   D. 795.02

REFERENCE: Brown, pp 97–99

94. A patient presents to the emergency department with ascites. A paracentesis was done.
   A. 789.30, 54.91
   B. 789.51, 54.91
   C. 789.59, 54.91
   D. 782.3, 54.91

REFERENCE: Brown, pp 97–99
              Ingenix, p 456

95. A patient is admitted with fever due to bacteremia.
   A. 780.61, 790.7
   B. 038.9
   C. 780.61
   D. 790.7, 780.61

REFERENCE: Brown, pp 97–99

96. A patient has urinary retention requiring the insertion of a Foley catheter.
   A. 788.21, 57.94
   B. 788.20, 57.93
   C. 788.20, 57.94
   D. 788.29, 57.93

REFERENCE: Brown, pp 97–99
              Ingenix, p 489

Injury and Poisoning

97. A patient has a fracture of the medial malleolus due to a fall down some steps. The fracture was treated with a closed reduction procedure.

    A. 824.1, E880.9, 79.05
    B. 824.0, E880.9, 79.06
    C. 824.0, 79.09
    D. 824.1, E880.1, 79.05

REFERENCE: Bowie and Schaffer, pp 325–328
               Brown, pp 413–414, 416
               Schraffenberger, pp 354–355
               Ingenix, p 617

98. A patient experienced a closed head injury. He was a passenger in a motor vehicle involved in a head-on collision with another motor vehicle.

    A. 959.01, E812.1
    B. 959.09, E812.2
    C. 959.01, E813.1
    D. 959.09, E813.1

REFERENCE: Brown, pp 405–408
               Schraffenberger, pp 367–368

99. A man appears with a gunshot wound to the abdomen. There is a moderate laceration of the liver. The patient stated that he was assaulted with a pistol.

    A. 864.00, E965.1
    B. 864.10, E965.0
    C. 864.13, E965.1
    D. 864.13, E965.0

REFERENCE: Brown, pp 405–408
               Schraffenberger, pp 359–360

100. A patient was admitted with third-degree burns to his upper back, which involved 20% of his body surface. There was an explosion and fire at his home.

    A. 942.25, 948.22, E890.2
    B. 942.44, 948.21, E895
    C. 942.34, 948.22, E890.3
    D. 942.24, 949.3, E897

REFERENCE: Brown, pp 433–436
               Schraffenberger, pp 363–364

101. A woman experienced third-degree burns to her thigh and second-degree burns to her foot. She stated that the burns were from hot liquid.

    A. 945.36, 945.22, E924.0
    B. 945.22, 945.36, E924.0
    C. 945.22, E924.0
    D. 945.29, 945.39, E924.0

REFERENCE: Brown, pp 433–436
               Schraffenberger, pp 363–364

102. A patient presents with a laceration of left wrist with injury to the radial nerve as a result of an accident, with embedded glass. The wrist laceration was repaired with sutures.

    A. 881.02, 86.59
    B. 881.12, E920.8, 86.59
    C. 955.3, E920.8, 86.59
    D. 881.12, 955.3, E920.8, 86.59

REFERENCE: Brown, pp 405–408, 421
               Schraffenberger, p 352
               Ingenix, pp 717–718

103. A 76-year-old female is admitted with tachycardia due to theophylline toxicity.
   A.   785.0, E942.1
   B.   995.20, E942.1
   C.   785.0, E944.1
   D.   995.20, E944.1

REFERENCE: Brown, pp 443–446
                Schraffenberger, pp 338–339

104. A patient suffered dizziness as a result of taking prescribed phenobarbital. The patient took his medication with beer.
   A.   780.4, 980.0, E860.0
   B.   967.0, 980.0, 780.4, E851, E860.0
   C.   967.0, 708.4, E851
   D.   780.4, E851, E860.0

REFERENCE: Brown, pp 443–446
                Schraffenberger, pp 382–383

105. A patient is experiencing pain in the hip due to a displaced hip prosthesis. The patient is admitted and undergoes a revision of the hip prosthesis.
   A.   996.49, 81.53
   B.   996.77, 81.53
   C.   719.45, 81.53
   D.   996.49, 719.45, 81.53

REFERENCE: Schraffenberger, pp 386–388
                Ingenix, p 645

106. A patient has postoperative hemorrhage, resulting in acute blood-loss anemia.
   A.   997.72, 285.1
   B.   999.1, 285.1
   C.   998.11, 285.1
   D.   998.11

REFERENCE: Brown, pp 152, 462
                Schraffenberger, p 389

V-Codes

107. A patient is admitted for colostomy takedown. The takedown procedure is performed.
   A.   V44.3, 46.52
   B.   569.60, 46.52
   C.   997.49, 46.52
   D.   V55.3, 46.52

REFERENCE: Brown, pp 83–85
                Schraffenberger, pp 447–448
                Ingenix, p 414

108. The patient is being admitted for a preoperative EKG on an outpatient basis. He is scheduled to have an elective cholecystectomy tomorrow for chronic cholecystitis and cholelithiasis. The EKG reveals atrial flutter.
   A.   574.10
   B.   V72.81, 51.23
   C.   V72.81, 574.10, 427.32
   D.   427.32

REFERENCE: Brown, p 88
                Schraffenberger, pp 457–459

109. The patient presents for a screening examination for lung cancer.
   A.   V72.82
   B.   162.9
   C.   V72.5
   D.   V76.0

REFERENCE: Brown, p 89
                Schraffenberger, p 459

110. A patient is admitted for observation for a head injury following a fall. The patient also suffered a minor laceration to the forehead. Head injury was ruled out.
    A. V71.4, 873.42, E888.9
    B. 873.42, E888.9
    C. 959.01, 873.42, E888.9
    D. V71.4, E888.9

REFERENCE: Brown, pp 86–87
                Schraffenberger, pp 260–361, 457

When the question has the ICD-9-CM codes and their respective narrative description, you should practice answering the question without using your coding book.

111. An elderly man was admitted through the emergency department for severe urinary retention. Upon study, it was determined that his hypertension was uncontrolled (215/108). Prior medical records show admission 8 weeks ago for the same problem. As per conditions on previous admission, his BPH is complicated by acute cystitis. He is noncompliant with medications. Medication for the hypertension was immediately started and his hypertension was quickly brought under control. Urinary retention was relieved by placement of a Foley catheter. Transurethral resection of the prostate was done.

401.0	Essential hypertension, malignant
401.9	Essential hypertension, unspecified benign or malignant
595.0	Acute cystitis
595.9	Cystitis, unspecified
600.00	Hypertrophy (benign) of prostate without urinary obstruction and other lower urinary tract symptoms (LUTS)
600.01	Hypertrophy (benign) of prostate with urinary obstruction and other lower urinary tract symptoms (LUTS)
600.3	Cyst of prostate
788.20	Retention of urine, unspecified
V15.81	Personal history of noncompliance with medical treatment
57.92	Dilation of bladder neck
57.94	Insertion of indwelling urinary catheter
60.29	Other transurethral prostatectomy
60.61	Local excision of lesion of prostate

    A. 600.01, 595.0, 788.20, 401.9, V15.81, 57.94, 60.29
    B. 600.3, 595.0, 401.0, V15.81, 57.92, 60.61
    C. 600.00, 595.9, 788.20, 401.9, V15.81, 57.94, 60.61
    D. 600.3, 595.0, 788.20, 401.0, V15.81, 57.94, 60.61

REFERENCE: Brown, pp 83–84, 97–98, 347-348
                Schraffenberger, pp 180–181, 251–252, 338–339

112. A 32-year-old female known to be HIV positive was admitted with lesions of the anterior trunk. Excisional biopsies of the skin lesions were positive for Kaposi's sarcoma. Further examination revealed thrush.

042	Human Immunodeficiency Virus (HIV) Disease
112.0	Candidiasis of mouth
176.0	Kaposi's sarcoma of skin
528.9	Other and unspecified diseases of the oral soft tissues
686.00	Pyoderma, unspecified
795.71	Nonspecific serological evidence of Human Immunodeficiency Virus (HIV)
86.11	Closed biopsy of skin and subcutaneous tissue
86.22	Excisional debridement of wound, infection, or burn

A. 042, 686.00, 112.0, 86.22   C. 795.71, 176.0, 528.9, 86.11
B. 042, 176.0, 112.0, 86.11   D. 795.71, 686.00, 528.9, 86.22

REFERENCE: Brown, pp 115–117
                    Schraffenberger, pp 82–84

113. A female patient was admitted with uncontrolled type 2 diabetes. She also had an abscessed diabetic ulcer of the foot that was treated with incision and drainage. The culture and sensitivity of the abscess shows growth of methicillin-susceptible *Staphylococcus aureus*. The patient was started on the appropriate antibiotic. The patient is on oral as well as injectional insulin for control of her diabetes.

041.11	Bacterial infection in conditions classified elsewhere and of unspecified site, methicillin-susceptible *staphylococcus aureus* (MSSA)
041.12	Methicillin-resistant *staphylococcus aureus* (MSRA)
041.19	Bacterial infection in conditions classified elsewhere and of unspecified site, other staphylococcus
250.82	Diabetes mellitus with other specified manifestations, type 2 or unspecified type, uncontrolled
250.83	Diabetes mellitus with other specified manifestations, type 1 (juvenile type), uncontrolled
682.7	Other cellulitis and abscess of foot, except toes
682.8	Other cellulitis and abscess of other specified sites
707.00	Chronic ulcer of skin, pressure ulcer, unspecified site
707.15	Ulcer of lower limbs, except pressure ulcer, of other part of foot (toes)
707.8	Chronic ulcer of other specified sites
V09.0	Infection with microorganisms resistant to penicillins
86.01	Aspiration of skin and subcutaneous tissue
86.04	Other incision with drainage of skin and subcutaneous tissue

A. 250.83, 682.8, V09.0, 86.04
B. 682.7, 682.8, 707.15, 041.19, 86.01
C. 682.8, 041.19, 250.82, 707.00, 86.04,
D. 250.82, 682.7, 707.15, 041.12, V09.0, 86.04

REFERENCE: Brown, pp 112, 121–126, 239–242
                    Schraffenberger, pp 79–80, 112–124, 292–294
                    Ingenix, p 712

114. A patient was admitted to a nursing home with acute respiratory failure due to congestive heart failure. Chest x-ray also showed pulmonary edema. Patient was intubated and placed on mechanical ventilation and expired the day after admission.

428.0	Congestive heart failure, unspecified
428.1	Left heart failure
428.20	Systolic heart failure, unspecified as to acute, chronic, or acute on chronic
518.4	Acute edema of lung, unspecified
518.81	Acute respiratory failure
518.84	Acute and chronic respiratory failure
96.71	Continuous invasive mechanical ventilation for less than 96 consecutive hours
96.04	Insertion of endotracheal tube

   A. 428.1, 518.84, 518.4, 96.71, 96.04
   B. 428.20, 428.0, 518.81, 518.4, 96.71, 96.04
   C. 518.81, 428.0, 96.71, 96.04
   D. 428.0, 518.4, 96.04, 96.71

REFERENCE: Brown, pp 189–192, 194–195
               Schraffenberger, pp 192–194, 224–226
               Ingenix, pp 793, 798

115. The patient has hypertensive heart disease and nephrosclerosis with end-stage renal disease. The patient had placement of arteriovenous fistula in his left wrist to prepare for the hemodialysis. Dialysis was also performed on this admission.

404.92	Hypertensive heart and chronic kidney disease, unspecified as malignant or benign, without heart failure and with chronic kidney disease Stage V or end-stage renal disease
404.93	Hypertensive heart and chronic kidney disease unspecified as malignant or benign, with heart failure and chronic kidney disease Stage V or end-stage renal disease
585.6	End-stage renal disease
585.9	Chronic kidney disease, unspecified
V56.0	Encounter for extracorporeal dialysis
39.27	Arteriovenostomy for renal dialysis
38.95	Venous catheterization for renal dialysis
39.95	Hemodialysis
54.98	Peritoneal dialysis

   A. 404.93, 585.9, 54.98, 39.27   C. 404.93, 585.6, 39.95, 39.27
   B. 404.92, 585.6, 39.95, 39.27   D. 404.92, 585.9, 38.95, 39.27

REFERENCE: Brown, pp 221–222
               Ingenix, pp 348–349, 352, 365

116. The patient has had abnormal heavy uterine bleeding and abdominal pain. There was bright red blood in the vagina and the right adnexa was enlarged. The woman was admitted. During surgery, a laparoscopy revealed a right follicular ovarian cyst. A laparoscopic ovarian cystectomy was performed. Following surgery, she was transfused two units of packed red blood cells for acute blood-loss anemia.

280.0	Iron-deficiency anemia secondary to blood loss (chronic)
285.1	Acute posthemorrhagic anemia
620.0	Follicular cyst of ovary
65.25	Other laparoscopic local excision or destruction of ovary
65.39	Other unilateral oophorectomy

A. 620.0, 285.1, 65.25
B. 620.0, 280.0, 65.39
C. 620.0, 285.1, 65.39
D. 620.0, 280.0, 65.25

REFERENCE: Brown, p 153
Schraffenberger, pp 135, 253
Ingenix, pp 530–531

117. Jane Doe is 6 weeks post-mastectomy for carcinoma of the breast. She is admitted for chemotherapy. What is the correct sequencing of the codes?
A. V58.11 (chemotherapy), 174.9 (malignant neoplasm of the breast), V45.71 (acquired absence of breast)
B. V58.11 (chemotherapy), V10.3 (personal history of malignant neoplasm of breast), V45.71 (acquired absence of breast)
C. V67.00 (follow-up exam after surgery), V58.11 (chemotherapy)
D. V10.3 (personal history of malignant neoplasm of breast)

REFERENCE: Brown, pp 391–396
Schraffenberger, pp 445–446, 449–450

118. The patient was admitted due to increasingly severe pain in his right arm, shoulder, and neck for the past 6 weeks. MRI tests showed herniation of the C5-C6 disc. Patient underwent cervical laminotomy and diskectomy for C5-C6 disc. The patient is currently being treated for COPD and CAD with a history of a PTCA.

414.00	Coronary atherosclerosis of unspecified type of vessel, native or graft
414.01	Coronary atherosclerosis of native coronary artery
492.8	Other emphysema
496	Chronic airway obstruction, not elsewhere classified
722.0	Displacement of cervical intervertebral disc without myelopathy
722.11	Displacement of thoracic intervertebral disc without myelopathy
V45.82	Percutaneous transluminal coronary angioplasty status
80.51	Excision of intervertebral disc
03.09	Other exploration and decompression of spinal canal

A. 722.0, 492.8, 414.01, V45.82, 80.51
B. 722.11, 496, 414.01, V45.82, 03.09, 80.51
C. 722.11, 492.8, 414.00, 03.09, 80.51
D. 722.0, 496, 414.01, V45.82, 80.51

REFERENCE: Brown, pp 186, 251–252, 337, 355
Schraffenberger, pp 190–193, 224, 304, 445–446
Ingenix, pp 99–100, 624–625

119. A 75-year-old man is admitted with acute cerebral embolism with infarction. He had hemiplegia and dysphagia. Physical therapy was given for the hemiplegia. The hemiplegia was resolved at the time of discharge.

342.90	Hemiplegia, unspecified, affecting unspecified side
434.11	Cerebral embolism with cerebral infarction
787.20	Dysphagia, unspecified
V57.1	Other physical therapy

   A. 434.11, 342.90, V57.1
   B. 434.11, 342.90, 787.20
   C. 434.11, 342.90
   D. 434.11, 342.90, 787.20, V57.1

REFERENCE: Brown, pp 343–345

Infectious and Parasitic Diseases

120. Patient is admitted to St. Mary's Hospital with hyperthermia, tachycardia, hypoxemia, and altered mental status. Urinalysis is positive for *E. coli* and blood cultures are negative. Patient is immediately started on broad-spectrum IV antibiotics. Physician documents urosepsis as the final diagnosis. The coder should
   A. report 599.0 (UTI) and 041.4 (*E. coli*).
   B. report 038.42 (septicemia due to *E. coli*) and 995.91 (SIRS-sepsis).
   C. report 038.42 (septicemia due to *E. coli*), 599.0 (UTI) and 995.91 (SIRS-sepsis).
   D. confer with physician for reporting 038.9 (unspecified septicemia) based on the clinical findings with 041.4 (*E. coli*) and 995.91 (SIRS-sepsis).

REFERENCE: Brown, pp 109–110
                Schraffenberger, pp 80–82

121. Six-year-old Alex attended a birthday party where hot dogs and potato salad were served for lunch. Several hours after returning home, Alex began vomiting and having severe diarrhea. Alex was admitted to the hospital for treatment of his vomiting and diarrhea and was diagnosed with salmonella food poisoning. Alex was given IV fluids for dehydration. Alex also has asthma, so he was given respiratory treatments while in the hospital.

003.9	Salmonella infection, unspecified
005.9	Food poisoning, unspecified
276.51	Dehydration
493.90	Asthma, unspecified, unspecified as to with status asthmaticus or with acute exacerbation
787.03	Vomiting alone
787.91	Diarrhea

   A. 003.9, 276.51, 493.90
   B. 005.9, 003.9, 276.51, 493.90
   C. 005.9, 276.51, 493.90
   D. 005.9, 003.9, 267.51, 787.03, 787.91, 493.90

REFERENCE: Schraffenberger, pp 78–79, 126, 222–224

122. A patient is admitted to the hospital with listlessness, fever, and persistent cough. Workup reveals HIV infection with HIV-related pneumonia. The patient is treated for pneumonia.

042	Human Immunodeficiency Virus (HIV) disease
486	Pneumonia, organism unspecified
795.71	Nonspecific serologic evidence of Human Immunodeficiency Virus (HIV)
V08	Asymptomatic Human Immunodeficiency Virus (HIV) infection status

A. 486, 042

B. 042, 486

C. 486, 795.71

D. 486, V08

REFERENCE: Brown, p 115

Schraffenberger, pp 82–85, 220

123. David was experiencing chronic fatigue and was experiencing flulike symptoms. Blood testing indicated that he had hepatitis C. A percutaneous liver biopsy was performed to determine the stage of the disease.

070.41	Acute viral hepatitis C with hepatic coma
070.51	Acute viral hepatitis C without mention of hepatic coma
487.1	Influenza with other respiratory manifestations
780.79	Other malaise and fatigue
50.11	Closed (percutaneous) (needle) biopsy of liver
50.12	Open biopsy of liver

A. 070.51, 487.1, 780.79, 50.12

B. 070.41, 50.11

C. 070.51, 487.1, 50.11

D. 070.51, 50.11

REFERENCE: Brown, pp 70–71, 107

Schraffenberger, p 79

Ingenix, p 491

124. A 40-year-old female suddenly develops a painful rash. A visit to her physician reveals she has shingles. She is experiencing a great amount of anxiety and stress, so her physician prescribes medication for the shingles and for the anxiety that occurred as a reaction to the stress.

053.8	Herpes zoster with unspecified complication
053.9	Herpes zoster without mention of complication
300.00	Anxiety state, unspecified
308.0	Predominant disturbance of emotions
308.3	Other acute reactions to stress

A. 053.9, 308.0

B. 053.9, 308.3, 300.00

C. 053.8, 300.00

D. 053.8, 308.0

REFERENCE: Brown, pp 107, 139–140

Schraffenberger, pp 79, 143

Neoplasms

125. James is admitted to the hospital for severe anemia that is a result of the chemotherapy treatments he is receiving for metastatic prostate cancer to bone. James receives blood transfusions and is discharged home.

185	Malignant neoplasm of prostate
198.5	Secondary malignant neoplasm, bone and bone marrow
285.22	Anemia in neoplastic disease
E933.1	Adverse effect of antineoplastic and immunosuppressive drugs

A. 185, 198.5, 285.22, E933.1
B. E933.1, 285.22
C. 285.22, E933.1
D. 285.22, 185, 198.5, E933.1

REFERENCE: Brown, pp 151, 153, 383–385
                          Schraffenberger, pp 103–111, 135

126. Mary had resection of the large bowel for carcinoma of the colon. She is admitted for further staging of her cancer and receives radiation therapy during this admission.

153.9	Malignant neoplasm of colon, unspecified
V10.05	Personal history of malignant neoplasm of large intestine
V58.0	Encounter for radiotherapy
V67.09	Follow-up examination following other surgery
92.29	Other radiotherapeutic procedure

A. 153.9, 92.29
B. V58.0, V10.05
C. V67.09, V58.0
D. V10.05, V58.0

REFERENCE: Brown, pp 382–383, 391–392

127. Jackie has developed a lesion on her right shoulder. A biopsy was obtained and was positive for malignant melanoma. She is now admitted for radical excision of the melanoma lesion and full-thickness skin graft.

172.6	Malignant melanoma of skin, upper limb, including shoulder
173.69	Malignant neoplasm of skin of upper limb, including shoulder
86.3	Other local excision or destruction of lesion or tissue of skin and subcutaneous tissue
86.4	Radical excision of skin lesion
86.63	Full-thickness skin graft to other sites

A. 172.6, 86.4, 86.63
B. 173.69, 86.4, 86.63
C. 173.69, 86.3, 86.63
D. 172.6, 86.3, 86.63

REFERENCE: Brown, pp 243, 377–379
                          Schraffenberger, p 103
                          Ingenix, pp 716–718

128. Richard is admitted for chemotherapy for leukemia. Chemotherapy is administered. Given this information,
    A. the leukemia code and a procedure code for the chemotherapy will be assigned.
    B. an admission for chemotherapy code and a chemotherapy procedure code will be assigned.
    C. an admission for chemotherapy code, a leukemia code, and a procedure code for the chemotherapy should be assigned and the principal diagnosis will be the admission for chemotherapy V code.
    D. an admission for chemotherapy code, a leukemia code, and a procedure code for the chemotherapy should be assigned and the principal diagnosis will be the leukemia code.

REFERENCE: Brown, pp 382–385
                Schraffenberger, p 111

129. Sophia has been diagnosed with metastatic carcinoma of lung, primary site breast. Simple mastectomy performed 2 years ago. What is the principal diagnosis?
    A. metastatic carcinoma of the lung
    B. carcinoma of breast
    C. history of carcinoma of breast
    D. status post-mastectomy

REFERENCE: Brown, pp 382–385
                Schraffenberger, pp 108–109

130. Given the following diagnosis: "Carcinoma of axillary lymph nodes and lungs, metastatic from breast." What is the primary cancer site(s)?
    A. axillary lymph nodes   C. breast
    B. lungs   D. both A and B

REFERENCE: Brown, pp 382–385
                Schraffenberger, pp 107–109

131. When is it appropriate to use category V10, history of malignant neoplasm?
    A. Primary malignancy recurred at the original site and adjunct chemotherapy is directed at the site.
    B. Primary malignancy has been eradicated and no adjunct treatment is being given at this time.
    C. Primary malignancy is eradicated and the patient is admitted for adjunct chemotherapy to primary site.
    D. Primary malignancy is eradicated; adjunct treatment is refused by the patient even though there is some remaining malignancy.

REFERENCE: Brown, pp 89–90
                Schraffenberger, pp 102–104

Endocrine, Nutritional, and Metabolic Diseases and Immunity Disorders

132. Ralph is a 96-year-old nursing home resident who is admitted for malnutrition. He has suffered a previous stroke that has left him with dysphagia. He is treated for malnutrition with hyperalimentation. He was also found to have hypokalemia that was treated with IV potassium replacement. On the day prior to discharge, Ralph underwent a PEG tube insertion.

263.9	Unspecified protein-calorie malnutrition
276.8	Hypopotassemia (Hypokalemia)
438.82	Dysphagia, late effect of cerebrovascular disease
787.20	Dysphagia, unspecified
43.11	Percutaneous endoscopic gastrostomy (PEG) insertion

A. 438.82, 263.9, 787.20, 43.11
B. 787.20, 276.8, 43.11
C. 263.9, 276.8, 438.82, 43.11
D. 263.9, 787.20, 276.8, 43.11

REFERENCE: Brown, pp 129, 343–344
               Schraffenberger, pp 122, 126, 198
               Ingenix, pp 391–392

133. Jessica has been diagnosed with hyperthyroidism due to toxic multinodular goiter with crisis. She also has hypertension and has a history of sick sinus syndrome with pacemaker insertion. Jessica has a partial thyroidectomy on this admission.

240.9	Goiter, unspecified
241.1	Nontoxic multinodular goiter
242.21	Toxic multinodular goiter with mention of thyrotoxic crisis or storm
401.0	Essential hypertension, malignant
401.9	Essential hypertension, unspecified benign or malignant
427.81	Sinoatrial node dysfunction
V45.01	Other postprocedural states, cardiac pacemaker
06.39	Other partial thyroidectomy
06.4	Complete thyroidectomy

A. 240.9, 401.0, 427.81, 06.4
B. 242.21, 401.9, 427.81, V45.01, 06.39
C. 240.9, 242.21, 401.9. V45.01, 06.4
D. 242.21, 401.9. V45.01, 06.39

REFERENCE: Brown, p 347
               Schraffenberger, pp 121–122, 180–182, 445–446
               Ingenix, p 120

134. Laura is 7 years old and has acute bronchitis and cystic fibrosis. She is admitted to ambulatory surgery for bronchoscopy.

277.00	Cystic fibrosis without mention of meconium ileus
277.01	Cystic fibrosis with meconium ileus
466.0	Acute bronchitis
33.23	Other bronchoscopy
33.24	Closed (endoscopic) biopsy of bronchus
96.56	Other lavage of bronchus and trachea

A. 466.0, 277.00, 33.23
B. 466.0, 277.01, 33.24

C. 277.00, 96.56, 33.23
D. 277.00, 33.23, 33.24, 96.56

REFERENCE: Brown, p 129
Schraffenberger, pp 113, 181
Ingenix, pp 378–379, 797

135. Estelle has had nausea and vomiting and is unable to eat. She develops dehydration and is subsequently admitted for rehydration with intravenous fluids.

276.51	Dehydration
787.01	Nausea with vomiting
787.02	Nausea alone
787.03	Vomiting alone

A. 276.51, 787.01
B. 276.51

C. 276.51, 787.02
D. 276.51, 787.02, 787.03

REFERENCE: Schraffenberger, p 112

136. A patient is admitted for treatment of peripheral vascular disease, renal failure, and diabetes mellitus. The coder would
A. assign codes for PVD, renal failure, and diabetes.
B. assign codes for diabetes with peripheral vascular and renal manifestations.
C. query physician for causal relationship between the PVD, renal failure, and diabetes.
D. assign codes of diabetes with PVD and a code for renal failure.

REFERENCE: Brown, pp 123–126

137. Lucy is admitted because of diabetic coma. She has type 2 diabetes with nephritic syndrome and gangrene of her toes, all due to her diabetes.

250.30	Diabetes mellitus with other coma, type 2 or unspecified type, not stated as uncontrolled
250.31	Diabetes mellitus with other coma, type 1 (juvenile type), not stated as uncontrolled
250.40	Diabetes mellitus with renal manifestations, type 2 or unspecified type, not stated as uncontrolled
250.41	Diabetes mellitus with renal manifestations, type 1 (juvenile type), not stated as uncontrolled
250.70	Diabetes mellitus with peripheral circulatory disorders, type 2 or unspecified type, not stated as uncontrolled
581.81	Nephrotic syndrome in diseases classified elsewhere (manifestation)
785.4	Gangrene

A. 250.30, 250.40, 581.81, 250.70, 785.4
B. 250.31, 581.81, 785.4
C. 250.30, 250.40, 581.81
D. 250.30, 250.41, 785.4

REFERENCE: Brown, pp 121–126
Schraffenberger, pp 122–124, 250

138. George has type 2 diabetes and is admitted in a coma with blood glucose of 876. He is diagnosed with diabetic ketoacidosis. George also has a diabetic cataract.

250.10	Diabetes mellitus with ketoacidosis, type 2 or unspecified type, not stated as uncontrolled
250.11	Diabetes mellitus with ketoacidosis, type 1 (juvenile type), not stated as uncontrolled
250.30	Diabetes mellitus with other coma, type 2 or unspecified type, not stated as uncontrolled
250.31	Diabetes mellitus with other coma, type 1 (juvenile type), not stated as uncontrolled
250.32	Diabetes mellitus with other coma, type 2 or unspecified type, uncontrolled
250.50	Diabetes mellitus with ophthalmic manifestations, type 2 or unspecified type, not stated as uncontrolled
250.51	Diabetes mellitus with ophthalmic manifestations, type 1 (juvenile type), not stated as uncontrolled
250.52	Diabetes mellitus with ophthalmic manifestations, type 2 or unspecified type, uncontrolled
366.41	Diabetic cataract (manifestation)
366.9	Unspecified cataract

A. 250.11, 250.31, 366.9
B. 250.10, 250.30, 250.50, 366.9
C. 250.32, 250.52, 366.41
D. 250.31, 250.51, 366.41

REFERENCE: Brown, pp 121–126
Schraffenberger, pp 122–124, 164

139. Spencer has hypercholesterolemia and is treated with medication.

> 272.0   Pure hypercholesterolemia
> 272.1   Pure hyperglyceridemia
> 272.3   Hyperchylomicronemia
> 272.8   Other disorders of lipoid metabolism

A. 272.0
B. 272.1
C. 272.3
D. 272.8

REFERENCE: Schraffenberger, p 121

140. Edward is diagnosed with syndrome of inappropriate antidiuretic hormone with resultant electrolyte imbalance.

> 253.6   Other disorders of neurophyophysis (syndrome of inappropriate secretion of antidiuretic hormone—ADH)
> 272.9   Unspecified disorder of lipoid metabolism
> 276.50   Volume depletion, unspecified
> 276.8   Hypopotassemia (hypokalemia)
> 276.9   Electrolyte and fluid disorders, not elsewhere classified

A. 276.50
B. 276.9, 272.9
C. 253.6, 276.9
D. 253.6. 276.8

REFERENCE: Schraffenberger, pp 121–126

Diseases of the Blood and Blood-Forming Organs

141. Ruth is admitted for an axillary lymph node biopsy to determine the cause of her chronic lymphadenitis. She is on medication for gout and atrial fibrillation.

> 274.9   Gout, unspecified
> 289.1   Chronic lymphadenitis
> 289.2   Nonspecific mesenteric lymphadenitis
> 427.31   Atrial fibrillation
> 40.11   Biopsy of lymphatic structure
> 40.23   Excision of axillary lymph node
> 40.51   Radical excision of axillary lymph nodes

A. 289.1, 274.9, 427.31, 40.11
B. 274.9, 289.2, 427.31, 40.11
C. 289.1, 427.31, 40.23
D. 289.1, 427.31, 274.9, 40.51

REFERENCE: Brown, pp 70–71
Schraffenberger, pp 126, 137–138, 194
Ingenix, pp 368–369, 371

142. Elizabeth has a history of von Willebrand's disease and frequently requires transfusions for chronic blood-loss anemia associated with her condition. She presents to the outpatient department for routine blood transfusion.

> 280.0   Iron-deficiency anemia secondary to blood loss (chronic)
> 280.1   Iron-deficiency anemia secondary to inadequate dietary iron intake
> 285.1   Acute posthemorrhagic anemia
> 286.4   Von Willebrand's disease
> 286.7   Acquired coagulation factor deficiency

A. 285.1, 286.4   C. 286.4, 280.1
B. 286.7, 286.4   D. 280.0, 286.4

REFERENCE: Brown, pp 151–153
               Schraffenberger, pp 132–136

143. Steven, a 7-year-old, is seen in the emergency department with severe joint pain. Following workup, it is discovered that he is having a severe crisis due to sickle cell anemia.

> 282.61   Sickle cell disease (Hb-SS disease without crisis)
> 282.62   Sickle cell disease (Hb-SS disease with crisis)
> 282.63   Sickle cell/Hb-C disease without crisis
> 282.69   Other sickle cell disease with crisis

A. 282.61   C. 282.63
B. 282.62   D. 282.69

REFERENCE: Bowie and Schaffer, p 145
               Brown, p 154
               Schraffenberger, p 132

144. Angela has just undergone orthopedic surgery. Documentation indicates that she lost 700 cc of blood during surgery. Her hemoglobin and hematocrit are monitored following surgery. Subsequently, she is transfused. The physician documents anemia as a secondary diagnosis. The coder would
    A. query the physician to clarify the type of anemia as acute blood loss.
    B. assign a code for unspecified anemia.
    C. assign a code for acute blood-loss anemia.
    D. not assign a code for anemia.

REFERENCE: Brown, p 152

145. Liza has been diagnosed with anemia. She is being admitted for a bone marrow aspiration to determine the specific type of anemia. The pathology report indicates that she has iron-deficiency anemia.

280.0	Iron-deficiency anemia secondary to blood loss (chronic)
280.8	Other specified iron-deficiency anemias
280.9	Iron-deficiency anemia, unspecified
41.31	Biopsy of bone marrow
41.38	Other diagnostic procedures on bone marrow
41.91	Aspiration of bone marrow from donor for transplant

A. 280.0, 41.38
B. 280.9, 41.31
C. 280.9, 41.91
D. 280.8, 41.38

REFERENCE: Bowie and Schaffer, pp 144–145
Brown, p 151
Ingenix, pp 377–378, 380

146. Peggy has thymic dysplasia with immunodeficiency.

254.0	Persistent hyperplasia of thymus
254.8	Other specified diseases of thymus gland
254.9	Unspecified disease of thymus gland
279.2	Combined immunity deficiency (thymic aplasia or dysplasia with immunodeficiency)
279.3	Unspecified immunity deficiency

A. 279.3, 254.8
B. 254.0
C. 279.2
D. 279.2, 254.9

REFERENCE: Brown, p 130

147. Aaron has suffered a hypoglycemic reaction due to alcohol intoxication. Hypoglycemia is treated.

250.80	Diabetes mellitus with other specified manifestations, type 2 or unspecified type, not stated as uncontrolled
251.2	Hypoglycemia, unspecified
303.90	Other and unspecified alcohol dependence, unspecified
305.00	Alcohol abuse, unspecified
995.29	Unspecified adverse effect of other drug, medicinal, and biological substance

A. 251.2, 305.00
B. 251.2, 303.90
C. 995.29, 303.90
D. 250.80, 305.00

REFERENCE: Brown, pp 128, 141–142

Mental Disorders

148. Joe is being admitted for treatment of chronic alcoholism. As a result of Joe's drinking he also has chronic alcoholic gastritis for which he receives medication. Joe is scheduled to spend 30 days in the inpatient rehab unit of Sunshine Hospital.

303.01	Acute alcoholic intoxication, continuous
303.90	Other and unspecified alcohol dependence, unspecified
303.91	Other and unspecified alcohol dependence, continuous
535.00	Acute gastritis without mention of hemorrhage
535.30	Alcoholic gastritis without mention of hemorrhage
535.31	Alcoholic gastritis with hemorrhage
94.61	Alcohol rehabilitation
94.62	Alcohol detoxification
94.63	Alcohol rehabilitation and detoxification

A. 303.01, 535.00, 94.63
B. 303.91, 535.00, 94.63
C. 303.90, 535.30, 94.61
D. 303.01, 303.90, 535.30, 94.63

REFERENCE: Brown, pp 141–142, 201
                        Schraffenberger, pp 234–235
                        Ingenix, pp 786–787

149. Sheila has paranoid alcoholic psychosis with chronic alcoholism, continuous. She is admitted for treatment of her psychosis.

291.5	Alcohol-induced psychotic disorder with delusions
303.91	Other and unspecified alcohol dependence, continuous
V57.89	Other specified rehabilitation procedure

A. 291.5, 303.91
B. 303.91, 291.5
C. V57.89, 303.91
D. 291.5, 303.91, V57.89

REFERENCE: Brown, pp 135, 141–142
                        Schraffenberger, pp 143, 148

150. Sybil has been admitted to Shady Acres Psychiatric facility for treatment of schizophrenia. Sybil is also manic depressive and has been noncompliant with her medications.

295.40	Schizophreniform disorder, unspecified
295.41	Schizophreniform disorder, subchronic
295.90	Unspecified schizophrenia, unspecified
296.7	Bipolar I disorder, most recent episode (or current) unspecified
296.80	Bipolar disorder, unspecified
296.89	Other bipolar disorders (manic-depressive psychosis, mixed type)
V15.81	Personal history, presenting hazards to health (noncompliance with medical treatment)

A. V15.81, 296.89, 295.40
B. 296.89, 295.41, V15.81
C. 296.7, 295.90
D. 295.90, 296.80, V15.81

REFERENCE: Brown, p 137

151. Allen is addicted to Vicodin. He has stopped taking the drug and is now having withdrawal symptoms. Allen has chronic back pain for which he has been prescribed the medication. He is admitted for treatment of his withdrawal symptoms.

292.0	Drug withdrawal
292.11	Drug-induced psychotic disorder with delusions
292.2	Pathological drug intoxication
304.00	Drug dependence, opioid type dependence, unspecified
304.91	Unspecified drug dependence, continuous
724.5	Backache, unspecified

A. 292.2, 724.5
B. 292.11, 292.2, 304.91

C. 292.0, 304.00, 724.5
D. 292.11, 304.91, 724.5

REFERENCE: Brown, pp 141–142
Schraffenberger, pp 143, 147–148

152. Acute epileptic twilight state with delirium.

293.0	Delirium due to conditions classified elsewhere (epileptic twilight state)
293.1	Subacute delirium
294.0	Amnestic disorder in conditions classified elsewhere
345.00	Generalized nonconvulsive epilepsy without mention of intractable epilepsy
780.02	Transient alteration of awareness

A. 293.0
B. 780.02

C. 293.1
D. 294.0, 345.00

REFERENCE: Brown, pp 164–165

153. Sally has been diagnosed with panic attacks and is prescribed Xanax. She has been taking the medication as prescribed by her physician for 3 days and is now having hallucinations. Her physician advises her to stop taking the medication and her symptoms abate. Her doctor determines that the hallucinations were due to the Xanax.

292.12	Drug-induced psychotic disorder with hallucinations
300.01	Panic disorder without agoraphobia
E939.4	Benzodiazepine-based tranquilizers

A. 292.12, E939.4, 300.01
B. 292.12

C. E939.4, 292.12
D. 300.01, 292.12

REFERENCE: Brown, pp 443–446
Schraffenberger, p 143

154. Lou has profound mental retardation due to mongolism.

317	Mild intellectual abilities
318.0	Moderate intellectual abilities
318.2	Profound intellectual abilities
758.0	Down's syndrome
759.0	Congenital anomaly of spleen

A. 318.2, 758.0
B. 318.0, 759.0
C. 758.0, 318.2
D. 317, 758.0

REFERENCE: Schraffenberger, pp 130, 283–284

Diseases of the Nervous System and Sense Organs

155. Mark has a long history of epilepsy. He is brought to the emergency department and is admitted with intractable epileptic seizures. Mark's epilepsy is the result of a head injury he suffered several years ago.

345.11	Generalized convulsive epilepsy with intractable epilepsy
345.10	Generalized convulsive epilepsy, without mention of intractable epilepsy
345.3	Grand mal status
345.91	Epilepsy, unspecified, with intractable epilepsy
780.39	Other convulsions
907.0	Late effect of intracranial injury without mention of skull fracture

A. 780.39, 907.0
B. 345.91, 907.0
C. 345.3
D. 345.10, 780.39

REFERENCE: Brown, pp 59–60, 164–165
Schraffenberger, pp 161–162

156. Jeff was in a car accident when he was 25 years old and suffered a spinal cord injury. As a result, he is a paraplegic and has neurogenic bladder. Jeff also has chronic ulcers of the buttocks. He is being seen for evaluation of his paraplegia.

344.1	Paraplegia
344.60	Cauda equina syndrome without mention of neurogenic bladder
596.53	Paralysis of bladder
596.54	Neurogenic bladder, not otherwise specified
707.00	Chronic pressure ulcer of skin, unspecified site
707.8	Chronic ulcer of other specified sites
907.2	Late effect of spinal cord injury

A. 344.1, 907.2, 596.54, 707.8
B. 344.60, 596.53, 707.00, 907.2
C. 344.1, 596.53, 907.2
D. 344.1, 596.54, 707.8

REFERENCE: Brown, pp 60, 425

157. Josephine has developed senile cataracts in both eyes. She is admitted for right extracapsular cataract extraction with synchronous lens insertion.

366.10	Senile cataract, unspecified
366.9	Unspecified cataract
13.59	Other extracapsular extraction of lens
13.71	Insertion of intraocular lens prosthesis at time of cataract extraction, one stage

A. 366.9, 13.71
B. 366.10, 13.59, 13.71

C. 366.9, 13.59, 13.71
D. 366.10, 13.59

REFERENCE: Brown, p 172
                       Schraffenberger, p 164
                       Ingenix, pp 172–174

158. A patient presents with diabetic macular or retinal edema.

250.50	Diabetes mellitus with ophthalmic manifestations, type 2 or unspecified type, not stated as uncontrolled
250.51	Diabetes mellitus with ophthalmic manifestations, type 1 (juvenile type), not stated as uncontrolled
362.01	Background diabetic retinopathy (manifestation)
362.02	Proliferative diabetic retinopathy (manifestation)
362.07	Diabetic macular edema

A. 250.51, 362.07, 360.02
B. 362.07, 250.51, 362.02

C. 250.50, 362.07, 362.01
D. 362.02, 362.07, 250.50

REFERENCE: Schraffenberger, pp 122–124, 163–164

159. A patient presents with bilateral sensorineural conductive hearing loss.

389.20	Mixed hearing loss, unspecified
389.21	Mixed hearing loss, unilateral
389.22	Mixed hearing loss, bilateral
389.9	Unspecified hearing loss

A. 389.22
B. 389.21

C. 389.9
D. 389.20

REFERENCE: Schraffenberger, p 165

Diseases of the Circulatory System

160. Madeline is diagnosed with bilateral carotid stenosis. She is being admitted for a bilateral endarterectomy. Madeline is also treated for Parkinson's disease and glaucoma.

332.0	Paralysis agitans (Parkinson's disease)
365.9	Unspecified glaucoma
433.30	Occlusion and stenosis of precerebral arteries, multiple and bilateral, without mention of cerebral infarction
38.12	Endarterectomy, other vessels of head and neck

A. 433.30, 38.12
B. 433.30, 38.12, 38.12

C. 433.30, 332.0, 365.9, 38.12
D. 433.30, 332.0, 365.9, 38.12, 38.12

REFERENCE: Brown, pp 172–173, 343–344
                       Schraffenberger, p 159, 164, 197
                       Ingenix, pp 341–342

161. Jonathan is admitted with bleeding prolapsed internal hemorrhoids and chronic constipation. The physician performed a rubber band ligation of the internal hemorrhoids.

455.1	Internal thrombosed hemorrhoids
455.2	Internal hemorrhoids with other complication
564.09	Other constipation
49.44	Destruction of hemorrhoids by cryotherapy
49.45	Ligation of hemorrhoids
49.46	Excision of hemorrhoids

A. 455.1, 564.09, 49.44
B. 455.1, 49.45
C. 455.2, 564.09 49.45
D. 455.1, 455.2, 49.45

REFERENCE: Schraffenberger, p 234
Ingenix, p 428

162. Frank has been diagnosed with sick sinus syndrome and is being admitted for dual chamber pacemaker and leads insertion. Frank also has type 2 diabetes on oral medication as well as insulin regimen. Surgery is carried out without complication.

250.00	Diabetes mellitus without mention of complication, type 2 or unspecified type, not stated as uncontrolled
250.01	Diabetes mellitus without mention of complication, type 1 (juvenile type), not stated as uncontrolled
427.81	Sinoatrial node dysfunction
V58.67	Long-term (current) use of insulin
37.70	Initial insertion of lead (electrode), not otherwise specified
37.71	Initial insertion of transvenous lead (electrode) into ventricle
37.72	Initial insertion of transvenous leads (electrode) into atrium and ventricle
37.82	Initial insertion of single-chamber device, rate responsive
37.83	Initial insertion of dual chamber device

A. 427.81, 250.00, V58.67, 37.72, 37.83
B. 427.81, 250.01, 37.71, 37.83
C. 427.81, 37.70, 37.83
D. 427.81, 250.00, 250.01, 37.72, 37.83

REFERENCE: Brown, pp 121–122, 358
Ingenix, pp 335–338

163. A patient is treated for congestive heart failure with pleural effusion. A therapeutic thoracentesis is performed.

428.0	Congestive heart failure, unspecified
511.9	Unspecified pleural effusion
34.04	Insertion of intercostal catheter for drainage
34.91	Thoracentesis

A. 511.9, 34.91
B. 428.0, 34.04
C. 428.0, 511.9
D. 428.0, 511.9, 34.91

REFERENCE: Brown, pp 189, 339–340
Schraffenberger, pp 192–193
Ingenix, pp 287–288, 296

164. A patient presents to the emergency department complaining of a severe headache. Workup revealed a ruptured berry aneurysm.

430	Subarachnoid hemorrhage
437.3	Cerebral aneurysm, nonruptured
784.0	Headache

A. 430
B. 784.0

C. 784.0, 430
D. 437.3

REFERENCE: Brown, pp 343–344

Diseases of the Respiratory System

165. Joseph has had cough, fever, and painful respirations for 2 days. He also has congestive heart failure and COPD. Joseph presents to the emergency department with severe shortness of breath, using accessory muscles to assist with breathing. Upon examination, Joseph is diagnosed with acute respiratory failure, congestive heart failure, pneumonia, and exacerbation of COPD. Joseph is intubated and placed on mechanical ventilation. He is weaned from the ventilator on the third day of admission. Two days later, he again goes into respiratory failure, requiring reintubation and placement on the ventilator. Fortunately, he is able to breathe on his own the following day, so was extubated.

428.0	Congestive heart failure, unspecified
486	Pneumonia, organism unspecified
491.21	Obstructive chronic bronchitis with (acute) exacerbation
496	Chronic airway obstruction, not elsewhere classified
518.81	Acute respiratory failure
96.04	Insertion of endotracheal tube
96.71	Continuous invasive mechanical ventilation for less than 96 consecutive hours
96.72	Continuous invasive mechanical ventilation for 96 consecutive hours or more

A. 428.0, 486, 496, 518.81, 96.04, 96.71
B. 518.81, 428.0, 491.21, 96.04, 96.71
C. 486, 428.0, 518.81, 491.21, 96.04, 96.72
D. 518.81, 486, 428.0, 491.21, 96.04, 96.71, 96.04, 96.71

REFERENCE: Bowie and Schaffer, p 216
Brown, pp 189–191, 194–195, 339–340
Schraffenberger, pp 192–193, 219, 223–224
Ingenix, pp 793, 798

166. Ronald is admitted for stenosis of his tracheostomy. He is a quadriplegic, C1-C4 secondary to spinal cord injury suffered in a diving accident. He has chronic respiratory failure and is maintained on mechanical ventilation. He undergoes revision of his tracheostomy.

344.00	Quadriplegia, unspecified
344.01	Quadriplegia, C1-C4, complete
518.83	Chronic respiratory failure
519.02	Mechanical complication of tracheostomy
519.09	Other tracheostomy complications
907.2	Late effect of spinal cord injury
V46.11	Dependence on respirator status (ventilator)
31.74	Revision of tracheostomy
31.79	Other repair and plastic operations on trachea
96.71	Continuous invasive mechanical ventilation for less than 96 consecutive hours
96.72	Continuous invasive mechanical ventilation for 96 consecutive hours or more

A. 518.83, 519.09, 907.2, 31.74
B. 344.01, 518.83, 519.02, 31.79, V46.11
C. 519.02, 344.01, 518.83, 907.2, V46.11, 31.74, 96.72
D. 519.02, 518.83, 907.2, 31.74

REFERENCE: Brown, pp 189–191, 194–195
               Schraffenberger, pp 161, 224–226, 446
               Ingenix, pp 270, 798–799

167. Jennifer presents to the emergency department with severe chest pain and shortness of breath. Chest x-ray revealed a secondary spontaneous pneumothorax. Jennifer also has acute bronchitis. The emergency department physician inserts a chest tube and Jennifer is admitted.

466.0	Acute bronchitis
491.20	Obstructive chronic bronchitis without exacerbation
491.21	Obstructive chronic bronchitis with (acute) exacerbation
512.0	Spontaneous tension pneumothorax
512.1	Iatrogenic pneumothorax
512.81	Primary spontaneous pneumothorax
512.82	Secondary spontaneous pneumothorax
34.01	Incision of chest wall
34.04	Insertion of intercostal catheter for drainage

A. 466.0, 512.82, 34.04   C. 466.0, 491.21, 512.1, 34.04
B. 512.0, 491.21, 34.01   D. 491.20, 466.0, 512.82, 34.01

REFERENCE: Schraffenberger, pp 217–218
               Ingenix, pp 287–288

168. Dale is admitted with emphysematous nodules. He undergoes, without complication, a wedge resection of the right upper lobe. Dale developed atelectasis postoperatively that required monitoring with portable chest x-rays and extended his length of stay.

492.8	Other emphysema
518.0	Pulmonary collapse (atelectasis)
518.89	Other diseases of lung, not elsewhere classified
997.39	Respiratory complications
32.29	Other local excision or destruction of lesions or tissue of lung
32.30	Thoracoscopic segmental resection of lung

   A. 518.89, 997.39, 32.30   C. 492.8, 997.39, 518.0, 32.29
   B. 997.39, 518.0, 518.89, 32.29   D. 518.89, 518.0, 32.29

REFERENCE: Brown, pp 188–189
                     Schraffenberger, pp 223, 387–390
                     Ingenix, pp 274–275

169. Agnes is admitted with cough, fever, and dysphagia. Chest x-ray shows infiltrates in both lower lobes. Sputum culture is positive for *Staphylococcus aureus*. Swallow study indicates that Agnes aspirates. Physician documents aspiration pneumonia and *Staphylococcus aureus* pneumonia. As a coder, you would assign codes for the following conditions in this proper sequence.
   A. *Staphylococcus aureus* pneumonia, dysphagia
   B. *Staphylococcus aureus* pneumonia, aspiration pneumonia
   C. Aspiration pneumonia, dysphagia
   D. Aspiration pneumonia, *Staphylococcus aureus* pneumonia, dysphagia

REFERENCE: Bowie and Schaffer, p 212
                     Brown, pp 181–183
                     Schraffenberger, p 219

170. This patient has pneumonia. She also has acute exacerbation of COPD.

486	Pneumonia, organism unspecified
491.20	Obstructive chronic bronchitis, without exacerbation
491.21	Obstructive chronic bronchitis, with (acute) exacerbation

   A. 491.21   C. 491.20, 486
   B. 486, 491.21   D. 486

REFERENCE: Brown, pp 181–182, 186
                     Schraffenberger, p 219

171. Matthew has acute and chronic maxillary sinusitis. He had a maxillary sinusectomy performed.

461.0	Acute maxillary sinusitis
461.2	Acute ethmoidal sinusitis
473.0	Chronic maxillary sinusitis
22.62	Excision of lesion of maxillary sinus with other approach

   A. 461.0, 22.62   C. 461.0, 473.0, 22.62
   B. 473.0, 22.62   D. 461.2, 22.62

REFERENCE: Schraffenberger, p 217
                     Ingenix, p 234

Diseases of the Digestive System

172. Grace has been having abdominal pain for several weeks and has been vomiting blood for 2 days. Her physician performs an esophagogastroduodenoscopy and biopsies a lesion in the duodenum. The pathology report indicates Grace has acute and chronic gastritis.

532.00	Acute duodenal ulcer with hemorrhage without mention of obstruction
535.01	Acute gastritis with hemorrhage
535.11	Chronic (atrophic) gastritis with hemorrhage
789.00	Abdominal pain, unspecified site
45.13	Esophagogastroduodenoscopy (EGD)
45.16	Esophagogastroduodenoscopy with closed biopsy

A. 532.00, 789.00, 45.13
B. 535.01, 789.00, 45.16
C. 535.01, 535.11, 789.00. 45.13
D. 535.01, 535.11, 45.16

REFERENCE: Brown, p 201
                        Ingenix, pp 404–405

173. Mary presents to the emergency department with complaints of chest pain. Myocardial infarction is ruled out; however, gastrointestinal studies indicate Mary is suffering from gastroesophageal reflux disease (GERD). Mary is given medication to relieve her symptoms and instructed to follow up with her physician.

410.91	Acute myocardial infarction, unspecified site, initial episode of care
530.81	Gastroesophageal reflux (GERD)
786.50	Chest pain, unspecified

A. 530.81
B. 786.50
C. 530.81, 410.91
D. 410.91, 786.50

REFERENCE: Brown, p 203

174. Crystal has been vomiting for 24 hours with complaint of right lower quadrant pain. Examination is suspicious for acute appendicitis. Crystal is taken to surgery and laparoscopic appendectomy is carried out. Pathological diagnosis is consistent with acute appendicitis. Crystal developed postoperative paralytic ileus.

540.0	Acute appendicitis with generalized peritonitis
540.9	Acute appendicitis without mention of peritonitis
560.1	Paralytic ileus
997.49	Digestive system complications
47.01	Laparoscopic appendectomy
47.09	Other appendectomy
47.11	Laparoscopic incidental appendectomy

A. 540.0, 997.49, 47.11
B. 540.0, 997.49, 47.09
C. 540.9, 997.49, 560.1, 47.01
D. 997.49, 560.1, 540.9, 47.09

REFERENCE: Brown, pp 210–211
                        Ingenix, pp 417–418

175. A patient presents with intestinal obstruction due to adhesions. He also has peripheral vascular disease and chronic urinary tract infections; both conditions were treated with oral medication.

443.9	Peripheral vascular disease, unspecified
560.81	Intestinal or peritoneal adhesions with obstruction (postoperative) (post infection)
560.89	Other specified intestinal obstruction
560.9	Unspecified intestinal obstruction
599.0	Urinary tract infection, site not specified

A. 560.81, 443.9, 599.0   C. 560.9, 443.9, 599.0
B. 560.9   D. 560.89, 443.9, 599.0

REFERENCE: Brown, pp 208, 217

176. This patient has chronic diarrhea associated with Crohn's disease. She also has protein-calorie malnutrition. She is admitted for bowel resection of the diseased colon.

263.9	Unspecified protein-calorie malnutrition
555.1	Regional enteritis, large intestine (Crohn's disease)
556.9	Ulcerative colitis, unspecified
787.91	Diarrhea
45.79	Other and unspecified partial excision of large intestine
45.94	Large-to-large intestinal anastomosis

A. 556.9, 263.9, 45.79, 45.94   C. 555.1, 787.91, 263.9, 45.79
B. 555.1, 263.9, 45.79   D. 556.9, 263.9, 45.79, 45.94

REFERENCE: Schraffenberger, p 236
                 Ingenix, pp 409–410

177. A patient is admitted with hepatic coma with ascites due to Laennec's cirrhosis.

571.2	Alcoholic cirrhosis of liver (Laennec's cirrhosis)
572.2	Hepatic encephalopathy (hepatic coma)
789.59	Other ascites

A. 572.2, 571.2, 789.59   C. 789.59, 572.2
B. 571.2, 789.59   D. 789.59, 572.2, 571.2

REFERENCE: Schraffenberger, p 234

Diseases of the Genitourinary System

178. Chantel is admitted with infertility secondary to pelvic peritoneal adhesions. She had a laparoscopic lysis of adhesions performed.

614.6	Pelvic peritoneal adhesions, female (postoperative) (post infection)
628.2	Infertility, female, of tubal origin
54.21	Laparoscopy
65.81	Laparoscopic lysis of adhesions of ovary and fallopian tube

A. 628.2, 614.6, 65.81   C. 614.6, 65.81, 54.21
B. 628.2, 54.21, 65.81   D. 614.6, 54.21

REFERENCE: Brown, p 208
                 Ingenix, pp 453, 535–536

179. Betsy has chronic pelvic inflammatory disease with dysmenorrhea. She undergoes a diagnostic laparoscopy.

    614.4   Chronic or unspecified parametritis and pelvic cellulitis
    625.3   Dysmenorrhea
    54.21   Laparoscopy
    54.4   Excision or destruction of peritoneal tissue

    A. 625.3, 54.21   C. 625.3, 614.4, 54.21
    B. 614.4, 54.4   D. 614.4, 625.3, 54.21

REFERENCE: Schraffenberger, p 253
                  Ingenix, pp 453–454

180. David has chronic interstitial cystitis. The physician performs a cystoscopy with biopsy.

    595.1   Chronic interstitial cystitis
    595.2   Other chronic cystitis
    599.0   Urinary tract infection, site not specified
    57.32   Other cystoscopy
    57.33   Closed (transurethral) biopsy of bladder

    A. 599.0, 57.32   C. 595.2, 57.32, 57.33
    B. 595.1, 57.33   D. 595.1, 599.0, 57.32

REFERENCE: Brown, p 217

181. Cynthia has fibrocystic disease of the breast and undergoes a needle biopsy of the breast.

    610.1   Diffuse cystic mastopathy (fibrocystic disease of breast)
    610.2   Fibroadenosis of breast
    610.3   Fibrosclerosis of breast
    610.9   Benign mammary dysplasia, unspecified
    85.11   Closed (percutaneous) (needle) biopsy of breast
    85.12   Open biopsy of breast

    A. 610.1, 85.11   C. 610.2, 85.11
    B. 610.3, 85.12   D. 610.9, 85.12

REFERENCE: Brown, p 229
                  Ingenix, pp 702–703

Complications of Pregnancy, Childbirth, and the Puerperium

182. Tammy has an intrauterine pregnancy and delivers a set of twins at 33 weeks. She had premature rupture of membranes. The spontaneous delivery of the premature twins was via a vertex presentation, and both infants were born alive.

644.20   Early onset of delivery, unspecified episode of care
644.21   Early onset of delivery, delivered, with or without mention of antepartum condition
651.01   Twin pregnancy, delivered, with or without mention of antepartum condition
658.11   Premature rupture of membranes, delivered, with or without mention of antepartum condition
659.11   Failed medical or unspecified induction, delivered, with or without mention of antepartum condition
V27.2   Outcome of delivery, twins, both liveborn
73.59   Other manually assisted delivery

  A.   644.21, 658.11, 651.01, V27.2, 73.59
  B.   644.20, 659.11, V27.2
  C.   644.20, 658.11, 651.02, 73.59
  D.   658.11, 651.01, V27.2, 73.59

REFERENCE: Brown, pp 269–275
                     Schraffenberger, pp 223, 230, 235–236
                     Ingenix, p 585

183. A pregnant patient was admitted to the hospital with uncontrolled diabetes mellitus. She has type 1 diabetes and was brought under control. The following code was assigned:

648.03   Other current conditions in the mother classifiable elsewhere but complicating pregnancy, childbirth or the puerperium, diabetes mellitus, antepartum condition, or complication

Which of the following describe why the coding is in error?
  A.   The incorrect fifth digit was used.
  B.   The condition should have been coded as gestational diabetes because she is pregnant.
  C.   An additional code describing the diabetes mellitus should be used.
  D.   Only the code for the diabetes mellitus should be used.

REFERENCE: Brown, pp 126–127, 276–277
                     Schraffenberger, pp 108–110

Disease of the Skin and Subcutaneous Tissue

184. Max is 80% bald. He is admitted for a hair transplant, which he undergoes without complication. Max is also treated for congestive heart failure and hypertension for which he is on medication.

401.9	Essential hypertension, unspecified benign or malignant
402.91	Hypertensive heart disease unspecified as to malignant or benign, with heart failure
428.0	Congestive heart failure, unspecified
704.00	Alopecia, unspecified
704.8	Other specified diseases of hair and hair follicles
86.64	Hair transplant

A. 704.00, 402.91, 86.64
B. 704.8, 401.9, 428.0, 86.64
C. 704.00, 401.9, 428.0, 86.64
D. 704.8, 402.91, 86.64

REFERENCE: Brown, pp 278, 339–340
Schraffenberger, pp 180–181, 192–194, 291
Ingenix, p 712

185. Melissa is status post mastectomy due to breast cancer. There has been no recurrence of the disease. She is admitted for insertion of unilateral breast implant.

174.9	Malignant neoplasm of breast (female), unspecified
V10.3	Personal history of malignant neoplasm of breast
V45.71	Acquired absence of breast and nipple
V51.0	Encounter for breast reconstruction following mastectomy
V58.42	Aftercare following surgery for neoplasm
85.53	Unilateral breast implant
85.54	Bilateral breast implant

A. V51.0, V10.3, 85.54
B. V58.42, V51.0, V45.71, V10.3, 85.53
C. V45.71, 174.9, 85.53
D. V51.0, V45.71, V10.3, 85.53

REFERENCE: Brown, pp 83–84, 89–90
Ingenix, p 707

186. Roscoe is 57 years old and has been diagnosed with gynecomastia. Roscoe also is on medication for temporal arteritis. Roscoe is admitted and bilateral mammectomy is performed. Roscoe's intravenous catheter infiltrates and he develops cellulitis at the IV site in the arm. This condition requires additional treatment.

446.5	Giant cell arteritis
611.1	Hypertrophy of breast
682.3	Other cellulitis and abscess upper arm and forearm
999.39	Infection following other infusion, injection, transfusion, or vaccination
85.34	Other unilateral subcutaneous mammectomy
85.36	Other bilateral subcutaneous mammectomy

A. 611.1, 85.36, 85.36
B. 611.1, 999.39, 446.5, 85.36
C. 611.1, 999.39, 682.3, 446.5, 85.36
D. 611.1, 682.3, 446.5, 85.34

REFERENCE: Brown, pp 462–464
Schraffenberger, pp 252, 292, 389–390
Ingenix, p 705

187. Brandon has an infected ingrown toenail that his physician removes.

681.11	Onychia and paronychia of toe
703.0	Ingrowing nail
77.89	Other partial ostectomy, other site
86.23	Removal of nail, nail bed, or nail fold
86.27	Debridement of nail, nail bed, or nail fold

    A. 703.0, 86.23   C. 681.11, 86.27

    B. 681.11, 86.23   D. 703.0, 86.23, 77.89

REFERENCE: Schraffenberger, p 291

                       Ingenix, pp 715–716

Disease of the Musculoskeletal System and Connective Tissue

188. Julia is an 80-year-old female with osteoporosis. She presents to the emergency department complaining of severe back pain. X-rays revealed pathological compression fractures of several vertebrae.

721.90	Spondylosis of unspecified site without mention of myelopathy
733.00	Osteoporosis, unspecified
733.13	Pathological fracture of vertebrae
805.8	Fracture of vertebral column without mention of spinal cord injury, unspecified, closed

    A. 733.13, 733.00   C. 721.90, 733.13

    B. 805.8, 733.00   D. 733.00, 733.13

REFERENCE: Brown, pp 255–256, 415

                       Schraffenberger, pp 305–306

189 Scott has a deformity of his left ring finger, due to an old tendon injury. He is admitted and undergoes a transfer of the flexor tendon from the distal phalanx to the middle phalanx.

727.82	Calcium deposits in tendon and bursa
736.20	Unspecified deformity of finger (acquired)
834.02	Closed dislocation of finger, interphalangeal (joint), hand
905.8	Late effect of tendon injury
82.55	Other change in hand muscle or tendon length
82.56	Other hand tendon transfer or transportation

    A. 727.82, 82.56   C. 834.02, 82.55

    B. 736.20, 905.8, 82.56   D. 727.82, 82.55

REFERENCE: Schraffenberger, p 305

                       Ingenix, p 664

190. Sara has Dupuytren's contracture of the right middle finger. She has an incision and division of the palmar fascia.

728.6	Contracture of palmar fascia (Dupuytren's contracture)
728.71	Plantar fascial fibromatosis
728.86	Necrotizing fasciaitis
82.12	Fasciotomy of hand
82.19	Other division of soft tissue of hand

A. 728.6, 82.12   C. 728.6, 82.19
B. 728.71, 82.19   D. 728.86, 82.12

REFERENCE: Schraffenberger, pp 304–305
               Ingenix, pp 659–660

191. Cheryl has had chronic worsening pain of her left knee from rheumatoid arthritis. She has decided to undergo a total knee replacement as recommended by her physician. The surgery goes well; however, she develops a urinary tract infection that requires an additional day of stay in the hospital.

599.0	Urinary tract infection, site not specified
714.0	Rheumatoid arthritis
714.31	Polyarticular juvenile rheumatoid arthritis, acute
715.96	Osteoarthrosis, unspecified whether generalized or localized, low leg
81.53	Revision of hip replacement, not otherwise specified
81.54	Total knee replacement

A. 715.96, 599.0, 81.54   C. 714.31, 81.53
B. 714.0, 599.0, 81.54   D. 714.31, 81.54

REFERENCE: Brown, pp 218, 251–252, 256–257
               Schraffenberger, pp 250–251, 303
               Ingenix, pp 645–650

Injury and Poisoning

192. A patient who is HIV positive and currently asymptomatic is admitted with a compound fracture of the tibia. The patient was treated previously for Pneumocystis carinii pneumonia. Given the following codes, which is the correct coding and sequencing?

042	Human Immunodeficiency Virus (HIV) disease
136.3	Pneumocystosis (pneumonia due to *Pneumocystis carinii*)
V08	Asymptomatic HIV infection status
823.80	Fracture of tibia alone, unspecified part, closed
823.90	Fracture of tibia alone, unspecified part, open

A. 823.90, V08   C. 823.80, V08, 136.3
B. 823.90, 042   D. 823.80, 042

REFERENCE: Brown, pp 115–116
               Schraffenberger, pp 80–81, 291

193. The diagnosis reads "first-, second-, and third-degree burns of the right arm." You would code:
    A. the first degree only.   C. the third degree only.
    B. the second degree only.   D. each degree of burn separately.

REFERENCE: Brown, pp 433–434
               Schraffenberger, pp 363–364

V Codes

194. A patient is admitted for elective cholecystectomy to treat chronic cholecystitis with cholelithiasis. Prior to administration of general anesthesia, the patient suffers cerebral thrombosis. The surgery is subsequently canceled. Code and sequence appropriately the codes.

434.00	Cerebral thrombosis, without mention of cerebral infarction
574.10	Calculus of gallbladder with other cholecystitis without mention of obstruction
V64.1	Surgical or other procedure not carried out because of contraindication
997.02	Iatrogenic cerebrovascular infarction or hemorrhage
51.22	Cholecystectomy

A.   997.02, 574.10, 51.22
B.   574.10, 434.00, V64.1

C.   997.02, 434.00, V64.1
D.   434.00, V64.1

REFERENCE: Brown, pp 72–73
                        Schraffenberger, pp 45–47, 197, 237
                        Ingenix, p 437

And Just a Few More Coding Questions for Practice

195. A physician lists the final diagnosis as diarrhea and constipation due to either irritable bowel syndrome or diverticulitis. The following codes are assigned:

562.10	Diverticulosis of colon without mention of hemorrhage
562.11	Diverticulitis of colon without mention of hemorrhage
564.00	Constipation, unspecified
564.1	Irritable bowel syndrome
787.91	Diarrhea

A.   564.1, 562.11
B.   562.10, 564.1

C.   564.00, 787.91, 564.1, 562.11
D.   564.1, 562.10, 564.00, 787.91

REFERENCE: Brown, pp 28–29
                        Schraffenberger, pp 234, 338–339

196. When an open biopsy is followed by a more extensive definitive procedure the coder reports
    A.   the open biopsy.
    B.   the extensive definitive procedure and the open biopsy.
    C.   no procedures.
    D.   the extensive definitive procedure.

REFERENCE: Brown, pp 70–71

197. In ICD-9-CM, when an exploratory laparotomy is performed followed by a therapeutic procedure, the coder reports
    A.   therapeutic procedure first, exploratory laparotomy second.
    B.   exploratory laparotomy, therapeutic procedure, closure of wound.
    C.   exploratory laparotomy first, therapeutic procedure second.
    D.   therapeutic procedure only.

REFERENCE: Brown, p 68

198. Codes from category 655, known or suspected fetal abnormality affecting the mother, should
    A. be assigned if the fetal conditions are documented.
    B. be assigned at the discretion of the physician.
    C. be assigned when they affect the management of the mother.
    D. never be assigned.

REFERENCE: Brown, p 276

199. There are a limited number of late effect codes in ICD-9-CM. When coding a residual condition where there is no applicable late effect code, one should code
    A. the residual condition followed by its cause.
    B. the cause followed by the residual condition.
    C. only the residual condition.
    D. only the cause of the residual condition.

REFERENCE: Brown, pp 59–60

200. A patient is admitted for a total hip replacement because of rheumatoid arthritis. Following admission, but prior to surgery, the patient develops congestive heart failure, which necessitates transfer to ICU. The hip replacement is canceled and the patient is treated for the heart failure. What is the principal diagnosis?
    A. congestive heart failure   C. hip replacement
    B. rheumatoid arthritis   D. canceled surgical procedure

REFERENCE: Brown, pp 72–73

201. According to the UHDDS guidelines, the principal procedure is performed for _____ rather than for _____.
    A. diagnostic or exploratory purposes; definitive treatment
    B. exploratory purposes; complications
    C. definitive treatment; diagnostic or exploratory purposes
    D. complications; definitive treatment

REFERENCE: Schraffenberger, p 65

202. A patient with diabetes is admitted to the hospital with acute gastrointestinal hemorrhage due to ulcer disease. In this case, the diabetes would be
    A. the principal diagnosis.
    B. a comorbid condition.
    C. a complication.
    D. irrelevant and not coded.

REFERENCE: Brown, pp 27–28
               Schraffenberger, p 65

203. Which of the following are considered late effects regardless of time?
    A. congenital defect
    B. nonunion, malunion, scarring
    C. fracture, burn
    D. poisoning

REFERENCE: Brown, p 425

204. When a patient is admitted in respiratory failure due to a chronic nonrespiratory condition
    A. the respiratory failure is the principal diagnosis.
    B. the chronic nonrespiratory problem is the principal diagnosis.
    C. only the respiratory failure is coded.
    D. only the chronic nonrespiratory condition is coded.

REFERENCE: Brown, pp 189–191
                Schraffenberger, pp 188–190

205. When Robert was discharged, his physician listed his diagnoses as congestive heart failure with acute pulmonary edema. You will code
    A. the CHF only.
    B. the edema only.
    C. both the CHF and the edema; sequence the CHF first.
    D. both the CHF and the edema; sequence the edema first.

REFERENCE: Brown, pp 27, 31

206. A patient was admitted with severe abdominal pain, elevated temperature, and nausea. The physical examination indicated possible cholecystitis. Acute and chronic pancreatitis secondary to alcoholism was recorded on the face sheet as the final diagnosis. The principal diagnosis is
    A. alcoholism.   C. cholecystitis.
    B. abdominal pain.   D. acute pancreatitis.

REFERENCE: Brown, pp 27, 30

207. A patient was admitted to the hospital with hemiplegia and aphasia. The hemiplegia and aphasia were resolved before discharge and the patient was diagnosed with cerebral thrombosis. What is the correct coding and sequencing?
    A. Hemiplegia; aphasia
    B. Cerebral thrombosis
    C. Cerebral thrombosis; hemiplegia; aphasia
    D. Hemiplegia; cerebral thrombosis; aphasia

REFERENCE: Brown, pp 27–28, 342–344

Use this information to answer questions 208–210:

Present on admission (POA) guidelines were established to identify and report diagnoses that are present at the time of a patient's admission. The reporting options for each ICD-9-CM code are
   A. Y = Yes
   B. N = No
   C. U = Unknown
   D. W = clinically undetermined
   E. Unreported/Not Used (Exempt from POA) reporting

208. The physician explicitly documents that a condition is not present at the time of admission.
   A. Y = Yes
   B. N = No
   C. U = Unknown
   D. W = clinically undetermined
   E. Unreported/Not Used (Exempt from POA) reporting

REFERENCE: Brown, pp 541–544

209. The physician documents that the patient has diabetes that was diagnosed prior to admission.
   A. Y = Yes
   B. N = No
   C. U = Unknown
   D. W = clinically undetermined
   E. Unreported/Not Used (Exempt from POA) reporting

REFERENCE: Brown, pp 541–544

210. The medical record documentation is unclear as to whether the condition was present on admission.
   A. Y = Yes
   B. N = No
   C. U = Unknown
   D. W = clinically undetermined
   E. Unreported/Not Used (Exempt from POA) reporting

REFERENCE: Brown, pp 541–544

Answer Key for ICD-9-CM Coding

1. D
2. B
3. A
4. C
5. D
6. C
7. D
8. C
9. A
10. B
11. C
12. B
13. A
14. D
15. B
16. A
17. C
18. B
19. D
20. B
21. A   Pain is a symptom that is integral to the sickle cell crisis and therefore is not coded.

22. D
23. B
24. D
25. D
26. B
27. A
28. C
29. B
30. D
31. C
32. B
33. A
34. C
35. B
36. D
37. D   Effective October 1, 2010 the *Official ICD-9-CM Coding Guidelines* state, "Additional codes should be assigned for any neurologic deficits associated with the acute CVA, regardless of whether or not the neurologic deficit resolves prior to discharge."

38. C
39. D

40. A
41. B
42. A
43. D
44. A
45. B
46. A
47. C
48. B
49. A
50. D
51. C
52. A
53. C
54. B   The physician should be asked if the blood loss should be added as a discharge diagnosis.

55. A
56. C
57. D
58. A
59. C
60. A
61. A
62. C
63. B
64. D
65. B
66. D
67. B
68. D
69. A
70. B
71. A
72. C
73. B
74. D
75. C
76. D
77. C
78. B
79. C
80. D
81. B   Newborn V-code is not assigned by the receiving facility when a newborn is transferred.

82. C
83. A

Answer Key for ICD-9-CM Coding

84. B
85. D
86. A
87. A
88. D
89. C
90. A
91. C
92. B
93. A
94. C
95. D
96. C
97. B
98. A
99. D
100. C
101. A
102. D
103. C
104. B
105. A
106. C
107. D
108. C
109. D
110. A
111. A
112. B
113. D
114. C
115. B
116. A
117. A
118. D
119. D   Effective October 1, 2010, the *Official ICD-9-CM Coding Guidelines* state, "Additional codes should be assigned for any neurologic deficits associated with the acute CVA, regardless of whether or not the neurologic deficit resolves prior to discharge."
120. D
121. A
122. B

123. D   Fatigue and flulike symptoms/signs of hepatitis would not be coded.
124. A
125. D
126. A
127. A
128. C
129. A
130. C
131. B
132. C
133. D   SSS would not be reported as a current condition because the pacemaker would have taken care of this condition.
134. A
135. B
136. C   The coder cannot assume a causal relationship between the diabetes and conditions that are usually related to the diabetes unless a physician confirms this relationship.
137. A
138. C   Diabetic ketoacidosis by definition is uncontrolled.
139. A
140. C
141. A
142. D
143. B
144. A
145. B
146. C
147. A
148. C   The term "continuous" refers to daily intake of large amounts of alcohol, or regular heavy drinking on weekends or days off. The coder should not assume to use the fifth digit "1" unless documented as continuous.
149. A
150. D
151. C
152. A
153. A
154. A

Answer Key for ICD-9-CM Coding

155. B

156. A

157. B

158. C

159. A

160. D

161. C

162. A

163. D

164. A

165. D   COPD (496) is a general term. It will present as chronic obstructive bronchitis.

166. C

167. A

168. C   The atelectasis is coded because it required monitoring and extended his length of stay.

169. D

170. B

171. C   The alphabetic index is misleading and directs the coder to use one code for acute and chronic sinusitis. The Tabular List, however, directs the coder to use two separate codes.

172. D

173. A

174. C   The note under category 997 instructs the coder to "use additional code to identify complication."

175. A

176. B

177. A

178. A

179. D

180. B

181. A

182. A

183. C

184. C

185. B

186. C

187. A

188. A

189. B

190. A

191. B

192. B   A "compound" fracture is considered an "open" fracture.

193. C   Code the highest degree burn ONLY of the same site.

194. B

195. C

196. B

197. D

198. C

199. C

200. B

201. C

202. B

203. B

204. A

205. A

206. D

207. C   Effective October 1, 2010, the *Official ICD-9-CM Coding Guidelines* state, "Additional codes should be assigned for any neurologic deficits associated with the acute CVA, regardless of whether or not the neurologic deficit resolves prior to discharge."

208. B

209. A

210. C

REFERENCES

Bowie, M., & Schaffer, R. (2012). *Understanding ICD-9-CM coding: A worktext* (3rd ed.). Clifton Park, NY: Delmar Cengage Learning.

Brown, F. (2012). *ICD-9-CM Coding handbook with answers.* Chicago: American Hospital Association (AHA).

Ingenix. (2012). *ICD-9-CM Expert for hospitals* (Vols. 1, 2 and 3). St. Louis, MO: Author.

Ingenix. (2012). *ICD-9-CM Procedures Answers to your toughest ICD-9-CM coding questions.* St. Louis, MO: Author.

Schraffenberger, L. A. (2012). *Basic ICD-9-CM coding.* Chicago: American Health Information Management Association (AHIMA).

ICD-9-CM Coding Competencies

Questions	CCS Competencies
1-210	Domain 2

VIII. CPT Coding

Lisa M. Delhomme, MHA, RHIA

Evaluation and Management

1. Patient is admitted to the hospital with acute abdominal pain. The attending medical physician requests a surgical consult. The consultant agrees to see the patient and conducts a comprehensive history and physical examination. To rule out pancreatitis, the physician orders lab work, along with an ultrasound of the gallbladder and an abdominal x-ray. Due to the various diagnosis possibilities and the tests reviewed, a moderate medical decision was made.

    A. 99244
    B. 99222

    C. 99254
    D. 99204

    REFERENCE: AMA (7th ed.), pp 49, 54–55
                          Green, pp 435–438
                          Johnson and Linker, pp 153–154
                          Smith, pp 215–216

2. An established patient returns to the physician's office for follow-up on his hypertension and diabetes. The physician takes the blood pressure and references the patient's last three glucose tests. The patient is still running above-normal glucose levels, so the physician decides to adjust the patient's insulin. An expanded history was taken and a physical examination was performed.

    A. 99213
    B. 99232

    C. 99202
    D. 99214

    REFERENCE: AMA (7th ed.), p 48
                          Green, pp 428–429
                          Johnson and Linker, p 149
                          Smith, p 214

3. Patient arrives in the emergency room via a medical helicopter. The patient has sustained multiple life-threatening injuries due to a multiple car accident. The patient goes into cardiac arrest 10 minutes after arrival. An hour and 30 minutes of critical care time is spent trying to stabilize the patient.

    A. 99285, 99288, 99291
    B. 99291, 99292

    C. 99291, 99292, 99285
    D. 99282

    REFERENCE: AMA (7th ed.), pp 57–58
                          Green, pp 439–441
                          Johnson and Linker, pp 155–157
                          Smith, pp 216–217

4. The physician provided services to a new patient who was in a rest home for an ulcerative sore on the hip. A problem-focused history and physical examination were performed and a straightforward medical decision was made.

    A. 99304
    B. 99325

    C. 99324
    D. 99334

    REFERENCE: AMA (7th ed.), p 55
                          Green, pp 443–444
                          Johnson and Linker, pp 158–159
                          Smith, p 218

5. A doctor provides critical care services in the emergency department for a patient in respiratory failure. He initiates ventilator management and spends an hour and 10 minutes providing critical care for this patient.

    A. 99281, 99291, 99292, 94002
    B. 99291, 99292, 94002
    C. 99291, 94002
    D. 99291

    REFERENCE: AMA (7th ed.), pp 57–58
    Green, pp 439–441
    Johnson and Linker, pp 155–157
    Smith, pp 216–217

6. Services were provided to a patient in the emergency room after the patient twisted her ankle stepping down from a curb. The emergency room physician ordered x-rays of the ankle, which came back negative for a fracture. A problem-focused history and physical examination were performed and ankle strapping was applied. A prescription for pain was given to the patient. Code the emergency room visit only.

    A. 99201
    B. 99282
    C. 99281
    D. 99211

    REFERENCE: AMA (7th ed.), pp 47–48
    Green, pp 438–439
    Johnson and Linker, pp 155–157
    Smith, p 216

7. An established patient was seen in her primary physician's office. The patient fell at home and came to the physician's office for an examination. Due to a possible concussion, the patient was sent to the hospital to be admitted as an observation patient. A detailed history and physical examination were performed and the medical decision was low complexity. The patient stayed overnight and was discharged the next afternoon.

    A. 99214, 99234
    B. 99214, 99218, 99217
    C. 99218
    D. 99218, 99217

    REFERENCE: AMA, 2015
    AMA (7th ed.), pp 48–49
    Green, pp 431–435
    Johnson and Linker, p 155
    Smith, pp 214–215

8. An out-of-town patient presents to a walk-in clinic to have a prescription refilled for a nonsteroidal anti-inflammatory drug. The physician performs a problem-focused history and physical examination with a straightforward decision.

    A. 99211
    B. 99201
    C. 99212
    D. 99202

    REFERENCE: AMA (7th ed.), pp 39, 48
    Frisch, pp 49–51
    Green, pp 411–412
    Johnson and Linker, p 149
    Smith, pp 195–196

9. An office consultation is performed for a postmenopausal woman who is complaining of spotting in the past 6 months with right lower-quadrant tenderness. A detailed history and physical examination were performed with a low-complexity medical decision.
   A. 99242
   B. 99243
   C. 99253
   D. 99254

REFERENCE: AMA (7th ed.), pp 39–40
Green, pp 435–438
Johnson and Linker, pp 153–154
Smith, pp 215–216

Anesthesia

10. Code anesthesia for upper abdominal ventral hernia repair.
    A. 00832
    B. 00750
    C. 00752
    D. 00830

REFERENCE: AMA (7th ed.), pp 82–83
Green, pp 483–485
Johnson and Linker, p 175
Smith, pp 249–252

11. Code anesthesia for total hip replacement.
    A. 01210
    B. 01402
    C. 01230
    D. 01214

REFERENCE: AMA (7th ed.), pp 82–83
Green, p 487
Smith, pp 249–252

12. Code anesthesia for vaginal hysterectomy.
    A. 00846
    B. 00944
    C. 00840
    D. 01963

REFERENCE: AMA (7th ed.), pp 82–83
Green, pp 484–485
Smith, pp 249–252

13. Code anesthesia for placement of vascular shunt in forearm.
    A. 01844
    B. 01850
    C. 00532
    D. 01840

REFERENCE: AMA (7th ed.), pp 82–83
Green, p 487
Smith, pp 249–252

14. Code anesthesia for decortication of left lung.
    A. 01638
    B. 00542
    C. 00546
    D. 00500

REFERENCE: AMA (7th ed.), pp 82–83
Green, p 483
Smith, pp 249–252

15. Code anesthesia for total shoulder replacement.
    A. 01760
    B. 01630
    C. 01402
    D. 01638

REFERENCE: AMA (7th ed.), pp 82–83
                Green, p 487
                Smith, pp 249–252

16. Code anesthesia for cesarean section.
    A. 00840
    B. 01961
    C. 00940
    D. 01960

REFERENCE: AMA (7th ed.), pp 82–83
                Green, p 489
                Smith, pp 249–252

17. Code anesthesia for procedures on bony pelvis.
    A. 00400
    B. 01170
    C. 01120
    D. 01190

REFERENCE: AMA (7th ed.), pp 82–83
                Green, p 487
                Smith, pp 249–252

18. Code anesthesia for corneal transplant.
    A. 00144
    B. 00140
    C. 00147
    D. 00190

REFERENCE: AMA (7th ed.), pp 82–83
                Green, p 481
                Smith, pp 249–252

Surgery—Integumentary System

19. Patient presents to the hospital for skin grafts due to previous third-degree burns. The burn eschar of the back was removed. Once the eschar was removed, the defect size measured 10 cm x 10 cm. A skin graft from a donor bank was placed onto the defect and sewn into place as a temporary wound closure.
    A. 15002, 15130
    B. 15002, 15271, 15272, 15272, 15272
    C. 15002, 15200
    D. 15002, 15273

REFERENCE: AMA, 2015

20. Patient presents to the operating room for excision of a 4.5-cm malignant melanoma of the left forearm. A 6 cm x 6 cm rotation flap was created for closure.
    A. 14021
    B. 11606, 14020
    C. 14301
    D. 11606, 15100

REFERENCE: AMA, 2015
                AMA (7th ed.), pp 103–104, 107
                Green, pp 517–521
                Smith, pp 72–76
                Smith (2), pp 26–27

21. Female patient has a percutaneous needle biopsy of the left breast lesion in the lower outer quadrant. Following the biopsy frozen section results, the physician followed this with an excisional removal of the same lesion.
    A. 19100, 19125
    B. 19100, 19120-LT
    C. 19120-LT
    D. 19100, 19120, 19120

    REFERENCE: AMA (7th ed.), p 115
                  Green, pp 535–536
                  Smith, p 79
                  Smith (2), p 30

22. Patient presents to the emergency room with lacerations of right lower leg that involved the fascia. Lacerations measured 5 cm and 2.7 cm.
    A. 11406, 11403
    B. 12034
    C. 12032, 12031
    D. 12032

    REFERENCE: AMA (7th ed.), p 107
                  Smith, pp 66–68
                  Smith (2), p 21

23. A 10-square-centimeter epidermal autograft to the face from the back.
    A. 15110
    B. 15115
    C. 15110, 15115
    D. 15120

    REFERENCE: AMA, 2015
                  AMA (7th ed.), pp 109–110
                  Smith (2), p 27

24. Nonhuman graft for temporary wound closure. Patient has a 5-cm defect on the scalp.
    A. 15275, 15276
    B. 15271
    C. 15275
    D. 15271, 15272

    REFERENCE: AMA, 2015

25. Patient is admitted for a blepharoplasty of the left lower eyelid and a repair for a tarsal strip of the left upper lid.
    A. 67917-E1, 15822-E2
    B. 67917-E1, 15820-E2
    C. 67917-E1
    D. 67917-E1, 15823-E2

    REFERENCE: AMA (7th ed.), pp 252–253
                  CPT Assistant, January 2005, p 46
                  Smith (2), p 165

26. Patient presents to the emergency room with lacerations sustained in an automobile accident. Repairs of the 3.3- cm skin laceration of the left leg that involved the fascia, 2.5- cm and 3- cm lacerations of the left arm involving the fascia, and 2.7 cm of the left foot, which required simple sutures, were performed. Sterile dressings were applied.
    A. 12032, 12032-59, 12031-59, 12002-59
    B. 12002, 12002-59
    C. 12034, 12002-59
    D. 13151, 12032-59, 12032-59, 12001-59

    REFERENCE: AMA (7th ed.), pp 106–108
                  Green, pp 524–526
                  Smith, pp 66–68
                  Smith (2), p 24

27. Patient presents to the operating room for excision of three lesions. The 1.5-cm and 2-cm lesions of the back were excised with one excision. The 0.5-cm lesion of the hand was excised. The pathology report identified both back lesions as squamous cell carcinoma. The hand lesion was identified as seborrheic keratosis.

    A. 11604, 11420   C. 11403, 11642, 11642
    B. 11402, 11420, 11403   D. 11602, 11402

REFERENCE: AMA (7th ed.), pp 101–104
                     CPT Assistant, November 2002, pp 5–6, 8
                     Green, pp 517–521
                     Smith, pp 61–62
                     Smith (2), pp 21–22

28. Patient presents to the radiology department where a fine-needle aspiration of the breast is performed utilizing computed tomography.

    A. 19085, 77012   C. 19125
    B. 19100   D. 10022, 77012

REFERENCE: AMA (7th ed.), pp 270, 330–331
                     CPT Assistant, November 2002, pp 2–3
                     Green, p 535
                     Smith (2), p 29

29. Patient presents to the operating room where a 3.2-cm malignant lesion of the shoulder was excised and repaired with simple sutures. A 2-cm benign lesion of the cheek was excised and was repaired with a rotation skin graft.

    A. 11604, 11442, 14040, 12001   C. 15002, 15120
    B. 14040, 11604   D. 17264, 17000, 12001

REFERENCE: AMA (7th ed.), pp 101–107
                     CPT Assistant, July 1999, pp 3–4
                     CPT Assistant, August 2002, p 5
                     CPT Assistant, November 2002, pp 5–8
                     Green, pp 517–520, 526–527
                     Smith, pp 61–62, 73–75
                     Smith (2), pp 26–27

30. Patient was admitted to the hospital for removal of excessive tissue due to massive weight loss. Liposuction of the abdomen and bilateral thighs was performed.

    A. 15830   C. 15877, 15879-50
    B. 15830, 15833, 15833   D. 15839

REFERENCE: AMA, 2015

Surgery—Musculoskeletal

31. Patient presents to the hospital with ulcer of the right foot. Patient is taken to the operating room where a revision of the right metatarsal head is performed.

    A. 28104-RT   B. 28111-RT
    C. 28288-RT   D. 28899-RT

REFERENCE: AMA, 2015

32. Patient presents to the emergency room following a fall. X-rays were ordered for the lower leg and results showed a fracture of the proximal left tibia. The emergency room physician performed a closed manipulation of the fracture with skeletal traction.
    A. 27532-LT
    B. 27536-LT
    C. 27530-LT
    D. 27524-LT

REFERENCE: Green, pp 565–568
              Smith, pp 84–85
              Smith (2), pp 42–44

33. Trauma patient was rushed to the operating room with multiple injuries. Open reduction with internal fixation of intertrochanteric femoral fracture, and open reduction of the tibial and fibula shaft with internal fixation was performed.
    A. 27245, 27759
    B. 20690
    C. 27248, 27756
    D. 27244, 27758

REFERENCE: Green, pp 565–568
              Smith, pp 84–85
              Smith (2), pp 42–44

34. Open I&D of a deep abscess of the cervical spine.
    A. 22010
    B. 22015
    C. 10060
    D. 10140

REFERENCE: AMA, 2015

35. Patient presents to the emergency room following an assault. Examination of the patient reveals blunt trauma to the face. Radiology reports that the patient suffers from a fracture to the frontal skull and a blow-out fracture of the orbital floor. Patient is admitted and taken to the operating room where a periorbital approach to the orbital fracture is employed and an implant is inserted.
    A. 21407, 21275
    B. 21387, 61330
    C. 21390
    D. 61340, 21401

REFERENCE: Smith, pp 84–85
              Smith (2), pp 42–44

36. Patient presents with a traumatic partial amputation of the second, third, and fourth fingers on the right hand. Patient was taken to the operating room where completion of the amputation of three fingers was performed with direct closure.
    A. 26910-F6, 26910-F7, 26910-F8
    B. 26843-RT
    C. 26951-F6, 26951-F7, 26951-F8
    D. 26550-RT

REFERENCE: AMA, 2015

37. Patient is brought to the emergency room following a shark attack. The paramedics have the patient's amputated foot. The patient is taken directly to the operating room to reattach the patient's foot.
    A. 28800
    B. 28200, 28208
    C. 28110
    D. 20838

REFERENCE: AMA, 2015

38. Patient presents to the hospital with a right index trigger finger. Release of the trigger finger was performed.
    A. 26060-F7
    B. 26055-F6
    C. 26170-F6
    D. 26110

REFERENCE: AMA, 2015

39. Patient had been diagnosed with a bunion. Patient was taken to the operating room where a simple resection of the base of the proximal phalanx along with the medial eminence was performed. Kirschner wire was placed to hold the joint in place.
    A. 28292
    B. 28290
    C. 28293
    D. 28294

REFERENCE: AMA, 2015
              AMA (7th ed.), pp 93–94, 132–135
              CPT Assistant, December 1995, pp 5–7
              Smith (2), pp 47–49

Surgery—Respiratory

40. Patient has a bronchoscopy with endobronchial biopsies of three sites.
    A. 31625, 31625, 31625
    B. 31625
    C. 31622, 31625
    D. 31622, 31625, 31625, 31625

REFERENCE: AMA (7th ed.), pp 139–141
              CPT Assistant, June 2004, p 11
              Green, pp 576–577
              Smith, pp 99–100
              Smith (2), p 61

41. Patient presents to the surgical unit and undergoes unilateral nasal endoscopy, partial ethmoidectomy, and maxillary antrostomy.
    A. 31254, 31256-51
    B. 31201, 31225-51
    C. 31290, 31267-51
    D. 31233, 31231-51

REFERENCE: AMA (7th ed.), pp 137–138
              CPT Assistant, January 1997, pp 4–6
              Green, pp 573–574
              Smith, p 93
              Smith (2), p 59

42. Patient has been diagnosed with metastatic laryngeal carcinoma. Patient underwent subtotal supraglottic laryngectomy with radical neck dissection.
    A. 31540
    B. 31367
    C. 31365
    D. 31368

REFERENCE: Green, pp 574–575

43. Patient was involved in an accident and has been sent to the hospital. During transport the patient develops breathing problems and, upon arrival at the hospital, an emergency transtracheal tracheostomy was performed. Following various x-rays, the patient was diagnosed with traumatic pneumothorax. A thoracentesis with insertion of tube was performed.
   A. 31603, 31612
   B. 31610, 32555
   C. 31603, 32555
   D. 31603, 32555

REFERENCE: AMA, 2015

44. Patient with laryngeal cancer has a tracheoesophageal fistula created and has a voicebox inserted.
   A. 31611
   B. 31580
   C. 31395
   D. 31502

REFERENCE: AMA, 2015

45. Upper lobectomy of the right lung with repair of the bronchus.
   A. 32480
   B. 32486
   C. 32320
   D. 32480, 32501

REFERENCE: AMA (7th ed.), pp 140–141
               Green, pp 578–579
               Smith (2), pp 61–62

46. Patient with a deviated nasal septum that was repaired by septoplasty.
   A. 30400
   B. 30620
   C. 30520
   D. 30630

REFERENCE: AMA, 2015

47. Lye burn of the larynx repaired by laryngoplasty.
   A. 31588
   B. 16020
   C. 31360
   D. 31540

REFERENCE: AMA, 2015

48. Bronchoscopy with multiple transbronchial right upper and right lower lobe lung biopsy with fluoroscopic guidance.
   A. 31628-RT, 76000-RT
   B. 31717-RT, 31632-RT
   C. 32405-RT
   D. 31628-RT, 31632-RT

REFERENCE: AMA (7th ed.), pp 139–140
               CPT Assistant, March 1999, p 3
               Green, pp 576–577
               Smith, pp 99–100
               Smith (2), p 61

49. Patient has recurrent spontaneous pneumothorax, which has resulted in a chemical pleurodesis by thoracoscopy.
   A. 32650
   B. 32310, 32601
   C. 32601
   D. 32960

REFERENCE: AMA, 2015

50. Laryngoscopic stripping of vocal cords for leukoplakia of the vocal cords.
    A. 31535
    B. 31540
    C. 31541
    D. 31570

REFERENCE: AMA (7th ed.), pp 137–138
              Green, pp 574–575
              Smith, p 97

Surgery—Cardiovascular System

51. Patient returns to the operating room following open-heart bypass for exploration of blood vessel to control postoperative bleeding in the chest.
    A. 35820
    B. 20101
    C. 35761
    D. 35905

REFERENCE: AMA, 2015

52. Patient undergoes construction of apical aortic conduit with an insertion of a single-ventricle ventricular assist device.
    A. 33404
    B. 33975
    C. 33977
    D. 33975, 33404

REFERENCE: CPT Assistant, January 2004, p 28

53. Patient presents to the operating room where a CABG x 3 is performed using the mammary artery and two sections of the saphenous vein.
    A. 33534, 33511
    B. 33534, 33518, 33511
    C. 33535
    D. 33533, 33518

REFERENCE: AMA (7th ed.), pp 155–158
              Green, pp 599–600
              Smith, p 108
              Smith (2), pp 74–75

54. Patient complains of recurrent syncope following carotid thromboendarterectomy. Patient returns 2 weeks after initial surgery and undergoes repeat carotid thromboendarterectomy.
    A. 33510
    B. 35301
    C. 35201
    D. 35301, 35390

REFERENCE: CPT Assistant, Winter 1993, p 3
              Smith (2), pp 78–79

55. Patient is admitted with alcohol cirrhosis and has a TIPS procedure performed.
    A. 35476, 36011, 36481
    B. 37183
    C. 37182
    D. 37140

REFERENCE: CPT Assistant, December 2003, pp 1–3

56. Eighty-year-old patient has carcinoma and presents to the operating room for placement of a tunneled implantable centrally inserted venous access port.
    A. 36558   C. 36561
    B. 36571   D. 36481

    REFERENCE: CPT Assistant, February 1999, pp 1–5
                    CPT Assistant, November 1999, pp 19–20
                    Green, pp 615–618
                    Smith, pp 112–114
                    Smith (2), pp 79–80

57. Patient presents to the operating room and undergoes an endovascular repair of an infrarenal abdominal aortic aneurysm utilizing a unibody bifurcated prosthesis.
    A. 34800, 34813   C. 34804
    B. 34802   D. 35081

    REFERENCE: AMA (7th ed.), pp 159–161
                    CPT Assistant, September 2002, p 4
                    CPT Assistant, February 2003, pp 2–4, 16
                    Green, p 620
                    Smith (2), pp 76–77

58. The physician punctures the left common femoral to examine the right common iliac.
    A. 36245   C. 36247
    B. 36246   D. 36140

    REFERENCE: AMA, 2015
                    AMA (7th ed.), pp 283–285

59. Patient has a history of PVD for many years and experiences chest pains. The patient underwent Doppler evaluation, which showed a common femoral DVT. Patient is now admitted for thromboendarterectomy.
    A. 35371   C. 37224
    B. 35372   D. 35256

    REFERENCE: AMA, 2015
                    Smith (2), pp 78–79

60. Patient undergoes percutaneous transluminal iliac artery balloon angioplasty.
    A. 37228   C. 37222
    B. 37220   D. 37224

    REFERENCE: AMA, 2015
                    Smith, p 114

Surgery—Hemic and Lymphatic Systems, Mediastinum, and Diaphragm

61. Patient has breast carcinoma and is now undergoing sentinel node biopsy. Patient was injected for sentinel node identification and two deep axillary lymph nodes showed up intensely. These two lymph nodes were completely excised. Path report was positive for metastatic carcinoma.
    A. 38525, 38790
    B. 38589
    C. 38308, 38790
    D. 38525, 38792

    REFERENCE: CPT Assistant, November 1998, pp 15–16
    CPT Assistant, July 1999, pp 6–12
    Green, p 624

62. Patient has a history of hiatal hernia for many years, which has progressively gotten worse. The decision to repair the hernia was made and the patient was sent to the operating room where the repair took place via the thorax and abdomen.
    A. 39545
    B. 43336
    C. 43332
    D. 39503

    REFERENCE: AMA, 2015

63. Patient has a bone marrow aspiration of the iliac crest and of the tibia.
    A. 38220, 38220-59
    B. 38221
    C. 38230
    D. 38220

    REFERENCE: AMA (7th ed.), pp 323–324
    CPT Assistant, January 2004, p 26
    Green, pp 623–624

64. Trauma patient is rushed to the operating room with multiple injuries. The patient had his spleen removed due to a massive rupture, with repair of the lacerated diaphragm.
    A. 38115, 39501
    B. 38120, 39599
    C. 38102, 39540
    D. 38100, 39501

    REFERENCE: AMA, 2015

65. Laparoscopic retroperitoneal lymph node biopsy.
    A. 38570
    B. 38780
    C. 49323
    D. 38589

    REFERENCE: AMA, 2015

66. Excision of mediastinal cyst.
    A. 11400
    B. 39200
    C. 17000
    D. 39400

    REFERENCE: AMA, 2015

67. Patient diagnosed with cystic hygroma of the axilla, which was excised.
    A. 38555
    B. 11400
    C. 38550
    D. 38300

    REFERENCE: AMA, 2015

68. Laparoscopy with multiple biopsies of retroperitoneal lymph nodes.
    A. 38570
    B. 38571
    C. 38570-22
    D. 38572

REFERENCE: AMA, 2015

69. Cannulation of the thoracic duct.
    A. 38794
    B. 36810
    C. 36260
    D. 38999

REFERENCE: AMA, 2015

70. Patient has been on the bone marrow transplant recipient list for 3 months. A perfect match was made and the patient came in and received a peripheral stem cell transplant.
    A. 38242
    B. 38230
    C. 38241
    D. 38240

REFERENCE: Green, pp 623–624

Surgery—Digestive System

71. Laparoscopic gastric banding.
    A. 43842
    B. 43843
    C. 43770
    D. 43771

REFERENCE: AMA, 2015

72. Patient presents with a history of upper abdominal pain. Cholangiogram was negative and patient was sent to the hospital for ERCP. During the procedure the sphincter was incised and a stent was placed for drainage.
    A. 43260, 43262, 43264
    B. 43262
    C. 43275
    D. 43274

REFERENCE: CPT Assistant, Spring 1994, pp 5–7
               Smith (2), pp 92–93

73. Patient presents to the emergency room with right lower abdominal pains. Emergency room physician suspects possible appendicitis. Patient was taken to the operating room where a laparoscopic appendectomy was performed. Pathology report was negative for appendicitis.
    A. 44950
    B. 44950, 49320
    C. 44970
    D. 44979

REFERENCE: AMA, 2015
               AMA (7th ed.), p 176
               Smith (2), p 97

74. Morbidly obese patient comes in for vertical banding of the stomach.
    A. 43848
    B. 43659
    C. 43842
    D. 43999

REFERENCE: CPT Assistant, May 1998, pp 5–6

75. Patient underwent anoscopy followed by colonoscopy. The physician examined the colon to 60 cm.
    A. 46600, 45378
    B. 46600, 45378-59
    C. 45378
    D. 45999

REFERENCE: Green, pp 650–652
               Smith, pp 121–122
               Smith (2), p 93

76. Injection snoreplasty for treatment of palatal snoring.
    A. 42299
    B. 42145
    C. 42999
    D. 40899

REFERENCE: CPT Assistant, December 2004, p 19

77. Patient arrives to the hospital and has a Nissen fundoplasty done laparoscopically.
    A. 43410
    B. 43415
    C. 43502
    D. 43280

REFERENCE: AMA, 2015
               Smith (2), p 97

78. Young child presents with cleft lip and cleft palate. This is the first attempt of repair, which includes major revision of the cleft palate and unilateral cleft lip repair.
    A. 42200, 40701
    B. 42225, 40700
    C. 42220, 40720
    D. 42215, 40700

REFERENCE: AMA, 2015

79. Patient has a history of chronic alcohol abuse with portal hypertension. Patient has been vomiting blood for the past 3 days and presented to his physician's office. Patient was sent to the hospital for evaluation and an EGD was performed. Biopsy findings showed gastritis, esophagitis, and bleeding esophageal varices, which were injected with sclerosing solution.
    A. 43235, 43244, 43204
    B. 43239, 43244
    C. 43239, 43243
    D. 43239, 43243, 43204

REFERENCE: AMA (7th ed.), pp 179–180
               Green, pp 641–645
               Smith, p 120
               Smith (2), p 92

Surgery—Urinary System

80. Patient is admitted for contact laser vaporization of the prostate. The physician performed a TURP and transurethral resection of the bladder neck at the same time.
    A. 52648
    B. 52648, 52450, 52500
    C. 52450, 53500
    D. 52648, 52450

REFERENCE: AMA (7th ed.), pp 197–198
               CPT Assistant, July 2005, p 15
               Smith (2), p 122

81. Patient comes to the hospital with a history of right flank pain. Urine tests are negative. Radiology examination reveals that the patient has renal cysts. Patient is now admitted for laparoscopic ablation of the cysts.

   A. 50541
   B. 50390
   C. 50280
   D. 50920

   REFERENCE: AMA (7th ed.), p 192
   CPT Assistant, November 1999, p 25
   CPT Assistant, May 2000, p 4
   CPT Assistant, October 2001, p 8
   CPT Assistant, January 2003, p 19

82. Patient has extensive bladder cancer. She underwent a complete cystectomy with bilateral pelvic lymphadenectomy and creation of ureteroileal conduit.

   A. 51575, 50820
   B. 50825, 51570, 38770
   C. 51595
   D. 51550, 38770

   REFERENCE: AMA, 2015

83. Patient presents to the hospital with right ureteral calculus. Patient is taken to the operating room where a cystoscopy with ureteroscopy is performed to remove the calculus.

   A. 52353
   B. 52310
   C. 51065
   D. 52352

   REFERENCE: Green, pp 664–665
   Smith, p 134
   Smith (2), pp 111–112

84. Female with 6 months of stress incontinence. Outpatient therapies are not working and the patient decides to have the problem fixed. Laparoscopic urethral suspension was completed.

   A. 51992
   B. 51990
   C. 51840
   D. 51845

   REFERENCE: CPT Assistant, November 1999, p 26
   CPT Assistant, May 2000, p 4
   CPT Changes: An Insider's View, 2000

85. Patient has ovarian vein syndrome and has ureterolysis performed.

   A. 58679
   B. 58660
   C. 52351
   D. 50722

   REFERENCE: AMA, 2015

86. Male patient has been diagnosed with benign prostatic hypertrophy and undergoes a transurethral destruction of the prostate by radiofrequency thermotherapy.

   A. 52648
   B. 53852
   C. 52601
   D. 53850

   REFERENCE: AMA (7th ed.), pp 197–198
   CPT Assistant, November 1997, p 20
   CPT Assistant, April 2001, p 4

87. Nephrectomy with resection of half of the ureter.
    A. 50220
    B. 50234
    C. 50230, 50650
    D. 50546

REFERENCE: AMA (7th ed.), p 192
              Green, pp 659–660

88. Male with urinary incontinence. Sling procedure was performed 6 months ago and now the patient has returned for a revision of the sling procedure.
    A. 53449
    B. 53442
    C. 53440
    D. 53431

REFERENCE: AMA, 2015

89. Excision of 2.5-cm bladder tumor with cystoscopy.
    A. 51550
    B. 51530
    C. 52235
    D. 51060

REFERENCE: AMA (7th ed.), pp 194–195
              Green, pp 644–645
              Smith, p 134

90. Closure of ureterocutaneous fistula.
    A. 50930
    B. 50920
    C. 57310
    D. 50520

REFERENCE: AMA, 2015

Surgery—Male Genital System

91. Removal of nephrostomy tube with fluoroscopic guidance.
    A. 50387
    B. 50389
    C. 99212
    D. 99213

REFERENCE: AMA, 2015
              AMA (7th ed.), p 196

92. Patient has been diagnosed with prostate cancer. Patient arrived in the operating room where a therapeutic orchiectomy is performed.
    A. 54560
    B. 54530
    C. 55899
    D. 54520

REFERENCE: CPT Assistant, October 2001, p 8
              Smith (2), p 122

93. Patient undergoes laparoscopic orchiopexy for intra-abdominal testes.
    A. 54650
    B. 54699
    C. 54692
    D. 55899

REFERENCE: CPT Assistant, November 1999, p 27
              CPT Assistant, May 2000, p 4
              CPT Assistant, October 2001, p 8
              Smith (2), p 122

94. Scrotal wall abscess drainage.
    A. 55100
    B. 55150
    C. 54700
    D. 55110

REFERENCE: AMA, 2015

95. Hydrocelectomy of spermatic cord.
    A. 55500
    B. 55000
    C. 55041
    D. 55520

REFERENCE: CPT Assistant, October 2001, p 8

96. Patient has been followed by his primary care physician for elevated PSA. Patient underwent prostate needle biopsy in the physician's office 2 weeks ago and the final pathology was positive for carcinoma. Patient is admitted for prostatectomy. The frozen section of the prostate and one lymph node is positive for prostate cancer with metastatic disease to the lymph node. Prostatectomy became a radical perineal with bilateral pelvic lymphadenectomy.
    A. 55845
    B. 55815
    C. 55815, 38562
    D. 38770

REFERENCE: Green, p 665
              Smith (2), p 122

97. Male presented to operating room for sterilization by bilateral vasectomy.
    A. 55200
    B. 55400
    C. 55250
    D. 55450

REFERENCE: CPT Assistant, June 1998, p 10
              CPT Assistant, July 1998, p 10

98. Laser destruction of penile condylomas.
    A. 54057
    B. 17106
    C. 17270
    D. 54055

REFERENCE: AMA, 2015
              Smith, p 139

99. First-stage repair for hypospadias with skin flaps.
    A. 54300
    B. 54308, 14040
    C. 54322
    D. 54304

REFERENCE: AMA, 2015

100. Priapism operation with spongiosum shunt.
    A. 54450
    B. 54352
    C. 54430
    D. 55899

REFERENCE: AMA, 2015

Surgery—Female Genital System

101. Patient was admitted to the hospital with sharp pelvic pains. A pelvic ultrasound was ordered and the results showed a possible ovarian cyst. The patient was taken to the operating room where a laparoscopic destruction of two corpus luteum cysts was performed.
   A. 49321
   B. 58925
   C. 58561
   D. 58662

   REFERENCE: AMA, 2015
                 Smith (2), p 534

102. Patient was admitted with a cystocele and rectocele. An anterior colporrhaphy was performed.
   A. 57250
   B. 57260
   C. 57240
   D. 57110

   REFERENCE: AMA, 2015

103. Patient has a Bartholin's gland cyst that was marsupialized.
   A. 54640
   B. 10060
   C. 58999
   D. 56440

   REFERENCE: AMA, 2015

104. Patient is at a fertility clinic and undergoes intrauterine embryo transplant.
   A. 58679
   B. 58322
   C. 58323
   D. 58974

   REFERENCE: AMA, 2015

105. Patient has been diagnosed with carcinoma of the vagina, and she has a radical vaginectomy with complete removal of the vaginal wall.
   A. 57107
   B. 57110
   C. 58150
   D. 57111

   REFERENCE: AMA, 2015
                 Smith (2), p 133

106. Patient has been diagnosed with uterine fibroids and undergoes a total abdominal hysterectomy with bilateral salpingo-oophorectomy.
   A. 58200
   B. 58150
   C. 58262
   D. 58150, 58720

   REFERENCE: AMA (7th ed.), pp 202–203
                 Green, pp 682–685
                 Johnson and Linker, p 380
                 Smith, pp 145–146
                 Smith (2), p 133

107. Hysteroscopy with D&C and polypectomy.
 A. 58563
 B. 58558
 C. 58120, 58100, 58555
 D. 58558, 58120

REFERENCE: AMA (7th ed.), pp 203–205
              Green, pp 682–685
              Smith, p 145
              Smith (2), p 132

108. Laparoscopic tubal ligation utilizing Endoloop.
 A. 58670
 B. 58615
 C. 58671
 D. 58611

REFERENCE: AMA (7th ed.), p 204
              Green, p 685

109. Laser destruction of extensive herpetic lesions of the vulva.
 A. 17106
 B. 17004
 C. 56515
 D. 56501

REFERENCE: AMA, 2015
              Smith (2), p 131

110. Patient undergoes hysteroscopy with excision uterine fibroids.
 A. 58545
 B. 58140
 C. 58561
 D. 58140, 49320

REFERENCE: AMA (7th ed.), pp 203–204
              Green, pp 683–685
              Smith, p 145
              Smith (2), p 132

Surgery—Maternity Care and Delivery

111. Attempted vaginal delivery in a previous cesarean section patient, which resulted in a repeat cesarean section.
 A. 59409
 B. 59612
 C. 59620
 D. 59514

REFERENCE: AMA (7th ed.), p 208
              Green, pp 686–690
              Smith, p 146

112. Patient is admitted to the hospital following an ultrasound at 25 weeks, which revealed fetal pleural effusion. A fetal thoracentesis was performed.
 A. 59074
 B. 32554
 C. 32555
 D. 76815

REFERENCE: AMA (7th ed.), p 206
              CPT Assistant, May 2004, pp 3–4

113. Patient in late stages of labor arrives at the hospital. Her OB physician is not able to make the delivery and the house physician delivers the baby vaginally. Primary care physician resumes care after delivery. Code the delivery.
    A. 59409
    B. 59612
    C. 59620
    D. 59400

REFERENCE: AMA (7th ed.), pp 208–209
              Green, pp 686–690
              Smith, p 146

114. Patient is 24 weeks pregnant and arrives in the emergency room following an automobile accident. No fetal movement or heartbeat noted. Patient is taken to the OB ward where prostaglandin is given to induce abortion.
    A. 59200
    B. 59855
    C. 59821
    D. 59410

REFERENCE: Green, pp 686–690

115. Patient is 6 weeks pregnant and complains of left-sided abdominal pains. Patient is suspected of having an ectopic pregnancy. Patient has a laparoscopic salpingectomy with removal of the ectopic tubal pregnancy.
    A. 59120
    B. 59200
    C. 59121
    D. 59151

REFERENCE: AMA, 2015
              AMA (7th ed.), p 206

116. Cesarean delivery with antepartum and postpartum care.
    A. 59610
    B. 59514
    C. 59400
    D. 59510

REFERENCE: AMA (7th ed.), pp 208–209
              Green, pp 686–690
              Smith, p 146

117. A pregnant patient has an incompetent cervix, which was repaired using a vaginal cerclage.
    A. 57700
    B. 57531
    C. 59320
    D. 59325

REFERENCE: AMA, 2015
              AMA (7th ed.), p 207

118. A D&C is performed for postpartum hemorrhage.
    A. 59160
    B. 58120
    C. 58558
    D. 58578

REFERENCE: AMA, 2015

119. Hysterotomy for hydatidifom mole and tubal ligation.
    A. 58285, 58600
    B. 58150, 58605
    C. 51900, 58605
    D. 59100, 58611

REFERENCE: AMA, 2015

120. D&C performed for patient with a diagnosis of incomplete abortion at 8 weeks.
    A. 59812
    B. 59820
    C. 58120
    D. 59160

REFERENCE: Green, p 690

Surgery—Endocrine System

121. Patient comes in for a percutaneous needle biopsy of the thyroid gland.
    A. 60000
    B. 60270
    C. 60699
    D. 60100

REFERENCE: CPT Assistant, June 1997, p 5

122. Laparoscopic adrenalectomy, complete.
    A. 60650
    B. 60650-50
    C. 60659
    D. 60540

REFERENCE: AMA, 2015

123. Left carotid artery excision for tumor of carotid body.
    A. 60650
    B. 60600
    C. 60605
    D. 60699

REFERENCE: AMA, 2015

124. Patient undergoes total thyroidectomy with parathyroid autotransplantation.
    A. 60240, 60512
    B. 60520, 60500
    C. 60260, 60512
    D. 60650, 60500

REFERENCE: Green, p 692

125. Unilateral partial thyroidectomy.
    A. 60252
    B. 60210
    C. 60220
    D. 60520

REFERENCE: Green, p 692

Surgery—Nervous System

126. Patient comes in through the emergency room with a wound that was caused by an electric saw. Patient is taken to the operating room where two ulna nerves are sutured.
    A. 64837
    B. 64892, 69990
    C. 64836, 64837
    D. 64856, 64859

REFERENCE: AMA, 2015
                    Smith (2), p 153

127. Laminectomy and excision of intradural lumbar lesion.
    A. 63272
    B. 63267
    C. 63282
    D. 63252

REFERENCE: AMA, 2015
                    Smith (2), p 149

128. Patient comes in for steroid injection for lumbar herniated disk. Marcaine and Aristocort were injected into the L2-L3 space.
    A. 64520
    B. 64483
    C. 62311
    D. 64714

REFERENCE: CPT Assistant, September 1997, p 10
               Smith, p 153
               Smith (2), p 148

129. Patient with Parkinson's disease is admitted for insertion of a brain neurostimulator pulse generator with one electrode array.
    A. 61885
    B. 61850, 61863
    C. 61888
    D. 61867, 61870

REFERENCE: AMA (7th ed.), pp 222–224
               CPT Assistant, June 2000, pp 4, 12
               CPT Assistant, April 2001, pp 8–9
               Smith (2), p 145

130. Patient has rhinorrhea, which requires repair of the CSF leak with craniotomy.
    A. 63707
    B. 63709
    C. 62100
    D. 62010

REFERENCE: AMA, 2015
               Smith (2), pp 143–144

131. Patient has metastatic brain lesions. Patient undergoes stereotactic radiosurgery gamma knife of two lesions.
    A. 61533
    B. 61500
    C. 61796, 61797
    D. 61796

REFERENCE: AMA, 2015
               AMA (7th ed.), pp 221–222

132. Patient has right sacroiliac joint dysfunction and requires a right S2-S3 paravertebral facet joint anesthetic nerve block with image guidance.
    A. 62311
    B. 64493
    C. 64490
    D. 64520

REFERENCE: AMA, 2015
               Smith (2), pp 152–153

133. Patient requires repair of a 6-cm meningocele.
    A. 63700
    B. 63709
    C. 63180
    D. 63702

REFERENCE: AMA, 2015
               Smith (2), pp 151–152

134. Patient comes in through the emergency room with a laceration of the posterior tibial nerve. Patient is taken to the operating room where the nerve requires transposition and suture.
   A. 64856
   B. 64831, 64832, 64876
   C. 64840, 64874
   D. 64834, 64859, 64872

REFERENCE: AMA, 2015
              Smith (2), p 153

Surgery—Eye and Ocular Adnexa

135. Patient returns to the physician's office complaining of obscured vision. Patient has had cataract surgery 6 months prior. Patient requires laser discission of secondary cataract.
   A. 66821
   B. 66940
   C. 67835
   D. 66830

REFERENCE: AMA (7th ed.), p 297
              Smith, pp 157–158
              Smith (2), pp 162–163

136. Patient undergoes enucleation of left eye, and muscles were reattached to an implant.
   A. 65135-LT
   B. 65105-LT
   C. 65730-LT
   D. 65103-LT

REFERENCE: AMA, 2015
              Smith (2), p 161

137. Patient suffers from strabismus and requires surgery. Recession of the lateral rectus (horizontal) muscle with adjustable sutures was performed.
   A. 67340, 67500
   B. 67314, 67320
   C. 67332, 67334
   D. 67311, 67335

REFERENCE: AMA, 2015
              AMA (7th ed.), p 253
              CPT Assistant, Summer 1993, p 20
              CPT Assistant, March 1997, p 5
              CPT Assistant, November 1998, p 1
              CPT Assistant, September 2002, p 10
              Smith, p 160
              Smith (2), p 165

138. Radial keratotomy.
   A. 92071
   B. 65855
   C. 65767
   D. 65771

REFERENCE: Green, pp 706–711
              Smith (2), pp 162–163

139. Correction of trichiasis by incision of lid margin.
   A. 67840
   B. 67830
   C. 67835
   D. 67850

REFERENCE: AMA, 2015
              Smith (2), p 165

140. Patient undergoes ocular resurfacing construction utilizing stem cell allograft from a cadaver.
   A. 67320   C. 68371
   B. 66999   D. 65781

REFERENCE: CPT Assistant, May 2004, pp 9–11
               Smith (2), pp 162–163

141. Aphakia penetrating corneal transplant.
   A. 65755   C. 65750
   B. 65730   D. 65765

REFERENCE: AMA, 2015
               AMA (7th ed.), pp 247–248
               Smith (2), pp 162–163

142. Lagophthalmos correction with implantation using gold weight.
   A. 67912   C. 67901
   B. 67911   D. 67121

REFERENCE: CPT Assistant, May 2004, p 12
               Smith (2), p 165

143. Lacrimal fistula closure.
   A. 68760   C. 68700
   B. 68761   D. 68770

REFERENCE: AMA, 2015
               AMA (7th ed.), pp 255–256
               Smith (2), pp 165–166

Surgery—Auditory

144. Patient comes into the office for removal of impacted earwax.
   A. 69210   C. 69222
   B. 69200   D. 69000

REFERENCE: AMA (7th ed.), p 257
               Green, pp 712–713
               Smith (2), p 120

145. Patient with a traumatic rupture of the eardrum. Repaired with tympanoplasty with incision of the mastoid. Repair of ossicular chain not required.
   A. 69641   C. 69642
   B. 69646   D. 69635

REFERENCE: AMA, 2015
               AMA (7th ed.), pp 258–259
               Smith (2), p 173

146. Patient came in for excision of a middle ear lesion.
    A. 11440
    B. 69540
    C. 69552
    D. 69535

REFERENCE: AMA, 2015
              Smith (2), p 173

147. Patient with chronic otitis media requiring eustachian tube catheterization.
    A. 69420
    B. 69424
    C. 69421
    D. 69799

REFERENCE: AMA, 2015
              AMA (7th ed.), p 258
              Smith (2), p 173

148. Modified radical mastoidectomy.
    A. 69511
    B. 69505
    C. 69635
    D. 69641

REFERENCE: AMA, 2015
              Smith (2), p 173

149. Decompression internal auditory canal.
    A. 69979
    B. 69915
    C. 69970
    D. 69960

REFERENCE: AMA, 2015
              Smith (2), pp 172–173

150. Myringoplasty.
    A. 69620
    B. 69635
    C. 69610
    D. 69420

REFERENCE: AMA (7th ed.), p 258
              CPT Assistant, March 2001, p 10

151. Insertion of cochlear device inner ear.
    A. 69711
    B. 69949
    C. 69930
    D. 69960, 69990

REFERENCE: AMA, 2015
              AMA (7th ed.), p 259
              Smith (2), p 173

152. Patient with Bell's palsy requiring a total facial nerve decompression.
    A. 64742
    B. 64771
    C. 69955
    D. 64864

REFERENCE: AMA, 2015
              Smith (2), p 173

153. Drainage of simple external ear abscess.
    A. 69000
    B. 69100
    C. 10060
    D. 69020

REFERENCE: CPT Assistant, October 1997, p 11
                        CPT Assistant, October 1999, p 10
                        Smith (2), p 173

Radiology

154. Administration of initial oral radionuclide therapy for hyperthyroidism.
    A. 78015
    B. 77402
    C. 78099
    D. 79005

REFERENCE: Green, pp 753–761

155. Patient comes into the outpatient department at the local hospital for an MRI of the cervical spine with contrast. Patient status post automobile accident.
    A. 72156
    B. 72142
    C. 72149
    D. 72126

REFERENCE: AMA (7th ed.), pp 277–278
                        Smith, pp 175–176

156. Obstetric patient comes in for a pelvimetry with placental placement.
    A. 74710
    B. 76946
    C. 76805
    D. 76825

REFERENCE: AMA, 2015

157. Patient comes into his physician's office complaining of wrist pain. Physician gives the patient an injection and sends the patient to the hospital for an arthrography. Code the complete procedure.
    A. 73115
    B. 73100
    C. 73110
    D. 25246, 73115

REFERENCE: AMA, 2015
                        AMA (7th ed.), pp 278–279

158. Patient has carcinoma of the breast and undergoes proton beam delivery of radiation to the breast with a single port.
    A. 77523
    B. 77432
    C. 77520
    D. 77402

REFERENCE: AMA (7th ed.), p 299
                        Green, pp 753–761
                        Smith, pp 178–180

159. CT scan of the head with contrast.
    A. 70460
    B. 70542
    C. 70551
    D. 70470

REFERENCE: AMA (7th ed.), p 274
                        Smith, pp 175–176

160. Patient undergoes x-ray of the foot with three views.
     A. 73620
     B. 3610
     C. 73630
     D. 27648; 73615

REFERENCE: Smith, pp 175–176

161. Unilateral mammogram with computer-aided detection with further physician review and interpretation.
     A. 77055, 77022
     B. 77055-22
     C. 77056-52, 77051
     D. 77055, 77051

REFERENCE: AMA, 2015
               AMA (7th ed.), pp 291–292
               Green, pp 751–752

162. Pregnant female comes in for a complete fetal and maternal evaluation via ultrasound.
     A. 76856
     B. 76805
     C. 76811
     D. 76810

REFERENCE: AMA (7th ed.), pp 286–287
               Green, p 750

163. Ultrasonic guidance for the needle biopsy of the liver. Code the complete procedure.
     A. 47000, 76942
     B. 47000, 76937
     C. 47000, 76999
     D. 47000, 77002

REFERENCE: AMA (7th ed.), p 281
               Green, p 750

Pathology and Laboratory

164. What code is used for a culture of embryos less than 4 days old?
     A. 89251
     B. 89272
     C. 89268
     D. 89250

REFERENCE: AMA (7th ed.), p 336
               CPT Assistant, April 2004, p 2
               CPT Assistant, May 2004, p 16
               CPT Assistant, June 2004, p 9
               Green, pp 790–791

165. Basic metabolic panel (calcium, total) and total bilirubin.
     A. 80048, 82247
     B. 80053
     C. 80053
     D. 82239, 80400, 80051

REFERENCE: AMA (7th ed.), p 309
               Green, p 778
               Smith, p 188

166. Huhner test and semen analysis.
   A. 89325
   B. 89258
   C. 89310
   D. 89300

REFERENCE: CPT Assistant, November 1997, p 36
             CPT Assistant, July 1998, p 10
             CPT Assistant, October 1998, p 1
             CPT Assistant, April 2004, p 3

167. Chlamydia culture.
   A. 87110
   B. 87106
   C. 87118
   D. 87109, 87168

REFERENCE: Green, pp 785–786

168. Partial thromboplastin time utilizing whole blood.
   A. 85732
   B. 85730
   C. 85245
   D. 85246

REFERENCE: AMA (7th ed.), p 323
             Smith, p 190

169. Pathologist bills for gross and microscopic examination of medial meniscus.
   A. 88300
   B. 88302, 88311
   C. 88325
   D. 88304

REFERENCE: AMA (7th ed.), p 334
             Green, pp 789–790
             Smith, p 190

170. Cytopathology of cervical Pap smear with automated thin-layer preparation utilizing computer screening and manual rescreening under physician supervision.
   A. 88175
   B. 88148
   C. 88160, 88141
   D. 88161

REFERENCE: AMA (7th ed.), p 329
             CPT Assistant, July 2003, p 9
             CPT Assistant, March 2004, p 4
             Green, pp 786–787

171. Pathologist performs a postmortem examination, including the brain, of an adult. Tissue is sent to the lab for microscopic examination.
   A. 88309
   B. 88025
   C. 88099
   D. 88028

REFERENCE: Green, p 486
             Smith, p 190

172. Clotting factor VII.
   A. 85220
   B. 85240
   C. 85362
   D. 85230

REFERENCE: Smith, p 190

Medicine Section

173. IV push of one antineoplastic drug.
    A. 96401
    B. 96409
    C. 96411
    D. 96413

REFERENCE: AMA (7th ed.), pp 418–419
              Green, pp 825–828
              Smith, pp 240–242

174. One-half hour of IV chemotherapy by infusion followed by IV push of a different drug.
    A. 96413
    B. 96413, 96411
    C. 96413, 96409
    D. 96409, 96411

REFERENCE: AMA (7th ed.), pp 417–418
              Green, pp 825–828
              Smith, pp 240–242

175. Caloric vestibular test using air.
    A. 92543, 92700
    B. 92543, 92543
    C. 92700
    D. 92543

REFERENCE: AMA (7th ed.), p 361
              CPT Assistant, November 2004, p 10

176. Patient presents to the emergency room with chest pains. The patient is admitted as a 23-hour observation. The cardiologist orders cardiac workup and the patient undergoes left heart catheterization via the left femoral artery with visualization of the coronary arteries and left ventriculography. The physician interprets the report. Code the heart catheterization.
    A. 93452, 93455
    B. 93452, 93458
    C. 93458
    D. 93459

REFERENCE: AMA, 2015

177. Patient with hematochromatosis had a therapeutic phlebotomy performed on an outpatient basis.
    A. 99195
    B. 36522
    C. 36514
    D. 99199

REFERENCE: AMA (7th ed.), p 307
              CPT Assistant, June 1996, p 10

178. A physician performs a PTCA with drug-eluting stent placement in the left anterior descending artery and angioplasty only in the right coronary artery.
    A. 92928-LD, 92929-RC
    B. 92928-LD, 92920-RC
    C. 92928-LD, 92920-RC
    D. 92920-RC, 92929-LD

REFERENCE: AMA (7th ed.), pp 366–367
              CPT Assistant, April 2005, p 14
              Smith, pp 231–234

179. Transesophageal echocardiography (TEE) with probe placement, image, and interpretation and report.
    A. 93307
    B. 93303, 93325
    C. 93312, 93313, 93314
    D. 93312

REFERENCE: AMA (7th ed.), pp 374–375
              CPT Assistant, December 1997, p 5
              CPT Assistant, January 2000, p 10

180. Which code listed below would be used to report an esophageal electrogram during an EPS?
    A. 93600
    B. 93615
    C. 93612
    D. 93616

REFERENCE: CPT Assistant, April 2004, p 9
              Smith, p 237

181. Cardioversion of cardiac arrhythmia by external forces.
    A. 92961
    B. 92950
    C. 92960
    D. 92970

REFERENCE: CPT Assistant, Summer 1993, p 13
              CPT Assistant, November 1999, p 49
              CPT Assistant, June 2000, p 5
              CPT Assistant, November 2000, p 9
              CPT Assistant, July 2001, p 11

182. Osteopathic manipulative treatment to three body regions.
    A. 98926
    B. 98941
    C. 97110
    D. 97012

REFERENCE: Green, p 830

183. Patient presents to the Respiratory Therapy Department and undergoes a pulmonary stress test. CO_2 production with O_2 uptake with recordings was also performed.
    A. 94450
    B. 94620
    C. 94002
    D. 94621

REFERENCE: CPT Assistant, November 1998, p 35
              CPT Assistant, January 1999, p 8
              CPT Assistant, August 2002, p 10

For the following questions, you will be utilizing the codes provided for the scenarios. You will need to code appropriate CPT-4 codes only.

184. Patient presents to the hospital for debridement of a diabetic ulcer of the left ankle. The patient has a history of recurrent ulcers. Medication taken by the patient includes Diabeta and the patient was covered in the hospital with insulin sliding scales. The decubitus ulcer was debrided down to the bone.

11043	Debridement, muscle and/or fascia (includes epidermis, dermis, and subcutaneous tissue, if performed); first 20 cm^2 or less
11044	Debridement, bone (includes epidermis, dermis, subcutaneous tissue, muscle and/or fascia, if performed); first 20 cm^2 or less
+11046	each additional 20 cm^2 thereof (List separately in addition to code for primary procedure.) (Use 11046 in conjunction with 11043.)
+11047	each additional 20 cm^2, or part thereof (List separately in addition to code for primary procedure.) (Use 11047 in conjunction with 11047.)

A. 11043, +11047
B. 11043, +11046

C. 11044
D. 11044, +11047

REFERENCE: AMA, 2015

185. Patient presents to the emergency room following a fall from a tree. X-rays were ordered for the left upper arm, which showed a fracture of the humerus shaft. The emergency room physician performed a closed reduction of the fracture and placed the patient in a long arm spica cast. Code the diagnoses and procedures, excluding the x-ray.

24500	Closed treatment of humeral shaft fracture; without manipulation
24505	Closed treatment of humeral shaft fracture; with manipulation, with or without skeletal traction
24515	Open treatment of humeral shaft fracture with plate/screws, with or without cerclage
29065	Application, cast; shoulder to hand (long arm) LT Left side

A. 24505-LT
B. 24515-LT
C. 24505-LT, 29065
D. 24500-LT

REFERENCE: AMA (7th ed.), pp 115, 134–135
             Green, p 563
             Smith, pp 84–85

186. Patient was admitted with hemoptysis and underwent a bronchoscopy with transbronchial lung biopsy. Following the bronchoscopy, the patient was taken to the operating room where a left lower lobe lobectomy was performed without complications. Pathology reported large cell carcinoma of the left lower lobe.

31625	Bronchoscopy with bronchial or endobronchial biopsy, with or without fluoroscopic guidance
31628	Bronchoscopy with transbronchial lung biopsy, with or without fluoroscopic guidance
32405	Biopsy, lung or mediastinum, percutaneous needle
32440	Removal of lung, total pneumonectomy
32480	Removal of lung, other than total pneumonectomy, single lobe (lobectomy)
32484	Removal of lung, other than total pneumonectomy, single segment (segmentectomy)

A. 31625
B. 31628, 32480

C. 32405, 32484
D. 32440

REFERENCE: AMA (7th ed.), pp 140–141
CPT Assistant, June 2001, p 10
CPT Assistant, June 2002, p 10
CPT Assistant, September 2004, p 9
Green, pp 576–580
Smith, p 100

187. Patient was admitted for right upper quadrant pain. Workup included various x-rays that showed cholelithiasis. Patient was taken to the operating room where a laparoscopic cholecystectomy was performed. During the procedure, the physician was unable to visualize through the ports and an open cholecystectomy was elected to be performed. An intraoperative cholangiogram was performed. Pathology report states acute and chronic cholecystitis with cholelithiasis.

47605	Cholecystectomy with cholangiography
47563	Laparoscopy, surgical; cholecystectomy with cholangiography

A. 47563
B. 47563, 47605
C. 47605

REFERENCE: AMA (7th ed.), p 187
Green, p 654

188. Patient presents to the emergency room complaining of right forearm/elbow pain after racquetball last night. Patient states that he did not fall, but overworked his arm. Past medical history is negative and the physical examination reveals the patient is unable to supinate. A four-view x-ray of the right elbow is performed and is negative. The physician signs the patient out with right elbow sprain. Prescription of Motrin is given to the patient.

73040	X-ray of shoulder, arthrography radiological supervision and interpretation
73070	X-ray of elbow, two views
73080	X-ray of elbow, complete, minimum of three views
99281	E/M visit to emergency room—problem-focused history, problem-focused exam, straightforward medical decision
99282	E/M visit to emergency room—expanded problem-focused history, expanded problem-focused exam, and medical decision of low complexity
-25	Significant, separately identifiable evaluation and management service by the same physician on the same day of the procedure or other service

   A. 73080
   B. 99281, 73070
   C. 73080, 99282, 73040
   D. 99281-25, 73080

REFERENCE: AMA, 2015
               AMA (7th ed.), pp 56–57, 275, 276
               Smith, pp 175–176, 216

189. A physician orders a lipid panel on a 54-year-old male with hypercholesterolemia, hypertension, and a family history of heart disease. The lab employee in his office performs and reports the total cholesterol and HDL cholesterol only.

80061	Lipid panel; this panel must include the following: Cholesterol, serum, total (82465); Lipoprotein, direct measurement, high density cholesterol (HDL cholesterol) (83718); Triglycerides (84478)
82465	Cholesterol, serum or whole blood, total
83718	Lipoprotein, direct measurement; high density cholesterol (HDL cholesterol)
84478	Triglycerides
-52	Reduced services

   A. 80061
   B. 80061-52
   C. 82465, 83718
   D. 82465, 84478

REFERENCE: AMA (7th ed.), p 308
               Green, p 788
               Smith, pp 188–189

190. Chronic nontraumatic rotator cuff tear. Arthroscopic subacromial decompression with coracoacromial ligament release, and open rotator cuff repair.

23410	Repair of ruptured musculotendinous cuff (e.g., rotator cuff); open, acute
23412	Repair of ruptured musculotendinous cuff (e.g., rotator cuff) open; chronic
29821	Arthroscopy, shoulder, surgical; synovectomy, complete
29823	Arthroscopy, shoulder, surgical; debridement, extensive
+29826	Arthroscopy, shoulder, surgical; decompression of subacromial space with partial acromioplasty, with coracoacromial ligament release (List separately in addition to code from primary procedure.)
29827	Arthroscopy, shoulder, surgical; with rotator cuff repair
-59	Distinct procedural service

A. 29823
B. 23412, 29826-59

C. 29826, 29821
D. 23410

REFERENCE: AMA (7th ed.), pp 135, 498
              Smith, p 88

191. The patient is on vacation and presents to a physician's office with a lacerated finger. The physician repairs the laceration and gives a prescription for pain control and has the patient follow up with his primary physician when he returns home. The physician fills out the superbill as a problem-focused history and physical examination with straightforward medical decision making. Also checked is a laceration repair for a 1.5-cm finger wound.

99201	New patient office visit with a problem-focused history, problem-focused examination and straightforward medical decision making
99212	Established patient office visit with a problem-focused history, problem-focused examination and straightforward medical decision making
12001	Simple repair of superficial wounds of scalp, neck, axillae, external genitalia, trunk and/or extremities (including hands and feet); 2.5 cm or less
13131	Repair, complex, forehead, cheeks, chin, mouth, neck, axillae, genitalia, hands and/or feet; 1.1 cm to 2.5 cm

A. 99212, 13131
B. 12001

C. 99212, 12001
D. 99201, 12001

REFERENCE: AMA (7th ed.), pp 107, 447–448
              Green, pp 428–429, 524–526
              Smith, pp 66–68, 195–196

192. A 69-year-old established female patient presents to the office with chronic obstructive lung disease, congestive heart failure, and hypertension. The physician conducts a comprehensive history and physical examination and makes a medical decision of moderate complexity. Physician admits the patient from the office to the hospital for acute exacerbation of CHF.

99212	Established office visit for problem-focused history and exam, straightforward medical decision making
99214	Established office visit for a detailed history and physical exam, moderate medical decision making
99222	Initial hospital care for comprehensive history and physical exam, moderate medical decision making
99223	Initial hospital care for comprehensive history and physical exam, high medical decision making

A. 99214
B. 99223
C. 99222
D. 99212

REFERENCE: AMA (7th ed.), p 48
Green, pp 432–435
Smith, pp 214–215

193. Established 42-year-old patient comes into your office to obtain vaccines required for his trip to Sri Lanka. The nurse injects intramuscularly the following vaccines: hepatitis A and B vaccines, cholera vaccine, and yellow fever vaccine. As the coding specialist, what would you report on the CMS 1500 form?
A. office visit, hepatitis A and B vaccine, cholera vaccine and yellow fever vaccine
B. office visit, intramuscular injection; HCPCS Level II codes
C. office visit; administration of two or more single vaccines; vaccine products for hepatitis A and B, cholera, and yellow fever
D. administration of two or more single vaccines; vaccine products for hepatitis A and B, cholera, and yellow fever

REFERENCE: Green, pp 802–804
Smith, p 226

194. Patient presents to the operating room where the physician performed, using imaging guidance, a percutaneous breast biopsy utilizing a rotating biopsy device.

19000	Puncture aspiration of cyst of breast
19081	Biopsy, breast, with imaging of the biopsy specimen, percutaneous; first lesion, including stereotactic guidance
19120	Excision of cyst, fibroadenoma, or other benign or malignant tumor, aberrant breast tissue, duct lesion, nipple or areolar lesion (except 19300), open, male or female, one or more lesions
19125	Excision of breast lesion identified by preoperative placement of radiological marker, open; single lesion
19283	Placement of breast localization device(s) (ed clip, metallic pellet, wire/needle, radioactive seeds), percutaneous; first lesion, including stereotactic guidance

A. 19081
B. 19125, 19283
C. 19120
D. 19000

REFERENCE: AMA (7th ed.), p 115
CPT Assistant, January 2001, pp 10–11
Green, pp 835–837
Smith, pp 79–80

195. Facelift utilizing the superficial musculoaponeurotic system (SMAS) flap technique.

15788	Chemical peel, facial; epidermal
15825	Rhytidectomy; neck with platysmal tightening (platysmal flap, P-flap)
15828	Rhytidectomy; cheek, chin, and neck
15829	Rhytidectomy; SMAS flap

A. 15825   C. 15829
B. 15788   D. 15828

REFERENCE: AMA, 2015
                  Green, pp 531–532

196. Tracheostoma revision with flap rotation.

31613	Tracheostoma revision; simple, without flap rotation
31614	Tracheostoma revision; complex, with flap rotation
31750	Tracheoplasty; cervical
31830	Revision of tracheostomy scar

A. 31830   C. 31614
B. 31750   D. 31613

REFERENCE: AMA, 2015

197. Blood transfusion of three units of packed red blood cells.

36430	Transfusion, blood or blood components
36455	Exchange transfusion; blood, other than newborn
36460	Transfusion, intrauterine, fetal

A. 36430   C. 36460
B. 36430, 36430, 36430   D. 36455

REFERENCE: AMA, 2015

198. Two-year-old patient returns to the hospital for cleft palate repair where a secondary lengthening procedure takes place.

40720	Plastic repair of cleft lip/nasal deformity; secondary, by re-creation of defect and reclosure
42145	Palatopharyngoplasty
42220	Palatoplasty for cleft palate; secondary lengthening procedure
42226	Lengthening of palate and pharyngeal flap

A. 40720   C. 42226
B. 42220   D. 42145

REFERENCE: AMA, 2015

199. Tonsillectomy on a 14-year-old.

42820	Tonsillectomy and adenoidectomy; under age 12
42821	Tonsillectomy and adenoidectomy; age 12 or over
42825	Tonsillectomy, primary or secondary; under age 12
42826	Tonsillectomy, primary or secondary; age 12 or over

A. 42820　　　　　　　　　　C. 42825
B. 42821　　　　　　　　　　D. 42826

REFERENCE:　Green, p 640

200. Laparoscopic repair of umbilical hernia.

49580	Repair umbilical hernia, under age 5 years, reducible
49585	Repair umbilical hernia, age 5 years or over, reducible
49652	Laparoscopy, surgical, repair, ventral, umbilical, spigelian or epigastric hernia (includes mesh insertion when performed); reducible
49654	Laparoscopy, surgical, repair, incisional hernia (includes mesh insertion when performed); reducible

A. 49580　　　　　　　　　　C. 49585
B. 49654　　　　　　　　　　D. 49652

REFERENCE:　AMA, 2015
　　　　　　　AMA (7th ed.), p 189

201. Ureterolithotomy completed laparoscopically.

50600	Ureterotomy with exploration or drainage (separate procedure)
50945	Laparoscopy, surgical ureterolithotomy
52325	Cystourethroscopy; with fragmentation of ureteral calculus
52352	Cystourethroscopy, with urethroscopy and/or pyeloscopy; with removal or manipulation of calculus (ureteral catheterization is included)

A. 52352　　　　　　　　　　C. 50600
B. 52325　　　　　　　　　　D. 50945

REFERENCE:　CPT Assistant, November 1999, p 26
　　　　　　　CPT Assistant, May 2000, p 4
　　　　　　　CPT Assistant, October 2001, p 8

202. Patient undergoes partial nephrectomy for carcinoma of the kidney.

50220	Nephrectomy, including partial ureterectomy, any open approach including rib resection
50234	Nephrectomy with total ureterectomy and bladder cuff; through same incision
50240	Nephrectomy, partial
50340	Recipient nephrectomy (separate procedure)

A. 50234　　　　　　　　　　C. 50340
B. 50220　　　　　　　　　　D. 50240

REFERENCE:　AMA (7th ed.), p 193
　　　　　　　Green, pp 659–660

203. Patient presents to the operating room for fulguration of bladder tumors. The cystoscope was inserted and entered the urethra, which was normal. Bladder tumors measuring approximately 1.5 cm were removed.

50957	Ureteral endoscopy through established ureterostomy, with or without irrigation, instillation, or ureteropyelography, exclusive of radiologic service; with fulguration and/or incision, with or without biopsy
51530	Cystotomy; for excision of bladder tumor
52214	Cystourethroscopy, with fulguration of trigone, bladder neck, prostatic fossa, urethra, or periurethral glands
52234	Cystourethroscopy, with fulguration (including cryosurgery or laser surgery) and/or resection of small bladder tumor(s) (0.5 up to 2.0 cm)

A. 52234   C. 52214
B. 50957   D. 51530

REFERENCE: AMA (7th ed.), pp 193–194
                     Green, pp 664–665
                     Smith, p 134

204. Excision of Cowper's gland.

53220	Excision or fulguration of carcinoma of urethra
53250	Excision of bulbourethral gland (Cowper's gland)
53260	Excision or fulguration; urethral polyp(s), distal urethra
53450	Urethromeatoplasty, with mucosal advancement

A. 53250
C. 53260
B. 53450
D. 53220

REFERENCE: AMA, 2015

205. Placement of double-J stent.

52320	Cystourethroscopy (including ureteral catheterization); with removal of ureteral calculus
52330	Cystourethroscopy; with manipulation, without removal of ureteral calculus
52332	Cystourethroscopy with insertion of indwelling ureteral stent (e.g., Gibbons or double-J type)
52341	Cystourethroscopy, with treatment of ureteral stricture (e.g., balloon dilation, laser electrocautery, and incision)

A. 52341   C. 52330, 52332
B. 52320   D. 52332

REFERENCE: AMA (7th ed.), pp 193–195
                     Green, pp 664–665
                     Smith, p 134

206. Litholapaxy, 3 cm calculus.

50590	Lithotripsy, extracorporeal shock wave
52317	Litholapaxy, simple or small (< 2.5 cm)
52318	Litholapaxy, complicated or large (over 2.5 cm)
52353	Cystourethroscopy, with ureteroscopy and/or pyeloscopy; with lithotripsy

A. 52353　　　　　　　　　　C. 52318
B. 50590　　　　　　　　　　D. 52317

REFERENCE:　AMA, 2015

207. Patient presented to the operating room where an incision was made in the epigastric region for a repair of ureterovisceral fistula.

50520	Closure of nephrocutaneous or pyelocutaneous fistula
50525	Closure of nephrovisceral fistula, including visceral repair; abdominal approach
50526	Closure of nephrovisceral fistula, including visceral repair; thoracic approach
50930	Closure of ureterovisceral fistula (including visceral repair)

A. 50526　　　　　　　　　　C. 50520
B. 50930　　　　　　　　　　D. 50525

REFERENCE:　AMA, 2015

208. Amniocentesis.

57530	Trachelectomy, amputation of cervix (separate procedure)
57550	Excision of cervical stump, vaginal approach
59000	Amniocentesis, diagnostic
59200	Insertion of cervical dilator (separate procedure)

A. 59000　　　　　　　　　　C. 57550
B. 59200　　　　　　　　　　D. 57530

REFERENCE:　AMA, 2015
　　　　　　　AMA (7th ed.), p 206

209. Patient is admitted to the hospital with facial droop and left-sided paralysis. CT scan of the brain shows subdural hematoma. Burr holes were performed to evacuate the hematoma.

61150	Burr hole(s) or trephine; with drainage of brain abscess or cyst
61154	Burr hole(s) with evacuation and/or drainage of hematoma, extradural or subdural
61156	Burr hole(s); with aspiration of hematoma or cyst, intracerebral
61314	Craniectomy or craniotomy for evacuation of hematoma, infratentorial; extradural or subdural

A. 61156　　　　　　　　　　C. 61154
B. 61314　　　　　　　　　　D. 61150

REFERENCE:　Green, p 695

210. Spinal tap.

62268	Percutaneous aspiration, spinal cord cyst or syrinx
62270	Spinal puncture, lumbar diagnostic
62272	Spinal puncture, therapeutic, for drainage of cerebrospinal fluid (by needle or catheter)
64999	Unlisted procedure, nervous system

A. 62272
B. 64999
C. 62268
D. 62270

REFERENCE: AMA, 2015
                          AMA (7th ed.), p 445

211. Injection of anesthesia for nerve block of the brachial plexus.

64413	Injection, anesthetic agent; cervical plexus
64415	Injection, anesthetic agent; brachial plexus, single
64510	Injection, anesthetic agent; stellate ganglion (cervical sympathetic)
64530	Injection, anesthetic agent; celiac plexus, with or without radiologic monitoring

A. 64415
B. 64413
C. 64530
D. 64510

REFERENCE: AMA (7th ed.), p 448
                          Green, p 703

212. SPECT bone imaging.

77080	Dual energy x-ray absorptiometry (DXA), bone density study, one or more sites; axial skeleton (e.g., hips, pelvis, spine)
76977	Ultrasound bone density measurement and interpretation, peripheral site(s), any method
78300	Bone and/or joint imaging; limited area
78320	Bone and/or joint imaging; tomographic (SPECT)

A. 76977
B. 78320
C. 77080
D. 76977

REFERENCE: AMA, 2015
                          AMA (7th ed.), pp 303–304
                          CPT Assistant, June 2003, p 11

213. Vitamin B_{12}

82180	Ascorbic acid (vitamin C), blood
82607	Cyanocobalamin (vitamin B_{12})
84590	Vitamin A
84591	Vitamin, not otherwise specified

A. 84590
B. 82180
C. 84591
D. 82607

REFERENCE: AMA, 2015
                          Green, p 782
                          Smith, p 190

214. Hepatitis C antibody.

86803	Hepatitis C antibody
86804	Hepatitis C antibody; confirmatory test (e.g., immunoblot)
87520	Infectious agent detection by nucleic acid (DNA or RNA); hepatitis C, direct probe technique
87522	Infectious agent detection by nucleic acid (DNA or RNA); hepatitis C, quantification

A. 86804
B. 86803

C. 87522
D. 87520

REFERENCE: AMA, 2015
              Green, p 784

215. Creatinine clearance.

82550	Creatine kinase (CK), (CPK); total
82565	Creatinine; blood
82575	Creatinine; clearance
82585	Cryofibrinogen

A. 82550
B. 82565

C. 82575
D. 82585

REFERENCE: Green, p 782
              Smith, p 190

216. Comprehensive electrophysiologic evaluation (EPS) with induction of arrhythmia.

93618	Induction of arrhythmia by electrical pacing
93619	Comprehensive electrophysiologic evaluation with right atrial pacing and recording, right ventricular pacing and recording, His bundle recording, including insertion and repositioning of multiple electrode catheters, without induction or attempted induction of arrhythmia
93620	Comprehensive electrophysiologic evaluation including insertion and repositioning of multiple electrode catheters with induction or attempted induction of arrhythmia; with right atrial pacing and recording, right ventricular pacing and recording, His bundle recording
+93623	Programmed stimulation and pacing after intravenous drug infusion (list separately in addition to code for primary procedure)
93640	Electrophysiologic evaluation of single- or dual-chamber pacing cardioverter-defibrillator leads including defibrillation threshold evaluation (induction of arrhythmia, evaluation of sensing and pacing for arrhythmia termination) at time of initial implantation or replacement

A. 93618, 93620
B. 93620

C. 93640, 93623
D. 93619, 93620

REFERENCE: AMA (7th ed.), p 149
              CPT Assistant, Summer 1994, p 12
              CPT Assistant, August 1997, p 9
              CPT Assistant, October 1997, p 10
              CPT Assistant, July 1998, p 10

217. Patient presents to the hospital for a two-view chest x-ray for a cough. The radiology report comes back negative. What would be the correct codes to report to the insurance company?

71010 Radiologic examination, chest; single view, frontal
71020 Radiologic examination, chest, two views, frontal and lateral
71035 Radiologic examination, chest, special views

A. 71010
B. 71020
C. 71035

REFERENCE: AMA, 2015
                         Schraffenberger, pp 338–339

Answer Key for CPT-4 Coding

1.	C		43.	C	
2.	A		44.	A	
3.	B		45.	D	
4.	C		46.	C	
5.	D		47.	A	
6.	C		48.	D	
7.	D		49.	A	
8.	B		50.	B	
9.	B		51.	A	
10.	C		52.	B	
11.	D		53.	D	
12.	B		54.	B	
13.	A		55.	C	
14.	B		56.	C	
15.	D		57.	C	
16.	B		58.	A	
17.	C		59.	A	
18.	A		60.	B	
19.	D	The supply of skin substitutes graft(s) should be reported separately.	61.	D	
			62.	B	
			63.	A	
20.	C		64.	D	
21.	C		65.	A	
22.	B		66.	B	
23.	B		67.	C	
24.	C	The supply of skin substitutes graft(s) should be reported separately.	68.	A	
			69.	A	
			70.	D	
25.	B		71.	C	
26.	C		72.	D	Radiology codes would be used for the supervision and interpretation.
27.	A	See Principles of CPT Coding 7th edition, pages 103–104. If two lesions are removed with one excision, only one excision code would be reported.			
			73.	C	
			74.	C	
			75.	C	
28.	D		76.	A	
29.	B		77.	D	
30.	C		78.	D	
31.	D		79.	C	
32.	A		80.	A	
33.	D		81.	A	
34.	A	Codes 10060 and 10140 are used for I&Ds of superficial abscesses.	82.	C	
			83.	D	
35.	C		84.	B	
36.	C		85.	D	
37.	D		86.	B	
38.	B		87.	A	
39.	A		88.	B	
40.	B		89.	C	
41.	A		90.	B	
42.	D		91.	B	

Answer Key for CPT-4 Coding

92.	D	
93.	C	
94.	A	
95.	A	
96.	B	
97.	C	
98.	A	
99.	D	
100.	C	
101.	D	
102.	C	
103.	D	
104.	D	
105.	D	
106.	B	
107.	B	
108.	C	
109.	C	
110.	C	
111.	C	
112.	A	
113.	A	
114.	B	
115.	D	
116.	D	
117.	C	
118.	A	
119.	D	When tubal ligation is performed at the same time as hysterotomy, use 58611 in addition to 59100.
120.	A	
121.	D	
122.	A	
123.	C	
124.	A	
125.	B	
126.	C	
127.	A	
128.	C	
129.	A	
130.	C	
131.	C	
132.	B	
133.	D	
134.	C	
135.	A	
136.	B	
137.	D	
138.	D	
139.	B	
140.	D	
141.	C	
142.	A	
143.	D	
144.	A	
145.	D	
146.	B	
147.	D	
148.	B	
149.	D	
150.	A	
151.	C	
152.	C	
153.	A	
154.	D	
155.	B	
156.	A	
157.	D	
158.	C	
159.	A	
160.	C	
161.	D	
162.	C	
163.	A	
164.	D	
165.	A	
166.	D	
167.	A	
168.	B	
169.	D	
170.	A	
171.	B	
172.	D	
173.	B	
174.	B	
175.	C	Use code 92543 when an irrigation substance is used.
176.	C	
177.	A	
178.	B	
179.	D	
180.	B	
181.	C	
182	A	

Answer Key for CPT-4 Coding

183. D

184. C

185. A   Casting is included in the surgical procedure.

186. B

187. C

188. D

189. C   In order to use the code for the panel, every test must have been performed.

190. B   Code both the arthroscopic procedure and the open procedure. Both need to be reported because there were two separate procedures. Modifier -59 must be added to code 29826 because it is a component of the comprehensive procedure 23412. That is allowed if an appropriate modifier is used per NCCI edits.

191. D

192. C   According to CPT guidelines, when a patient is admitted to the hospital on the same day as an office visit, the office visit is not billable.

193. D   According to the CPT coding and guidelines for vaccines, only a separate identifiable Evaluation Management code may be billed in addition to the vaccine. In this scenario, the patient was seen only for his vaccines. This guideline immediately eliminates all the other answers.

194. A

195. C

196. C

197. A   Report this code only once no matter how many units were given.

198. B

199. D

200. D

201. D

202. D

203. A

204. A

205. D

206. C

207. B

208. A

209. C

210. D

211. A

212. B

213. D

214. B

215. C

216. B

217. B

REFERENCES

American Medical Association (AMA). *CPT assistant.* Chicago: Author.

American Medical Association (AMA). (2013). *Principles of CPT coding* (7th ed.). Chicago: Author.

American Medical Association (AMA). (2014). *Physician's current procedural terminology (CPT) 2015 professional edition.* Chicago: Author.

Green, M. (2014). *3-2-1 Code It!* (4th ed.). Clifton Park, NY: Delmar Cengage Learning.

Hazelwood, A. & Venable, C. (2013). *ICD-9-CM and ICD-10-CM coding and reimbursement for physician services.* Chicago: American Health Information Management Association (AHIMA).

Johnson, S. L. & Linker, R. (2013). *Understanding medical coding: A comprehensive guide* (3rd ed.). Clifton Park, NY: Delmar Cengage Learning.

Smith, G. (2014). *Basic current procedural terminology and HCPCS coding, 2014 edition.* Chicago: American Health Information Management Association (AHIMA).

Smith, G. (2) (2011). *Coding surgical procedures: Beyond the basics.* Clifton Park, NY. Delmar Cengage Learning.

CPT Coding Competencies

Questions	CCS Competencies
1-203	Domain 2

IX. CCS Case Study Coding Review

CCS CASE STUDY

Working these case studies should help you in identifying your strengths and weaknesses in coding cases. The following is a list of a few resources for coding instructions and the latest official guidelines for coding:

- ICD-9-CM codebook
- ICD-9-CM Official Guidelines for coding and reporting
- Coding Clinic for ICD-9-CM (AHA)
- Coding Clinic for HCPCS (AHA)
- CPT codebook (AMA)
- CPT Assistant (AMA)

Use ICD-9-CM (Volumes 1–3) for coding inpatient diagnoses and procedures. Code diagnoses for ambulatory care records using ICD-9-CM (Volumes 1 and 2). Code ambulatory procedures using CPT coding.

There are plenty of coding cases in this section to help you practice taking the medical record case coding portion of the CCS Examination. For each of these coding cases, the coding system (ICD-9-CM and/or CPT) and number of codes necessary for each coding system will be given. The spaces for codes on the answer sheet reflect the number and type of codes necessary.

As always, refer to the latest information about the examination that is provided in your examination packet and online at http://www.AHIMA.org.

INPATIENT CODING INSTRUCTIONS

TIP: Refer to the Inpatient information provided in the Examination Study Strategies and Resources, Coding Review, and ICD-9-CM sections in this book before coding the CCS inpatient cases.

1. Follow UHDDS definitions, ICD-9-CM instructional notations and conventions, and current coding guidelines to assign correct ICD-9-CM diagnostic and procedural codes to hospital inpatient medical records.

2. In sequencing the ICD-9-CM codes, list the principal diagnosis first for inpatient cases.

3. Code other diagnoses that coexist at the time of admission, that develop subsequently, or that affect the treatment received and/or the length of stay. These represent additional conditions that affect patient care in terms of
   - Requiring clinical evaluation, therapeutic treatment, or diagnostic procedures
   - Extending length of hospital stay, or
   - Increased nursing care and/or monitoring
   Examples
      - Present on admission (POA) conditions
      - Conditions that develop subsequent to admission
      - Chronic diseases requiring active intervention during the hospital visit
      - Chronic systemic or generalized conditions that may have a bearing on the management of the patient (e.g., blindness)
      - Status post previous surgeries or conditions that are likely to recur and that may have an effect on patient management

4. Do not code
   - Localized conditions that have no effect on patient management
   - Status post previous surgeries or conditions that have no effect on patient management
   - Abnormal findings (laboratory, x-ray, pathologic, and other diagnostic testing results) unless documentation from the physician of their clinical significance
   - Signs or symptoms that are characteristic of a diagnosis
   - Any social history condition(s) that have no bearing on patient management

5. Do not assign
   - M-codes (Morphology codes)
   - E-codes except those to identify the cause or substance for an adverse effect of a drug that is correctly prescribed and properly administered (E850-E982)

6. Code all procedures that fall within the code range of 00.01–86.99, but do not code 57.94 (Foley catheter).

7. Do not code procedures that fall within the code range 87.01–99.99, but do code these:

Cholangiograms	87.51–87.54
Retrogrades, urinary systems	87.74 and 87.76
Arteriography and angiography	88.40–88.58
Radiation therapy	92.21–92.29
Psychiatric therapy	94.24–94.27
Alcohol/drug detoxification and rehabilitation	94.61–94.69
Insertion of endotracheal tube	96.04
Other lavage of bronchus and trachea	96.56
Mechanical ventilation	96.70–96.72
ESWL	98.51–98.59
Chemotherapy	99.25

AMBULATORY CARE CODING INSTRUCTIONS

TIP: Refer to the outpatient information provided in the Examination Study Strategies and Resources, Coding Review, and CPT and ICD-9-CM coding sections in this book before beginning coding of the CCS outpatient cases.

1. To select diagnoses, conditions, problems, or other reasons for care that require ICD-9-CM coding in an ambulatory care visit or encounter either in a hospital clinic, outpatient surgical area, emergency room, physician's office, or other ambulatory care setting: apply ICD-9-CM instructional notations and conventions; current approved Coding Guidelines for Outpatient Services; and "Diagnostic Coding and Reporting Requirements for Physician Billing" (*Coding Clinic for ICD-9-CM*, Fourth quarter 1995 and 1996).

2. In sequencing the ICD-9-CM codes, the first listed code should describe the condition chiefly responsible for the outpatient services provided during the encounter.

3. Code the secondary diagnoses as follows:

    -   Code and report chronic diseases that are treated on an ongoing basis as many times as the patient receives treatment and care for the condition(s).
    -   Code all documented conditions that coexist at the time of the encounter that require or affect patient care, treatment, or management.
    -   Do not code conditions previously treated that no longer exist.

4. Do not assign

    -   E-codes except for those that identify the causative substance for an adverse effect of a drug that is correctly prescribed and properly administered (E850-E982)
    -   M-codes
    -   ICD-9-CM procedure codes

5. Assign CPT codes for all surgical procedures that fall in the surgery section (regardless of payer).

6. Assign CPT codes from the following sections ONLY IF indicated on the case cover sheet:

    -   Anesthesia
    -   Medicine
    -   Evaluation and management services
    -   Radiology
    -   Laboratory and pathology

7. Assign CPT/HCPCS modifiers for hospital-based facilities, if applicable (regardless of payer).

8. Do not assign HCPCS Level II (alphanumeric) codes.

Code ICD-9-CM Diagnoses ONLY
(Nine diagnosis codes will be needed)

Case Study 1

Inpatient Face Sheet

Admit Date: 1/06/2015

Discharge Date: 1/10/2015

Sex: Female

Age: 64

Disposition: Home

Admitting Diagnoses:
1. Neutropenic sepsis
2. Status postchemotherapy for non-Hodgkin's lymphoma
3. Hypertension

Discharge Diagnoses:
1. Pancytopenia with neutropenic sepsis secondary to chemotherapy
2. Non-Hodgkin's lymphoma
3. Hypoalbuminemia
4. Hypertension

Case Study 1

Discharge Summary

Admitted: 1/06/2015
Discharge: 1/10/2015

ADMISSION DIAGNOSES:

1. Neutropenic sepsis
2. Status postchemotherapy for non-Hodgkin's lymphoma
3. Hypertension

DISCHARGE DIAGNOSES:

1. Pancytopenia with neutropenic sepsis secondary to chemotherapy
2. Non-Hodgkin's lymphoma
3. Hypoalbuminemia
4. Hypertension

HISTORY:

This is a 64-year-old female with non-Hodgkin's lymphoma, currently undergoing chemotherapy. The patient was evaluated by Oncology in follow-up and found to be neutropenic as well as febrile.

PHYSICAL EXAMINATION:

Vital Signs:	Blood pressure 132/90. Temperature was 102.
HEENT:	Dry oral mucous membranes. No thrush or herpetic lesions.
Neck:	Supple, no adenopathy.
Lungs:	Clear.
Heart:	Slightly tachycardiac, no murmur.
Abdomen:	Soft, nontender.
Extremities:	Pulses bilateral. Decreased muscle tone.

LABORATORY DATA:

Chemistries revealed total protein 5.8, albumin 2.4. Calcium 7.3, 7.6. The follow-up chem-7 revealed CO_2 of 25, chloride 111. Admission white blood cell count was 0.1, hemoglobin 11.2, hematocrit 32.8, red cell indices were normal. The platelet count was 14,000. The last blood count revealed white blood cell count of 3,500. The hemoglobin was 11.4, hematocrit 34.3, red cell indices remained normal. The urinalysis was pale in color and clear with trace protein noted, nitrite negative, leukocyte esterase negative. The urine culture showed no growth. Blood culture showed no growth.

RADIOLOGY:

The chest x-ray showed no acute process.

Case Study 1

Discharge Summary

Continued:

HOSPITAL COURSE:
The patient was admitted after follow-up with her oncologist. She was found to be febrile and neutropenic; rule out sepsis. The patient was admitted and placed in isolation. Cultures were obtained, and the patient was placed on IV Fortaz as well as IV gentamicin. The patient had pancytopenia with a drop in her platelet count, and the patient was given platelet transfusion, blood transfusions, and IV fluids for dehydration. The patient had a mild reaction to the transfusion and was given IV steroids as well as Benadryl. The patient was started on Neupogen injections on November 7. The patient again received platelet and blood transfusion on November 7 and additional platelet transfusion on November 11. The patient's white blood cell count was increasing, and she was less clinically septic. IV antibiotics were converted to oral Cipro. Her isolation was discontinued, and she remained afebrile. The patient's platelets counts continued to be low; however, this will be managed as an outpatient.

DISCHARGE MEDICATIONS:
Floxin 400 mg twice daily.
Mycostatic swish and swallow 5 mL three times daily.

Patient is discharged in improved condition.
Diet and activity as tolerated.
The patient will follow-up with me in my office in 1 week.

Case Study 1

History and Physical

CHIEF COMPLAINT: Neutropenic sepsis.

HISTORY OF PRESENT ILLNESS:

This is 64-year-old white female with a known history of non-Hodgkin's lymphoma. The patient has been treated with chemotherapy and, on evaluation by Oncology, was found to be febrile and neutropenic. She was felt to be clinically septic. There was also evidence of significant neutropenia. The patient was admitted to the Oncology floor for antibiotic therapy, monitoring of her blood counts, medications to raise her white and hemoglobin counts, and to be placed in reverse isolation.

PAST MEDICAL HISTORY: Non-Hodgkin's lymphoma and hypertension.

SOCIAL HISTORY: Nonsmoker, no alcohol use.

FAMILY HISTORY: Positive for cancer and heart disease.

REVIEW OF SYSTEMS: Negative.

PHYSICAL EXAMINATION:
Vital Signs: Blood pressure 132/90, respirations 28, temperature 102.
HEENT: Negative except for dry oral mucous membranes. No thrush or herpetic lesions.
Neck: Supple, no carotid bruit. No evidence of adenopathy.
Lungs: Clear.
Cardiac: Slightly tachycardic, but no murmur.
Abdomen: Soft, nontender, positive bowel sounds.
Extremities: Bilateral pulses. Poor muscle tone. No evidence of deep venous thrombosis or cellulitis.

ASSESSMENT:
1. Neutropenic sepsis, status postchemotherapy.
2. Non-Hodgkin's lymphoma.

PLAN:
1. Admit and place in reverse isolation.
2. Intravenous hydration.
3. Intravenous antibiotics.
4. Continue present medications.
5. Follow blood counts.

Case Study 1

Progress Notes:

1/6: Admit Note: Patient with non-Hodgkin's lymphoma admitted to isolation for neutropenic sepsis secondary to chemotherapy.

1/7: S: "Feel better today."
 O: Vital signs stable, WBCs 0.1, platelets 14,000, temperature 101.3, blood and urine cultures negative.
 A: Responding to antibiotics, still dehydrated.
 P: Continue IV fluids and antibiotics. Transfuse platelets and PRBCs. Begin Neupogen injections.

1/8: S: No complaints.
 O: Vitals stable, temp 99.8, transfusion reaction last night requiring IV steroids and Benadryl.
 A: Continued improvement, responded well to steroids and Benadryl for transfusion reaction.
 P: Continue current meds, transfuse PRBCs and platelets tomorrow.

1/9: S: "I feel great."
 O: WBC at 3,500, platelets at 14,000, afebrile, vitals stable.
 A: Less clinically septic, tolerated transfusions well with no adverse reaction.
 P: Discontinue isolation, change antibiotics to p.o. Discontinue IV fluids.

1/10: S: "I want to go home."
 O: Afebrile, platelets still low.
 A: Ready for discharge, will manage platelets as an outpatient.
 P: Discharge home.

Orders:

1/6: 1. Admit to reverse isolation.
 2. IV fluids at 83 mL/h with IV Fortaz and gentamicin.
 3. Urine and blood cultures.
 4. Chemistry profile.
 5. CBC, WBC.
 6. Type and cross 4 units.
 7. PA and lateral CXR
 8. Vitals q. shift.

1/7: 1. Begin daily Neupogen injections.
 2. Transfuse 2 units PRBCs and platelets.

1/8: Continue with current treatment.

1/9: 1. Transfuse 2 units PRBCs and platelets.
 2. Discontinue isolation.
 3. Discontinue IV fluids when finished and switch to p.o. antibiotics.

1/10: Discharge home.

Case Study 1

Answer Sheet

DIAGNOSES	ICD-9-CM CODES					
Principal Diagnosis				.		
DX 2				-		
DX 3				-		
DX 4				-		
DX 5				-		
DX 6				-		
DX 7				-		
DX 8				-		
DX 9				-		

Code ICD-9-CM Diagnoses and Procedures
(Five diagnosis codes and three procedure codes will be needed)

Case Study 2

Inpatient Face Sheet

Admit Date: 1/11/2015

Discharge Date: 1/15/2015

Sex: Female

Age: 50

Disposition: Home

Admit Diagnoses:
1. Right upper lobe lesion
2. Asthmatic bronchitis
3. Depression

Discharge Diagnoses:
1. Non–small-cell carcinoma right upper lobe
2. Metastasized to hilar and thoracic lymph nodes
3. Chronic obstructive pulmonary disease
4. Depression

Procedures:
1. Flexible bronchoscopy
2. Right upper lobe lobectomy with diagnostic biopsies

Case Study 2

Discharge Summary

Admitted: 1/11/2015
Discharged: 1/15/2015

DISCHARGE DIAGNOSES:
1. Non–small-cell carcinoma right upper lobe of lung with metastasis to hilar and thoracic lymph nodes
2. Chronic obstructive pulmonary disease
3. Depression

PROCEDURES PERFORMED:
1. Flexible bronchoscopy
2. Right upper lobe lobectomy

HISTORY OF PRESENT ILLNESS:
This is a 50-year-old female with a 3 cm lesion in the right upper lobe. She had an episode of bronchitis in January. Subsequent chest x-ray revealed a lesion in the right upper lobe. A CAT scan of the chest was performed, and the presence of the lesion in the right upper lobe was confirmed.

HOSPITAL COURSE:
The patient underwent flexible bronchoscopy with right upper lobectomy on November 11, 2010. The findings were a 3 cm lesion in the right upper lobe with metastasis to the lymph nodes. The patient tolerated the procedure well. Vital signs remained stable. There was minimal chest tube drainage. She was advanced to a regular diet the second postoperative day.

LABORATORY DATA:
Routine laboratory work on admission showed potassium of 4, BUN 10, creatinine 0.6. WBCs 8.8, hemoglobin 13.7, and hematocrit 38.2. Platelet count 288,000. The urinalysis was negative. PT was 10.1. Discharge laboratory was unchanged with the exception of BUN 12, creatinine 0.9. Hemoglobin 11.3 and hematocrit 34.2.

EKG: Sinus rhythm.

IMAGING: The preoperative chest x-ray showed a 3 cm suspicious nodule in the right upper lobe with chronic obstructive pulmonary disease. Postoperative chest x-ray showed good expansion of the right middle and lower lobes.

The patient was discharged on the fourth postoperative day in satisfactory condition. Regular diet as tolerated. She is to limit activity for the next 3 weeks. She will follow-up in my office in 1 week.

Discharge medications include: Vicodin 1 tablet p.o. q4h prn for pain. Elavil 150 mg h.s., Ventolin 2 puffs q.i.d.

Case Study 2

History and Physical

CHIEF COMPLAINT: Right upper lobe lesion.

HISTORY OF PRESENT ILLNESS:
This is a 50-year-old female with a 3 cm lesion in the right upper lobe. She had an episode of bronchitis in January. Subsequent chest x-ray revealed a lesion in the right upper lobe. A CAT scan of the chest was performed, and the presence of the lesion in the right upper lobe was confirmed. The patient is admitted at this time for a bronchoscopy and right thoracotomy.

REVIEW OF SYSTEMS:
Patient denies hematemesis, melena, and angina pectoris. There is no complaint of syncope, claudication, or edema.

HEENT:	No masses. Pupils equal, round, reactive to light. No oral cavity lesions. No evidence of JVD; thyroid is not enlarged. No carotid bruits.
Chest:	Symmetrical.
Lungs:	Clear to auscultation and percussion. No wheezing.
Heart:	No murmurs, no gallops, regular rhythm.
Abdomen:	No masses, no organomegaly.
Extremities:	No cyanosis, clubbing, or edema. Good peripheral pulses.

PAST MEDICAL HISTORY:
She has asthmatic bronchitis and has been hospitalized twice in the past for bronchitis. Patient is currently treated for depression. She has no history of diabetes mellitus, hypertension, myocardial infarction, or neurological deficits. She has had no surgeries.

MEDICATIONS: Elavil 150 mg h.s., Ventolin 2 puffs q.i.d.

ALLERGIES: None known.

SOCIAL HISTORY: She smokes two packs of cigarettes per day and has smoked for 30 years.

FAMILY HISTORY: Noncontributory.

IMPRESSION:
1. Right upper lobe lesion
    a. Rule out bronchogenic carcinoma.
    b. Rule out benign lesion.

2. Asthmatic bronchitis
3. Depression

PLAN: Patient is admitted for bronchoscopy and right thoracotomy with right upper lobectomy. The procedures and the risks involved were fully explained to the patient and all questions answered. An informed consent was signed by the patient.

Case Study 2

Operative Report

DATE OF OPERATION:	1/11/2015
PREOPERATIVE DIAGNOSIS:	Right upper lobe lesion
POSTOPERATIVE DIAGNOSIS:	Carcinoma of the right upper lobe with metastasis to hilar and thoracic lymph nodes
SURGEON:	Hector Gonzalez, MD
OPERATIVE PROCEDURE:	1. Flexible bronchoscopy 2. Right upper lobe lobectomy

INDICATIONS: Female patient with a 3 cm lesion centrally located in the right upper lobe.

FINDINGS:

The bronchoscopy was negative. On thoracotomy there was a 3 cm lesion centrally located in the right upper lobe. There were positive nodes in the hilar and thoracic lymph nodes.

DESCRIPTION OF PROCEDURE:

Under general anesthesia, the flexible bronchoscope was introduced through both lumen of the endotracheal tube. The carina was normal. Both the right and left bronchial trees were visualized down to the subsegmental level. There was no evidence of endobronchial lesions. The bronchoscopy was negative.

After prepping and draping the operative area, a right posterolateral thoracotomy was made. The incision was deepened through the skin, subcutaneous tissue, and latissimus dorsi muscle. The serratus anterior muscles were retracted anteriorly, and the chest was entered through the fifth intercostal space. On exploration of the right lung there was a 3 cm lesion centrally located in the right upper lobe. A right total lobectomy was performed based on the above findings. Surrounding lymph nodes were inspected and diagnostic biopsies were obtained from both the hilar and surrounding thoracic nodes.

Frozen section was positive for non–small-cell carcinoma. The bronchial resection margin was negative for tumor. The inferior pulmonary ligament was taken all of the way up to the inferior pulmonary vein. The bronchial stump was checked up to a pressure of 35 mm Hg and there was no air leak. Hemostasis was again secured. A chest tube was placed through a separate stab wound and secured to the skin with 0 silk. The incision was closed using #2 Vicryl pericostal sutures, #1 Vicryl for the latissimus dorsi muscle, 2-0 Vicryl for the subcutaneous tissue, and staples for the skin.

The estimated blood loss was less than 200 mL. The patient tolerated the procedure very well and was taken to the recovery room in good condition with stable vital signs.

Case Study 2

Progress Notes:

1/11:   Admit Note: A 50-year-old female found to have a 3 cm lesion in the right upper lobe. She is admitted at this time for flexible bronchoscopy and right thoracotomy.

1/12:   S: Complains of incisional pain.
        O: Vital signs stable, labs within normal limits, minimal chest tube drainage.
        A: Post-op CXR shows good expansion of right middle and lower lobes.
        P: Patient doing well from surgical standpoint, will remove chest tube in a.m.

1/13:   S: Less pain, depressed with diagnosis.
        O: Vitals remain stable, afebrile, good lung sounds.
        A: Progressing nicely.
        P: Advance to full diet, increase ambulation.

1/14:   S: Feels better today.
        O: Afebrile, vital signs stable, labs look good.
        A: Incisions clean and dry with no redness.
        P: Possible discharge tomorrow.

1/15:   S: Ready to go home.
        O: Discharge labs and CXR within normal limits.
        A: Incisions healing well.
        P: Discharge patient.

Orders:

1/11:   1.   Admit patient.
        2.   Have consents signed for flexible bronchoscopy and right thoracotomy.
        3.   Place pre-op diagnostics on chart.

1/12:   1.   Ambulate patient.
        2.   Repeat CXR.
        3.   Repeat labs.

1/13:   1.   Advance to full diet.
        2.   Increase ambulation.

1/14:   No new orders.

1/15:   Discharge patient.

Case Study 2

Answer Sheet

DIAGNOSES	ICD-9-CM CODES					
Principal Diagnosis				-		
DX 2				-		
DX 3				-		
DX 4						
DX 5						

PROCEDURES	ICD-9-CM CODES				
PP 1			-		
PX 2			-		
PX 3			-		

Code ICD-9-CM Diagnoses and Procedures
(Twelve diagnosis codes and one procedure code will be needed)

Case Study 3

Inpatient Face Sheet

Admit Date:	1/10/2015
Discharge Date:	1/15/2015
Sex:	Male
Age:	55
Disposition:	Home with home health care

Admitting Diagnoses:
1. Diabetic ulcer
2. Uncontrolled diabetes, type 1
3. Chronic renal failure
4. Pneumonia

Discharge Diagnoses:
1. Diabetic ulcer
2. Uncontrolled diabetes with peripheral circulatory disease
3. Pneumonia
4. Anemia
5. Chronic renal failure

Procedure:
1. Excisional debridement decubitus ulcer

Case Study 3

Discharge Summary

Admitted: 1/10/2015
Discharged: 1/15/2015

ADMITTING DIAGNOSES:
1. Diabetic ulcer
2. Uncontrolled diabetes
3. Chronic renal failure
4. Pneumonia

DISCHARGE DIAGNOSES:
1. Diabetic ulcer
2. Uncontrolled diabetes with peripheral circulatory disease, type 1
3. Pneumonia
4. Anemia
5. Chronic renal failure

PROCEDURE:
1. Excisional debridement decubitus ulcer

HISTORY:
This is a 55-year-old male who was admitted through the emergency room for elevated blood sugars and a necrotic heel ulcer of the left foot. The patient was admitted for control of his blood sugars and treatment of the heel ulcer.

PAST MEDICAL HISTORY:
This patient has a long history of type 1 diabetes, chronic kidney failure, coronary artery disease of the native artery with history of CABG, and peripheral vascular disease with subsequent below knee amputation of the right leg.

HOSPITAL COURSE:
The patient was admitted to the hospital and started on intravenous antibiotic therapy. The patient was placed on sliding scale insulin therapy as well as wound care for the heel necrosis. The patient's left heel ulcer was debrided of all necrotic tissue on January 11. There was no cellulitis of the foot; however, there were multiple areas of skin breakdown on the foot. The patient had no feeling in his left foot, secondary to severe diabetic neuropathy. The patient was continued on local wound care and antibiotic therapy. The patient's renal failure was monitored and fluids restricted. The patient's chest x-ray was positive for left lower lobe pneumonia. Sputum culture was not ordered because the patient was already on intravenous antibiotic therapy for the skin ulcer.

Case Study 3

Discharge Summary

Continued:

LABORATORY DATA:
Hemoglobin 9.4, hematocrit 29.6, WBC 8,600, platelet count 336,000. Urinalysis was normal except for a small amount of bacteria, and proteinuria. Sodium was 130, potassium 4.1, chloride 92, CO_2 32, glucose 270, BUN 53, and creatinine 3.2.

DISCHARGE MEDICATIONS:
70/30 insulin in the morning and 20 units in the evening
Cardizem CD 180 mg once daily
Imdur 60 mg once a day
Lasix 80 mg once a day
Pepcid 20 mg twice a day
Paxil 10 mg three times a day
Nitrostat prn
Patient is prescribed Floxin once daily times 7 days

The patient was felt to have reached maximum benefit of hospitalization and was discharged home in fair condition. He will be followed by home health care for wound care and monitoring of his diabetes as well as chronic renal failure. He is to continue with a 1,800 ADA diet. His activity is limited due to his wheelchair. He is to have no weight bearing on his left foot. He will follow up in my office in 10 days.

Case Study 3

History and Physical

CHIEF COMPLAINT: Diabetic ulcer left foot, elevated blood sugars.

HISTORY OF PRESENT ILLNESS:
This is a 55-year-old white male who presented to the emergency room because of high blood sugars. This patient has a long history of type 1 diabetes. He also has chronic kidney failure due to his diabetes. This gentleman also has a history of coronary artery disease, CABG, and myocardial infarction in 1998. He has diabetic peripheral vascular disease with a history of below the knee amputation of his right leg. He presently has an open necrotic area on the left foot, most likely due to PVD.

PAST MEDICAL HISTORY:
He denies hypertension, shortness of breath. Significant past history is detailed above.

PAST SURGICAL HISTORY: See above.

ALLERGIES: None known.

MEDICATIONS:
70/30 insulin in the morning and 20 units in the evening, Cardizem CD 180 mg once daily, Imdur 60 mg once a day, Lasix 80 mg once a day, Pepcid 20 mg twice a day, Paxil 10 mg three times a day, Nitrostat as needed.

SOCIAL HISTORY:
Patient lives with his wife. He does not smoke or drink. Patient is disabled due to his chronic illness.

FAMILY HISTORY: Noncontributory.

PHYSICAL EXAMINATION:

Vital Signs:	Temperature 97.7, pulse 77, respirations 20, blood pressure 146/62.
HEENT:	Unremarkable.
Neck:	Carotid bruit. The neck is supple.
Heart:	Regular rate and rhythm.
Lungs:	Clinically clear.
Abdomen:	Soft, nontender, no organomegaly.
Extremities:	Right below the knee amputation. There is a necrotic area on the left heel and an open ulcer on the left foot.

Case Study 3

History and Physical

Continued:

DIAGNOSTIC DATA:

The patient's labs that have been done show a hemoglobin of 9.4, hematocrit of 29.6, white blood count 8.6, platelet count 336,000. Urinalysis is abnormal with 25–50 RBCs, 50–100 WBCs, small amount of bacteria, glycosuria, and proteinuria. Chemistry: sodium 130, potassium 4.1, chloride 92, CO_2 31, anion gap is 11, glucose 260. BUN 53 and creatinine 3.2. Blood cultures and urine cultures have been ordered. The patient has been started on Floxin 400 twice a day. He had a CT scan of the head, which is negative.

His EKG reveals right bundle branch block with right axis deviation, bifascular block, right bundle branch block with left posterior fascicular block.

IMPRESSION:
1. Uncontrolled diabetes.
2. Atherosclerotic cardiovascular heart disease (native artery).
3. Diabetic peripheral vascular disease with left heel and foot ulcer and neuropathy.
4. Carotid stenosis.
5. Status post right below the knee amputation.
6. End-stage renal disease.

Case Study 3

Progress Notes:

1/10: Admit Note: 55-year-old diabetic male admitted for elevated blood sugars and necrotic heel ulcer of left foot. Patient has a long history of type 1 diabetes, PVD with BKA right in 1995. Patient has CRF, not yet requiring dialysis.

1/11: S: Complains only of chest pain from coughing.
       O: Glucose under better control with sliding scale coverage, last accucheck is 203, renal stable, BUN 57, and creatinine 3.8.
       A: Foot ulcers debrided at bedside of necrotic tissue.
       P: Continue IV antibiotics and wound care for ulcers.

1/12: S: Feeling better.
       O: BS at 189, BUN/creatinine at 54/3.6, CXR shows clearing of infiltrates.
       A: Foot healing nicely, respiratory status improving.
       P: Continue current treatment plan.

1/13   S: No complaints.
       O: BS leveling, now at 160. Renal status is stable.
       A: Patient is improving, foot ulcer is healing well.
       P: DC IV fluids when completed and start on PO meds.

1/14: S: Patient is ready to go home.
       O: Wounds look good, BS now in good control, renal status stable.
       A: Patient can be discharged tomorrow, reaching maximum medical improvement.
       P: Will plan discharge tomorrow.

1/15: Discharge note: Patient will be followed by home health care for wound care and monitoring of type 1 diabetes and renal failure.

Orders:

1/10: 1. Admit patient.
       2. CBC, WBC, Chem profile, CXR, EKG.
       3. IV antibiotics.
       4. Sliding scale insulin, accuchecks q2h.
       5. Whirlpool therapy for ulcers.

1/11: 1. Debridement tray at bedside.
       2. Continue with wound care treatment.

1/12: 1. Adjust sliding scale.
       2. Repeat labs and CXR.

1/13: 1. DC IVs when finished.
       2. Switch to Floxin 400 mg twice daily.

1/14:   Repeat labs.

1/15:   Discharge home with home health care.

Case Study 3

Answer Sheet

DIAGNOSES	ICD-9-CM CODES					
Principal Diagnosis				-		
DX 2				-		
DX 3				-		
DX 4				-		
DX 5				-		
DX 6				-		
DX 7				-		
DX 8				-		
DX 9				-		
DX 10				-		
DX 11				-		
DX 12				-		

PROCEDURES	ICD-9-CM CODES				
PP 1			-		

**Code ICD-9-CM Diagnoses and Procedures
(Three diagnosis codes and two procedure codes will be needed)**

Case Study 4

Inpatient Face Sheet

Admitted: 11/18/2014

Discharged: 11/21/2014

Sex: Male

Age: 68

Disposition: Home

Admitting Diagnoses:
1. Severe anemia
2. Hypertension
3. SOB, rule out cardiac origin
4. Atrial fibrillation

Discharge Diagnoses:
1. Severe blood loss anemia
2. Atrial fibrillation
3. Hypertension

Procedures:
1. Esophagogastroduodenoscopy
2. Colonoscopy

<u>**Case Study 4**</u>

Discharge Summary

Admitted: 11/18/2014
Discharged: 11/21/2014

ADMITTING DIAGNOSES:
1. Severe anemia
2. Hypertension
3. SOB, rule out cardiac origin
4. Atrial fibrillation

DISCHARGE DIAGNOSES:
1. Severe blood loss anemia
2. Atrial fibrillation
3. Hypertension

PROCEDURES PERFORMED:
1. Esophagogastroduodenoscopy
2. Colonoscopy

HISTORY OF PRESENT ILLNESS:
Patient presented to my office with complaints of shortness of breath and fatigue. Patient was found to have severe anemia and immediately admitted to the hospital as an inpatient. Patient did not have complaints of abdominal pain or indicate melena or hemoptysis.

PAST MEDICAL HISTORY:
Treatment for hypertension and atrial fibrillation. On Lanoxin and Lopressor.

HOSPITAL COURSE:
The patient was admitted with severe anemia. Patient was transfused 4 units of packed red blood cells with improvement in H/H. Patient was placed on telemetry for cardiac monitoring. Gastrointestinal workup revealed no source of bleed, and patient will be followed as an outpatient for further workup. The patient tolerated the EGD and colonoscopy without complaints or complications.

The patient is discharged home in good condition. Activity and diet as tolerated. He will follow up with me in my office in 1 week.

Case Study 4

History and Physical

CHIEF COMPLAINT: Fatigue and shortness of breath.

HISTORY OF PRESENT ILLNESS:
This 68-year-old male presented to the office complaining of shortness of breath and fatigue for 3 days duration. Blood test performed in the office revealed hemoglobin of 7.3 and hematocrit of 24.3. The patient denies blood in stool and test done in the office was negative. Also denies any abdominal pain or hemoptysis. Patient was admitted from the office with diagnosis of anemia.

PAST MEDICAL HISTORY:
He is currently treated for hypertension and atrial fibrillation.

PAST SURGICAL HISTORY: Remote appendectomy.

ALLERGIES: None known.

MEDICATIONS: Lanoxin and Lopressor.

FAMILY HISTORY: Noncontributory.

SOCIAL HISTORY:
Patient is married and lives with his wife. Quit smoking in 1985 and uses alcohol socially.

REVIEW OF SYSTEMS:
Integument: Skin warm, dry, and pale.
HEENT: Unremarkable.
Respiratory: Clear to auscultation. Admits to SOB.
Cardiac: Regular rhythm.
Abdomen: Soft, bowel sounds present, no masses.
Rectal: Deferred as performed in office.
Extremities: Pedal pulses bilaterally, no clubbing, or edema.

IMPRESSION:
1. Severe anemia.
2. Shortness of breath, rule out cardiac origin.
3. Hypertension.
4. Atrial fibrillation.

PLAN:
1. Admit to telemetry under Dr. Emilia Warren's services.
2. Cardiac consult with Dr. Lee.
3. Rule out blood loss anemia.

Case Study 4

Cardiac Consult

Date of Consult: 11/18/2014
Consulting Physician: Dr. Ashanti Lee
Requesting Physician: Dr. Emalia Warren

REASON FOR CONSULTATION: Shortness of breath.

HISTORY OF PRESENT ILLNESS:
I am asked to see this patient for evaluation of shortness of breath to rule out cardiac origin. See history and physical for complete details.

PHYSICAL EXAMINATION:
Skin: Warm and dry.
HEENT: Unremarkable.
Chest: Clear breath sounds. No SOB at this time.
Cardiac: Rhythm shows atrial fibrillation.
Abdomen: Soft, good bowel sounds, no tenderness
Extremities: Good pedal pulses, no edema.
Vital Signs: Blood pressure 140/93. Heart rate 80. Respirations 12. Temperature 99.2.

LABORATORY DATA: Electrolytes good. CPKs and Troponin normal. CBC revealed H/H to be 8.9/32.4 after transfusion on admission.

CHEST X-RAY: Normal.

EKG: Atrial fibrillation.

IMPRESSION:
1. Atrial fibrillation.
2. Hypertension.
3. SOB, no cardiac origin, probable due to severe anemia.

PLAN:
1. Continue telemetry for one more day in light of atrial fibrillation.
2. Control hypertension.
3. Continue treatment of anemia.

Case Study 4

Procedure Note

Date:	11/19/2014
PREOPERATIVE DIAGNOSIS:	Severe anemia
POSTOPERATIVE DIAGNOSIS:	Severe anemia
PROCEDURE:	Esophagogastroduodenoscopy
SURGEON:	Dr. Carlos Waldron

DESCRIPTION OF PROCEDURE:

The esophagogastroscope was inserted through the oropharynx and taken down to the second portion of the duodenum, which was normal. The antrum and fundus of the stomach revealed no pathology. There was a small hiatal hernia noted.

The scope was removed and the patient tolerated the procedure without complication.

FINDINGS:

Normal findings, other than small hiatal hernia. No bleeding noted.

Case Study 4

Procedure Note

Date of Procedure:	11/19/2014
Preoperative Diagnosis:	Severe anemia
Postoperative Diagnosis:	Severe anemia
Surgeon:	Makena Mitchell, MD
Procedure:	Colonoscopy
Indications:	Severe anemia, r/o lower GI bleed as source.

DESCRIPTION OF PROCEDURE:
Following IV sedation, the colonoscope was inserted into the rectum and advanced to the left colon and beyond the splenic flexure and into the ascending colon and into the cecum. The entire colon was normal with no signs of bleeding. The scope was gradually withdrawn, and the patient tolerated the procedure well.

Case Study 4

Progress Notes:

11/18:   Admit note: Severe anemia in a 68-year-old male. Patient complains of SOB and fatigue for several days. Cardiac consult with Dr. Lee to rule out cardiac source for SOB. Will transfuse 2 units PRBCs now and run serial CBCs. Telemetry to monitor heart rate, control hypertension until cardiac origin for SOB ruled out. Will schedule patient for GI workup.

11/19:   S: Less SOB and fatigued, no complaints.
            O: Hypertension under good control, as well as heart rate.
            A: H/H now at 9.3/34.5.
            P: Patient schedule for EGD and colonoscopy later today. Will transfuse 2 more units of PRBCs prior to scope.

11/20:   S: No complaints follow EGD and colonoscopy. No SOB and no fatigue.
            O: Anemia, likely due to blood loss, but no source of bleeding found.
            A: Tolerated scopes; upper and lower anatomy normal. H/H continues to rise.
            P: Monitor H/H one more day and plan for discharge tomorrow.

11/21:   S: No complaints. Feels well.
            O: Labs within normal limits, vital signs stable.
            A: Blood loss anemia, with no identified source.
            P: Discharge home and follow as an outpatient for possible additional workup to determine source of bleed.

Orders:

11/18:
1. Admit patient to telemetry.
2. Vitals q. 12 hours.
3. Two units PRBCs now.
4. Standard lab orders.
5. H/H q. 12 hours.
6. Consult Dr. Lee, Cardiology.
7. GI workup for bleeding source.
8. Prep for colonoscopy.

11/19:
1. EGD and colonoscopy today.
2. Transfuse 2 units PRBCs.
3. Continue with H/H monitoring.

11/20:   Continue monitoring H/H.

11/21:   Discharge home.

Case Study 4

Answer Sheet

DIAGNOSES	ICD-9-CM CODES					
Principal Diagnosis				-		
DX 2				-		
DX 3				-		

PROCEDURES	ICD-9-CM CODES				
PP 1			-		
PX 2			-		

Code ICD-9-CM Diagnoses and Procedures
(Eight diagnosis codes and one procedure code will be needed)

Case Study 5

Inpatient Face Sheet

Admit Date: 1/15/2015

Discharge Date: 1/18/2015

Sex: Male

Age: 53

Disposition: Home

Admit Diagnoses:
1. Upper GI bleeding
2. Alcohol abuse

Discharge Diagnoses:
1. Alcoholic gastritis with hemorrhage
2. Alcoholic cirrhosis
3. Obesity
4. Chronic obstructive pulmonary disease

Procedure:
1. Esophagogastroduodenoscopy

Case Study 5

Discharge Summary

Admitted: 1/15/2015
Discharged: 1/18/2015

DISCHARGE DIAGNOSIS:
1. Acute upper gastrointestinal bleeding secondary to gastritis
2. Alcoholic cirrhosis
3. Obesity

HISTORY:
This is a 53-year-old white male who presented to the emergency room on the day of admission after vomiting bright red blood. The patient had an onset of nausea early in the morning and he had bright red vomitus and brownish vomitus later and then passed a black stool. The patient has a long-standing history of alcohol abuse, and he is a heavy smoker.

His initial hemoglobin was 14.5, hematocrit 42.4; later this dropped to 13.1 and 37.6.

PAST HISTORY:
Significant for chronic smoking and alcohol abuse. Patient has a history of hernia repair in the past.

MEDICATIONS:
Patient is taking Pepcid 20 mg, Darvon, and hydrochlorothiazide.

ALLERGIES: None known.

PHYSICAL EXAMINATION:
A large, well-developed, and obese male in no acute distress. NG tube was passed. The patient's abdomen is soft and nontender. The patient's liver was down about four fingerbreadths. The patient's initial bilirubin was 3.4, SGOT 103, alkaline phosphatase 269, albumin was down to 2.2, and the prothrombin time was 14.5.

HOSPITAL COURSE:
Upper GI endoscopy revealed lower esophagitis and gastritis. The patient had no duodenal ulcers. The patient's bleeding stopped, and he was maintained on IV fluids the first 2 days of admission, followed by removal of NG tube and placed on a clear liquid diet, followed by bland, low-fat diet. The patient has made progressive improvement.

Case Study 5

Discharge Summary

Continued:

The patient had hepatitis C drawn and results have not been reported as yet. The patient's hemoglobin is stabilized at about 12 g. The patient's white count has remained normal, mean corpuscular volume is enlarged and compatible with alcohol liver disease. The patient's PT was elevated after vitamin K, this returned to a more normal level of 12.9. The patient's blood chemistries have been maintained. His electrolytes on the day of discharge revealed a sodium 137, potassium 3.5, BUN 6; creatinine was 0.8 and the remainder of the values within normal limits. His alkaline phosphatase is slightly high at 176. SGOT 75. Bilirubin still high at 3.4.

The patient's abdominal sonogram revealed thickening of the gallbladder wall with irregularity in the neck region. There were no visualized stones. There was no dilatation of the cystic or hepatic duct. The patient's chest x-ray revealed clear lung fields.

The patient has been informed that he has cirrhosis. The patient is discharged home in improved condition. He has been encouraged to stop smoking and drinking. He will be continued on Pepcid 20 mg and a multivitamin each day. Activity and diet as tolerated. He will follow up in my office in 1 week.

Case Study 5

History and Physical

CHIEF COMPLAINT:
Throwing up blood, dark tarry stool, and diarrhea for a few weeks.

HISTORY OF PRESENT ILLNESS:

The patient is a 53-year-old white male with no significant medical problems except a history of depression. He is a chronic smoker with COPD. His only surgery was a hernia repair 20 years ago. The patient was brought to the emergency room following several episodes of bright red vomitus. His hemoglobin and hematocrit is stable at 14.5/43.4. His guaiac was positive. NG tube was inserted and was positive for guaiac, and he was throwing up coffee-ground emesis, and he was admitted for upper GI.

PAST MEDICAL HISTORY:
Significant for depression, alcohol abuse, chronic smoker, arthritis.

MEDICATIONS:
He is taking Pepcid 20 mg, Darvon, and hydrochlorothiazide.

ALLERGIES: None known.

SOCIAL HISTORY:
He is married. Smokes two packs of cigarettes per day and drinks six to seven drinks nightly.

FAMILY HISTORY: Not significant.

PHYSICAL EXAMINATION:
He is alert and oriented x3. NG tube is passed through his nose. He is not in acute distress.
Vital signs are stable. Temp 98.5, blood pressure 125/60, pulse 88, respiration rate 20.

HEENT:	Pupils equal and reactive to light. Extraocular muscles intact, anicteric sclerae. No lesions on the scalp.
Neck:	Supple. No thyromegaly. No JVD. He has NG tube through his nose and bloodstain on his NG tube.
Chest:	Clear to auscultation. No rales. No wheezing.
Heart:	S1 and S2 audible. Regular rhythm.
Abdomen:	Bulky, but is soft and nontender. Bowel sounds positive. No hepatosplenomegaly.
Extremities:	Trace edema. Nontender calf muscles of his legs.

DIAGNOSTIC DATA:
WBC 3.9, hemoglobin 14.5, hematocrit 43 and platelets 197. PT 14.5, INR 1.5, PTT 30. Sodium 138, potassium 3.8, chloride 98, bicarb 32, BUN 7, creatinine 0.8, and glucose 105. He had low albumin 2.2, low protein 6.3, low calcium 8.7, and albumin/globulin ratio of 0.5.

EKG showed normal sinus rhythm and nonspecific T-wave changes. Chest x-ray is negative.

IMPRESSION:
A 53-year-old white male with a known history of depression, alcohol abuse, and chronic smoker admitted with upper GI bleed. Patient has had a NG tube inserted in the emergency room as well as being started on intravenous Pepcid. Patient also has depression and will continue his Paxil.

Case Study 5

Procedure Note

Date of Procedure: 1/16/2015
Preoperative Diagnosis: Upper GI bleeding
Postoperative Diagnosis: 1. Alcoholic gastritis
                                     2. Esophagitis
Surgeon: Huan Jing, MD
Procedure: Complete endoscopy to descending duodenum

An informed consent was obtained after which the patient underwent sedation and continuous monitoring of pulse oximetry and vital signs.

With the patient in the left lateral decubitus position, the video gastroscope was carefully advanced under direct visualization through the upper esophageal sphincter. Esophageal examination revealed esophagitis of the distal esophagus.

The scope was advanced into the stomach. Moderate gastritis was noted. Retroflexion revealed normal angularis, lesser curvature, and fundus of the stomach. The instrument was advanced across the pylorus into the duodenal bulb, which was unremarkable. The descending duodenum was also normal.

As the endoscope was being withdrawn, careful examination revealed no other findings. Patient appeared to tolerate the procedure well and was sent to the recovery area in stable condition.

His GI bleeding appears to have originated from gastritis and esophagitis. There was no active bleeding noted at this time. This is suspected to be secondary to alcohol.

Case Study 5

Progress Notes:

1/15: Admit Note: Patient presented to the emergency room after vomiting bright red blood. Patient has a long history of alcohol abuse. Patient had a NG tube inserted in the ER and was started on IV fluids. Patients H/H remains stable at this point. Will continue to monitor. Lab studies are significant for alcoholic liver disease.

1/16: S: Feels better, is hungry.
O: Patient's labs are within normal levels other than indicating chronic liver disease.
A: Patient tolerated EGD. There was no evidence of active bleeding, but bleeding source was presumed to be hemorrhagic gastritis secondary to alcohol.
P: Remove NG tube and place on clear liquid diet.

1/17: S: Patient feels improved, no complaints of abdominal pain.
O: Vital signs stable, afebrile.
A: Tolerating clear liquids.
P: Advance to soft diet.

1/18: S: No complaints.
O: Vitals stable, H/H WNL.
A: Patient much improved.
P: Discharge patient home.

Orders:

1/15: 1. Admit patient to service of Haley Renee, MD.
2. Keep on bed rest.
3. Monitor H/H.
4. Continue IV fluids at 85 mL/h.

1/16: 1. For EGD this afternoon.
2. Continue with current treatment.
3. Remove NG tube.
4. Clear liquid diet.
5. Ambulate with assistance.

1/17: 1. Repeat labs.
2. Advance to soft diet.

1/18: Discharge patient home.

Case Study 5

Answer Sheet

DIAGNOSES	ICD-9-CM CODES					
Principal Diagnosis				-		
DX 2				-		
DX 3				-		
DX 4				-		
DX 5				-		
DX 6				-		
DX 7				-		
DX 8				-		

PROCEDURE	ICD-9-CM CODE				
PP 1			-		

Code ICD-9-CM Diagnoses and Procedures
(Six diagnosis codes and four procedure codes will be needed)

Case Study 6

Inpatient Face Sheet

Admit Date: 11/27/2014
Discharge Date: 11/30/2014
Sex: Female
Age: 72
Disposition: Home

Admitting Diagnosis:
1. Chest pain, rule out acute coronary artery disease

Discharge Diagnoses:
1. Coronary artery disease
2. Unstable angina
3. Atrial fibrillation
4. Second-degree AV block
5. Status post percutaneous transluminal coronary angioplasty

Procedures:
1. Diagnostic left-heart catheterization, percutaneous transluminal coronary angioplasty, coronary angiograms

Case Study 6

Discharge Summary

Admitted: 11/27/2014
Discharged: 11/30/2014

ADMITTING DIAGNOSES:
1. Chest pain, rule out acute coronary artery disease

DISCHARGE DIAGNOSES:
1. Chest pain, acute intermediate coronary syndrome
2. History of arteriosclerosis of the native coronary vessels
3. Atrial fibrillation
4. Second-degree atrioventricular block

PROCEDURE PERFORMED:
1. Left-heart catheterization, selective coronary angiography, percutaneous transluminal coronary angioplasty.

HOSPITAL COURSE:

This is a 72-year-old female with a history of coronary artery disease, status post percutaneous transluminal coronary angioplasty several months ago. She came in with acute intermediate coronary syndrome. A myocardial infarction was ruled out. In view of these events, it was decided to perform a diagnostic heart catheterization and possible percutaneous transluminal coronary angioplasty versus bypass surgery.

A diagnostic heart catheterization was performed and showed the following: the left main coronary artery was open, the left anterior descending artery was open, and there was a previous stent in the circumflex system, which had no obstruction. There was a totally occluded distal right coronary artery. There was some collateral circulation filling the right coronary artery. In view of this, it was felt that the patient would benefit from percutaneous transluminal coronary angioplasty, so the patient received IV heparin, ReoPro, and intracoronary nitroglycerin, and we were able to open the distal right coronary artery with balloon angioplasty.

The patient began ambulation the day after the above procedure. The patient is stable at discharge. Discharge to home on atenolol 25 mg once a day, Monopril 10 mg once a day, and aspirin. She will follow a low-cholesterol, low-fat diet. She is to follow up in my office in 1 week.

Case Study 6

History and Physical

CHIEF COMPLAINT: Chest pain.

HISTORY OF PRESENT ILLNESS:
This is a 72-year-old white female with a history of coronary artery disease, status post percutaneous transluminal coronary angioplasty and stent implantation last summer, who has been taking Tenormin 50 mg once a day, Monopril 10 mg once a day, one aspirin a day, and nitroglycerin prn. She experienced an episode of palpitation and lightheadedness last night, and this morning she started having chest pain. The patient called 911 and the EMS staff found her with a very fast rhythm, heart rate of 160 per minute accompanied by atrial fibrillation. She denied any prior history of palpitations and denies chest pains prior to this episode. The patient denies diabetes mellitus or high blood pressure. She denies history of myocardial infarction in the past. She has a strong family history of coronary artery disease. She denies alcohol or smoking.

PAST MEDICAL HISTORY: The past history is only pertinent for coronary artery disease and low HDL, postmenopausal.

PAST SURGICAL HISTORY: History of back surgery.

ALLERGIES: Sulfa.

REVIEW OF SYSTEMS: See history of present illness. Patient denies paroxysmal nocturnal dyspnea, orthopnea, leg swelling, fatigue, or loss of consciousness.

PHYSICAL EXAMINATION:
General Appearance: Patient is alert, cooperative, and in no acute distress.

Vital Signs:	Her heart rhythm is regular. Telemetry shows a second-degree atrioventricular block, Mobitz type I, with beats 2 and 4, 2:3 conduction. No electrocardiogram evidence of ischemia.
Head and Neck:	Neck is supple. No jugular venous distention, no carotid bruits.
Lungs:	Clear.
Heart:	Irregular rate and rhythm. No murmur, gallop, or rub.
Abdomen:	Soft, nontender. Bowel sounds present. No tenderness on rebound.
Extremities:	No cyanosis or edema. Bilateral peripheral pulses.

ASSESSMENT:
1. Prolonged chest pain, rule out acute coronary artery disease.
2. Mobitz type I second-degree atrioventricular block.
3. Coronary artery disease, status post stent implantation 8 months ago.

PLAN:
1. Admit to telemetry. Obtain cardiac enzymes and serial electrocardiograms.
2. Hold Tenormin and place on Norvasc and nitrates.
3. Cardiac catheterization and electrophysiology study.

Case Study 6

Procedure Note

Date: 11/27/2014
Procedure: Left-heart catheterization
                                        Selective coronary angiography
                                        PTCA of distal right coronary artery
Pre Operative Diagnosis: Unstable angina r/o CAD
Post Operative Diagnosis: CAD
Surgeon: Chao Cheng, MD

Procedure Note:

A diagnostic left-heart catheterization was performed and showed the following: the left main coronary artery was open, the left anterior descending artery was open, and there was a previous stent in the circumflex system, which had no obstruction. There was a totally occluded distal right coronary artery. There was some collateral circulation filling the right coronary artery. In view of this, it was felt that the patient would benefit from percutaneous transluminal coronary angioplasty, so the patient received IV heparin, ReoPro, and intracoronary nitroglycerin, and we were able to open the distal right coronary artery with balloon angioplasty. There was no clot formation or dissection. The patient returned to the floor in stable condition.

Case Study 6

Progress Notes

11/27: S: Chest pain.
O: EKG and enzymes negative for AMI.
A: Unstable angina, probable coronary occlusion.
P: Heart cath. and possible PTCA.

11/28: S: Patient feels great, no chest pain.
O: Labs within normal limits, EKG stable; patient ambulating.
A: CAD.
P: Observe a few more days.

11/29: S: No chest pain, wants to go home.
O: Vitals stable, heart sounds good, regular rhythm.
A: Patient is stable, continues to do well.
P: Plan discharge for a.m.

11/30: S: "Never felt better."
O: CXR clear, labs and vitals within normal limits.
A: Patient stable for discharge.
P: Discharge now.

Orders

11/27: 1. Admit patient to telemetry.
2. Vitals q4h.
3. Prepare for left-heart catheterization and possible PTCA.
4. Continue home medications.
5. Serial EKGs.
6. Cardiac enzymes.
7. Cardiac diet
8. Hold Tenormin, place on Norvasc and IV nitrates.

11/28: Ambulate.

11/29: Discontinue all IVs.

11/30: Discharge patient.

Case Study 6

Answer Sheet

DIAGNOSES	ICD-9-CM CODES					
Principal Diagnosis				-		
DX 2				-		
DX 3				-		
DX 4				-		
DX 5				-		
DX 6				-		

PROCEDURES	ICD-9-CM CODES				
PP 1			-		
PX 2			-		
PX 3			-		
PX 4			-		

Code ICD-9-CM Diagnoses ONLY
(Six diagnosis codes will be needed)

Case Study 7

Inpatient Face Sheet

Admit Date: 12/02/2014
Discharge Date: 12/05/2014
Sex: Male
Age: 81
Disposition   Home

Admitting Diagnoses:
1. Unstable angina
2. Aortic stenosis
3. Atrial fibrillation

Discharge Diagnoses:
1. Acute anterior wall MI
2. Moderate aortic stenosis
3. Chronic atrial fibrillation
4. Herpes zoster
5. Hypertension

Case Study 7

Discharge Summary

Admitted: 12/02/2014
Discharged: 12/05/2014

ADMITTING DIAGNOSES:
1. Unstable angina
2. Aortic stenosis
3. Atrial fibrillation

DISCHARGE DIAGNOSES:
1. Acute myocardial infarction, anterior wall
2. Moderate aortic stenosis
3. Chronic atrial fibrillation
4. Herpes zoster
5. Hypertension

HISTORY: This 81-year-old Hispanic male presented to the emergency room complaining of chest pain that began that morning. Upon walking to retrieve his newspaper he began having discomfort in the chest as well as the right jaw. The pain was relieved with rest and was not associated with any sweating, syncope, or palpitations.

PHYSICAL EXAMINATION:
Vital Signs: Blood pressure 136/60. Heart rate was 100 to 120.

Heart: There was II/VI systolic murmur in the pericardium.

HOSPITAL COURSE: Following admission, the cardiac enzymes showed a CPK of 100, Troponin was positive at 4.6, and the relative index was 5.4. Digoxin level was 1.7. The BUN, creatinine, and electrolytes were unremarkable. The prothrombin time initially was 24.2, and prior to discharge, it was 15.1 with an INR of 1.6.

The admission electrocardiogram showed atrial fibrillation with rapid ventricular response and was positive for new anterior wall infarction. Chest x-ray showed a left lower lobe infiltrate but no obvious pneumonia.

This patient was seen by Dr. Maddie Kendall of Cardiology who concurred with the diagnosis of acute myocardial infarction with the elevation of Troponin and the patient's pain. The patient's hospital course was benign. He was maintained on Imdur 30 mg daily, Metoprolol 50 mg in the morning and 25 mg in the evening. He was also maintained on Nitro-Dur initially, which was then changed to Imdur. Anticoagulation was continued.

The patient stabilized, having no further symptoms. Patient was discharged home on Imdur 60 mg twice daily, Lanoxin 0.25 mg daily, and Coumadin. Continue Zovirax for herpes zoster. Diet is low fat, low cholesterol, and low sodium. No strenuous activity. Patient to follow up in my office in 1 week.

Case Study 7

History and Physical

CHIEF COMPLAINT: Chest pain and right jaw pain.

HISTORY OF PRESENT ILLNESS:
Patient began having chest and right jaw pain upon walking to get his newspaper. The pain lasted about 10–15 minutes but was relieved with rest. There was no associated sweating, palpitation, or syncope.

PAST MEDICAL HISTORY:
Irregular heartbeats and a history of myocardial infarction in 1965.

PAST SURGICAL HISTORY:
Includes tonsillectomy; appendectomy; cataract surgery and hernia repair, all remote.

CURRENT MEDICATIONS:
Digoxin 0.25 mg daily, Lopressor 25 mg twice daily, Imdur 30 mg daily, Coumadin 5 mg daily.

FAMILY HISTORY:
Noncontributory.

REVIEW OF SYSTEMS:
Unremarkable.

PHYSICAL EXAMINATION:
Admission evaluation revealed blood pressure of 136/60, heart rate from 100 to 120, temperature of 98.3.

HEENT:	Unremarkable.
Neck:	Supple, bilateral carotid bruits, no adenopathy.
Lungs:	Clear.
Heart:	S1 and S2 is normal, grade 2/6 systolic murmur all over the pericardium.
Abdomen:	Soft, nontender.
Extremities:	No edema of the feet.

PLAN:
1. Admit patient to coronary care.
2. Continue intravenous nitroglycerin drip.
3. Serial cardiograms and enzymes.

Case Study 7

Progress Notes:

12/2:   Admit Note: Patient admitted through the emergency room with chest pain. EKG revealed new infarct of anterior wall. Patient placed in CCU for cardiac monitoring and IV nitro.

12/3:   S: Patient feels well, no more chest pain.
       O: Vitals stable, cardiac enzymes within normal limits.
       A: Evolving inferior AMI.
       P: Continue monitoring.

12/4:   S: No chest pain, wants to go home.
       O: IVs discontinued, patient started on Imdur.
       A: Patient doing well from cardiac standpoint.
       P: Plan discharge for tomorrow.

12/5:   S: Ready for discharge.
       O: Vitals stable, heart rhythm regular.
       A: Tolerating change in meds.
       P: Discharge patient.

Orders:

12/2:
1. Admit to coronary care.
2. Follow CCU protocol.
3. IV nitro.
4. Continue home meds.
5. Cardiac enzymes.
6. Serial EKGs.
7. Cardiac diet.
8. Chemistry profile.
9. Dig level.
10. PT level.

12/3:
1. Cardiac enzymes
2. Transfer to PCU
3. Continue home meds.
4. Ambulate with assistance.

12/4:
1. Discontinue IVs.
2. Start on Imdur 60 mg twice daily.

12/5:   Discharge patient.

Case Study 7

Answer Sheet

DIAGNOSES	ICD-9-CM CODES					
Principal Diagnosis				-		
DX 2				-		
DX 3				-		
DX 4				-		
DX 5				-		
DX 6				-		

Code ICD-9-CM Diagnoses ONLY
(Four diagnosis codes)

Case Study 8

Inpatient Face Sheet

Admit Date:	12/18/2014
Discharge Date:	12/22/2014
Sex:	Female
Age:	74
Disposition:	Home with home health care

Admitting Diagnoses:
1. Chronic obstructive pulmonary disease with upper respiratory infection
2. Hypertension
3. Thoracoabdominal aneurysm

Discharge Diagnoses:
1. Acute exacerbation of chronic obstructive lung disease
2. Hypertension
3. Thoracoabdominal aneurysm

Case Study 8

Discharge Summary

Admitted: 12/18/2014

Discharged: 12/22/2014

ADMITTING DIAGNOSIS:
1. COPD with upper respiratory infection

DISCHARGED DIAGNOSIS:
1. Acute exacerbation of chronic obstructive lung disease
2. Hypertension
3. Thoracoabdominal aneurysm

HISTORY:
This is a 74-year-old female who was admitted for exacerbation of chronic obstructive pulmonary disease. Please see details of history and physical.

PAST MEDICAL HISTORY:
This patient has a history of COPD. She has had GI bleeding secondary to AVM in the past. She has a history of GI reflux and hypertension. She has a large thoracoabdominal aneurysm; however is not a surgical candidate due to her severe COPD.

HOSPITAL COURSE:
The patient was admitted and placed on intravenous steroids and intravenous antibiotics with Claforan, oxygen, inhalation therapy, and mucolytics. Her chest tightness and wheezing gradually improved with the medications and respiratory therapy.

IMAGING: The chest x-ray was clear other than the thoracic aneurysm. Her follow-up x-ray was also clear.

EKG: Sinus rhythm with left ventricular hypertrophy type changes.

LABORATORY DATA: Oxygen saturation on 2 L revealed 94% to 98%, and on room air she desaturated to 90%. The biochemical profile showed a BUN of 17, creatinine of 1.1, potassium 3.5, sugar 136. The liver function tests were normal. CBC showed a white count of 10.2, hemoglobin 13, and hematocrit of 39.

DISCHARGE MEDICATIONS: Cough syrup including Ventolin solution, Benadryl elixir, and Tylenol with codeine elixir 2 teaspoons q.i.d. Cefzil 250 1 b.i.d. for 7 days. Humibid LA 2 b.i.d. Tagamet 400 mg b.i.d. Provera 2.5 mg daily. Senokot 25 at h.s. Nebulizer with Atrovent and Albuterol q.i.d. Ativan 1 b.i.d. as needed. Home oxygen at 2 L.

The patient is discharged home in stable condition. She will be followed by home health care. Diet and activity as tolerated. She will follow up in my office in 1 week.

Case Study 8

History and Physical

CHIEF COMPLAINT: Increased shortness of breath.

HISTORY OF PRESENT ILLNESS: This is a 74-year-old white female admitted to the hospital with dyspnea. The patient has a known history of COPD and has been controlled with medications at home. She has not been on home oxygen. One week ago, she had acute onset of a respiratory infection with wheezing and increasing shortness of breath. She was seen in the office and started on antibiotics and steroids. However, she returned to the office today with worsening symptoms and inability to sleep because of her breathing problems and acute dyspnea.

PAST MEDICAL HISTORY: COPD with previous smoking history. She has had a history of GI bleed secondary to AVM. She has GI reflux and hypertension. She has a large thoracoabdominal aneurysm.

SOCIAL HISTORY: Married. No alcohol and currently not smoking.

MEDICATIONS: Humibid LA 2 b.i.d, Tagamet 400 mg b.i.d, Provera 2.5-mg daily, Senokot 25 at h.s. Nebulizer with Atrovent and albuterol q.i.d. Ativan. Diazide one a day. Aerobid two puffs b.i.d. Multivitamin, and Biaxin 500 mg b.i.d.

ALLERGIES: None known.

REVIEW OF SYSTEMS: No chest pains, palpitations, no complaints of stomach, bowel, or urinary symptoms.

PHYSICAL EXAMINATION: Acutely ill female. She is dyspneic, using accessory muscles for respiration with a respiratory rate of 28. Pulse is 100. O$_2$ was 92% on room air. She has audible wheezing.

Neck:	No JVD.
Lungs:	Diffuse inspiratory and expiratory wheezing and diminished breath sounds overall.
Cardiac:	Sounds were obscured.
Abdomen:	Soft. Palpable aortic consistent with aneurysm.
Extremities:	Without edema.
Heart:	Has had a murmur in the past.
Chest X-ray:	Enlargement of thoracic aneurysm. No infiltrates.

IMPRESSION: Severe COPD with secondary bronchitis and worsening pulmonary status, unresponsive to outpatient treatment.

PLAN: Patient is to be placed on oxygen. She is admitted for intravenous antibiotics, breathing treatments, and respiratory care. She will be placed on intravenous steroids.

Case Study 8

Progress Notes:

12/18:   Admit Note: 74-year-old female admitted for acute exacerbation of COPD. Patient was tried on outpatient antibiotics and steroid therapy without relief. She requires acute hospital care for IV antibiotics and respiratory care.

12/19:   S: Breathing is easier.
           O: CXRs clear, breathing is easier.
           A: Chest tightness and wheezing improving.
           P: Continue with IV Claforan and respiratory care.

12/20:   S: Feeling much better.
           O: Respiratory status improving. Vital signs stable, afebrile.
           A: Patient continues to improve.
           P: Continue current treatment plan.

12/21:   S: Feels good.
           O: Afebrile, vitals stable. Labs within normal limits.
           A: Good respiratory improvement.
           P: DC IVs. Case Management for discharge planning.

12/22:   S: Anxious to go home.
           O: Vitals good, afebrile, lungs clear.
           A: Ready for discharge.
           P: Discharge patient today.

Orders:

12/18:   1. Admit patient to service of Elizabeth Ann, MD.
         2. CXR.
         3. IV Claforan.
         4. Respiratory care.
         5. CBC, WBC, liver function studies, Chem profile.

12/19:   Continue with current orders.

12/20:   Add Tylenol with codeine elixir 2 teaspoons q.i.d.

12/21:   1. DC IV fluids.
         2. Make arrangements for home O_2.

12/22:   Discharge patient home with home health care.

Case Study 8

Answer Sheet

DIAGNOSES	ICD-9-CM CODES					
Principal Diagnosis				-		
DX 2				-		
DX 3				-		
DX 4				-		

Code ICD-9-CM Diagnoses and Procedures
(Eight diagnosis codes and five procedure codes)

Case Study 9

Inpatient Face Sheet

Admit Date: 11/24/2014

Discharge Date: 12/01/2014

Sex: Female

Age: 70

Disposition: Home

Admitting Diagnoses:
1. Acute abdominal pain, rule out diverticular disease
2. History of hypertension

Discharge Diagnoses:
1. Perforated sigmoid colon secondary to diverticulitis
2. Dense intra-abdominal adhesions
3. Hypertension
4. Postoperative atelectasis
5. Acute pharyngitis
6. Small bowel defect requiring resection

Procedures Performed:
1. Hartmann's procedure, lysis of adhesions, small bowel resection, colostomy
2. Flexible sigmoidoscopy

Case Study 9

Discharge Summary

Admitted: 11/24/2014

Discharged: 12/01/2014

ADMITTING DIAGNOSES:

1. Acute abdominal pain, probably due to diverticular disease
2. History of hypertension

DISCHARGE DIAGNOSIS:

1. Perforated sigmoid colon secondary to diverticulitis
2. Dense intra-abdominal adhesions
3. Hypertension
4. Pulmonary atelectasis, persistent postoperative
5. Acute pharyngitis

PROCEDURES:

1. Hartmann's procedure, lysis of adhesions, small bowel resection
2. Flexible sigmoidoscopy

HISTORY OF PRESENT ILLNESS:

This is a 70-year-old white woman who had, on the day of admission, undergone an outpatient colonoscopy. The physician was unable to advance the scope past the sigmoid colon and felt she had a perforated bowel secondary to diverticulitis. She has had a history of numerous episodes of diverticulitis.

PAST MEDICAL HISTORY: Hypertension, hysterectomy, appendectomy.

MEDICATIONS ON ADMISSION: Inderal-LA and aspirin.

ALLERGIES: None known.

PHYSICAL EXAMINATION:

Reveals an elderly white woman with tenderness in the left lower quadrant of the abdomen.

LABORATORY DATA:

The admission laboratory data were within normal limits with the exception of low hematocrit of 34, hemoglobin 11.8, and elevated globulin 3.9. Postoperatively, white count was over 19,000, transiently returning to normal in 2 days. The hemoglobin dropped to 10.1 with hematocrit of 29.7.

RADIOLOGY REPORTS:

Gastrografin enema findings were suggestive of perforation at the level of the rectosigmoid at a point where the patient had extensive diverticula.

Case Study 9

Discharge Summary

Continued:

Chest x-ray revealed pneumomediastinum and subcutaneous emphysema, but no pneumothorax. There was air in the retroperitoneum. The follow-up chest x-rays showed nasogastric tube in satisfactory position with decreased subcutaneous emphysema within the neck and decreased pericardial air collection since the prior study, and development of small bilateral effusions on November 11. The abdominal x-rays showed a large amount of free retroperitoneal air and air in the mediastinum.

HOSPITAL COURSE:
The patient was admitted and started on intravenous antibiotics with Unasyn and tobramycin combination.

The patient was seen in consult by gastrologist who felt she probably had an acute sigmoid perforation secondary to diverticular disease. He felt she would benefit with Gastrografin enema, especially to determine whether she could be treated conservatively or not. The procedure was completed with the findings as mentioned above. It was felt she would require resection.

She was taken to the operating room where the above procedures were performed. The patient tolerated the procedure well under general anesthesia. The estimated blood loss was less than 100 mL with no replacement. The pathology report revealed diverticulosis with diverticulitis and perforation of the small bowel.

Postoperatively, the wound was healing nicely. The colostomy was noted to be viable. She was transferred to the surgical floor on November 25. She was having the expected amount of abdominal discomfort postsurgery. She also complained of sore throat and was started on Cepacol throat lozenges. The intravenous fluids and medications were continued.

The colostomy was not functioning over the first few days. There was minimal drainage from the nasogastric tube. Reglan was added. Breath sounds were decreased over the right lower lobe on November 28. The chest x-ray revealed atelectasis. CXRs were done daily and the RLL was reexpanded on November 30.

The colostomy began functioning on November 29. Intravenous fluids were discontinued. Intravenous Lasix was given. Her diet was increased with toleration. Activity was increased and medications were changed to p.o.

The patient improved significantly in the next several days, and she was stable enough to be discharged. She will be followed in the office in 1 week. She is discharged on Duricef 500 mg b.i.d. and Tylox one q4h prn soft diet and activity as tolerated.

Case Study 9

History and Physical

CHIEF COMPLAINT: Abdominal pain.

HISTORY OF PRESENT ILLNESS:
The patient is a 70-year-old white female who has undergone attempted colonoscopy this morning. There was difficulty in negotiating the sigmoid colon and the patient developed tenderness post colonoscopy. Abdominal x-rays revealed free air as well as mediastinal air.

PAST MEDICAL HISTORY: Hypertension, hysterectomy, appendectomy.

MEDICATIONS ON ADMISSION: Inderal-LA and aspirin.

ALLERGIES: None known.

PHYSICAL EXAMINATION:
Well-developed, well-nourished, 70-year-old white female in moderate distress.

REVIEW OF SYSTEMS:

Cardiac:	Normal sinus rhythm.
Pulmonary:	Clear.
HEENT:	Within normal limits.
Abdomen:	Soft with left lower quadrant pain and some distention.
Extremities:	Bilateral pedal pulses.

Patient will be admitted for conservative management in hopes of avoiding surgery. She will receive intravenous antibiotic and bowel rest.

Case Study 9

Procedure Note

DATE OF PROCEDURE: 11/24/2014

PROCEDURE: Attempted full colonoscopy

SURGEON: Aaron Nair, MD

INDICATION: Abdominal pain with history of diverticular disease

DESCRIPTION OF PROCEDURE:

With the patient in the left lateral position under direct luminal vision, a complete colonoscopy was attempted, but the Olympus colonoscope was only advanced up to 30 cm inside the sigmoid. The findings were as follows:

1. Rectum and anal canal: Internal hemorrhoids are seen in circumferential fashion, not bleeding at the time. No evidence of masses, lesions, angioma, or polyps seen in the rectal area.
2. Rectosigmoid junction, sigmoid, and descending colon: Extensive sigmoid diverticulosis with significant peridiverticulitis and spasm appreciated in a highly redundant sigmoid.

In view of the fact that the diverticular process was so extensive and the sigmoid extremely redundant, the advancement of the scope beyond this area was difficult and hence the procedure was terminated.

The patient returned to the floor in stable condition.

FINAL IMPRESSION:

1. Extensive sigmoid diverticulosis with diverticulitis and spasm.
2. Redundant sigmoid.
3. Internal hemorrhoids.

Case Study 9

Procedure Note

DATE OF PROCEDURE:	11/24/2014
PREOPERATIVE DIAGNOSIS:	Perforated sigmoid colon
POSTOPERATIVE DIAGNOSIS:	1. Perforated sigmoid colon
	2. Dense intra-abdominal adhesions
PROCEDURE:	1. Hartmann's procedure
	2. Lysis of adhesions
	3. Small bowel resection
SURGEON:	Amadeusz Worton, MD

FINDINGS: Moderately large perforation of the sigmoid colon approximately 2 cm in diameter with pelvic phlegmon. Dense intra-abdominal adhesions requiring extensive lysis taking 2 hours.

DESCRIPTION OF PROCEDURE:

The patient was taken to the operating suite and placed in the supine position. After adequate induction of general anesthesia the patient was prepped and draped in sterile fashion. A midline incision was made and the abdomen was entered. Dense adhesions were encountered requiring extensive sharp dissection.

The area of transection in the proximal sigmoid was dissected out circumferentially. The mesentery was taken down between Kelly clamps. Rectosigmoid was mobilized. The distal sigmoid was dissected out circumferentially and a roticulator placed across this. A stapler was fired, the bowel was transected.

Small bowel adhesions were lysed. One area was extremely thin, resulting in a serosal defect, which required resection. An area in the mid jejunum was dissected out circumferentially both proximally and distally. The intervening mesentery was serially cross-clamped between Kelly clamps. The vessels were ligated with 2-0 silks. G.A. was fired across both sides. Functional end-to-end anastomosis was then performed.

The abdomen was irrigated with copious amounts of fluid. A Jackson-Pratt drain was placed in the pelvis. Attention was then directed toward closure. The proximal defect was made in the left lower quadrant. Transected colon was brought out through the colostomy defect without difficulty. Upon adequate sponge, needle, lap, and instrument count the abdominal wound was closed with running #2 Prolene suture.

The subcutaneous tissue was irrigated with copious amounts of antibiotic solution. The cautery was utilized for hemostasis. The skin was loosely approximated. A Jackson-Pratt drain was secured with a 3-0 Nylon. A sterile dressing was applied and attention turned toward maturation of the colostomy.

The colon was secured to the fascia with three interrupted 3-0 Vicryl sutures. The colon was than transected and the colostomy matured in the usual fashion with interrupted 3-0 Vicryl sutures. The colostomy appliance was placed and the patient was taken to the recovery room, having tolerated the procedure well.

Case Study 9

Progress Notes:

11/24: Admit Note: Patient admitted following attempted colonoscopy. Physician was unable to advance the scope past the sigmoid colon and felt she had perforated bowel secondary to diverticulitis. This patient has a long history of diverticulitis. Laboratory data is within normal limits with the exception of H/H of 11.8/34. Patient was taken to surgery for resection of bowel. She tolerated the procedure well with minimal blood loss. The pathology report revealed diverticulitis and bowel perforation.

11/25: S: Incisional pain.
   O: H/H dropped to 10.1/29.7, WBC 19,000, vital signs stable.
   A: Good postoperative course so far.
   P: Continue present treatment.

11/26: S: Less surgical pain.
   O: WBCs coming down, now at 14,000, vitals stable, incisions clean and dry.
   A: Continues to improve.
   P: Begin ambulation, maintain liquid diet.

11/27: S: Complaining of sore throat.
   O: WBCs normal, incisions healing nicely, colostomy still not functioning but viable.
   A: Acute pharyngitis.
   P: Continue all meds; add Cepacol lozenges for sore throat.

11/28: S: Throat still sore, some surgical pain.
   O: Minimal NG drainage, decreased breath sounds RLL.
   A: Wound healing nicely, possible atelectasis.
   P: Get CXR to evaluate atelectasis.

11/29: S: Feels better, throat less sore.
   O: CXR shows persistent post-op atelectasis RLL, colostomy beginning to function.
   A: Good post-op course.
   P: Advance diet; remove NG tube, CXR daily.

11/30: S: More comfortable with NG tube out.
   O: CXR improved, RLL expanded, tolerating diet.
   A: Continues to improve, colostomy functioning nicely.
   P: Plan for discharge tomorrow.

12/01: S: Ready to go home.
   O: Wounds clean and dry, afebrile, tolerating diet.
   A: Good post-op recovery.
   P: Discharge today.

Case Study 9

Orders:

11/24: 1. Admit patient and prep for bowel resection.
      2. Transfer to SICU following surgery.
      3. Follow unit protocol.
      4. Vitals q4h.
      5. IV Unasyn and tobramycin.
11/25: 1. Transfer to surgical floor.
      2. Continue all current meds and treatment.
      3. Cepacol throat lozenges for sore throat.
11/26: 1. Portable CXR.
      2. Continue all orders.
11/27: CXR daily.
11/28: Advance diet.
11/29: Remove NG tube.
11/30: Discontinue IVs.
12/01: Discharge.

Case Study 9

Answer Sheet

DIAGNOSES	ICD-9-CM CODES					
Principal Diagnosis				.		
DX 2				.		
DX 3				.		
DX 4				.		
DX 5				.		
DX 6				.		
DX 7				.		
DX 8				.		

PROCEDURES	ICD-9-CM CODES				
PP 1			.		
PX 2			.		
PX 3			.		
PX 4			.		
PX 5			.		

Code ICD-9-CM Diagnoses and Procedures
(Four diagnosis codes and two procedure codes will be needed)

Case Study 10

Inpatient Face Sheet

Admitted: 12/14/2014

Discharged: 12/17/2014

Sex: Female

Age: 35

Disposition: Home

Admitting Diagnosis:
1. Ovarian cyst

Discharge Diagnoses:
1. Ovarian cyst
2. Postoperative blood loss
3. Urinary tract infection

Procedures:
1. Total abdominal hysterectomy
2. Bilateral salpingo-oophorectomy
3. Exploratory laparotomy

Case Study 10

Discharge Summary

Admitted: 12/14/2014

Discharged: 12/17/2014

DISCHARGE DIAGNOSES:
1. Ovarian cyst
2. Uterine adhesions
3. Urinary tract infection
4. Postoperative anemia

PROCEDURES PERFORMED:
1. Exploratory laparotomy
2. Hysterectomy
3. Bilateral salpingo-oophorectomy

HISTORY:
This 35-year-old female has experienced pelvic pain for 3 months duration. Pelvic ultrasound revealed a right ovarian cystic mass. She was admitted for elective surgery.

PAST MEDICAL HISTORY:
Refer to History and Physical for complete history.

HOSPITAL COURSE:
Patient underwent exploratory laparotomy that revealed a benign cyst of the right ovary and adhesions of the uterus requiring hysterectomy and bilateral salpingo-oophorectomy. She tolerated the surgery without complication. Postoperative course was significant for postoperative anemia, requiring transfusion of PRBCs. She also was noted to have elevated temperature and cultures indicated a urinary tract infection. She was already on IV antibiotics postsurgery that would also cover the UTI. She progressed well, in spite of the anemia and the UTI, and she was discharged in good condition on December 17. She was given a prescription for antibiotics and iron pills. Activity as tolerated; however, no driving for 2 weeks. Diet as tolerated. She is to see me in 3 days for postoperative follow-up and staple removal.

Case Study 10

History and Physical

CHIEF COMPLAINT: Pelvic pain.

HISTORY OF PRESENT ILLNESS:

This 35-year-old gravida 3, para 3, has complained of pelvic pain for 3 months duration. Pelvic ultrasound revealed her right ovary to be enlarged with a large cystic mass. She is admitted today for elective exploratory laparotomy. The patient understands that she may require a hysterectomy and possible salpingo-oophorectomy.

PAST MEDICAL HISTORY: Negative, except for childbirth.

PAST SURGICAL HISTORY: No surgeries.

SOCIAL HISTORY: Nonsmoker, nondrinker.

FAMILY HISTORY: Noncontributory.

ALLERGIES: Penicillin.

MEDICATIONS: None.

REVIEW OF SYSTEMS:

HEENT: Within normal limits.

Neck: Supple. No lymphadenopathy.

Heart: Regular rhythm, no murmurs.

Lungs: Clear to auscultation.

Abdomen: Soft. Good bowel sounds. Pelvic pain on palpation.

Rectal: Deferred.

Extremities: Within normal limits.

IMPRESSION:
1.   Ovarian cyst.

PLAN:
1.   Exploratory laparotomy.

Case Study 10

Procedure Note

Date of Procedure:	12/14/2014
Preoperative Diagnosis:	Ovarian cyst, right
Postoperative Diagnosis:	Right ovarian cyst
Surgeon:	Dr. Ajambo Odehiambo
Anesthesiologist:	Dr. Cedric Alger
Procedure:	Exploratory laparotomy
	Hysterectomy, bilateral salpingo-oophorectomy

DESCRIPTION OF PROCEDURE:

Following administration of general anesthesia, the patient's abdomen was prepped and draped in sterile manner. A midline incision was done below the umbilicus to the pubis symphysis and then taken down to the fascia. The muscles were separated and the peritoneum was cut, taking care to avoid the bladder and bowel. There was a large cystic mass on the right ovary measuring 6 × 8 centimeters. The right ovary and tube with the cyst intact were removed. The left tube and ovary were removed in similar fashion. The decision was made to perform a hysterectomy and this was carried out without complications. All bleeders were ligated using 0-Vicryl. The pelvic cavity was irrigated with saline. The abdomen was then closed using 2-0 Dexon and the skin was closed using staples. The patient tolerated the procedure and was discharged to the recovery room in good condition.

Estimated blood loss: 400 mL

Pathology Report

Specimens:

1. Uterus dense adhesions
2. Left ovary and fallopian tube
3. Right ovary and fallopian tube with cystic mass

Microscopic Diagnosis:

1. Uterus:
   Mild chronic cervicitis
2. Left fallopian tube and ovary:
   Atrophic ovary with normal fallopian tube
3. Right fallopian tube and ovary:
   Normal right tube and benign cyst of the ovary

Case Study 10

Progress Notes:

12/14: Patient admitted to surgical floor following exploratory laparotomy, hysterectomy, and bilateral salpingo-oophorectomy. Patient tolerated the procedure well. Is fully awake and complains of moderate surgical pain. Patient will remain NPO until the evening meal and then will have a soft diet. Ambulate upon full recovery from anesthesia.

12/14: S: Moderate pain.
     O: Incision clean and dry, vital signs good. H/H 9.8/35.4. Was 12.9/42.3 on admission. Temp elevated to 101.2.
     A: Probable post-op anemia.
     P: Monitor H/H, continue with present pain medication.

12/15: S: Feels okay.
     O: Incision clean and dry, vitals good. H/H dropped to 8.10/32.2. Temp still elevated 100.1.
     A: Possible occult infection.
     P: Will culture to r/o infection. Continue to monitor H/H.

12/16: S: Complains of minor pain at operative site.
     O: Vital signs good. H/H at 10.9/39.8 after transfusion. Temperature 99.9.
     A: Urine culture revealed UTI. Treated with antibiotics. Ambulating freely, progressing well.
     P: Change to p.o. antibiotics, monitor H/H, probable discharge tomorrow.

12/17: S: Feels well, ready to go home.
     O: Incision healing well, vital signs good. H/H at 11.2/42.1. Temperature normal.
     A: Ready for discharge.
     P: Discharge home; follow up in office in 1 week.

Orders:

12/14: 1. Admit patient to surgical floor from recovery.
     2. Standard postoperative orders.
     3. Vital signs q.6 hours.
12/15: 1. Blood and urine cultures to rule out infection.
     2. Transfuse 2 units PRBCs.
     3. Continue with IV antibiotics.
12/16: 1. Change IV antibiotics to p.o.
     2. Continue to monitor H/H.
12/17: Discharge home.

Case Study 10

Answer Sheet

DIAGNOSE	ICD-9-CM CODE					
Principal Diagnosis				-		
DX 2				-		
DX 3				-		
DX 4				-		

PROCEDURES	ICD-9-CM CODES				
PP 1			-		
PX 2			-		

Code ICD-9-CM Diagnosis Code and CPT Codes for Procedure(s) and Radiology
(One diagnosis code and two CPT codes will be needed)

Case Study 11

Emergency Room Visit Face Sheet

Date of Service:	01/01/2015
Age:	25
Sex:	Female
Admitting Diagnosis:	Injury to left wrist
Discharge Diagnosis:	Sprain left wrist
Disposition:	Home

Case Study 11

Emergency Room Visit

DATE OF SERVICE: 1/01/2015

HISTORY OF PRESENT ILLNESS:
Initial encounter for a 25-year-old female who was at work today when a bread tray fell on her left wrist. She has persistent pain in the area, which is exacerbated with moving the wrist and hand. She describes the pain as very severe.

PAST MEDICAL HISTORY: Noncontributory.

ALLERGIES: None.

PHYSICAL EXAMINATION:

General:	Well-developed, well-nourished female in moderate distress. Vitals are stable.
Skin:	Warm and dry.
HEENT:	Unremarkable.
Chest:	Symmetrical.
Extremities:	The left wrist is tender and mildly swollen, especially over the distal ulna with no gross deformity. Normal range of motion against resistance with moderate pain. No abrasions or lacerations. Normal distal neurosensory examination. The remainder of the extremity examination is within normal limits.
Neurological:	She is awake, alert, and oriented times three with no focal neurologic deficits.

RADIOLOGY EXAMINATION:
The patient was taken to the x-ray room where the wrist was x-rayed. No acute fractures appreciated in the AP and lateral views.

IMPRESSION: Left wrist sprain.

The patient was placed in a padded splint and was given a prescription for Darvocet. She will follow up with her physician next week.

Case Study 11

Answer Sheet

DIAGNOSE	ICD-9-CM CODE					
First Listed DX				-		

PROCEDURES	CPT CODES					MODIFIERS (If Applicable)		
PR 1						-		
PR 2						-		

Note: E&M codes are assigned, when applicable, for outpatient clinic and emergency department visits. Because each hospital facility has its own unique system to assign the appropriate E&M codes, the appropriate codes would range from 99281 to 99285 with modifier -25 for this case.

Code ICD-9-CM Diagnoses Codes
(Two diagnosis codes will be needed)

Case Study 12

Emergency Room Visit Face Sheet

Date of Service: 01/15/2015

Age: 7

Sex: Male

Admitting Diagnosis: Fever, abdominal pain, vomiting

Discharge Diagnosis: Acute pyelonephritis due to *E. coli*
                            Nausea and vomiting

Disposition: Home

Case Study 12

Emergency Room Visit

Date: 01/15/2015

HISTORY OF PRESENT ILLNESS:
This is a 7-year-old boy who is brought to the emergency room by his parents. He has been running an elevated temperature for the past 12 hours; the high was 103. He also complains of stomach pains and vomiting. The parents are very concerned.

PAST MEDICAL HISTORY: Negative.

ALLERGIES: None.

MEDICATIONS: None.

SOCIAL HISTORY: Patient lives with his parents.

PHYSICAL EXAMINATION:

General: Well-developed, well-nourished child who is lethargic and pale. His temperature is 101. Pulse 110. Respirations 28.

HEENT: Eyes are normal. There is a minimal amount of inflammation of the tonsils. Ears, nose, and mouth are normal.

Neck: Supple.

Skin: Negative.

Chest: Lungs sounds are normal.

Heart: Normal rhythm with no murmurs appreciated.

Abdomen: Diffuse tenderness. No masses or organomegaly noted.

Neurological: Normal.

Extremities: Normal.

RADIOLOGY EXAMINATION: Renal x-ray was normal.

LABORATORY REPORTS:
Labs normal except for urinalysis, which was positive for *E. coli* > 100,000.

IMPRESSION:
1. Acute pyelonephritis.
2. Nausea and vomiting.
3. Discharged with Bactrim and will follow up with his physician.

Case Study 12

Answer Sheet

DIAGNOSES	ICD-9-CM CODES					
First Listed DX				-		
DX 2				-		

Note: E&M codes are assigned, when applicable, for outpatient clinic and emergency department visits. Because each hospital facility has its own unique system to assign the appropriate E&M codes, the appropriate codes would range from 99281 to 99285 for this case.

Code ICD-9-CM Diagnoses Code
(One diagnosis code will be needed)

Case Study 13

Emergency Room Visit Face Sheet

Date of Service:	01/02/2015
Age:	65
Sex:	Female
Admitting Diagnosis:	Nose bleed
Discharge Diagnosis:	Recurrent nosebleed
Disposition:	Home

Case Study 13

Emergency Room Visit

DATE OF SERVICE: 01/02/2015

HISTORY OF PRESENT ILLNESS:
Patient presents to the emergency room with a history of waking up with her nose bleeding. This is the second occurrence of epistaxis that she has had. She states that the bleeding has resolved. Denies that she takes any aspirin.

PHYSICAL EXAMINATION:

HEENT: Normal tympanic membranes. The examination of the nares shows evidence of former bleeding site, it is now resolved. Oropharynx is normal.

Neck: Supple, no bruits.

Lungs: Clear.

IMPRESSION: Recurrent nosebleed.

The patient is to return to her primary physician if bleeding reoccurs.

Case Study 13

Answer Sheet

DIAGNOSES	ICD-9-CM CODES					
First Listed DX				-		

Note: E&M codes are assigned, when applicable, for outpatient clinic and emergency department visits. Because each hospital facility has its own unique system to assign the appropriate E&M codes, the appropriate codes would range from 99281 to 99285 for this case.

Code ICD-9-CM Diagnoses Code
(One diagnosis code will be needed)

Case Study 14

Emergency Room Visit Face Sheet

Date of Service: 01/17/2015

Age: 58

Sex: Male

Admitting Diagnosis: Indigestion

Discharge Diagnosis: Dyspepsia

Disposition: Home

Case Study 14

Emergency Room Visit

DATE OF EMERGENCY ROOM VISIT: 01/17/2015

HISTORY OF PRESENT ILLNESS:
Patient has complaints of indigestion for the past month. The indigestion occurs after eating heavy meals and/or physical exertion. The duration of pain lasts about 20 minutes. He states that he has had a previous cholecystectomy approximately 2 years ago.

There is no shortness of breath, nausea, vomiting, bloody stools, or sweating. There is a family history of heart disease with his father having bypass surgery in his 60s. His mother died of an MI 3 years ago. The patient has a history of smoking but is currently on the patch to help him stop. He does not exercise regularly. He denied any chest pains or cough. GU, Musc., Neuro, Skin, Eyes are negative.

PHYSICAL EXAMINATION:

Vitals:	Blood pressure 140/80, P 76, Resp. 16. Temperature is normal.
HEENT:	Head is normocephalic. No masses or lesions noted on the eyes. Oral mucosa is normal. Throat is normal.
Neck:	No distention of jugular vein.
Lungs:	Clear bilaterally to percussions and auscultation. No rubs, rales, or wheezing noted.
Heart:	Normal sinus rhythm. No rubs, gallops, or murmurs. Carotid arteries, abdominal artery and femoral arteries are normal. No bruits noted. Pedal pulses normal. No peripheral edema noted.
Abdomen:	No masses, tenderness, organomegaly.
Neurological:	Normal.
Extremities:	No clubbing, cyanosis, ischemia, or edema noted. Gait is steady. Good range of motion in all extremities.

PLAN:
At this point, the patient will not be placed on prescriptions. It was suggested that he take an over-the-counter antacid like Pepcid or Axid to help prevent heartburn. It was recommended that the patient make an appointment with his physician to follow up.

Case Study 14

Answer Sheet

DIAGNOSES	ICD-9-CM CODES					
First Listed DX				-		

Note: E&M codes are assigned, when applicable, for outpatient clinic and emergency department visits. Because each hospital facility has its own unique system to assign the appropriate E&M codes, the appropriate codes would range from 99281 to 99285 for this case.

Code ICD-9-CM Diagnoses Codes and CPT Procedure Code
(Four diagnosis codes and one procedure code will be needed)

Case Study 15

Ambulatory Care

Face Sheet

Date of Service: 01/15/2015

Age: 62

Sex: Male

Admitting Diagnoses: Urinary retention

Postoperative Diagnoses: Benign prostatic hypertrophy

Procedure: 1. Cystoscopy

                           2. Transurethral resection of the prostate

Discharge Disposition: Home

Case Study 15

History and Physical

DATE OF ADMISSION: 01/15/2015

ADMITTING DIAGNOSIS: Urinary Retention

HISTORY OF PRESENT ILLNESS:
This is a 62-year-old male who has been experiencing increasing signs of urinary retention with urgency and difficulty with urination.

PAST MEDICAL HISTORY:
Positive for severe COPD, requiring home oxygen at 2.5 L. Patient is also on steroids for COPD. Past history of myocardial infarction with coronary artery disease. Patient underwent cardiac catheterization but is not considered a surgical candidate.

ALLERGIES: None known.

MEDICATIONS:
Albuterol one dose four times a day; Theo-Dur 200 mg twice a day; Cardizem CD 120 mg once a day.

SOCIAL HISTORY: Significant for smoking two packs a day for 45 years. Occasional alcohol use.

FAMILY HISTORY: Noncontributory.

PHYSICAL EXAMINATION:

General:	The patient is awake, alert, and oriented.
HEENT:	Pupils are equal and react to light and accommodation. Extraocular muscles are intact.
Respiratory:	Prolonged expiratory phase. Scattered wheezes.
Cardiovascular:	Regular rate and rhythm. No murmurs, rubs, or gallops.
Abdomen:	Soft, nontender. Bowel sounds are present. No organomegaly.
Extremities:	No edema, cyanosis, or clubbing.
Neurologic:	Nonfocal.

PLAN:
Patient is admitted to ambulatory surgery for cystoscopy and possible transurethral resection of the prostate.

Case Study 15

Operative Report

Date of Operation:	01/15/2015
Preoperative Diagnosis:	Urinary retention
Postoperative Diagnosis:	Benign prostatic hypertrophy
	Incomplete bladder emptying
Operation:	Laser coagulation of the prostate
Surgeon:	Dai Ngyun, Jr., MD
Anesthesiologist:	Earl Kenna, MD
Anesthesia:	Spinal

DESCRIPTION OF PROCEDURE:

The patient was placed on the operating table in the lithotomy position after spinal anesthesia was given. External genitalia was prepped and draped in the sterile manner.

A 21-French cystoscope was introduced within the bladder. The bladder was carefully inspected, and there was no evidence of tumor. There was mild trabeculations in both ureteral orifices. At this time, the resectoscope was introduced and resection of the lateral lobes of the prostate was done, allowing complete opening of the prostatic urethra. All of the prostatic chips were removed from the bladder. The bladder was coagulated and completely smoothed out with the VaporTrode. An 18-French Foley catheter was inserted into the bladder and left indwelling.

The patient tolerated the procedure well and was sent to the recovery room in satisfactory condition.

The patient will be discharged home when fully recovered with Foley in place. Patient will see me in my office tomorrow for removal of the Foley.

Pathology Report

TISSUES:	Prostate tissue
PREOPERATIVE DIAGNOSIS:	Urinary retention
POSTOPERATIVE DIAGNOSIS:	Benign prostatic hypertrophy

GROSS DESCRIPTION:

Specimen received in formalin labeled "prostate tissue" consists of 9.0 × 9.0 × 2.5 cm, 40 g aggregate of multiple irregular rubbery gray-white, tan-yellow, and tan-pink tissue. Representative sections (40 chips) are submitted.

MICROSCOPIC DIAGNOSIS:

Prostate tissue:	Benign hyperplasia in 36 chips
	Foci of adenocarcinoma in four chips

Case Study 15

Progress Note:

The patient was taken to the OR where under spinal anesthesia; a cystoscopy and transurethral resection of the prostate was performed. The patient tolerated the procedure well and was transferred to the recovery room in satisfactory condition. Pathology report showed BPH and foci of adenocarcinoma in four chips.

Orders:

Standard postoperative orders.

Discharge from the recovery room when stable.

Vital signs q. 15 minutes x 4, q. 30 minutes x 2, then q. 1 hour until discharge.

Vicodin, 40 mg one tablet prn for pain.

Macrobid b.i.d. for 1 week.

Discharge patient home when fully recovered and stable with Foley indwelling.

Patient is to return to my office tomorrow for follow-up and Foley removal.

Case Study 15

Answer Sheet

DIAGNOSES	ICD-9-CM CODES					
First Listed DX				-		
DX 2				-		
DX 3				-		
DX 4				-		

PROCEDURE	CPT CODES					MODIFIERS (If Applicable)		
PR 1						-		

Code ICD-9-CM Diagnosis Code and CPT Codes for Procedure(s)
(Three diagnosis codes and one procedure code will be needed)

Case Study 16

Ambulatory Care

Face Sheet

Date of Service:	01/17/2015
Age:	52
Sex:	Male
Admitting Diagnosis:	Chest pain
Discharge Diagnoses:	Coronary artery disease, native artery
	Angina
	History of coronary artery bypass grafting
Procedures:	Left-heart catheterization
Disposition:	Home

Case Study 16

History and Physical

DATE OF ADMISSION: 01/17/2015

HISTORY OF PRESENT ILLNESS:
This is a 52-year-old male with a history of angina for which he underwent four-vessel coronary surgical revascularization. This was performed last December. He had a left internal mammary artery to the left anterior descending coronary artery, sequential saphenous vein graft to the obtuse marginal and diagonal vessels and a saphenous vein graft to the right coronary artery. His left ventricular function was normal.

More recently he has been having problems with chest pain. For this reason, he is now brought back to the cardiac catheterization laboratory for reevaluation.

ALLERGIES: Demerol and Biaxin.

LABORATORY DATA:
His laboratory studies reveal normal electrolytes, BUN, creatinine, and a mildly depressed hemoglobin and hematocrit of 13 and 38.8, respectively, with normochromic, normocytic indices. The platelet count is normal. PT and PTT are normal.

ELECTROCARDIOGRAM: Demonstrates sinus bradycardia and otherwise is normal.

PHYSICAL EXAMINATION:

Vital signs:	Stable.
General:	Well-developed, well-nourished male in no acute distress. Patient is oriented times three. Skin is warm and dry. Pupils round and equal. Neck supple; trachea is midline.
Chest:	Clear to auscultation and percussion.
Heart:	Normal sinus rhythm. No rubs or gallops appreciated.
Abdomen:	Soft without distention. There is no guarding or rebound. No organomegaly.
Extremities:	Unremarkable.

Further decisions will be based on cardiac catheterization test results. He is agreeable to proceed. He is aware of the risks that include bleeding, infection, heart attack, rhythm disturbance, death, stroke, reaction to dye, or damage to nerve or blood vessel.

He is aware of the alternatives of cardiac catheterization, which would include medical therapy and possibly stress testing. He is agreeable to catheterization.

Case Study 16

Cardiac Catheterization Report

Date of Catheterization:	01/17/2015
Procedure:	Cardiac catheterization
Preoperative Diagnosis:	Chest pain
	History of angina
Postoperative Diagnosis:	Coronary artery disease
Surgeon:	Marta Senka, MD
Assistant:	Salali Phillips, MD

Cardiac Catheterization Procedure:

The patient was brought to the cardiac catheterization laboratory n.p.o. with a peripheral intravenous line in place. The right groin was prepped and draped in the usual fashion. Local anesthesia was obtained with Xylocaine 2%.

Utilizing a modified Seldinger technique, the right femoral artery was entered percutaneously and a #5 French side-arm sheath was placed. Utilizing Judkin's technique and left and right 4 bend Judkin's catheters and a #5 French 110 cm pigtail catheter, left-heart catheterization was completed.

Upon completion, the arterial catheter and sheath were removed and hemostasis was achieved by direct pressure applied to the right groin. The patient tolerated the procedure well and left in stable condition.

IMPRESSION:
1. Severe native multivessel coronary arterial disease. Total occlusion of the proximal left anterior descending coronary artery after the first septal and first diagonal vessels.
2. Anatomically obstructive stenosis in the obtuse marginal vessel; 3 in its proximal and midportions.
3. Total occlusion of the mid right coronary artery.
4. Patent LIMA graft to the left anterior descending coronary artery.
5. Patent sequential saphenous vein graft to the diagonal vessel and OM-3 vessel. Small diseased diagonal vessel demonstrated.
6. Patent saphenous vein graft to the distal right coronary artery. Approximate 60%–70% stenosis in the midportion of the posterior descending coronary artery.
7. Normal left ventricular size and systolic contractile pattern.
8. Mildly elevated left ventricular end-diastolic pressure 16 mm Hg.

Case Study 16

Progress Note

1/17   Patient admitted for left-heart catheterization. Aware of risks and benefits. Agreeable to proceed.

1/17   LHC completed via right femoral approach. Tolerated well. SVG to Diag./OM patent. Stenosis at level of Diagonal at SVG. SVG–RCA patent. LIMA to LAD patent. Normal LV. Severe native CAD. Films to be reviewed. D/C home today.

Physician Orders:

1/17
1. NPO after MN except for meds.
2. D5 1/2 NSS with 10 mEq. KCL/l at 75 cc/hour on admit.
3. Pre-op meds.
4. Benadryl 50 mg p.o.
5. Tagamet 300 mg.
6. Consent for right- and left-heart catheterization.
7. Diet: Cardiac.

1/17
1. Darvocet –100 tab p.o. q. 4–6 hours PRN pain.
2. Tylenol #3 one tab p.o. q4h PRN pain if unrelieved by Darvocet
3. Maintain IV at 150 mL/hour x 4 hours, then Heplock.
4. Resume diet.
5. Bed rest for 3 hours, then bathroom privileges.
6. Blood pressure in right arm, pulse, respirations q. 15 minutes x 2; q. 30 minutes x2; q1h x 2 or until stable; the q4h. Call physician if heart rate 50 or > 100 systolic BP.
7. Check pulses distal to catheterization site q. 15 minutes x 2; q. 30 minutes x 2; q1h x 2; then q4h. Notify physician of loss of palpable pulse, complaint, or pain or coldness in distal extremity.
8. Check dressing for bleeding and hematoma q. 15 minutes x 2; q. 30 minutes x 2; then q1h x 2 and PRN.
9. Discharge when patient is stable.

Case Study 16

Answer Sheet

DIAGNOSES				ICD-9-CM CODES		
First Listed DX					-	-
DX 2					-	
DX 3					-	

PROCEDURE	CPT CODES					MODIFIERS (If Applicable)	
PR 1						-	

Code ICD-9-CM Diagnosis Codes and CPT Codes for Procedure(s)
(Two diagnosis codes and one procedure code will be needed)

Case Study 17

Ambulatory Care

Face Sheet

Date of Service:	01/18/2015
Age:	23
Sex:	Male
Admitting Diagnosis:	Injury to right knee
Discharge Diagnosis:	Tear medical meniscus right knee
Procedure:	Arthroscopy Medial meniscectomy
Disposition:	Home

Case Study 17

History and Physical

DATE OF ADMISSION: 01/18/2015

ADMITTING DIAGNOSIS: Twisting injury right knee

HISTORY OF PRESENT ILLNESS:
This patient was playing baseball 2 weeks ago when he sustained an injury to his right knee sliding into a base. Patient was seen in the emergency room (initial encounter) where x-rays were negative for any fractures. Patient has been keeping his leg elevated and keeping weight off it as much as possible.

PAST MEDICAL HISTORY: Negative.

ALLERGIES: None.

MEDICATIONS: None.

SOCIAL HISTORY: Patient smoked one pack a day for 10 years; alcohol, none.

PHYSICAL EXAMINATION:

General:	Well-developed, well-nourished male.
HEENT:	No gross lesions noted. Pupils round and equal. No icterus. No masses or thyroidomegaly. Oropharynx negative.
Neck:	No masses or thyroidomegaly.
Chest:	Clear to auscultation and percussion.
Heart:	Normal rhythm.
Abdomen:	No masses or rebound tenderness.
Extremities:	Right knee with recurrent swelling, locking and catching. 2+ effusion. Left knee is normal.

PLAN:
Patient will be admitted for 1-day surgery for arthroscopy of the right knee.

Case Study 17

Operative Report

Date of Operation:	01/18/2015
Preoperative Diagnosis:	Right knee medial meniscus tear
Postoperative Diagnosis:	Right knee medial meniscus tear
Operation:	Arthroscopic medial meniscectomy
Surgeon:	Edmundo Diego, MD
Anesthesia:	General
Anesthesiologist:	Branden Godfrey, MD

INDICATIONS:

This patient has a twisting injury to the right knee. He has had recurrent swelling, locking, catching involving the knee, 2+ effusion.

PROCEDURE:

The patient was taken to the operating room, and general anesthesia was induced without complications. A well-padded pneumatic tourniquet was placed to the right upper thigh. The right leg was prepped and draped in the normal fashion. Diagnostic arthroscopy was performed. The findings are as listed below.

Under direct visualization, a medial portal was established. The posterior horn of the medial meniscus was debrided. A shaver was then introduced and taken back to a stable rim. The rest of the knee was then probed, and the findings are listed below.

The scope was then withdrawn and the wound closed with #4-0 Vicryl. The patient tolerated the procedure well and was transferred to the recovery room.

FINDINGS:
1. Patello-femoral joint: No articular cartilage change.
2. Medial compartment: Grade 1 changes of the mediofemoral condyle, posterior horn degenerative meniscus tear.
3. Anterior cruciate ligament and posterior cruciate ligament intact.
4. Lateral compartment, no articular cartilage changes noted. Lateral meniscus is intact. A fissure is seen within the tibial surface.

Case Study 17

Progress Notes

Patient has a twisting injury to the right knee with recurrent swelling, locking, and catching. Patient was taken to the operating room where an arthroscopic medical meniscectomy was performed. Patient will be discharged with crutches and will make a follow-up appointment in 2 weeks.

Orders:

1. Standard postoperative orders.
2. Discharge from recovery room when stable.
3. Urinary catheterization if patient unable to void post-op x 1; then call physician.
4. Elevate right knee 20 degrees. Ice packs for 15 minutes then discontinue. Repeat x 1 hour.
5. Vital signs q. 15 minutes x 4; then q. 30 minutes x 2; then q. 1 hour until discharge.
6. Tylenol 500 mg q4h for pain.
7. Start on soft diet.
8. Discharge when patient is stable.

Case Study 17

Answer Sheet

DIAGNOSES		ICD-9-CM CODES					
First Listed DX					-		
DX 2					-		

PROCEDURE		CPT CODES				MODIFIERS (If Applicable)	
PR 1						-	

| Code ICD-9-CM Diagnosis Codes and CPT Codes for Procedures |
| (Four diagnosis codes and two procedure codes will be needed) |

Case Study 18

Ambulatory Care

Face Sheet

Date of Service: 01/03/2015

Age: 71

Sex: Female

Admitting Diagnosis: Scalp masses

Discharge Diagnoses: Sebaceous cyst, scalp

                           Hypertension

                           Chronic obstructive pulmonary disease

Procedure: Excision scalp masses x 2

Disposition: Home

Case Study 18

History and Physical

DATE OF ADMISSION: 01/03/2015

ADMITTING DIAGNOSIS: Scalp mass

HISTORY OF PRESENT ILLNESS:
Patient is returning for recurrent scalp masses. She had one removed approximately 1 year ago and now has two more.

PAST MEDICAL HISTORY:
Scalp mass, 1 year ago. Patient has a history of hypertension and COPD.

ALLERGIES: Sulfa.

MEDICATIONS: Tenormin and Alupent.

SOCIAL HISTORY:
She smoked 1/2 pack a day for 12 years; alcohol, social. She is retired and her hobbies include reading, gardening, and bingo.

PHYSICAL EXAMINATION:

General: Patient weighs 185. She is 5'6½" tall. BP 148/78. Pulse 80. Patient appears generally in good health considering her weight and history of COPD.

Head: Mass on the vertex of the scalp with another mass located in the right posterior occipital region.

HEENT: Pupils are equal, round, and reactive to light and accommodation. Extraocular muscles are intact. Fundi are poorly visualized.

Neck: Thyroid not palpable. No jugular venous distention.

Chest: Lungs showed resonant breath sounds equally with left basilar rales.

Heart: Regular rate and rhythm, no murmurs.

Abdomen: No masses or rebound tenderness.

Extremities: Normal with good reflexes.

PLAN:
Admit to day surgery for removal of scalp masses.

Case Study 18

Operative Report

Date of Operation:	01/03/2015
Preoperative Diagnosis:	Scalp mass x 2
Postoperative Diagnosis:	Scalp mass x 2
Operation:	Excision of scalp mass x 2
Surgeon:	Fairuza Padma, MD
Anesthesia:	Monitored anesthesia care
Anesthesiologist:	Jaden Allen, MD
Estimated Blood Loss:	Minimal
Drains:	None
Complications:	None

PROCEDURE:

Patient is taken to the operating room with her informed consent. She is prepped and draped in the usual manner. IV sedation is administered, and then local, using 1% lidocaine.

The first mass measuring 2 cm was on the vertex of the scalp. There is a scar here from a previous excision and a mass just posterior to it. The scar was excised through a 2 cm transverse incision with an elliptical incision, and she was found to have a sebaceous cyst, which was adherent to the scar and also tracking posteriorly. This was excised in its entirety. The wound was closed with 2-0 Prolene in an interrupted fashion.

Next, a 2.5 cm mass is located in the right posterior occipital region, and this area was anesthetized with 1% lidocaine and a 2.5 cm transverse incision made over this through the skin and subcutaneous tissue, and this mass is circumferentially dissected and excised.

The wound was closed with 3-0 Vicryl in interrupted fashion for the subcu, and we had a good skin closure with this. Steri-Strips and Benzoin applied. The patient tolerated the procedure well. She was written a prescription for Vicodin one q4h prn for pain.

Case Study 18

Pathology Report

Date:	01/03/2015
Physician:	Nicholle Atticus, MD
Preoperative Diagnosis:	Scalp mass x 2
Surgical Procedure:	Excision of scalp mass x 2
Postoperative Diagnosis:	Scalp mass x 2
Specimen(s):	1. Scalp mass
	2. Scalp mass
GROSS:	There are two containers.

Container number one, labeled "scalp mass," consists of an ovoid firm mass of smooth surfaced tissue with overall dimensions of 2 × 1.5 × 0.5 cm. The specimen is marked with India ink, bisected and entirely submitted in cassette "1."

Container number two, labeled "scalp mass," consists of multiple portions of yellow-gray-white soft tissue in aggregate 3 × 1.5 × 0.3 cm and totally submitted in cassette "2."

GROSS AND MICROSCOPIC EXAMINATION:

Mass from scalp:	(Specimen #1)	Sebaceous cyst
Mass from scalp:	(Specimen #2)	Sebaceous cyst

Case Study 18

Progress Notes:

Patient had removal of two scalp lesions. Tolerated procedure well. No complications. Will follow up in my office in 2 weeks. Normal diet, regular activities.

Orders:

1. Standard postoperative orders.
2. Discharge from recovery room when stable.
3. Urinary catheterization if patient unable to void post-op x 1; then call physician.
4. Vital signs q. 15 minutes x 4; then q. 30 minutes x 2; then q. 1 hour until discharge.
5. Tylenol 500 mg q4h for pain.
6. Start on soft diet.
7. Discharge when patient is stable.

Case Study 18

Answer Sheet

DIAGNOSES	ICD-9-CM CODES					
First Listed DX				-		
DX 2				-		
DX 3				-		
DX 4				-		

PROCEDURES	CPT CODES					MODIFIERS (If Applicable)		
PR 1						-		
PR 2						-		

> **Code ICD-9-CM Diagnosis Codes and Procedure Codes**
> **(Four diagnosis codes and three procedure codes will be needed)**

Case Study 19

Inpatient Face Sheet

Admit Date:	1/15/2015
Discharge Date:	1/17/2015
Sex:	Female
Age:	46
Disposition:	Home

Admitting Diagnoses:
1. Herniated cervical disk
2. Neck and right arm pain
3. Asthma

Discharge Diagnoses:
1. Herniated C7-T1 disk
2. Radiculopathy secondary to above
3. Asthma
4. Respiratory distress secondary to morphine

Procedures:
1. Cervical fusion, anterior
2. Excision of C7-T1

Case Study 19

History and Physical

CHIEF COMPLAINT: Neck and arm pain.

HISTORY OF PRESENT ILLNESS:

This 46-year-old female is referred by her primary care physician, Dr. Adrianna Ross, due to neck and right arm pain that she attributes to a whiplash-type injury sustained during a fall while using her roller blades in March of last year. She has been treated medically by her PCP without resolution of her symptoms. She was seen by Dr. Alexander Warren who ordered EMG nerve conduction velocity testing and subsequent MRI. Patient describes her pain as radiating into the right shoulder, down the back of the arm, with pain in the fingers. The pain is on the right side and is made worse by moving her neck. Patient denies any other pain.

PAST MEDICAL HISTORY:

MEDICATIONS: Flexeril and Vicodin for pain and occasional inhaler for asthma.

ALLERGIES: None known.

OPERATIONS: Appendectomy in 1979.

REVIEW OF SYSTEMS:
Vital Signs: Temperature 98.7, pulse 73, respirations 18, blood pressure 117/78.

HEENT: Unremarkable.

Neck: Decreased range of motion due to pain.

Heart: Regular rate and rhythm.

Lungs: Clear.

Abdomen: Soft, nontender.

Extremities: Decreased grip on the right as compared to the left.

SOCIAL HISTORY:
Single, nondrinker, nonsmoker. Lives with two teen-aged children.

FAMILY HISTORY: Noncontributory.

ASSESSMENT:
Review of MRI demonstrates herniated disk on the right at C7-T1.

C8 radiculopathy secondary to C7-T1herniated disk.

PLAN: Diskectomy.

<u>Case Study 19</u>

Procedure Note

DATE: 1/15/2015

PREOPERATIVE DIAGNOSIS:	C7-T1 herniated disk, right
POSTOPERATIVE DIAGNOSIS:	C7-T1 herniated disk, right
PROCEDURE:	C7-T1 microdiskectomy and fusion with
	Allograft and premier plate system
SURGEON:	Dr. Anika Miller
ASSISTANT:	Dr. Dagnar Mallard
ANESTHESIA:	General

INDICATIONS: The patient is a 46-year-old female with neck and right arm pain, found to have a large herniated disk.

DESCRIPTION OF PROCEDURE: The patient was inducted with general anesthesia and placed supine on the operating table. The neck was prepped and draped in the usual manner. A transverse skin incision was made low in the neck from the sternocleidomastoid to the midline. The platysmas was cut sharply. Dissection was carried down to the space between carotid sheath laterally, esophagus and trachea medially. Prevertebral fascia was opened. Appropriate level was identified by x-ray. Longus colli muscles were cauterized, elevated, and retracted. Then posts were drilled in the body of C7 and T1, and the disk spaced was distracted. It was opened initially with a #15 blade and interspace rongeurs. Microscope was brought into the field, and a dissection was carried down to the posterior longitudinal ligament and the dura was exposed transversely. Herniated fragment was found in the right lateral gutter.

A foraminotomy was carried out, giving exposure to the initial part of the C8 nerve. Once this was accomplished, and it felt to be well decompressed, the wound was irrigated out. An allograft was fashioned with slightly more height on the left than on the right, as this is where some extra bone was removed. This was tapped into place, the posts were removed, the holes were waxed, and an appropriate size 25 mm fusion premier plate was put into place and screwed into place. The compression devise was used to give some compression on the bone. Once this was accomplished, the wound was irrigated and closed with 3-0 coated Vicryl in the platysma and 4-0 coated Vicryl in the skin.

The patient tolerated the procedure well without complications.

ESTIMATED BLOOD LOSS: 100 mL.

Case Study 19

Progress Notes:

1/15:   Admit Note: Patient admitted with complaint of neck pain radiating to the right arm. MRI revealed a herniated C7-T1 disk. Patient is admitted for elective diskectomy. The procedure, alternative therapy, and the accompanying risks have been discussed and she desires the procedure.

1/15:   Operative Note:

        Pre-op: C7-T1 HNP
        Post-op: Same
        Operation: C7-T1 diskectomy
        Surgeon: Dr. Miller
        Assistant: Dr. Millard
        Anesthesia: General

    Patient was given morphine postoperatively in the recovery room. Patient immediately suffered respiratory distress as a result of the morphine. Narcan was administered with immediate results. Patient was observed for an additional 2 hours postrecovery with no further adverse effects. She was transferred to the floor alert and oriented with no further signs of complications.

1/15:   S: Patient feeling well, only complaint of incisional pain.
         O: Respiratory rate normal with no signs of distress.
         A: Neurological stable.
         P: Patient advised of allergy to morphine and instructed to never allow administration of morphine.

1/16:   S: No complaints.
         O: Afebrile, vital signs stable.
         A: Upper extremity strength good, sutures intact without redness.
         P: Discharge tomorrow.

1/17:   Discharge Note: Patient admitted on January 15 for elective diskectomy C7-T1. Patient tolerated surgery well. Patient developed respiratory distress as a result of morphine given postoperatively in the recovery room. Respiratory distress quickly reversed with administration of Narcan. Patient's vital signs and laboratory values were within normal limits throughout hospitalization. Incision is healing well with sutures intact. Patient is stable from a neurological standpoint with good upper extremity strength. She is to follow up with me in 3 weeks. Activity as tolerated; however, she is to do no lifting. Discharge home in good condition.

Case Study 19

Orders:

1/15:   Preoperative Orders:

    1.   Admit to Dr. Rosen.

    2.   Complete following tests 2 days pre-op:
          CBC
          C/C UA
          PT/PTT
          Type and screen
          Chem basic
          Chest x-ray
          EKG

    3.   Pre-op per anesthesia.

    4.   Start IV 1,000 mL D_5LR prior to surgery.

    5.   Bilateral thigh-high TED hose.

    6.   NPO.

1/15:   PACU Standing Orders

    1.   Vital signs every 5 minutes for 15 minutes, then every 15 minutes until discharged from PACU.

    2.   Oxygen via nasal cannula at 3–5 L/minute.

    3.   May discontinue oxygen when stable.

    4.   Check operative site every 30 minutes.

    5.   Maintain IV with D_5LR 500 mL while in PACU.

    6.   Discharge from PACU when discharge criteria met.

1/16:   1.   Incentive spirometer q. 2 hours.

1/17:   1.   D/C home.

    2.   F/U 3 weeks.

Case Study 19

Answer Sheet

DIAGNOSES	ICD-9-CM CODES					
Principal Diagnosis				-		
DX 2				-		
DX 3				-		
DX 4				-		

PROCEDURES	ICD-9-CM CODES			
PP 1			-	
PX 2			-	
PX 3			-	

Code ICD-9-CM Diagnosis Code
(One diagnosis code will be needed)

Case Study 20

Inpatient Face Sheet

Admit Date: 1/14/2015

Discharge Date: 1/15/2015

Sex: Female

Age: 24

Disposition: Home

Admitting Diagnosis: Preterm labor

Discharge Diagnosis: Preterm labor

Case Study 20

Labor and Delivery History and Physical

HISTORY: Patient is a 24-year-old female, gravida 2, para 0, abortus 0, who had her prenatal care at the Women's Clinic. She presented to Labor and Delivery with the complaint of abdominal pain and cramps. Her membrane is intact.

LMP: EGA of 31.4 weeks. Ultrasound at 6 weeks. No complications during this pregnancy.

PAST MEDICAL HISTORY: Noncontributory.

PAST SURGICAL HISTORY: None.

MEDICINE: None during pregnancy.

ALLERGIES: No known allergies.

PRENATAL LABS: Rh+, Rubella BL, VDRL NR, GC–, Chlamydia–, Pap–, AB Screen 0, Hepatitis Screen–, Diabetic Screen 153.

PHYSICAL EXAMINATION:

Vital signs:	BP 135/82, Temp. 98.4, Pulse 102, Resp 21, FHTs 145.
General:	No acute diseases.
HEENT:	No asymmetry.
Neck:	No asymmetry.
Heart:	Regular rate and rhythm.
Lungs:	Clear to auscultation bilaterally.
Abdomen:	Soft, nontender, nondistended, + bowel sounds.
Extremities:	No edema.
Neuro:	No deficits.
Cervix:	1/th.
Presenting Part:	VTX/FFN+.

Impression: 24-year-old G2P00 at 31.4 weeks with PTL

PLAN:		
	1.	Admit
	2.	U/S

Case Study 20

Progress Notes:

1/14:   Admit Note: Patient admitted to Labor and Delivery with preterm labor at 31.4 weeks' gestation. Patient immediately started on magnesium sulfate.

    S: Patient denies HA/CP/SOB/CTX/RUQ pain.
    O: VS 121/73, P 87, FHT: 135–141, + accelerations.
    A: 24-year-old at 31.4 weeks with PTL.
    P: Follow Mg levels, perform US.

1/15:   S: Patient reports that pain is completely gone.
    O: PE, WNL. FHT: 150's, + accels, − decels.
    A: PTL with Mg tocolysis, US indicates fetus at 1,698 g, cervix closed.
    P: DC today, strict bed rest with BRP, follow-up at clinic in 1 week.

Orders:

1/14:   1.   Admit to L&D with PTL at 31.4 weeks.
    2.   CBC and clean-catch UA.
    3. $MgSO_4$ per protocol–5 g loading dose/then 2 g/hour.
    4.   Fetal monitor.
    5.   US.
    6.   Strict bed rest.
    7.   Clear liquid diet.

1/15:   1.   DC $MgSO_4$.
    2.   Transfer to antepartum.
    3.   If patient remains stable throughout the day, may discharge this evening.

Case Study 20

Answer Sheet

DIAGNOSES	ICD-9-CM CODES					
Principal Diagnosis				-		

Code ICD-9-CM Diagnosis Codes
(Five diagnosis codes will be needed)

Case Study 21

Inpatient Face Sheet

Admit Date: 12/12/2014

Discharge Date: 12/18/2014

Sex: Female

Age: 75

Disposition: Home

Admitting Diagnoses:
1. Asthmatic bronchitis
2. Pneumonia
3. Supraventricular tachycardia
4. Chronic diastolic heart failure

Discharge Diagnoses:
1. Pneumonia
2. Asthmatic bronchitis
3. Supraventricular tachycardia
4. Chronic diastolic heart failure
5. Tobacco use

Procedures: None

Case Study 21

Discharge Summary

ADMTTED: 12/12/2014

DISCHARGED: 12/18/2014

ADMITTING DIAGNOSES:
1. Asthmatic bronchitis, rule out pneumonia
2. Supraventricular tachycardia

DISCHARGE DIAGNOSES:
1. Pneumonia
2. Asthmatic bronchitis
3. Supraventricular tachycardia
4. Chronic diastolic heart failure
5. Tobacco use

CHIEF COMPLAINT: Shortness of breath, history of asthma, possible pneumonia, fever.

HISTORY OF PRESENT ILLNESS: A 75-year-old female presented to the emergency room with the above complaints. She had been treated as an outpatient by her primary care physician, Dr. Nicholas Magee. She failed to improve with Zithromax. The patient has a past history of bronchial asthma, supraventricular arrhythmia, and chronic diastolic heart failure. Her cardiologist is Dr. Benjamin William and her pulmonologist is Dr. Victoria Stamper. On 3/23/2014, the patient had a cardiac catheterization with findings of minimal coronary artery disease.

PHYSICAL EXAMINATION: On exam today, the patient is short of breath with congestion noted in the head and chest, expiratory wheezing, rales, and rhonchi throughout. No edema. For complete physical details, please see History and Physical.

HOSPITAL COURSE: The patient was admitted and given intravenous fluids, placed on telemetry monitoring, started on intravenous steroids, which were subsequently tapered, pan cultured, and had a pulmonary medicine consult. Chest x-ray shows pneumonia.

Consultation with Dr. Stamper of pulmonary medicine was performed.

RADIOLOGY REPORTS:
PA and lateral chest x-ray of December 12, showed left lower lobe pneumonia. Follow-up PA and lateral chest x-ray on 12/15 showed clear, but hyperexpanded lungs compatible with the patient's clinical history of asthma, no evidence of focal consolidation pneumonia compared to the chest x-ray of 12/13, which showed slight improvement of left lower lobe pneumonia and hiatal hernia.

LABORATORY DATA: On admission, glucose 116, sodium 135, potassium 3.5, blood urea nitrogen 11, creatinine 1.4, calcium 8.4. On 12/15 glucose 125, sodium 137, potassium 3,9, blood urea nitrogen 19, creatinine 1.5, calcium 8.5. On admission, white blood cell count was 22,300 with a hemoglobin 13.9, hematocrit 42, platelets 210,000. White blood cell count had decreased on 12/15 to 12,900 with a hemoglobin of 12.7, hematocrit 37.7, platelets 266,000. Blood culture negative.

Case Study 21

Discharge Summary

Continued:

HOSPITAL COURSE: The patient presented with shortness of breath, cough, and congestion, following outpatient care for respiratory infection. She has a history of asthma. She was admitted and placed on intravenous antibiotics, supplemental oxygen, nebulizer therapy with bronchodilators and intravenous steroids. She also was found to have sinusitis, pneumonia.

The patient was felt to have reached maximum medical improvement on December 17 and was cleared for discharge. The patient was given the instructions and advice and will go home with the medications and the nebulizer treatments of albuterol and saline four times a day.

DISCHARGE MEDICATIONS:
1. Levaquin 250 mg once a day for 7 days.
2. Claritin 10 mg, one tablet daily.
3. Nasonex nasal spray, two sprays each nostril daily.
4. Potassium chloride spray, three or four times a day.
5. Lanoxin 0.125 mg daily.
6. Lasix.

Case Study 21

History and Physical

ADMISSION DATE: 12/12/2014

CHIEF COMPLAINT: Shortness of breath, history of asthma, possible pneumonia, fever.

HISTORY: This 75-year-old female presented to the emergency room with the above complaints. She was initially seen by her primary care physician when Zithromax failed to improve her symptoms. The patient was found to have possible infiltrate on chest x-ray, pyrexia, and was admitted for further evaluation and treatment.

The past medical history includes bronchial asthma, history of supraventricular arrhythmia, and palpitation.

PREVIOUS CONSULTANTS: Dr. Benjamin William and Dr. Victoria Stamper.

PROCEDURES: On 10/23/2011, the patient had cardiac catheterization with findings of minimal coronary artery disease with recommendation for medical management.

PRESENT MEDICATIONS: The present medications include Lanoxin 0.25 mg daily, Nasonex nasal spray, and Claritin D 24-hour tablet.

Additional medical history includes asthmatic bronchitis and respiratory allergies.

PAST SURGERY: Cataracts.

SOCIAL HISTORY: The patient admits to cigarette smoking. She has never been married and has no children.

ALLERGIES: None known.

SYSTEMS REVIEW:
INTEGUMENT:	Denies rashes, seborrhea, or psoriasis.
HEENT:	Denies any problems chewing, tasting, hearing, or swallowing.
RESPIRATORY:	Admits to shortness of breath, asthma, and dyspnea on exertion.
GASTROINTESTINAL:	Unremarkable.

FAMILY HISTORY: The family history includes two brothers and two sisters. One brother deceased. One brother has asthma. Parents are deceased. Mother died at age 82 from a stroke and father died at age 85 from a stroke.

Case Study 21

History and Physical

Continued:

PHYSICAL EXAMINATION: The physical examination reveals a well-nourished, well-hydrated, Caucasian female with no complaints, alert and cooperative, mild respiratory stridor.

LUNGS:	Full aeration, expiratory wheezing bilaterally.
CARDIOVASCULAR:	S1 and S2 regular. No palpitations perceived at this time. No irregular rhythm noted on auscultation by this examiner. There is no jugular venous distention.
ABDOMEN:	The abdomen is soft, nontender. No guarding, rebound, or rigidity.

IMPRESSION AT THIS TIME: Asthmatic bronchitis, rule out pneumonia.

RECOMMENDATION: Intravenous fluids, intravenous steroids, intravenous Levaquin, panculture, pulmonary medicine consult.

CONDITION AT THIS TIME: Guarded.

Case Study 21

Consultation

DATE: 12/12/2014

REQUESTING PHYSICIAN: Dr. Magee

CONSULTING PHYSICIAN: Dr. Stamper

This is a 75-year-old female who has a long-standing history of asthma since the age of 8 who was not doing well for the past few days with increased shortness of breath, cough, and congestion. She saw Dr. Magee who gave her Zithromax, which did not help her symptoms. Then she developed increased fever, cough, and congestion, so she came to the emergency room where she was noted to have questionable pneumonia and bronchitis and bronchospasm. She was admitted to the hospital for further treatment.

PAST MEDICAL HISTORY: The past medical history is positive for long-standing asthma, COPD exacerbation requiring recurrent hospitalization, and history of allergic rhinitis. She also has a history of postnasal drip, chronic wheezing, shortness of breath, and tachycardia.

SOCIAL HISTORY: Past history of smoking. Does not abuse alcohol. She lives alone.

FAMILY HISTORY: Parents died of stroke in their 80s. One brother had asthma.

MEDICATIONS PRIOR TO ADMISSION: The patient's medications prior to admission included Vioxx 25 mg once a day, Ablution inhaler, Claritin 10 mg once a day, Serevent inhaler, Flonase inhaler and nasal spray.

ALLERGIES: None known.

REVIEW OF SYSTEMS: Otherwise negative.

PHYSICAL EXAMINATION: Alert white female who is in acute distress, tachycardic and tachypneic, she is short of breath. Temperature 100.4, pulse 120, respirations 20, blood pressure 140/98, saturation 88%, on admission. Last vitals: temperature 97, pulse 99, respirations 20, blood pressure 150/80.

HEENT:	Negative except some sinus tenderness and postnasal drip.
NECK:	No jugular venous distention.
LUNGS:	Bilateral diffuse rhonchi and wheezes.
HEART:	Regular rhythm, tachycardia, no gallops or murmur.
ABDOMEN:	The abdomen is soft, nontender.
EXTREMITIES:	No edema.

Case Study 21

Consultation

Continued:

Chest x-ray was reviewed; there is no definite infiltrate except some basilar atelectasis, early infiltrate cannot be ruled out. Arterial blood gas: pH 7.45, pCO_2 30, pO_2 73 on 2 L nasal cannula. White blood count 18.1, hemoglobin 13.9. Comprehensive metabolic panel essentially unremarkable. Bilirubin 1.67. Digoxin 0.49.

ASSESSMENT:
1. Bronchial asthma
2. Bronchitis
3. No definite pneumonia; however, cannot be ruled out
4. Basilar atelectasis
5. Tachycardia due to above

RECOMMENDATION: Intravenous Solu-Medrol, intravenous antibiotics, oxygen, nebulizer treatment, sinus x-rays, and follow closely.

Case Study 21

Answer Sheet

DIAGNOSES	ICD-9-CM CODES					
Principal Diagnosis				-		
DX 2				-		
DX 3				-		
DX 4				-		
DX 5				-		

> ## Code ICD-9-CM Diagnosis Codes
> ### (12 diagnosis codes will be needed)

Case Study 22

Inpatient Face Sheet

Admit Date: 11/25/2014

Discharge Date: 12/02/2014

Age: 78

Sex: Male

Disposition: Home

Admit Diagnoses:
1. Dyspnea, rule out pulmonary embolism
2. History of deep venous thrombosis
3. Chronic renal insufficiency
4. Dizziness, possibly benign positional vertigo, rule out other causes

Discharge Diagnoses:
1. Dyspnea on exertion, confirmed secondary to pulmonary embolism
2. Mild congestive heart failure, chronic systolic
3. History of chronic renal failure
4. Diabetes mellitus type 1
5. Diabetic neuropathy

Procedure Performed: None

Case Study 22

Discharge Summary

ADMITTED: 11/25/2014

DISCHARGED: 12/02/2014

ADMITTING DIAGNOSES:
1. Dyspnea, rule out pulmonary embolism
2. History of deep venous thrombosis
3. Chronic renal insufficiency
4. Dizziness, possibly benign positional vertigo, rule out other causes

DISCHARGE DIAGNOSES:
1. Dyspnea on exertion, confirmed secondary to pulmonary embolism
2. Mild congestive heart failure, chronic systolic
3. History of chronic renal failure
4. Diabetes mellitus type 1
5. Diabetic neuropathy
6. Chronic obstructive pulmonary disease
7. Dizziness: etiology likely multifactorial, patient started on Meclizine
8. History of tobacco depedence

HISTORY: This is a 78-year-old gentleman with the above-mentioned medical problems who came to the emergency room at this time with light-headedness, dizziness, wooziness, drunk feeling, not sure of his steps. He was having increasing shortness of breath and does have a history of deep venous thrombosis and pulmonary emboli.

PERTINENT EXAM: Blood pressure 123/80, pulse rate 109, respirations 16, temperature 96.

HEENT:	Unremarkable.
NECK:	No jugular venous distention.
LUNGS:	A few crepitations, no wheezing.
HEART:	Regular. No murmur.
ABDOMEN:	Distended, soft, nontender.
EXTREMITIES:	2–3 + edema.

LABORATORY: White blood cell account 11,500, left shift differential. Other counts were normal. Follow-up hemoglobin 11.1, hematocrit 32.9. Baseline INR normal. Chemistries: sodium 135, blood urea nitrogen 35, creatinine 1.8, alkaline phosphatase 80. AST/ALT levels initially normal. Follow-up blood sugar 198–200. Urinalysis: yellow and hazy appearance, microscopic blood noted, protein noted, nitrite negative, leukocyte esterase a small amount detected. Urine culture suggested a contaminated specimen.

Chest film revealed some prominent interstitial markings and possible congestive heart failure.

Case Study 22

Discharge Summary

Continued:

Computed tomography brain scan shows mild atrophy. Ventilation perfusion lung scan revealed an intermediate probability for pulmonary embolism. Electrocardiogram—sinus rhythm, sinus tachycardia. Arterial blood gases on 2 L nasal cannula, pH 7.41, pCO_2 33.1, pO_2 98.8, bicarb 20.8, and saturation is 97.5%.

HOSPITAL COURSE: The patient admitted with increasing weakness, dyspnea, and hypoxemia and dizziness at this time as well. There is no evidence of acute cerebrovascular accident. Computed tomography brain scan revealing chronic changes, nothing acute.

Ultimately the patient was found to have a pulmonary embolism and started on subcutaneous Lovenox injection, 1 mg/kg subcutaneous every 12 hours and then Coumadin started as well. Daily prothrombin time, INR evaluations were obtained, and Coumadin doses were titrated accordingly. We were able to confirm the suspicion with a computed tomography scan and pulmonary angiogram. The patient was continued on anticoagulation, as well as treatment for heart failure with ace inhibitor therapy. He had reached the maximal hospital benefit and was discharged on December 2, 2010.

MEDICATIONS ON DISCHARGE:
1. Humulin 75/25 15 units twice daily
2. Xanax 0.25 mg three times a day
3. Celexa 30 mg at h.s.
4. Coumadin 10 mg daily
5. Protonix 40 mg a day
6. Prinivil 40 mg daily
7. Meclizine

DIET: 1,800 ADA, low fat, low salt.

OTHER THERAPEUTIC MEASURES: The patient reached maximum therapeutic benefit from his hospital admission. He was discharged with his medications and diet as listed.

ACTIVITY: As tolerated.

Case Study 22

History and Physical

ADMITTED: 11/25/2014

CHIEF COMPLAINT: Dizziness, lightheadedness, and shortness of breath on exertion.

HISTORY OF PRESENT ILLNESS: This is 78-year-old gentleman who has a history of multiple medical problems. He came into the emergency room because he was feeling dizzy, lightheaded, woozy, and kind of drunk. He could not be sure of his steps. He has also been complaining of increased shortness of breath on exertion. He does have chronic dyspnea on exertion due to multiple medical problems including obesity, deep venous thrombosis; however, he feels that his symptoms are worse than before.

PAST MEDICAL HISTORY: His history is positive for multiple medical problems. He has history of hypertension, diabetes mellitus type 1, deep venous thrombosis. He has been on Coumadin for quite some time because of deep venous thrombosis.

SOCIAL HISTORY: He smoked cigarettes but quit smoking 25 years ago. He does not drink alcohol. He is married, lives with his wife.

ALLERGIES: None.

REVIEW OF SYSTEMS: As mentioned earlier; other than that, is unremarkable. He does not have any chest pain, denies any shortness of breath on exertion. He has no cough, hemoptysis, fever, or chills. No nausea or vomiting, abdominal pain, diarrhea, or urinary burning or hematuria at this time.

MEDICATIONS: Protonix 40 mg once a day, and insulin 75/25 Humalog, 35 units in the morning and 35 units in the evening.

PHYSICIAL EXAMINATION:

GENERAL APPEARANCE: Elderly white gentleman who is in no respiratory distress, but gets short of breath on exertion.

VITAL SIGNS: Blood pressure 123/80 on admission, pulse 109, respirations 16, temperature 96, oxygen saturation 98%.

HEENT:	Head, ears, eyes, nose, and throat were negative.
NECK:	No jugular venous distention.
LUNGS:	There are a few crepitations, no wheezing, rhonchi, or rales.
HEART:	Regular rhythm, no gallops or murmur.
ABDOMEN:	The abdomen is distended, soft, nontender.
EXTREMITIES:	There are 2–3 + edema.

Case Study 22

History and Physical

Continued:

LABORATORY DATA: The pertinent laboratories include on admission, urinalysis positive for white blood cells and 2+ bacteria. White blood cell count 11.5, hemoglobin 12.4. Comprehensive metabolic panel is unremarkable, except blood urea nitrogen 35, creatinine 1.8. Troponin I 0.05. Prothrombin time and partial thromboplastin time normal, partial thromboplastin time 54. D-dimer positive. Chest x-ray: Basal atelectasis, otherwise unremarkable. There is some interstitial marking. Computerized tomography scan of the brain was unremarkable. Urine culture: multiple species, could be contaminated.

ASSESMENT:
1. Shortness of breath on exertion, which could be related to obesity, chronic obstructive pulmonary disease, asthma, bronchitis, rule out pulmonary emboli, especially with the history of deep venous thrombosis.
2. History of deep venous thrombosis and renal insufficiency.
3. Dizziness, rule out benign positional vertigo, orthostatic hypotension, rule out bleeding, cerebrovascular accident, etc.

RECOMMENDATIONS:
1. Computerized tomography scan of brain.
2. Neurology consultation.
3. Orthostatic check of blood pressure and pulse.
4. Check complete blood count, chemistry, and other laboratories.
5. Get pulmonary CT angiogram to rule out pulmonary emboli.
6. Check oxygen saturation on exertion.
7. Give nebulizer treatment and oxygen, insulin, and other medications as before.

Case Study 22

Consultation

DATE: 11/26/2014

REQUESTING PHYSICIAN: Dr. Chase William

CONSULTING PHYSICIAN: Dr. Lynn Pagano

HISTORY OF PRESENT ILLNESS: The patient is a 78-year-old white male with past history of diabetes mellitus type 1, history of hypertension, who was admitted to the hospital with dizziness.

He denied any fall, any loss of consciousness, denied any slurring of the speech, he denied any weakness focally.

PAST MEDICAL HISTORY: Hypertension, diabetes mellitus type 1.

MEDICATIONS: He is on clonidine, Norvasc, Protonix, and insulin.

NEUROLOGICAL EXAMINATION:

GENERAL APPEARANCE: On examination, the patient is pleasant, awake, alert, oriented times three.

VITAL SIGNS: Temperature 98 degrees, blood pressure 133/74, pulse is 94 beats per minute.

HEENT: There is equal eye movement, reactive to light. No nystagmus, no carotid bruit. The left visual field is normal. No neck rigidity, no Kernig or Brudzinski sign.

CRANIAL NERVES: The cranial nerves are unremarkable. Palatal movement is intact with tongue midline. Corneal and gag reflexes are intact.

MOTOR SYSTEM: Normal tone and power, 5/5 in all four extremities proximally and distally. There is decreased pinprick and touch in bilateral upper and lower extremities distally, with decreased position and vibration. Deep tendon reflexes +2 in the lower extremities, +1 knee jerk, and absent ankle jerk, and absent ankle jerk. Plantar is both down going.

CEREBELLAR: Finger-to-nose, heel-to-shin normal. Speech is clear, alert, with normal naming, normal comprehensions, normal reading.

Case Study 22

Consultation

Continued:

LABORATORY DATA: Urinalysis: Hazy and many bacteria 2+, Chemistry: Sodium 135, potassium 4.8, blood urea nitrogen 35, creatinine 0.8, sugar 149, alkaline phosphatase 580, globulin 4.5. White blood cell count 11.5, hemoglobin 12.5, hematocrit 36.5, platelet count 268.

IMPRESSION:

The patient has hypertension, diabetes mellitus type 1, with severe peripheral neuropathy with complaints of feeling dizziness, lightheaded, without any acute focal motor or sensory deficit, without any nystagmus:

1. Rule out benign positional vertigo.
2. Rule out cardiac arrhythmia versus gastrointestinal, which is unlikely.
3. Rule out orthostatic hypotension.

RECOMMENDATIONS:
1. Computerized tomography scans of the head.
2. Meclezine 25 mg p.o. b.i.d.
3. Physical therapy, occupational therapy for gait training.
4. Diabetic control.
5. Check for orthostatic blood pressure every 6 hours.

Case Study 22

Answer Sheet

DIAGNOSES	ICD-9-CM CODES					
Principal Diagnosis				-		
DX 2				-		
DX 3				-		
DX 4				-		
DX 5				-		
DX 6				-		
DX 7				-		
DX 8				-		
DX 9				-		
DX 10				-		
DX 11				-		
DX 12				-		

Code ICD-9-CM Diagnosis Codes and CPT Procedure Codes
(Two diagnosis codes and three CPT codes will be needed)

Case Study 23

Ambulatory Services

Face Sheet

Patient Name: Nathan Jenkins

Date of Visit: 01/17/2015

Age: 45

Insurance: HMO

Case Study 23

History and Physical

DATE: 01/17/2015

CHIEF COMPLAINT: Palpitations

PRESENT ILLNESS: This is a 45-year-old male who had visited the emergency room at Sun City Hospital on January 6, 2015, for rapid palpitations. He has had three episodes of sudden, rapid palpitations. Usually, they break on their own. The last episode lasted 18 hours. Patient was given Cardizem without any response. He usually is completely asymptomatic, although he feels poorly the day afterward.

The arrhythmia seen on the electrocardiogram at Sun City Hospital was most consistent with classical flutter. Holter monitor was performed, which was normal. Ablation was recommended to the patient.

PAST MEDICAL HISTORY: Borderline hypertension, but he is not treated for it. No history of diabetes or pulmonary disease.

FAMILY HISTORY: Negative.

SOCIAL HISTORY: Denies cigarette use.

PHYSICAL EXAMINATION:

GENERAL: Overweight male in no acute distress. Blood pressure is high at 138/80; pulse is regular at 160 beats per minute.

NECK: Neck is supple without evidence of bruits. There is no thyromegaly.

CHEST: Clear to auscultation.

HEART: Cardiac examination revealed a normal S1 S2 without murmurs.

ABDOMEN: Benign.

EXTREMITIES: No evidence of clubbing, cyanosis, or edema.

His electrocardiogram at Sun City Hospital showed classical atrial flutter at 103 beats per minute.

IMPRESSION: The patient's arrhythmia is fairly classic for atrial flutter.

PLAN: Patient is to be admitted as an outpatient for ablation.

Case Study 23

Operative Report

Date of Operation:	January 17, 2015
Preoperative Diagnosis:	Atrial Flutter
Postoperative Diagnosis:	1. Typical atrioventricular reentrant tachycardia
	2. Classic type I atrial flutter

Operation:

1. Full electrophysiologic study with coronary sinus catheter
2. Follow-up programmed stimulation with isoproterenol
3. Electrical cardioversion of atrial flutter
4. Radiofrequency catheter ablation of the slow AV nodal pathway
5. Radiofrequency catheter ablation of the atrial flutter

Medications given: Heparin 1,000 units per hour
Isoproterenol 2 mcg per minute

Findings:

1. Baseline normal sinus nodal and His-Purkinje function. Ventricular function was not completely studied. The corrected sinus nodal recovery time measured 154 milliseconds at baseline. The H-V interval measured 53 milliseconds at baseline.

2. On isoproterenol 2 mcg per minute, reproducible induced typical AV nodal reentrant tachycardia with a cycle length of 260 milliseconds (231 beats per minute) was induced by double atrial electric stimuli at the high right atrium. This produces systolic blood pressure of 83 mm Hg. The arrhythmia was terminated with ventricular burst pacing at 230 milliseconds. Dual AV nodal pathways were evident at baseline with a fast AV nodal effective refractory period measuring 500/310; the slow AV nodal effective refractory period measured 500/350/220.

3. Successful radiofrequency catheter ablation of the slow AV nodal pathway was accomplished after three applications of radiofrequency energy of 50 watts/60 degrees centigrade to the roof of the coronary sinus OS. Junctional tachycardia occurred within 6 seconds of radiofrequency application.

4. After slow AV nodal pathway ablation, antegrade AV nodal block measured 300 milliseconds. The AV nodal effective refractory period measured 400/240 and no slow AV nodal conduction could be seen. No inducible AV nodal reentrant tachycardia despite double atrial electric stimuli on isoproterenol 2 mcg per minute AV nodal refractoriness.

5. Induced atrial fibrillation with rapid atrial pacing at 230 milliseconds at the high right atrium on isoproterenol 2 mcg per minute; this organized to classic type I atrial flutter.

6. Successful creation of bidirectional conduction block was accomplished across the isthmus of the tricuspid annulus and inferior vena cava, coronary sinus os of the inferior vena cava, coronary sinus os of the tricuspid annulus. Conduction block was proven using coronary sinus os and low right atrial pacing.

Impression:

1. Inducible typical atrioventricular nodal reentrant tachycardia
2. Inducible atrial flutter, classic type I

Case Study 23

Progress Notes:

Feels good
BP 140/84
Groins healing well
Cardiac normal
Will discharge home

Physician Orders:

1. Supine bed rest for 4 hours keeping left and right legs straight.
2. May elevate HOB no greater than 30 degrees.
3. Vital signs every 15 minutes x 4, every 30 minutes x 4, every hour x 4.
4. Change IV to Heplock.
5. 12 lead EKG.
6. Percocet 1–2 p.o. q6.

Discharge Instructions:
1. Discharge home when stable.
2. ASA 325 mg daily.
3. Follow up with me in 1 month.
4. Regular diet and activity.

Case Study 23

Answer Sheet

DIAGNOSES	ICD-9-CM CODES					
First Listed DX					-	
DX 2					-	

PROCEDURES	CPT CODES				MODIFIERS (If Applicable)		
PR 1						-	
PR 2						-	
PR 3						-	

Code ICD-9-CM Diagnosis Codes and CPT Procedure Codes
(Two diagnosis codes and two procedure codes will be needed)

Case Study 24

Ambulatory Surgery

Face Sheet

Name: Elizabeth Cooper

Date: 01/03/2015

Age: 72

Insurance: Medicare

<u>Case Study 24</u>

History and Physical

DATE OF ADMISSION: 01/03/2015

HISTORY OF PRESENT ILLNESS:
Mrs. Cooper is returning to our office for follow-up of lightheadedness. The patient has been doing well since her last visit. She has not experienced any syncope or near syncope. No chest pain or pressure, PND, orthopnea, or dyspnea on exertion.

MEDICATIONS: She is taking aspirin 81 mg daily and Celexa 10 mg daily.

REVIEW OF SYSTEMS: General: No fevers or chills. Respiratory: No wheezing, cough, or shortness of breath. GI: No complaints. GU: No complaints. Extremities: No edema or other problems.

PREVIOUS TESTING RESULTS: Stress nuclear study showed an area of septal and also apical thinning with improvements in counts on delay. There was some motion artifact; however, one has to be concerned about the possibility of ischemia in this region, which would appear to be, if present, LAD. LV function was normal, and there appears to be LVH. Of concern, the patient did not exercise a great distance, got about 3 minutes on Bruce protocol, and had a dip near her starting blood pressure at peak exercise.

Holter monitor showed short runs of paroxysmal SVT versus atrial fibrillation up to 150 beats per minute. Echocardiogram showed normal LV function, mild to moderate MR, mild TR. I am concerned with the stress nuclear study showing a question of LAD ischemia and the fact that her blood pressure at peak exercise dropped back near starting level.

PHYSICAL EXAMINATION:
VITAL SIGNS:	BP: 144/60; P: 72 and regular.
NECK:	No JVD.
LUNGS:	Clear bilaterally.
CARDIAC:	Regular rate and rhythm. Grade 1/6 right upper sternal border systolic murmur and a positive S4.
ABDOMEN:	Soft, nontender and benign.
EXTREMITIES:	Femoral pulses appear to be 2+ without bruits. Distal extremities unremarkable. No significant edema.
NEUROLOGIC:	Alert and oriented, grossly appears nonfocal.

IMPRESSION:
1. Coronary artery disease. Based on nuclear described above, I suspect there may be LAD coronary artery disease.
2. Mild to moderate MR by echo.
3. Probable hypertension.

PLAN:
1. Patient will be scheduled for outpatient cardiac catheterization.
2. Continue aspirin at this point.

Case Study 24

Procedure

Date of Procedure:	01/03/2015
Preoperative Diagnosis:	Coronary artery disease
Postoperative Diagnosis:	Coronary artery disease of mid lateral anterior descending artery
Procedure:	Left heart catheterization
	Coronary arteriograms
	Left ventriculography
	PTCA with stent

Patient was taken to the cardiac catheterization lab and was prepped and draped in the usual sterile manner. The right femoral artery was entered using the percutaneous technique. Left coronary arteriograms were performed using #6 French, JL4 catheters. Left ventriculography was performed using #6 French, JR4 catheters. Right coronary arteriograms were performed using #6 French, JR4.

#6 French sheath was sutured to right groin. Heparinized NaCl via pressure bag attached to #6 French sheath. The injection fraction was 79%.

Then #6 French RFA & FRV flex sheaths were placed. GFXB 3.5 guide & PT Graphix wire was used to cross lesion. IV NTG given. ACT baseline = 133. IV heparin 3 units given. Mid left anterior descending lesion was predilated with 2.5 × 20 mm Maverick balloon. Stented with 2.5 × 18 mm Bx Velocity stent immediately distal to diagonal. Post dilated with 2.75 × 15 mm Maverick balloon with 14 bars with good opposition.

Results: Residual 0%–5%. Side branch: Diagonal not jeopardized.

Complications: None.

Case Study 24

Progress Notes:

1/03   Heart catheterization showed 90% stenosis of LAD. PTCA was performed with insertion of 2.5 × 18 mm B × Velocity stent. Patient tolerated procedure well.

1/04   No problems or complications from catheterization. Pulses OK. Abdomen soft. No bleeding from femoral site.

Physician Orders:

1/03

1.   Right groin check, right DP pulse q. 15 minutes × 4, then q. 30 minutes x 4; then q4h.
2.   Monitor femoral artery line, swan if applicable.
3.   NPO until fully alert, then liquids, then advance as tolerated to cardiac diet.
4.   Bed rest with right leg extended; loose protective device right ankle. May elevate HOB 30 degrees while sheaths in.
5.   Bed rest x 8 hours after sheaths out, then out of bed with assistance.
6.   IV D5 1/2 NS at 125 mL/hour x 8 hours.
7.   Tridil 10 mcg/minute per standard concentration. Wean at 6 a.m.
8.   Uncoated ASA 325 mg PO q. a.m.
9. O_2 at 2 L/minute via nasal cannula prn, SOB, or O_2 sats < 90%. Oximeter if O_2 in use.

1/04

1.   Discharge patient.
2.   Script for Plavix 75 mg p.o. OD × 1 month.
3.   Follow up with me in 2 weeks.

Case Study 24
Answer Sheet

DIAGNOSES			ICD-9-CM CODES			
First Listed DX					-	
DX 2					-	

PROCEDURES	CPT CODES					MODIFIERS (If Applicable)	
PR 1						-	
PR 2						-	

Code ICD-9-CM Diagnoses
(Three diagnosis codes will be needed)

Case Study 25

Emergency Room Visit

Face Sheet

Date of Service:	01/14/2015
Age:	78
Sex:	Female
Admitting Diagnosis:	Nausea and vomiting
Discharge Diagnosis:	Gastroenteritis, giardia
	Dehydration
	Arthritis
Disposition:	Home

Case Study 25

Emergency Room Visit

DATE OF ADMISSION: 01/14/2015

HISTORY:
This elderly female was brought to the emergency room today when she was out with some friends and developed nausea and vomiting. She also developed diarrhea last night. She has a slight fever and appears to be somewhat dehydrated. She was started on an IV in the emergency room.

PAST MEDICAL HISTORY:
She has had the usual childhood diseases. She has a history of arthritis. History of cataract extraction of the left eye.

ALLERGIES: No apparent allergies.

MEDICATIONS: She is on no medications.

SOCIAL HISTORY: She is a widow who lives alone.

PHYSICAL EXAMINATION:

GENERAL:	Well-developed, well-nourished female in no acute distress. Blood pressure is 100/74, pulse 70, temperature of 101, respirations 18.
HEAD:	Normocephalic.
EYES:	There is an opacity, right eye. Aphakia in the left.
NECK:	Supple. No bruits.
SKIN:	Negative.
CHEST:	Few scattered rhonchi.
HEART:	Normal rhythm. No murmurs appreciated.
ABDOMEN:	Slightly distended with tenderness. Bowel sounds present.
EXTREMITIES:	Negative.

IMPRESSION:
1. Gastroenteritis
2. Slight dehydration
3. Arthritis

The patient was discharged in good condition. No further nausea and vomiting. Patient was given a prescription for Flagyl 500 mg t.i.d. for 10 days.

LABORATORY EXAMINATION

Special Laboratory Examination: Stool.

Results: Stool shows moderate amount of Giardia lamblia cysts.

Case Study 25

Answer Sheet

DIAGNOSES	ICD-9-CM CODES					
First Listed DX				-		
DX 2				-		
DX 3				-		

Code ICD-9-CM Diagnoses and CPT Procedures
(Four diagnosis codes and one procedure code will be needed)

Case Study 26

Ambulatory Surgery

Face Sheet

Date of Service:	01/09/2015
Age:	61
Sex:	Male
Admitting Diagnosis:	Dyspepsia
	Dysphagia
Discharge Diagnoses:	Candidal esophagitis
	Acute and chronic gastritis
	Helicobacter
Procedure:	Esophagogastroduodenoscopy with biopsies

Case Study 26

History and Physical

DATE OF ADMISSION: 01/09/2015

ADMITTING DIAGNOSIS: Dyspepsia and dysphagia.

HISTORY OF PRESENT ILLNESS:
This gentleman has been complaining of dyspepsia for the past month. Now has developed difficulty in swallowing. Patient was treated conservatively with Riopan. With the difficulty in swallowing we will proceed with an esophagogastroduodenoscopy.

PAST MEDICAL HISTORY: History of basal cell carcinoma of the back, hypertension now not treated, diabetes.

ALLERGIES: None.

MEDICATIONS: Riopan and Glucotrol.

SOCIAL HISTORY: Patient does not smoke, alcohol is minimal.

PHYSICIAL EXAMINATION:

GENERAL:	This is an obese male. Vital signs are within normal limits.
HEENT:	Extraocular movements are intact. No evidence of cataracts. Dysphagia and dyspepsia.
NECK:	Without bruits, masses, or adenopathy.
CHEST:	Clear to auscultation bilaterally without any crackles or wheezes.
HEART:	Regular rate and rhythm. No murmurs or gallops.
ABDOMEN:	Without hernias, masses, or hepatosplenomegaly. Bowel sound present in all four quadrants.
NEUROLOGICAL:	Normal.
EXTREMITIES:	Unremarkable.

PLAN:
Patient will be admitted to 1-day surgery for an esophagogastroduodenoscopy.

Case Study 26

Operative Report

Date of Operation: 01/09/2015

Preoperative Diagnosis: 1. Dyspepsia
                            2. Dysphagia

Postoperative Diagnosis: 1. Candidal esophagitis, biopsies taken for confirmation.
                            2. Upper GI endoscopy was otherwise unremarkable. Gastric biopsies were taken to exclude *Helicobacter pylori* infection.

Operation: Esophagogastroduodenoscopy

Surgeon: Rodney Verne, MD

Assistant: V. G. Smith, MD

Anesthesia: Demerol 50 mg intravenous, Versed 6 mg intravenous

Instrument: Olympus video gastroscope

PROCEDURE:

The risks and benefits of the procedure were explained to the patient and informed consent was obtained. The patient was placed in the left lateral decubitus position. Flexible video endoscope was gently advanced through the circopharyngeus into the esophagus. There are typical changes of candidal esophagitis in the mid and distal esophagus. Photographs and biopsies were taken. The GE junction was located at 38 cm from the incisors. Retroflexed views in the cardia showed no fundic mass.

The endoscope was placed in the forward viewing position and advanced from the greater curvature to the antrum, and there was no evidence of ulceration or mass. The pylorus was patent. The duodenal bulb is nondeformed and free of ulceration. Postbulbar duodenum is unremarkable. The endoscope was then withdrawn back into the stomach. Gastric biopsies were taken to exclude *Helicobacter pylori,* and the procedure was terminated. The patient tolerated the procedure well without evident complications.

RECOMMENDATIONS:
1. Await results of pathologic findings.
2. Diflucan therapy 100 mg daily x 3 weeks for treatment of candidiasis.
3. The patient will follow up with her primary physician.

Case Study 26

Pathology Report

Date:	01/09/2015
Physician:	Rodney Verne, MD
Preoperative Diagnosis:	Dyspepsia/dysphagia
Surgical Procedure:	EGD
Postoperative Diagnosis:	Candidal, esophagitis
Specimen(s):	1. Esophageal biopsy 2. Gastric biopsy
GROSS:	There are two containers.

Container number one, labeled "biopsy esophagus," consists of fragments of gray-white soft tissue. In aggregate, these measure $0.3 \times 0.3 \times 0.2$ cm and are submitted in cassette "1."

Container number two, labeled "biopsy gastric," consists of two fragments of gray-tan soft tissue in aggregate $0.3 \times 0.2 \times 0.2$ cm. Submitted in cassette "2."

GROSS AND MICROSCOPIC EXAMINATION:

Biopsy of esophagus: Esophagitis.

COMMENT:
Special stain for fungal organisms is positive with fungal elements consistent with candidal esophagitis.

Gastric biopsies: Acute and chronic gastritis.

COMMENT:
Special stain for *Helicobacter* organism is strongly positive.

Case Study 26

Progress Notes:

Patient has a history of dyspepsia and dysphagia for a month. Taken to endoscopy room where an esophagogastroscopy was performed. Biopsies showed esophagitis, acute and chronic gastritis with *Helicobacter* present. Patient tolerated the procedure well.

Orders:

1. Standard postoperative orders.
2. Vital signs q. 15 minutes × 4; then q. 30 minutes × 2; then q. 1 hour until discharge.
3. Start on soft diet.
4. Discharge when patient is stable.

Case Study 26

Answer Sheet

DIAGNOSES	ICD-9-CM CODES					
First Listed DX				-		
DX 2				-		
DX 3				-		
DX 4				-		

PROCEDURES	CPT CODES					MODIFIERS (If Applicable)		
PR 1						-		

Code the ICD-9-CM Diagnosis Codes and CPT E&M Code
(Two diagnosis codes and one CPT code will be needed)

Case Study 27

Skilled Nursing Facility Visit

Face Sheet

Patient Name:	Cora Wilkinson
Admission Date:	01/15/2015
Age:	68
Sex:	Female
Insurance:	Medicare

Case Study 27

Skilled Nursing Facility Visit

ADMISSION DATE: 01/15/2015

HISTORY OF PRESENT ILLNESS:
This is a follow-up visit for this 68-year-old female. She was admitted to Oakdale Nursing Home 10 days ago with cellulitis of the left foot. She was placed in Oakdale for IV therapy of her cellulitis. She is recovering well, and the infection is about gone. She has a history of type 1 diabetes.

Allergies: None.

MEDICATIONS: Insulin 70/30, IV Vancomycin.

REVIEW OF SYSTEMS: Normal.

PHYSICAL EXAMINATION:
GENERAL: Well-developed, well-nourished female in no acute distress. BP 128/75. Pulse: 80, regular and strong. Respirations: 12, unlabored and regular. Temperature: normal. Height: 5 foot.

HEENT: Normal. No lesions noted.

SKIN: Left foot shows slight reddening on the upper surface. Infection had decreased significantly. All other areas are normal.

PLAN:
Patient is doing well and will be taken off IV Vancomycin.
She will be discharged home tomorrow and will be given a prescription for penicillin.
She is to follow up in my office in 1 week.

Case Study 27

Answer Sheet

DIAGNOSES	ICD-9-CM CODES				
First Listed DX				-	
DX 2				-	

PROCEDURES	CPT CODES				MODIFIERS (If Applicable)	
PR 1					-	

Code ICD-9-CM Diagnoses and CPT Procedures
(Two diagnosis codes and one CPT code will be needed)

Case Study 28

Ambulatory Surgery

Face Sheet

Patient's Name:	Georgia Phillips
Date of Visit:	01/17/2015
Age:	52
Sex:	Female
Insurance:	Medicare

Case Study 28

History and Physical

DATE OF ADMISSION: 01/17/2015

HISTORY OF PRESENT ILLNESS:
The patient has a history of bilateral breast cysts, and in a follow-up mammogram, a mass was discovered in the left breast. Patient also has some dimpling in the area demonstrated on mammogram in the upper outer quadrant.

PAST MEDICAL HISTORY: Patient has a history of mitral valve prolapse.

ALLERGIES: Demerol and Biaxin.

MEDICATIONS: V-Tabs prior to procedures for her mitral valve prolapse.

PHYSICAL EXAMINATION:
VITAL SIGNS: BP 146/80; respiration's 17; pulse 77; temperature 99.

SKIN: Warm and dry.

EYES: The pupils are equal, round, reactive to light and accommodation.

               Sclera is clear.

NECK: Supple. No masses, scars, or bruits.

LUNGS: Clear to auscultation and percussion.

HEART: Normal sinus rhythm. No murmurs or gallops.

BREASTS: Breasts are symmetrical. There is an area of slight skin retraction on the upper outer quadrant of the left breast. There is some thickness in the area. No other masses felt. No axillary lymphadenopathy.

EXTREMITIES: Good distal pulses.

PLAN:
Patient will be brought to the ambulatory surgical center for a left breast biopsy.

Case Study 28

Operative Report

Date of Operation:	01/17/2015
Preoperative Diagnosis:	Left Breast Mass
Postoperative Diagnosis:	Infiltrating ductal cell carcinoma left breast
Procedure Performed:	Excision of left breast mass
Surgeon:	Cheryl Bottom, MD
Assistant:	Jon Actor, MD

PROCEDURE:

The patient was placed on the supine position where anesthesia was administered. The left breast was prepped and draped in the usual sterile manner.

A transverse incision was made along the mass and was carried down through the skin and subcutaneous tissue. A firm mass was identified and was sharply excised from the surrounding breast tissue. Bleeding was controlled with electrocautery.

The wound was closed using interrupted sutures of 3-0 Vicryl for the deep layer. The subcutaneous tissue was closed with interrupted suture of 3-0 Vicryl and the skin was closed 4-0 Monocryl. Dressing was applied. The patient tolerated the procedure well.

Case Study 28

Pathology Report

Date:	01/17/2015
Physician:	Cheryl Bottom, MD
Preoperative Diagnosis:	Left breast mass
Surgical Procedure:	Excision left breast mass
Postoperative Diagnosis:	Infiltrating ductal carcinoma
Specimen(s):	Left breast mass

GROSS:
Received directly from the operating room is a 4 × 3 × 3 cm ovoid pink-tan to yellow fibroadipose tissue, which is firm.

GROSS AND MICROSCOPIC EXAMINATION:
Excisional biopsy of left breast.

Invasive ductal carcinoma, 2.3 cm, histologic grade 2, nuclear grade 2, mitotic grade 1.

Focal lymph vascular space invasion is noted.

Diffuse fibrocystic changes are also noted.

Case Study 28

Progress Notes and Physician Orders

Progress Notes:

Patient has a left breast mass and was taken to the operating room where an excisional biopsy of the mass was performed. Pathology report is pending final determination, but preliminary report is ductal carcinoma.

Physician Orders:

<u>Preoperative Orders</u>

Diet: NPO

Consent to read: Excision left breast mass

Ancef 1 g IV before surgery

<u>Postoperative Orders</u>

Vicodin 1 q6h prn

Liquids as tolerated

Discharge when criteria are met

Case Study 28

Answer Sheet

DIAGNOSES	ICD-9-CM CODES					
First Listed DX				-		
DX 2				-		

PROCEDURES	CPT CODES				MODIFIERS (If Applicable)		
PR 1						-	

Code ICD-9-CM Diagnoses
(8 diagnosis codes will be needed)

Case Study 29

Inpatient Face Sheet

Admit Date: 1/13/2015

Discharge Date: 1/16/2015

Sex: Female

Age: 86

Disposition: Home with home health care

Admitting Diagnoses:
1. Cellulitis, left lower extremity
2. Acute exacerbation of chronic obstructive pulmonary disease
3. Coronary artery disease
4. Hypothyroidism

Discharge Diagnoses:
1. Cellulitis left lower extremity
2. Acute exacerbation of chronic obstructive pulmonary disease
3. Coronary artery disease
4. Hypothyroidism
5. Gastroesophageal reflux disease
6. Depression
7. Degenerative joint disease

Case Study 29

Discharge Summary

Admitted: 1/13/2015

Discharged: 1/16/2015

DISCHARGE DIAGNOSES:
1. Cellulitis of the left lower extremity
2. Acute exacerbation of chronic obstructive pulmonary disease
3. Coronary artery disease
4. Hypothyroidism
5. Gastroesophageal reflux disease
6. Depression
7. Degenerative joint disease

HISTORY OF PRESENT ILLNESS:
Please see admission history and physical examination. This is an 86-year-old female with a 75-pack/year smoking history and severe chronic obstructive pulmonary disease who is seen for recurrent cellulitis in the left lower extremity, which has not responded to outpatient oral antibiotic and diuretic treatment.

HOSPITAL COURSE:
She was treated with intravenous Lasix, Aldactone, potassium supplement, bronchodilator treatment, Solu-Medrol, and intravenous Claforan. The inflammation of the left lower extremity resolved over the next few days. Her wheezing improved, and at rest her lungs were clear. With minimal exertion, she was noted to have wheezing and desaturation with O_2 saturation dropping to 84% on room air. She was advised to have home oxygen therapy.

The edema of the lower extremities resolved, and she will be continued on oral Lasix and Aldactone. The patient is discharged home with home health care to follow. Oxygen 2 L via nasal cannula. Her condition is improved.

DISCHARGE MEDICATIONS:
1. Imdur 60 mg 1/2 tablet q. a.m.
2. Synthroid 0.125 mg q.i.d.
3. Albuterol 2.5 mg plus Atrovent 500 mg via nebulizer q3h.
4. K-Dur 20 mEq b.i.d.
5. Aldactone 25 mg b.i.d.
6. Lasix 80 mg q. a.m. and noon
7. Flovent 220 4 puffs b.i.d. with aerochamber
8. Biaxin 250 mg b.i.d. times 3 days
9. Accolate 20 mg b.i.d.
10. Effexor XR 75 mg q.i.d. for depression

Diet: no added salt. Activity as tolerated.

Plan: She will follow up in my office in 10 days.

Case Study 29

History and Physical

DATE: 1/13/2015

CHIEF COMPLAINT: Swelling, redness, and heat of the left lower extremity.

HISTORY OF PRESENT ILLNESS:
Patient was seen in my office for swelling, erythema, and heat of the left lower extremity and started on oral antibiotics and diuretics as an outpatient. She has not responded to outpatient treatment, therefore, is admitted for inpatient therapy.

PAST MEDICAL HISTORY:
Surgeries include thyroidectomy, total hip replacement, and appendectomy. She also has severe COPD, hypothyroidism, peptic ulcer disease, diverticulosis, coronary artery disease, and mild congestive heart failure.

MEDICATIONS:
Current medications include Synthroid 0.125 mg q.i.d., Imdur 60 mg one-half tablet q.i.d., Azmacort 2 puffs q.i.d., potassium chloride 10 mEq t.i.d., Aldactone 25 mg b.i.d., Lasix 80 mg b.i.d., Colace 100 mg b.i.d., Accolate 20 mg b.i.d., albuterol 2.5 mg plus Atrovent 500 mcg nebulizer q3h.

ALLERGIES: Iodine.

FAMILY HISTORY: Noncontributory.

SOCIAL HISTORY: Previous smoker, no tobacco currently. No alcohol.

REVIEW OF SYSTEMS:

History of gastroesophageal reflux disease, peptic ulcer disease, and osteoarthritis.

PHYSICAL EXAMINATION:

VITAL SIGNS:	Blood pressure 168/70, pulse 96, temperature 99.5, respirations 30. She is wheezing and appears dyspneic.
HEENT:	Unremarkable.
NECK:	Thyroidectomy scar, carotids 2+. No JVD.
CHEST:	Wheezing bilaterally.
CARDIOVASCULAR:	Regular rate and rhythm.
ABDOMEN:	Benign.
EXTREMITIES:	Pitting edema both lower extremities, left greater than right. Left anterior shin is hot, red, and indurated.
NEUROLOGIC:	Unremarkable.

Case Study 29

History and Physical

Continued:

LABORATORY DATA:
Electrolytes are normal. Potassium 4.1. White count 9.5, hemoglobin 12.5. Urinalysis is clear. Chest x-ray shows slight atelectasis in the right base, chronic obstructive pulmonary disease. No acute infiltrates nor congestive heart failure noted. Electrocardiogram shows sinus rhythm, right bundle branch block, nonspecific ST-T changes.

ASSESSMENT:
1. Cellulitis, left lower extremity
2. Acute exacerbation of COPD
3. Coronary artery disease
4. Hypothyroidism
5. Degenerative joint disease
6. Gastroesophageal reflux disease

PLAN:
Admit for intravenous antibiotics, diuresis, and pulmonary rehab.

Case Study 29

Progress Notes:

1/13:   Admit Note: 86-year-old female was seen in my office 1 week ago with recurrent cellulitis of her left foot. She was placed on antibiotics and diuretics; however, has had no response to outpatient therapy. She is now admitted for aggressive treatment.

1/14:   S: Complains only of leg pain and SOB.

          O: Afebrile, vital signs stable, wheezing with minimal exertion.

          A: Leg looks better, less redness. COPD is severe, will probably require home O_2.

          P: Continue with present treatment.

1/15:   S: Feeling much better, able to ambulate some but easily tires.

          O: Labs within normal limits, vitals remain stable, still with SOB and wheezing on exertion.

          A: Leg has responded well to IV medications.

          P: DC IV and start on p.o. Biaxin.

1/16:   S: Patient desires discharge.

          O: Afebrile, vital signs stable.

          A: Leg looks much better.

          P: Discharge patient.

Orders:

1/13:   1.   Admit patient to service of Sarah Stamper, MD.

          2.   IV Lasix and Claforan.

          3.   Respiratory treatments.

          4.   WBC, CBC, EKG, CXR.

1/14:   Continue current treatment regime.

1/15:   1.   Increase ambulation.

          2.   DC IV fluids.

          3.   Biaxin 500 mg p.o. twice daily.

1/16:   Discharge patient with home health care.

Case Study 29

Answer Sheet

DIAGNOSES	ICD-9-CM CODES					
Principal Diagnosis				-		
DX 2				-		
DX 3				-		
DX 4				-		
DX 5				-		
DX 6				-		
DX 7				-		
DX 8				-		

Code ICD-9-CM Diagnoses
(Seven diagnosis codes will be needed)

Case Study 30

Inpatient Face Sheet

Admit Date: 1/10/2015

Discharge Date: 1/13/2015

Sex: Female

Age: 79

Disposition: ACLF

Admitting Diagnoses:
1. Syncope
2. Hypertension
3. Chronic obstructive pulmonary disease
4. Hyperlipidemia
5. Congestive heart failure

Discharge Diagnoses:
1. Syncope, undetermined etiology
2. Chronic obstructive pulmonary disease
3. Congestive heart failure
4. Hypertension
5. Hyperlipidemia

Case Study 30

Discharge Summary

ADMITTED: 1/10/2015

DISCHARGED: 1/13/2015

DISCHARGE DIAGNOSES:

1. Syncope, undetermined etiology
2. Malnourishment
3. CHF
4. COPD
5. Hypertension
6. Hyperlipidemia

PROCEDURES: None

HISTORY OF PRESENT ILLNESS:

Patient presented to the emergency department (initial encounter) with complaint of weakness and feeling of passing out for 2 days duration. Patient was admitted to telemetry to rule out cardiac origin of syncope. Patient is also under current treatment for COPD, CHF, hypertension, and hyperlipidemia.

HOSPITAL COURSE:

Patient was continued on home medications for treatment of chronic illnesses as documented above. Lab values were within normal limits with the exception of low protein and albumin, indicative of mild malnourishment. In addition, the lipids were elevated. Patient was started on Ensure to address the malnourishment, and Pravacol was increased to 40 mg per day to bring the lipids under control. EKG and ECHO were insignificant in determining a cause of the syncope. The patient's hypertension, COPD, and CHF remained under control while the patient was in the hospital. In light of not finding a cause of the syncope and the patient's weakened state from the malnourishment, it was recommended that she enter an ACLF temporarily until her strength returned and she was able to return to her own home. She was in agreement with this, and arrangements were made for discharge to an ACLF. She is to follow a high-protein, low-fat diet and continue with ensure. Activity as tolerated.

Case Study 30

History and Physical

DATE: 1/10/2015

CHIEF COMPLAINT: Weakness and syncope.

HISTORY OF PRESENT ILLNESS:

This 79-year-old woman presented to the emergency room with complaints of weakness and syncope. She was accompanied by a friend who provided most of the current history. The friend states that the patient has had several episodes of "passing out" in the last 2 days. The patient has not fallen during these episodes so there has been no injury as a result of these syncopal episodes.

PAST MEDICAL HISTORY:
Significant for COPD for which she uses inhalers and nebulizer treatment. Also is treated for hypertension, CHF, and high cholesterol. Patient has had a hysterectomy and cholecystectomy.

FAMILY HISTORY:
Mother deceased at 82 years of age with a myocardial infarction. Father deceased at 45 due to coal miner's disease. Patient has no siblings.

SOCIAL HISTORY: 100 pack/year smoking history, quit in 1995. No alcohol use.

MEDICATIONS: Lasix, Pravacol, potassium, and Cardizem.

ALLERGIES: None known.

PHYSICAL EXAMINATION: Blood pressure 110/75, pulse 88, respirations 18, temperature 98.2. Patient appears malnourished.

REVIEW OF SYSTEMS:
HEENT: Pupils equal and reactive to light. Pale conjunctiva. Moist mucous membranes.
NECK: Supple without masses.
LUNGS: Decreased breath sounds.
HEART: Regular rate and rhythm.
ADOMEN: Soft, nontender. Bowel sounds present.
EXTREMITIES: No cyanosis or clubbing.

IMPRESSION:
1. Syncope, etiology to be determined
2. Hypertension
3. COPD
4. Hyperlipidemia
5. CHF

PLAN:
1. Admit to telemetry.
2. Continue with home meds.

Case Study 30

Progress Notes:

1/10:   Admit Note: Patient admitted via emergency room to telemetry for syncope, undetermined etiology. Patient to continue with home meds for CHF, COPD, hypertension, and hyperlipidemia.

1/11:   S: No syncope while here.

O: EKG showed sinus rhythm with RBBB. ECHO WNL Chest x-ray, no CHF, known COPD. Hypertension under control. Vital signs good. Chem profile significant for low protein and albumin with HDL of 281.

A: No cardiac reason for syncope. Patient is malnourished.

P: Continue with current treatment. Add Ensure to diet as a supplement.

1/12:   S: No complaints. No further syncopal episodes.

O: Rhythm remains unchanged. Condition stable.

A: Repeat labs within normal limits, except for protein and albumin, which are still low.

P: Case management to arrange transfer to ACLF until patient can return home.

1/13:   Discharge Note: No cardiac or chemical explanation for syncope. Patient to be discharged to an ACLF until she can return to her own home. Continue with dietary supplement in light of mild malnourishment.

Orders:

1/10:   1.   Admit patient to service of Dr. James Mitchell, per Dr. Lyle Douglas, emergency room physician.

2.   Place patient on telemetry.

3.   Chem profile, CBC.

4.   Continue with patient's home medications.

5.   EKG, chest x-ray, ECHO.

1/11.   1.   Repeat labs.

2.   Provide patient with Ensure.

3.   Case management to assist with discharge plans.

1/12:   1.   Discontinue telemetry.

2.   Arrange transfer to ACLF tomorrow.

1/13:   Discharge today to ACLF.

Case Study 30

Answer Sheet

DIAGNOSES	ICD-9-CM CODES					
Principal Diagnosis				-		
DX 2				-		
DX 3				-		
DX 4				-		
DX 5				-		
DX 6				-		
DX 7				-		

**Code ICD-9-CM Diagnoses and Procedure Codes
(Seven diagnosis codes and one procedure code will be needed)**

Case Study 31

Inpatient Face Sheet

Admit Date: 1/01/2015

Discharge Date: 1/13/2015

Age: 79

Sex: Male

Disposition: Home with home health care

Admission Diagnoses:
1. Acute bronchial asthma in exacerbation
2. Hypoxemia, hypercapnia
3. Suspected chronic obstructive pulmonary disease
4. Rule out pulmonary embolism
5. Hypertension
6. Hyperlipidemia

Discharge Diagnoses:
1. Acute bronchial asthma with acute exacerbation
2. Tracheobronchitis
3. Chronic hypoxemia
4. Suspect underlying chronic obstructive pulmonary disease
5. History of hypertension
6. Hyperlipidemia

Procedures Performed:
1. Broncoscopy with biopsies and lavage

Case Study 31

Discharge Summary

ADMITTED: 1/01/2015

DISCHARGED: 1/13/2015

DISCHARGE DIAGNOSES:
1. Acute bronchial asthma with acute exacerbation
2. Tracheobronchitis
3. Chronic hypoxemia
4. Suspect underlying chronic obstructive pulmonary disease
5. History of hypertension
6. Hyperlipidemia

ADMITTING DIAGNOSES:
1. Acute bronchial asthma in exacerbation
2. Hypoxemia, hypercapnia
3. Suspected chronic obstructive pulmonary disease
4. Rule out pulmonary embolism
5. Hypertension
6. Hyperlipidemia

PROCEDURE:
1. Bronchoscopy with lavage and biopsy

HISTORY OF PRESENT ILLNESS:
This is a 79-year-old male patient with above-mentioned medical problems who now presents with increasing shortness of breath, cough, wheezing, and respiratory distress. He has been on multiple bronchodilators and inhaled steroids, including Flovent, nebulizer, theophylline, and a small dose of prednisone.

HOSPITAL COURSE:
This patient was admitted with increasing shortness of breath. He was not responding to outpatient medical therapy. He was placed on albuterol nebulized respiratory treatment and started on a short course of pulse intravenous steroids, given mucolytics, expectorants, and continued on theophylline. He was cultured and placed on intravenous Claforan initially, empirically; he was otherwise continued on treatment for hypertension. At this initial encounter, a therapeutic bronchoscopy was performed with evidence of thick, purulent mucous plugs widespread on both sides, some narrowing of the left lower lobe bronchus also noted with some inflammation. Biopsies were negative for malignancy. He was continued on Mucomyst at this point, nebulized respiratory treatments, chest physiotherapy, and intravenous Solu-Medrol.

Following several days of aggressive treatment, he started to improve and was less short of breath, bronchospasm was resolving, and was discharged on January 13.

Case Study 31

Discharge Summary

Continued:

PERTINENT EXAM: Audible wheezing, coughed continuously, tachycardic, tachypneic, afebrile.

VITAL SIGNS: Blood pressure stable.
HEENT: Revealed postnasal drip.
NECK: No jugular venous distention.
LUNGS: Diffuse wheezing, rhonchi and rales.
HEART: Regular.
ABDOMEN: Soft.
EXTREMITIES: No edema.

REVIEW OF LABORATIORY DATA:

The bronchoscopy cytology revealed no malignancy. The arterial blood gases on room air: pH 7.48, pCO$_2$ 36, pO$_2$ 56, bicarb 26.4, and saturation 92.3%. Complete blood count: white blood cell count 9,800. Hemoglobin 15, hematocrit 47.1, and platelet count normal. Follow-up complete blood count remained stable. Chemistries—blood urea nitrogen 17, creatinine 1.4. Troponin I normal on a serial basis. Albumin 2.4 to 3.3. Liver functions normal. Theophylline level 19.2. Urinalysis: yellow and clear; microscopic blood noted, protein negative, nitrite negative, leukocyte esterase a small amount detected. Sputum revealed *Candida*. Urine culture: no growth. Sputum for acid-fast bacilli: test still pending at this time although smears were negative. The chest revealed a new hazy opacity of the left mid lung, in the lower lung area, possibly fusion or atelectasis. This persisted on follow-up.

Electrocardiogram: sinus rhythm, sinus tachycardia. While on telemetry the patient was in sinus rhythm.

MEDICATIONS ON DISCHARGE:
1. Prednisone 30 mg daily for 4 days, then 20 mg daily for 4 days, then 10 mg daily
2. Flovent 220 mcg three puffs twice daily
3. Albuterol treatments four times daily
4. Norvasc 5 mg daily
5. Lasix 40 mg half tablet daily
6. Potassium 10 mEq daily
7. Nasonex spray two puffs daily
8. Theophylline 200 mg twice daily

ACITIVITY: As tolerated.

Case Study 31

History and Physical

ADMISSION DATE: 1/01/2015

CHIEF COMPLAINT: Shortness of breath, wheezing, cough, and chest congestion.

HISTORY OF PRESENT ILLNESS:
This is a 79-year-old male with multiple admissions for respiratory problems and exacerbation of asthma. Presented to the emergency room because of increasing shortness of breath, cough, wheezing, and respiratory distress. Apparently he has been on multiple bronchodilators and inhaled steroids, including Flovent, nebulizer, theophylline, and a small dose of prednisone a day. In spite of the outpatient treatment, his symptoms continued to worsen. He was admitted to the hospital for further treatment.

PAST MEDICAL HISTORY:
Past medical history is positive for long-standing bronchial asthma with chronic exacerbation, steroid-dependent asthma. He also had history of tracheobronchitis, hypertension, and hyperlipidemia.

MEDICATIONS AT HOME:
Flovent 220 micrograms two puffs twice a day, but he is not using regularly. Nebulizer four times a day, Norvasc 5 mg once a day, Lasix 40 mg ½ tablet once a day, potassium 10 mEq once a day, calcium t.i.d., theophylline 200 mg b.i.d., and prednisone 5 mg once a day.

ALLERGIES: None.

SOCIAL HISTORY: Does not smoke. Never smoked.

REVIEW OF SYSTEMS:

HEENT:	Revealed postnasal drip.
NECK:	No jugular venous distension.
LUNGS:	Bilateral diffuse wheezing, rhonchi, and rales.
HEART:	Regular rhythm.
ABDOMEN:	Soft.
EXTREMITIES:	No edema.
GASTROINTESTINAL:	No gastritis, gastroesophageal reflux, occasional indigestion, no ulcer.
RESPIRATORY:	As mentioned in the history.
CARDIAC:	History of hypertension, but no history of angina, coronary artery disease. Does not have any chest pain. He had an echocardiogram in 2001, which was normal with ejection fraction of 60%.
MUSCULOSKELETAL:	Negative.
NEUROLOGIC:	Negative for stroke, transient ischemic attack, headache, dizziness, or syncope.
GENITOURINARY:	Negative. The rest of review of systems is negative.

Case Study 31

History and Physical

Continued:

PHYSICAL EXAMINATION:
Elderly male who is in acute distress with audible wheeze. He coughs continuously. He is tachycardiac, tachypneic, afebrile. Vitals stable otherwise.

The labs, x-rays, and so on, were reviewed.

IMPRESSION:
1. Acute bronchial asthma and exacerbation.
2. Severe hypoxemia, hypercapnia. Rule out due to chronic obstructive pulmonary disease, bronchospasm. Rule out other causes, such as pulmonary embolism.

PLAN: Will give IV steroids, IV antibiotics, nebulizer treatment, and oxygen.
Get a spiral CT scan to rule out pulmonary emboli.
Continue other treatment, and will follow him closely.

Case Study 31

Procedure Report

DATE: 1/02/2015

ENDOSCOPIST: Dr. Brandon Douglas

PROCEDURE: Bronchoscopy with diagnostic biopsy

INDICATION: Left lower lobe collapse, due to mucous plug

ANESTHESIA: Dr. Jeffrey Cottrell

DESCRIPTION OF PROCEDURE:

After the anesthesiologist anesthetized the patient, the Olympus bronchoscope was introduced through the bite block into the oral cavity. The upper airway was seen and was unremarkable. Cords were sprayed with Xylocaine. The scope was passed through the cords into the trachea, which was free of lesion. Carina was sharp. The scope was passed into the right mid stem bronchus. The upper lobe and middle lobe segments were seen. They are remarkable for thick purulent mucous plugging of all the bronchial segments. Aggressive lavage with saline and Mucomyst were done. In spite of that, mucous plugs were quite thick, and it required manual removal of the mucous plugs through the scope. Subsequently the scope was withdrawn back to the left main stem, and left upper lobe, lingual lobe, and subsegments were seen. They were also remarkable for severe mucous plugs, which were removed manually. After complete evacuation of mucous plugs was done, bronchial segments were visualized again, and there was some narrowing of left lower segment with some inflamed, swollen mucosa. Diagnostic biopsies were done from that segment. Bronchial washings were done and sent for cytology and culture.

The patient tolerated the procedure well.

FINDINGS: Thick, purulent mucous pluggings were widespread on both sides. There was some narrowing of left lower lobe bronchus with inflamed, swollen mucosa with smooth margin.

SPECIMENS: Biopsies were done from left lobe bronchus. Washing was done. Bronchoscopic lavage was done using saline and Mucomyst, and all the mucous plugs were removed.

Case Study 31

Pathology Report

DATE: 1/02/2015

SPECIMEN TYPE: CYTO

SURGICAL PATHOLOGY/CYTOPATHOLOGY REPORT

PRE-OP DIAGNOSIS: Left lower lobe collapse
Inflamed swollen bronchial mucosa left lower lobe

POST-OP DIAGNOSIS: Left lower lobe collapse
Inflamed swollen bronchial mucosa left lower lobe

SPECIMEN(S)

BRONCHIAL WASHING MATERIAL:

GROSS DESCRIPTION:
Received 8 cc of hemorrhagic fluid in the laboratory. Two smears and 1 cell block are prepared for cytological evaluation.

MICROSCOPIC DESCRIPTION:
Microscopic examination of the specimen reveals groups of and single epithelial cells that appear poorly preserved, displaying nuclear enlargement, hyperchromasia, increased N/C bronchial columnar, metaplastic, and reserve cells: pulmonary macrophages, mixed inflammatory cells, necrotic debris, and fungal elements.

CYTOPATHOLOGICAL DIAGNOSIS:

BRONCHIAL WASHING:

Poorly preserved dysplastic epithelial cells present.

Candida species identified.

Case Study 31

SURGICAL PATHOLOGY/CYTOPATHOLOGY REPORT

PRE-OP DIAGNOSIS: Left lower lobe collapse: Inflamed swollen bronchial mucosa left lower lobe.

POST-OP DIAGNOSIS: Left lower lobe collapse: Inflamed swollen bronchial mucosa left lower lobe.

SPECIMEN(S):
  Lung, left lower lobe–biopsy × 4

  GROSS DESCRIPTION:
  The specimen consists of four fragments of tan tissue ranging from 0.1 up to 0.6 cm in greatest dimension. Entirely submitted.

  MICROSCOPIC DIAGNOSIS:

  BIOPSY OF LEFT LOWER LOBE: Mild nonspecific chronic bronchitis with hypertrophy of the submucosal glands and thickening of the subepithelial basement membrane.

  No tumor present.

FINAL DIAGNOSIS:
  BIOPSY OF LEFT LOWER LOBE:

  Minute detached fragment of dysplastic epithelium.

  Mild nonspecific chronic bronchitis with hypertrophy of submucosal glands and thickened subepithelial basement membrane.

Case Study 31

Answer Sheet

DIAGNOSES	ICD-9-CM CODES					
Principal Diagnosis				-		
DX 2				-		
DX 3				-		
DX 4				-		
DX 5				-		
DX 6				-		
DX 7				-		

PROCEDURES	ICD-9-CM CODES				
PP 1			-		

Code ICD-9-CM Diagnosis and Procedure Code
(One diagnosis code and one procedure code will be needed)

Case Study 32

Inpatient Face Sheet

ADMIT DATE: 01/02/2015

DISCHARGE DATE: 01/10/2015

AGE: 47

SEX: M

DISPOSITION: Home

ADMISSION DIAGNOSES:
1. Low back pain
2. L5-S1 radiculopathy

DISCHARGE DIAGNOSIS:
1. Herniated nucleus pulposus right-sided at L5-S1

OPERATION/PROCEDURE:
1. Lumbar laminectomy at L5 and S1
2. Right-sided L5-S1 micro-diskectomy
3. Use of operating microscope

Case Study 32

History and Physical

ADMISSION DATE: 01/02/2015

REASON FOR ADMISSION: The patient is a 47-year-old gentleman who presented with severe back pain.

HISTORY OF PRESENT ILLNESS:
The patient is a 47-year-old gentleman seen in my office in a severe state of pain. It was suspected that the patient had radiculopathy. The patient was sent for a MRI. The radiologist reported a very large disk herniation with right-sided disk protrusion and early extrusion of the disk material at L5-S1 with compression of the thecal sac.

MEDICATIONS PRIOR TO ADMISSION:
The patient's medications prior to admission included Tylenol #3, Decadron, and Vicodin.

ALLERGIES: The patient has no known allergies.

SOCIAL HISTORY:
The patient is married and lives with his wife. The patient has a history of smoking one pack of cigarettes per day. The patient has a history of drinking alcoholic beverages occasionally.

REVIEW OF SYSTEMS:
The patient denied a history of chest pain. The patient denied a history of chest pressure. The patient denied a history of chest tightness. The patient denied a history of difficulty breathing.

PHYSICAL EXAMINATION:

VITAL SIGNS: The patient's vital signs on admission were stable.

NECK: The neck was supple. There was no jugular venous distention. There were no carotid bruits.

LUNGS: The lungs were clear to auscultation and percussion. There were no signs of consolidation.

HEART: The heart was normal.

ABDOMEN: The abdomen was soft and nontender. The bowel sounds were positive.

EXTREMITIES: The examination of the extremities was negative for cyanosis, clubbing, or edema.

NEUROLOGICAL: The cranial nerves II through XII appeared to be intact. The tone was normal. The power was five by five in the upper extremities. The power was decreased in the right lower extremity secondary to maybe being in pain. The sensation on the right side revealed only one plus at the knee and ankle jerks. The straight leg raising was positive.

PLAN: Consultation with neurology and surgical consultation will be requested.

Case Study 32

Consultation

REQUESTING PHYSICIAN: Dr. Rosie Wags

DATE: 01/02/2015

CONSULTING PHYSICIAN: Dr. Zachary Service

CHIEF COMPLAINT: Right lower extremity pain

HISTORY OF PRESENT ILLNESS: This is a 47-year-old gentleman who has a past medical history significant for bulging disk at L5-L1. The patient was having this pain and was ultimately relieved with medication as well as chiropractic manipulation. The patient had magnetic resonance imaging done yesterday, which showed he had a bulging disk at L5-S1 on the right side. At the time of the examination, the patient is awake, alert, and oriented x 4. He denied any lower extremity weakness but complained of right lower extremity pain at the L5-S1 nerve root distribution. He denied any bowel or bladder dysfunction.

PAST MEDICAL HISTORY: No significant past medical history.

MEDICATIONS: Vicodin, Tylenol #3, Soma, Decadron.

SOCIAL HISTORY: Smokes one pack of cigarettes per day. Denies any alcohol use.

REVIEW OF SYSTEMS: Completely reviewed and was negative.

PHYSICAL EXAMINATION: This is a 47-year-old gentleman lying in bed in no acute distress.

HEAD:	Norma cephalic, traumatic.
ENT:	Within normal limits.
NECK:	Supple. No bruits are auscultated. No adenopathy.
CHEST:	Clear to auscultation.
HEART:	Regular rate and rhythm. No murmurs, rubs, or gallops.
ABDOMEN:	Positive bowel sounds, nontender, no distended. No organomegaly.
EXTREMITIES:	No cyanosis, edema, or clubbing.
NEUROLOGIC:	The patient is alert and oriented x 3. Cranial nerves II–XII are grossly intact. Pupils are equal, round, and react to light and accommodation. Extraocular movements are intact. Cerebellar function is intact. Motor/sensory exam is intact.

There is negative Babinski. No pronator drift. Strength is 5/5 in all extremities in all ranges of motion. There was a positive straight-leg raise on the right. There was evidence of a decreased reflex knee jerk on the right, which was 1+. MRI scan of the lumbar spine revealed L5-S1 right-sided disk herniation.

IMPRESSION: Low back pain. L5-S1 radiculopathy.

RECOMMENDATIONS:
1. The patient is stable.
2. Continue current care.
3. Suggest an epidural steroid injection as well as physical therapy at this time.

Case Study 32

Consultation

REQUESTING PHYSICIAN: Dr. Rosie Wags

DATE: 01/02/2015

CONSULTING PHYSICIAN: Dr. Liza Gaige

REASON FOR CONSULTATION:

The patient is a 47-year-old gentleman who presented with lower back pain.

HISTORY OF PRESENT ILLNESS:

The patient is a 47-year-old gentleman whose past medical history was significant for a history of a bulging disk in 1994 at L5 and S1. He subsequently had a MRI that revealed L5 and S1, herniated disk. The patient was then admitted to the hospital for further management. A neurological consultation was then requested. At this time the patient is still having lower back pain with some pain radiating to the right lower extremity, all the way to the toes. The patient denied a history of chest pain. The patient denied a history of shortness of breath. There is no history of nausea or vomiting. The patient denied a history of dysphagia.

PAST MEDICAL AND SURGICAL HISTORY:

The patient has a history of a fall with lower back pain.

MEDICATIONS PRIOR TO ADMISSION:

The patient's medications prior to admission included Vicodin and Tylenol #3 and Soma and Decadron.

ALLERGIES: The patient has no known allergies.

SOCIAL HISTORY:

The patient has a history of smoking approximately one pack of cigarettes per day. The patient has a history of drinking alcoholic beverages occasionally.

PHYSICAL EXAMINATION:

GENERAL APPEARANCE: On examination the patient is awake, alert, and oriented times three.

NEUROLOGICAL: Extraocular movements were intact. Pupils are equal, round, and reactive to light and accommodation. There was no nystagmus. There were no carotid bruits. The visual fields were within normal limits. There was no Kernig sign. There was no Brudzinski sign. The cranial nerves II through XII appeared to be intact. The tongue was midline. The corneal reflex was intact. The gag reflex was intact. Motor system revealed tone was normal. Power was five by five in left upper extremity and the right upper extremity. The power in the lower extremities was five by five distally but three plus to four by five because of the severe pain proximally. The sensory examination revealed normal pin prick, touch, and temperature. Normal position. Normal vibration. The reflexes were plus one at the right knee jerk and ankle jerk. The straight leg raising was a stronger positive in the right lower extremity than in the left lower extremity. The patient can walk but with a limp. The patient cannot walk on heel and tiptoes.

Case Study 32

Consultation

Continued:

LABORATORY INVESTIGATIONS:
The magnetic resonance imaging of the lumbar spine revealed L5-S1 central and right-side herniated disk.

IMPRESSION:
1. Severe lower back pain.
2. Severe radicular pain mainly of the right lower extremity secondary to herniated disk.
3. L5-S1 radiculopathy.
4. Straight leg raising positive.
5. Right knee jerk plus one, decreased compared to the left knee jerk.

RECOMMENDATION:
1. Immediate lumbar laminectomy

Case Study 32

Operative Report

DATE: 01/03/2015

SURGEON: Dr. Liza Gaige

PREOPERATIVE DIAGNOSIS:

1. Herniated nucleus pulposus right sided at L5-S1.

POSTOPERATIVE DIAGNOSIS:

1. Herniated nucleus pulposus right sided at L5-S1.

OPERATION/PROCEDURE:

Lumbar laminectomy at L5 and S1, right sided.

L5-S1 diskectomy.

ASSISTANT: Dr. Jeff Cottrell

COMPLICATIONS: There were no complications.

ANESTHESIA: General endotracheal anesthesia.

ESTIMATED BLOOD LOSS: Less than 50 cc.

INDICATIONS FOR THE PROCEDURE:
This is a young gentleman with intractable right sciatica of 8 years duration who has failed conservative treatment. The patient is now being taken to surgery for decompression and removal of the disk. The risks of the surgery and the limitations of the surgery were explained to the patient and the patient's wife at length. They understand the risks and wish to proceed with procedure.

DESCRIPTION OF THE OPERATION:
Intravenous lines were started. Thigh-high TED and compression boots were placed on the lower extremities. The patient received general endotracheal anesthesia. The patient was placed in the prone position resting on the Wilson frame. All the pressure points were appropriately padded. The area in the lumbar spine was shaved, prepped, and draped in the usual sterile manner. An incision was made in the spinous process of L5 to S1 inclusive using the subperiosteal dissection. The lamina of right L5 and S1 were exposed. Intraoperative x-ray confirmed our level. Using the Anspach drill we thinned out the lamina arch to the level of the ligamentum flavum. We then proceeded to do the laminotomy of L5 on the right side of the inferior two-thirds and superior two-thirds of S1. This exposed the nerve root going out. The nerve root was retracted slightly medially. There was a large anterior compression of the nerve root pushing the nerve root posteriorly. Slightly moving the nerve root medially, we exposed the big rent in the angelus fibrosis, entered this big defect, and the diskectomy was performed.

Case Study 32

Operative Report

Continued:

There was a large disk herniation that had broken through the angelus and into the posterior part of the vertebral body of L5-S1. Once the diskectomy was performed, the wound was irrigated thoroughly using antibiotic solution. With a small nerve hook we went ahead and looked for any residual fragments, and there were none. The wound was then irrigated thoroughly using a copious amount of antibiotic solution. The wound was closed in serial layers using #0-Vicryl in an interrupted fashion on the muscle and fascial layers. We used #2-0 Vicryl sutures to close the subcutaneous tissues. We used #2-0 Nurolon vertical and multilocking sutures for the skin. All the sponge and needle counts were reported correct at the end of the procedure. The patient tolerated the procedure well. The patient was extubated in the operating room and was taken to the recovery room in stable condition moving all extremities.

SURGICAL PATHOLOGY REPORT

ACUTE HERNIATED DISK L5-S1

SPECIMENS(S)   DISK NOS.—L5-S1

GROSS DESCRIPTION:

The specimen consists of multiple irregular fragments of fibrocartilaginous tissue weighing approximately 5 g in aggregate.

Representative sections are submitted in a single cassette for decalcification and processing.

MICROSCOPIC DIAGNOSIS:

Degenerated fibrocartilaginous tissue consistent with intervertebral disk. Clinically herniated disk L5-S1.

Case Study 32

Answer Sheet

DIAGNOSES			ICD-9-CM CODES			
Principal Diagnosis				-		

PROCEDURE		ICD-9-CM CODES			
PP 1			-		

X. CCS Case Study Coding Review Answer Key

Case Study Answer Key

Case 1

Diagnoses	ICD-9-CM Codes					
Principal Diagnosis 　　　Unspecified septicemia	0	3	8	-	9	
DX 2　SIRS, due to noninfectious process without acute organ 　　　dysfunction	9	9	5	-	9	3
DX 3　Non-Hodgkin's lymphoma	2	0	2	-	8	0
DX 4　Dehydration	2	7	6	-	5	1
DX 5　Pancytopenia anemia	2	8	4	-	1	1
DX 6　Adverse effect of antineoplastic	E9	3	3	-	1	
DX 7　Hypertension	4	0	1	-	9	
DX 8　Hypoalbuminemia	2	7	3	-	8	
DX 9　Transfusion reaction	9	9	9	-	8	9

Case 2

Diagnoses	ICD-9-CM Codes					
Principal Diagnosis 　　　Malignant neoplasm upper lobe, lung	1	6	2	-	3	
DX 2　Secondary malignancy thoracic lymph nodes	1	9	6	-	1	
DX 3　Asthmatic bronchitis	4	9	3	-	2	0
DX 4　Depression NOS	3	1	1	-		
DX 5　Tobacco use disorder	3	0	5	-	1	

Procedures	ICD-9-CM Codes						
PP 1　Right upper lobectomy	3	2	-	4	9	-	
PX 2　Flexible bronchoscopy	3	3	-	2	2	-	
PX 3　Diagnostic biopsy lymph nodes	4	0	-	1	1	-	

Case Study Answer Key

Case 3

Diagnoses	ICD-9-CM Codes					
Principal Diagnosis Diabetes mellitus, type 1 with peripheral circulatory disorder, uncontrolled	2	5	0	-	7	3
DX 2 Diabetic ulcer of heel and midfoot	7	0	7	-	1	4
DX 3 Chronic renal failure	5	8	5	-	9	
DX 4 Pneumonia	4	8	6	-		
DX 5 Type 1 diabetes, uncontrolled with polyneuropathy	2	5	0	-	6	3
DX 6 Type 1 diabetes, uncontrolled with renal manifestations	2	5	0	-	4	3
DX 7 Peripheral vascular disease due to diabetes	4	4	3	-	8	1
DX 8 Diabetic polyneuropathy	3	5	7	-	2	
DX 9 Anemia	2	8	5	-	9	
DX 10 Below the knee amputation status	V	4	9	-	7	5
DX 11 Coronary atherosclerosis of native coronary artery	4	1	4	-	0	1
DX 12 Aortocoronary bypass status	V	4	5	-	8	1

Procedure	ICD-9-CM Codes					
PP 1 Excisional debridement	8	6	-	2	2	-

Case 4

Diagnoses	ICD-9-CM Codes				
Principal Diagnosis Blood loss anemia	2	8	0	-	0	
DX 2 Atrial fibrillation	4	2	7	-	3	1
DX 3 Hypertension	4	0	1	-	9	

Procedures	ICD-9-CM Codes					
PP 1 Colonoscopy	4	5	-	2	3	-
PX 2 Esophagogastroduodenoscopy	4	5	-	1	3	-

Case Study Answer Key

Case 5

Diagnoses	ICD-9-CM Codes					
Principal Diagnosis Alcoholic gastritis with hemorrhage	5	3	5	-	3	1
DX 2 Chronic airway obstruction	4	9	6	-		
DX 3 Alcohol abuse	3	0	3	-	9	0
DX 4 Tobacco use disorder	3	0	5	-	1	
DX 5 Depression	3	1	1	-		
DX 6 Obesity, unspecified	2	7	8	-	0	0
DX 7 Alcoholic cirrhosis	5	7	1	-	2	
DX 8 Esophagitis	5	3	0	-	1	0

Procedure	ICD-9-CM Codes						
PP 1 Esophagogastroduodenoscopy	4	5	-	1	3	-	

Case 6

Diagnoses	ICD-9-CM Codes					
Principal Diagnosis Coronary artery disease, native artery	4	1	4	-	0	1
DX 2 Unstable angina	4	1	1	-	1	
DX 3 Atrial fibrillation	4	2	7	-	3	1
DX 4 Second-degree atrioventricular block	4	2	6	-	1	3
DX 5 History of percutaneous transluminal coronary angioplasty	V	4	5	-	8	2
DX 6 Family history of cardiovascular disease	V	1	7	-	4	9

Procedures	ICD-9-CM Codes						
PP 1 PTCA, single vessel	0	0	-	6	6	-	
PX 2 Procedure on single vessel	0	0	-	4	0	-	
PX 3 Left heart catheterization	3	7	-	2	2	-	
PX 4 Coronary angiography	8	8	-	5	7	-	

Case 7

Diagnoses	ICD-9-CM Codes					
Principal Diagnosis Anterior wall myocardial infarction, initial episode	4	1	0	-	1	1
DX 2 Atrial fibrillation	4	2	7	-	3	1
DX 3 Aortic valve stenosis	4	2	4	-	1	
DX 4 Herpes zoster	0	5	3	-	9	
DX 5 Hypertension	4	0	1	-	9	
DX 6 Old myocardial infarction	4	1	2	-		

Case Study Answer Key

Case 8

Diagnoses	ICD-9-CM Codes					
Principal Diagnosis Acute exacerbation of COPD	4	9	1	-	2	1
DX 2 Hypertension	4	0	1	-	9	
DX 3 Thoracoabdominal aneurysm	4	4	1	-	7	
DX 4 Gastroesophageal reflux disease	5	3	0	-	8	1

Case 9

Diagnoses	ICD-9-CM Codes					
Principal Diagnosis Diverticulitis of colon	5	6	2	-	1	1
DX 2 Postoperative atelectasis	9	9	7	-	3	9
DX 3 Atelectasis	5	1	8	-	0	
DX 4 Peritoneal adhesions	5	6	8	-	0	
DX 5 Hypertension	4	0	1	-	9	
DX 6 Acute pharyngitis	4	6	2	-		
DX 7 Spasm, sigmoid	5	6	4	-	8	9
DX 8 Internal hemorrhoids	4	5	5	-	0	

Procedures	ICD-9-CM Codes						
PP 1 Sigmoidectomy	4	5	-	7	6	-	
PX 2 Colostomy	4	6	-	1	0	-	
PX 3 Partial resection of small bowel	4	5	-	6	2	-	
PX 4 Lysis of adhesion	5	4	-	5	9	-	
PX 5 Flexible sigmoidoscopy	4	5	-	2	4	-	

Case 10

Diagnoses	ICD-9-CM Codes				
Principal Diagnosis Ovarian cyst	6	2	0	-	2
DX 2 Acute blood loss anemia	2	8	5	-	1
DX 3 Urinary tract infection	5	9	9	-	0
DX 4 Intrauterine synechiae	6	2	1	-	5

Procedures	ICD-9-CM Codes					
PP 1 Hysterectomy	6	8	-	4	9	-
PX 2 Bilateral salpingo-oophorectomy	6	5	-	6	1	-

Case Study Answer Key

Case 11

Diagnoses	ICD-9-CM Codes					
First listed DX Sprain, wrist, unspecified site	8	4	2	-	0	0

Procedures	CPT Codes					Modifiers (If Appropriate)		
PR 1 Application of short arm splint (forearm to hand); static	2	9	1	2	5	-	L	T
PR 2 X-ray, wrist, two views	7	3	1	0	0	-	L	T

Case 12

Diagnoses	ICD-9-CM Codes					
First listed DX Acute pyelonephritis, without lesion	5	9	0	-	1	0
DX 2 *Escherichia coli*	0	4	1	-	4	9

Case 13

Diagnoses	ICD-9-CM Codes				
First listed DX Epistaxis	7	8	4	-	7

Case 14

Diagnoses	ICD-9-CM Codes				
First listed DX Dyspepsia	5	3	6	-	8

Case Study Answer Key

Case 15

Diagnoses	ICD-9-CM Codes					
First listed DX Benign prostatic hypertrophy	6	0	0	-	0	1
DX 2 Malignant neoplasm of prostate	1	8	5	-		
DX 3 Coronary artery disease, native artery	4	1	4	-	0	1
DX 4 Chronic airway obstruction	4	9	6	-		
Additional DX Retention of urine, unspecified	7	8	8		2	0
Additional DX Incomplete bladder emptying	7	8	8		2	1
Additional DX Supplemental oxygen	V	4	6		2	

Note: As per instructions, only four DX will be coded. These additional DX were added for your study convenience.

Procedure	CPT Codes					Modifier (If Appropriate)		
PR 1 Laser coagulation of prostate	5	2	6	4	7	-		

Case 16

Diagnoses	ICD-9-CM Codes					
First listed DX Coronary artery disease of native artery	4	1	4	-	0	1
DX 2 Angina pectoris	4	1	3	-	9	
DX 3 History of coronary artery bypass graft	V	4	5	-	8	1

Procedure	CPT Codes					Modifier (If Appropriate)		
PR 1 Left heart catheterization with catheter placement in bypass graft	9	3	4	5	9	-		

Case 17

Diagnoses	ICD-9-CM Codes					
First listed DX Tear medial meniscus	8	3	6	-	0	-
DX 2 Tobacco use disorder	3	0	5	-	1	-

Procedure	CPT Codes					Modifier (If Appropriate)		
PR 1 Arthroscopic medial meniscectomy	2	9	8	8	1	-	R	T

Case Study Answer Key

Case 18

Diagnoses	ICD-9-CM Codes					
First listed DX Sebaceous cyst	7	0	6	-	2	
DX 2 Hypertension	4	0	1	-	9	
DX 3 Chronic airway obstruction	4	9	6	-		
DX 4 Tobacco use disorder	3	0	5	-	1	

Procedures	CPT Codes					Modifier (If Appropriate)	
PR 1 Excision of cyst 2 cm	1	1	4	2	2	-	
PR 2 Excision of cyst 2.5 cm	1	1	4	2	3	-	

Case 19

Diagnoses	ICD-9-CM Codes					

Principal Diagnosis
    Displacement of cervical intervertebral disk without
    myelopathy
	7	2	2	-	0	

DX 2 Dyspnea and respiratory abnormality	7	8	6	-	0	9
DX 3 Opiates/narcotics causing adverse effects in therapeutic use	E9	3	5	-	2	
DX 4 Asthma, unspecified	4	9	3	-	9	0

Procedures	ICD-9-CM Codes					
PP 1 Cervical fusion, anterior technique	8	1	-	0	2	-
PX 2 Excision of intervertebral disk	8	0	-	5	1	-
PX 3 Fusion of 2–3 vertebrae	8	1	-	6	2	-

Case 20

Diagnoses	ICD-9-CM Codes					
Principal Diagnosis Threatened premature labor, antepartum condition	6	4	4	-	0	3

Case Study Answer Key

Case 21

Diagnoses	ICD-9-CM Codes					
Principal Diagnosis Pneumonia	4	8	6	-		
DX 2 Asthma, unspecified type with acute exacerbation	4	9	3	-	9	2
DX 3 Cardiac dysrhythmia	4	2	7	-	8	9
DX 4 Chronic diastolic heart failure	4	2	8	-	3	2
DX 5 Tobacco use disorder	3	0	5	-	1	

Case 22

Diagnoses	ICD-9-CM Codes					
Principal Diagnosis Pulmonary embolism	4	1	5	-	1	9
DX 2 Chronic systolic congestive heart failure	4	2	8	-	2	2
DX 3 Hypertensive renal disease with failure	4	0	3	-	9	0
DX 4 Type 1 diabetes with neurological manifestations	2	5	0	-	6	1
DX 5 Diabetic neuropathy	3	5	7	-	2	
DX 6 Deep-vein thrombophlebitis	4	5	3	-	4	0
DX 7 Dizziness	7	8	0	-	4	
DX 8 Chronic airway obstruction	4	9	6	-		
DX 9 Chronic kidney disease, unspecified	5	8	5	-	9	
DX 10 Obesity	2	7	8	-	0	0
DX 11 Long-term (current) use of insulin	V	5	8	-	6	7
DX 12 History of tobacco use	V	1	5	-	8	2

Case 23

Diagnoses	ICD-9-CM Codes					
First listed DX Other specified cardiac dysrhythmia	4	2	7	-	8	9
DX 2 Atrial flutter	4	2	7	-	3	2

Procedures	CPT Codes					Modifier (If Appropriate)		
PR 1 Comprehensive EPS	9	3	6	2	0	-		
PR 2 Intracardiac catheter ablation	9	3	6	5	0	-		
PR 3 Programmed stimulation and pacing	9	3	6	2	3	-		

Case Study Answer Key

Case 24

Diagnoses		ICD-9-CM Codes					
First listed DX Coronary artery disease of native artery		4	1	4	-	0	1
DX 2 Mitral valve disorder		4	2	4	-	0	

Procedures	CPT Codes					Modifier (If Appropriate)		
PR 1 LD stent placement	9	2	9	2	8	-	L	D
PR 2 Catheter placement in coronary artery(s) for coronary angiography, including injection(s) for coronary angiography, imaging supervision and interpretation; with left heart catheterization including injection(s) for left ventriculography when performed	9	3	4	5	8	-		

Case 25

Diagnoses		ICD-9-CM Codes					
First listed DX Giardiasis		0	0	7	-	1	
DX 2 Dehydration (volume depletion)		2	7	6	-	5	1
DX 3 Arthropathy, unspecified site		7	1	6	-	9	0

Case 26

Diagnoses		ICD-9-CM Codes					
First listed DX Candidal esophagitis		1	1	2	-	8	4
DX 2 Acute gastritis, without hemorrhage		5	3	5	-	0	0
DX 3 Atrophic gastritis, without hemorrhage		5	3	5	-	1	0
DX 4 *Helicobacter pylori* (bacterial infection)		0	4	1	-	8	6

Procedure	CPT Codes					Modifier (If Applicable)		
PR 1 Esophagogastroduodenoscopy with biopsies	4	3	2	3	9	-		

Case Study Answer Key

Case 27

Diagnoses	ICD-9-CM Codes					
First listed DX Other cellulitis and abscess, of foot, except toes	6	8	2	-	7	
DX 2 Type 1 diabetes mellitus, without mention of complication, not stated as uncontrolled	2	5	0	-	0	1

Procedure	CPT Codes					Modifier (If Applicable)	
PR 1 Nursing home visit	9	9	3	0	7	-	

Case 28

Diagnoses	ICD-9-CM Codes					
First listed DX Malignant neoplasm of female breast, upper-outer quadrant	1	7	4	-	4	
DX 2 Mitral valve disorder	4	2	4	-	0	

Procedure	CPT Codes					Modifier (If Applicable)	
PR 1 Excision of breast mass	1	9	1	2	0	-	L	T

Case 29

Diagnoses	ICD-9-CM Codes					
Principal Diagnosis Cellulitis and abscess of foot	6	8	2	-	7	
DX 2 Acute exacerbation of chronic obstructive pulmonary disease	4	9	1	-	2	1
DX 3 Coronary atherosclerosis, of native artery	4	1	4	-	0	1
DX 4 Hypothyroidism, postsurgical	2	4	4	-	0	
DX 5 Osteoarthrosis, unspecified whether generalized or localized, site unspecified	7	1	5	-	9	0
DX 6 Gastroesophageal reflux	5	3	0	-	8	1
DX 7 Depressive disorder, not elsewhere classified	3	1	1	-		
DX 8 History of tobacco use	V	1	5	-	8	2

Case Study Answer Key

Case 30

Diagnoses	ICD-9-CM Codes					
Principal Diagnosis Syncope and collapse	7	8	0	-	2	
DX 2 Malnourishment of mild degree	2	6	3	-	1	
DX 3 Congestive heart failure, unspecified	4	2	8	-	0	
DX 4 Chronic airway obstruction	4	9	6	-		
DX 5 Essential hypertension, unspecified	4	0	1	-	9	
DX 6 Hyperlipidemia, unspecified	2	7	2	-	4	
DX 7 History of tobacco use	V	1	5	-	8	2

Case 31

Diagnoses	ICD-9-CM Codes					
Principal Diagnosis Chronic obstructive asthma with acute exacerbation	4	9	3	-	2	2
DX 2 Tracheobronchitis, not specified as acute or chronic	4	9	0	-		
DX 3 Hypertension	4	0	1	-	9	
DX 4 Hyperlipidemia, unspecified	2	7	2	-	4	
DX 5 Foreign body in main bronchus	9	3	4	-	1	
DX 6 Inhalation/ingestion causing obstruction of respiratory tract	E9	1	2	-		
DX 7 Infection, Candida, of unspecified site	1	1	2	-	9	

Procedure	ICD-9-CM Codes						
PP 1 Bronchoscopy with closed (endoscopic) biopsy	3	3	-	2	4	-	

Case 32

Diagnoses	ICD-9-CM Codes					

Principal Diagnosis
    Herniated lumbar intervertebral disk, without
    myelopathy
	7	2	2	-	1	0

Procedure	ICD-9-CM Codes						
PP 1 Excision of intervertebral disk	8	0	-	5	1	-	

XI. CCS Mock Exam
Mock Exam 1 Section 1 and Section 2
Mock Exam 2 Section 1 and Section 2

CCS Mock Examination 1 Section 1 Part 1

1. Your organization is sending confidential patient information across the Internet using technology that will transform the original data into unintelligible code that can be re-created by authorized users. This technique is called
   A. a firewall.
   B. validity processing.
   C. a call-back process.
   D. data encryption.

2. As part of a concurrent record review, you need to locate the initial plan of action based on the attending physician's initial assessment of the patient. You can expect to find this documentation either within the body of the history and physical or in the
   A. doctor's admitting progress note.
   B. nurse's admit note.
   C. review of systems.
   D. discharge summary.

3. Employing the SOAP style of progress notes, choose the "assessment" statement from the following:
   A. Patient states low back pain with sciatica is as severe as it was on admission.
   B. Patient moving about very cautiously and appears to be in pain.
   C. Adjust pain medication; begin physical therapy tomorrow.
   D. Sciatica unimproved with hot pack therapy.

4. You have been hired to work with a computer-assisted coding initiative. The technology that you will be working with is
   A. electronic data interchange.
   B. intraoperability.
   C. message standards.
   D. natural language processing.

5. A final progress note is appropriate as a discharge summary for a hospitalization in which the patient
   A. dies within 24 hours of admission.
   B. has no comorbidities or complications during this episode of care.
   C. was admitted within 30 days with the same diagnosis.
   D. was an obstetric admission with a normal delivery and no complications.

6. In reviewing a medical record for coding purposes, the coder notes that the discharge summary has not yet been transcribed. In its absence, the best place to look for the patient's response to treatment and documentation of any complications that may have developed during this episode of care is in the
   A. doctors' progress note section.
   B. operative report.
   C. history and physical.
   D. doctors' orders.

7. You would expect to find documentation regarding the assessment of an obstetric patient's lochia, fundus, and perineum on the
   A. prenatal record.
   B. labor record.
   C. delivery room record.
   D. postpartum record.

8. A patient is admitted through the emergency department with diabetes mellitus. Three days after admission, the physician documents uncontrolled diabetes mellitus. What is the "present on admission" (POA) indicator for uncontrolled diabetes mellitus?
   A. "Y"
   B. "U"
   C. "W"
   D. "N"

SAMPLE MS-DRG REPORT		
MS-DRG IDENTIFIER	RELATIVE WEIGHT	NUMBER OF PATIENTS WITH THIS
A	1.234	12
B	3.122	10
C	2.165	19
D	5.118	16

9. Based on the sample MS-DRG report above, what is the case-mix index for this facility?
    A. 42.26275
    B. 2.965807
    C. 11.639
    D. 2.90975

10. The special form that plays the central role in planning and providing care at nursing, psychiatric, and rehabilitation facilities is the
    A. interdisciplinary patient care plan.
    B. medical history and review of systems.
    C. interval summary.
    D. problem list.

11. What legal term is used in describing sexual harassment in reference to unwelcome sexual advances, requests for sexual favors, and verbal or physical conduct of a sexual nature made in return for job benefits?
    A. res ipsa loquitur
    B. qui tam
    C. quid pro quo
    D. respondeat superior

12. Your facility would like to improve physician documentation in order to allow improved coding. As coding supervisor, you have found it very effective to provide the physicians with
    A. a copy of the facility coding guidelines, along with written information on improved documentation.
    B. the UHDDS and information on where each data element is collected and/or verified in your facility.
    C. regular in-service presentations on documentation, including its importance and tips for improvement.
    D. feedback on specific instances when improved documentation would improve coding.

WATERSIDE HOSPITAL CODING PRODUCTIVITY WEEK ENDING JANUARY			
EMPLOYEE NUMBER	INPATIENT	OUTPATIENT PROCEDURE	OUTPATIENT OBSERVATION OR EMERGENCY RECORDS
425	120	35	16
426	48	89	95
427	80	92	4
428	65	109	16

13. The performance standard for coders is 28–33 workload units per day. Workload units are calculated as follows:

   Inpatient records = 1 workload unit
   Outpatient surgical procedure records = 0.75 workload units
   Outpatient observation/Emergency records = 0.50 workload units

   One week's productivity information is shown in the table above. What percentage of the coders is meeting the productivity standards?
   A. 100%
   B. 75%
   C. 50%
   D. 25%

14. Which of the following diagnoses or procedures would prevent the normal delivery code, 650, from being assigned?
   A. occiput presentation
   B. single liveborn
   C. episiotomy
   D. low forceps

15. Which of the following are considered late effects regardless of time?
   A. congenital defect
   B. nonunion
   C. nonhealing fracture
   D. poisoning

16. Patient is admitted for elective cholecystectomy for treatment of chronic cholecystitis with cholelithiasis. Prior to administration of general anesthesia, patient suffers cerebral thrombosis. Surgery is subsequently canceled. Code and sequence the coding from the following codes.

434.00	Cerebral thrombosis without cerebral infarction
574.10	Calculus of gallbladder with other cholecystitis without mention of obstruction V64.1
	Surgical or other procedure not carried out because of contraindication
997.02	Iatrogenic cerebrovascular infarction or hemorrhage
51.22	Cholecystectomy

   A. 997.02, 574.10, 51.22
   B. 574.10, 434.00, V64.1
   C. 997.02, 434.00, V64.1
   D. 434.00, V64.1

17. Some ICD-9-CM codes are exempt from POA reporting because they
   A. represent circumstances regarding the health care encounter or factors influencing health status that do not represent a current disease or injury.
   B. are always present on admission.
   C. are both A and B.
   D. represent V codes and E codes.

18. Which of these conditions are always considered "present on admission" (POA)?
   A. congenital conditions
   B. E codes
   C. acute conditions
   D. possible, probable, or suspected conditions

19. When coding multiple wound repairs in CPT,
   A. only the most complex repair is reported.
   B. only the least complex repair is reported.
   C. up to nine individual repair codes may be reported.
   D. all wound repairs are coded with the most complex reported first.

20. Which of the following is vital for determining why the reimbursement from an insurance company is less than that which was expected?
    A. a CPT codebook
    B. the remittance advice
    C. talking to the patient
    D. knowledge of the individual insurance company's policies

21. Four people were seen in your Emergency Department yesterday. Which one will be coded as a poisoning?

    Robert: diagnosed with digitalis intoxication
    Gary: had an allergic reaction to a dye administered for a pyelogram
    David: developed syncope after taking Contac pills with a double scotch
    Brian: had an idiosyncratic reaction between two properly administered prescription drugs

    A. Robert   C. David
    B. Gary   D. Brian

22. Present on Admission (POA) apply to
    A. inpatient reporting of diagnosis codes.
    B. outpatient reporting of procedure codes.
    C. inpatient reporting of diagnosis and procedure codes.
    D. outpatient reporting of diagnosis and procedure codes.

23. Using the ICD-10-CM code structure, which of the following would be used for "right upper quadrant abdominal tenderness"?
    A. 108.11   C. R10.811
    B. R10811.11   D. 1.0811

24. Which of the following scenarios identifies a pathologic fracture?
    A. greenstick fracture secondary to fall from a bed
    B. compression fracture of the skull after being hit with a baseball bat
    C. vertebral fracture with cord compression following a car accident
    D. compression fracture of the vertebrae as a result of bone metastasis

25. All of the following signs/symptoms suggest gram-negative pneumonia EXCEPT
    A. fever.   C. purulent sputum.
    B. patchy infiltrate.   D. decreased leukocyte count.

26. During her hospitalization for her third delivery, Janet had a sterilization procedure performed. When the record is coded, the V code for sterilization, V25.2 is
    A. not used.
    B. used and sequenced as the principal diagnosis.
    C. used and sequenced as a secondary diagnosis.
    D. the only code used.

27. Ensuring that data have been modified or accessed only by individuals who are authorized to do so is a function of data
    A. accuracy.   C. integrity.
    B. validity.   D. quality.

28. Which of the following statements is true?
    A. A surgical procedure may include one or more surgical operations.
    B. The terms *surgical operation* and *surgical procedure* are synonymous.
    C. A surgical operation may include one or more surgical procedures.
    D. The term *surgical procedure* is an incorrect term and should not be used.

29. Security devices that form barriers between routers of a public network and a private network to protect access by unauthorized users are called
    A. data translators.   C. data manipulation engines.
    B. passwords.   D. firewalls.

30. The Joint Commission requires that all medical records be completed within _____ following patient discharge.
    A. 30 days   C. 7 days
    B. 14 days   D. 90 days

31. You are conducting an educational session on benchmarking. You tell your audience that the key to benchmarking is to use the comparison to
    A. implement your QI process.
    B. make recommendations for improvement to the other department or organization.
    C. improve your department's processes.
    D. compare your department with another.

32. Which of the following procedures can be identified as "destruction" of lesions?
    A. removal of skin tags   C. laser removal of condylomata
    B. shaving of skin lesion   D. paring of hyperkeratotic lesion

33. A _____ is a collection of information or data that is organized in such a way that its contents can be queried and relationships created.
    A. database   C. record
    B. field   D. table

34. Staging
    A. refers to the monitoring of incidence and trends associated with a disease.
    B. is continued medical surveillance of a case.
    C. is a system for documenting the extent or spread of cancer.
    D. designates the degree of differentiation of cells.

35. Which diagnosis should be listed first when sequencing inpatient codes using the UHDDS?
    A. primary diagnosis   C. significant diagnosis
    B. principal diagnosis   D. admitting diagnosis

36. Which of the following would NOT require HCPCS/CPT codes?
    A. hospital ambulatory surgery visit   C. clinic visit
    B. hospital outpatient visit   D. hospital inpatient procedure

37. Patient was seen in the emergency department with lacerations on the left arm. Two lacerations, one 7 cm and one 9 cm, were closed with layered sutures.

12002	Simple repair of superficial wounds of scalp, neck, axillae, external genitalia, trunk and/or extremities (including hands and feet); 2.6 cm to 7.5 cm
12004	Simple repair of superficial wounds of scalp, neck, axillae, external genitalia, trunk, and/or extremities (including hands and feet); 7.6 cm to 12.5 cm
12035	Layer closure of wounds of scalp, axillae, trunk, and/or extremities (excluding hands and feet); 12.6 cm to 20 cm
12045	Layer closure of wounds of neck, hands, feet, and/or external genitalia; 12.6 cm to 20 cm

A. 12045

B. 12035

C. 12002, 12004

D. 12004

38. Patient was seen for excision of two interdigital neuroma from the left foot.

28080	Excision, interdigital (Morton) neuroma, single, each
64774	Excision of neuroma; cutaneous nerve, surgically identifiable
64776	Excision of neuroma; digital nerve, one or both, same digit

A. 64774

B. 64776

C. 28080

D. 28080, 28080

39. Patient was seen today for regular hemodialysis. No problems reported; patient tolerated procedure well.

90935	Hemodialysis procedure with single physician evaluation
90937	Hemodialysis procedure requiring repeated evaluation(s) with or without substantial revision of dialysis prescription
90945	Dialysis procedure other than hemodialysis (e.g., peritoneal dialysis, hemofiltration, or other continuous renal replacement therapies), with single physician evaluation
+99354	Prolonged service in the office or other outpatient setting requiring direct (face-to-face) contact beyond the usual service, first hour (List separately in addition to code for office or other outpatient Evaluation and Management service.)

A. 90937

B. 99354

C. 90945

D. 90935

40. Office visit for 43-year-old male, new patient, with no complaints. Patient is applying for life insurance and requests a physical examination. A detailed health and family history was obtained, and a basic physical was done. Physician completed life insurance physical form at patient's request. Blood and urine were collected.

99381	Initial comprehensive preventive medicine evaluation and management of an individual including an age and gender appropriate history, examination, counseling/anticipatory guidance/risk factor reduction interventions, and the ordering of appropriate laboratory/diagnostic procedures, new patient; infant (age under 1 year)
99386	Initial comprehensive preventive medicine evaluation and management of an individual including an age and gender appropriate history examination, counseling/anticipatory guidance/risk factor reduction interventions, and the ordering of appropriate laboratory/diagnostic procedures, new patient; 40–64 years
99396	Periodic comprehensive preventive medicine reevaluation and management of an individual including an age and gender appropriate history, examination, counseling/anticipatory guidance/risk factor reduction interventions, and the ordering of appropriate laboratory/diagnostic procedures, established patient; 40–64 years
99450	Basic life and/or disability examination that includes completion of a medical history following a life insurance pro forma

A. 99450
B. 99386
C. 99396
D. 99381

41. A quantitative drug assay was performed for a patient to determine digoxin level.

80050	General health panel
80101	Drug screen, qualitative; single drug class method (e.g., immunoassay, enzyme assay), each drug class
80162	Digoxin (therapeutic drug assay, quantitative examination)
80166	Doxepin (therapeutic drug assay, quantitative examination)

A. 80101
B. 80050
C. 80166
D. 80162

42. Provide the CPT code for anesthesia services for the transvenous insertion of a pacemaker.

00530	Anesthesia for permanent transvenous pacemaker insertion
00560	Anesthesia for procedures on heart, pericardial sac, and great vessels of chest; without pump oxygenator
33202	Insertion of epicardial electrode(s); by open incision
33206	Insertion of new or replacement of permanent pacemaker with transvenous electrode(s); atrial

A. 00560
B. 33202, 00530
C. 00530
D. 33206, 00560

43. A 4-year-old had a repair of an incarcerated inguinal hernia. This is the first time this child has been treated for this condition.

49496	Repair initial inguinal hernia full-term infant, under age 6 months, or preterm infant over 50 weeks postconception age and under 6 months at the time of surgery with or without hydrocelectomy; incarcerated or strangulated
49501	Repair initial inguinal hernia, age 6 months to under 5 years, with or without hydrocelectomy; incarcerated or strangulated
49521	Repair recurrent inguinal hernia, any age; incarcerated or strangulated
49553	Repair initial femoral hernia, any age; incarcerated or strangulated

A. 49553
B. 49496
C. 49521
D. 49501

44. The patient had a thrombectomy, without catheter, of the peroneal artery, by leg incision.

34203	Embolectomy or thrombectomy, with or without catheter; popliteal-tibio-peroneal artery, by leg incision
35226	Repair blood vessel, direct; lower extremity
35302	Thromboendarterectomy, including patch graft, if performed, superficial femoral artery
37799	Unlisted procedure, vascular surgery

A. 34203
B. 37799
C. 35302
D. 35226

45. A patient with lung cancer and bone metastasis is seen for complex treatment planning by a radiation oncologist.

77263	Therapeutic radiology treatment planning; complex
77290	Therapeutic radiology simulation-aided field setting; complex
77315	Teletherapy, isodose plan (whether hand or computer calculated); complex (mantle or inverted Y, tangential ports, the use of wedges, compensators, complex blocking, rotational beam, or special beam considerations)
77334	Treatment devices, design and construction; complex (irregular blocks, special shields, compensators, wedges, molds, or casts)

A. 77315
B. 77263
C. 77290
D. 77334

46. An established patient was seen by a physician in her office for DTaP vaccine and Hib.

90471	Immunization administration (includes percutaneous, intradermal, subcutaneous, or intramuscular injections); one vaccine (single or combination vaccine/toxoid)
90700	Diphtheria, tetanus toxoids, and acellular pertussis vaccine (DTaP), when administered to individuals younger than 7 years, for intramuscular use
90720	Diphtheria, tetanus toxoids, and whole cell pertussis vaccine and Hemophilus influenza B vaccine (DTP-Hib), for intramuscular use
90721	Diphtheria, tetanus toxoids, and acellular pertussis vaccine and Hemophilus influenza B vaccine (DTaP-Hib), for intramuscular use
90748	Hepatitis B and Hemophilus influenza B vaccine (Hep B-Hib), for intramuscular use
99211	Office or other outpatient visit for the evaluation and management of an established patient, which may not require the presence of a physician. Usually, the presenting problem(s) are minimal. Typically, 5 minutes are spent performing or supervising these services

A. 90721
B. 90720, 90471

C. 90700, 90748, 99211
D. 90471, 90721

47. Which of the following is NOT coded separately from a coronary artery bypass procedure?
   A. upper extremity vein
   B. upper extremity artery
   C. saphenous vein
   D. femoropopliteal portion of a vein

48. If the same condition is described as both acute and chronic, and separate subentries exist in the ICD-9-CM alphabetic index at the same indentation level,
   A. they should both be coded, acute sequenced first.
   B. they should both be coded, chronic sequenced first.
   C. only the acute condition should be coded.
   D. only the chronic condition should be coded.

49. A patient was sent to the surgeon's office as requested by the patient because the insurance company requires a second opinion regarding surgery. The patient has been complaining of lower back pain for over a year due to a herniated disk. The patient presents to the surgeon's office where a detailed history and physical examination was performed. Medical records from the primary care physician and the physical therapist were reviewed along with the tests performed in the office. Low medical decision making was made. A copy of the surgeon's reports was sent to the insurance company.
   A. 99242–32
   B. 99243
   C. 99253–32
   D. 99203–32

50. Patient arrives in the emergency room via a medical helicopter. The patient has sustained multiple life-threatening injuries due to a multiple car accident. The patient goes into cardiac arrest upon arrival. An hour and 30 minutes of critical care time is spent trying to stabilize the patient.

99282   Emergency department visit for the evaluation and management of a patient, which requires these three key components:
   • An expanded problem focused history;
   • An expanded problem focused examination; and
   • Medical decision making of low complexity.
Counseling and/or coordination of care with other providers or agencies are provided consistent with the nature of the problem(s) and the patient's and/or family's needs.
Usually, the presenting problem(s) are of low to moderate severity.

99285   Emergency department visit for the evaluation and management of a patient, which requires these three key components within the constraints imposed by the urgency clinical condition and/or mental status:
   • A comprehensive history;
   • A comprehensive examination; and
   • Medical decision making of high complexity.
Counseling and/or coordination of care with other providers or agencies are provided consistent with the nature of the problem(s) and the patient's and/or family's needs.
Usually, the presenting problem(s) are of high severity and pose an immediate significant threat to life or physiologic function.

99288   Physician direction of emergency medical systems (EMS) emergency care, advanced life support

99291   Critical care, evaluation and management of the critically ill or critically injured patient; first 30–74 minutes

+99292   Each additional 30 minutes (list separately in addition to code for primary service)

A. 99285, 99288, 99291
B. 99291, 99292
C. 99291, 99292, 99285
D. 99282

51. Patient presents with a diabetic ulcer that needs to be debrided. The patient was taken to the operating room where debridement of the muscle took place.

11011   Debridement including removal of foreign material associated with open fracture(s) and, or dislocation(s); skin, subcutaneous tissue, muscle fascia, and muscle

11043   Debridement, muscle, and/or fascia (includes epidermis, dermis, and subcutaneous tissue, if performed); first 20 sq cm or less

11400   Excision, benign lesion including margins, except skin tag (unless listed elsewhere), trunk, arms or legs; excised diameter 0.5 cm or less

15999   Unlisted procedure, excision pressure ulcer (for free skin graft to close ulcer or donor site, see 15002 et seq)

A. 15999
B. 11400
C. 11011
D. 11043

52. Excision 2-cm subcutaneous soft tissue lipoma of the back. (Code for diagnoses using ICD-9-CM. Code for procedure using CPT.)

214.1	Lipoma of other skin and subcutaneous tissue
216.5	Benign neoplasm of the skin of the trunk except scrotum
216.9	Benign neoplasm of the skin, site unspecified
11600	Excision, malignant lesion, trunk, arms, or legs, lesion diameter 0.5 cm or less
21556	Excision, tumor, soft tissue of neck or anterior thorax; subfascial (e.g., intramuscular); less than 5 cm
21925	Biopsy, soft tissue of back or flank; deep
21930	Excision, tumor, soft tissue of back or flank, subcutaneous; less than 3 cm

A. 216.5, 11600

B. 214.1, 21925

C. 216.9, 21556

D. 214.1, 21930

53. Patient presents to the hospital and undergoes a posterior L1-L5 spinal fusion for scoliosis with placement of a Harrington rod. Code using CPT.

22612	Arthrodesis, posterior or posteriorlateral technique, single level; lumbar (with lateral transverse technique, when performed
22800	Arthrodesis, posterior, for spinal deformity, with or without cast; up to 6 vertebral segments.
+22840	Posterior nonsegmental instrumentation (e.g., Harrington rod technique, pedicle fixation across one interspace, atlantoaxial transarticular screw fixation, sublaminar wiring at C1, facet screw fixation) (list separately in addition to code for primary procedure)
+22841	Internal spinal fixation by wiring spinous processes (list separately in addition to code for primary procedure)
+22842	Posterior segmental instrumentation (e.g., pedicle fixation, dual rods with multiple hooks and sublaminar wires); 3–6 vertebral segments (list separately in addition to code for primary procedure)
+22846	Anterior instrumentation; 4–7 vertebral segments (list separately in addition to code for primary procedure)

A. 22800, 22846

B. 22800, 22842

C. 22800, 22840

D. 22612, 22800, 22841

54. Patient has tear of the medial meniscus with loose bodies in the medial compartment of the left knee that was repaired by arthroscopic medial meniscectomy, shaving and trimming of meniscal rim, resection of synovium, and removal of the loose bodies. (Code using CPT procedure codes.)

27331	Arthrotomy, knee; including joint exploration, biopsy, or removal of loose or foreign bodies
27333	Arthrotomy, knee; medial and lateral
29800	Arthroscopy, temporomandibular joint, diagnostic, with or without synovial biopsy (separate procedure)
29804	Arthroscopy, temporomandibular joint, surgical; (for open procedures, use 21010)
29819	Arthroscopy, shoulder, surgical; with removal of loose body or foreign body (for open procedure, see 23040–23044, 23107)
29874	Arthroscopy, knee, surgical; for removal of loose body or foreign body (e.g., osteocondritis dissecans fragmentation, chondral fragmentation)
29881	Arthroscopy, knee, surgical; with meniscectomy (medial OR lateral, including any meniscal shaving)
LT	Left side

A. 29804

B. 27333-LT, 27331-LT

C. 29800-LT, 29819-LT

D. 29881-LT

55. Single lung transplant without cardiopulmonary bypass. (Code for physician using CPT procedure codes only.)

32652	Thoracoscopy, surgical; with total pulmonary decortication, including intrapleural pneumonolysis
32850	Donor pneunomectomy(s) (including cold preservation), from cadaver donor
32851	Lung transplant, single; without cardiopulmonary bypass
32852	Lung transplant, single; with cardiopulmonary bypass

A. 32850

B. 32652

C. 32852

D. 32851

56. Patient has a year history of mitral valve regurgitation and now presents for a mitral valve replacement with bypass. (Code for physician using CPT procedure codes only.)

33425	Valvuloplasty, mitral valve, with cardiopulmonary bypass
33430	Replacement, mitral valve, with cardiopulmonary bypass
33460	Valvectomy, tricuspid valve, with cardiopulmonary bypass
35231	Repair blood vessel with vein graft; neck

A. 33430

B. 33460

C. 33425

D. 35231

57. Patient has breast carcinoma and is now undergoing complete axillary lymphadenectomy. (Code for physician using CPT procedure codes only.)

38525	Biopsy or excision of lymph nodes; open, deep axillary node(s)
38562	Limited lymphadenectomy for staging (separate procedure); pelvic and para-aortic
38740	Axillary lymphadenectomy; superficial
38745	Axillary lymphadenectomy; complete

A. 38525
B. 38740
C. 38562
D. 38745

58. Patient presents to the GI lab for a colonoscopy. During the colonoscopy, polyps were discovered in the ascending colon and in the transverse colon. Polyps in the ascending colon were removed via hot biopsy forceps, and the polyps in the transverse colon were removed by snare technique.

211.3	Benign neoplasm of colon
44392	Colonoscopy through stoma; with removal of polyps, hot biopsy forceps
44394	Colonoscopy through stoma; with removal of polyps, snare technique
45355	Colonoscopy, transabdominal via colotomy
45383	Colonoscopy, with ablation of polyps, not by hot biopsy forceps or snare technique
45384	Colonoscopy with removal of polyps, hot biopsy forceps
45385	Colonoscopy with removal of polyps, snare technique
-59	Distinct procedural service

A. 211.3, 45355
B. 211.3, 45384, 45385-59
C. 211.3, 44392, 44394-59
D. 211.3, 45355, 45383-59

59. Patient came to the hospital ambulatory surgical center for repair of incisional hernia. This is the second time the patient has developed this problem. The hernia was repaired with Gore-Tex graft. Choose the appropriate ICD-9-CM and CPT codes.

550.10	Inguinal hernia, with obstruction, without gangrene, unilateral or unspecified
553.20	Ventral hernia, unspecified without obstruction or gangrene
553.21	Incisional hernia, without obstruction or gangrene
49520	Repair recurrent inguinal hernia, any age, reducible
49560	Repair initial incisional or ventral hernia, reducible
49565	Repair recurrent incisional or ventral hernia, reducible
+49568	Implantation of mesh or other prosthesis for incisional or ventral hernia repair or mesh for closure of debridement for necrotizing soft tissue infection. (List separately in addition to code for the incisional or ventral hernia repair.)

A. 553.21, 49565, 49568
B. 553.20, 553.21, 49520, 49568
C. 550.10, 49565
D. 550.10, 553.20, 49560, 49568

60. Female with 6 months of stress incontinence. Laparoscopic urethral suspension was completed. Choose the appropriate ICD-9-CM and CPT codes.

625.6	Urinary stress incontinence female
788.30	Urinary incontinence, unspecified
788.32	Urinary stress incontinence male
51840	Anterior vesicourethropexy or urethropexy (e.g., Marshall-Marchetti-Krantz, Burch); simple
51845	Abdominovaginal vesical neck suspension with or without endoscopic control
51990	Laparoscopy, surgical; urethral suspension for stress incontinence
51992	Laparoscopy, surgical; sling operation for stress incontinence

    A. 788.30, 51992   C. 788.32, 51840
    B. 625.6, 51990   D. 788.30, 51845

61. A patient is diagnosed with psychogenic paroxysmal tachycardia.
    A. 427.2, 316   C. 427.1, 306.2
    B. 306.2, 427.1   D. 316, 427.2

62. A patient is diagnosed with Alzheimer's disease with dementia.
    A. 331.0, 294.8   C. 331.0, 294.10
    B. 294.8   D. 331.0

63. A patient has end-stage kidney disease, which resulted from malignant hypertension.
    A. 403.01, 585.6   C. 403.00
    B. 585.9, 401.0   D. 401.0, 585.9

64. A patient presents with dermatitis due to prescription topical antibiotic cream used as directed by physician.
    A. 692.4   C. 692.3
    B. 692.3, E930.9   D. 692.3, E930.1

65. A patient presents with cervical spina bifida with hydrocephalus.
    A. 741.02   C. 741.01
    B. 741.93   D. 741.91

66. An infant has hypoglycemia with mother with diabetes.
    A. 251.2   C. 775.0
    B. 775.1   D. 251.1

67. A woman has a Pap smear that detected cervical high-risk human papillomavirus (HPV). The DNA test was positive.
    A. 795.05   C. 795.04
    B. 795.09   D. 795.02

68. A patient suffered dizziness as a result of taking prescribed phenobarbital. The patient took his medication with beer.
    A. 780.4, 980.0, E860.0
    B. 967.0, 980.0, 780.4, E851, E860.0
    C. 967.0, 708.4, E851
    D. 80.4, E851, E860.0

69. The patient presents for a screening examination for lung cancer.
    A. V72.82
    B. 162.9
    C. V72.5
    D. V76.0

70. The diagnosis is as follows: "Carcinoma of axillary lymph nodes and lungs, metastatic from breast." Given this, which are the primary cancer site(s)?
    A. axillary lymph nodes
    B. lungs
    C. breast
    D. both A and B

71. Robert Thompson was seen in the outpatient department with a chronic cough and the record states "rule out lung cancer." What should be coded as the patient's diagnosis?
    A. chronic cough
    B. observation and evaluation without need for further medical care
    C. diagnosis of unknown etiology
    D. lung cancer

72. A patient who is taking the drug Antivert may have a diagnosis of
    A. dizziness.
    B. urinary tract infection.
    C. arthritis.
    D. congestive heart failure.

73. The use of radioactive sources placed into a tumor-bearing area to generate high-intensity radiation is termed
    A. stereotactic radiation treatment.
    B. proton beam treatment.
    C. brachytherapy.
    D. external beam radiation.

74. A patient has a total abdominal hysterectomy with bilateral salpingectomy. The coder selected the following codes:

    | 58150 | Total abdominal hysterectomy (corpus and cervix), with or without removal of tube(s) with or without removal of ovary(s) |
    | 58700 | Salpingectomy, complete or partial unilateral or bilateral (separate procedure) |

    This type of coding is referred to as
    A. upcoding.
    B. unbundling.
    C. maximizing.
    D. optimization.

75. Which of the following is classified as a poisoning in ICD-9-CM?
    A. syncope due to Contac pills and a three-martini lunch
    B. digitalis intoxication
    C. reaction to dye administered for pyelogram
    D. idiosyncratic reaction between various drugs

76. Laparoscopic removal and replacement of both a gastric band and the subcutaneous port components.
    A. 43774, 43659
    B. 43659
    C. 43773
    D. 43848

77. Laryngoscopic submucosal removal of nonneoplastic lesion of the vocal cord with graft reconstruction. An operating microscope was used.
    A. 31546, 69990
    B. 31546, 20926
    C. 31546
    D. 31546, 20926-51

78. Laparoscopic takedown of the splenic flexure and a partial colectomy with anastomosis.
    A. 44140, 44213
    B. 44204
    C. 44213
    D. 44204, 44213

79. Laparoscopic gastric restrictive procedure and placement of adjustable gastric band.
    A. 43770
    B. 43800
    C. 43845
    D. 43846

80. High-energy ESW of the lateral humeral epicondyle using general anesthesia.
    A. 0019T
    B. 0101T
    C. 0102T
    D. 28890

81. A 32-year-old patient has a colonoscopy with removal of three polyps by snare. Moderate sedation was used and provided by the physician. The intraservice time was 30 minutes.
    A. 45385, 45385-51, 45385-51
    B. 45385, 99144
    C. 45385
    D. 45385, 45385-51, 45385-51, 99144

CCSA MOCK Exam Part 1 Section 1

ANSWER   EXPLANATION

1. D

REFERENCE: McWay, p 321

2. A A clinical impression and an intended course of action are either entered in the physical examination or provided in the admission note. The admission note provides an overview of the patient and adds any relevant information that is not included in the history and physical examination.

REFERENCE: Green and Bowie, pp 145–148

3. D Progress note elements written in the acronym "SOAP" style are:

    S—subjective, records what the patient states is the problem

    O—objective, records what the practitioner identifies through the history, physical examination, and diagnostic tests

    A—assessment, combines the subjective and objective into a conclusion

    P—plan, what approach is going to be taken to resolve the problem

REFERENCE: Abdelhak, p 119
                 Green and Bowie, pp 90–92
                 LaTour, Eichenwald-Maki, and Oachs, pp 256–257
                 Sayles, p 126

4. D

REFERENCE: McWay, p 132
                 LaTour and Eichenwald-Maki, pp 54, 400, 615

5. D A final note may substitute for a discharge summary for patients admitted for less than 48 hours with minor problems, uncomplicated deliveries, and for normal neonates.

REFERENCE: Abdelhak, p 113
                 Green and Bowie, pp 142–144
                 LaTour, Eichenwald-Maki, and Oachs, p 251

6. A The physician releasing the patient should write a final note of summary of the patient's course of treatment, stating the patient's condition at discharge, and instructions for the patient's activity, diet, and medications, as well as any follow-up appointments or instructions. If a patient expires, the final notes describe the circumstances regarding the death, the findings, the cause of death, and whether or not an autopsy was performed.

REFERENCE: Green, pp 14–16
                 LaTour, Eichenwald-Maki, and Oachs, p 442
                 Sayles, p 85

7. D The postpartum record contains information about the condition of the mother after delivery and includes an assessment of the lochia and conditions of the breasts, fundus, and perineum.

REFERENCE: Abdelhak, p 113
                 Green and Bowie, p 182

CCSA MOCK Exam Answer Key

ANSWER   EXPLANATION

8. D   Not all of the components of the combination code for diabetes mellitus, uncontrolled, were present on admission. The diabetes mellitus was present on admission, but it was not "uncontrolled" until 3 days after admission.
   A. "Y" = yes, present on admission
   B. "U" = no information in the record
   C. "W" = clinically undetermined
   D. "N" = no, not present on admission

REFERENCE: Bowie, pp 130–132
                  Bowie and Schaffer, pp 326–327
                  Brown, pp 542–544

9. B CALCULATION:

Step 1: Multiply each row (relative weight × number of patients). Step 2: Sum the totals of each row (169.051).

Step 3: Divide the total relative weight sums (169.051) by the total number of patients (57)

$$\frac{169.051 \text{ total relative weight}}{57 \text{ total patients seen}} = 2.965807$$

REFERENCE: Green and Bowie, pp 316–317
                  LaTour, Eichenwald-Maki, and Oachs, pp 470, 496–498
                  McWay (2014), p 165
                  Sayles, p 499

10. A The interdisciplinary care plan is the foundation around which patient care is organized. It contains input from the unique perspective of each discipline involved. It includes an assessment, statement of goals, identification of specific activities, or strategies to achieve those goals and periodic assessment of goal attainment.

REFERENCE: Abdelhak, p 142
                  LaTour, Eichenwald-Maki, and Oachs, p 254
                  Sayles, pp 111–112, 114

11. C

REFERENCE: McWay, p 294

12. D

REFERENCE: Abdelhak, pp 197–199
                  LaTour, Eichenwald-Maki, and Oachs, pp 243, 442, 470
                  Sales, pp 121, 292–293, 306–307

CCSA MOCK Exam Answer Key

ANSWER   EXPLANATION

13. A   Employee number 425: $120 + (35 \times 0.75) + (16 \times 0.5) = 154.25$

                    $154.25/5 = 30.85$ average work units per day

        Employee number 426: $48 + (89 \times 0.75) + (95 \times 0.5) = 162.25$

                    $162.25/5 = 32.45$ average work units per day

        Employee number 427: $80 + (92 \times 0.75) + (4 \times 0.5) = 151$

                    $151/5 = 30.2$ average work units per day

        Employee number 428: $65 + (109 \times 0.75) + (16 \times 0.5) = 154.75$

                    $154.75/5 = 30.95$ average work units per day

REFERENCE: Abdelhak, pp 19, 621–622
                     McWay, pp 209–214

14. D

REFERENCE: Bowie and Schaffer, pp 260–263
                     Brown, pp 272–273
                     Johnson and Linker, pp 54–55

15. B

REFERENCE: Brown, p 425
                     Johnson and Linker, pp 77–78

16. D

REFERENCE: Bowie and Schaffer, 64
                     Brown, pp 72–73
                     Green, pp 136–137

17. C

REFERENCE: Brown, pp 542–544
                     Johnson and Linker, p 79

18. A

REFERENCE: Bowie and Schaffer, pp 73–74
                     Brown, pp 542–544
                     Green and Bowie, pp 326–327
                     LaTour, Eichenwald-Maki, and Oachs, pp 443, 921, 940
                     Sayles, p 439

19. D

REFERENCE: Bowie, p 144
                     Green, pp 524–526
                     Johnson and Linker, pp 442–443

20. B

REFERENCE: Green, p 688
                     Green and Rowell, pp 8, 83–87
                     Johnson and Linker, pp 539–540

CCSA MOCK Exam Answer Key

ANSWER   EXPLANATION

21. C   The condition should be coded as a poisoning when there is an interaction of an over-the-counter drug and alcohol. Answers A, B, and D are adverse effects of a correctly administered prescription drug.

REFERENCE: Bowie and Schaffer, pp 36, 335
                Brown, p 446
                Johnson and Linker, pp 73–75

22. A

REFERENCE: Bowie and Schaffer, pp 73–74
                Brown, pp 542–544
                Green and Bowie, pp 326–327
                LaTour, Eichenwald-Maki, and Oachs, pp 443, 921, 940
                Sayles, p 439

23. C   All ICD-10-CM codes start with an alphabetic character. The basic code structure consists of three digits and then a decimal point. Most codes contain a maximum of six characters with a few chapters having a seventh character.

REFERENCE: Bowie and Schaffer, p 556
                Brown, pp 482, 493–498

24. D

REFERENCE: Bowie and Schaffer, p 289
                Brown, p 255
                Green, pp 201, 549
                Johnson and Linker, pp 24, 255–256

25. D

REFERENCE: Brown, p 182

26. C

REFERENCE: Brown, p 28
                Koch, p 180
                LaTour, Eichenwald-Maki, and Oachs, p 496
                Sayles, p 498

27. C

REFERENCE: Green and Bowie, p 281
                LaTour, Eichenwald-Maki, and Oachs, pp 50–51, 89, 161–164,187, 229–230, 907
                Sayles, pp 326–327

28. C   A surgical operation is one or more surgical procedures performed at one time for one patient using a common approach or for a common purpose.

REFERENCE: LaTour, Eichenwald-Maki, and Oachs, p 496
                Sayles, p 498

CCSA MOCK Exam Answer Key

ANSWER   EXPLANATION

29. D

REFERENCE: Koch, p 180
McWay, pp 312, 422
LaTour, Eichenwald-Maki, and Oachs, p 496
Sayles, p 1042

30. A

REFERENCE: LaTour. Eichenwald-Maki, and Oachs, pp 100–102
McWay, pp 312, 422

31. C Benchmarking involves comparing your department to other departments or organizations known to be excellent in one or more areas. The success of benchmarking involves finding out how the other department functions and then incorporating their ideas into your department.

REFERENCE: Abdelhak, p 452
LaTour, Eichenwald-Maki, and Oachs, p 708
McWay (2014), p 179
Sayles, pp 449, 1222

32. C

REFERENCE: Bowie, pp 130–131
Green, pp 533–534
Johnson and Linker, pp 216–217

33. A

REFERENCE: McWay, pp 169–170

34. C *Staging* is a term used to refer to the progression of cancer. In accessing most types of cancer, a method (staging) is used to determine how far the cancer has progressed. The cancer is described in terms of how large the main tumor is, the degree to which it has invaded surrounding tissue, and the extent to which it has spread to lymph glands or other areas of the body. Staging not only helps to assess the outlook but also determine the most appropriate treatment.

REFERENCE: Abdelhak, p 488
LaTour, Eichenwald-Maki, and Oates, pp 371, 949

35. B According to the UHDDS, the principal diagnosis is to be sequenced first.

REFERENCE: Bowie and Schaffer, p 66
Johnson and Linker, p 17

36. D The hospital inpatient procedure would not be coded using HCPCS/CPT codes. Hospital inpatient visit diagnoses and procedures are coded using ICD-9-CM codes.

REFERENCE: Bowie, pp 9, 445
Green, p 240
Johnson and Linker, pp 11–12
LaTour, Eichenwald-Maki, and Oachs, pp 394–470, 919
Sayles, pp 200–202, 1212

CCSA MOCK Exam Answer Key

ANSWER   EXPLANATION

37. B   The sizes of the layered wound repairs of the same body area are added together in order to select the correct CPT code.

REFERENCE: AMA, pp 131–132
                    Bowie, pp 119–121
                    Green, pp 524–526
                    Johnson and Linker, pp 120–122

38. D   Look up in CPT code book under foot, neuroma.

REFERENCE: AMA CPT (2014)
                    AMA, pp 131–132
                    Bowie, pp 119–121
                    Green, pp 524–526
                    Johnson and Linker, pp 120–122

39. D   *Dialysis* is the main term to be referenced in the CPT manual index.

REFERENCE: AMA, p 405
                    Bowie, p 432
                    Bowie and Schaffer (2013), pp 429–431
                    Green, pp 808–810
                    Johnson and Linker, pp 432–434

40. A   The codes in this subsection are used to report evaluations for life or disability insurance baseline information.

REFERENCE: AMA, pp 88–90
                    AMA CPT (2014), p 38
                    Bowie, pp 77–79
                    Green, p 448
                    Johnson and Linker, pp 161–165

41. D

REFERENCE: AMA, pp 362–365
                    Bowie (2015), p 222
                    Green, p 779
                    Johnson and Linker, 418

42. C

REFERENCE: AMA, pp 99–103
                    Bowie (2015), pp 90–92
                    Green, pp 482–484
                    Johnson and Linker, pp 175–178

43. D

REFERENCE: AMA, pp 362–365
                    Bowie, p 222
                    Green, p 779
                    Johnson and Linker, 418

CCSA MOCK Exam Answer Key

ANSWER   EXPLANATION

44. A

REFERENCE: AMA, pp 269, 282, 344, 345
                Bowie, pp 73–74
                Green, p 606
                Johnson and Linker, p 17

45. B

REFERENCE: AMA, pp 269, 282, 344–345
                AMA CPT (2014)
                Bowie, pp 408–409
                Green, pp 753–756
                Johnson and Linker, p 403

46. D   If immunization is the only service that the patient receives, then two codes are used to report the service. The immunization administration code is first, and then the code for the vaccine/toxoid.

REFERENCE: AMA, pp 394–395
                AMA CPT (2014)
                Bowie, p 429
                Green, pp 802–804
                Johnson and Linker, p 429

47. C   The saphenous vein is included in the code for the CABG.

REFERENCE: AMA, pp 195–196
                AMA, CPT (2014), pp 185–187
                Bowie, p 206
                Bowie and Schaffer, p 219
                Green, pp 599–560
                Johnson and Linker, p 316

48. A

REFERENCE: Bowie and Schaffer, p 61
                Brown, pp 57–58
                Johnson and Linker, p 79

49. D

REFERENCE: AMA, pp 53, 491
                AMA CPT (2014)
                Bowie, p 42
                Green, p 428
                Johnson and Linker, pp 149–154

50. B

REFERENCE: AMA, pp 37, 68–71
                AMA CPT (2014)
                Bowie, p 65
                Green, pp 439–441
                Johnson and Linker, pp 155–157

CCSA MOCK Exam Answer Key

ANSWER   EXPLANATION

51. D

REFERENCE: AMA, pp 120–122
                Bowie, p 13
                Johnson and Linker, p 218

52. D   Excision of lipomas code to excision of soft tissue.

REFERENCE: Bowie, p 152
                Bowie and Schaffer, pp 109–115
                AMA CPT (2014), p 111

53. C

REFERENCE: AMA, pp 160–162
                AMA CPT (2014), pp 118–119
                Bowie, pp 150–151
                Green, pp 558, 561–562
                Johnson and Linker, pp 275–276

54. D   If debridement or shaving of articular cartilage and meniscectomy are performed in the same
         compartment of the knee, then code only 29881.

REFERENCE: AMA, pp 171–172
                CPT Assistant, April 2001, pp 5–7, 12
                CPT Assistant, April 2003, pp 12, 14
                Green, p 565
                Johnson and Linker, pp 268–271

55. D

REFERENCE: AMA, p 182
                Bowie, p 186
                CPT Assistant, Winter 1993, p 2
                Green, pp 579–580

56. A   valvuloplasty is a plastic surgery repair of a valve.

REFERENCE: AMA, p 195
                AMA CPT (2014), p 181
                Bowie, p 205
                Green, p 598
                Johnson and Linker, p 315

57. D

REFERENCE: AMA, p 195
                AMA CPT (2014), p 181
                Bowie, p 205
                Green, p 598
                Johnson and Linker, p 315

CCSA MOCK Exam Answer Key

ANSWER   EXPLANATION

58. B   According to CPT Assistant, when a colonoscopy with a polypectomy is performed by two different techniques, both techniques are coded.

REFERENCE: AMA CPT (2014), p 286
                    Bowie, p 267
                    Bowie and Schaffer, p 109
                    Green, pp 650–651
                    Johnson and Linker, p 188

59. A   The mesh is reported as an additional code. The hernia is considered recurrent because this documentation states this is the second hernia.

REFERENCE: AMA, pp 121, 229–230
                    AMA CPT (2014), pp 300–302
                    Bowie, pp 272–273
                    Bowie and Schaffer, pp 227–228
                    Green, p 656

60. B   There are two different ICD-9-CM codes for stress incontinence; one for males and one for females.

REFERENCE: AMA CPT (2014), p 315
                    Bowie, p 293
                    Bowie and Schaffer, pp 245–246
                    Green, p 694
                    Johnson and Linker, pp 194–195

61. D

REFERENCE: Bowie, p 200
                    Bowie and Schaffer, pp 158, 171
                    Brown, p 139

62. C

REFERENCE: Bowie and Schaffer, p 170
                    Brown, p 136

63. A

REFERENCE: Bowie and Schaffer, pp 195
                    Brown, pp 219–220

64. B

REFERENCE: Bowie and Schaffer, p 274
                    Brown, pp 239–240

65. C

REFERENCE: Bowie and Schaffer, p 295
                    Brown, p 307

66. C

REFERENCE: Bowie and Schaffer, pp 310–311
                    Brown, pp 313, 320–321

CCSA MOCK Exam Answer Key

ANSWER   EXPLANATION

67. A

REFERENCE: Bowie and Schaffer, p 319
                  Brown, pp 97–99

68. B

REFERENCE: Bowie and Schaffer, pp 35–36
                  Brown, pp 443–446

69. D

REFERENCE: Bowie and Schaffer, p 352
                  Brown, p 89

70. C

REFERENCE: Bowie and Schaffer, pp 112–117
                  Brown, pp 382–385

71. A

REFERENCE: Schraffenberger (2012), p 339

72. A   Antivert is used for the management of nausea and dizziness associated with motion sickness
         and in vertigo associated with diseases affecting the vestibular system.

REFERENCE: Nobles, p 543

73. C

REFERENCE: Bowie, p 410
                  Johnson and Linker, p 401

74. B

REFERENCE: Johnson and Linker, p 628
                  McWay, pp 67, 356

75. A   A reaction due to mixing drugs and alcohol is coded as a poisoning.

REFERENCE: Bowie, pp 443–444
                  Bowie and Schaffer, pp 34–36
                  Johnson and Linker, pp 73–74

76. B

REFERENCE: CPT Assistant, June 2006, p 16

77. C

REFERENCE: CPT Assistant, May 2006, pp 16–17

78. D

REFERENCE: AMA, p 214
                  CPT Assistant, April 2006, p 19

79. A

REFERENCE: AMA, pp 221–222
                  CPT Assistant, April 2006, p 2

CCSA MOCK Exam Answer Key

ANSWER   EXPLANATION

80. C

REFERENCE: AMA, p 24
                CPT Assistant, March 2006, p 2

81. C   CPT designates certain procedures as including moderate sedation; therefore, moderate sedation is
        included in the code for the removal of polyps.

REFERENCE: AMA, pp 216, 224
                AMA CPT (2014)
                CPT Assistant, February 2006, pp 9–10

Section 2

1. A 40-year-old female suddenly develops a painful rash. A visit to her physician reveals she has shingles. She is experiencing a great amount of anxiety and stress, so her physician prescribes medication for the shingles and for the anxiety that occurred as a reaction to the stress.

    Select TWO of the following options:

A.	053.8	Herpes zoster with unspecified complication
B.	053.9	Herpes zoster without mention of complication
C.	300.00	Anxiety state, unspecified
D.	308.0	Predominant disturbance of emotions
E.	308.3	Other acute reactions to stress

2. Edward is diagnosed with syndrome of inappropriate antidiuretic hormone with resultant electrolyte imbalance.

    Select TWO of the following options:

A.	253.6	Other disorders of neurophyophysis (syndrome of inappropriate secretion of antidiuretic hormone—ADH)
B.	272.9	Unspecified disorder of lipoid metabolism
C.	276.50	Volume depletion, unspecified
D.	276.8	Hypopotassemia (hypokalemia)
E.	276.9	Electrolyte and fluid disorders, not elsewhere classified

3. Aaron has suffered a hypoglycemic reaction due to alcohol intoxication. Hypoglycemia is treated.

    Select TWO of the following options:

A.	250.80	Diabetes mellitus with other specified manifestations, type 2 or unspecified type, not stated as uncontrolled
B.	251.2	Hypoglycemia, unspecified
C.	303.90	Other and unspecified alcohol dependence, unspecified
D.	305.00	Alcohol abuse, unspecified
E.	995.29	Unspecified adverse effect of other drug, medicinal, and biological substance

4. Lou has profound mental retardation due to mongolism.

    Select TWO of the following options:

A.	317	Mild intellectual abilities
B.	318.0	Moderate intellectual abilities
C.	318.2	Profound intellectual abilities
D.	758.0	Down's syndrome
E.	759.0	Congenital anomaly of spleen

5. Mary underwent percutaneous transluminal atherectomy and balloon angioplasty of one coronary artery and percutaneous transluminal atherectomy only of another coronary artery.

Select TWO of the following options:

A.	92982	Percutaneous transluminal coronary balloon angioplasty; single vessel
B.	+92984	Percutaneous transluminal coronary balloon angioplasty; each additional vessel
C.	92995	Percutaneous transluminal coronary atherectomy, by mechanical or other method, with or without balloon angioplasty; single vessel
D.	+92996	Percutaneous transluminal coronary atherectomy, by mechanical or other method, with or without balloon angioplasty; each additional vessel
E.	92980	Transcatheter placement of an intracoronary stent(s), percutaneous, with or without therapeutic intervention, any method; single vessel

6. Rob had two lesions removed from his arm. The physician removed a 1-cm lesion with 0.3-cm margins and a 2-cm lesion with 0.5-cm margins. Pathology report on both specimens showed basal cell carcinoma. Defects were repaired with simple closure.

Select TWO of the following options:

A.	11601	Excision, malignant lesion including margins, trunk, arms, or legs; excised diameter 0.6 to 1 cm
B.	11602	Excision, malignant lesion including margins, trunk, arms, or legs; excised diameter 1.1 to 2 cm
C.	11603	Excision, malignant lesion including margins, trunk, arms, or legs; excised diameter 2.1 to 3 cm
D.	11606	Excision, malignant lesion including margins, trunk, arms, or legs; excised diameter over 4 cm
E.	12002	Simple repair of superficial wounds of extremities; 2.6 to 7.5 cm

7. Patient complains of frequent temporal headaches and the physician suspects temporal arteritis. Patient underwent temporal artery biopsy.

Select TWO of the following options:

A.	784.0	Headache
B.	446.5	cell arteritis
C.	37600	Ligation; external carotid artery
D.	37609	Ligation or biopsy, temporal artery
E.	37615	Ligation, major artery (e.g., post-traumatic, rupture); neck

8. Patient came to the hospital from a local nursing home for a PEG tube placement via EGD. Patient had neurogenic dysphagia and dominant hemiplegia due to prior CVA.

Select FOUR of the following options:

A.	436	Acute, but ill-defined, cerebrovascular disease
B.	438.21	Late effect of CVA with hemiplegia affecting dominant side
C.	438.81	Late effect of CVA with apraxia
D.	438.82	Late effect of CVA with dysphagia
E.	787.29	Dysphagia, neurogenic
F.	43219	Esophagoscopy, rigid or flexible with insertion of plastic tube or stent
G.	43246	Upper gastrointestinal endoscopy of esophagus, stomach, and either the duodenum and/or jejunum with directed placement of percutaneous gastrostomy tube
H.	44372	Small intestine endoscopy, enteroscopy beyond second portion of duodenum with placement of percutaneous jejunostomy tube

CCS MOCK Exam 1 Section 2 Exam Answer Key

1. A and D

REFERENCE: Brown, pp 107, 139–140

2. A and E

REFERENCE: Brown, pp 128, 141–142

3. B and D

REFERENCE: Brown, pp 128, 141–142

4. C and D

REFERENCE:

5. C and D

REFERENCE: AMA (6th ed.), pp 419–424

6. B and C

REFERENCE: Green, pp 493–496

7. A and D

REFERENCE: AMA, 2012

8. D, B, E, and G

REFERENCE: AMA (6th ed.), pp 220, 228
               Brown, pp 343–344

REFERENCES

Abdelhak, M., Grostick, S., Hanken, M. A. & Jacobs, E. (Eds.). (2012). *Health information: Management of a strategic resource* (5th ed.). St. Louis, MO: Saunders Elsevier.

AMA CPT Assistant American Medical Association (AMA). *CPT assistant.* Chicago: Author.

AMA, American Medical Association (AMA). (2010). *Principles of CPT coding.* Chicago: Author.

AMA CPT (2014) American Medical Association (AMA). (2014). *Physicians' current procedural terminology (CPT) professional edition.* Chicago: Author.

Bowie, M. (2014). *Understanding procedural coding: A worktext.* Clifton Park, NY: Delmar Cengage Learning.

Bowie, M. & Schaffer, L. (2014). *Understanding ICD-9-CM coding: A worktext.* Clifton Park, NY: Delmar Cengage Learning.

Brown, F. (2012). *ICD-9-CM coding handbook 2011 with answers.* Chicago: American Hospital Association (AHA) Press.

Green, M. (2013). *3-2-1 Code it!* (3rd ed.). Clifton Park, NY: Delmar Cengage Learning.

Green, M. A. & Bowie, M. J. (2011). *Essentials of health information management: Principles and practices.* Clifton Park, NY: Delmar Cengage Learning.

INGENIX. (2012). *ICD-9-CM expert for hospitals* (Vol. 1, 2 & 3). Salt Lake City, UT: Author.

Johnson, S. L. & Linker, R. (2013). *Understanding medical coding: A comprehensive guide* (3rd ed.). Clifton Park, NY: Delmar Cengage Learning.

Jones, B. D. (2011). *Comprehensive medical terminology* (4th ed.). Clifton Park, NY: Delmar Cengage Learning.

Koch, G. (2008). *Basic allied health statistics and analysis* (3rd ed.). Clifton Park, NY: Delmar Cengage Learning.

LaTour, K. & Eichenwald-Maki, S. (2010). *Health information management concepts: Principles and practice* (3rd ed.). Chicago: American Health Information Management Association (AHIMA).

McWay, D. C. (2008). *Today's health information management: An integrated approach.* Clifton Park, NY: Delmar Cengage Learning.

Neighbors, M. & Tannehill-Jones, R. (2010). *Human diseases* (3rd ed.). Clifton Park, NY: Delmar Cengage Learning.

Sormunen, C. (2013). *Terminology for allied health professionals* (7th ed.). Clifton Park, NY: Delmar Cengage Learning.

CCS Mock Examination 2 Section 1

Question	CCS Domains							
	1	2	3	4	5	6	7	8
1						X		
2	X							
3	X							
4						X		
5		X						
6	X							
7	X							
8				X				
9		X						
10	X							
11							X	
12					X			
13					X			
14		X						
15		X						
16		X						
17			X					
18			X					
19		X						
20					X			
21		X						
22			X					
23		X						
24		X						
25	X							
26		X						
27	X							
28							X	
29						X		
30					X			
31					X			
32		X						
33						X		
34	X							
35				X				
36	X							
37		X						
38		X						
39		X						
40		X						
41		X						
42		X						
43		X						
44		X						

CCS Mock Examination 2 Section 1

Question	CCS Domains							
	1	2	3	4	5	6	7	8
45		X						
46			X					
47		X						
48		X						
49			X					
50			X					
51			X					
52		X						
53			X					
54		X						
55		X						
56			X					
57			X					
58		X						
59		X						
60		X						
61		X						
62		X						
63		X						
64		X						
65		X						
66		X						
67		X						
68		X						
69		X						
70		X						
71			X					
72		X						
73	X							
74			X					
75		X						
76		X						
77		X						
78		X						
79		X						
80			X					
81		X						

CCS Mock Examination 1 Section 2

Question	CCS Domains							
	1	2	3	4	5	6	7	8
1								
2								
3								
4								
5								
6								
7								
8								

CCS Mock Exam 2 Section 1 Multiple Choice Questions

1. Chronic otitis media with bilateral myringotomy and tube insertion using local anesthesia (Code ICD-9-CM for diagnoses and CPT for procedures.)

381.00	Acute nonsuppurative otitis media, unspecified
381.05	Acute allergic mucoid otitis media
382.9	Unspecified otitis media
69400	Eustachian tube inflation, transnasal; with catheterization
69405	Eustachian tube catheterization, transtympanic
69420	Myringotomy including aspiration and/or eustachian tube inflation
69433	Tympanostomy (requiring insertion of ventilating tube), local or topical anesthesia
-50	Bilateral procedure

   A. 382.9, 69420-50
   B. 382.9, 69433-50
   C. 381.05, 69405-50
   D. 381.00, 69400-50

2. A coworker complained of the sudden onset of chest pain and was admitted. A myocardial infarction was ruled out. You would code
   A. the myocardial infarction as if it were an established condition.
   B. both the infarction and the chest pain and sequence the infarction first.
   C. as an impending myocardial infarction.
   D. only the chest pain.

3. A 32-year-old female, known to be HIV positive, was admitted with lesions of the anterior trunk. Excisional biopsies of the skin lesions were positive for Kaposi's sarcoma. Further examination revealed thrush.

042	Human immunodeficiency virus (HIV) disease
795.71	Nonspecific serological evidence of HIV
176.0	Kaposi's sarcoma, skin
686.00	Pyoderma, unspecified
112.0	Candidiasis of mouth
528.9	Other and unspecified diseases of the oral soft tissues
86.11	Biopsy of the skin and subcutaneous tissue
86.22	Excisional debridement of the skin and subcutaneous tissue (wound, infection, or burn)

   A. 042, 686.00, 112.0, 86.22
   B. 042, 176.0, 112.0, 86.11
   C. 795.71, 176.0, 528.9, 86.11
   D. 795.71, 686.00, 528.9, 86.22

4. An 89-year-old male is admitted to the hospital from a nursing home. He was confused and had hypotension, a temperature of 103.5, and obvious dehydration. Blood cultures were negative; however, the urine culture was positive for *E. coli*. The physician documents the final diagnosis as septicemia, septic shock, UTI due to *E. coli*, and dehydration.

038.9	Septicemia, unspecified
041.49	*E. coli*
276.51	Dehydration
298.9	Psychosis, unspecified
458.9	Hypotension, unspecified
599.0	UTI, site not specified
780.60	Fever, unspecified
785.52	Septic shock
995.92	Severe sepsis

   A. 599.0, 458.9, 041.49, 780.60, 276.51
   B. 038.9, 995.92, 785.52, 599.0, 041.49, 276.51
   C. 599.0, 038.9, 041.49, 276.51, 995.92
   D. 038.9, 276.51, 041.49, 780.60, 995.92

5. Mary is 6 weeks post mastectomy for carcinoma of the breast. She is admitted for chemotherapy. What is the correct sequencing of the codes?

174.9	Malignant neoplasm of the female breast, unspecified site
V10.3	Personal history of malignant neoplasm of breast
V58.11	Encounter for antineoplastic chemotherapy
V67.00	Follow-up examination following surgery, unspecified

   A. V58.11, 174.9   C. V67.00, V58.11
   B. V58.11, V10.3   D. V10.3

6. Chip is 35 years old and has been previously diagnosed with lung cancer. He has been receiving chemotherapy and radiation. He develops seizures and is admitted. Workup revealed metastasis of the lung cancer to the brain.

V10.11	Personal history of malignant neoplasm of the bronchus and lung
V10.85	Personal history of malignant neoplasm of the brain
162.9	Malignant neoplasm of the bronchus/lung, unspecified site
191.9	Malignant neoplasm of the brain, unspecified
197.0	Secondary malignant neoplasm of lung
198.3	Secondary malignant neoplasm of brain and spinal cord
780.39	Other convulsions (seizures, not otherwise specified)

   A. 780.39, 191.9, 197.0, V10.11   C. 780.39, V10.11, V10.85
   B. 780.39, 198.3, 162.9   D. 198.3, 162.9, 780.39

7. Which of the following is coded as an adverse effect in ICD-9-CM?
   A. tinnitus due to allergic reaction after administration of ear drops
   B. mental retardation due to intracranial abscess
   C. rejection of transplanted kidney
   D. nonfunctioning pacemaker due to defective soldering

8. Mitch was admitted directly from his physician's office for dehydration. Mitch has had gastroenteritis for several days which has resulted in dehydration and requires intravenous hydration. Mitch also has chronic kidney disease and is at high risk for acute or chronic kidney failure. Two days following admission, Mitch develops acute renal failure. Mitch also has hypertension.

276.51	Dehydration
401.9	Essential hypertension, unspecified benign or malignant
403.90	Hypertensive chronic kidney disease stage I through stage IV, or unspecified, unspecified benign, or malignant
403.91	Hypertensive chronic kidney disease stage V or end-stage renal disease, unspecified benign, or malignant
584.9	Acute kidney failure, unspecified
585.9	Chronic kidney disease, unspecified
586	Renal failure, unspecified

A. 584.9, 403.90, 276.51
B. 276.51, 584.9, 585.9, 403.90
C. 403.91, 276.51
D. 276.51, 586, 584.9, 401.9

9. Aunt Elsie is brought to the hospital for increased confusion. She is subsequently diagnosed with Alzheimer's disease with dementia and cerebral atherosclerosis. Aunt Elsie is also treated for hypertension and hypothyroidism.

244.9	Unspecified acquired hypothyroidism
294.10	Dementia in conditions classified elsewhere without behavioral disturbance (manifestation)
294.11	Dementia in conditions classified elsewhere with behavioral disturbance (manifestation)
331.0	Alzheimer's disease
401.9	Essential hypertension, unspecified benign or malignant
437.0	Cerebral atherosclerosis

A. 437.0, 294.10, 244.9, 401.9
B. 294.10, 401.9, 244.9
C. 331.0, 244.9, 401.9, 294.11
D. 331.0, 294.10, 437.0, 244.9, 401.9

10. The patient was admitted due to increasingly severe pain in his right arm, shoulder, and neck for the past 6 weeks. MRI tests showed herniation of the C5–C6 disc. Patient underwent cervical laminotomy and diskectomy of the C5–C6 disc. The patient is currently being treated for COPD and CAD with a history of a PTCA.

722.0	Displacement of cervical intervertebral disc without myelopathy
722.71	Intervertebral disc disorder with myelopathy, cervical region
492.8	Other emphysema
496	Chronic airway obstruction, not elsewhere classified
414.01	Coronary atherosclerosis of native coronary artery
414.00	Coronary atherosclerosis of unspecified type of vessel, native or graft
V45.82	Percutaneous transluminal coronary angioplasty status
80.51	Excision of intervertebral disc
03.09	Other exploration and decompression of spinal canal (Decompression, laminotomy)

A. 722.0, 492.8, 414.01, V45.82, 80.51
B. 722.71, 496, 414.01, V45.82, 03.09, 80.51
C. 722.71, 492.8, 414.00, 03.09, 80.51
D. 722.0, 496, 414.01, V45.82, 80.51

11. Tom is admitted with acute chest pain. Final diagnoses listed include acute pulmonary edema with congestive heart failure, subendocardial anterior wall myocardial infarction, hypertensive heart disease, and chronic obstructive pulmonary disease.

410.11	Acute myocardial infarction, of other anterior wall, initial episode of care
410.71	Acute subendocardial infarction, initial episode of care
402.90	Hypertensive heart disease, without heart failure, unspecified benign or malignant
402.91	Hypertensive heart disease, with heart failure, unspecified benign or malignant
428.1	Congestive heart failure, unspecified
428.2	Left heart failure
496	Chronic airway obstruction, not elsewhere classified
518.4	Acute edema of lung, unspecified

A. 410.71, 402.91, 496, 428.0
B. 410.11, 428.0, 518.4, 402.91, 496, 428.0
C. 410.71, 410.11, 402.91, 518.4, 496, 428.0
D. 410.11, 428.0, 402.90, 518.4, 496, 428.0

12. Patient was admitted from the nursing home in acute respiratory failure that was due to congestive heart failure. Chest x-ray also showed acute pulmonary edema. Patient was intubated and placed on mechanical ventilation and expired the day after admission.

428.1	Congestive heart failure, unspecified
428.2	Left heart failure
518.4	Acute edema of lung, unspecified
518.81	Acute respiratory failure
518.84	Acute and chronic respiratory failure
96.04	Insertion of endotrachial tube
96.71	Continuous invasive mechanical ventilation for less than 96 consecutive hours

A. 428.1, 518.84, 518.4, 96.71, 96.04
B. 428.1, 428.0, 518.81, 518.4, 96.71, 96.04
C. 518.81, 428.0, 96.71, 96.04
D. 428.0, 518.4, 96.04, 96.71

13. Diverticulitis large bowel with abscess; right hemicolectomy with colostomy performed.

562.10	Diverticulosis of colon (without mention of hemorrhage)
562.11	Diverticulitis of colon (without mention of hemorrhage)
569.5	Abscess of intestine
45.73	Open and other right hemicolectomy
45.74	Open and other resection of transverse colon
46.03	Exteriorization of large intestine (loop colostomy)
46.10	Colostomy, not otherwise specified
46.11	Temporary colostomy

A. 562.10, 45.74, 46.03   C. 562.11, 569.5, 45.73, 46.10
B. 562.11, 45.73, 46.03   D. 562.11, 569.5, 45.74, 46.11

14. Patient has bilateral inguinal hernias; the left is indirect and the right is direct. He has repair of both hernias with mesh prosthesis.

550.90	Inguinal hernia, without mention of obstruction or gangrene, unilateral or unspecified (not specified as recurrent)
550.91	Inguinal hernia, without mention of obstruction or gangrene, unilateral or unspecified, recurrent
550.92	Inguinal hernia, without mention of obstruction or gangrene, bilateral (not specified as recurrent)
53.1	Other and open unilateral repair of direct inguinal hernia
53.2	Other and open unilateral repair of indirect inguinal hernia
53.16	Other and open bilateral repair of inguinal hernia, one direct and one indirect, with graft or prosthesis

A. 550.91, 550.92, 53.16   C. 550.92, 53.16
B. 550.90, 53.1, 53.2   D. 550.92, 53.1, 53.2

15. Vaginal delivery of a full-term liveborn infant. Patient undergoes episiotomy with repair and post delivery elective tubal ligation.

648.91	Other current conditions in the mother classifiable elsewhere, but complicating pregnancy, childbirth, or puerperium, delivered with or without mention of antepartum condition
650	Normal delivery
V25.2	Encounter for contraceptive management, sterilization
V27.0	Single liveborn
66.32	Other bilateral ligation and division of fallopian tubes
73.59	Other manually assisted delivery
73.6	Episiotomy (with subsequent repair)

A. 650, V25.2, V27.0, 73.6, 66.32   C. 650, V27.0, 66.32
B. 648.91, V27.0, 73.6, 66.32   D. 650, V27.0, 73.59, 66.32

16. Incomplete abortion complicated by excessive hemorrhage; dilation and curettage performed.

285.1	Acute blood loss anemia
634.11	Spontaneous abortion complicated by delayed or excessive hemorrhage, incomplete
634.12	Spontaneous abortion complicated by delayed or excessive hemorrhage, complete
634.91	Spontaneous abortion without complication, incomplete
69.02	Dilation and curettage following delivery or abortion
69.09	Other dilation and curettage

A. 634.12, 69.09   C. 634.11, 69.02
B. 634.12, 285.1, 69.09   D. 634.91, 69.02

17. John has chronic ulcers of the calf and back. Both ulcers are excisionally debrided, and the ulcer of the back has a split-thickness skin graft.

707.12	Ulcer of calf
707.8	Chronic ulcer of other specified sites
86.22	Excisional debridement of wound, infection, or burn
86.69	Skin graft

A. 707.12, 707.8, 86.22, 86.22, 86.69   C. 707.8, 86.22, 86.69
B. 707.12, 707.8, 86.22   D. 707.8, 86.22, 86.22, 86.69

18. The physician has documented the final diagnoses as acute myocardial infarction, COPD, CHF, hypertension, atrial fibrillation, and status postcholecystectomy. The following conditions should be reported:

401.1	Essential Hypertension, benign
401.9	Essential Hypertension, unspecified
402.91	Hypertensive heart disease, unspecified as to malignant or benign, with heart failure
410.91	Acute myocardial infarction, unspecified site, initial episode of care
427.31	Atrial fibrillation
428.0	Congestive heart failure, unspecified
496	Chronic obstructive pulmonary disease
V45.79	Acquired absence of organ

    A. 410.91, 496, 402.91, 427.31, V45.79
    B. 410.91, 496, 428.0, 401.9, 427.31
    C. 410.91, 496, 428.0, 401.9, 427.31, V45.79
    D. 410.91, 496, 428.0, 401.1, 427.31

19. Which of the following is the term describing a woman who has delivered one child?
    A. primipara   C. nulligravida
    B. primigravida   D. paragravida

20. HPV or human papillomavirus is
    A. caused by the spirochete *Treponema pallidum*.
    B. a vaginal inflammation that is caused by a protozoan parasite.
    C. also known as genital warts.
    D. characterized by painful urination and an abnormal discharge.

21. A marked loss of bone density and increase in bone porosity is
    A. lumbago.   C. spondylitis.
    B. osteoarthritis.   D. osteoporosis.

22. The blood disorder in which red blood cells lack the normal ability to produce hemoglobin is called
    A. aplastic anemia.   C. pernicious anemia.
    B. hemolytic anemia.   D. thalassemia.

23. Which diagnostic technique records the patient's heart rates and rhythms over a 24-hour period?
    A. echocardiography   C. Holter monitor
    B. electrocardiography D. angiocardiography

24. The physician's office note states: "Counseling visit, 15 minutes counseling in follow-up with a patient newly diagnosed with diabetes." If the physician reports code 99214, which piece of documentation is missing to substantiate this code?
    A. chief complaint   C. exam
    B. history   D. total length of visit

25. A patient initially consulted with Dr. Vasseur at the request of Dr. Meche, the patient's primary care physician. Dr. Vasseur examined the patient, prescribed medication, and ordered tests. Additional visits to Dr. Vasseur's office for continuing care would be assigned from which E/M section?
    A. Office and other outpatient services, new patient
    B. Office and other outpatient services, established patient
    C. Office or other outpatient consultations, new or established patient
    D. Confirmatory consultations, new or established patient

26. In order to correctly code a hernia repair, the coder needs to know all of the following EXCEPT
    A. type of hernia.
    B. whether the hernia is strangulated or incarcerated.
    C. age of the patient.
    D. whether the patient is obese or not.

27. According to CPT, a biopsy of the breast that involves removal of only a portion of the lesion for pathologic examination is
    A. percutaneous.   C. excisional.
    B. incisional.   D. punch.

28. A patient is seen in the emergency department following an accident. The physician documents that the wound required multiple layers and extensive undermining. According to CPT definitions, this type of repair would be classified as
    A. complex.   C. simple.
    B. intermediate.   D. advancement flap.

29. The discharge diagnosis for this inpatient encounter is "rule out myocardial infarction." The coder would assign
    A. a code for a myocardial infarction.
    B. a code for the patient's symptoms.
    C. a code for an impending myocardial infarction.
    D. no code for this condition.

30. _____ is a defect characterized by four anatomical abnormalities within the heart that results in poorly oxygenated blood being pumped to the body.
    A. atrial septal defect   C. tetralogy of Fallot
    B. patent ductus arteriosus   D. coarctation of the aorta

31. Urinary frequency, urgency, nocturia, incontinence, and hesitancy are all symptoms of
    A. BPH.   C. salpingitis.
    B. end-stage kidney disease. D. genital prolapse.

32. Down syndrome, Edwards syndrome, and Patau syndrome are all examples of ____ defects.
    A. musculoskeletal   C. genitourinary tract
    B. chromosomal   D. digestive system

33. The type of anemia caused by a failure of the bone marrow to produce red blood cells is
    A. acute blood-loss anemia. C. iron-deficiency anemia.
    B. sickle cell anemia.   D. aplastic anemia.

34. A patient has major surgery and sees the surgeon 10 days later for an unrelated E/M service. Indicate the modifier that should be attached to the E/M code for the service provided.

A. –24
B. –25
C. –59
D. –79

35. Patient presents to the hospital for a three-view x-ray of the right shoulder. The diagnosis is shoulder pain, and the radiology report states the patient has a dislocated shoulder. What would be the correct codes to report to the insurance company?

719.41	Shoulder pain
831.00	Closed dislocation shoulder, unspecified
831.01	Closed dislocation shoulder, anterior
73020	Radiologic examination, shoulder; one view
73030	Radiologic examination, shoulder; complete, minimum of two views
73060	Radiologic examination; humerus, minimum of two views
RT	Right side

A. 831.00, 73060-RT
B. 719.41, 73020-RT
C. 831.01, 73030-RT
D. 831.00, 73030-RT

36. Male patient has been diagnosed with benign prostatic hypertrophy and undergoes a transurethral destruction of the prostate by radiofrequency thermotherapy. (Code ICD-9-CM for diagnoses and CPT for procedures.)

600.00	Hypertrophy (benign of prostate) without urinary obstruction and other lower urinary tract symptoms (LUTS)
52601	Transurethral electrosurgical resection of prostate including control of postoperative bleeding, complete (vasectomy, meatotomy, cystourethroscopy, urethral calibration and/or dilation, and internal urethrotomy are included)
52648	Laser vaporization of prostate, including control of postoperative bleeding, complete (vasectomy, meatotomy, cystourethroscopy, urethral calibration and/or dilation, internal urethrotomy, and transurethral transection of the prostate are included if performed)
53850	Transurethral destruction of prostate tissue; by microwave thermotherapy
53852	Transurethral destruction of prostate tissue; by radiofrequency thermotherapy

A. 600.00, 52648
B. 600.00, 53852
C. 600.00, 52601
D. 600.00, 53850

37. Hysteroscopy with D&C and polypectomy. (Code CPT for procedures.)

58100	Endometrial sampling (biopsy) with or without endocervical sampling (biopsy), without cervical dilation, any method (separate procedure)
58120	Dilation and curettage, diagnostic and/or therapeutic (nonobstetrical)
58555	Hysteroscopy, diagnostic (separate procedure)
58558	Hysteroscopy, surgical; with sampling (biopsy) of endometrium and/or polypectomy, with or without D&C
58563	Hysteroscopy, surgical; with endometrial ablation (e.g., endometrial resection, electrosurgical ablation, thermoablation)

A. 58563
B. 58558
C. 58120, 58100, 58555
D. 58558, 58120

38. Cesarean delivery with antepartum and postpartum care. (Code CPT for procedures.)

59400	Routine obstetric care, including antepartum care, vaginal delivery (with or without episiotomy and/or forceps), and postpartum care
59510	Routine obstetric care including antepartum care, cesarean delivery, and postpartum care
59514	Cesarean delivery only
59610	Routine obstetric care including antepartum care, vaginal delivery (with or without episiotomy and/or forceps) and postpartum care, after previous cesarean delivery

A. 59610
B. 59514
C. 59400
D. 59510

39. D&C for missed abortion, first trimester. (Code CPT for procedures.)

59820	Treatment of missed abortion, completed surgically; first trimester
59840	Induced abortion, by dilation and curettage
59850	Induced abortion, by one or more intra-amniotic injections (amniocentesis injections) including hospital admission and visits, delivery of fetus and secundines
59855	Induced abortion, by one or more vaginal suppositories (e.g., prostaglandin), with or without cervical dilation (e.g., laminaria), including hospital admission and visits, delivery of fetus and secundines

A. 59840
B. 59850
C. 59855
D. 59820

40. Total transcervical thymectomy. (Code CPT for procedures.)

60200	Excision of cyst or adenoma of thyroid, or transection of isthmus
60240	Thyroidectomy, total or complete
60520	Thymectomy, partial or total; transcervical approach (separate procedure)
60540	Adrenalectomy, partial or complete, or exploration of adrenal gland with or without biopsy, transabdominal, lumbar or dorsal (separate procedure)

A. 60520
B. 60540
C. 60240
D. 60200

41. Patient with carpal tunnel comes in for an open carpal tunnel release. (Code ICD-9-CM for diagnoses and CPT for procedures.)

354.0	Carpal tunnel syndrome
64721	Neuroplasty and/or transposition; median nerve at carpal tunnel
64892	Nerve graft (includes obtaining graft), single strand, arm or leg; up to 4 cm length
64905	Nerve pedicle transfer; first stage
64999	Unlisted procedure, nervous system

A. 354.0, 64999   C. 354.0, 64905
B. 354.0, 64721   D. 354.0, 64892

42. Lumbar laminectomy (one segment) for decompression of spinal cord. (Code CPT for procedures.)

62263	Percutaneous lysis of epidural adhesions using solution injection (e.g., hypertonic saline, enzyme) or mechanical means (e.g., catheter) including radiologic localization (includes contrast when administered), multiple adhesiolysis sessions; 2 or more days
63005	Laminectomy, with exploration and/or decompression of spinal cord and/or cauda equina, without facetectomy, foraminotomy, or diskectomy (e.g., spinal stenosis), one or two vertebral segments; lumbar except for spondylolisthesis
63030	Laminotomy (hemilaminectomy), with decompression of nerve root(s), including partial facetectomy, foraminotomy, and/or excision of herniated intervertebral disk; one interspace, lumbar
63170	Laminectomy with myelotomy (e.g., Bischof or DREZ type), cervical, thoracic, or thoracolumbar

A. 63005   C. 63170
B. 62263   D. 63030

43. Phacoemulsification of left cataract with IOL implant and subconjunctival injection. (Code ICD-9- CM for diagnosis and CPT for procedures.)

366.9	Unspecified cataract
66940	Removal of lens material; extracapsular
66983	Intracapsular cataract extraction with insertion of intraocular lens prosthesis (one-stage procedure)
66984	Extracapsular cataract removal with insertion of intraocular lens prosthesis (one-stage procedure) manual or mechanical technique (e.g., irrigation and aspiration or phacoemulsification)
68200	Subconjunctival injection

A. 366.9, 66940-LT   C. 366.9, 66984-LT
B. 366.9, 66983, 68200   D. 366.9, 66984-LT, 68200-LT

44. When a patient is admitted because of a primary neoplasm with metastasis, and treatment is directed toward the secondary neoplasm only,
    E. code only the primary neoplasm as the principal diagnosis.
    F. the primary neoplasm is coded as the principal diagnosis and the secondary neoplasm is coded as an additional diagnosis.
    G. the secondary neoplasm is coded as the principal diagnosis, and the primary neoplasm is coded as an additional diagnosis.
    H. code only the secondary neoplasm as the principal diagnosis.

45. A document that acknowledges patient responsibility for payment if Medicare denies the claim is a(n)
    A. explanation of benefits.
    B. remittance advice.
    C. advance beneficiary notice.
    D. CMS-1500 claim form.

46. The patient sees a participating (PAR) provider and has a procedure performed after meeting the annual deductible. If the Medicare-approved amount is $200, how much is the patient's out-of-pocket expense?
    A. $0
    B. $20
    C. $40
    D. $100

47. The purpose of the Correct Coding Initiative is to
    A. increase fines and penalties for bundling services into comprehensive CPT codes.
    B. restrict Medicare reimbursement to hospitals for ancillary services.
    C. teach coders how to unbundle codes.
    D. detect and prevent payment for improperly coded services.

48. CMS delegates its daily operations of the Medicare and Medicaid programs to
    A. the office of the Inspector General.
    B. the PRO in each state.
    C. the National Center for Vital and Health Statistics.
    D. Medicare administrative contractor (MAC).

49. The _____ are the organizations that contract with Medicare to perform reviews of medical records with the corresponding Medicare claims to detect and correct improper payments.
    A. Atlas Systems
    B. medical outcomes study
    C. recovery audit contractors (RACs)
    D. adjusted clinical groups (ACGs) system

50. Which of the following could influence a facility's case mix?
    A. changes in DRG weights
    B. changes in the services offered by a facility
    C. accuracy of coding
    D. all of the above

51. The chargemaster relieves the coders from coding repetitive services that require little, if any, formal documentation analysis. This is called
    A. grouping.
    B. hard coding.
    C. soft coding.
    D. mapping.

52. The practice of using a code that results in a higher payment to the provider than the code that more accurately reflects the service provided is known as
    A. unbundling.
    B. upcoding.
    C. optimizing.
    D. downcoding.

53. The APC payment system is based on what coding system(s)?
    A. AMA's CPT codes
    B. CPT and ICD-9-CM diagnosis and procedure codes
    C. ICD-9-CM diagnosis and procedure codes
    D. CPT/HCPCS codes

54. Which of the following contains a list of coding edits developed by CMS in an effort to promote correct coding nationwide and to prevent the inappropriate unbundling of related services?
    A. National Coverage Determination (NCD)
    B. National Correct Coding Initiative (NCCI)
    C. CPT Assistant
    D. Healthcare Common Procedure Coding System (HCPCS)

55. A(n) _____ form is used to record the patient's diagnoses and the services performed for a particular visit. It also includes codes (CPT, HCPCS, and ICD-9-CM) used specifically by that physician's office.
    A. authorization
    B. ABN (Advance Beneficiary Notice)
    C. superbill
    D. EOB (Explanation of Benefits)

56. What is the term used to describe the adjusting of the dollar amount due from the patient or insurance company to reflect a zero balance due on the claim?
    A. authorization
    B. write-off
    C. rebill
    D. outstanding

57. In ICD-9-CM, when an exploratory laparotomy is performed followed by a therapeutic procedure, the coder reports
    A. therapeutic procedure first, exploratory laparotomy second.
    B. exploratory laparotomy, therapeutic procedure, closure of wound.
    C. exploratory laparotomy first, therapeutic procedure second.
    D. therapeutic procedure only.

58. In the CPT coding system, when there is no code to properly represent the work performed by the provider, the coder must use this code.
    A. not otherwise specified
    B. not elsewhere classifiable
    C. unlisted procedure
    D. miscellaneous code

59. The physician listed the discharge diagnoses as congestive heart failure with acute pulmonary edema. You will code
    A. the CHF only.
    B. the edema only.
    C. both the CHF and the edema; sequence the CHF first.
    D. both the CHF and the edema; sequence the edema first.

60. If any part of a combination code was not "present on admission" (POA), assign the POA indicator of
A. "Y."
C. "W."
B. "U."
D. "N."

61. Patient presents a pathological fracture of the femur due to metastatic bone cancer. Patient has a history of lung cancer. Only the fracture is treated.

162.9	Malignant neoplasm of bronchus and lung, unspecified
198.5	Secondary malignant neoplasm of bone and bone marrow
733.14	Pathologic fracture of neck of femur
821.00	Closed fracture of unspecified part of femur
V10.11	Personal history of malignant neoplasm of bronchus and lung

A. 198.5, 733.14, V10.11
C. 821.00, 198.5, V10.11
B. 733.14, 198.5, V10.11
D. 821.00, 198.5, 162.9

62. Liveborn infant, born in hospital, cleft palate and lip

749.20	Cleft palate with cleft lip, unspecified
V30.00	Single liveborn, born in hospital, without mention of c-section
27.54	Repair of cleft lip
27.62	Correction of cleft palate

A. 749.20, 27.54, 27.62
C. V30.00, 749.20
B. 749.20
D. V30.00

63. A participating (PAR) physician is one who
A. can bill 115% above the Medicare Fee Schedule.
B. signs an agreement to participate in the Medicare program and agrees to accept whatever Medicare pays for a provider or service.
C. receives 5% less than other non-PAR physicians.
D. submits claim forms using ICD-9-CM procedure codes.

64. The _____ are reported for all levels of care.
A. AMA's CPT codes
B. CPT diagnosis and procedure codes
C. ICD-9-CM diagnosis and procedure codes
D. CPT/HCPCS codes

65. When is it appropriate to use category V10, history of malignant neoplasm?
A. Primary malignancy recurred at original site and adjunct chemotherapy is directed at the site.
B. Primary malignancy has been eradicated and no adjunct treatment is being given at this time.
C. Primary malignancy eradicated and the patient is admitted for adjunct chemotherapy to primary site.
D. Primary malignancy is eradicated; adjunct treatment is refused by patient even though there is some remaining malignancy.

66. Spencer has hypercholesterolemia and is treated with medication.

272.0   Pure hypercholesterolemia
272.1   Pure hyperglyceridemia
272.3   Hyperchylomicronemia
272.8   Other disorders of lipoid metabolism

A. 272.0   C. 272.3
B. 272.1   D. 272.8

67. Peggy has thymic dysplasia with immunodeficiency.

254.0   Persistent hyperplasia of thymus
254.8   Other specified diseases of thymus gland
254.9   Unspecified disease of thymus gland
279.2   Combined immunity deficiency (thymic aplasia or dysplasia with immunodeficiency)
279.3   Unspecified immunity deficiency

A. 279.3, 254.8   C. 279.2
B. 254.0   D. 279.2, 254.9

68. Acute epileptic twilight state with delirium.

293.0   Delirium due to conditions classified elsewhere (epileptic twilight state)
293.1   Subacute delirium
294.0   Amnestic disorder in conditions classified elsewhere
345.00 Generalized nonconvulsive epilepsy without mention of intractable epilepsy
780.02 Transient alteration of awareness

A. 293.0   C. 293.1
B. 780.02   D. 294.0, 345.00

69. A patient presents with bilateral sensorineural conductive hearing loss.

389.20 Mixed hearing loss, unspecified
389.21 Mixed hearing loss, unilateral
389.22 Mixed hearing loss, bilateral
389.9   Unspecified hearing loss

A. 389.22   C. 389.9
B. 389.21   D. 389.20

70. The diagnosis reads "first-, second-, and third-degree burns of the right arm." You would code
A. the first degree only.   C. the third degree only.
B. the second degree only.   D. each degree of burn separately.

71. A physician lists the final diagnosis as diarrhea and constipation due to either irritable bowel syndrome or diverticulitis. The following codes are assigned:

562.10	Diverticulosis of colon without mention of hemorrhage
562.11	Diverticulitis of colon without mention of hemorrhage
564.00	Constipation, unspecified
564.1	Irritable bowel syndrome
787.91	Diarrhea

   A. 564.1, 562.11
   B. 562.10, 564.1
   C. 564.00, 787.91, 564.1, 562.11
   D. 564.1, 562.10, 564.00, 787.91

72. Codes from category 655, known or suspected fetal abnormality affecting the mother, should
   A. be assigned if the fetal conditions are documented.
   B. be assigned at the discretion of the physician.
   C. be assigned when they affect the management of the mother.
   D. never be assigned.

73. There are a limited number of late effect codes in ICD-9-CM. When coding a residual condition where there is no applicable late effect code, one should code
   A. the residual condition followed by its cause.
   B. the cause followed by the residual condition.
   C. only the residual condition.
   D. only the cause of the residual condition.

74. In the diagnosis "first-, second-, and third-degree burns of the chest wall," a code is required for
   A. the first-degree burn only.
   B. the second-degree burn only.
   C. the third-degree burn only.
   D. for each first-, second-, and third-degree burn.

75. In regards to quality of coding, the degree to which the codes selected accurately reflect the diagnoses and procedures refers to
   A. reliability.
   B. validity.
   C. completeness.
   D. timeliness.

76. Which code represents an HCPCS Level II National Code?
   A. W0166
   B. 99281
   C. A2615
   D. 66680

77. Repair of retinal detachment with vitrectomy.

67040	Vitrectomy, mechanical, pars plana approach; with endolaser panretinal photocoagulation
67105	Repair of retinal detachment, one or more sessions; photocoagulation, with or without drainage of subretinal fluid
67108	Repair of retinal detachment; with vitrectomy, any method, with or without air or gas tamponade, focal endolaser photocoagulation, cryotherapy, drainage of subretinal fluid, scleral buckling, and/or removal of lens by same technique
67112	Repair of retinal detachment; by sclera l buckling or vitrectomy, on patient having previous ipsilateral retinal detachment repair(s) using scleral buckling or vitrectomy techniques

A. 67112
B. 67105
C. 67108
D. 67040

78. Excision of thyroid adenoma.

60100	Biopsy thyroid, percutaneous core needle
60200	Excision of cyst or adenoma of thyroid, or transection of isthmus
60210	Partial thyroid lobectomy, unilateral; with or without isthmusectomy
60280	Excision of thyroglossal duct cyst or sinus

A. 60210
B. 60200
C. 60280
D. 60100

79. Closure of traumatic kidney injury.

13100	Repair, complex trunk, 1.1 cm to 2.5 cm
50400	Pyeloplasty (Foley Y-pyeloplasty), plastic operation on renal pelvis, with or without plastic operation on ureter, nephropexy, nephrostomy, pyelostomy or ureteral splinting; simple
50500	Nephrorrhaphy, suture of kidney wound or injury
50520	Closure of nephrocutaneous or pyelocutaneous fistula

A. 50520
B. 13100
C. 50500
D. 50400

80. Excision of simple internal and external hemorrhoids.

46221	Hemorrhoidectomy, internal, by rubber band ligation(s)
46255	Hemorrhoidectomy, internal and external, single column/group
46260	Hemorrhoidectomy, internal and external, two or more columns/groups
46945	Hemorrhoidectomy, internal, by ligation other than rubber band, single hemorrhoid, column/group

A. 46255
B. 46945
C. 46221
D. 46260

81. Patient presents to the operating room for a secondary Achilles tendon repair.

27599	Unlisted procedure, femur or knee
27650	Repair, primary, open or percutaneous, ruptured Achilles tendon
27654	Repair, secondary, Achilles tendon, with or without graft
27698	Repair, secondary, disrupted ligament, ankle, collateral (e.g., Watson–Jones procedure)

A. 27599

B. 27654

C. 27650

D. 27698

CCS Mock 2 Part 1 Answer Key

ANSWER   EXPLANATION

1. B   CPT notes immediately following code 69433 instruct the coder to report 69433 with modifier -50 for a procedure performed bilaterally.

REFERENCE: AMA CPT (2014), p 399
                Bowie, p 390
                Bowie and Schaffer, pp 178–179
                Green, pp 681–682

2. D

REFERENCE: Bowie and Schaffer, p 69
                Brown, p 57
                Green, p 249
                Johnson and Linker, p 35

3. B   The medical term for thrush is candidiasis.

REFERENCE: Bowie, pp 95–96, 144–148, 539
                Brown, pp 115–117
                Green, pp 127–130

4. B

REFERENCE: Bowie and Schaffer, pp 92–95, 242
                Brown, pp 109–112
                Green, pp 148–151

5. A   The cancer is coded as a current condition as long as the patient is receiving adjunct therapy.

REFERENCE: Bowie and Schaffer, p 120
                Brown, pp 391–392
                Green, pp 153, 161
                Johnson and Linker, pp 63–64

6. D   Additional conditions that may not be routinely associated with a disease process should be coded when present. Seizures are not routinely associated with cancer; therefore, it is coded.

REFERENCE: Bowie and Schaffer, pp 116–117, 317–318
                Brown, pp 384–385
                Green, pp 154–162
                Johnson and Linker, pp 62–64

7. A

REFERENCE: Bowie and Schaffer, pp 36, 334–337
                Brown, pp 443–444
                Green, pp 99, 211–212, 217
                Johnson and Linker, p 75

8. B

REFERENCE: Bowie and Schaffer, pp 240–241
                Green, pp 178–179, 188, 207–209
                Johnson and Linker, pp 79–82

CCS Mock Exam Answer Key

ANSWER	EXPLANATION

9. D

REFERENCE: Bowie and Schaffer, pp 121–130, 170, 191–193, 200–201
Brown, p 347
Green, pp 176–183
Johnson and Linker, pp 79–82

10. D   When a patient has no known history of CABG and is diagnosed with coronary artery disease (CAD) with no mention of a specific vessel, it is appropriate to assign code 414.01 (coronary atherosclerosis of native coronary artery) since there is no history of prior bypass surgery.

REFERENCE: Bowie and Schaffer, pp 197, 214–215, 287, 344, 350
Brown, pp 89–90, 186–187, 252, 343–344

11. A   Subendocardial MI takes precedence over the anatomical site unless there were two separate acute MIs. Acute pulmonary edema is included in the code for congestive heart failure (CHF).

REFERENCE: Bowie and Schaffer, pp 197, 214–215, 287, 344, 530
Brown, pp 186, 333–334, 339–340, 347–348
Johnson and Linker, pp 43–44

12. C   Acute pulmonary edema is included in the code for congestive heart failure (CHF).

REFERENCE: Bowie and Schaffer, pp 194–195, 197–198, 214
Brown, pp 189–191, 339–340
Green, pp 182–183
Johnson and Linker, p 41

13. C

REFERENCE: Bowie and Schaffer, pp 229–230, 468
Brown, p 205

14. C

REFERENCE: Bowie and Schaffer, pp 227, 474
Brown, p 209
Johnson and Linker, pp 192–193

15. A

REFERENCE: Bowie and Schaffer, pp 260, 347, 507, 518
Johnson and Linker, pp 53–56

16. C

REFERENCE: Bowie and Schaffer, pp 255, 509
Brown, pp 291–294
Johnson and Linker, pp 56, 343, 353–354

17. A

REFERENCE: Brown, pp 241–242, 244
Bowie and Schaffer, pp 275, 539–540

CCS Mock Exam Answer Key

ANSWER	EXPLANATION

18. B Category V45.7x acquired absence of organ is intended to be used for patient care where the absence of an organ affects treatment.

REFERENCE: Bowie and Schaffer, pp 191, 197, 200, 214
Brown, pp 186, 333–334, 339–340, 347–348

19. A

REFERENCE: Jones, p 808

20. C

REFERENCE: Jones, p 716
Neighbors and Tannehill-Jones, p 370
Scott and Fong, p 470
Sormunen, pp 511, 515

21. D

REFERENCE: Neighbors and Tannehill-Jones, p 100
Scott and Fong, pp 113–114
Sormunen, p 154

22. D

REFERENCE: Jones, p 335
Neighbors and Tannehill-Jones, p 138
Scott and Fong, pp 250–251

23. C

REFERENCE: Scott and Fong, p 270
Sormunen, p 221

24. D In order to use time as a factor in determining the appropriate E/M code, the total time spent with the patient, as well as the amount of time spent in counseling, must be recorded.

REFERENCE: AMA CPT (2014), pp 7–8
Bowie, p 57
Johnson and Linker, pp 141–143

25. B Consultation codes can no longer be coded when the physician has taken an active part in the continued care of the patient.

REFERENCE: AMA CPT (2014), p 90
Bowie, pp 61–63
Green, p 436
Johnson and Linker, pp 153–154

26. D

REFERENCE: Bowie and Schaffer, pp 474, 475
Johnson and Linker, pp 192–193

27. B

REFERENCE: AMA CPT (2014), p 90
Bowie, p 115
Johnson and Linker, pp 218–219

CCS Mock Exam Answer Key

ANSWER	EXPLANATION

28. A

REFERENCE: AMA CPT (2014), pp 75–77
                           Johnson and Linker, pp 224–225

29. A When a diagnosis is preceded by the phrase "rule out" in the inpatient setting, the condition is coded as though it is confirmed.

REFERENCE: Bowie, p 67
                           Johnson and Linker, p 35

30. C

REFERENCE: Jones, p 409
                           Neighbors and Tannehill-Jones, p 444

31. A

REFERENCE: Bowie and Schaffer (2012), pp 243–245
                           Brown, pp 225–226
                           Neighbors and Tannehill-Jones, p 376

32. B

REFERENCE: Bowie and Schaffer, p 301
                           Scott and Fong, p 483

33. D

REFERENCE: Bowie and Schaffer, pp 144–147
                           Brown, p 153

34. A

REFERENCE: AMA CPT (2014), p 639
                           Bowie, p 17
                           Green, p 387
                           Johnson and Linker, p 452

35. D

REFERENCE: AMA CPT (2014), p 413
                           Bowie, pp 402–403
                           Bowie and Schaffer, p 359
                           Brown, pp 97–98

36. B

REFERENCE: AMA, pp 241–242
                           Bowie, p 295
                           Brown, pp 225–226
                           Green, p 665

CCS Mock Exam Answer Key

ANSWER	EXPLANATION

37. B

REFERENCE: AMA, p 250
Bowie, p 323
Green, p 683
Johnson and Linker, pp 380–381

38. D

REFERENCE: AMA, p 256
Bowie, pp 334–336
Green, p 683
Johnson and Linker, pp 346–348

39. D

REFERENCE: AMA, pp 258–259
Bowie, p 337
Green, p 690
Johnson and Linker, pp 353–354

40. A

REFERENCE: Bowie, p 347
Green, p 692

41. B

REFERENCE: AMA, p 492
Bowie, p 364
Green, p 704

42. A

REFERENCE: AMA, pp 154, 163
Bowie, p 363
Green, p 699
Johnson and Linker, pp 275–276

43. C Subconjunctival injections are included in 66984.

REFERENCE: AMA, pp 297, 302
Bowie, pp 373–376
Brown, p 172
CPT Assistant, Fall 1992, pp 5, 8
CPT Assistant, February 2001, p 7
CPT Assistant, November 2003, p 11
Green, pp 708–709
Johnson and Linker, pp 200–201

44. C

REFERENCE: Brown, pp 382–386
Green, p 156
Johnson and Linker, pp 60–64

CCS Mock Exam Answer Key

ANSWER	EXPLANATION

45. C

REFERENCE: Green, p 886

46. C   Medicare pays 80%, or $160, and the patient pays 20%, or $40.

REFERENCE: Green, p 852

47. D

REFERENCE: Green, p 324
                Johnson and Linker, pp 624–626

48. D   Medicare administrative contractor is the new name for the previously termed carriers and fiscal intermediaries.

REFERENCE: Green, pp 879–880

49. C

REFERENCE: Green, p 850

50. D

REFERENCE: Green, p 689

51. B

REFERENCE: Green, pp 870–872

52. B

REFERENCE: Green and Bowie, p 324
                Johnson and Linker, p 657

53. D

REFERENCE: Green, pp 863–864
                Green and Bowie, p 314

54. B

REFERENCE: Green, pp 2, 395–398
                Johnson and Linker, p 118

55. C

REFERENCE: Green, pp 870, 872
                Green and Bowie, pp 191, 200, 304, 318
                Johnson and Linker, pp 553–554

56. B   This bad debt is subsequently deleted from the balance as a "write-off" to adjust to a zero balance.

REFERENCE: Green and Rowell, p 95

57. D

REFERENCE: Bowie and Schaffer, p 374
                Brown, p 68
                Green, p 266

CCS Mock Exam Answer Key

ANSWER	EXPLANATION

58. C

REFERENCE: AMA, pp 29, 323
AMA CPT (2013), pp 59–60
Bowie, p 107
Green, pp 412

59. A Acute pulmonary edema is included in the code for congestive heart failure (CHF).

REFERENCE: Bowie, p 62
Brown, pp 339–340
Green, pp 103, 134
Johnson and Linker, p 26

60. D

REFERENCE: Bowie, pp 73–74
Brown, pp 541–544
Green, p 861

61. B

REFERENCE: Bowie and Schaffer, pp 116–117
Brown, pp 255, 318, 383
Johnson and McHugh, pp 55–60, 252–253

62. C Procedure codes are not assigned unless there is documentation that a procedure was performed.

REFERENCE: Bowie and Schaffer, pp 299, 307
Brown, pp 307, 319
Johnson and McHugh, pp 56–58

63. B

REFERENCE: Green and Rowell, p 64

64. C

REFERENCE: Bowie and Schaffer, p 5
Green and Bowie, p 314

65. B

REFERENCE: Bowie and Schaffer, pp 116–117
Brown, pp 89–90

66. A

REFERENCE: Bowie and Schaffer, p 134

67. C

REFERENCE: Bowie and Schaffer, p 134
Brown, p 130

CCS Mock Exam Answer Key

ANSWER	EXPLANATION

68. A

REFERENCE: Bowie and Schaffer, p 156
Brown, pp 164–165

69. A

REFERENCE: Bowie and Schaffer, p 178

70. C

REFERENCE: Bowie and Schaffer, pp 331–334
Brown, pp 433–434

71. C

REFERENCE: Bowie and Schaffer, pp 66–67
Brown, pp 28–29

72. C

REFERENCE: Bowie and Schaffer, pp 254–255
Brown, p 276

73. C

REFERENCE: Bowie and Schaffer, p 65
Brown, pp 59–60

74. B

REFERENCE: Bowie and Schaffer, pp 331–334

75. B

REFERENCE: Green, p 19

76. C   HCPCS Level I codes are five-digit (numeric) codes found in the CPT book. HCPCS Level II National Codes are alphanumeric starting with letters A–V. HCPCS Level III Local Codes are alphanumeric starting with letters W–Z. Level III codes were eliminated as of December 31, 2003.

REFERENCE: Green, pp 341–356
Johnson and Linker, p 11

77. C

REFERENCE: AMA (6th ed.), p 298
Bowie, p 377
CPT Assistant, October 2002, p 8

78. B

REFERENCE: AMA CPT (2014)
Bowie, p 346

79. C

REFERENCE: AMA CPT (2014)
Bowie, p 284

CCS Mock Exam Answer Key

ANSWER   EXPLANATION

80. A

REFERENCE: AMA CPT (2014)
                Bowie, p 268

81. B

REFERENCE: AMA CPT (2014)
                Bowie, p 154

Section 2 Multiple-Selection Questions

1. This patient has pneumonia. She also has acute exacerbation of COPD.

   Select TWO of the following options:
A.	486	Pneumonia, organism unspecified
B.	491.20	Obstructive chronic bronchitis, without exacerbation
C.	491.21	Obstructive chronic bronchitis, with (acute) exacerbation

2. A patient presents with intestinal obstruction due to adhesions. He also has peripheral vascular disease and chronic urinary tract infections; both conditions were treated with oral medication.

   Select THREE of the following options:
A.	443.9	Peripheral vascular disease, unspecified
B.	560.81	Intestinal or peritoneal adhesions with obstruction (postinfection)
C.	560.89	Other specified intestinal obstruction
D.	560.9	Unspecified intestinal obstruction
E.	599.0	Urinary tract infection, site not specified

3. Brandon has an infected ingrown toenail. He also has hypertension.

   Select TWO of the following options:
A.	681.11	Onychia and paronychia of toe
B.	703.0	Ingrowing nail
C.	401.9	Essential hypertension, unspecified

4. Julia is an 80-year-old female with osteoporosis. She presents to the emergency department complaining of severe back pain. X-rays revealed pathological compression fractures of several vertebrae.

   Select TWO of the following options:
A.	721.90	Spondylosis of unspecified site without mention of myelopathy
B.	733.00	Osteoporosis, unspecified
C.	733.13	Pathological fracture of vertebrae
D.	805.8	Fracture of vertebral column without mention of spinal cord injury, unspecified, closed

5. IV infusion of chemotherapy for 2 hours.

   Select TWO of the following options:
A.	96365	IV infusion, for therapy, prophylaxis, or diagnosis; initial, up to 1 hour
B.	+ 96366	IV infusion, for therapy, prophylaxis, or diagnosis; each additional hour
C.	96413	Chemotherapy administration, intravenous infusion; up to 1 hour, single or initial substance/drug
D.	+ 96415	Chemotherapy administration, intravenous infusion; each additional hour

6. Patient underwent repair of a recurrent ventral hernia with implantation of mesh.

   Select TWO of the following options:
   A. 49560 Repair initial incisional or ventral hernia; reducible
   B. 49565 Repair recurrent incisional or ventral hernia; reducible
   C. 49566 Repair recurrent incisional or ventral hernia; incarcerated or strangulated
   D. +49568 Implantation of mesh or other prosthesis for open incisional or ventral hernia repair or mesh for closure of debridement for necrotizing soft tissue infection

7. Patient presents with breast mass. Using imaging guidance, the surgeon places a metallic clip to identify the lesion, then performs a fine needle aspiration with imaging guidance.

   Select TWO of the following options:
   A. 10022 Fine-needle aspiration, with imaging guidance
   B. 19102 Biopsy of breast; percutaneous, needle core, using imaging guidance
   C. 19125 Excision of a breast lesion identified by preoperative placement of a radiologic marker, open; single lesion
   D. +19295 Image guided placement, metallic localization clip, percutaneous, during breast biopsy/aspiration

8. Mother brings in her 1-year-old for the influenza split virus vaccine. Physician discusses merits of the vaccine with the mother.

   Select TWO of the following options:
   A. 90460 Immunization administration through 18 years of age via any route of administration, with counseling by physician; first or only component of each vaccine
   B. 90471 Immunization administration; 1 vaccine
   C. 90657 Influenza virus vaccine, split virus, when administered to children 6–35 months of age, for intramuscular use
   D. 90664 Influenza virus vaccine, pandemic formulation, live, for intranasal use

CCS Mock 2 Section 2 Answer Key

1. A and C

    REFERENCE: Bowie and Schaffer, pp 68, 212, 214–215
                      Brown, pp 181–182, 186

2. B, A, and E   560.81 should be coded as the principal or first listed diagnosis.

    REFERENCE: Bowie and Schaffer, pp 201, 229, 242
                      Brown, pp 208, 217

3. B and C

    REFERENCE: Bowie and Schaffer, pp 191–192, 275

4. C and B   733.13 should be coded as the principal or first listed diagnosis.

    REFERENCE: Bowie and Schaffer, pp 287–789
                      Brown, pp 255–256, 415

5. C and D

    REFERENCE: AMA (6th ed.), pp 464, 466
                      Bowie, p 439
                      Green, pp 827–828

6. B and D

    REFERENCE: Bowie, pp 727–728
                      Green, pp 655–666

7. A and D

    REFERENCE: Bowie, pp 111–112, 132–133
                      Green, pp 514, 535–537

8. A and C

    REFERENCE: AMA CPT (2014)
                      Green, pp 802–803
                      Bowie, pp 428-429

REFERENCES

American Medical Association (AMA). *CPT assistant*. Chicago: Author.

American Medical Association (AMA). (2014). *Physicians' current procedural terminology (CPT) professional edition*. Chicago: Author.

American Medical Association (AMA). (2014). *Principles of CPT coding*. Chicago: Author.

Bowie, M. (2014). *Understanding procedural coding: A worktext*. Clifton Park, NY: Delmar Cengage Learning.

Bowie, M. & Schaffer, L. (2014). *Understanding ICD-9-CM coding: A worktext*. Clifton Park, NY: Delmar Cengage Learning.

Brown, F. (2012). *ICD-9-CM coding handbook 2011 with answers*. Chicago: American Hospital Association (AHA) Press.

Green, M. (2014). *3-2-1 Code it!* (2nd ed.). Clifton Park, NY: Delmar Cengage Learning.

Green, M. A. & Bowie, M. J. (2011). *Essentials of health information management: Principles and practices*. Clifton Park, NY: Delmar Cengage Learning.

INGENIX. (2013). *ICD-9-CM expert for hospitals* (Vol. 1, 2 & 3). Salt Lake City, UT: Author.

Johnson, S. L. & Linker, R. (2013). Understanding medical coding: A comprehensive guide (3rd ed.). Clifton Park, NY: Delmar Cengage Learning.

Jones, B. D. (2011). *Comprehensive medical terminology* (4th ed.). Clifton Park, NY: Delmar Cengage Learning.

Neighbors, M. & Tannehill-Jones, R. (2010). *Human diseases* (3rd ed.). Clifton Park, NY: Delmar Cengage Learning.

Sormunen, C. (2013). *Terminology for allied health professionals* (7th ed.). Clifton Park, NY: Delmar Cengage Learning.

CCS Mock Examination 2 Section 1

Question	CCS Domains							
	1	2	3	4	5	6	7	8
1		X						
2			X					
3		X						
4		X						
5		X						
6		X						
7		X						
8		X						
9		X						
10		X						
11		X						
12		X						
13		X						
14		X						
15		X						
16		X						
17		X						
18		X						
19	X							
20	X							
21	X							
22	X							
23	X							
24	X							
25			X					
26	X							
27			X					
28	X							
29			X					
30	X							
31	X							
32	X							
33	X							
34			X					
35		X						
36		X						
37		X						
38								
38		X						
39		X						
40		X						
41		X						
42		X						

CCS Mock Examination 2 Section 1

Question	CCS Domains							
	1	2	3	4	5	6	7	8
43		X						
44			X					
45					X			
46			X					
47					X			
48					X			
49						X		
50					X			
51			X					
52				X				
53				X				
54					X			
55				X				
56					X			
57				X				
58				X				
59			X					
60			X					
61		X						
62		X						
63				X				
64			X					
65			X					
66		X						
67		X						
68		X						
69		X						
70			X					
71		X						
72			X					
73			X					
74			X					
75					X			
76	X							
77		X						
78		X						
79		X						
80		X						
81		X						

CCS Mock Examination 1 Section 2

Question	CCS Domains							
	1	2	3	4	5	6	7	8
1		X						
2		X						
3		X						
4		X						
5		X						
6		X						
7		X						
8		X						

XII. CCS Mock Exam Section 3 Coding Cases

CCS MOCK EXAMINATION SECTION 3

As stated earlier in the book, Section 3 of the CCS Examination consists of twelve (12) coding cases. The mock exam in this book contains twelve (12) cases to code. Use ICD-9-CM (Volumes 1–3) for coding inpatient diagnoses and procedures. Code diagnoses for outpatient/ambulatory care records using ICD-9-CM (Volumes 1 and 2). Code ambulatory procedures using CPT coding.

For each of the 12 coding cases, the coding system (ICD-9-CM and or CPT) and the number of codes necessary for each coding system will be given. The spaces for codes on the answer sheet reflect the number and type of codes necessary.

As always, refer to the latest information about the examination that is provided in your examination packet and online at http://www.AHIMA.org.

INPATIENT CODING INSTRUCTIONS

1. Follow UHDDS definitions, ICD-9-CM instructional notations and conventions, and current coding guidelines to assign correct ICD-9-CM diagnostic and procedural codes to hospital inpatient medical records.

2. In sequencing the ICD-9-CM codes, list the principal diagnosis first.

3. Code other diagnoses that coexist at the time of admission, that develop subsequently, or that affect the treatment received and/or the length of stay. These represent additional conditions that affect patient care in terms of:
   - requiring clinical evaluation, therapeutic treatment, diagnostic procedures, or
   - extending length of hospital stay, or
   - increased nursing care and/or monitoring

   Examples:
   - Present on admission (POA) conditions
   - Conditions that develop subsequent to admission
   - Chronic diseases requiring active intervention during the hospital visit
   - Chronic systemic or generalized conditions that may have a bearing on the management of the patient (e.g., blindness)
   - Status post previous surgeries or status post previous conditions that are likely to recur and that may have an effect on patient management

4. Do not code:
   - Localized conditions that have no effect on patient management
   - Status post previous surgeries or conditions that have no effect on patient management
   - Abnormal findings (laboratory, x-ray, pathologic, and other diagnostic testing results) unless documentation from the physician is present
   - Signs or symptoms that are characteristic of a diagnosis
   - Any social history condition(s) that have no bearing on patient management

5. Do not assign:
    - M-codes (Morphology codes)
    - E-codes except those to identify the cause or substance for an adverse effect of a drug that is correctly prescribed and properly administered (E850–E982)

6. Code all procedures that fall within the code range of 00.01 through 86.99, but do not code 57.94 (Foley catheter).

7. Do not code procedures that fall within the code range 87.01 through 99.99, but code procedures in the following ranges:

Cholangiograms	87.51–87.54
Retrogrades, urinary systems	87.74 and 87.76
Arteriography and angiography	88.40–88.58
Radiation therapy	92.21–92.29
Psychiatric therapy	94.24–94.27
Alcohol/drug detoxification and rehabilitation	94.61–94.69
Insertion of endotracheal tube	96.04
Other lavage of bronchus and trachea	96.56
Mechanical ventilation	96.70–96.72
ESWL	98.51–98.59
Chemotherapy	99.25

AMBULATORY CARE CODING INSTRUCTIONS

1. To select diagnoses, conditions, problems, or other reasons for care that requires ICD-9-CM coding in an ambulatory care visit or encounter either in a hospital clinic, outpatient surgical area, emergency room, physician's office, or other ambulatory care setting: apply ICD-9-CM instructional notations and conventions; current approved Coding Guidelines for Outpatient Services; and "Diagnostic Coding and Reporting Requirements for Physician Billing" (*Coding Clinic for ICD-9-CM*, Fourth quarter 1995 and 1996).

2. In sequencing ICD-9-CM diagnoses codes, the first code shown for the case should describe the condition chiefly responsible for the outpatient services provided during the encounter.

3. Code the secondary diagnoses as follows:
   - Code and report chronic diseases that are treated on an ongoing basis as many times as the patient receives treatment and care for the condition(s).
   - Code all documented conditions that coexist at the time of the encounter, that require or affect patient care, treatment, or management.
   - Do not code conditions previously treated that no longer exist.

4. Do not assign:
   - E-codes, except for those that identify the causative substance for an adverse effect of a drug that is correctly prescribed and properly administered (E850–E982)
   - M-codes
   - ICD-9-CM procedure codes
   - HCPCS Level II (alphanumeric) codes

5. Assign CPT codes for all surgical procedures that fall in the surgery section.

6. Assign CPT codes from the following sections ONLY IF indicated on the case cover sheet:
   - Anesthesia
   - Medicine
   - Evaluation and management services
   - Radiology
   - Laboratory and pathology

7. Assign CPT/HCPCS modifiers for hospital-based facilities if applicable (regardless of payer).

8. Do not assign HCPCS Level II (alphanumeric) codes.

Code ICD-9-CM Diagnoses and Procedures
(Seven diagnosis codes and two procedure codes will be needed)

Mock Examination Case 1
INPATIENT FACE SHEET

Admit Date: 12/14/14

Discharge Date: 12/16/14

Age: 89

Sex: Female

Disposition: Home

Admit Diagnoses:
Lower abdominal pain and nausea possibly due to partial small bowel obstruction.
History of colon resection for cancer with elevated CEA of 23.1. Rule out recurrence of cancer.

Discharge Diagnoses:
1. Diverticulosis
2. Benign colon polyp

Procedure:
Colonoscopy with polypectomy and biopsy

Mock Examination Case 1
HISTORY AND PHYSICAL

ADMITTED: 12/14/14

CHIEF COMPLAINT: Abdominal pain, nausea, and vomiting.

HISTORY OF PRESENT ILLNESS: This is an 89-year-old woman who has been complaining of abdominal pain, vomiting, and nausea for several weeks. She is admitted at this time for further evaluation, including colonoscopy. The patient has a history of colon cancer with an elevated CEA, suggesting recurrence of cancer.

PAST HISTORY: The patient had colon resection in June 2001 for colon cancer. She had her left lung resected in July 1997 for carcinoma. In addition, she has had coronary artery bypass graft in 2000 for severe coronary artery disease. She has known hypertension and osteoporosis with L1 compression fracture.

MEDICATIONS: Metoprolol 100 mg b.i.d., Cardizem 180 mg daily, and Cardura.

ALLERGIES: No known allergies.

SOCIAL HISTORY: The patient is widowed and lives alone. She does not smoke cigarettes or drink alcohol.

FAMILY HISTORY: There is a strong family history of arteriosclerotic heart disease and myocardial infarction.

REVIEW OF SYSTEMS: The patient has had intermittent diarrhea over the past years, since the time of her colon surgery. She has had episodes where her abdomen becomes distended and hard.

PHYSICAL EXAMINATION:

General: On physical examination the patient is a pleasant, alert, 89-year-old woman in no distress.

HEENT: Shows capillary reflexes. Her extraocular movements are normal. There is no pallor, icterus. Ears and throat are unremarkable. Neck is supple and free of masses. There is no jugular venous distension in the neck.

Chest: Symmetrical.

Lungs: Lung fields are clear.

Heart: Heart sounds are regular with no significant murmurs.

Abdomen: Firm. Bowel sounds are active. There is some diffuse low abdominal tenderness, most noted in the right lower quadrant. There is no rebound tenderness. There are no apparent masses.

Extremities: Show 2 plus edema.

Assessment: The patient is an 89-year-old woman with known colon cancer and recurrent episodes of abdominal pain and vomiting over the past several weeks. The case has been discussed with her gastroenterologist, Dr. Angela Gaige. She is admitted at this time for continued intravenous fluid hydration, colonoscopy, and diagnostic workup.

Mock Examination Case 1
CONSULTATION

DATE: 12/14/14

REQUESTING PHYSICIAN: Dr. Bronwyn Mills

CONSULTING PHYSICIAN: Dr. David Clark

REASON FOR CONSULTATION:
Evaluation of patient with lower abdominal pain, nausea, and vomiting.

HISTORY:
This 89-year-old woman is referred for further evaluation of lower abdominal pain, nausea, and vomiting. Her bowel movements are erratic and range from being constipated with no bowel movement for several days to loose bowel movements. She has lost about 3 pounds over the past month.

She underwent CT scan of the abdomen and pelvis on November 24, revealing a dilated bile duct. Her liver enzymes, however, were normal and HIDA scan revealed no evidence of obstruction, and thus it was felt that the dilation of the bile duct was physiologic and did not represent obstruction. She had a CEA of 23.1 on November 23.

PAST MEDICAL HISTORY:
Colon resection for cancer of the colon in June 2001.
Coronary artery bypass graft in 2000.

MEDICATIONS IN THE HOSPITAL: Pepcid 20 mg IV q. 12 h.; nitroglycerin q.i.d.; atenolol 25 mg p.o. b.i.d.

ALLERGIES: None known.

SOCIAL HISTORY: Cigarettes: smoked until 1989.

FAMILY HISTORY: Negative for cancer.

PHYSICAL EXAMINATION:

General Appearance:	Pleasant cooperative woman, who appears to be in moderate distress due to her abdominal symptoms.
HEENT:	Normocephalic, traumatic. No scleral icterus.
Neck:	Supple. No lymphadenopathy or enlarged thyroid.
Lungs:	Clear.
Heart:	Regular rate and rhythm. No murmurs, rubs, or gallops.
Abdomen:	Moderately tender and moderately distended in the lower abdomen. No hepatosplenomegaly.
Rectal:	No masses. Firm stool. Negative for occult blood.
Extremities:	No cyanosis, clubbing, or edema.
Neurologic:	Alert and oriented × 3. Grossly nonfocal.

Mock Examination Case 1
CONSULTATION

Continued:

LABORATORY: 12/14/14, glucose 113, BUN 25, creatinine 1.3.

The remainder of the CMP, amylase, and lipase are within normal range. CBC within normal range.

Abdominal series on December 13 reveals possible partial small bowel obstruction and possible persistent pleural effusion.

IMPRESSION:

Lower abdominal pain and nausea possibly due to partial small bowel obstruction.

History of colon resection for cancer with elevated CEA of 23.1. Rule out recurrence of cancer.

Dilated common bile duct, but normal liver enzymes and HIDA scan on recent admission suggesting no physiological obstruction.

PLAN:

Colonoscopy advised.

Repeat CEA.

Clear liquid diet.

Mock Examination Case 1
PROCEDURE NOTE

Date of Procedure: 12/15/14

Preoperative Diagnosis: Abdominal pain, nausea, vomiting, history of colon cancer

Postoperative Diagnoses: Marked diverticulosis

                                        Small internal hemorrhoid

                                        Benign polyp

Surgeon: Dr. David Clark

Procedure: Colonoscopy with biopsy

DESCRIPTION OF PROCEDURE:
Following IV sedation, the colonoscope was inserted into the rectum and advanced to the left colon and beyond to the splenic flexure and into the ascending colon and into the cecum. A 5 mm polyp at the level of previous anastomosis was removed with snare and additional biopsies were taken at the sigmoid level. The patient tolerated the procedure well.

Mock Examination Case 1
Answer Sheet

DIAGNOSES	ICD-9-CM CODES					
Principal Diagnosis				.		
DX 2				-		
DX 3				-		
DX 4				-		
DX 5				-		
DX 6				-		
DX 7				-		

PROCEDURES	ICD-9-CM CODES				
PP 1			-		
PX 2			-		

Code ICD-9-CM Diagnoses and CPT Procedures
(Three diagnosis codes and one procedure code will be needed)

Mock Examination Case 2
Ambulatory Surgery Face Sheet

DATE OF ADMISSION: 01/16/15

AGE: 45

SEX: Female

ADMITTING DIAGNOSIS: Carpal tunnel syndrome, left wrist

DISCHARGE DIAGNOSES:

        Carpal tunnel syndrome, left wrist

        Type 1 diabetes mellitus

        Hypertension

PROCEDURE: Decompression of medial nerve, left wrist

DISPOSITION: Home

Mock Examination Case 2
History and Physical

DATE OF ADMISSION: 01/16/15

ADMITTING DIAGNOSIS: Carpal tunnel syndrome left wrist.

HISTORY OF PRESENT ILLNESS:

This patient has been complaining of left wrist pain for approximately 1 year. She has been receiving physical therapy for 6 months, and it does not seem to be helping. She is a transcriptionist and does repetitive computer work. She has been wearing bilateral wrist supports, which have helped to some extent.

PAST MEDICAL HISTORY:

The patient has a history of T&A; hysterectomy 2 years ago; history of type 1 diabetes; and hypertension. She does not complain of chest pain or shortness of breath.

ALLERGIES: No apparent allergies.

MEDICATIONS: Patient takes Humulin 70/30 and Zestril.

SOCIAL HISTORY: Noncontributory.

PHYSICAL EXAMINATION:

General:	This is a well-developed, well-nourished female in no acute distress.
Head:	Normocephalic.
Neck:	Supple. No masses. Carotid pulse is palpable. Trachea is in midline.
Skin:	Negative.
Chest:	Clear to auscultation and percussion.
Heart:	No murmurs, gallops, or rubs.
Abdomen:	Negative.
Extremities:	Left wrist has weakness. Unable to touch thumb and little finger together. There is a prominent mass on the palmar aspect of the left wrist.

PLAN:

Patient will be seen at the ambulatory surgery center for carpal tunnel surgery.

Mock Examination Case 2
Operative Report

Date of Operation:	01/16/15
Preoperative Diagnosis:	Carpal tunnel syndrome left wrist
Postoperative Diagnosis:	Carpal tunnel syndrome left wrist
Operation:	Decompression of medial nerve, left wrist
Surgeon:	E.B. Mannion, MD
Anesthesia:	Bier block
Estimated Blood Loss:	Less than 500 mL

PROCEDURE:

Under Bier block anesthesia, preparation was done with Betadine scrub, Betadine solution, and sterile draping was done. Curvilinear incision was made based on the lunar side of the longitudinal wrist crease and carried up to the proximal flexor wrist crease. This was carried through subcutaneous tissue. Range retractors were inserted. The median nerve was visualized at the proximal edge of the transverse carpal ligament. The nerve was protected, and using curved dissecting scissors, the transverse carpal ligament was sectioned under direct vision. The nerve was quite compressed. After the ligament had been sectioned, the wound was closed with interrupted 5-0 nylon sutures, and sterile dressings were applied. The patient tolerated the procedure well, and circulation to the extremity was intact at the completion of the procedure.

Mock Examination Case 2

Progress Notes:

Patient was taken to the operating room for carpal tunnel repair. Patient tolerated the procedure well. No apparent complications are noted. Patient will be discharged when stable and should follow up in my office in 2 weeks.

Orders:

1. Standard postoperative orders.
2. Discharge patient from recovery room when stable.
3. Vital signs q. 15 minutes × 4; then q. 30 minutes × 2; then q1h until discharge.
4. Tylenol 500 mg q. 4 for pain.
5. Discharge when patient is stable.

Mock Examination Case 2
Answer Sheet

DIAGNOSES				ICD-9-CM CODES		
First Listed DX					-	
DX 2					-	
DX 3					-	

PROCEDURE			CPT CODES		MODIFIERS (If Applicable)	
PR 1					-	

Code ICD-9-CM Diagnoses and CPT Procedures
(One diagnosis code and one procedure code will be needed)

Mock Examination Case 3
Emergency Room Visit Face Sheet

Date of Visit: 01/15/15

Age: 25

Sex: Male

Admitting Diagnosis: Laceration, right hand

Discharge Diagnosis: Laceration, right hand

Disposition: Home

Mock Examination Case 3
Emergency Room Visit

DATE OF SERVICE: 01/15/15

HISTORY OF PRESENT ILLNESS:

This is a 25-year-old male who cut his hand while opening a can. Patient stated that he cut his hand and just came to the closest emergency room.

PAST MEDICAL HISTORY: Noncontributory.

MEDICATIONS: None.

REVIEW OF SYSTEMS: All normal.

PHYSICAL EXAMINATION:

General:	Healthy appearing male in mild distress.
Skin:	Warm and dry.
Lungs:	Clear.
Extremities:	Normal range of motion times four. The dorsal right hand has a 1.5 cm laceration, which is superficial with no deep structure involvement.

The right hand was prepped with Betadine and anesthetized with 1% plain Xylocaine. The wound was irrigated with saline and explored. No evidence of foreign body. The wound was closed with four interrupted sutures of #6-0 Ethilon. A sterile dressing was applied.

IMPRESSION: Right hand laceration.

The patient was given a prescription for Erythromycin 500 mg q.i.d., and he is to take Tylenol for pain.

Patient is to schedule a follow-up visit in 12 days for suture removal.

Mock Examination Case 3
Answer Sheet

DIAGNOSES	ICD-9-CM CODES					
First Listed DX				-		

PROCEDURE	CPT CODES					MODIFIERS (If Applicable)		
PR 1						-		

Note: E&M codes are assigned, when applicable, for outpatient clinic and emergency department visits. Because each hospital facility has its own unique system to assign the appropriate E&M codes, the appropriate codes would range from 99281 to 99285 for this case.

Code ICD-9-CM Diagnoses and CPT Procedures
(Two diagnosis codes and two procedure codes will be needed)

Mock Examination Case 4
Ambulatory Care Face Sheet

Date of Admission: 01/16/15

Date of Discharge: 01/16/15

Age: 46

Sex: Female

ADMITTING DIAGNOSIS: Nasal obstruction

DISCHARGE DIAGNOSES:

                           1.   Bilateral hypertrophic turbinates

                           2.   Nasoseptal spur

PROCEDURE: Functional internal nasal reconstruction

DISPOSITION: Home

**Mock Examination Case 4
History and Physical**

DATE OF ADMISSION: 01/16/15

ADMITTING DIAGNOSIS: Nasal obstruction

HISTORY OF PRESENT ILLNESS:

This patient has been complaining of nasal obstruction for several months. She also had a left nasal polyp and a Caldwell-Luc done many years ago. She has been given antihistamines and decongestants, but these have not rectified her condition.

PAST MEDICAL HISTORY:
Caldwell-Luc many years ago. No other significant problems.

ALLERGIES: None.

MEDICATIONS: Antihistamine and decongestant.

SOCIAL HISTORY: Patient smokes 1/2 pack per day; alcohol, social. Hobbies include gardening, reading, and sailing.

PHYSICAL EXAMINATION:

General:	Well-developed, well-nourished female in no acute distress.
HEENT:	Head is normocephalic. She has a spur on the right in the inferior turbinates bilaterally, which are obstructed and hypertrophic.
Chest:	Clear to auscultation and percussion.
Heart:	Normal rhythm.
Abdomen:	Negative.
Neurological:	Normal.
Extremities:	Normal.

PLAN:
The patient will be admitted to 1-day surgery for functional intranasal surgery for bilateral hypertrophic turbinates and nasoseptal spur.

Mock Examination Case 4
Operative Report

Date of Operation:	01/16/15
Preoperative Diagnoses:	
	1. Bilateral hypertrophic turbinates
	2. Nasoseptal spur
Postoperative Diagnosis:	Same
Operation:	Functional internal nasal reconstruction
Surgeon:	Carlos Earl, III, MD
Anesthesia:	General
Anesthesiologist:	C.V. Wilkinson, MD
Estimated Blood Loss:	Less than 500 mL
Complications:	None

PROCEDURE:

The patient was taken to the surgical suite and prepped and draped in the usual fashion. General anesthesia was given, both nasal cavities were packed, and the anterior aspect of the septum and both inferior turbinates were infiltrated with 1% Xylocaine with 1:40,000 epinephrine solution.

The nose was inspected, and the patient was found to have a septal spur on the right side, which was obstructing her nasal passages. Both interior turbinates were hypertrophic.

An incision was made along the caudal end of the septum and was carried down to the perichondrium and dissected posteriorly and inferiorly. The second incision was then made 1.5 cm beyond the first one, and the mucoperichondrium on the opposite side was dissected posteriorly and inferiorly. The septal cartilage was not detached from the maxillary crest, and the nasal process of the palatine bone on that side was removed. The vomer was fractured and left intact.

With the obstructing cartilaginous and bony portion corrected, the septal mucosa was placed back and was closed. A left inferior turbinoplasty was then carried out, making an incision from the anterior-superior aspect down to the anterior-inferior. The turbinate bone was dissected medially and laterally and was removed. The nasal cavity was packed, and attention was turned to the other side, where an incision was made and the turbinate bone was dissected medially and posteriorly. Some of the bone was removed.

Bilateral nasal splints were placed, and bilateral nasal packing was placed inferiorly. The patient was transferred to the recovery room in satisfactory condition. No apparent complications noted.

Mock Examination Case 4

Progress Notes:

Patient was taken to the operating room for functional internal nasal reconstruction. Patient tolerated the procedure well. Nasal packs are in place. No apparent complication from the surgery or anesthesia is noted. Patient will be discharged when stable and is to follow up in my office tomorrow.

Orders:

1. Standard postoperative orders.
2. Discharge patient from recovery room when stable.
3. Vital signs q. 15 minutes × 4; then q. 30 minutes × 2; then q1h until discharge.
4. Urinary catheterization × 1, if patient unable to void.
5. Start on soft diet.
6. Check nasal packings prior to leaving for excessive bleeding.
7. Discharge when patient is stable.

Mock Examination Case 4
Answer Sheet

DIAGNOSES	ICD-9-CM CODES					
First Listed DX				-		
DX 2				-		

PROCEDURES	CPT CODES				MODIFIERS (If Applicable)		
PR 1					-		
PR 2					-		

Code ICD-9-CM Diagnoses and CPT Procedure(s) Codes for ER Visit
(Two diagnosis codes and two procedure codes will be needed)

Mock Examination Case 5
Emergency Room Report Face Sheet

Patient's Name: Nancy Jean

Date of Visit: 01/16/15

Age: 40

Sex: Female

Insurance: Commercial

Mock Examination Case 5
Emergency Room Report

DATE OF ADMISSION: 01/16/15

CHIEF COMPLAINT: Severe headache, nausea, and vomiting.

HISTORY:

This 40-year-old female was seen in the emergency room for complaints of headache, neck pain, nausea, and vomiting, with the possibility of viral meningitis. At the time, my impression was that it probably was a viral syndrome, and a spinal tap was done to rule out viral meningitis. The spinal tap was unremarkable, and a CT scan of the head was also performed and was unremarkable.

PAST MEDICAL HISTORY:	Noncontributory.
ALLERGIES:	None.
MEDICATIONS:	None.
SOCIAL HISTORY:	Noncontributory.

PHYSICAL EXAMINATION:

General:	At present, examination reveals her to be in moderate distress due to her headache.
HEENT:	Markedly photophobia. No gross lesions noted. Pupils round and reactive. Trachea midline.
Chest:	Lungs clear to auscultation and percussion.
Heart:	Murmurs not noted.
Abdomen:	Soft, no organomegaly.
Neurological:	Examination includes the cranial nerve, motor, sensory, gait and station, deep tendon reflexes, and cerebellum, which were unremarkable. No nuchal rigidity noted. No Brudzinski or Kernig's signs.
Extremities:	All pulses palpable.
PROCEDURE:	Spinal tap
	CT scan of head
LABORATORY RESULTS:	CSF showed 1 WBC and 1 RBC, glucose 33, protein 27.

IMPRESSION:
1. Viral syndrome
2. Headache

Patient is discharged from the emergency room and is to follow up with her physician.

A prescription of Demerol 50 mg p.o. q.i.d. was given.

Mock Examination Case 5
Answer Sheet

DIAGNOSES	ICD-9-CM CODES					
First Listed DX				-		
DX 2				-		

PROCEDURES	CPT CODES					MODIFIERS (If Applicable)		
PR 1						-		
PR 2						-		

Note: E&M codes are assigned, when applicable, for outpatient clinic and emergency department visits. Because each hospital facility has its own unique system to assign the appropriate E&M codes, the appropriate codes would range from 99281 to 99285 for this case.

Code ICD-9-CM Diagnoses and CPT Procedures
(One diagnosis code and one procedure code will be needed)

Mock Examination Case 6
Ambulatory Surgery Face Sheet

Patient's Name:	Sally Hunter
Date of Visit:	01/16/15
Age:	45
Sex:	Female
Insurance:	Commercial

Mock Examination Case 6
Ambulatory Surgery History and Physical

DATE OF ADMISSION: 01/16/15

ADMITTING DIAGNOSIS: Eyes turn out.

HISTORY OF PRESENT ILLNESS:
This is the first visit for this patient, who is being admitted for ambulatory surgery. Patient will undergo eye muscle surgery in hopes of recapturing and maintaining binocular function.

PAST MEDICAL HISTORY:
The patient's eyes began to turn out in early childhood, and she underwent surgery for correction at the age of 7. Progression of the disease has now resulted in the patient only being able to use one eye at a time.

ALLERGIES: None.

MEDICATIONS: None.

FAMILY HISTORY: No familial disorders known.

REVIEW OF SYSTEMS: Review of systems is unremarkable.

PHYSICAL EXAMINATION:

General:	Patient is alert, cooperative, and in no acute distress. BP 120/80; Respirations 17; Pulse 77.
HEENT:	Head is normocephalic. Tympanic membranes clear. Nose, throat, and mouth are normal. No inflammation is noted.
Neck:	Supple with no masses palpated.
Eyes:	Visual acuity 20/20 OU with correction. Fundus is normal. Exotropia 30 prism diopters at distance, 20 prism diopters at near. Sensory testing reveals binocular function when the amount of strabismus is corrected with prisms, otherwise suppression OS.
Chest:	Clear to auscultation and percussion.
Heart:	Normal sinus rhythm without murmur, gallop, or rub.
Skin:	Clear.
Extremities:	Full range of motion. Normal peripheral pulses.
Neurological:	Cranial nerves II through XII and deep tendon reflexes equal and symmetrical.
PLAN:	Strabismus surgery under general anesthesia.

Mock Examination Case 6
Ambulatory Surgery Operative Report

DATE OF OPERATION:	01/16/15
PREOPERATIVE DIAGNOSIS:	Exotropia
POSTOPERATIVE DIAGNOSIS:	Exotropia
PROCEDURE PERFORMED:	Recession, lateral rectus muscle, 6 mm OU
SURGEON:	E.B. Mannion, MD
ASSISTANT SURGEON:	Carlos Earl, III, MD
ANESTHESIOLOGIST:	Jim Wilkins, MD

PROCEDURE:

Under general endotracheal anesthesia, the patient's adnexa were prepped with Betadine. The patient was draped under sterile conditions. Forced ductions were performed and found to be negative, OU. A small wire lid speculum with solid teeth was applied OD. The right eye was rotated superonasally, and an inferotemporal incision was made at the conjunctiva and tendon capsule in the cul-de-sac region with Westcott scissors. The right lateral rectus muscle was isolated on a muscle hook and brought out through the incision site. A double-arm suture of 6-0 Vicryl on a #29 spatula needle was placed through the muscle at its insertion and locked at both ends. The muscle was removed from the globe and reinserted into the sclera 6 mm from the original insertion site as measured with calipers. The conjunctiva was repositioned in its original position without suturing.

The lid speculum was transferred to the patient's left eye for an identical technique. The left lateral rectus muscle was recessed 6 mm.

At the completion of the surgery, several drops of Maxitrol were instilled OU, and the patient left the operating room in good condition. No apparent complications noted.

Mock Examination Case 6
Progress Notes and Orders

Progress Notes:

Patient was taken to the operating room for strabismus surgery. Patient tolerated the procedure well, and no apparent complications were noted. The patient will be discharged when stable and when discharge criteria have been met. The patient is to follow up in my office tomorrow.

Physician Orders:

A.M. admit on 01/16/15.

Patient to sign op permit.

Postoperative Orders

Discharge when alert and stable.

IV orders per anesthesia.

Tylenol #3 q4h prn.

Vistaril 50 mg q4h for nausea.

Cold moist compress to both eyes prn drainage.

Mock Examination Case 6
Answer Sheet

DIAGNOSES		ICD-9-CM CODES					
First Listed DX					-		

PROCEDURE	CPT CODES					MODIFIERS (If Applicable)		
PR 1						-		

Code ICD-9-CM Diagnoses and CPT Procedures
(Two diagnosis codes and one procedure code will be needed)

Mock Examination Case 7
Ambulatory Surgery

Patient's Name:	Bonnie Bonn
Date of Visit:	01/06/15
Age:	71
Sex:	Female
Insurance:	Medicare

Mock Examination Case 7
History and Physical

DATE OF ADMISSION: 01/06/15

HISTORY OF PRESENT ILLNESS:
This 71-year-old female has been hospitalized for symptomatic slow heart rate and atrial fibrillation. Echocardiogram did show evidence of enlarged left atrium, and the patient has been taking Coumadin for over a month. Patient also had electrocardioversion and was converted but did revert into atrial fibrillation. Patient is not taking any medications for the complete AV block, and it was felt that a pacemaker would be the best option for the patient.

PAST MEDICAL HISTORY: Noncontributory.

SOCIAL HISTORY: Patient is married and lives with her husband. Does not smoke or drink alcohol.

PHYSICAL EXAMINATION:
General: Well-developed female in no acute distress.
HEENT: Within normal limits.
Heart: Complete AV block and atrial fibrillation. No murmurs noted.
Lungs: Clear to auscultation.
Abdomen: Soft, nontender.
Urogential: Denies problems.
Extremities: Within normal limits. Full range of motion.

PLAN:
Patient will be admitted for a pacemaker.

Mock Examination Case 7
Operative Report

Date of Operation:	01/06/15
Preoperative Diagnosis:	AV Block
	Atrial Fibrillation
Postoperative Diagnosis:	AV Block
	Atrial Fibrillation
Operation:	Implantation of a DDIR mode-switching permanent pacemaker and leads
Surgeon:	David Pool, MD
Assistant:	Kent David, MD
Anesthesia:	Versed 6 mg IV, 1% Xylocaine

PROCEDURE:

The left infraclavicular area was prepped and draped in the usual manner, and the area was infused with 1% Xylocaine. A pacemaker pocket was formed with the incision made parallel to the left clavicle, down to the level of the prepectoral fascia. The left subclavian vein was then easily cannulated and, over a guide wire, two 7-French sheaths were passed without difficulty. Through these sheaths, a Medtronic model lead was fastened to the right ventricular apex and fixed into position. Through the other sheath, a Medtronic model lead was passed to the right atrial appendage and fixed into position. After adequate endocardiac anchoring was ensured, threshold testing on these leads were performed.

R waves measured 10.2 mV. Ventricular capture occurred down to amplitude of 0.4 volt, and a pulse width of 0.5 msec, measuring a current of 0.7 MA. The 5-volt resistance was measured at 707 ohms. On the atrial lead, atrial fibrillation waves measured 1.5 to 3.8 mV. Atrial impedance measured 536 ohms. We could not test capture due to the presence of the atrial fibrillation. Once in these positions, the leads were anchored using the anchoring sleeves with two 2-Ethibond sutures, then a purse string suture was placed around the leads to prevent back bleeding.

The patient tolerated the procedure well without any complications.

Mock Examination Case 7

Progress Note:

The patient was admitted for a permanent pacemaker for a complete AV block and atrial fibrillation. The patient was taken to the operating room where a pacemaker was inserted. No complications from the procedure were noted. The patient is to be discharged when discharge criteria have been met and will follow up in my office in a week.

Physician Orders:
Routine vital signs.
Place on cardiac monitor until discharge.
Diet as tolerated.
Up with assistance.
IV D5RL at 83 mL/h. Change to heparin lock with flush when tolerating p.o. fluids well.
M.S. 4–10 mg IM for severe pain q. 3–4 h prn.
Discharge when patient is stable.

Mock Examination Case 7
Answer Sheet

DIAGNOSES	ICD-9-CM CODES					
First Listed DX				-		
DX 2				-		

PROCEDURE	CPT CODES					MODIFIERS (If Applicable)	
PR 1						-	

Code ICD-9-CM Diagnoses and Procedures
(Seven diagnosis codes and two procedure codes will be needed)

Mock Examination Case 8
Inpatient Face Sheet

Admit Date: 12/25/14

Discharge Date: 12/29/14

Sex: Female

Age: 35

Disposition: Home

ADMITTING DIAGNOSES:
1. Induction of labor
2. Severe pre-eclampsia
3. Intrauterine growth retardation

DISCHARGE DIAGNOSES:
1. Severe pre-eclampsia
2. Accelerated hypertension
3. Intrauterine growth retardation
4. Preterm at 36 weeks

PROCEDURE: Primary low transverse c-section

Mock Examination Case 8
Discharge Summary

Admitted: 12/25/14

Discharged: 12/29/14

ADMITTING DIAGNOSES:
1. Induction of labor
2. Severe pre-eclampsia
3. IUGR

DISCHARGE DIAGNOSES:
1. Severe pre-eclampsia
2. Accelerated hypertension
3. IUGR

Patient is a 35-year-old, gravida 3, para 2, admitted for induction due to severe pre-eclampsia and late decelerations. She was admitted for induction and began on Pitocin. However, due to persistent late decelerations, patient underwent a primary low flap transverse cesarean section with delivery of a 4-pound, 12-ounce liveborn male with 6, 9 Apgars.

There were no postoperative problems other than accelerated hypertension, for which the patient was started on Apresoline and Aldomet. Last blood pressure reading was 180/90. Discharge hemoglobin and hematocrit were 11.3 and 32.4, and platelet count was 122. The platelet count had been as low as 94,000. The patient's magnesium levels when she was on magnesium ranged between 4.5 and 4, her electrolytes were normal, alkaline phosphatase 262 and 304. The hemoglobin and hematocrit on admission were 13 and 37, platelet count was 158,000. The PT and PTT were normal. The urinalysis was negative.

The patient was discharged in satisfactory condition with diet and activity as tolerated. Patient will continue to take Aldomet and Apresoline. I will see the patient in my office in 1 week for staple removal.

Mock Examination Case 8
History and Physical

HISTORY OF PRESENT ILLNESS:

The patient is a 35-year-old gravida 3, para 2, due date 12/25/14, whom I saw in my office with blood pressure of 154/104, 150/98, 2+ protein. She was immediately sent to the hospital for admission for induction of labor.

ANTEPARTUM HISTORY:

She has had two vaginal deliveries in the past. Her ultrasound was consistent with dates. Her group B Strep was negative. She has a history of hypertension.

PAST MEDICAL HISTORY: Usual childhood diseases.

FAMILY HISTORY: Noncontributory.

ALLERGIES: None known.

PHYSICAL EXAMINATION:

Vital Signs:	Blood pressure ranged from 154/90 to 168/104.
HEENT:	Within normal limits.
Chest:	Clear to percussion and auscultation.
Heart:	Normal sinus rhythm.
Breasts:	Without masses or discharge.
Abdomen:	Gravid.
Extremities:	Without clubbing or cyanosis. There was +1 edema. Reflexes were +2.
Cervical:	Cervical examination revealed 1 cm.

She was admitted and Pitocin was started. Decreased variability and occasional late decelerations were noted. Pitocin was once again stopped. She began having contractions on her own with recurrent late decelerations. Oxygen was started. She was turned on her side, and the late decels continued. Magnesium was started at 6 g and then 1 g an hour for the pre-eclampsia. There was no response to the medication; consequently the patient will undergo a primary low transverse c-section.

Mock Examination Case 8
Procedure Note

Date:	12/25/14
PREOPERATIVE DIAGNOSES:	Intrauterine pregnancy 36 weeks, pre-eclampsia, fetal distress
POSTOPERATIVE DIAGNOSES:	Intrauterine pregnancy 36 weeks, severe pre-eclampsia, persistent late decelerations with intrauterine growth retardation
PROCEDURE:	Primary low transverse c-section
SURGEON:	Nicolas Todd, M.D.
ANESTHESIA:	Spinal

The patient was taken to the operating room. After adequate level of spinal anesthesia, Foley catheter was inserted. She was prepped and draped in the usual sterile fashion.

A Pfannenstiel incision was made, taken down through the subcutaneous tissue to the fascia. The fascia was scored and taken transversely. Rectus muscle was split. The peritoneum was opened.

The uterus was incised in a low transverse manner with delivery of 6–9 Apgar live born male. The cord was noted to be thin. The placenta was delivered. It was noted to be small. Uterus, tubes, and ovaries were noted to be normal. The uterus was closed in two separate layers with running locked 0 chromic. Posterior peritoneum was closed with 0 chromic. The uterus was placed back into the abdomen; anterior peritoneum was closed with 0 chromic. The fascia was closed with running 0 Vicryl, and the skin was closed with staples.

ESTIMATED BLOOD LOSS:	600 mL
FLUIDS RECEIVED:	Ringer's lactate

The patient tolerated the procedure well and left the recovery room in satisfactory condition.

Mock Examination Case 8

Progress Notes:

12/25: Admit note: Gravida 3, para 2, 35-year-old white female admitted for induction of labor due to severe pre-eclampsia. Patient was admitted directly from my office. She is at 36 weeks' gestation by dates. There is evidence of IUGR also. Patient has had a benign prenatal course with the exception of hypertension. Patient was started on Pitocin without success. There were persistent late decelerations noted and patient was transferred to surgical suite for immediate c-section. Patient delivered a 4-pound, 12-ounce liveborn male infant.

12/26: S: Feels well, other than surgical pain.

      O: BP 160/95.

      A: Incision clean and dry, no redness or tenderness.

      P: Continue BP meds, advance diet and activity.

12/27: S: Feeling well.

      O: Good post-op course, BP 168/104.

      A: Accelerated hypertension.

      P: Continue meds.

12/28: S: No pain, ambulating.

      O: BP better, but still high at 150/98.

      A: Continues with elevated BP.

      P: Doing well, will discharge.

12/29: S: Ready for home.

      O: Vitals stable, except BP, afebrile, incisions healing.

      A: Hypertension.

      P: Discharge, follow hypertension as outpatient.

Orders

12/25: 1.   Admit patient to obstetrics.

      2.   IV Pitocin for induction.

      3.   Monitor BP q. 15 min.

      4.   CBC, WBC, Chem profile.

      5.   Magnesium IV.

12/25:   Prep for c-section.

12/26: 1.   Continue IV fluids.

      2.   Start patient on Apresoline and Aldomet for BP control.

      3.   Advance diet.

12/27: 1.   Continue BP meds.

      2.   Discontinue IVs.

12/28:   Continue meds.

12/29:   Discharge.

Mock Examination Case 8
Answer Sheet

DIAGNOSES	ICD-9-CM CODES					
Principal Diagnosis				.		
DX 2				-		
DX 3				-		
DX 4				-		
DX 5				-		
DX 6				-		
DX 7				-		

PROCEDURES	ICD-9-CM CODES				
PP 1			-		
PX 2			-		

Code ICD-9-CM Diagnoses and Procedures
(14 diagnosis codes and 2 procedure codes will be needed)

Mock Examination Case 9
Inpatient Face Sheet

Admit Date:	12/24/14
Discharge Date:	12/27/14
Sex:	Male
Age:	84
Disposition:	Expired

ADMITTING DIAGNOSES:
1. Pneumonia secondary to possible community-acquired strep pneumonia
2. Respiratory failure and hypoxia secondary to pneumonia
3. New onset atrial fibrillation
4. History of liver cirrhosis with splenomegaly and some ascites
5. History of myeloproliferative disorder

DISCHARGE DIAGNOSES:
1. Respiratory failure
2. Streptococcus pneumonia
3. Atrial fibrillation
4. Alcoholic liver cirrhosis
5. Hepatorenal syndrome
6. Streptococcal septicemia
7. Septic shock
8. Urinary tract infection, *Escherichia coli*
9. Uremia
10. Hypertension
11. Hypoglycemia

Mock Examination Case 9
Discharge Summary

Admitted: 12/24/14

Expired: 12/27/14

ADMITTING DIAGNOSES:
1. Pneumonia secondary to possible community-acquired strep pneumonia
2. Respiratory failure and hypoxia secondary to pneumonia
3. New onset atrial fibrillation
4. History of liver cirrhosis with splenomegaly and some ascites
5. History of myeloproliferative disorder

DISCHARGE DIAGNOSES:
1. Septic shock with multiorgan failure
2. Streptococcal pneumonia and respiratory failure
3. *Escherichia coli* urosepsis
4. Hypoglycemia secondary to sepsis and cirrhosis of the liver
5. New onset atrial fibrillation
6. Hepatorenal syndrome

HISTORY OF PRESENT ILLNESS AND HOSPITAL COURSE:

The patient is an 84-year-old white male who is admitted to the hospital after complaining of shortness of breath, cough with productive sputum, fever and chills, and pain below the breast area. In the emergency room his temperature was 98.3, blood pressure was 140/80, pulse was 140. Patient was noted to be in atrial fibrillation with rapid ventricular rate and required Digoxin intravenous push and procainamide and cardioversion. Patient went into respiratory failure with hypoxia, requiring intubation and ventilator assistance. Patient was also noted to be severely neutropenic and acidotic in acute renal failure. Patient was seen in the emergency room by cardiology for new onset of atrial fibrillation and cardioverted for this.

The patient's white blood cell count remained 1,700 the day after admission, and his echocardiogram Doppler studies showed that he had a left ejection fraction of 60%, mild mitral regurgitation, and tricuspid regurgitation. His prothrombin time was 12, and partial thromboplastic time was 41. His BUN and creatinine went up to 67/2.6, and his hemoglobin and hematocrit remain within normal limits. His calcium did drop to 7.8 along with a decreased albumin. His chest x-ray shows right-sided opacity secondary to his pneumonia. Blood cultures grew gram-positive cocci in chains.

Impression on December 25, the patient was having Streptococcus pneumonia with multiorgan failure. The patient did have a history of cirrhosis of the liver and splenomegaly and pancytopenia. Patient was started on intravenous dopamine and intravenous hydration because of decreased urine output and increasing renal functions and possible hepatorenal syndrome. The patient remained lethargic, responding to deep painful stimuli. The patient's urine grew *Escherichia coli* and blood cultures grew *Streptococcus pneumoniae* pneumonia. His white count increased to 23,900 with Neupogen. His BUN and creatinine went up to 86/4.4. The patient remained hypoglycemic and required D5 and D10 drips. The patient continued to be hypertensive in renal failure and acidotic.

In spite of the aggressive treatment and continued ventilator assistance, the patient expired on 12/27/14.

Mock Examination Case 9
History and Physical

CHIEF COMPLAINT: The patient was admitted through the emergency room after complaining of increased shortness of breath and productive cough.

HISTORY OF PRESENT ILLNESS:

Patient was well until 2 days prior to admission when he began having shortness of breath, productive cough, fever, and chills. He also complained of pain beneath the breast area. The patient was brought to the emergency room by EMS. In the emergency room the patient's temperature was 98.3, blood pressure was 140/80, pulse was 140. Patient was in atrial fibrillation with rapid ventricular response and was treated with Digoxin 0.5 mg intravenous push and procainamide. Patient also required cardioversion at 100–200 joules. The patient was also noted to be in acute respiratory distress with hypoxia, requiring intubation and ventilator assistance. The patient's blood work revealed severe neutropenia, acidosis, and renal failure.

At present the patient is sedated and most of the history is taken from his wife and from previous charts.

PAST MEDICAL HISTORY:

Includes cirrhosis of the liver, likely secondary to excessive alcohol intake. There is also a history of myeloproliferative disorder and a history of ascites. There is no prior history of atrial fibrillation, heart disease, diabetes, gastrointestinal disease, or neurological symptoms.

SOCIAL HISTORY: History of excessive alcohol intake and former smoker.

FAMILY HISTORY: Strong history of colon cancer.

ALLERGIES: None known.

PHYSICAL EXAMINATION: Presently intubated, sedated, and unresponsive.

HEENT:	Pupils equal and reactive to light, nonicterus, nonpallor. Orally intubated.
Neck:	Supple, no lymphadenopathy, and no jugular venous distention.
Lungs:	No rales, no rhonchi.
Heart:	S1 and S2, no murmur or gallop.
Abdomen:	Distended, possible ascites present.
Extremities:	Mild peripheral edema, no rash or ulcers noted.

LABORATORY DATA:

Blood gas revealed pH 7.33, pCO_2 34 and pO_2 of 51, and saturation of 86%. The patient's urinalysis is consistent with leukocyte esterase small amount, nitrite negative. His white blood cell count is 0.8, hemoglobin 10.6, hematocrit 31.8, and platelet count 79,000. His sodium is 137, potassium 4.2, chloride 102, glucose 88, BUN 60, creatinine 2.3, and CPK 63. Alkaline phosphatase 142, SGOT 185, bilirubin 1.8. Prothrombin time is 13, INR is 1.1, and partial thromboplastin time is 42.

Mock Examination Case 9
History and Physical

Continued:

IMPRESSION:

1. Pneumonia secondary to community-acquired strep pneumonia
2. Respiratory failure secondary to pneumonia
3. New onset atrial fibrillation
4. History of cirrhosis of the liver with splenomegaly and ascites
5. History of myeloproliferative syndrome with pancytopenia

PLAN:

1. Patient is admitted to intensive care, intubated, and on ventilator.
2. Patient has already been started on broad-spectrum intravenous antibiotic.

Mock Examination Case 9

Progress Notes:

12/24: Admit Note: Elderly white gentleman admitted through the emergency room in acute respiratory failure, pneumonia, sepsis, and septic shock. He also has new onset of atrial fibrillation that required cardioversion in the ER. The patient was intubated and placed on the ventilator. The patient required digoxin and procainamide IV push in the ER.

12/25: S: Unresponsive.

     O: Lethargic, responds to deep painful stimuli. UA positive for *Escherichia coli*, blood positive for strep. BUN/creatinine 86/4.4, decreased urine output, BP 210/130.

     A: Sepsis, UTI, acute renal failure, multiorgan failure, prognosis grave.

     P: IV dopamine and hydration, continue present vent settings.

12/26: S: Unresponsive.

     O: White count increasing with Neupogen injections, renal labs worsening, patient less responsive, now hypoglycemic.

     A: Respiratory and multiorgan failure, renal failure, hepatorenal syndrome. Prognosis is poor.

     P: Provide supportive care.

12/27: S: Unresponsive.

     O: Patient rapidly declining.

     A: Poor prognosis.

     P: Continue supportive care.

Orders:

12/24: 1. Admit patient to CCU.

     2. Follow CCU protocol.

     3. Respiratory services to maintain vent.

     4. Strict I&O.

12/25: 1. IV dopamine and hydration.

     2. Add Neupogen injections.

     3. Continue present vent settings.

     4. Repeat all labs.

12/26: 1. Add D_5 and D_{10} drips for hypoglycemia.

     2. Continue all previous orders.

Mock Examination Case 9
Answer Sheet

DIAGNOSES	ICD-9-CM CODES					
Principal Diagnosis				.		
DX 2				-		
DX 3				-		
DX 4				-		
DX 5				-		
DX 6				-		
DX 7				-		
DX 8				-		
DX 9				-		
DX 10				-		
DX 11				-		
DX 12				-		
DX 13				-		
DX 14				-		

PROCEDURES	ICD-9-CM CODES				
PP 1			-		
PX 2			-		

Code ICD-9-CM Diagnoses
(12 diagnosis codes will be needed)

Mock Examination Case 10
Inpatient Face Sheet

Admit Date: 12/25/14

Discharge Date: 12/30/14

Sex: Female

Age: 82

Disposition: Skilled Nursing Facility for Rehab

ADMITTING DIAGNOSES:
1. Cerebral infarction
2. Hypertension
3. Atrial fibrillation
4. Osteoarthritis

DISCHARGE DIAGNOSES:
1. Left middle cerebral artery occlusion with cerebral infarction
2. Atrial fibrillation
3. Mitral regurgitation
4. Urinary tract infection
5. Pacemaker in situ
6. Bilateral carotid artery disease
7. Hypertension
8. Osteoarthritis
9. Right hemiplegia

Mock Examination Case 10
Discharge Summary

Admitted: 12/25/14

Discharge: 12/30/14

DISCHARGE DIAGNOSES:
1. Left middle cerebral artery occlusion with cerebral infarction
2. Atrial fibrillation
3. Mitral regurgitation
4. Urinary tract infection
5. Pacemaker in situ
6. Bilateral carotid artery disease
7. Hypertension
8. Osteoarthritis

HISTORY OF PRESENT ILLNESS:
This 82-year-old white female was found on the floor at her home. She had right-sided weakness, stool incontinence, and garbled speech. The CAT scan was positive for infarction with left basal ganglia hemorrhage.

HISTORY AND PHYSICAL: See H&P.

MEDICATIONS: Lanoxin.

ALLERGIES: Sulfa.

PHYSICAL EXAMINATION: Elderly white female, hypertensive 196/73. Pale subconjunctival and nail beds. Garbled speech with weakness on the right.

LABORATORY DATA:
The patient's admission laboratory data were within normal limits with the exception of hemoglobin 16.5, hematocrit 48.8; 100 mg of protein, a large amount of occult blood, and 5 to 9 red blood cells on urinalysis; elevated globulin of 4.2, alkaline phosphatase 161, CPK 346. The Lanoxin was subtherapeutic at 0.6. Drug screening was negative. During hospitalization there was a transient mild leukocytosis of 14,700 and hemoglobin returned to normal. Sedimentation rate was elevated at 39 on December 26. The PTT rose to therapeutic and vacillated throughout.
A repeat urinalysis revealed a large amount of leukocytes, continued occult blood, and red blood cells up to 50+ with 20 to 29 white blood cells and moderate bacteria. Urine culture revealed *Escherichia coli.*

Mock Examination Case 10
Discharge Summary

Continued:

The sodium dropped as low as 126 but rebounded to 132 by December 28. The globulin returned to normal. The albumin dropped slightly below normal. The alkaline phosphatase returned to normal. The CPK levels steadily decreased to 213 and 186 with CK-MB remaining within normal limits.

RADIOLOGY REPORTS:

The chest x-ray revealed cardiomegaly; several calcified granuloma in the right upper, mid, and lower lung zones; left-sided pacemaker in satisfactory position; and no acute changes.

The CAT scan of the brain, noncontrast, showed acute left middle cerebral artery infarction with hemorrhage within the left basal ganglia. A repeat CAT scan was unchanged.

A KUB showed nasogastric tube in satisfactory position, nonspecific bowel gas pattern. A repeat KUB did reveal the nasogastric tube to be coiled in the stomach on December 29.

A carotid duplex Doppler examination showed moderate bilateral carotid occlusive disease with plaquing at the right carotid bifurcation, left common carotid, and carotid bifurcation, but no evidence of flow-restricting lesion, stenosis of less than 35%, external carotid stenosis approaching 40% to 50%, antegrade vertebral artery blood flow bilaterally, no change since January of this year.

An echocardiogram revealed hypokinetic septal and apical wall motion, aortic valve sclerosis, mitral annular calcification, and moderate mitral regurgitation.

An electrocardiogram revealed pacemaker rhythm with rate of 58 per minute, left ventricular hypertrophy, ST-T abnormalities, Q waves in V1 and V2, diffuse T-wave abnormalities, consistent with ischemia. The subsequent repeats showed atrial fibrillation with transient rapid ventricular response and premature ventricular contractions.

HOSPITAL COURSE:

The patient was admitted on December 25. She was started on routine and intensive care unit orders, neuro checks, Lanoxin, Decadron intravenously, multivitamins, intravenous hydration.

It was noted by neurological consult that the patient had two cerebrovascular accidents with the atrial fibrillation as the likely source. Anticoagulation was initiated cautiously after blood pressure was brought under control. Intravenous Nipride was begun for blood pressure control. Heparin was begun. Catapres was added for additional blood pressure control, and Decadron was also added.

Mock Examination Case 10
Discharge Summary

Continued:

The patient remained afebrile other than intermittent temperatures of 100.

The patient was evaluated by speech pathology. She was noted to have severe receptive and fluent aphasia. Speech therapy will be initiated.

Nasogastric tube was inserted for administration of medications due to lack of poor oral intake and dysphagia with some aspiration potential noted on video swallow study. Following improvement in the patient's condition, nasogastric tube was removed and diet was adjusted. Dysphagia cleared by discharge.

The patient began to improve but remained aphasic and with right-sided hemiplegia. It was decided that she would require intensive rehab, so she was transferred to a rehab facility for continued physical, speech, and occupational therapy. Patient is to be continued on pureed diet.

DISCHARGE MEDICATIONS:
Catapres TTS Patch 0.4 mg patch q. week
Lanoxin 0.125 mg daily
Norvasc 5 mg daily
Multivitamins one daily
Floxin 200 mg q12h times 5 days

Mock Examination Case 10
History and Physical

CHIEF COMPLAINT: Garbled speech and right-sided weakness.

HISTORY OF PRESENT ILLNESS:
This 82-year-old white female was found on the floor by her neighbors and brought to the emergency room via EMS. A CAT scan of the brain was completed, which revealed a left MCA infarct with hemorrhage into the left basal ganglia.

CURRENT MEDICATIONS: Lanoxin.

PAST MEDICAL HISTORY: Positive for hypertension, atrial fibrillation, and degenerative osteoarthritis.

SOCIAL HISTORY: Nonsmoker, occasional alcohol.

PHYSICAL EXAMINATION: Elderly white female who is in acute distress. She has garbled speech.

REVIEW OF SYSTEMS:
Vital Signs: Blood pressure 199/73, pulse 78, respiratory rate of 18, afebrile.
HEENT: Pupils equal and reactive to light, sclera is not icteric. Subconjunctival is pale.
Lungs: Clear.
Heart: Regular sinus rhythm with an irregular rate.
Abdomen: Soft, benign. No organomegaly or mass to palpation.
Extremities: No edema, no varicosity. Nail beds are pale.
Neuro logical: Good DTR, negative Babinski.

IMPRESSION: Acute cerebrovascular accident.

PLAN:
1. Admit to intensive care.
2. Serial electrocardiograms and cardiac enzymes.
3. Neuro checks q2h.
4. Carotid duplex.
5. Echo to heart, EEG.

Mock Examination Case 10
Progress Notes:

12/25: Admit Note: Patient admitted with left MCA infarction. Patient also has severe hypertension. Please see H&P for complete details.

12/26: S: Noncommunicative.

O: Sed rate elevated to 39, rest of lab data within normal limits. Carotid Doppler revealed bilateral occlusive disease, but not of any clinical significance.

A: Patient still aphasic with right-sided paralysis.

P: Repeat CT of brain and do KUB, ECHO.

12/27: S: Remains aphasic.

O: BP remains high, but slowly coming under control, NG tube in good position per KUB. Repeat CT of brain unchanged since CT at admission CT. ECHO revealed moderate mitral regurgitation.

A: Patient is slowly improving.

P: Transfer to neuro floor. Add Catapres for additional BP control.

12/28: S: Feels better after transfer out of ICU.

O: BP better controlled. Repeat UA positive for *Escherichia coli*. Some strength returning on right side. Sodium dropped to 126.

A: UTI, hyponatraemia, dysphagia clearing.

P: Remove NG tube and advance diet. Start Cipro p.o. 500 mg for UTI. Monitor sodium level.

12/29: S: No new complaints.

O: Labs improving, vitals stable.

A: Tolerating advanced diet.

P: Discharge planning for intensive rehab, patient agreeable.

12/30: S: Ready for transfer to rehab.

O: Patient's condition is stable. BP better controlled. Sodium level normal.

A: Patient will continue with speech and physical therapy at rehabilitation center.

P: Transfer patient.

Mock Examination Case 10
Orders:

12/25: 1. Admit to ICU.
      2. Neuro checks q2h.
      3. Serial EKGs and cardiac enzymes.
      4. CXR.
      5. ICU protocol.
      6. Carotid Doppler.
      7. IV Decadron, Lanoxin, Nipride, and fluids at 83 mL/h.

12/26: 1. Repeat CT brain.
      2. KUB, ECHO.
      3. Continue present meds.
      4. Repeat UA.

12/27: 1. Add Catapres.
      2. Have speech pathology evaluated.

12/28: 1. Remove NG tube, advance diet.
      2. Cipro for UTI.

12/29: Case management for discharge planning.

12/30: Transfer to rehab.

Mock Examination Case 10
Answer Sheet

DIAGNOSES	ICD-9-CM CODES					
Principal Diagnosis				.		
DX 2				-		
DX 3				-		
DX 4				-		
DX 5				-		
DX 6				-		
DX 7				-		
DX 8				-		
DX 9				-		
DX 10				-		
DX 11				-		
DX 12				-		

Code ICD-9-CM Diagnoses and Procedures
(10 diagnosis codes and 2 procedure codes will be needed)

Mock Examination Case 11
Inpatient Face Sheet

Admit Date: 12/06/14

Discharge Date: 12/10/14

Sex: Male

Age: 60

Disposition: Home health care

ADMITTING DIAGNOSES:
1. Fracture right hip
2. Ascites
3. Decubitus ulcer

DISCHARGE DIAGNOSES:
1. Intertrochanteric fracture right hip
2. Decubitus ulcer
3. Ascites in alcoholic liver cirrhosis
4. Hyperammonemia
5. Chronic obstructive pulmonary disease
6. Right lower quadrant abdominal mass, etiology unknown

PROCEDURES:
1. Closed reduction with internal fixation of fracture of right hip
2. Paracentesis

Mock Examination Case 11
DISCHARGE SUMMARY

ADMITTED: 12/06/14
DISCHARGED: 12/10/14

DISCHARGE DIAGNOSES:
1.   Intertrochanteric fracture right hip
2.   Severe COPD
3.   Chronic alcoholic cirrhosis with massive ascites
4.   Right lower quadrant abdominal mass, etiology unknown

PROCEDURES:
1.   Closed reduction with internal fixation of right hip
2.   Paracentesis

HOSPITAL COURSE:
This elderly gentleman had a fall at home resulting in an intertrochanteric fracture of the right hip. He was transported to the emergency room and placed in Buck's traction. The patient was typed and crossed for six units of blood. He received two units preoperatively. On postoperative day 2, he underwent paracentesis for removal of 2.5 L of ascites. The postoperative course was complicated by a rise in ammonia. This came down with Lactulose. The patient also has two open areas, stage II decubitus on his coccyx and buttock. The bases are clean and dry. These are being treated with Duoderm.

On the day of discharge his ammonia was 47. He is comfortable and ambulating with a walker. His abdomen is less tense. He is afebrile and vital signs are stable. The hip wound is healing. He is discharged on Percodan and routine medications of Lasix 40 mg b.i.d., Aldactone 100 mg q.i.d. with K-Dur 20 mEq in the morning and 10 mEq in the evening.

He is discharged on a low-salt diet with moderate fluid restriction.

He will be seen by home health care. The patient will see me in my office in 10 days and will undergo a colonoscopy in 4 to 6 weeks to investigate the abdominal mass.

Mock Examination Case 11
History and Physical

CHIEF COMPLAINT: Fell at home, presents now with hip pain.

HISTORY OF PRESENT ILLNESS:
This is a 60-year-old male who fell at home this morning with immediate pain in the right hip. There was no loss of consciousness. In the emergency room he was found to have an intertrochanteric fracture. He is admitted to the hospital for definitive evaluation and treatment.

PAST MEDICAL HISTORY:
Significant for long-standing alcoholic liver disease with cirrhosis and ascites. He was found to have a right lower quadrant mass by his gastroenterologist.

ALLERGIES: Tylenol PM.

MEDICATIONS: Lasix 40 mg b.i.d., Aldactone 100 mg q.i.d. with K-Dur 10 mEq b.i.d., low-salt diet, moderate fluid restriction to 1,200 mL q.i.d.

SOCIAL HISTORY: No alcohol in the past 5 years. One pack of tobacco per day. Patient is retired.

PHYSICAL EXAMINATION: Blood pressure 110/70, pulse 88, marked muscle wasting.

REVIEW OF SYSTEMS:
HEENT:	Within normal limits.
Neck:	Supple, no adenopathy.
Chest:	Clear.
Abdomen:	Marked ascites, liver spans about 2–3 fingers below costal margin and is firm.
Extremities:	Patient is in Buck's traction with foreshortening of the right leg.

LABORATORY DATA:
Random blood sugar 145, alkaline phosphatase 179. Bilirubin and SGOT are normal. The white blood cell count is 15,400, hemoglobin of 8.8 with a hematocrit of 26.2, MCV is 72, MCHC is 23.9.

IMPRESSION:
1. Fall resulting in an intertrochanteric fracture in the right hip
2. Chronic cirrhosis
3. COPD, with tobacco dependency
4. Right lower quadrant abdominal mass, will work up

PLAN:
1. Type and cross 6 units, transfuse 2
2. Gastrointestinal consult regarding paracentesis
3. Closed reduction with internal fixation of fracture of hip

Mock Examination Case 11
Procedure Note

DATE OF PROCEDURE: 12/06/14

PREOPERATIVE DIAGNOSIS: Intertrochanteric fracture, right hip

POSTOPERATIVE DIAGNOSIS: Intertrochanteric fracture, right hip

SURGEON: Alexander Warren, M.D.

ANESTHESIA: Spinal

ANESTHESIOLOGIST: Norma Jean, M.D.

ESTIMATED BLOOD LOSS: 350 mL

No replacement

DESCRIPTION OF PROCEDURE:

After satisfactory induction of spinal anesthesia with the patient lying on the fracture table, traction applied to the right lower extremity with internal rotation, reducing the fracture. The left leg abducted to allow the image intensifier to come into view in both AP and lateral positions.

Standard lateral incision was made taken through the skin and subcutaneous tissue, the fascia slit longitudinally. The vastus lateralis split longitudinally, coming along the proximal aspect of the femur. Guide wire inserted in good position, both AP and lateral. This was then reamed to accept the 95 mm barrel screw. A 135 degree four-hole plate was attached. The titanium cortical side screws were inserted. Good fixation was obtained.

The area was irrigated with saline and antibiotic solution. A medium set screw was put in place. Constavac drain was inserted through a separate puncture site. Vastus lateralis was closed with interrupted 0 Vicryl suture, the fascia with interrupted 0 Vicryl suture, the subcutaneous tissue with 00 Vicryl, and the skin with staples. Neosporin, Adaptic, bulky 4 × 4s, ABDs, and Mefix dressing applied.

The patient tolerated the procedure well and left the operating room in good condition.

Mock Examination Case 11
Progress Notes:

12/6:   Admit Note: Patient is admitted via the emergency room after suffering a fall at home resulting in intertrochanteric fracture of the right femur. Patient was a former drinker, now has liver cirrhosis and ascites. Patient is also a smoker with COPD. Patient is admitted for definitive treatment of hip fracture. Admitting H/H is 10.8/37.2, will T&C six units and transfuse two prior to surgery.

12/7:   S: Only complaint is surgical pain.

   O: H/H is stable, will not require blood transfusions. Abdomen is very tense. Stable respiratory status. No shortness of breath and good lung sounds.

   A: Ascites, stable from surgical standpoint.

   P: Begin ambulation with minimal weight bearing, will do paracentesis tomorrow.

12/8:   S: No complaints.

   O: Vital signs stable, afebrile, incision clean and dry, ammonia elevated.

   A: Paracentesis with removal of 2.5 L ascitic fluid.

   P: Continue ambulation, give Lactulose for elevated ammonia.

12/9:   S: Doing well.

   O: Vitals stable, ammonia level within normal limits, abdomen less tense, afebrile.

   A: Good postoperative recovery.

   P: Will plan discharge for tomorrow.

12/10:   Patient to be discharged home with home health care.

Orders:

12/6: 1.   Admit patient.

   2.   Continue Buck's traction.

   3.   Prepare for surgery this afternoon.

   4.   Cross and type six units, transfuse two prior to surgery.

   5.   Respiratory treatments prior to surgery.

   6.   CBC, WBC, Chem profile.

12/7: 1.   Incentive spirometer q4h.

   2.   Begin ambulation.

   3.   Ammonia level.

12/8: 1.   Paracentesis tray to bedside.

   2.   Lactulose for elevated ammonia level.

12/9:   Continue with current orders.

12/10:   Discharge home with home health care.

Mock Examination Case 11
Answer Sheet

DIAGNOSES	ICD-9-CM CODES					
Principal Diagnosis				.		
DX 2				-		
DX 3				-		
DX 4				-		
DX 5				-		
DX 6				-		
DX 7				-		
DX 8				-		
DX 9				-		
DX 10				-		

PROCEDURES	ICD-9-CM CODES				
PP 1			-		
PX 2			-		

Code ICD-9-CM Diagnoses and Procedures
(Seven diagnosis codes will be needed)

Mock Examination Case 12
Inpatient Face Sheet

Admit Date: 1/02/15

Discharge Date: 1/05/15

Sex: Female

Age: 42

Disposition: Transfer to Psychiatric Facility

Admitting Diagnoses:
1. Drug overdose
2. Diet-controlled diabetes
3. Peripheral vascular disease

Discharge Diagnoses:
1. Accidental overdose of Haldol and Xanax
2. Diet-controlled diabetes
3. Peripheral vascular disease

Mock Examination Case 12
Discharge Summary

Admitted: 1/02/15

Discharged: 1/05/15

DISCHARGE DIAGNOSES:
1. Accidental poisoning of Haldol and Xanax
2. Type 2 diabetes
3. Peripheral vascular disease
4. Depression

HISTORY:

This 42-year-old female was admitted to intensive care following overdose of Haldol and Xanax. Patient is currently treated for depression. See History and Physical for complete details.

HOSPITAL COURSE:

This patient was admitted to the intensive care unit following ingestion of Haldol and Xanax. Patient was given IV fluids and Narcan to counteract the overdose of medication. She responded well to the Narcan and the day following admission was more alert and less confused. She remained in the ICU for 1 additional day until she was transferred to the medical floor. Her laboratory results were within normal limits on transfer to the medical unit. The patient denied a suicide attempt; however, in light of her ongoing depression, she is being transferred to the psychiatric facility for continued treatment. Her condition from a medical standpoint was stable upon transfer.

Mock Examination Case 12
History and Physical

CHIEF COMPLAINT:
This patient was brought to my office by her friend who had stopped by her home because she was unable to reach her by phone. The friend states that the patient was exhibiting inappropriate behavior and told her that she had taken some pills. I sent the patient to the hospital as a direct admission because of her mental status changes and possible drug overdose.

HISTORY OF PRESENT ILLNESS:
Upon presentation to my office, the patient had become lethargic and was becoming difficult to arouse. She has a known history of depression and was treated with antidepressants. It is unknown at this time if she has overmedicated herself with the antidepressants. This patient has a history of peripheral vascular disease and diet-controlled diabetes.

ALLERGIES: None.

PAST MEDICAL HISTORY: As indicated above.

CURRENT MEDICATIONS: Haldol and Xanax.

SOCIAL HISTORY: Lives alone. No tobacco or alcohol use.

REVIEW OF SYSTEMS:

General:	Well-developed, somewhat unkempt woman. She is confused. Somewhat lethargic and difficult to arouse and then becomes combative.
Vital signs:	Temperature of 99.9, blood pressure 120/90, pulse 118, respirations at 21.
HEENT:	Within normal limits.
Neck:	No lymphadenopathy.
Cardiac:	Sinus tachycardia.
Lungs:	Clear to auscultation.
Abdomen:	No masses, bowel sounds present.
Extremities:	No cyanosis, edema, or clubbing.
Skin:	Unremarkable.

IMPRESSION:
1. Drug overdose, Haldol and Xanax.
2. Peripheral vascular disease.
3. Type 2 diabetes.

PLAN:
1. Admit patient to intensive care.
2. Standing ICU orders.
3. Drug screen.

Mock Examination Case 12

Progress Notes:

1/2: Admit Note: Patient admitted to intensive care for suspected drug overdose of Haldol and Xanax. Prescriptions had been issued 2 days ago. Multiple dosages were missing from the bottles and drug screen is positive for antidepressants. Patient has been under treatment for depression. Monitor patient in ICU.

1/3: S: Patient does not recall what brought her to the hospital.

O: Patient awake, less confused, vital signs improved, labs improving.

A: Patient somewhat improved.

P: Continue ICU monitoring and with current meds and IVs. Case management to arrange transfer to psychiatric facility when medically stable.

1/4: S: Feels much better, but admits to feeling depressed. Denied suicide attempt.

O: Patient more alert today. Vital signs good. All labs WNL.

A: Transfer out of ICU today.

P: Transfer to psych hospital in the morning.

1/5: Discharge Note: Patient is medically stable for transfer to psychiatric facility following overdose of Haldol and Xanax.

Orders:

1/2: 1. Admit to ICU.
2. Standing ICU orders.
3. IV NS at 125 mL/h.
4. Narcan IV.
5. Accuchecks q4h.
6. Drug screen.

1/3: 1. Decrease IV rate to 75 mL/h.
2. Case management for discharge planning.

1/4: 1. Transfer to medical floor.
2. DC IVs.

1/5: Transfer to psychiatric facility under the care of Dr. Sierra Seybolt.

Mock Examination Case 12
Answer Sheet

DIAGNOSES	ICD-9-CM CODES					
Principal Diagnosis				.		
DX 2				-		
DX 3				-		
DX 4				-		
DX 5				-		
DX 6				-		
DX 7				-		

XIII. CCS Mock Exam Answer Key

Mock Examination Answer Key
Case 1

Diagnoses	ICD-9-CM Codes					
Principal Diagnosis Diverticulosis of colon	5	6	2	.	1	0
DX 2 Benign neoplasm colon-sigmoid	2	1	1	.	3	
DX 3 Personal history of colon cancer	V	1	0	.	0	5
DX 4 Osteoporosis, unspecified	7	3	3	.	0	0
DX 5 Postcoronary artery bypass status	V	4	5	.	8	1
DX 6 Personal history of lung carcinoma	V	1	0	.	1	1
DX 7 Essential hypertension, unspecified	4	0	1	.	9	

Procedures	ICD-9-CM Codes						
PP 1 Colonoscopy with polypectomy	4	5	.	4	2	-	
PX 2 Colonoscopy with closed (endoscopic) biopsy of large intestine	4	5	.	2	5	-	

Case 2

Diagnoses	ICD-9-CM Codes					
First Listed DX Carpal tunnel syndrome	3	5	4	.	0	
DX 2 Type 1 diabetes mellitus, without mention of complication, not stated as uncontrolled	2	5	0	.	0	1
DX 3 Essential hypertension, unspecified	4	0	1	.	9	

Procedure	CPT Codes					Modifiers (If Applicable)		
PR 1 Decompression of medial nerve, left wrist	6	4	7	2	1	-	L	T

Case 3

Diagnoses	ICD-9-CM Codes					
First Listed DX Open wound of hand except finger(s) alone, without mention of complication	8	8	2	.	0	

Procedure	CPT Codes					Modifiers (If Applicable)		
PR 1 Simple repair of superficial wound 2.5 cm or less	1	2	0	0	1	-		

Mock Examination Answer Key

Case 4

Diagnoses		ICD-9-CM Codes					
First Listed DX Hypertrophy of nasal turbinates		4	7	8	.	0	
DX 2 Other diseases of nasal cavity and sinuses		4	7	8	.	1	9

    * Although it is not mandatory, you could also code for Tobacco use disorder (305.1).

Procedures	CPT Codes					Modifiers (If Applicable)		
PR 1 Nasal reconstruction	3	0	5	2	0	-		
PR 2 Excision nasoseptal spur	3	0	1	3	0	-		

Case 5

Diagnoses		ICD-9-CM Codes					
First Listed DX Unspecified viral infection		0	7	9	.	9	9
DX 2 Headaches		7	8	4	.	0	

Procedures	CPT Codes					Modifiers (If Applicable)		
PR 1 Spinal tap	6	2	2	7	0	-		
PR 2 CT scan, head, without contrast	7	0	4	5	0	-		

Note: E&M codes are assigned, when applicable, for outpatient clinic and emergency department visits. Because each hospital facility has its own unique system to assign the appropriate E&M codes, the appropriate codes would range from 99281 to 99285 with modifier –25 for this case.

Case 6

Diagnoses		ICD-9-CM					
First Listed DX Exotropia, unspecified		3	7	8	.	1	0

Procedure	CPT Codes					Modifiers (If Applicable)		
PR 1 Strabismus surgery, recession, lateral rectus muscle	6	7	3	1	1	-	5	0

Mock Examination Answer Key

Case 7

Diagnoses	ICD-9-CM Codes					
First Listed DX Atrioventricular block, complete	4	2	6	.	0	
DX 2 Atrial fibrillation	4	2	7	.	3	1

Procedure	CPT Codes				Modifiers (If Applicable)		
PR 1 Insertion pacemaker with dual leads	3	3	2	0	8	-	

Mock Examination Answer Key

Case 8

Diagnoses	ICD-9-CM Codes					
Principal Diagnosis Abnormality in fetal heart rate, delivered	6	5	9	.	7	1
DX 2 Pre-eclampsia or eclampsia superimposed on pre-existing hypertension, delivered	6	4	2	.	7	1
DX 3 Malignant essential hypertension	4	0	1	.	0	
DX 4 Mother with single liveborn	V	2	7	.	0	
DX 5 Poor fetal growth, affecting management of mother, delivered	6	5	6	.	5	1
DX 6 Elderly multigravida, delivered	6	5	9	.	6	1
DX 7 Elderly on set of delivery, delivered	6	4	4	.	2	1

Procedures	ICD-9-CM Codes					
PP 1 Low cervical Cesarean section	7	4	.	1	-	
PX 2 Medical induction of labor	7	3	.	4	-	

Mock Examination Answer Key

Case 9

Diagnoses	ICD-9-CM Codes					
Principal Diagnosis Streptococcal septicemia	0	3	8	.	2	
DX 2 Systemic inflammatory response syndrome	9	9	5	.	9	2
DX 3 Septic shock	7	8	5	.	5	2
DX 4 Alcoholic liver cirrhosis	5	7	1	.	2	
DX 5 Hepatorenal syndrome	5	7	2	.	4	
DX 6 Acute respiratory failure	5	1	8	.	8	1
DX 7 Streptococcus pneumonia	4	8	1	.		
DX 8 Urinary tract infection	5	9	9	.	0	
DX 9 Bacterial infection in conditions classified elsewhere and of unspecified site, *E. coli*	0	4	1	.	4	9
DX 10 Atrial fibrillation	4	2	7	.	3	1
DX 11 Alcohol dependence	3	0	3	.	9	0
DX 12 Acute renal failure	5	8	4	.	9	
DX 13 Essential hypertension, unspecified	4	0	1	.	9	
DX 14 Hypoglycemia	2	5	1	.	2	

Procedures	ICD-9-CM Codes						
PP 1 Continuous mechanical ventilation less than 96 consecutive hours	9	6	.	7	1	-	
PX 2 Insertion of endotracheal tube	9	6	.	0	4	-	

Case 10

Diagnoses	ICD-9-CM Codes					

Principal Diagnosis
    Unspecified cerebral artery occlusion with cerebral
    infarction
	4	3	4	.	9	1

DX 2 Urinary tract infection	5	9	9	.	0	
DX 3 Atrial fibrillation	4	2	7	.	3	1
DX 4 Mitral regurgitation, not otherwise specified	4	2	4	.	0	
DX 5 Hyposmolality and/or hyponatremia	2	7	6	.	1	

DX 6   Occlusion and stenosis of precerebral arteries,
    multiple and bilateral, without mention of
    cerebral infarction
	4	3	3	.	3	0

DX 7 Hemiplegia, unspecified, affecting unspecified site	3	4	2	.	9	0
DX 8 Essential hypertension, unspecified	4	0	1	.	9	
DX 9 Aphasia	7	8	4	.	3	
DX 10 Bacterial infection in conditions classified elsewhere and of unspecified site, *E. coli*	0	4	1	.	4	9
DX 11 Pacemaker (other postprocedural status)	V	4	5	.	0	1
DX 12 Dysphagia	7	8	7	.	2	0

Mock Examination Answer Key

Case 11

Diagnoses		ICD-9-CM Codes					
Principal Diagnosis Closed fracture of neck of femur, intertrochanteric section	8	2	0	.		2	1
DX 2 Chronic obstructive pulmonary disease	4	9	6	.			
DX 3 Alcoholic liver cirrhosis	5	7	1	.	2		
DX 4 Ascites	7	8	9	.	5	9	
DX 5 Hyperammonemia	2	7	0	.	6		
DX 6 Abdominal mass, right lower quadrant	7	8	9	.	3	3	
DX 7 Decubitus ulcer, buttock	7	0	7	.	0	5	
DX 8 Decubitus ulcer, other site (coccyx)	7	0	7	.	0	9	
DX 9 Pressure ulcer, stage II	7	0	7	.	2	2	
DX 10 Tobacco use disorder	3	0	5	.	1		

Procedures		ICD-9-CM Codes					
PP 1 Closed reduction, internal fixation femur	7	9	.	1	5	-	
PX 2 Paracentesis	5	4	.	9	1	-	

Mock Examination Answer Key

Case 12

Diagnoses		ICD-9-CM Codes					
Principal Diagnosis Poisoning, Haldol	9	6	9	.	2		
DX 2 Accidental poisoning	E8	5	3	.	1		
DX 3 Poisoning, Xanax	9	6	9	.	4		
DX 4 Accidental poisoning	E8	5	3	.	2		
DX 5 Depressive disorder	3	1	1	.			
DX 6 Type 2 diabetes	2	5	0	.	0	0	
DX 7 Peripheral vascular disease, unspecified	4	4	3	.	9		

APPENDIX A
PHARMACOLOGY

The most common prescription drugs with examples of diagnoses

Analgesics
acetaminophen w/codeine (Tylenol #2, #3, #4) mild to moderate pain
Advil (ibuprofen) mild to moderate pain
aspirin, enteric coated (salicylate) reduces fever, relieves mild to moderate pain
Dilaudid (hydromorphine HCl) moderate to severe pain
Feldene (piroxicam) NSAID
hydrocodone w/APAP (Lortab 2.5) pain, moderate to severe; antitussives/expectorants, back pain
ibuprofen (Advil, Motrin) NSAID, arthritis, osteoarthritis; rheumatoid arthritis, dysmenorrhea; mild to moderate pain, fever; gout
Lortab (hydrocodone w/APAP) moderate to severe pain, expectorant
Motrin (ibuprofen) mild to moderate pain
oxycodone pain
Oxycotin (oxycodone hydrochloride) opioid analgesic
piroxicam (Feldene) NSAID
tramadol (Ultram) moderate to severe pain
Tylenol #2, #3, #4 (acetaminophen w/codeine) mild to moderate pain
Ultram (tramadol) short-term pain

Antibacterial
amoxicillin (AMOXIL) antibiotic; broad-spectrum antibacterial drug, urinary tract infections, strep throat
Amoxil (amoxicillin) antibiotic; broad-spectrum antibacterial drug
Augmentin (amoxicilln with clavulanate potassium) treats certain bacterial infections of the ears, lungs, sinus, skin, and urinary tract
Avelox (moxifloxacin hydrochloride) for susceptible strains of designated microorganisms
Bactroban (mupirocin) topical antibiotic
cephalexin, USP (Keflex) antibiotic–antibacterial
ciprofloxacin (Cipro) antibacterial (drug-resistant bacteria)
Cipro (ciprofloxacin) antibacterial (drug-resistant bacteria)
clindamycin (Cleocin) antibacterial
doxycycline hyclate (Vibra-Tabs) antibacterial (drug-resistant bacteria)
erythromycin (Ery-Tab, Erythrocin) macrolide antibiotic
Flagyl (metronidazole) trichomoniasis
Keflex (cephalexin, USP) antibacterial antibiotic
levofloxacin (Levaquin) antibacterial (drug-resistant bacteria)
Levaquin (levofloxacin) antibacterial (drug-resistant bacteria), acute bacterial sinusitis
metronidazole tabs (Fagyl) trichomoniasis
minocycline (Solodyn) used to treat moderate to severe acne
mupirocin (Bactroban) topical antibiotic
Omnicef (cefdinir) drug-resistant bacteria
Penicillin VK infections
Solodyn (minocycline HCl) used to treat moderate to severe acne
tetracycline HCl (Sumycin, Panmycin) antibiotic
Vibra-Tabs (doxycycline hyclate, USP) antibacterial (drug-resistant bacteria)

Anti-inflammatory

Anaprox (naproxen) relieves pain and swelling

Asacol (mesalamine) GI anti-inflammatory (5-aminosalicylic acid derivate)

Celebrex (celecoxib) osteoarthritis, rheumatoid arthritis

celecoxib (Celebrex) osteoarthritis and rheumatoid arthritis, adenomatous colorectal polyps

diclofenac (Voltaren) osteoarthritis, rheumatoid arthritis

Humira (adalimumab) rheumatoid arthritis, chronic plaque psoriasis, Crohn's disease, pain relief and reduces inflammation caused by a number of autoimmune diseases

Indocin (indomethacin) relieves pain, swelling, and joint stiffness

Lidoderm (lidocaine-transdermal) topical analgesic

Lortab (hydrocodone bitartrate and acetaminophen) relieves moderate to moderately severe pain

Medrol (methylprednisolone) reduces swelling and redness

methylprednisolone (Medrol) inflammatory disorders

Mobic (meloxicam) osteoarthritis and rheumatoid arthritis

Motrin (ibuprofen) relieves pain and swelling

Nalfon (fenoprofen calcium) reduces pain, swelling, and joint stiffness from arthritis

naproxen (Anaprox) NSAID, mild to moderate pain, osteoarthritis, rheumatoid arthritis, dysmenorrhea, gout, ankylosing spondylitis, fever

prednisone (Deltasone) inflammatory disorders, adrenal insufficiency, MS relapsing, pneumocystic pneumonia, asthma, inflammatory bowel disease

Ultram (tramadol hydrochloride) juvenile rheumatoid arthritis, rheumatoid arthritis, chronic fatigue syndrome

Voltaren (diclofenac) osteoarthritis, rheumatoid arthritis

Antifungal

Nystatin (Nystatin oral) antifungal agent

Nystatin (Nystop) topical antifungal cream

Antineoplastic

Arimidex (anastrozole) treats breast cancer

anastrozole (Arimidex) treats breast cancer

Gleevec (imatinib mesylate) treats certain types of cancer (e.g., chronic myeloid leukemia, gastrointestinal stromal tumors, and myelodysplastic/myeloproliferative diseases). Stops or slows growth of cancer cells (tumors); causes cancer cells to die

imatinib (Gleevec) treats certain types of cancer (e.g., chronic myeloid leukemia, gastrointestinal stromal tumors, and myelodysplastic/myeloproliferative diseases). Stops or slows growth of cancer cells (tumors); causes cancer cells to die

Nolvadet (tamoxifen citrate) antineoplastic agent, SERM, estrogen receptor antagonist

tamoxifen citrate (Nolvadet) antineoplastic agent, SERM, estrogen receptor antagonist

Antiviral

acyclovir (Zovirax) decreases pain and speed healing of sores or blisters from varicella (chickenpox), herpes zoster (shingles), and outbreaks of genital herpes

Afluria (influenza vaccine) active immunization against influenza disease

Atripla (evavirenz/emtricitabine/tenofovir disoproxil fumarate) HIV in adults

Norvir (ritonavir) anti-HIV medication

Reyataz (atazanavir) HIV protease inhibitors

Tamiflu (oseltamivir phosphate) antiviral

Truvada (emtricitabine and tenofovir) HIV treatment

Zostavax (shingle vaccine) herpes zoster (shingles) for age 50 and over

Cardiovascular

Accupril (quinapril) hypertension (HTN)

Aggrenox (aspirin and dypyridamole) reduces risk of strokes in patients who have had blood clots

Aldomet (methyldopa) HTN

Altace (ramipril) reduces risk of MI, stroke, HTN

Amodarone (cordarone, pacerone) antiarrhythmic

amlodipidine (Norvasc) angina, essential HTN (calcium channel blocker)

Atacand (candesartan cilexetil) antihypertensive

atenolol (Tenomin) angina pectoris, essential HTN, myocardial infarction

atorvastatin (Lipitor) hypercholesterolemia, hyperlipidemia; dysbetalipoproteinemia

Avalide (irbesartan-hydrochlorothiazide) HTN

Avapro (irbesartan) HTN

Azor (amlodipine and olmesartan medoxomil) HTN

benazepril (Lotensin) HTN, congestive heart failure (CHF)

Benicar (olmesartan medoxomil) HTN

Bystolic (nebivolol) beta-blocker HTN

Caduet (amlodipine besylate with atorvastatin) antihypertensive

Cardura (doxazosin) HTN

Catapres (clonidine HCl) HTN

Clonidine high blood pressure

clopidogrel bisulfate (Plavix) reduction of atherothrombotic events

Coreg (carvedilol) congestive heart failure

Coumadin (warfarin sodium) anticoagulant venous thrombosis, pulmonary embolism

Cozaar (losartan potassium) HTN

Crestor (rosuvastatin calcium) cholesterol

Digoxin (lanoxin) heart failure, irregular heartbeat (chronic atrial fibrillation)

Digitek heart failure

Diovan (valsartan) hypertension, heart failure, postmyocardial infarction

doxazosin (Cardura) HTN, BPH

Dyazide (triamterene/HCTZ) diuretic, HTN

Effient (prasugrel) reduces risk of heart-related events or blood clots in stent

Enalapril maleate (Vasotec) hypertension

enalapril (Vasotec) HTN, CHF, acute MI, nephropathy, asymptomatic left ventricular dysfunction

Exforge (amlodipine and valsaran) HTN

furosemide (Lasix) diuretic, peripheral and pulmonary edema, hypercalcemia, kidney failure

Gemfibrozil high serum triglyceride

Hyzaar (losartan potassium-hydrochlorithiazide) HTN

Imdur (isosorbide mononitrate) angina

Inderal (propranolol HCl) beta-blocker, antihypertensive

isosorbide mononitrate (Imdur, ISMO) angina

ISMO (isosorbide mononitrate) angina

lanoxin (Digoxin) CHF, atrial fibrillation/flutter, paroxysmal atrial tachycardia

Lasix (furosemide) CHF, HTN, diuretic

Lipitor (atorvastatin) high cholesterol

lisinopril (Prinivil, Zestril) HTN, CHF, acute MI

Lopressor (metoprolol) HTN

Lotensin (benazepril) HTN

Lotrel (amlodipine besylate and benazepril HCl) HTN

Lovaza (omega-3-acid ethyl esters) antihyperlipidemic

metoprolol tartrate (Lopressor, Toprol XL) HTN, CHF, acute MI, angina

Cardiovascular (continued)

Mevacor (lovastatin) cholesterol-lowering agent

Miscardis HCT (telmisartan with hydrochlorothiazide)

Minipress (prazosin HCl) HTN

nebivolol (Bystolic) beta-blocker HTN

nifedipine ER (Procardia, Adalat) angina

Nitrostat (nitroglycerin) angina pectoris due to coronary artery disease

Norvasc (amlodipine besylate) HTN

Plavix (clopidogrel bisulfate) reduces risk of atherothrombotic events, heart attack, stroke, peripheral vascular disease

Pradaxa (dabigatran etexilae mesylate) blood thinner, reduces risk of strokes and blood clots in atrial fibrillation

Pravachol (pravastatin sodium) hypercholesterolemia, hyperlipidemia, dysbetalipoproteinemia

Prinivil (lisinopril) HTN

quinapril (Accupril) hypertension, CHF

ramipril (Altace) reduces risk of MI, stroke, hypertension

Ranexa (ranolazine) antianginal medication

simvastatin (Zocor) hypercholesterolemia, hypertriglyceridemia, dysbetalipoproteinemia

Toprol XL (metoprolol) HTN

triamterene/HCTZ (Dyazide) diuretic, hypertension, peripheral edema

Tricor (penofibrate) hypercholesterolemia

Trizac (diltiazem hydrochloride) hypertension

valsartan (Diovan) HTN

Vasotec (enalapril) HTN

verapamil angina, hypertension, supraventricular arrhythmia, atrial fibrillation/flutter, migraine prophylaxis

Vytorin (ezetimibe with simvastatin) cholesterol

warfarin (Coumadin) anticoagulation

Welchol (colsevelam Hcl) lowers cholesterol and A1C level

Xarelto (rivaroxaban) DVT and PE, aids with stroke prevention in atrial fibrillation

Zestril (lisinopril) HTN

Zetia (ezetimibe) primary hypercholesterolemia

Zocor (simvastatin) high cholesterol

Electrolytes

K-Dur (potassium chloride) hypokalemia, prevention of hypokalemia

Klor-Con (potassium chloride) hypokalemia, prevention of hypokalemia

potassium chloride (K-Dur, Klor-Con) hypokalemia, prevention of hypokalemia

Endocrinology

Actos (pioglitazone hydrochloride) DM type 2

Aldactone (spironolactone) hyperaldosteronism

allopurinol (Zyloprim) gout

Byetta (exenatide) antidiabetic (incretin mimetic)

DiaBeta (glyburide) DM type 2

Estrace (estrogen) reduces menopausal symptoms

glipizide (Glucotrol XL) DM type 2

Glucophage XR (metformin hydrochloride) diabetes

Glucotrol XL (glipizide) DM type 2

glyburide (DiaBeta, Micronase) DM type 2

Humalog (insulin lispro, rDNA origin) diabetes

Humulin N (insulin isophane [rDNA origin]) DM

Endocrinology (continued)

Janumet (sitagliptin/metaformin HCI) DM type 2
Januvia (sitagliptin) DM type 2
Lantus (insulin glargine [rDNA origin] injection) DM type 1
Levemir (insulin determir [rDNAorigin]) injection to control high blood sugar in DM
Levothroid (levothyroxine) hypothyroidism
levothyroxine (Levoxyl, Synthroid, Levothroid) hypothyroidism, myxedema coma, thyroid cancer
Levoxyl (levothyroxine sodium) hypothyroidism, pituitary TSH suppression
metformin (Glucophage) DM type 2
methylprednisolone endocrine disorders, rheumatic disorders
Micronase (glyburide) DM type 2
NovoLog (insulin) antidiabetic
Onglyza (saxagliptin) DM type 2
Synthroid (levothyroxine) hypothyroidism
Trajenta (linagliptin) DM type 2
Uloric (febuxostat) lowers uric acid levels, gout
Victoza (liraglutide [rDNA origin] injection) adults with type 2 DM

Gastrointestinal

Aciphex (rabeprazole sodium) erosive or ulcerative GERD
Amitiza (lubiprosone) chronic idiopathic constipation (CIC)
Dexilant (dexlansoprazole) proton pump inhibitor GERD
esomeprazole magnesium (Nexium) GERD
Humira (adalimumab) injection, Crohn's disease
Lomotil (diphenoxylate) diarrhea
metoclopramide (Reglan) GERD
Nexium (esomeprazole magnesium) GERD
omeprazole (Prilosec) GERD, erosive esophagitis, gastric/duodenal ulcer, *H. pylori*
pantoprazole sodium (Protonix) GERD
Pepcid (famotidine) GERD, duodenal ulcer
Prevacid (lansoprazole) GERD
Prilosec (omeprazole) GERD
Protonix (pantoprazole sodium) GERD, stomach ulcers, heartburn
Xantac (ranitidine HCl) duodenal ulcer, gastric ulcer

Genitourinary

allopurinol (Zyloprim) prophylaxis for gout, urate nephropathy, calcium oxalate calculi
Aviane contraceptive
Avodart (dutasteride) prostate anti-inflammatory
azithromycin (Zithromax) chlamydia
Cialis (tadalifil) erectile dysfunction
conjugated estrogens (Premarin, Prempro) antineoplastics; cancer of breast and prostate, menopause; osteoporosis prevention; ovarian failure; primary atrophic vaginitis
Detrol (tolterodine tartrate) overactive bladder, urinary incontinence
Diflucan (fluconazole) vaginal yeast infections
Ditropan (oxybutynin chloride) urinary antispasmodic agent
Estrace (estradiol) reduces menopausal symptoms
estradiol (Estrace) vasomotor symptoms, atrophic vaginitis, osteoporosis prevention, palliative treatment for breast cancer and prostate cancer
Flomax (tamsulosin hydrochloride) benign prostatic hyperplasia
fluconazole (Diflucan) vaginal candidiasis, oropharyngeal and esophageal candidiasis, cryptococcal meningitis

Genitourinary (continued)

Demadex (torsemide) loop diuretic
Levitra (vardenafil HCl) erectile dysfunction
Lo Loestrin Fe (norethindrone acetate and ethinyl estradiol) contraceptive
medroxyprogesterone (Provera) HRT, amenorrhea, dysfunctional uterine bleeding
norgestimate/ethinyl estradiol (Ortho Tri-Cyclen) oral contraceptive
Nuvaring (etonogestrel/ethinyl estradiol vaginal ring) contraceptive
Ortho Evra (norelgestromin/ethinyl estradiol) contraceptive
Ortho Tri-Cy Lo 28 (norgestimate/ethinyl estradiol) contraceptive
Premarin (conjugated estrogens) vasomotor symptoms and vaginal atrophy due to
    menopause, breast cancer, prostate cancer
Prempro (conjugated estrogens/medroxyprogesterone) reduces menopausal symptoms
Provera (medroxyprogesterone) restores normal menstrual periods
Pyridium (phenazopyridine HCl) urinary tract analgesic
Septra (trimethoprim/sulfametoxazole) antibacterial bladder infections
sildenafil citrate (Viagra) erectile dysfunction
trimethoprim/sulfametoxazole (Septra) antibacterial bladder infections
Trisprintec (Ortho Tri-Cyclen) (norgestimate/ethinyl estradiol) contraceptive
Valtrex (valacyclovir hydrochloride) herpes zoster, genital herpes
Vesicare (solifenacin succinate) anticholinergic agent (urinary bladder modifier)
Viagra (sildenafil citrate) erectile dysfunction
Yasmin (drospirenone and ethinyl estradiol) contraceptive
Zithromax (azithromycin) treat STD (chlamydia)
Zyloprim (allopurinol) gout, kidney stones

Immunology and Allergy

Adrenalin (epinephrine) allergies
Allegra (fexofenadine hydrochloride) allergies, hay fever
Astelin (azelastine hydrochloride) allergic rhinitis
CellCept (mycophenolate mofetil) lowers body's immune system, used to prevent body
    rejecting a kidney, liver, or heart transplant
Cetirizine (Zyrtec) allergies
Chlor-Trimeton (chlorapheneramine maleate) allergies
Clarinex (desloratadine) seasonal allergic rhinitis
Dimetane (brompheniramine maleate) allergies
fexofenadine (Allegra) allergic rhinitis, chronic urticaria
Flonase (fluticasone propionate) allergic rhinitis, sleep apnea
fluticasone proprionate (Flonase) allergic rhinitis, sleep apnea
Humira Pen (aldalimumab injection) reduces pain and swelling due to arthritis, psoriasis,
    blocks a protein tumor necrosis factor (TNF)
momentasone nasal (Nasonex) seasonal and year-round allergy symptoms of the nose
mycophenolate mofetil (CellCept) lowers body's immune system, used to prevent body
    rejecting a kidney, liver, or heart transplant
Nasacort (triamcinolone acetonide, USP) seasonal and perennial allergic rhinitis
Nasonex (mometasone nasal) seasonal and year-round allergy symptoms of the nose
Rhinocort Aqua (budesonide nasal spray) antiallergy
Prograf (tacrolimus) lowers immune system to prevent rejection of transplanted organ
promethazine (Phenergan) allergic symptoms, nausea, motion sickness
Singular (montelukast sodium) allergic rhinitis
tacrolimus (Prograf) lowers immune system to prevent rejection of transplanted organ
Tussionex (chlorpheniramine with hydrocodone) antihistamine/antitussive
Zyrtec (cetirizine) allergic rhinitis, chronic urticaria

Musculoskeletal

Actonel (risedronate sodium) osteoporosis
alendronate (Fosamax) osteoporosis, Paget's disease
Baclofen (lioresal, kemstro) skeletal muscle relaxant
Boniva (ibandronate sodium) osteoporosis in postmenopausal women
carisoprodol (Soma) muscle spasm
cyclobenzaprine (Flexeril) muscle spasm
Evista (raloxifene hydrochloride) osteoporosis
Flexeril (cyclobenzaprine) muscle spasm, sciatica
Fosamax (alendronate sodium) osteoporosis
Skelaxin (metaxalone) acute, painful musculoskeletal conditions
Soma (carisoprodol) treats pain and discomfort from muscle injuries

Neurological

Aricept (donepezil hydrochloride) mild to moderate dementias of the Alzheimer's type
benztropine mesylate (Cogentin) treats tremors, symptoms of Parkinson's disease
clonazepam (Klonopin) neuralgia, absence seizures, epilepsy, panic attacks
Depakote (divalproex) seizure disorders, psychiatric conditions, prevents migraines
Dilantin (phenytoin sodium) seizures
divalproex (Depakote) seizure disorder, mania, migraine prophylaxis
Exelon (rivastigmine tartrate) treats function and cognition in Alzheimer's patients
gabapentin (Neurontin) partial seizures, neuropathic pain, postherpetic neuralgia in adults, epilepsy
Imitrex (sumatriptan succinate) hemiplegic or basilar migraine
Keppra (levetiracetam) partial onset seizures due to epilepsy
Klonopin (clonazepam) seizure disorders and panic attacks
Lamictal (lamotrigine) epilepsy
Lyrica (pregablalin) neurolopathic pain, postherpetic neuralgia, partial onset seizures, fibromyalgia
Mirapex (pramipexol dihydrochloride) anti-Parkinson's agent–dopamine agonist
Namenda (memantine HCl) agent for Alzheimer's dementia (NMDA receptor antagonist)
Neurontin (gabapentin) controls seizures, nerve pain
Requip (ropinirole HCl) anti-Parkinson's agent–dopamine agonist
Trileptal (oxcarbazepin) antiepileptic
Topamax (topiramate) epilepsy

Optical

Alphagan-P (brimonidine tartrate) glaucoma
Cosopt (dorzolamide hydrochloride and timolol maleate) reduces intraocular pressure in ocular hypertension, glaucoma
Combigan (brimonidine tartrate/timolol maleate) reduces intraocular pressure (IOP) in patients with glaucoma or ocular hypertension
Lotemax (loteprednol etabonate) internal and external inflammation of the eye
Lumigan (bimatoprost) glaucoma
Pataday (**Patanol**) (olopatadine) allergic conjunctivitis
TobraDex (tobramycin and dexamethasone) antibiotic ophthalmic corticosteroid
Travatan (travoprost) antiglaucoma agent (ophthalmic prostaglandin)
Vigamox (moxifloxacin hydrochloride) bacterial conjunctivitis
Xalatan (latanoprost) reduces intraocular pressure, glaucoma

Psychiatric

Abilify (aripiprazole) schizophrenia
Adderall ADHD
alprazolam (Xanax) anxiety, panic disorder
Ambien (zolpidem tartrate) sleep disorders, insomnia
amitriptyline (Elavil, Endep) depression, chronic pain
Ativan (lorazepam) anxiety
bupropion HCl (Wellbutrin SR) major depressive disorder
Budisol (butabarbital sodium) sedative or hypnotic, insomnia
Celexa (citalopram) depression
Citalopram (Celexa) depression
Concerta (methylphenidate HCl extended release) ADHD
Cymbalta (duloxetine hydrochloride) suicidal tendencies and depression
Desyrel (trazodone) depression
diazepam (Valium) anxiety, alcohol withdrawal stress, muscle spasm, seizure disorder, status epilepticus
Effexor XR (venlafaxine hydrochloride) major depressive disorder
Elavil (amitriptyline) depression, fibromyalgia
Endep (amitriptyline) depression
escitapropram oxalate (Lexapro) antidepressant
fluoxetine hydrochloride (Prozac) bulimia nervosa, depression, obsessive-compulsive disorder, social anxiety disorder
Focalin XR (dexmethylphenidate HCl) ADHD
Geodon (ziprasidone hydrochloride) antipsychotic schizophrenia, bipolar disorder
Haldol (haloperidol) treats mental/mood disorders
hydroxyzine (Atarax) anxiety, psychoneurosis
Lexapro (escitapropram oxalate) antidepressant, anxiety
lisdexamfetamine (Vyvanse) ADHD
lorazepam (Ativan) anxiety, panic attacks, depression
Lunesta (eszopiclone) non-BZD (nonbenzodiazepines drug) hypnotic
modafinil (Provigil) sleep disorders
nortriptyline (Pamelor) depression
Privigil (modafinil) sleep disorders
paroxetine (Paxil) anxiety, panic disorder, depression, obsessive-compulsive disorder
Paxil (paroxetine) panic attacks, depression, obsessive-compulsive disorder, post-traumatic stress disorder (PTSD)
Pristiq (desvenlafaxine) depression
Prozac (fluoxetine) depression, obsessive-compulsive disorder, panic attacks, bulimia, premenstrual syndrome
Restoril (temazepam) insomnia
Risperdal (risperidone) schizophrenia
Seroquel (quetiapine fumarate) treatment of bipolar mania
sertraline (Zoloft) anxiety, panic disorder, depression, obsessive-compulsive disorder
Strattera (atomoxetine HCl) ADHD
trazodone (Desyrel) depression
Valium (diazepam) anxiety
venlafaxine (Effexor EX) depression, anxiety
Viibryd (vilazodone HCl) major depressive disorder (MDD)
Vyvanse (lisdexamfetamine) ADHD
Wellbutrin SR (bupropion HCl) major depressive disorder
Xanax (alprazolam) anxiety and panic disorders

Psychiatric (continued)

ziprasidone hydrochloride (Geodon) antipsychotic schizophrenia, bipolar disorder
Zoloft (sertraline hydrochloride) depression, panic attacks, post-traumatic stress disorder
zolpidem (Ambien) insomnia
Zyprexa (olanzapine) dementia-related psychosis

Respiratory

Advair Diskus (fluticasone propionate) treatment of asthma
Advair HFA (fluticasone propionate and saleterol) asthma
albuterol (Proventil, Ventolin) asthma
Asmanex Twisthaler (mometasone furoate) maintenance treatment for asthma
Combivent Respimat (ipratropium bromide/albuterol) COPD
Dulera (mometasone furolate dehydrate) asthma control
Flovent HFA (fluticasone propionate) asthma
fluticasone propionate (Flovent) asthma
montelukast (Singular) asthma
Proair HFA (albuterol sulfate inhalation aerosol) asthma
Proventil HFA (albuterol) asthma
Symbicort (budesonide and formoterol) prevents bronchospasm in patients with asthma or
    COPD
Singulair (montelukast) asthma
Spiriva (tiotropium bromide inhalation powder) bronchospasm associated with COPD
Tussionex (pennkinetic) cough and upper respiratory symptoms with allergy or cold
Ventolin (albuterol) asthma
Xopenex (levalbuterol HCl) antiasthmatic (beta 2 agonist)

Smoking Cessation

Chantix (varenicline) aid to smoking cessation
Narcotic Cessation Suboxone (buprenorphide and naloxone) treats narcotic (opiate)
    addiction

Common Abbreviations

Always use with caution! Abbreviations may have multiple meanings.

a	before
ac, a.c.	before meals
AD	right ear
ad lib	as desired
alt dieb	alternate days
alt hr	alternate hours
alt noc	alternate nights
am, AM	morning
amt	amount
ante	before
aq	aqueous (water)
AS	left ear
AU	both ears
Ba	barium
bid, b.i.d.	two times a day
bin	two times a night
C	100
c, w/	with
cap(s)	capsule(s)
cc	cubic centimeter
CHF	congestive heart failure
d	day
Dx	diagnosis
D_5W	5% dextrose in water
D/C, dc	discontinue
dil	dilute
disp	dispense
DM	diabetes mellitus
dr	dram
elix	elixir
emul	emulsion
et	and
ext	extract/external
FDA	Food and Drug Administration
Fe	iron
Fl	fluid
G	gauge
g, GM, gm, gr	gram(s)
gal	gallon
gt, gtt	drop(s)
H	hour/hypodermic
HRT	hormone replacement therapy
Hs, h.s.	hour of sleep (bedtime)
HTN	hypertension
IM	intramuscular
Inj	injection
IU	international units
IV	intravenous

IVPB	IV piggyback (2nd line)
K	potassium
kg	kilogram
L	liter
Liq	liquid
mcg	microgram
mg	milligram(s)
ml, mL	milliliter(s)
mm	millimeter
NaCl 0.9%	normal saline
NKA	no known allergy
NKDA	no known drug allergy
noc, noct	night
non rep	do not repeat
NPO	nothing by mouth
NS	normal saline
NSAID	nonsteroidal anti-inflammatory drug(s)
O	pint
od	once day/daily
OD	right eye
om	every morning
OTC	over the counter
Oz, oz	ounce
Pc, p.c.	after meals
PCA	patient-controlled analgesia, patient-controlled administration
PCN	penicillin
PDR	Physician's Desk Reference
per	with
PM, pm	evening
PRN, prn	as needed as necessary
PO, po, p.o.	by mouth
pt	pint, patient
pulv	powder
Q, q	every
q2h	every 2 hours
qAM	every morning
qd, q.d.	every day
qh, q.h.	every hour
qh.s.	every bedtime
qid, q.i.d.	four times a day
qns	quantity not sufficient
qPM	every evening
qs, q.s.	as much as needed, sufficient quantity
Rx	prescription

Common Abbreviations
(continued)

SC, sc, sq, subc, subq. Subcutaneous
Sig, sig .... let be labeled as follows, directions
SL .... sublingual
SOB .... shortness of breath
susp .... suspension
T, tbsp .... tablespoon
tab .... tablet
tid, t.i.d. .... three times a day
TO .... telephone order
Top, top .... apply topically
tsp .... teaspoon
TX .... treatment
ut, diet, UD .... as directed
wt .... weight

BE ALERT FOR SOUNDALIKES

Drug names may be similar in sound as well as spelling. It is important to be alert when referring to drugs. For example:

Celebrex..................... NSAID
vs
Cerebyx........... anticonvulsant

DiaBeta ....oral hypoglycemic
vs
Zebeta beta-adrenergic blocker

Paxil .... antidepressant
vs
Taxol .... antineoplastic

REFERENCES FOR PHARMACOLOGY

Spratto, G. R. (2013). *Delmar health care drug handbook.* Clifton Park, NY: Delmar Cengage Learning.

Woodrow, R. (2015). *Essentials of pharmacology for health occupations* (7th ed.). Clifton Park, NY: Delmar Cengage Learning.

Web sites for Pharmacology: http://www.rxlist.com/script/main/hp.asp
http://www.epocrates.com/
http://www.fda.gov/drugs/
http://pdr.net/
http://mayoclinic.com/

HEMATOLOGY/COAGULATION

Complete Blood Count
Use: basic blood evaluation
AKA: CBC, CBC with differential
Note: usually includes Hct, Hgb, WBC counts and differential, platelet count, and often RBC count

Erythrocyte Count
AKA: RBC count (red blood cell)
High: acute hepatitis, acute MI, PID, rheumatoid arthritis
Low: anemias, leukemias, and following severe hemorrhage

Hematocrit
Use: determines the percent of whole blood composed of red blood cells
AKA: Hct, HCT, PVC
High: dehydration, Addison's disease, polycythemia due to dehydration, and shock
Low: anemia, severe hemorrhage

Hemoglobin
Use: measures Hgb in the blood
AKA: Hb, Hgb
High: dehydration, pernicious anemia, sickle cell anemia, thalassemia, polycythemia, obstructive pulmonary diseases, CHF
Low: excessive fluid intake, iron-deficiency anemia, pregnancy

Hemoglobin, Glycated
Use: monitors blood sugar control
AKA: HbA1C, GHb, DM control index
Note: Abnormal results over time indicate inadequate control

Leukocyte Count
AKA: WBC Count (white blood cell)
High: acute infections, leukemias, acute hemorrhage
Low: chemotherapy, shock, cachexia

Partial Thromboplastin Time
Use: measures intrinsic clotting time
AKA: APTT, activated
High: cirrhosis, leukemia, vitamin K deficiency, hemophilia

Low: extensive ca, early stages of disseminated intravascular coagulation

Platelet Count
Use: dx a bleeding disorder or bone marrow disease
High: iron-deficiency anemia, postop patients, malignancies, polycythemia
Low: acute leukemia, aplastic anemia, thrombocytopenic purpura

Prothrombin Time
Use: monitors blood-thinning medications used to prevent blood clots
AKA: PT, Pro Time
Prolonged: severe liver damage, heparin use, low vitamin K diet, colitis, chronic diarrhea

Reticulocyte Count
Use: measures percent of reticulocytes (slightly immature red blood cells)
High: need for RBCs, hemolytic anemias, acute or severe bleeding
Low: bone marrow failure (toxicity, tumor, fibrosis, infection), cirrhosis, iron deficiency, radiation therapy

Sedimentation Rate
Use: monitors inflammatory and malignant diseases and acute MI
AKA: erythrocyte sedimentation rate, sed rate, ESR
High: pregnancy, menstruation, infectious diseases, tissue damage

SERUM ELECTROLYTES

AKA: "Lytes"
Note: essential to normal metabolism, exists as acids, bases, and salts

Calcium, Total
Use: blood test to screen/monitor diseases of bone or calcium regulation (diseases of parathyroid and kidneys)
AKA: Ca^{+2}, Ca^{++}, serum calcium

SERUM ELECTROLYTES (continued)

High: metastatic ca of bone, lung, breast, Paget's disease, hyperparathyroidism, excess vitamin D
Low: severe pancreatitis, renal insufficiency, uremia, malabsorption, osteomalacia, hypoparathyroidism

Chloride
AKA: Cl
High: renal insufficiency, necrosis, dehydration, renal tubular acidosis, Cushing's syndrome, hyperventilation
Low: CHF, chronic renal failure, diabetic acidosis, diarrhea, excessive sweating, emphysema

Magnesium
AKA: Mg^{+2}
High: renal insufficiency, use of antacids with magnesium
Low: chronic alcoholism, chronic diarrhea, hepatic insufficiency

Phosphorus
AKA: PO4
High: renal insufficiency, healing fx, hypoparathyroidism, excess vitamin D
Low: chronic alcoholism, ketoacidosis, hyperalimentation, hyperparathyroidism

Potassium
AKA: K
High: renal insufficiency, adrenal insufficiency, Addison's disease, hypoventilation
Low: chronic diarrhea, vomiting or malabsorption syndrome, diabetic acidosis, chronic kidney disease, use of thiazide diuretics

Sodium
AKA: NA
High: (hypernatremia) excessive dietary intake, Cushing's disease, excessive sweating, diabetes insipidus
Low: (hyponatremia) ascites, CHF, insufficient intake, diarrhea, vomiting, SIADH (syndrome of inappropriate diuretic hormone), diuretic use, chronic renal insufficiency, excessive water intake, peripheral edema, pleural effusion

SERUM/URINE/STOOL

Acid Phosphatase
High: metastatic ca of bone, prostatic ca, some liver diseases, MI, pulmonary embolism, hepatobiliary diseases, hyperparathyroidism

Alanine Aminotransferase
Use: screens for liver disease
AKA: ALT, SGPT
High: acute hepatitis, liver necrosis

Albumin
Use: screens for liver or kidney disease or evaluates nutritional status
AKA: ALB
Note: Albumin is a protein
High: shock, dehydration, multiple myeloma
Low: malnutrition, malabsorption, acute or chronic glomerulonephritis, cancers, leukemia, hepatitis, cirrhosis, hepatocellular necrosis

Alkaline Phosphatase
Use: screens/monitors treatment for liver or bone disorders
AKA: ALP, alk phos
High: biliary duct obstruction, hyperparathyroidism, healing fx, rickets, osteomalacia, neoplastic bone disorders, liver diseases

Ammonia
AKA: NH^{4+}
Note: particularly toxic to the brain; can cause confusion and lethargy
High: CHF, liver failure, GI bleed, leukemia, pericarditis

Amylase
Use: blood test to diagnose/monitor pancreatic disease (blood)
Note: amylase is an enzyme that helps digest glycogen and starch
High: acute pancreatitis, ca of the pancreas, ovaries, or lungs, mumps, intestinal obstruction
Low: acute and chronic hepatitis, cirrhosis, toxemia of pregnancy

SERUM/URINE/STOOL (continued)

Anion Gap
Use: dx and tx of acidosis
High: lactic acidosis, diabetic ketoacidosis, alcoholic ketoacidosis, starvation, renal failure
Low: multiple myeloma, chronic vomiting, hyperaldosteronism

Arterial Blood Gases
AKA: ABGs
Abnormal Results: respiratory, metabolic or renal diseases, trauma

Aspartate Aminotransferase
Use: detects liver damage
AKA: AST, SGOT
High: acute MI, liver disease, diseases of skeletal muscles

Bilirubin, Total
Use: screens/monitors liver disorders
Note: bilirubin is a product of hemoglobin breakdown, causes jaundice
High: acute/chronic hepatitis, gallstones, toxic reaction to drugs/chemicals, infectious mononucleosis

Blood Urea Nitrogen
Use: evaluates kidney function and dialysis effectiveness
AKA: BUN
High: GI hemorrhage, dehydration, renal insufficiency
Low: hepatic failure, cachexia

Carbon Dioxide, Total
AKA: CO_2
High: respiratory diseases, vomiting, intestinal obstruction
Decreased: acidosis, nephritis, diarrhea

Carcinoembryonic Antigen
Use: dx cancer and monitor tx
AKA: CEA
High: colon, breast, lung, pancreatic, thyroid ca, also heavy smoking

Cholesterol, Total
Use: screens for heart disease
High: MI, uncontrolled DM, hypothyroidism, atherosclerosis, hypercholesterolemia, hyperlipidemia
Low: acute MI, pernicious anemia, malnutrition, liver disease, sepsis, malabsorption

Creatinine
Use: evaluates kidney function and tx
High: dehydration, diabetic nephropathy, kidney disease

Creatine (Phospho) Kinase
Use: evaluates muscle damage
AKA: CPK, CK
High: acute MI, muscular dystrophies, muscle injury, CNS trauma, stroke

Globulin
Use: protein evaluation
AKA: CPK, CK
High: hepatic disease, plasma cell neoplasms, lupus, malaria

Glucose
Use: diagnoses and manages DM
AKA: GTT glucose tolerance test
High: DM, IV therapy, hyperthyroidism, hyperpituitarism, liver diseases, nephritis
Low: hyperinsulinism, hyperthyroidism, Addison's disease

Iron
AKA: Fe
High: anemias, liver disease
Low: iron-deficiency anemia, excessive fluid intake, pregnancy

Lactose Dehydrogenase
AKA: LDH
High: acute MI, infectious hepatitis, malignant tumors and widespread ca, hemolytic and pernicious anemias, acute leukemias
Low: x-ray irradiation

Oxygen Saturation
AKA: oximetry, O_2
High: hyperventilation
Low: inadequate O_2 inspiration, hypoxic lung diseases, hypoxic cardiac diseases, severe hypoventilation

Prostate-Specific Antigen
AKA: PSA
High: BPH, prostate ca, prostatism

Stool Guaiac Test
Use: detects hidden blood in stool
AKA: hemoccult
Abnormal Results: NSAIDs, colon polyps, colon ca, GI tumors, esophagitis, gastritis, inflammatory bowel disease, peptic ulcer

Thyrotropin
AKA: THS
Abnormal Findings: hyperthyroidism, hypothyroidism, depression, acute starvation, pregnancy, old age

Thyroxine
AKA: T_4
High: Graves' disease, toxic thyroid adenoma, acute thyroiditis
Low: cretinism, myxedema, pituitary or iodine insufficiency, hypothalamic failure, renal failure, Cushing's disease, cirrhosis, advanced cancer

Triglycerides
AKA: TG
High: hyperlipidemias, hypothyroidism, poorly controlled DM, nephrotic syndrome, hypertension, alcoholic cirrhosis, pregnancy, MI
Low: malabsorption syndrome, malnutrition, hyperthyroidism

Uric Acid
High: gout, leukemia, renal insufficiency, polycythemia, pneumonia
Low: acute hepatitis

Viral Load
Use: severity of immune system damage, monitors HIV status and treatment
AKA: CD4 lymphocyte count
Low below 350 mL: herpes simplex, herpes zoster, TB
Low below 200 mL: pneumocystis carinii pneumonia
Low below 100 mL: AIDS dementia
Low below 50 mL: cytomegalovirus

COMMON ABBREVIATIONS

AKA	also known as
ca, Ca	cancer, calcium
CHF	congestive heart failure
DM	diabetes mellitus
Dx	diagnosis
fx	fracture
GI	gastrointestinal
HIV	human immunodeficiency virus
IV	intravenous
MI	myocardial infarction
NIDDM	non−insulin-dependent DM
NSAID	nonsteroidal anti-inflammatory
tx	treatment

REFERENCES FOR LAB TESTING

Daniels, R. (2010). *Delmar's guide to laboratory and diagnostic tests* (2nd ed.). Clifton Park, NY: Delmar Cengage Learning.

Estridge, B. H., & Reynolds, A. P. (2012). *Basic clinical laboratory techniques* (6th ed.). Clifton Park, NY: Delmar Cengage Learning.

Ridley, J. (2011). *Essentials of clinical laboratory science.* Clifton Park, NY: Delmar Cengage Learning.

ONLINE RESOURCES:
Lab Tests Online
 http://www.labtestsonline.org/

Labcorp (Laboratory Corporation of America)
 https://www.labcorp.com/wps/portal/provider/testmenu/

Laboratory testing
 http://www.thedoctorsdoctor.com/laboratory_testing.htm

MedlinePlus
 http://www.nlm.nih.gov/medlineplus/laboratorytests.html

Test Reference
 http://www.testreference.net/

ICD-9-CM Official Guidelines for Coding and Reporting
Partial Code Freeze for ICD-9-CM and ICD-10

The ICD-9-CM Coordination and Maintenance Committee implemented a partial freeze of the ICD-9-CM and ICD-10 (ICD-10-CM and ICD-10-PCS) codes prior to the implementation of ICD-10. The partial freeze is scheduled to end one year after the implementation of ICD-10. There was considerable support for this partial freeze. On April 1, 2014, the Protecting Access to Medicare Act of 2014 (PAMA) (Pub. L. No. 113-93) was enacted, which said that the Secretary may not adopt ICD-10 prior to October 1, 2015. Accordingly, the U.S. Department of Health and Human Services issued a final rule on August 4, 2014, that changed the compliance date for ICD-10 from October 1, 2014, to October 1, 2015. The final rule also requires HIPAA covered entities to continue to use ICD-9-CM through September 30, 2015. Links to the final rule are provided at http://www.cms.gov/Medicare/Coding/ICD10/Statute_Regulations.html.

The partial freeze will be implemented as follows:

• The last regular, annual updates to both ICD-9-CM and ICD-10 code sets were made on October 1, 2011.

• On October 1, 2012, October 1, 2013, and October 1, 2014, there were only limited code updates to both the ICD-9-CM and ICD-10 code sets to capture new technologies and diseases as required by section 503(a) of Pub. L. 108-173.

• On October 1, 2015, there will be only limited code updates to ICD-10 code sets to capture new technologies and diagnoses as required by section 503(a) of Pub. L. 108-173. There will be no updates to ICD-9-CM, as it will no longer be used for reporting.

• On October 1, 2016 (one year after implementation of ICD-10), regular updates to ICD-10 will begin.

The ICD-9-CM Coordination and Maintenance Committee will continue to meet twice a year during the partial freeze. At these meetings, the public will be asked to comment on whether or not requests for new diagnosis or procedure codes should be created based on the criteria of the need to capture a new technology or disease. Any code requests that do not meet the criteria will be evaluated for implementation within ICD-10 on and after October 1, 2016, once the partial freeze has ended.

Note: There are no new or revised or deleted ICD-9-CM diagnosis codes effective for October 1, 2012. There are no revised or deleted ICD-9-CM procedure codes effective for October 1, 2012. The final addendum which describes all changes to the procedure part of ICD-9-CM is posted on the CMS webpage at: www.cms.hhs.gov/ICD9ProviderDiagnosticCodes .

Procedure Code **Description**
00.95*   Injection or infusion of glucarpidase

Notes:

* This procedure code was discussed at the March 5, 2012 ICD-9-CM Coordination and Maintenance Committee meeting and was not finalized in time to include in the FY 2013 IPPS/LTCH PPS proposed rule. However, it will be implemented on October 1, 2012.

ICD-9-CM Official Guidelines for Coding and Reporting
Effective October 1, 2011
Narrative changes appear in bold text
Items underlined have been moved within the guidelines since October 1, 2010

The Centers for Medicare and Medicaid Services (CMS) and the National Center for Health Statistics (NCHS), two departments within the U.S. Federal Government's Department of Health and Human Services (DHHS) provide the following guidelines for coding and reporting using the International Classification of Diseases, 9th Revision, Clinical Modification (ICD-9-CM). These guidelines should be used as a companion document to the official version of the ICD-9-CM as published on CD-ROM by the U.S. Government Printing Office (GPO).

These guidelines have been approved by the four organizations that make up the Cooperating Parties for the ICD-9-CM: the American Hospital Association (AHA), the American Health Information Management Association (AHIMA), CMS, and NCHS. These guidelines are included on the official government version of the ICD-9-CM, and also appear in *"Coding Clinic for ICD-9-CM"* published by the AHA.

These guidelines are a set of rules that have been developed to accompany and complement the official conventions and instructions provided within the ICD-9-CM itself. The instructions and conventions of the classification take precedence over guidelines. These guidelines are based on the coding and sequencing instructions in Volumes I, II and III of ICD-9-CM, but provide additional instruction. Adherence to these guidelines when assigning ICD-9-CM diagnosis and procedure codes is required under the Health Insurance Portability and Accountability Act (HIPAA). The diagnosis codes (Volumes 1-2) have been adopted under HIPAA for all healthcare settings. Volume 3 procedure codes have been adopted for inpatient procedures reported by hospitals. A joint effort between the healthcare provider and the coder is essential to achieve complete and accurate documentation, code assignment, and reporting of diagnoses and procedures. These guidelines have been developed to assist both the healthcare provider and the coder in identifying those diagnoses and procedures that are to be reported. The importance of consistent, complete documentation in the medical record cannot be overemphasized. Without such documentation accurate coding cannot be achieved. The entire record should be reviewed to determine the specific reason for the encounter and the conditions treated.

The term encounter is used for all settings, including hospital admissions. In the context of these guidelines, the term provider is used throughout the guidelines to mean physician or any qualified health care practitioner who is legally accountable for establishing the patient's diagnosis. Only this set of guidelines, approved by the Cooperating Parties, is official.

The guidelines are organized into sections. Section I includes the structure and conventions of the classification and general guidelines that apply to the entire classification, and chapter-specific guidelines that correspond to the chapters as they are arranged in the classification. Section II includes guidelines for selection of principal diagnosis for non-outpatient settings. Section III includes guidelines for reporting additional diagnoses in non-outpatient settings. Section IV is for outpatient coding and reporting.

Section I. Conventions, general coding guidelines and chapter specific guidelines

The conventions, general guidelines and chapter-specific guidelines are applicable to all health care settings unless otherwise indicated. The conventions and instructions of the classification take precedence over guidelines.

A. Conventions for the ICD-9-CM

The conventions for the ICD-9-CM are the general rules for use of the classification independent of the guidelines. These conventions are incorporated within the index and tabular of the ICD-9-CM as instructional notes. The conventions are as follows:

1. Format:

The ICD-9-CM uses an indented format for ease in reference

2. Abbreviations

a. Index abbreviations

NEC   "Not elsewhere classifiable"
This abbreviation in the index represents "other specified" when a specific code is not available for a condition the index directs the coder to the "other specified" code in the tabular.

b. Tabular abbreviations

NEC   "Not elsewhere classifiable"
This abbreviation in the tabular represents "other specified". When a specific code is not available for a condition the tabular includes an NEC entry under a code to identify the code as the "other specified" code.
(See Section I.A.5.a. "Other" codes").

NOS   "Not otherwise specified"
This abbreviation is the equivalent of unspecified.
(See Section I.A.5.b., "Unspecified" codes)

3. Punctuation

[ ]   Brackets are used in the tabular list to enclose synonyms, alternative wording or explanatory phrases. Brackets are used in the index to identify manifestation codes.
(See Section I.A.6. "Etiology/manifestations")

( )   Parentheses are used in both the index and tabular to enclose supplementary words that may be present or absent in the statement of a disease or procedure without affecting the code number to which it is assigned. The terms within the parentheses are referred to as nonessential modifiers.

: Colons are used in the Tabular list after an incomplete term which needs one or more of the modifiers following the colon to make it assignable to a given category.

4. Includes and Excludes Notes and Inclusion terms

Includes: This note appears immediately under a three-digit code title to further define, or give examples of, the content of the category.

Excludes: An excludes note under a code indicates that the terms excluded from the code are to be coded elsewhere. In some cases the codes for the excluded terms should not be used in conjunction with the code from which it is excluded. An example of this is a congenital condition excluded from an acquired form of the same condition. The congenital and acquired codes should not be used together. In other cases, the excluded terms may be used together with an excluded code. An example of this is when fractures of different bones are coded to different codes. Both codes may be used together if both types of fractures are present.

Inclusion terms: List of terms is included under certain four and five digit codes. These terms are the conditions for which that code number is to be used. The terms may be synonyms of the code title, or, in the case of "other specified" codes, the terms are a list of the various conditions assigned to that code. The inclusion terms are not necessarily exhaustive. Additional terms found only in the index may also be assigned to a code.

5. Other and Unspecified codes

a. "Other" codes

Codes titled "other" or "other specified" (usually a code with a 4th digit 8 or fifth-digit 9 for diagnosis codes) are for use when the information in the medical record provides detail for which a specific code does not exist. Index entries with NEC in the line designate "other" codes in the tabular. These index entries represent specific disease entities for which no specific code exists so the term is included within an "other" code.

b. "Unspecified" codes

Codes (usually a code with a 4th digit 9 or 5th digit 0 for diagnosis codes) titled "unspecified" are for use when the information in the medical record is insufficient to assign a more specific code.

6. Etiology/manifestation convention ("code first", "use additional code" and "in diseases classified elsewhere" notes)

Certain conditions have both an underlying etiology and multiple body system manifestations due to the underlying etiology. For such conditions, the ICD-9-CM has a coding convention that requires the underlying condition be sequenced first followed by the manifestation. Wherever such a combination exists, there is a "use additional code" note at the etiology code, and a "code first" note at the manifestation code. These instructional notes indicate the proper sequencing order of the codes, etiology followed by manifestation.

In most cases the manifestation codes will have in the code title, "in diseases classified elsewhere." Codes with this title are a component of the etiology/ manifestation convention. The code title indicates that it is a manifestation code. "In diseases classified elsewhere" codes are never permitted to be used as first listed or principal diagnosis codes. They must be used in conjunction with an underlying condition code and they must be listed following the underlying condition.

There are manifestation codes that do not have "in diseases classified elsewhere" in the title. For such codes a "use additional code" note will still be present and the rules for sequencing apply.

In addition to the notes in the tabular, these conditions also have a specific index entry structure. In the index both conditions are listed together with the etiology code first followed by the manifestation codes in brackets. The code in brackets is always to be sequenced second.

The most commonly used etiology/manifestation combinations are the codes for Diabetes mellitus, category 250. For each code under category 250 there is a use additional code note for the manifestation that is specific for that particular diabetic manifestation. Should a patient have more than one manifestation of diabetes, more than one code from category 250 may be used with as many manifestation codes as are needed to fully describe the patient's complete diabetic condition. The category 250 diabetes codes should be sequenced first, followed by the manifestation codes.

"Code first" and "Use additional code" notes are also used as sequencing rules in the classification for certain codes that are not part of an etiology/ manifestation combination.
See - Section I.B.9. "Multiple coding for a single condition".

7. "And"

The word "and" should be interpreted to mean either "and" or "or" when it appears in a title.

8. "With"

The word "with" should be interpreted to mean "associated with" or "due to" when it appears in a code title, the Alphabetic Index, or an instructional note in the Tabular List.

The word "with" in the alphabetic index is sequenced immediately following the main term, not in alphabetical order.

9. "See" and "See Also"

The "see" instruction following a main term in the index indicates that another term should be referenced. It is necessary to go to the main term referenced with the "see" note to locate the correct code.

A "see also" instruction following a main term in the index instructs that there is another main term that may also be referenced that may provide additional index entries that may be useful. It is not necessary to follow the "see also" note when the original main term provides the necessary code.

B. General Coding Guidelines

1. Use of Both Alphabetic Index and Tabular List

Use both the Alphabetic Index and the Tabular List when locating and assigning a code. Reliance on only the Alphabetic Index or the Tabular List leads to errors in code assignments and less specificity in code selection.

2. Locate each term in the Alphabetic Index

Locate each term in the Alphabetic Index and verify the code selected in the Tabular List. Read and be guided by instructional notations that appear in both the Alphabetic Index and the Tabular List.

3. Level of Detail in Coding

Diagnosis and procedure codes are to be used at their highest number of digits available.

ICD-9-CM diagnosis codes are composed of codes with 3, 4, or 5 digits. Codes with three digits are included in ICD-9-CM as the heading of a category of codes that may be further subdivided by the use of fourth and/or fifth digits, which provide greater detail.

A three-digit code is to be used only if it is not further subdivided. Where fourth-digit subcategories and/or fifth-digit subclassifications are provided, they must be assigned. A code is invalid if it has not been coded to the full number of digits required for that code. For example, Acute myocardial infarction, code 410, has fourth digits that describe the location of the infarction (e.g., 410.2, Of inferolateral wall), and fifth digits that identify the episode of care. It would be incorrect to report a code in category 410 without a fourth and fifth digit.

ICD-9-CM Volume 3 procedure codes are composed of codes with either 3 or 4 digits. Codes with two digits are included in ICD-9-CM as the heading of a category of codes that may be further subdivided by the use of third and/or fourth digits, which provide greater detail.

4. Code or codes from 001.0 through V91.99

The appropriate code or codes from 001.0 through V91.99 must be used to identify diagnoses, symptoms, conditions, problems, complaints or other reason(s) for the encounter/visit.

5. Selection of codes 001.0 through 999.9

The selection of codes 001.0 through 999.9 will frequently be used to describe the reason for the admission/encounter. These codes are from the section of ICD-9-CM for the classification of diseases and injuries (e.g., infectious and parasitic diseases; neoplasms; symptoms, signs, and ill-defined conditions, etc.).

6. Signs and symptoms

Codes that describe symptoms and signs, as opposed to diagnoses, are acceptable for reporting purposes when a related definitive diagnosis has not been established (confirmed) by the provider. Chapter 16 of ICD-9-CM, Symptoms, Signs, and Ill-defined conditions (codes 780.0 - 799.9) contain many, but not all codes for symptoms.

7. Conditions that are an integral part of a disease process

Signs and symptoms that are associated routinely with a disease process should not be assigned as additional codes, unless otherwise instructed by the classification.

8. Conditions that are not an integral part of a disease process

Additional signs and symptoms that may not be associated routinely with a disease process should be coded when present.

9. Multiple coding for a single condition

In addition to the etiology/manifestation convention that requires two codes to fully describe a single condition that affects multiple body systems, there are other single conditions that also require more than one code. "Use additional code" notes are found in the tabular at codes that are not part of an etiology/manifestation pair where a secondary code is useful to fully describe a condition. The sequencing rule is the same as the etiology/manifestation pair - "use additional code" indicates that a secondary code should be added.

For example, for infections that are not included in chapter 1, a secondary code from category 041, Bacterial infection in conditions classified elsewhere and of unspecified site, may be required to identify the bacterial organism causing the infection. A "use additional code" note will normally be found at the infectious disease code, indicating a need for the organism code to be added as a secondary code.

"Code first" notes are also under certain codes that are not specifically manifestation codes but may be due to an underlying cause. When a "code first" note is present and an underlying condition is present the underlying condition should be sequenced first.

"Code, if applicable, any causal condition first", notes indicate that this code may be assigned as a principal diagnosis when the causal condition is unknown or not applicable. If a causal condition is known, then the code for that condition should be sequenced as the principal or first-listed diagnosis.

Multiple codes may be needed for late effects, complication codes and obstetric codes to more fully describe a condition. See the specific guidelines for these conditions for further instruction.

10.   Acute and Chronic Conditions

If the same condition is described as both acute (subacute) and chronic, and separate subentries exist in the Alphabetic Index at the same indentation level, code both and sequence the acute (subacute) code first.

11.   Combination Code

A combination code is a single code used to classify:
Two diagnoses, or
A diagnosis with an associated secondary process (manifestation)
A diagnosis with an associated complication

Combination codes are identified by referring to subterm entries in the Alphabetic Index and by reading the inclusion and exclusion notes in the Tabular List.

Assign only the combination code when that code fully identifies the diagnostic conditions involved or when the Alphabetic Index so directs. Multiple coding should not be used when the classification provides a combination code that clearly identifies all of the elements documented in the diagnosis. When the combination code lacks necessary specificity in describing the manifestation or complication, an additional code should be used as a secondary code.

12.   Late Effects

A late effect is the residual effect (condition produced) after the acute phase of an illness or injury has terminated. There is no time limit on when a late effect code can be used. The residual may be apparent early, such as in cerebrovascular accident cases, or it may occur months or years later, such as that due to a previous injury. Coding of late effects generally requires two codes sequenced in the following order: The condition or nature of the late effect is sequenced first. The late effect code is sequenced second.

Exceptions to the above guidelines are those instances where the late effect code has been expanded (at the fourth and fifth-digit levels) to include the manifestation(s) **or the classification instructs otherwise.** The code for the acute phase of an illness or injury that led to the late effect is never used with a code for the late effect.

13. Impending or Threatened Condition

Code any condition described at the time of discharge as "impending" or "threatened" as follows:

If it did occur, code as confirmed diagnosis.

If it did not occur, reference the Alphabetic Index to determine if the condition has a subentry term for "impending" or "threatened" and also reference main term entries for "Impending" and for "Threatened."

If the subterms are listed, assign the given code.

If the subterms are not listed, code the existing underlying condition(s) and not the condition described as impending or threatened.

14. Reporting Same Diagnosis Code More than Once

Each unique ICD-9-CM diagnosis code may be reported only once for an encounter. This applies to bilateral conditions or two different conditions classified to the same ICD-9-CM diagnosis code.

15. Admissions/Encounters for Rehabilitation

When the purpose for the admission/encounter is rehabilitation, sequence the appropriate V code from category V57, Care involving use of rehabilitation procedures, as the principal/first-listed diagnosis. The code for the condition for which the service is being performed should be reported as an additional diagnosis.

Only one code from category V57 is required. Code V57.89, Other specified rehabilitation procedures, should be assigned if more than one type of rehabilitation is performed during a single encounter. A procedure code should be reported to identify each type of rehabilitation therapy actually performed.

16. Documentation for BMI and Pressure Ulcer Stages

For the Body Mass Index (BMI) and pressure ulcer stage codes, code assignment may be based on medical record documentation from clinicians who are not the patient's provider (i.e., physician or other qualified healthcare practitioner legally accountable for establishing the patient's diagnosis), since this information is typically documented by other clinicians involved in the care of the patient (e.g., a dietitian often documents the BMI and nurses often documents the pressure ulcer stages). However, the associated diagnosis (such as overweight, obesity, or pressure ulcer) must be documented by the patient's provider. If there is conflicting medical record documentation, either from the same clinician or different clinicians, the patient's attending provider should be queried for clarification.

The BMI and pressure ulcer stage codes should only be reported as secondary diagnoses. As with all other secondary diagnosis codes, the BMI and pressure ulcer stage codes should only be assigned when they meet the definition of a reportable additional diagnosis (see Section III, Reporting Additional Diagnoses).

17. Syndromes

Follow the Alphabetic Index guidance when coding syndromes. In the absence of index guidance, assign codes for the documented manifestations of the syndrome.

18. Documentation of Complications of care

Code assignment is based on the provider's documentation of the relationship between the condition and the care or procedure. The guideline extends to any complications of care, regardless of the chapter the code is located in. It is important to note that not all conditions that occur during or following medical care or surgery are classified as complications. There must be a cause-and-effect relationship between the care provided and the condition, and an indication in the documentation that it is a complication. Query the provider for clarification, if the complication is not clearly documented.

C. Chapter-Specific Coding Guidelines

In addition to general coding guidelines, there are guidelines for specific diagnoses and/or conditions in the classification. Unless otherwise indicated, these guidelines apply to all health care settings. Please refer to Section II for guidelines on the selection of principal diagnosis.

1. Chapter 1: Infectious and Parasitic Diseases (001-139)

a. Human Immunodeficiency Virus (HIV) Infections

1) Code only confirmed cases

Code only confirmed cases of HIV infection/illness. This is an exception to the hospital inpatient guideline Section II, H.

In this context, "confirmation" does not require documentation of positive serology or culture for HIV; the provider's diagnostic statement that the patient is HIV positive, or has an HIV-related illness is sufficient.

2) Selection and sequencing of HIV codes

(a) Patient admitted for HIV-related condition

If a patient is admitted for an HIV-related condition, the principal diagnosis should be 042, followed by additional diagnosis codes for all reported HIV-related conditions.

(b) Patient with HIV disease admitted for unrelated condition

If a patient with HIV disease is admitted for an unrelated condition (such as a traumatic injury), the code for the unrelated condition (e.g., the nature of injury code) should be the principal diagnosis. Other diagnoses would be 042 followed by additional diagnosis codes for all reported HIV-related conditions.

(c) Whether the patient is newly diagnosed

Whether the patient is newly diagnosed or has had previous admissions/encounters for HIV conditions is irrelevant to the sequencing decision.

(d) Asymptomatic human immunodeficiency virus

V08 Asymptomatic human immunodeficiency virus [HIV] infection, is to be applied when the patient without any documentation of symptoms is listed as being "HIV positive," "known HIV," "HIV test positive," or similar terminology. Do not use this code if the term "AIDS" is used or if the patient is treated for any HIV-related illness or is described as having any condition(s) resulting from his/her HIV positive status; use 042 in these cases.

(e) Patients with inconclusive HIV serology

Patients with inconclusive HIV serology, but no definitive diagnosis or manifestations of the illness, may be assigned code 795.71, Inconclusive serologic test for Human Immunodeficiency Virus [HIV].

(f) Previously diagnosed HIV-related illness

Patients with any known prior diagnosis of an HIV-related illness should be coded to 042. Once a patient has developed an HIV-related illness, the patient should always be assigned code 042 on every subsequent admission/encounter. Patients previously diagnosed with any HIV illness (042) should never be assigned to 795.71 or V08.

(g) **HIV Infection in Pregnancy, Childbirth and the Puerperium**

During pregnancy, childbirth or the puerperium, a patient admitted (or presenting for a health care encounter) because of an HIV-related illness should receive a principal diagnosis code of 647.6X, Other specified infectious and parasitic diseases in the mother classifiable elsewhere, but complicating the pregnancy, childbirth or the puerperium, followed by 042 and the code(s) for the HIV-related illness(es). Codes from Chapter 15 always take sequencing priority.

Patients with asymptomatic HIV infection status admitted (or presenting for a health care encounter) during pregnancy, childbirth, or the puerperium should receive codes of 647.6X and V08.

(h) **Encounters for testing for HIV**

If a patient is being seen to determine his/her HIV status, use code V73.89, Screening for other specified viral disease. Use code V69.8, Other problems related to lifestyle, as a secondary code if an asymptomatic patient is in a known high risk group for HIV. Should a patient with signs or symptoms or illness, or a confirmed HIV related diagnosis be tested for HIV, code the signs and symptoms or the diagnosis. An additional counseling code V65.44 may be used if counseling is provided during the encounter for the test.

When a patient returns to be informed of his/her HIV test results use code V65.44, HIV counseling, if the results of the test are negative.

If the results are positive but the patient is asymptomatic use code V08, Asymptomatic HIV infection. If the results are positive and the patient is symptomatic use code 042, HIV infection, with codes for the HIV related symptoms or diagnosis. The HIV counseling code may also be used if counseling is provided for patients with positive test results.

b. Septicemia, Systemic Inflammatory Response Syndrome (SIRS), Sepsis, Severe Sepsis, and Septic Shock

1)   SIRS, Septicemia, and Sepsis

      (a)   The terms *septicemia* and *sepsis* are often used interchangeably by providers, however they are not considered synonymous terms. The following descriptions are provided for reference but do not preclude querying the provider for clarification about terms used in the documentation:

          (i) Septicemia generally refers to a systemic disease associated with the presence of pathological microorganisms or toxins in the blood, which can include bacteria, viruses, fungi or other organisms.

          (ii) Systemic inflammatory response syndrome (SIRS) generally refers to the systemic response to infection, trauma/burns, or other insult (such as cancer) with symptoms including fever, tachycardia, tachypnea, and leukocytosis.

          (iii)Sepsis generally refers to SIRS due to infection.

          (iv)Severe sepsis generally refers to sepsis with associated acute organ dysfunction.

      (b)   **The Coding of SIRS, sepsis and severe sepsis**

The coding of SIRS, sepsis and severe sepsis requires a minimum of 2 codes: a code for the underlying cause (such as infection or trauma) and a code from subcategory 995.9 Systemic inflammatory response syndrome (SIRS).

          (i) The code for the underlying cause (such as infection or trauma) must be sequenced before the code from subcategory 995.9 Systemic inflammatory response syndrome (SIRS).

          (ii) Sepsis and severe sepsis require a code for the systemic infection (038.xx, 112.5, etc.) and either code 995.91, Sepsis, or 995.92, Severe sepsis. If the causal organism is not documented, assign code 038.9, Unspecified septicemia.

(iii) Severe sepsis requires additional code(s) for the associated acute organ dysfunction(s).

(iv) If a patient has sepsis with multiple organ dysfunctions, follow the instructions for coding severe sepsis.

(v) Either the term sepsis or SIRS must be documented to assign a code from subcategory 995.9.

(vi) See Section I.C.17.g), Injury and poisoning, for information regarding systemic inflammatory response syndrome (SIRS) due to trauma/burns and other non-infectious processes.

(c)   Due to the complex nature of sepsis and severe sepsis, some cases may require querying the provider prior to assignment of the codes.

2)   Sequencing sepsis and severe sepsis

(a)   **Sepsis and severe sepsis as principal diagnosis**

If sepsis or severe sepsis is present on admission, and meets the definition of principal diagnosis, the systemic infection code (e.g., 038.xx, 112.5, etc) should be assigned as the principal diagnosis, followed by code 995.91, Sepsis, or 995.92, Severe sepsis, as required by the sequencing rules in the Tabular List. Codes from subcategory 995.9 can never be assigned as a principal diagnosis. A code should also be assigned for any localized infection, if present.

If the sepsis or severe sepsis is due to a postprocedural infection, see Section I.C.1.b.10 for guidelines related to sepsis due to postprocedural infection.

(b)   **Sepsis and severe sepsis as secondary diagnoses**

When sepsis or severe sepsis develops during the encounter (it was not present on admission), the systemic infection code and code 995.91 or 995.92 should be assigned as secondary diagnoses.

(c)   **Documentation unclear as to whether sepsis or severe sepsis is present on admission**

Sepsis or severe sepsis may be present on admission but the diagnosis may not be confirmed until sometime after admission. If the documentation is not clear whether the sepsis or severe sepsis was present on admission, the provider should be queried.

3) Sepsis/SIRS with Localized Infection

If the reason for admission is both sepsis, severe sepsis, or SIRS and a localized infection, such as pneumonia or cellulitis, a code for the systemic infection (038.xx, 112.5, etc) should be assigned first, then code 995.91 or 995.92, followed by the code for the localized infection. If the patient is admitted with a localized infection, such as pneumonia, and sepsis/SIRS doesn't develop until after admission, see guideline I.C.1.b.2.b).

If the localized infection is postprocedural, *see Section I.C.1.b.10 for guidelines related to sepsis due to postprocedural infection.*

Note: The term urosepsis is a nonspecific term. If that is the only term documented then only code 599.0 should be assigned based on the default for the term in the ICD-9-CM index, in addition to the code for the causal organism if known.

4) Bacterial Sepsis and Septicemia

In most cases, it will be a code from category 038, Septicemia, that will be used in conjunction with a code from subcategory 995.9 such as the following:

(a) **Streptococcal sepsis**

If the documentation in the record states streptococcal sepsis, codes 038.0, Streptococcal septicemia, and code 995.91 should be used, in that sequence.

(b) **Streptococcal septicemia**

If the documentation states streptococcal septicemia, only code 038.0 should be assigned, however, the provider should be queried whether the patient has sepsis, an infection with SIRS.

5) Acute organ dysfunction that is not clearly associated with the sepsis

If a patient has sepsis and an acute organ dysfunction, but the medical record documentation indicates that the acute organ dysfunction is related to a medical condition other than the sepsis, do not assign code 995.92, Severe sepsis. An acute organ dysfunction must be associated with the sepsis in order to assign the severe sepsis code. If the documentation is not clear as to whether an acute organ dysfunction is related to the sepsis or another medical condition, query the provider.

6) **Septic shock**

    (a) **Sequencing of septic shock and postprocedural septic shock**

Septic shock generally refers to circulatory failure associated with severe sepsis, and, therefore, it represents a type of acute organ dysfunction.

For cases of septic shock, the code for the systemic infection should be sequenced first, followed by codes 995.92, **Severe sepsis** and 785.52, **Septic shock or 998.02, Postoperative septic shock**. Any additional codes for other acute organ dysfunctions should also be assigned. As noted in the sequencing instructions in the Tabular List, the code for septic shock cannot be assigned as a principal diagnosis.

    (b) **Septic shock and postprocedural septic shock without documentation of severe sepsis**

Since septic shock indicates the presence of severe sepsis, code 995.92, Severe sepsis, **can be** assigned with code 785.52, Septic shock, **or code 998.02 Postoperative shock, septic,** even if the term severe sepsis is not documented in the record.

7) **Sepsis and septic shock complicating abortion and pregnancy**

Sepsis and septic shock complicating abortion, ectopic pregnancy, and molar pregnancy are classified to category codes in Chapter 11 (630-639).
See section I.C.11.i.7. for information on the coding of puerperal sepsis.

8) **Negative or inconclusive blood cultures**

Negative or inconclusive blood cultures do not preclude a diagnosis of septicemia or sepsis in patients with clinical evidence of the condition, however, the provider should be queried.

9) **Newborn sepsis**

See Section I.C.15.j for information on the coding of newborn sepsis.

10) Sepsis due to a Postprocedural Infection

   (a) Documentation of causal relationship

   As with all postprocedural complications, code assignment is based on the provider's documentation of the relationship between the infection and the procedure.

   (b) Sepsis due to postprocedural infection

   In cases of postprocedural sepsis, the complication code, such as code 998.59, Other postoperative infection, or 674.3x, Other complications of obstetrical surgical wounds should be coded first followed by the appropriate sepsis codes (systemic infection code and either code 995.91 or 995.92). An additional code(s) for any acute organ dysfunction should also be assigned for cases of severe sepsis.

   See Section see Section I.C.1.b.6 if the sepsis or severe sepsis results in postprocedural septic shock.

   (c) Postprocedural infection and postprocedural septic shock

   In cases where a postprocedural infection has occurred and has resulted in severe sepsis and postprocedural septic shock, the code for the precipitating complication such as code 998.59, Other postoperative infection, or 674.3x, Other complications of obstetrical surgical wounds should be coded first followed by the appropriate sepsis codes (systemic infection code and code 995.92). Code 998.02, Postoperative septic shock, should be assigned as an additional code. In cases of severe sepsis, an additional code(s) for any acute organ dysfunction should also be assigned.

11) External cause of injury codes with SIRS

   Refer to Section I.C.19.a.7 for instruction on the use of external cause of injury codes with codes for SIRS resulting from trauma.

12) Sepsis and Severe Sepsis Associated with Non-infectious Process

   In some cases, a non-infectious process, such as trauma, may lead to an infection which can result in sepsis or severe sepsis. If sepsis or severe sepsis is documented as associated with a non-infectious condition, such as a burn or serious injury, and this condition meets the definition for principal diagnosis, the code for the non-infectious condition should be sequenced first, followed by the code for the systemic infection and either code 995.91, Sepsis, or 995.92, Severe sepsis. Additional codes for any associated acute organ dysfunction(s) should also be assigned for cases of severe sepsis. If the sepsis or severe sepsis meets the definition of principal diagnosis, the systemic infection and sepsis codes should be sequenced before the non-infectious condition. When both the associated non-infectious condition and the sepsis or severe sepsis meet the definition of principal diagnosis, either may be assigned as principal diagnosis.

See Section I.C.1.b.2.a. for guidelines pertaining to sepsis or severe sepsis as the principal diagnosis.

Only one code from subcategory 995.9 should be assigned. Therefore, when a non-infectious condition leads to an infection resulting in sepsis or severe sepsis, assign either code 995.91 or 995.92. Do not additionally assign code 995.93, Systemic inflammatory response syndrome due to non-infectious process without acute organ dysfunction, or 995.94, Systemic inflammatory response syndrome with acute organ dysfunction.

See Section I.C.17.g for information on the coding of SIRS due to trauma/burns or other non-infectious disease processes.

c. **Methicillin Resistant *Staphylococcus aureus* (MRSA) Conditions**

1) **Selection and sequencing of MRSA codes**

   (a) **Combination codes for MRSA infection**
   When a patient is diagnosed with an infection that is due to methicillin resistant *Staphylococcus aureus* (MRSA), and that infection has a combination code that includes the causal organism (e.g., septicemia, pneumonia) assign the appropriate code for the condition (e.g., code 038.12, Methicillin resistant Staphylococcus aureus septicemia or code 482.42, Methicillin resistant pneumonia due to Staphylococcus aureus). Do not assign code 041.12, Methicillin resistant Staphylococcus aureus, as an additional code because the code includes the type of infection and the

MRSA organism. Do not assign a code from subcategory V09.0, Infection with microorganisms resistant to penicillins, as an additional diagnosis.

See Section C.1.b.1 for instructions on coding and sequencing of septicemia.

(b) **Other codes for MRSA infection**

When there is documentation of a current infection (e.g., wound infection, stitch abscess, urinary tract infection) due to MRSA, and that infection does not have a combination code that includes the causal organism, select the appropriate code to identify the condition along with code 041.12, Methicillin resistant Staphylococcus aureus, for the MRSA infection. Do not assign a code from subcategory V09.0, Infection with microorganisms resistant to penicillins.

(c) **Methicillin susceptible Staphylococcus aureus (MSSA) and MRSA colonization**

The condition or state of being colonized or carrying MSSA or MRSA is called colonization or carriage, while an individual person is described as being colonized or being a carrier. Colonization means that MSSA or MSRA is present on or in the body without necessarily causing illness. A positive MRSA colonization test might be documented by the provider as "MRSA screen positive" or "MRSA nasal swab positive".

Assign code V02.54, Carrier or suspected carrier, Methicillin resistant Staphylococcus aureus, for patients documented as having MRSA colonization. Assign code V02.53, Carrier or suspected carrier, Methicillin susceptible Staphylococcus aureus, for patient documented as having MSSA colonization. Colonization is not necessarily indicative of a disease process or as the cause of a specific condition the patient may have unless documented as such by the provider.

Code V02.59, Other specified bacterial diseases, should be assigned for other types of staphylococcal colonization (e.g., S. *epidermidis, S. saprophyticus).* Code V02.59 should not be assigned for colonization with any type of *Staphylococcus aureus* (MRSA, MSSA).

(d) **MRSA colonization and infection**

If a patient is documented as having both MRSA colonization and infection during a hospital admission, code V02.54, Carrier or suspected carrier, Methicillin resistant *Staphylococcus aureus*, and a code for the MRSA infection may both be assigned.

2. Chapter 2: Neoplasms (140-239)

General guidelines

Chapter 2 of the ICD-9-CM contains the codes for most benign and all malignant neoplasms. Certain benign neoplasms, such as prostatic adenomas, may be found in the specific body system chapters. To properly code a neoplasm it is necessary to determine from the record if the neoplasm is benign, in-situ, malignant, or of uncertain histologic behavior. If malignant, any secondary (metastatic) sites should also be determined.

The neoplasm table in the Alphabetic Index should be referenced first. However, if the histological term is documented, that term should be referenced first, rather than going immediately to the Neoplasm Table, in order to determine which column in the Neoplasm Table is appropriate. For example, if the documentation indicates "adenoma," refer to the term in the Alphabetic Index to review the entries under this term and the instructional note to "see also neoplasm, by site, benign." The table provides the proper code based on the type of neoplasm and the site. It is important to select the proper column in the table that corresponds to the type of neoplasm. The tabular should then be referenced to verify that the correct code has been selected from the table and that a more specific site code does not exist. *See Section I. C. 18.d.4. for information regarding V codes for genetic susceptibility to cancer.*

a. Treatment directed at the malignancy

If the treatment is directed at the malignancy, designate the malignancy as the principal diagnosis.

The only exception to this guideline is if a patient admission/encounter is solely for the administration of chemotherapy, immunotherapy or radiation therapy, assign the appropriate V58.x code as the first-listed or principal diagnosis, and the diagnosis or problem for which the service is being performed as a secondary diagnosis.

b. Treatment of secondary site

When a patient is admitted because of a primary neoplasm with metastasis and treatment is directed toward the secondary site only, the secondary neoplasm is designated as the principal diagnosis even though the primary malignancy is still present.

c. Coding and sequencing of complications

Coding and sequencing of complications associated with the malignancies or with the therapy thereof are subject to the following guidelines:

1) Anemia associated with malignancy

When admission/encounter is for management of an anemia associated with the malignancy, and the treatment is only for anemia, the appropriate anemia code (such as code 285.22, Anemia in neoplastic disease) is designated as the principal diagnosis and is followed by the appropriate code(s) for the malignancy.

Code 285.22 may also be used as a secondary code if the patient suffers from anemia and is being treated for the malignancy.

If anemia in neoplastic disease and anemia due to antineoplastic chemotherapy are both documented, **assign codes for both conditions.**

2) Anemia associated with chemotherapy, immunotherapy and radiation therapy

When the admission/encounter is for management of an anemia associated with chemotherapy, immunotherapy or radiotherapy and the only treatment is for the anemia, the anemia is sequenced first. The appropriate neoplasm code should be assigned as an additional code.

3) Management of dehydration due to the malignancy

When the admission/encounter is for management of dehydration due to the malignancy or the therapy, or a combination of both, and only the dehydration is being treated (intravenous rehydration), the dehydration is sequenced first, followed by the code(s) for the malignancy.

4) Treatment of a complication resulting from a surgical procedure

When the admission/encounter is for treatment of a complication resulting from a surgical procedure, designate the complication as the principal or first-listed diagnosis if treatment is directed at resolving the complication.

d. Primary malignancy previously excised

When a primary malignancy has been previously excised or eradicated from its site and there is no further treatment directed to that site and there is no evidence of any existing primary malignancy, a code from category V10, Personal history of malignant neoplasm, should be used to indicate the former site of the malignancy. Any mention of extension, invasion, or metastasis to another site is coded as a secondary malignant neoplasm to that site. The secondary site may be the principal or first-listed with the V10 code used as a secondary code.

e. Admissions/Encounters involving chemotherapy, immunotherapy and radiation therapy

1) Episode of care involves surgical removal of neoplasm

When an episode of care involves the surgical removal of a neoplasm, primary or secondary site, followed by adjunct chemotherapy or radiation treatment during the same episode of care, the neoplasm code should be assigned as principal or first-listed diagnosis, using codes in the 140-198 series or where appropriate in the 200-203 series.

2) Patient admission/encounter solely for administration of chemotherapy, immunotherapy and radiation therapy

If a patient admission/encounter is solely for the administration of chemotherapy, immunotherapy or radiation therapy assign code V58.0, Encounter for radiation therapy, or V58.11, Encounter for antineoplastic chemotherapy, or V58.12, Encounter for antineoplastic immunotherapy as the first-listed or principal diagnosis. If a patient receives more than one of these therapies during the same admission more than one of these codes may be assigned, in any sequence.

The malignancy for which the therapy is being administered should be assigned as a secondary diagnosis.

3) Patient admitted for radiotherapy/chemotherapy and immunotherapy and develops complications

When a patient is admitted for the purpose of radiotherapy, immunotherapy or chemotherapy and develops complications such as uncontrolled nausea and vomiting or dehydration, the principal or first-listed diagnosis is V58.0, Encounter for radiotherapy, or V58.11, Encounter for antineoplastic chemotherapy, or V58.12, Encounter for antineoplastic immunotherapy followed by any codes for the complications.

f. Admission/encounter to determine extent of malignancy

When the reason for admission/encounter is to determine the extent of the malignancy, or for a procedure such as paracentesis or thoracentesis, the primary malignancy or appropriate metastatic site is designated as the principal or first-listed diagnosis, even though chemotherapy or radiotherapy is administered.

g. Symptoms, signs, and ill-defined conditions listed in Chapter 16 associated with neoplasms

Symptoms, signs, and ill-defined conditions listed in Chapter 16 characteristic of, or associated with, an existing primary or secondary site malignancy cannot be used to replace the malignancy as principal or first-listed diagnosis, regardless of the number of admissions or encounters for treatment and care of the neoplasm.

h. Admission/encounter for pain control/management

See Section I.C.6.a.5 for information on coding admission/encounter for pain control/management.

i. Malignant neoplasm associated with transplanted organ

A malignant neoplasm of a transplanted organ should be coded as a transplant complication. Assign first the appropriate code from subcategory 996.8, Complications of transplanted organ, followed by code 199.2, Malignant neoplasm associated with transplanted organ. Use an additional code for the specific malignancy.

3. Chapter 3: Endocrine, Nutritional, and Metabolic Diseases and Immunity Disorders (240-279)

a. Diabetes mellitus

Codes under category 250, Diabetes mellitus, identify complications/manifestations associated with diabetes mellitus. A fifth-digit is required for all category 250 codes to identify the type of diabetes mellitus and whether the diabetes is controlled or uncontrolled.

See I.C.3.a.7 for secondary diabetes

1) Fifth-digits for category 250:

The following are the fifth-digits for the codes under category 250:

0   type II or unspecified type, not stated as uncontrolled
1   type I, [juvenile type], not stated as uncontrolled
2   type II or unspecified type, uncontrolled

3   type I, [juvenile type], uncontrolled

The age of a patient is not the sole determining factor, though most type I diabetics develop the condition before reaching puberty. For this reason type I diabetes mellitus is also referred to as juvenile diabetes.

2)   Type of diabetes mellitus not documented

If the type of diabetes mellitus is not documented in the medical record the default is type II.

3)   Diabetes mellitus and the use of insulin

All type I diabetics must use insulin to replace what their bodies do not produce. However, the use of insulin does not mean that a patient is a type I diabetic. Some patients with type II diabetes mellitus are unable to control their blood sugar through diet and oral medication alone and do require insulin. If the documentation in a medical record does not indicate the type of diabetes but does indicate that the patient uses insulin, the appropriate fifth-digit for type II must be used. For type II patients who routinely use insulin, code V58.67, Long-term (current) use of insulin, should also be assigned to indicate that the patient uses insulin. Code V58.67 should not be assigned if insulin is given temporarily to bring a type II patient's blood sugar under control during an encounter.

4)   Assigning and sequencing diabetes codes and associated conditions

When assigning codes for diabetes and its associated conditions, the code(s) from category 250 must be sequenced before the codes for the associated conditions. The diabetes codes and the secondary codes that correspond to them are paired codes that follow the etiology/manifestation convention of the classification *(See Section I.A.6., Etiology/manifestation convention)*. Assign as many codes from category 250 as needed to identify all of the associated conditions that the patient has. The corresponding secondary codes are listed under each of the diabetes codes.

(a)   Diabetic retinopathy/diabetic macular edema

Diabetic macular edema, code 362.07, is only present with diabetic retinopathy. Another code from subcategory 362.0, Diabetic retinopathy, must be used with code 362.07. Codes under subcategory 362.0 are diabetes manifestation codes, so they must be used following the appropriate diabetes code.

5) **Diabetes mellitus in pregnancy and gestational diabetes**

   (a) For diabetes mellitus complicating pregnancy, see Section I.C.11.f., Diabetes mellitus in pregnancy.

   (b) For gestational diabetes, see Section I.C.11, g., Gestational diabetes.

6) **Insulin pump malfunction**

   (a) **Underdose of insulin due insulin pump failure**

   An underdose of insulin due to an insulin pump failure should be assigned 996.57, Mechanical complication due to insulin pump, as the principal or first listed code, followed by the appropriate diabetes mellitus code based on documentation.

   (b) **Overdose of insulin due to insulin pump failure**

   The principal or first listed code for an encounter due to an insulin pump malfunction resulting in an overdose of insulin, should also be 996.57, Mechanical complication due to insulin pump, followed by code 962.3, Poisoning by insulins and antidiabetic agents, and the appropriate diabetes mellitus code based on documentation.

7) **Secondary Diabetes Mellitus**

   Codes under category 249, Secondary diabetes mellitus, identify complications/manifestations associated with secondary diabetes mellitus. Secondary diabetes is always caused by another condition or event (e.g., cystic fibrosis, malignant neoplasm of pancreas, pancreatectomy, adverse effect of drug, or poisoning).

   (a) **Fifth-digits for category 249:**

   A fifth-digit is required for all category 249 codes to identify whether the diabetes is controlled or uncontrolled.

   (b) **Secondary diabetes mellitus and the use of insulin**

   For patients who routinely use insulin, code V58.67, Long-term (current) use of insulin, should also be assigned. Code V58.67 should not be assigned if insulin is given temporarily to bring a patient's blood sugar under control during an encounter.

(c)   **Assigning and sequencing secondary diabetes codes and associated conditions**

When assigning codes for secondary diabetes and its associated conditions (e.g. renal manifestations), the code(s) from category 249 must be sequenced before the codes for the associated conditions. The secondary diabetes codes and the diabetic manifestation codes that correspond to them are paired codes that follow the etiology/manifestation convention of the classification. Assign as many codes from category 249 as needed to identify all of the associated conditions that the patient has. The corresponding codes for the associated conditions are listed under each of the secondary diabetes codes. For example, secondary diabetes with diabetic nephrosis is assigned to code 249.40, followed by 581.81.

(d)   **Assigning and sequencing secondary diabetes codes and its causes**

The sequencing of the secondary diabetes codes in relationship to codes for the cause of the diabetes is based on the reason for the encounter, applicable ICD-9-CM sequencing conventions, and chapter-specific guidelines.

If a patient is seen for treatment of the secondary diabetes or one of its associated conditions, a code from category 249 is sequenced as the principal or first-listed diagnosis, with the cause of the secondary diabetes (e.g. cystic fibrosis) sequenced as an additional diagnosis.

If, however, the patient is seen for the treatment of the condition causing the secondary diabetes (e.g., malignant neoplasm of pancreas), the code for the cause of the secondary diabetes should be sequenced as the principal or first-listed diagnosis followed by a code from category 249.

   (i)   **Secondary diabetes mellitus due to pancreatectomy**

For postpancreatectomy diabetes mellitus (lack of insulin due to the surgical removal of all or part of the pancreas), assign code 251.3, Postsurgical hypoinsulinemia. Assign a code from subcategory 249, Secondary diabetes mellitus and a code from subcategory V88.1, Acquired absence of pancreas as additional codes. Code also any diabetic manifestations (e.g. diabetic nephrosis 581.81).

(ii) Secondary diabetes due to drugs

Secondary diabetes may be caused by an adverse effect of correctly administered medications, poisoning or late effect of poisoning.
See section I.C.17.e for coding of adverse effects and poisoning, and section I.C.19 for E code reporting.

4. Chapter 4: Diseases of Blood and Blood Forming Organs (280-289)

a. Anemia of chronic disease

Subcategory 285.2, Anemia in chronic illness, has codes for anemia in chronic kidney disease, code 285.21; anemia in neoplastic disease, code 285.22; and anemia in other chronic illness, code 285.29. These codes can be used as the principal/first listed code if the reason for the encounter is to treat the anemia. They may also be used as secondary codes if treatment of the anemia is a component of an encounter, but not the primary reason for the encounter. When using a code from subcategory 285 it is also necessary to use the code for the chronic condition causing the anemia.

1) Anemia in chronic kidney disease

When assigning code 285.21, Anemia in chronic kidney disease, it is also necessary to assign a code from category 585, Chronic kidney disease, to indicate the stage of chronic kidney disease.
See I.C.10.a. Chronic kidney disease (CKD).

2) Anemia in neoplastic disease

When assigning code 285.22, Anemia in neoplastic disease, it is also necessary to assign the neoplasm code that is responsible for the anemia. Code 285.22 is for use for anemia that is due to the malignancy, not for anemia due to antineoplastic chemotherapy drugs. Assign **the appropriate code** for anemia due to antineoplastic chemotherapy.
See I.C.2.c.1 Anemia associated with malignancy.
See I.C.2.c.2 Anemia associated with chemotherapy, immunotherapy and radiation therapy.

5. **Chapter 5: Mental Disorders (290-319)**

Reserved for future guideline expansion

6. **Chapter 6: Diseases of Nervous System and Sense Organs (320-389)**

a. Pain - Category 338

1) General coding information

Codes in category 338 may be used in conjunction with codes from other categories and chapters to provide more detail about acute or chronic pain and neoplasm-related pain, unless otherwise indicated below.

If the pain is not specified as acute or chronic, do not assign codes from category 338, except for post-thoracotomy pain, postoperative pain, neoplasm related pain, or central pain syndrome.

A code from subcategories 338.1 and 338.2 should not be assigned if the underlying (definitive) diagnosis is known, unless the reason for the encounter is pain control/ management and not management of the underlying condition.

(a) Category 338 Codes as Principal or First-Listed Diagnosis

Category 338 codes are acceptable as principal diagnosis or the first-listed code:

- When pain control or pain management is the reason for the admission/encounter (e.g., a patient with displaced intervertebral disc, nerve impingement and severe back pain presents for injection of steroid into the spinal canal). The underlying cause of the pain should be reported as an additional diagnosis, if known.

- When an admission or encounter is for a procedure aimed at treating the underlying condition (e.g., spinal fusion, kyphoplasty), a code for the underlying condition (e.g., vertebral fracture, spinal stenosis) should be assigned as the principal diagnosis. No code from category 338 should be assigned.

- When a patient is admitted for the insertion of a neurostimulator for pain control, assign the appropriate pain code as the principal or first listed diagnosis. When an admission or encounter is for a procedure aimed at treating the underlying condition and a neurostimulator is inserted for pain control during the same admission/encounter, a code for the underlying condition should be assigned as the principal diagnosis and the appropriate pain code should be assigned as a secondary diagnosis.

(b) **Use of Category 338 Codes in Conjunction with Site Specific Pain Codes**

(i) Assigning Category 338 Codes and Site-Specific Pain Codes

Codes from category 338 may be used in conjunction with codes that identify the site of pain (including codes from chapter 16) if the category 338 code provides additional information. For example, if the code describes the site of the pain, but does not fully describe whether the pain is acute or chronic, then both codes should be assigned.

(ii) Sequencing of Category 338 Codes with Site-Specific Pain Codes

The sequencing of category 338 codes with site-specific pain codes (including chapter 16 codes), is dependent on the circumstances of the encounter/admission as follows:

- If the encounter is for pain control or pain management, assign the code from category 338 followed by the code identifying the specific site of pain (e.g., encounter for pain management for acute neck pain from trauma is assigned code 338.11, Acute pain due to trauma, followed by code 723.1, Cervicalgia, to identify the site of pain).

- If the encounter is for any other reason except pain control or pain management, and a related definitive diagnosis has not been established (confirmed) by the provider, assign the code for the specific site of pain first, followed by the appropriate code from category 338.

2) **Pain due to devices, implants and grafts**

Pain associated with devices, implants or grafts left in a surgical site (for example painful hip prosthesis) is assigned to the appropriate code(s) found in Chapter 17, Injury and Poisoning. Use additional code(s) from category 338 to identify acute or chronic pain due to presence of the device, implant or graft (338.18-338.19 or 338.28-338.29).

3) **Postoperative Pain**

Post-thoracotomy pain and other postoperative pain are classified to subcategories 338.1 and 338.2, depending on whether the pain is acute or chronic. The default for post-thoracotomy and other postoperative pain not specified as acute or chronic is the code for the acute form.

> Routine or expected postoperative pain immediately after surgery should not be coded.

(a) **Postoperative pain not associated with specific postoperative complication**

Postoperative pain not associated with a specific postoperative complication is assigned to the appropriate postoperative pain code in category 338.

(b) **Postoperative pain associated with specific postoperative complication**

Postoperative pain associated with a specific postoperative complication (such as painful wire sutures) is assigned to the appropriate code(s) found in Chapter 17, Injury and Poisoning. If appropriate, use additional code(s) from category 338 to identify acute or chronic pain (338.18 or 338.28). If pain control/management is the reason for the encounter, a code from category 338 should be assigned as the principal or first-listed diagnosis in accordance with *Section I.C.6.a.1.a above.*

(c) **Postoperative pain as principal or first-listed diagnosis**

Postoperative pain may be reported as the principal or first-listed diagnosis when the stated reason for the admission/encounter is documented as postoperative pain control/management.

(d) **Postoperative pain as secondary diagnosis**

Postoperative pain may be reported as a secondary diagnosis code when a patient presents for outpatient surgery and develops an unusual or inordinate amount of postoperative pain.

The provider's documentation should be used to guide the coding of postoperative pain, as well as *Section III. Reporting Additional Diagnoses* and *Section IV. Diagnostic Coding and Reporting in the Outpatient Setting.*

See Section II.I.2 for information on sequencing of diagnoses for patients admitted to hospital inpatient care following post-operative observation.

See Section II.J for information on sequencing of diagnoses for patients admitted to hospital inpatient care from outpatient surgery.

See Section IV.A.2 for information on sequencing of diagnoses for patients admitted for observation.

4)   **Chronic pain**

Chronic pain is classified to subcategory 338.2. There is no time frame defining when pain becomes chronic pain. The provider's documentation should be used to guide use of these codes.

5)   **Neoplasm Related Pain**

Code 338.3 is assigned to pain documented as being related, associated or due to cancer, primary or secondary malignancy, or tumor. This code is assigned regardless of whether the pain is acute or chronic.

This code may be assigned as the principal or first-listed code when the stated reason for the admission/encounter is documented as pain control/pain management. The underlying neoplasm should be reported as an additional diagnosis.

When the reason for the admission/encounter is management of the neoplasm and the pain associated with the neoplasm is also documented, code 338.3 may be assigned as an additional diagnosis.

See Section I.C.2 for instructions on the sequencing of neoplasms for all other stated reasons for the admission/encounter (except for pain control/pain management).

6) **Chronic pain syndrome**

This condition is different than the term "chronic pain," and therefore this code should only be used when the provider has specifically documented this condition.

b. Glaucoma

1) **Glaucoma**

For types of glaucoma classified to subcategories 365.1-365.6, an additional code should be assigned from subcategory 365.7, Glaucoma stage, to identify the glaucoma stage. Codes from 365.7, Glaucoma stage, may not be assigned as a principal or first-listed diagnosis.

2) **Bilateral glaucoma with same stage**

When a patient has bilateral glaucoma and both are documented as being the same type and stage, report only the code for the type of glaucoma and one code for the stage.

3) **Bilateral glaucoma stage with different stages**

When a patient has bilateral glaucoma and each eye is documented as having a different stage, assign one code for the type of glaucoma and one code for the highest glaucoma stage.

4) **Bilateral glaucoma with different types and different stages**

When a patient has bilateral glaucoma and each eye is documented as having a different type and a different stage, assign one code for each type of glaucoma and one code for the highest glaucoma stage.

5) **Patient admitted with glaucoma and stage evolves during the admission**

If a patient is admitted with glaucoma and the stage progresses during the admission, assign the code for highest stage documented.

6) **Indeterminate stage glaucoma**

Assignment of code 365.74, Indeterminate stage glaucoma, should be based on the clinical documentation. Code 365.74 is used for glaucomas whose stage cannot be clinically determined. This code should not be confused with code 365.70, Glaucoma stage, unspecified. Code

365.70 should be assigned when there is no documentation regarding the stage of the glaucoma.

7. Chapter 7: Diseases of Circulatory System (390-459)

a. Hypertension

Hypertension Table

The Hypertension Table, found under the main term, "Hypertension", in the Alphabetic Index, contains a complete listing of all conditions due to or associated with hypertension and classifies them according to malignant, benign, and unspecified.

1) Hypertension, Essential, or NOS

Assign hypertension (arterial) (essential) (primary) (systemic) (NOS) to category code 401 with the appropriate fourth digit to indicate malignant (.0), benign (.1), or unspecified (.9). Do not use either .0 malignant or .1 benign unless medical record documentation supports such a designation.

2) Hypertension with Heart Disease

Heart conditions (425.8, 429.0-429.3, 429.8, 429.9) are assigned to a code from category 402 when a causal relationship is stated (due to hypertension) or implied (hypertensive). Use an additional code from category 428 to identify the type of heart failure in those patients with heart failure. More than one code from category 428 may be assigned if the patient has systolic or diastolic failure and congestive heart failure.

The same heart conditions (425.8, 429.0-429.3, 429.8, 429.9) with hypertension, but without a stated causal relationship, are coded separately. Sequence according to the circumstances of the admission/encounter.

3) Hypertensive Chronic Kidney Disease

Assign codes from category 403, Hypertensive chronic kidney disease, when conditions classified to category 585 or code 587 are present with hypertension. Unlike hypertension with heart disease, ICD-9-CM presumes a cause-and-effect relationship and classifies chronic kidney disease (CKD) with hypertension as hypertensive chronic kidney disease.

Fifth digits for category 403 should be assigned as follows:
- 0 with CKD stage I through stage IV, or unspecified.
- 1 with CKD stage V or end stage renal disease.

The appropriate code from category 585, Chronic kidney disease, should be used as a secondary code with a code from category 403 to identify the stage of chronic kidney disease.

See Section I.C.10.a for information on the coding of chronic kidney disease.

4) **Hypertensive Heart and Chronic Kidney Disease**

Assign codes from combination category 404, Hypertensive heart and chronic kidney disease, when both hypertensive kidney disease and hypertensive heart disease are stated in the diagnosis. Assume a relationship between the hypertension and the chronic kidney disease, whether or not the condition is so designated. Assign an additional code from category 428, to identify the type of heart failure. More than one code from category 428 may be assigned if the patient has systolic or diastolic failure and congestive heart failure.

Fifth digits for category 404 should be assigned as follows:
- 0 without heart failure and with chronic kidney disease (CKD) stage I through stage IV, or unspecified
- 1 with heart failure and with CKD stage I through stage IV, or unspecified
- 2 without heart failure and with CKD stage V or end stage renal disease
- 3 with heart failure and with CKD stage V or end stage renal disease

The appropriate code from category 585, Chronic kidney disease, should be used as a secondary code with a code from category 404 to identify the stage of kidney disease.
See Section I.C.10.a for information on the coding of chronic kidney disease.

5) **Hypertensive Cerebrovascular Disease**

First assign codes from 430-438, Cerebrovascular disease, then the appropriate hypertension code from categories 401-405.

6) **Hypertensive Retinopathy**

Two codes are necessary to identify the condition. First assign the code from subcategory 362.11, Hypertensive retinopathy, then the appropriate code from categories 401-405 to indicate the type of hypertension.

7) **Hypertension, Secondary**

Two codes are required: one to identify the underlying etiology and one from category 405 to identify the hypertension.

Sequencing of codes is determined by the reason for admission/encounter.

8)   Hypertension, Transient

Assign code 796.2, Elevated blood pressure reading without diagnosis of hypertension, unless patient has an established diagnosis of hypertension. Assign code 642.3x for transient hypertension of pregnancy.

9)   Hypertension, Controlled

Assign appropriate code from categories 401-405. This diagnostic statement usually refers to an existing state of hypertension under control by therapy.

10)   Hypertension, Uncontrolled

Uncontrolled hypertension may refer to untreated hypertension or hypertension not responding to current therapeutic regimen. In either case, assign the appropriate code from categories 401-405 to designate the stage and type of hypertension. Code to the type of hypertension.

11)   Elevated Blood Pressure

For a statement of elevated blood pressure without further specificity, assign code 796.2, Elevated blood pressure reading without diagnosis of hypertension, rather than a code from category 401.

b. Cerebral infarction/stroke/cerebrovascular accident (CVA)

The terms stroke and CVA are often used interchangeably to refer to a cerebral infarction. The terms stroke, CVA, and cerebral infarction NOS are all indexed to the default code 434.91, Cerebral artery occlusion, unspecified, with infarction.

Additional code(s) should be assigned for any neurologic deficits associated with the acute CVA, regardless of whether or not the neurologic deficit resolves prior to discharge.

See Section I.C.18.d.3 for information on coding status post administration of tPA in a different facility within the last 24 hours.

c. Postoperative cerebrovascular accident

A cerebrovascular hemorrhage or infarction that occurs as a result of medical intervention is coded to 997.02, Iatrogenic cerebrovascular infarction or hemorrhage. Medical record documentation should clearly specify the cause- and-effect relationship between the medical intervention and the cerebrovascular accident in order to assign this code. A secondary code from the code range 430-432 or from a code from subcategories 433 or 434 with a fifth digit of "1" should also be used to identify the type of hemorrhage or infarct.

This guideline conforms to the use additional code note instruction at category 997. Code 436, Acute, but ill-defined, cerebrovascular disease, should not be used as a secondary code with code 997.02.

d. Late Effects of Cerebrovascular Disease

1) **Category 438, Late Effects of Cerebrovascular disease**

   Category 438 is used to indicate conditions classifiable to categories 430-437 as the causes of late effects (neurologic deficits), themselves classified elsewhere. These "late effects" include neurologic deficits that persist after initial onset of conditions classifiable to 430-437. The neurologic deficits caused by cerebrovascular disease may be present from the onset or may arise at any time after the onset of the condition classifiable to 430-437.

   Codes in category 438 are only for use for late effects of cerebrovascular disease, not for neurologic deficits associated with an acute CVA.

2) **Codes from category 438 with codes from 430-437**

   Codes from category 438 may be assigned on a health care record with codes from 430-437, if the patient has a current cerebrovascular accident (CVA) and deficits from an old CVA.

3) **Code V12.54**

   Assign code V12.54, Transient ischemic attack (TIA), and cerebral infarction without residual deficits (and not a code from category 438) as an additional code for history of cerebrovascular disease when no neurologic deficits are present.

e. Acute myocardial infarction (AMI)

1) **ST elevation myocardial infarction (STEMI) and non ST elevation myocardial infarction (NSTEMI)**

   The ICD-9-CM codes for acute myocardial infarction (AMI) identify the site, such as anterolateral wall or true posterior wall. Subcategories 410.0-410.6 and 410.8 are used for ST elevation myocardial infarction (STEMI). Subcategory 410.7, Subendocardial infarction, is used for non ST elevation myocardial infarction (NSTEMI) and nontransmural MIs.

2) **Acute myocardial infarction, unspecified**

Subcategory 410.9 is the default for the unspecified term acute myocardial infarction. If only STEMI or transmural MI without the site is documented, query the provider as to the site, or assign a code from subcategory 410.9.

3) **AMI documented as nontransmural or subendocardial but site provided**

If an AMI is documented as nontransmural or subendocardial, but the site is provided, it is still coded as a subendocardial AMI. If NSTEMI evolves to STEMI, assign the STEMI code. If STEMI converts to NSTEMI due to thrombolytic therapy, it is still coded as STEMI.

See Section I.C.18.d.3 for information on coding status post administration of tPA in a different facility within the last 24 hours.

8. Chapter 8: Diseases of Respiratory System (460-519)

See I.C.17.f. for ventilator-associated pneumonia.

a. Chronic Obstructive Pulmonary Disease [COPD] and Asthma

1) **Conditions that comprise COPD and Asthma**

The conditions that comprise COPD are obstructive chronic bronchitis, subcategory 491.2, and emphysema, category 492. All asthma codes are under category 493, Asthma. Code 496, Chronic airway obstruction, not elsewhere classified, is a nonspecific code that should only be used when the documentation in a medical record does not specify the type of COPD being treated.

2) **Acute exacerbation of chronic obstructive bronchitis and asthma**

The codes for chronic obstructive bronchitis and asthma distinguish between uncomplicated cases and those in acute exacerbation. An acute exacerbation is a worsening or a decompensation of a chronic condition. An acute exacerbation is not equivalent to an infection superimposed on a chronic condition, though an exacerbation may be triggered by an infection.

3) Overlapping nature of the conditions that comprise COPD and asthma

Due to the overlapping nature of the conditions that make up COPD and asthma, there are many variations in the way these conditions are documented. Code selection must be based on the terms as documented. When selecting the correct code for the documented type of COPD and asthma, it is essential to first review the index, and then verify the code in the tabular list. There are many instructional notes under the different COPD subcategories and codes. It is important that all such notes be reviewed to assure correct code assignment.

4) Acute exacerbation of asthma and status asthmaticus

An acute exacerbation of asthma is an increased severity of the asthma symptoms, such as wheezing and shortness of breath. Status asthmaticus refers to a patient's failure to respond to therapy administered during an asthmatic episode and is a life threatening complication that requires emergency care. If status asthmaticus is documented by the provider with any type of COPD or with acute bronchitis, the status asthmaticus should be sequenced first. It supersedes any type of COPD including that with acute exacerbation or acute bronchitis. It is inappropriate to assign an asthma code with 5th digit 2, with acute exacerbation, together with an asthma code with 5th digit 1, with status asthmatics. Only the 5th digit 1 should be assigned.

b. Chronic Obstructive Pulmonary Disease [COPD] and Bronchitis

1) Acute bronchitis with COPD

Acute bronchitis, code 466.0, is due to an infectious organism. When acute bronchitis is documented with COPD, code 491.22, Obstructive chronic bronchitis with acute bronchitis, should be assigned. It is not necessary to also assign code 466.0. If a medical record documents acute bronchitis with COPD with acute exacerbation, only code 491.22 should be assigned. The acute bronchitis included in code 491.22 supersedes the acute exacerbation. If a medical record documents COPD with acute exacerbation without mention of acute bronchitis, only code 491.21 should be assigned.

c. Acute Respiratory Failure

1) Acute respiratory failure as principal diagnosis

Acute respiratory failure, may be assigned as a principal diagnosis when it is the condition established after study to be chiefly responsible for occasioning the admission to the hospital, and the selection is supported by the Alphabetic Index and Tabular List. However, chapter-specific coding guidelines (such as obstetrics, poisoning, HIV, newborn) that provide sequencing direction take precedence.

2) Acute respiratory failure as secondary diagnosis

Respiratory failure may be listed as a secondary diagnosis if it occurs after admission, or if it is present on admission, but does not meet the definition of principal diagnosis.

3) Sequencing of acute respiratory failure and another acute condition

When a patient is admitted with respiratory failure and another acute condition, (e.g., myocardial infarction, cerebrovascular accident, aspiration pneumonia), the principal diagnosis will not be the same in every situation. This applies whether the other acute condition is a respiratory or nonrespiratory condition. Selection of the principal diagnosis will be dependent on the circumstances of admission. If both the respiratory failure and the other acute condition are equally responsible for occasioning the admission to the hospital, and there are no chapter-specific sequencing rules, the guideline regarding two or more diagnoses that equally meet the definition for principal diagnosis *(Section II, C.)* may be applied in these situations.

If the documentation is not clear as to whether acute respiratory failure and another condition are equally responsible for occasioning the admission, query the provider for clarification.

d. Influenza due to certain identified viruses

Code only confirmed cases of avian influenza (codes 488.01-488.02, 488.09, Influenza due to identified avian influenza virus), **2009** H1N1 influenza virus (codes 488.11-488.12, 488.19), **or novel influenza A (codes 488.81-488.82, 488.89, Influenza due to identified novel influenza A virus).** This is an exception to the hospital inpatient guideline Section II, H. (Uncertain Diagnosis).

In this context, "confirmation" does not require documentation of positive laboratory testing specific for avian, **2009 H1N1** or novel influenza **A virus**. However, coding should be based on the provider's diagnostic statement that the patient has avian **influenza, 2009 H1N1 influenza,** or novel influenza **A.**

If the provider records "suspected" or "possible" or "probable" avian, **2009 H1N1,** or novel influenza **A,** the appropriate influenza code from category 487, **Influenza** should be assigned. A code from category 488, Influenza due to certain identified influenza viruses, should not be assigned.

9. Chapter 9: Diseases of Digestive System (520-579)

Reserved for future guideline expansion

10. Chapter 10: Diseases of Genitourinary System (580-629)

a. Chronic kidney disease

1) Stages of chronic kidney disease (CKD)

The ICD-9-CM classifies CKD based on severity. The severity of CKD is designated by stages I-V. Stage II, code 585.2, equates to mild CKD; stage III, code 585.3, equates to moderate CKD; and stage IV, code 585.4, equates to severe CKD. Code 585.6, End stage renal disease (ESRD), is assigned when the provider has documented end-stage-renal disease (ESRD).

If both a stage of CKD and ESRD are documented, assign code 585.6 only.

2) Chronic kidney disease and kidney transplant status

Patients who have undergone kidney transplant may still have some form of CKD, because the kidney transplant may not fully restore kidney function. Therefore, the presence of CKD alone does not constitute a transplant complication. Assign the appropriate 585 code for the patient's stage of CKD and code V42.0. If a transplant complication such as failure or rejection is documented, see section I.C.17.f.2.b for information on coding complications of a kidney transplant. If the documentation is unclear as to whether the patient has a complication of the transplant, query the provider.

3) Chronic kidney disease with other conditions

Patients with CKD may also suffer from other serious conditions, most commonly diabetes mellitus and hypertension. The sequencing of the CKD code in relationship to codes for other contributing conditions is based on the conventions in the tabular list.
See I.C.3.a.4 for sequencing instructions for diabetes.

See I.C.4.a.1 for anemia in CKD.
See I.C.7.a.3 for hypertensive chronic kidney disease.
See I.C.17.f.2.b, Kidney transplant complications, for
instructions on coding of documented rejection or failure.

11. Chapter 11: Complications of Pregnancy, Childbirth, and the Puerperium (630-679)

a. General Rules for Obstetric Cases

1) Codes from chapter 11 and sequencing priority

Obstetric cases require codes from chapter 11, codes in the range 630-679, Complications of Pregnancy, Childbirth, and the Puerperium. Chapter 11 codes have sequencing priority over codes from other chapters. Additional codes from other chapters may be used in conjunction with chapter 11 codes to further specify conditions. Should the provider document that the pregnancy is incidental to the encounter, then code V22.2 should be used in place of any chapter 11 codes. It is the provider's responsibility to state that the condition being treated is not affecting the pregnancy.

2) Chapter 11 codes used only on the maternal record

Chapter 11 codes are to be used only on the maternal record, never on the record of the newborn.

3) Chapter 11 fifth-digits

Categories 640-649, 651-676 have required fifth-digits, which indicate whether the encounter is antepartum, postpartum and whether a delivery has also occurred.

4) Fifth-digits, appropriate for each code

The fifth-digits, which are appropriate for each code number, are listed in brackets under each code. The fifth-digits on each code should all be consistent with each other. That is, should a delivery occur all of the fifth-digits should indicate the delivery.

b. Selection of OB Principal or First-listed Diagnosis

1) Routine outpatient prenatal visits

For routine outpatient prenatal visits when no complications are present codes V22.0, Supervision of normal first pregnancy, and V22.1, Supervision of other normal pregnancy, should be used as the first-listed diagnoses. These codes should not be used in conjunction with chapter 11 codes.

2) Prenatal outpatient visits for high-risk patients

For routine prenatal outpatient visits for patients with high-risk pregnancies, a code from category V23, Supervision of high-risk pregnancy, should be used as the first-listed diagnosis. Secondary chapter 11 codes may be used in conjunction with these codes if appropriate.

3) Episodes when no delivery occurs

In episodes when no delivery occurs, the principal diagnosis should correspond to the principal complication of the pregnancy, which necessitated the encounter. Should more than one complication exist, all of which are treated or monitored, any of the complications codes may be sequenced first.

4) When a delivery occurs

When a delivery occurs, the principal diagnosis should correspond to the main circumstances or complication of the delivery. In cases of cesarean delivery, the selection of the principal diagnosis should be the condition established after study that was responsible for the patient's admission. If the patient was admitted with a condition that resulted in the performance of a cesarean procedure, that condition should be selected as the principal diagnosis. If the reason for the admission/encounter was unrelated to the condition resulting in the cesarean delivery, the condition related to the reason for the admission/encounter should be selected as the principal diagnosis, even if a cesarean was performed.

5) Outcome of delivery

An outcome of delivery code, V27.0-V27.9, should be included on every maternal record when a delivery has occurred. These codes are not to be used on subsequent records or on the newborn record.

c. Fetal Conditions Affecting the Management of the Mother

1) Codes from categories 655 and 656

Codes from categories 655, Known or suspected fetal abnormality affecting management of the mother, and 656, Other known or suspected fetal and placental problems affecting the management of the mother, are assigned only when the fetal condition is actually responsible for modifying the management of the mother, i.e., by requiring diagnostic studies, additional observation, special care, or termination of pregnancy. The fact that the fetal condition exists does not justify assigning a code from this series to the mother's record.

See I.C.18.d. for suspected maternal and fetal conditions not found

2) In utero surgery

In cases when surgery is performed on the fetus, a diagnosis code from category 655, Known or suspected fetal abnormalities affecting management of the mother, should be assigned identifying the fetal condition. Procedure code 75.36, Correction of fetal defect, should be assigned on the hospital inpatient record.

No code from Chapter 15, the perinatal codes, should be used on the mother's record to identify fetal conditions. Surgery performed in utero on a fetus is still to be coded as an obstetric encounter.

d. HIV Infection in Pregnancy, Childbirth and the Puerperium

During pregnancy, childbirth or the puerperium, a patient admitted because of an HIV-related illness should receive a principal diagnosis of 647.6X, Other specified infectious and parasitic diseases in the mother classifiable elsewhere, but complicating the pregnancy, childbirth or the puerperium, followed by 042 and the code(s) for the HIV-related illness(es).

Patients with asymptomatic HIV infection status admitted during pregnancy, childbirth, or the puerperium should receive codes of 647.6X and V08.

e. Current Conditions Complicating Pregnancy

Assign a code from subcategory 648.x for patients that have current conditions when the condition affects the management of the pregnancy, childbirth, or the puerperium. Use additional secondary codes from other chapters to identify the conditions, as appropriate.

f. Diabetes mellitus in pregnancy

Diabetes mellitus is a significant complicating factor in pregnancy. Pregnant women who are diabetic should be assigned code 648.0x, Diabetes mellitus complicating pregnancy, and a secondary code from category 250, Diabetes mellitus, or category 249, Secondary diabetes to identify the type of diabetes.

Code V58.67, Long-term (current) use of insulin, should also be assigned if the diabetes mellitus is being treated with insulin.

g. Gestational diabetes

Gestational diabetes can occur during the second and third trimester of pregnancy in women who were not diabetic prior to pregnancy. Gestational diabetes can cause complications in the pregnancy similar to those of pre-existing diabetes mellitus. It also puts the woman at greater risk of developing diabetes after the pregnancy. Gestational diabetes is coded to 648.8x, Abnormal glucose tolerance. Codes 648.0x and 648.8x should never be used together on the same record.

Code V58.67, Long-term (current) use of insulin, should also be assigned if the gestational diabetes is being treated with insulin.

h. Normal Delivery, Code 650

1) Normal delivery

Code 650 is for use in cases when a woman is admitted for a full-term normal delivery and delivers a single, healthy infant without any complications antepartum, during the delivery, or postpartum during the delivery episode. Code 650 is always a principal diagnosis. It is not to be used if any other code from chapter 11 is needed to describe a current complication of the antenatal, delivery, or perinatal period. Additional codes from other chapters may be used with code 650 if they are not related to or are in any way complicating the pregnancy.

2) Normal delivery with resolved antepartum complication

Code 650 may be used if the patient had a complication at some point during her pregnancy, but the complication is not present at the time of the admission for delivery.

3) V27.0, Single liveborn, outcome of delivery

V27.0, Single liveborn, is the only outcome of delivery code appropriate for use with 650.

i. The Postpartum and Peripartum Periods

1) Postpartum and peripartum periods

The postpartum period begins immediately after delivery and continues for six weeks following delivery. The peripartum period is defined as the last month of pregnancy to five months postpartum.

2) Postpartum complication

A postpartum complication is any complication occurring within the six-week period.

3) **Pregnancy-related complications after 6 week period**

Chapter 11 codes may also be used to describe pregnancy-related complications after the six-week period should the provider document that a condition is pregnancy related.

4) **Postpartum complications occurring during the same admission as delivery**

Postpartum complications that occur during the same admission as the delivery are identified with a fifth digit of "2." Subsequent admissions/encounters for postpartum complications should be identified with a fifth digit of "4."

5) **Admission for routine postpartum care following delivery outside hospital**

When the mother delivers outside the hospital prior to admission and is admitted for routine postpartum care and no complications are noted, code V24.0, Postpartum care and examination immediately after delivery, should be assigned as the principal diagnosis.

6) **Admission following delivery outside hospital with postpartum conditions**

A delivery diagnosis code should not be used for a woman who has delivered prior to admission to the hospital. Any postpartum conditions and/or postpartum procedures should be coded.

7) **Puerperal sepsis**

Code 670.2x, Puerperal sepsis, should be assigned with a secondary code to identify the causal organism (e.g., for a bacterial infection, assign a code from category 041, Bacterial infections in conditions classified elsewhere and of unspecified site). A code from category 038, Septicemia, should not be used for puerperal sepsis. Do not assign code 995.91, Sepsis, as code 670.2x describes the sepsis. If applicable, use additional codes to identify severe sepsis (995.92) and any associated acute organ dysfunction.

j. Code 677, Late effect of complication of pregnancy

1)   Code 677

Code 677, Late effect of complication of pregnancy, childbirth, and the puerperium is for use in those cases when an initial complication of a pregnancy develops a sequelae requiring care or treatment at a future date.

2)   After the initial postpartum period

This code may be used at any time after the initial postpartum period.

3)   Sequencing of Code 677

This code, like all late effect codes, is to be sequenced following the code describing the sequelae of the complication.

k. Abortions

1)   Fifth-digits required for abortion categories

Fifth-digits are required for abortion categories 634-637. Fifth digit assignment is based on the status of the patient at the beginning (or start) of the encounter. Fifth-digit 1, incomplete, indicates that all of the products of conception have not been expelled from the uterus. Fifth-digit 2, complete, indicates that all products of conception have been expelled from the uterus.

2)   Code from categories 640-649 and 651-659

A code from categories 640-649 and 651-659 may be used as additional codes with an abortion code to indicate the complication leading to the abortion.

Fifth digit 3 is assigned with codes from these categories when used with an abortion code because the other fifth digits will not apply. Codes from the 660-669 series are not to be used for complications of abortion.

3)   Code 639 for complications

Code 639 is to be used for all complications following abortion. Code 639 cannot be assigned with codes from categories 634-638.

4)   Abortion with Liveborn Fetus

When an attempted termination of pregnancy results in a liveborn fetus assign code 644.21, Early onset of delivery, with an appropriate code from category V27, Outcome of Delivery. The procedure code for the attempted termination of pregnancy should also be assigned.

5) **Retained Products of Conception following an abortion**

Subsequent admissions for retained products of conception following a spontaneous or legally induced abortion are assigned the appropriate code from category 634, Spontaneous abortion, or 635 Legally induced abortion, with a fifth digit of "1" (incomplete). This advice is appropriate even when the patient was discharged previously with a discharge diagnosis of complete abortion.

12. Chapter 12: Diseases Skin and Subcutaneous Tissue (680-709)

a. Pressure ulcer stage codes

1) **Pressure ulcer stages**

Two codes are needed to completely describe a pressure ulcer: A code from subcategory 707.0, Pressure ulcer, to identify the site of the pressure ulcer and a code from subcategory 707.2, Pressure ulcer stages.

The codes in subcategory 707.2, Pressure ulcer stages, are to be used as an additional diagnosis with a code(s) from subcategory 707.0, Pressure Ulcer. Codes from 707.2, Pressure ulcer stages, may not be assigned as a principal or first-listed diagnosis. The pressure ulcer stage codes should only be used with pressure ulcers and not with other types of ulcers (e.g., stasis ulcer).

The ICD-9-CM classifies pressure ulcer stages based on severity, which is designated by stages I-IV and unstageable.

2) **Unstageable pressure ulcers**

Assignment of code 707.25, Pressure ulcer, unstageable, should be based on the clinical documentation. Code 707.25 is used for pressure ulcers whose stage cannot be clinically determined (e.g., the ulcer is covered by eschar or has been treated with a skin or muscle graft) and pressure ulcers that are documented as deep tissue injury but not documented as due to trauma. This code should not be confused with code 707.20, Pressure ulcer, stage unspecified. Code 707.20 should be assigned when there is no documentation regarding the stage of the pressure ulcer.

3) **Documented pressure ulcer stage**

Assignment of the pressure ulcer stage code should be guided by clinical documentation of the stage or documentation of the terms found in the index. For clinical terms describing the stage that are not found in the index, and there is no documentation of the stage, the provider should be queried.

4)   Bilateral pressure ulcers with same stage

When a patient has bilateral pressure ulcers (e.g., both buttocks) and both pressure ulcers are documented as being the same stage, only the code for the site and one code for the stage should be reported.

5)   Bilateral pressure ulcers with different stages

When a patient has bilateral pressure ulcers at the same site (e.g., both buttocks) and each pressure ulcer is documented as being at a different stage, assign one code for the site and the appropriate codes for the pressure ulcer stage.

6)   Multiple pressure ulcers of different sites and stages

When a patient has multiple pressure ulcers at different sites (e.g., buttock, heel, shoulder) and each pressure ulcer is documented as being at different stages (e.g., stage 3 and stage 4), assign the appropriate codes for each different site and a code for each different pressure ulcer stage.

7)   Patients admitted with pressure ulcers documented as healed

No code is assigned if the documentation states that the pressure ulcer is completely healed.

8)   Patients admitted with pressure ulcers documented as healing

Pressure ulcers described as healing should be assigned the appropriate pressure ulcer stage code based on the documentation in the medical record. If the documentation does not provide information about the stage of the healing pressure ulcer, assign code 707.20, Pressure ulcer stage, unspecified.

If the documentation is unclear as to whether the patient has a current (new) pressure ulcer or if the patient is being treated for a healing pressure ulcer, query the provider.

9)   Patient admitted with pressure ulcer evolving into another stage during the admission

If a patient is admitted with a pressure ulcer at one stage and it progresses to a higher stage, assign the code for highest stage reported for that site.

13. Chapter 13: Diseases of Musculoskeletal and Connective Tissue (710-739)

a. Coding of Pathologic Fractures

1) Acute Fractures vs. Aftercare

Pathologic fractures are reported using subcategory 733.1, when the fracture is newly diagnosed. Subcategory 733.1 may be used while the patient is receiving active treatment for the fracture. Examples of active treatment are: surgical treatment, emergency department encounter, evaluation and treatment by a new physician.

Fractures are coded using the aftercare codes (subcategories V54.0, V54.2, V54.8 or V54.9) for encounters after the patient has completed active treatment of the fracture and is receiving routine care for the fracture during the healing or recovery phase. Examples of fracture aftercare are: cast change or removal, removal of external or internal fixation device, medication adjustment, and follow up visits following fracture treatment.

Care for complications of surgical treatment for fracture repairs during the healing or recovery phase should be coded with the appropriate complication codes.

Care of complications of fractures, such as malunion and nonunion, should be reported with the appropriate codes.

See Section I. C. 17.b for information on the coding of traumatic fractures.

14. Chapter 14: Congenital Anomalies (740-759)

a. Codes in categories 740-759, Congenital Anomalies

Assign an appropriate code(s) from categories 740-759, Congenital Anomalies, when an anomaly is documented. A congenital anomaly may be the principal/first listed diagnosis on a record or a secondary diagnosis.

When a congenital anomaly does not have a unique code assignment, assign additional code(s) for any manifestations that may be present.

When the code assignment specifically identifies the congenital anomaly, manifestations that are an inherent component of the anomaly should not be coded separately. Additional codes should be assigned for manifestations that are not an inherent component.

Codes from Chapter 14 may be used throughout the life of the patient. If a congenital anomaly has been corrected, a personal history code should be used to identify the history of the anomaly. Although present at birth, a congenital anomaly may not be identified until later in life. Whenever the condition is diagnosed by the physician, it is appropriate to assign a code from codes 740-759.

For the birth admission, the appropriate code from category V30, Liveborn infants, according to type of birth should be sequenced as the principal diagnosis, followed by any congenital anomaly codes, 740-759.

15. Chapter 15: Newborn (Perinatal) Guidelines (760-779)

For coding and reporting purposes the perinatal period is defined as before birth through the 28th day following birth. The following guidelines are provided for reporting purposes. Hospitals may record other diagnoses as needed for internal data use.

a. General Perinatal Rules

1) Chapter 15 Codes

They are <u>never</u> for use on the maternal record. Codes from Chapter 11, the obstetric chapter, are never permitted on the newborn record. Chapter 15 code may be used throughout the life of the patient if the condition is still present.

2) Sequencing of perinatal codes

Generally, codes from Chapter 15 should be sequenced as the principal/first-listed diagnosis on the newborn record, with the exception of the appropriate V30 code for the birth episode, followed by codes from any other chapter that provide additional detail. The "use additional code" note at the beginning of the chapter supports this guideline. If the index does not provide a specific code for a perinatal condition, assign code 779.89, Other specified conditions originating in the perinatal period, followed by the code from another chapter that specifies the condition. Codes for signs and symptoms may be assigned when a definitive diagnosis has not been established.

3) Birth process or community acquired conditions

If a newborn has a condition that may be either due to the birth process or community acquired and the documentation does not indicate which it is, the default is due to the birth process and the code from Chapter 15 should be used. If the condition is community-acquired, a code from Chapter 15 should not be assigned.

4) **Code all clinically significant conditions**

All clinically significant conditions noted on routine newborn examination should be coded. A condition is clinically significant if it requires:

- clinical evaluation; or
- therapeutic treatment; or
- diagnostic procedures; or
- extended length of hospital stay; or
- increased nursing care and/or monitoring; or
- has implications for future health care needs

Note: The perinatal guidelines listed above are the same as the general coding guidelines for "additional diagnoses", except for the final point regarding implications for future health care needs. Codes should be assigned for conditions that have been specified by the provider as having implications for future health care needs. Codes from the perinatal chapter should not be assigned unless the provider has established a definitive diagnosis.

b. Use of codes V30-V39

When coding the birth of an infant, assign a code from categories V30-V39, according to the type of birth. A code from this series is assigned as a principal diagnosis, and assigned only once to a newborn at the time of birth.

c. Newborn transfers

If the newborn is transferred to another institution, the V30 series is not used at the receiving hospital.

d. Use of category V29

1) Assigning a code from category V29

Assign a code from category V29, Observation and evaluation of newborns and infants for suspected conditions not found, to identify those instances when a healthy newborn is evaluated for a suspected condition that is determined after study not to be present. Do not use a code from category V29 when the patient has identified signs or symptoms of a suspected problem; in such cases, code the sign or symptom.

A code from category V29 may also be assigned as a principal code for readmissions or encounters when the V30 code no longer applies. Codes from category V29 are for use only for healthy newborns and infants for which no condition after study is found to be present.

2) V29 code on a birth record

A V29 code is to be used as a secondary code after the V30, Outcome of delivery, code.

e. Use of other V codes on perinatal records

V codes other than V30 and V29 may be assigned on a perinatal or newborn record code. The codes may be used as a principal or first-listed diagnosis for specific types of encounters or for readmissions or encounters when the V30 code no longer applies.

See Section I.C.18 for information regarding the assignment of V codes.

f. Maternal Causes of Perinatal Morbidity

Codes from categories 760-763, Maternal causes of perinatal morbidity and mortality, are assigned only when the maternal condition has actually affected the fetus or newborn. The fact that the mother has an associated medical condition or experiences some complication of pregnancy, labor or delivery does not justify the routine assignment of codes from these categories to the newborn record.

g. Congenital Anomalies in Newborns

For the birth admission, the appropriate code from category V30, Liveborn infants according to type of birth, should be used, followed by any congenital anomaly codes, categories 740-759. Use additional secondary codes from other chapters to specify conditions associated with the anomaly, if applicable.
Also, see Section I.C.14 for information on the coding of congenital anomalies.

h. Coding Additional Perinatal Diagnoses

1) Assigning codes for conditions that require treatment

Assign codes for conditions that require treatment or further investigation, prolong the length of stay, or require resource utilization.

2) Codes for conditions specified as having implications for future health care needs

Assign codes for conditions that have been specified by the provider as having implications for future health care needs.

Note: This guideline should not be used for adult patients.

3) **Codes for newborn conditions originating in the perinatal period**

Assign a code for newborn conditions originating in the perinatal period (categories 760-779), as well as complications arising during the current episode of care classified in other chapters, only if the diagnoses have been documented by the responsible provider at the time of transfer or discharge as having affected the fetus or newborn.

i. Prematurity and Fetal Growth Retardation

Providers utilize different criteria in determining prematurity. A code for prematurity should not be assigned unless it is documented. The 5th digit assignment for codes from category 764 and subcategories 765.0 and 765.1 should be based on the recorded birth weight and estimated gestational age.

A code from subcategory 765.2, Weeks of gestation, should be assigned as an additional code with category 764 and codes from 765.0 and 765.1 to specify weeks of gestation as documented by the provider in the record.

j. Newborn sepsis

Code 771.81, Septicemia [sepsis] of newborn, should be assigned with a secondary code from category 041, Bacterial infections in conditions classified elsewhere and of unspecified site, to identify the organism. A code from category 038, Septicemia, should not be used on a newborn record. Do not assign code 995.91, Sepsis, as code 771.81 describes the sepsis. If applicable, use additional codes to identify severe sepsis (995.92) and any associated acute organ dysfunction.

16. Chapter 16: Signs, Symptoms and Ill-Defined Conditions (780-799)

Reserved for future guideline expansion

17. Chapter 17: Injury and Poisoning (800-999)

a. Coding of Injuries

When coding injuries, assign separate codes for each injury unless a combination code is provided, in which case the combination code is assigned. Multiple injury codes are provided in ICD-9-CM, but should not be assigned unless information for a more specific code is not available. These traumatic injury codes are not to be used for normal, healing surgical wounds or to identify complications of surgical wounds.

The code for the most serious injury, as determined by the provider and the focus of treatment, is sequenced first.

1) Superficial injuries

Superficial injuries such as abrasions or contusions are not coded when associated with more severe injuries of the same site.

2) Primary injury with damage to nerves/blood vessels

When a primary injury results in minor damage to peripheral nerves or blood vessels, the primary injury is sequenced first with additional code(s) from categories 950-957, Injury to nerves and spinal cord, and/or 900-904, Injury to blood vessels. When the primary injury is to the blood vessels or nerves, that injury should be sequenced first.

b. Coding of Traumatic Fractures

The principles of multiple coding of injuries should be followed in coding fractures. Fractures of specified sites are coded individually by site in accordance with both the provisions within categories 800-829 and the level of detail furnished by medical record content. Combination categories for multiple fractures are provided for use when there is insufficient detail in the medical record (such as trauma cases transferred to another hospital), when the reporting form limits the number of codes that can be used in reporting pertinent clinical data, or when there is insufficient specificity at the fourth-digit or fifth-digit level. More specific guidelines are as follows:

1) Acute Fractures vs. Aftercare

Traumatic fractures are coded using the acute fracture codes (800-829) while the patient is receiving active treatment for the fracture. Examples of active treatment are: surgical treatment, emergency department encounter, and evaluation and treatment by a new physician.

Fractures are coded using the aftercare codes (subcategories V54.0, V54.1, V54.8, or V54.9) for encounters after the patient has completed active treatment of the fracture and is receiving routine care for the fracture during the healing or recovery phase. Examples of fracture aftercare are: cast change or removal, removal of external or internal fixation device, medication adjustment, and follow up visits following fracture treatment.

Care for complications of surgical treatment for fracture repairs during the healing or recovery phase should be coded with the appropriate complication codes.

Care of complications of fractures, such as malunion and nonunion, should be reported with the appropriate codes.

Pathologic fractures are not coded in the 800-829 range, but instead are assigned to subcategory 733.1. *See Section I.C.13.a for additional information.*

2)   Multiple fractures of same limb

Multiple fractures of same limb classifiable to the same three-digit or four-digit category are coded to that category.

3)   Multiple unilateral or bilateral fractures of same bone

Multiple unilateral or bilateral fractures of same bone(s) but classified to different fourth-digit subdivisions (bone part) within the same three-digit category are coded individually by site.

4)   Multiple fracture categories 819 and 828

Multiple fracture categories 819 and 828 classify bilateral fractures of both upper limbs (819) and both lower limbs (828), but without any detail at the fourth-digit level other than open and closed type of fractures.

5)   Multiple fractures sequencing

Multiple fractures are sequenced in accordance with the severity of the fracture. The provider should be asked to list the fracture diagnoses in the order of severity.

c.   Coding of Burns

Current burns (940-948) are classified by depth, extent and by agent (E code). Burns are classified by depth as first degree (erythema), second degree (blistering), and third degree (full-thickness involvement).

1)   Sequencing of burn and related condition codes

Sequence first the code that reflects the highest degree of burn when more than one burn is present.

a.   When the reason for the admission or encounter is for treatment of external multiple burns, sequence first the code that reflects the burn of the highest degree.

b.   When a patient has both internal and external burns, the circumstances of admission govern the selection of the principal diagnosis or first-listed diagnosis.

c. When a patient is admitted for burn injuries and other related conditions such as smoke inhalation and/or respiratory failure, the circumstances of admission govern the selection of the principal or first-listed diagnosis.

2)   Burns of the same local site

Classify burns of the same local site (three-digit category level, 940-947) but of different degrees to the subcategory identifying the highest degree recorded in the diagnosis.

3)   Non-healing burns

Non-healing burns are coded as acute burns.
Necrosis of burned skin should be coded as a non-healed burn.

4)   Code 958.3, Posttraumatic wound infection

Assign code 958.3, Posttraumatic wound infection, not elsewhere classified, as an additional code for any documented infected burn site.

5)   Assign separate codes for each burn site

When coding burns, assign separate codes for each burn site. Category 946 Burns of Multiple specified sites, should only be used if the location of the burns are not documented. Category 949, Burn, unspecified, is extremely vague and should rarely be used.

6)   Assign codes from category 948, Burns

Burns classified according to extent of body surface involved, when the site of the burn is not specified or when there is a need for additional data. It is advisable to use category 948 as additional coding when needed to provide data for evaluating burn mortality, such as that needed by burn units. It is also advisable to use category 948 as an additional code for reporting purposes when there is mention of a third-degree burn involving 20 percent or more of the body surface.

In assigning a code from category 948:

Fourth-digit codes are used to identify the percentage of total body surface involved in a burn (all degree).

Fifth-digits are assigned to identify the percentage of body surface involved in third-degree burn.

Fifth-digit zero (0) is assigned when less than 10 percent or when no body surface is involved in a third-degree burn.

Category 948 is based on the classic "rule of nines" in estimating body surface involved: head and neck are assigned nine percent, each arm nine percent, each leg 18 percent, the anterior trunk 18 percent, posterior trunk 18 percent, and genitalia one percent. Providers may change these percentage assignments where necessary to accommodate infants and children who have proportionately larger heads than adults and patients who have large buttocks, thighs, or abdomen that involve burns.

7) Encounters for treatment of late effects of burns

Encounters for the treatment of the late effects of burns (i.e., scars or joint contractures) should be coded to the residual condition (sequelae) followed by the appropriate late effect code (906.5-906.9). A late effect E code may also be used, if desired.

8) Sequelae with a late effect code and current burn

When appropriate, both a sequelae with a late effect code, and a current burn code may be assigned on the same record (when both a current burn and sequelae of an old burn exist).

d. Coding of Debridement of Wound, Infection, or Burn

Excisional debridement involves surgical removal or cutting away, as opposed to a mechanical (brushing, scrubbing, washing) debridement.

For coding purposes, excisional debridement is assigned to code 86.22.

Nonexcisional debridement is assigned to code 86.28.

e. Adverse Effects, Poisoning and Toxic Effects

The properties of certain drugs, medicinal and biological substances or combinations of such substances, may cause toxic reactions. The occurrence of drug toxicity is classified in ICD-9-CM as follows:

1) Adverse Effect

When the drug was correctly prescribed and properly administered, code the reaction plus the appropriate code from the E930-E949 series. Codes from the E930-E949 series must be used to identify the causative substance for an adverse effect of drug, medicinal and biological substances, correctly prescribed and properly administered. The effect, such as tachycardia, delirium, gastrointestinal hemorrhaging, vomiting, hypokalemia, hepatitis, renal failure, or respiratory failure, is

coded and followed by the appropriate code from the
E930-E949 series.

Adverse effects of therapeutic substances correctly prescribed
and properly administered (toxicity, synergistic reaction, side
effect, and idiosyncratic reaction) may be due to (1) differences
among patients, such as age, sex, disease, and genetic factors,
and (2) drug-related factors, such as type of drug, route of
administration, duration of therapy, dosage, and bioavailability.

2) **Poisoning**

(a) **Error was made in drug prescription**

Errors made in drug prescription or in the
administration of the drug by provider, nurse, patient,
or other person, use the appropriate poisoning code
from the 960-979 series.

(b) **Overdose of a drug intentionally taken**

If an overdose of a drug was intentionally taken or
administered and resulted in drug toxicity, it would be
coded as a poisoning (960-979 series).

(c) **Nonprescribed drug taken with correctly prescribed
and properly administered drug**

If a nonprescribed drug or medicinal agent was taken in
combination with a correctly prescribed and properly
administered drug, any drug toxicity or other reaction
resulting from the interaction of the two drugs would be
classified as a poisoning.

(d) **Interaction of drug(s) and alcohol**

When a reaction results from the interaction of a
drug(s) and alcohol, this would be classified as
poisoning.

(e) **Sequencing of poisoning**

When coding a poisoning or reaction to the improper
use of a medication (e.g., wrong dose, wrong substance,
wrong route of administration) the poisoning code is
sequenced first, followed by a code for the
manifestation. If there is also a diagnosis of drug abuse
or dependence to the substance, the abuse or
dependence is coded as an additional code.
*See Section I.C.3.a.6.b. if poisoning is the result of
insulin pump malfunctions and Section I.C.19 for
general use of E-codes.*

3) Toxic Effects

(a) **Toxic effect codes**

When a harmful substance is ingested or comes in contact with a person, this is classified as a toxic effect. The toxic effect codes are in categories 980-989.

(b) **Sequencing toxic effect codes**

A toxic effect code should be sequenced first, followed by the code(s) that identify the result of the toxic effect.

(c) **External cause codes for toxic effects**

An external cause code from categories E860-E869 for accidental exposure, codes E950.6 or E950.7 for intentional self-harm, category E962 for assault, or categories E980-E982, for undetermined, should also be assigned to indicate intent.

f. Complications of care

1) General guidelines for complications of care

(a) **Documentation of complications of care**

See Section I.B.18. for information on documentation of complications of care.

(b) **Use additional code to identify nature of complication**

An additional code identifying the complication should be assigned with codes in categories 996-999, Complications of Surgical and Medical Care NEC, when the additional code provides greater specificity as to the nature of the condition. If the complication code fully describes the condition, no additional code is necessary.

2) Transplant complications

(a) **Transplant complications other than kidney**

Codes under subcategory 996.8, Complications of transplanted organ, are for use for both complications and rejection of transplanted organs. A transplant complication code is only assigned if the complication affects the function of the transplanted organ. Two codes are required to fully describe a transplant complication, the appropriate code from subcategory

996.8 and a secondary code that identifies the complication.

Pre-existing conditions or conditions that develop after the transplant are not coded as complications unless they affect the function of the transplanted organs.

See I.C.18.d.3) for transplant organ removal status

See I.C.2.i for malignant neoplasm associated with transplanted organ.

(b)   **Kidney transplant complications**

Patients who have undergone kidney transplant may still have some form of chronic kidney disease (CKD) because the kidney transplant may not fully restore kidney function. Code 996.81 should be assigned for documented complications of a kidney transplant, such as transplant failure or rejection or other transplant complication. Code 996.81 should not be assigned for post kidney transplant patients who have chronic kidney (CKD) unless a transplant complication such as transplant failure or rejection is documented. If the documentation is unclear as to whether the patient has a complication of the transplant, query the provider.

Conditions that affect the function of the transplanted kidney, other than CKD, should be assigned code 996.81, Complications of transplanted organ, Kidney, and a secondary code that identifies the complication.

For patients with CKD following a kidney transplant, but who do not have a complication such as failure or rejection, *see section I.C.10.a.2, Chronic kidney disease and kidney transplant status*.

3)   **Ventilator associated pneumonia**

(a)   **Documentation of Ventilator associated Pneumonia**

As with all procedural or postprocedural complications, code assignment is based on the provider's documentation of the relationship between the condition and the procedure.

Code 997.31, Ventilator associated pneumonia, should be assigned only when the provider has documented ventilator associated pneumonia (VAP). An additional code to identify the organism (e.g., Pseudomonas aeruginosa, code 041.7) should also be assigned. Do not assign an additional code from categories 480-484 to identify the type of pneumonia.

Code 997.31 should not be assigned for cases where the patient has pneumonia and is on a mechanical ventilator but the provider has not specifically stated that the pneumonia is ventilator-associated pneumonia.

If the documentation is unclear as to whether the patient has a pneumonia that is a complication attributable to the mechanical ventilator, query the provider.

(b) **Patient admitted with pneumonia and develops VAP**

A patient may be admitted with one type of pneumonia (e.g., code 481, Pneumococcal pneumonia) and subsequently develop VAP. In this instance, the principal diagnosis would be the appropriate code from categories 480-484 for the pneumonia diagnosed at the time of admission. Code 997.31, Ventilator associated pneumonia, would be assigned as an additional diagnosis when the provider has also documented the presence of ventilator associated pneumonia.

g. SIRS due to Non-infectious Process

The systemic inflammatory response syndrome (SIRS) can develop as a result of certain non-infectious disease processes, such as trauma, malignant neoplasm, or pancreatitis. When SIRS is documented with a noninfectious condition, and no subsequent infection is documented, the code for the underlying condition, such as an injury, should be assigned, followed by code 995.93, Systemic inflammatory response syndrome due to noninfectious process without acute organ dysfunction, or 995.94, Systemic inflammatory response syndrome due to non-infectious process with acute organ dysfunction. If an acute organ dysfunction is documented, the appropriate code(s) for the associated acute organ dysfunction(s) should be assigned in addition to code 995.94. If acute organ dysfunction is documented, but it cannot be determined if the acute organ dysfunction is associated with SIRS or due to another condition (e.g., directly due to the trauma), the provider should be queried.

When the non-infectious condition has led to an infection that results in SIRS, *see Section I.C.1.b.12 for the guideline for sepsis and severe sepsis associated with a non-infectious process.*

18. Classification of Factors Influencing Health Status and Contact with Health Service (Supplemental V01-V91)

Note: The chapter specific guidelines provide additional information about the use of V codes for specified encounters.

a. Introduction

ICD-9-CM provides codes to deal with encounters for circumstances other than a disease or injury. The Supplementary Classification of Factors Influencing Health Status and Contact with Health Services (V01.0 - V91.99) is provided to deal with occasions when circumstances other than a disease or injury (codes 001-999) are recorded as a diagnosis or problem.

There are four primary circumstances for the use of V codes:

1) A person who is not currently sick encounters the health services for some specific reason, such as to act as an organ donor, to receive prophylactic care, such as inoculations or health screenings, or to receive counseling on health related issues.

2) A person with a resolving disease or injury, or a chronic, long-term condition requiring continuous care, encounters the health care system for specific aftercare of that disease or injury (e.g., dialysis for renal disease; chemotherapy for malignancy; cast change). A diagnosis/symptom code should be used whenever a current, acute, diagnosis is being treated or a sign or symptom is being studied.

3) Circumstances or problems influence a person's health status but are not in themselves a current illness or injury.

4) Newborns, to indicate birth status

b. V codes use in any healthcare setting

V codes are for use in any healthcare setting. V codes may be used as either a first listed (principal diagnosis code in the inpatient setting) or secondary code, depending on the circumstances of the encounter. Certain V codes may only be used as first listed, others only as secondary codes.
See Section I.C.18.e, V Codes That May Only be Principal/First-Listed Diagnosis.

c. V Codes indicate a reason for an encounter

They are not procedure codes. A corresponding procedure code must accompany a V code to describe the procedure performed.

d. Categories of V Codes

1) Contact/Exposure

Category V01 indicates contact with or exposure to communicable diseases. These codes are for patients who do not show any sign or symptom of a disease but have been exposed to it by close personal contact with an infected individual or are in an area where a disease is epidemic. These codes may be used as a first listed code to explain an encounter for testing, or, more commonly, as a secondary code to identify a potential risk.

Codes V15.84 – V15.86 describe contact with or (suspected) exposure to asbestos, potentially hazardous body fluids, and lead.

Subcategories V87.0 – V87.3 describe contact with or (suspected) exposure to hazardous metals, aromatic compounds, other potentially hazardous chemicals, and other potentially hazardous substances.

2) Inoculations and vaccinations

Categories V03-V06 are for encounters for inoculations and vaccinations. They indicate that a patient is being seen to receive a prophylactic inoculation against a disease. The injection itself must be represented by the appropriate procedure code. A code from V03-V06 may be used as a secondary code if the inoculation is given as a routine part of preventive health care, such as a well-baby visit.

3) Status

Status codes indicate that a patient is a carrier of a disease, has the sequelae or residual of a past disease or condition, or has another factor influencing a person's health status. This includes such things as the presence of prosthetic or mechanical devices resulting from past treatment. A status code is informative, because the status may affect the course of treatment and its outcome. A status code is distinct from a history code. The history code indicates that the patient no longer has the condition.

A status code should not be used with a diagnosis code from one of the body system chapters, if the diagnosis code includes the information provided by the status code. For example, code V42.1, Heart transplant status, should not be used with code 996.83, Complications of transplanted heart. The status code does not provide additional information. The complication code indicates that the patient is a heart transplant patient.

The status V codes/categories are:

V02	Carrier or suspected carrier of infectious diseases Carrier status indicates that a person harbors the specific organisms of a disease without manifest symptoms and is capable of transmitting the infection.
V07.5X	Use of agents affecting estrogen receptors and estrogen level This code indicates when a patient is receiving a drug that affects estrogen receptors and estrogen levels for prevention of cancer.
V08	Asymptomatic HIV infection status This code indicates that a patient has tested positive for HIV but has manifested no signs or symptoms of the disease.
V09	Infection with drug-resistant microorganisms This category indicates that a patient has an infection that is resistant to drug treatment. Sequence the infection code first.
V21	Constitutional states in development
V22.2	Pregnant state, incidental This code is a secondary code only for use when the pregnancy is in no way complicating the reason for visit. Otherwise, a code from the obstetric chapter is required.
V26.5x	Sterilization status
V42	Organ or tissue replaced by transplant
V43	Organ or tissue replaced by other means
V44	Artificial opening status
V45	Other postsurgical states Assign code V45.87, Transplant organ removal status, to indicate that a transplanted organ has been previously removed. This code should not be assigned for the encounter in which the transplanted organ is removed. The complication necessitating removal of the transplant organ should be assigned for that encounter.

See section I.C17.f.2. for information on the coding of organ transplant complications.

Assign code V45.88, Status post administration of tPA (rtPA) in a different facility within the last 24 hours prior to admission to the current facility, as a secondary diagnosis when a patient is received by transfer into a facility and documentation indicates they were administered tissue plasminogen activator (tPA) within the last 24 hours prior to admission to the current facility.

This guideline applies even if the patient is still receiving the tPA at the time they are received into the current facility.

The appropriate code for the condition for which the tPA was administered (such as cerebrovascular disease or myocardial infarction) should be assigned first.

Code V45.88 is only applicable to the receiving facility record and not to the transferring facility record.

V46	Other dependence on machines
V49.6	Upper limb amputation status
V49.7	Lower limb amputation status

Note: Categories V42-V46, and subcategories V49.6, V49.7 are for use only if there are no complications or malfunctions of the organ or tissue replaced, the amputation site or the equipment on which the patient is dependent.

V49.81	Asymptomatic postmenopausal status (age-related) (natural)
V49.82	Dental sealant status
V49.83	Awaiting organ transplant status
V49.86	Do not resuscitate status

This code may be used when it is documented by the provider that a patient is on do not resuscitate status at any time during the stay.

V49.87	Physical restraint status

This code may be used when it is documented by the provider that a patient has been put in restraints during the current encounter. Please note that this code should not be reported when it is documented by the provider that a patient is temporarily restrained during a procedure.

V58.6x	Long-term (current) drug use

Codes from this subcategory indicate a patient's continuous use of a prescribed drug (including such things as aspirin therapy) for the long-term treatment of a condition or for prophylactic use. It is not for use for patients who have addictions to drugs. This subcategory is not for use of medications for detoxification or maintenance programs to prevent withdrawal symptoms in patients with drug dependence (e.g., methadone maintenance for opiate dependence). Assign the appropriate code for the drug dependence instead.

Assign a code from subcategory V58.6, Long-term (current) drug use, if the patient is receiving a medication for an extended period as a prophylactic measure (such as for the prevention of deep vein thrombosis) or as treatment of a chronic condition (such as arthritis) or a disease requiring a lengthy course of treatment (such as cancer). Do not assign a code from subcategory V58.6 for medication being administered for a brief period of time to treat an acute illness or injury (such as a course of antibiotics to treat acute bronchitis).

V83 Genetic carrier status

Genetic carrier status indicates that a person carries a gene, associated with a particular disease, which may be passed to offspring who may develop that disease. The person does not have the disease and is not at risk of developing the disease.

V84 Genetic susceptibility status

Genetic susceptibility indicates that a person has a gene that increases the risk of that person developing the disease.

Codes from category V84, Genetic susceptibility to disease, should not be used as principal or first-listed codes. If the patient has the condition to which he/she is susceptible, and that condition is the reason for the encounter, the code for the current condition should be sequenced first. If the patient is being seen for follow-up after completed treatment for this condition, and the condition no longer exists, a follow-up code should be sequenced first, followed by the appropriate personal history and genetic susceptibility codes. If the purpose of the encounter is genetic counseling associated with procreative management, a code from subcategory V26.3, Genetic counseling and testing, should be assigned as the first-listed code, followed by a code from category V84. Additional codes should be assigned for any applicable family or personal history.

*See Section I.C. 18.d.14 for information on
prophylactic organ removal due to a genetic
susceptibility.*

V85	Body Mass Index (BMI)
V86	Estrogen receptor status
V88	Acquired absence of other organs and tissue
V90	Retained foreign body

4) **History (of)**

There are two types of history V codes, personal and family. Personal history codes explain a patient's past medical condition that no longer exists and is not receiving any treatment, but that has the potential for recurrence, and therefore may require continued monitoring. The exceptions to this general rule are category V14, Personal history of allergy to medicinal agents, and subcategory V15.0, Allergy, other than to medicinal agents. A person who has had an allergic episode to a substance or food in the past should always be considered allergic to the substance.

Family history codes are for use when a patient has a family member(s) who has had a particular disease that causes the patient to be at higher risk of also contracting the disease.

Personal history codes may be used in conjunction with follow-up codes and family history codes may be used in conjunction with screening codes to explain the need for a test or procedure. History codes are also acceptable on any medical record regardless of the reason for visit. A history of an illness, even if no longer present, is important information that may alter the type of treatment ordered.

The history V code categories are:

V10	Personal history of malignant neoplasm
V12	Personal history of certain other diseases
V13	Personal history of other diseases Except: V13.4, Personal history of arthritis, and subcategory V13.6, Personal history of congenital (corrected) malformations. These conditions are life-long so are not true history codes.
V14	Personal history of allergy to medicinal agents
V15	Other personal history presenting hazards to health Except: **Codes** V15.7, Personal history of contraception; **V15.84, Contact with and (suspected) exposure to asbestos; V15.85, Contact with and (suspected) exposure to**

> potentially hazardous body fluids; V15.86,
> Contact with and (suspected) exposure to lead.

V16   Family history of malignant neoplasm
V17   Family history of certain chronic disabling diseases
V18   Family history of certain other specific diseases
V19   Family history of other conditions
V87   Other specified personal exposures and history presenting hazards to health

> **Except: Subcategories V87.0, Contact with and (suspected) exposure to hazardous metals; V87.1, Contact with and (suspected) exposure to hazardous aromatic compounds; V87.2, Contact with and (suspected) exposure to other potentially hazardous chemicals; and V87.3, Contact with and (suspected) exposure to other potentially hazardous substances**

5) **Screening**

Screening is the testing for disease or disease precursors in seemingly well individuals so that early detection and treatment can be provided for those who test positive for the disease. Screenings that are recommended for many subgroups in a population include: routine mammograms for women over 40, a fecal occult blood test for everyone over 50, an amniocentesis to rule out a fetal anomaly for pregnant women over 35, because the incidence of breast cancer and colon cancer in these subgroups is higher than in the general population, as is the incidence of Down's syndrome in older mothers.

The testing of a person to rule out or confirm a suspected diagnosis because the patient has some sign or symptom is a diagnostic examination, not a screening. In these cases, the sign or symptom is used to explain the reason for the test.

A screening code may be a first listed code if the reason for the visit is specifically the screening exam. It may also be used as an additional code if the screening is done during an office visit for other health problems. A screening code is not necessary if the screening is inherent to a routine examination, such as a pap smear done during a routine pelvic examination.

Should a condition be discovered during the screening then the code for the condition may be assigned as an additional diagnosis.

The V code indicates that a screening exam is planned. A procedure code is required to confirm that the screening was performed.

The screening V code categories:
V28   Antenatal screening
V73-V82   Special screening examinations

6)   Observation

There are three observation V code categories. They are for use in very limited circumstances when a person is being observed for a suspected condition that is ruled out. The observation codes are not for use if an injury or illness or any signs or symptoms related to the suspected condition are present. In such cases the diagnosis/symptom code is used with the corresponding E code to identify any external cause.

The observation codes are to be used as principal diagnosis only. The only exception to this is when the principal diagnosis is required to be a code from the V30, Live born infant, category. Then the V29 observation code is sequenced after the V30 code. Additional codes may be used in addition to the observation code but only if they are unrelated to the suspected condition being observed.

Codes from subcategory V89.0, Suspected maternal and fetal conditions not found, may either be used as a first listed or as an additional code assignment depending on the case. They are for use in very limited circumstances on a maternal record when an encounter is for a suspected maternal or fetal condition that is ruled out during that encounter (for example, a maternal or fetal condition may be suspected due to an abnormal test result). These codes should not be used when the condition is confirmed. In those cases, the confirmed condition should be coded. In addition, these codes are not for use if an illness or any signs or symptoms related to the suspected condition or problem are present. In such cases the diagnosis/symptom code is used.

Additional codes may be used in addition to the code from subcategory V89.0, but only if they are unrelated to the suspected condition being evaluated.

Codes from subcategory V89.0 may not be used for encounters for antenatal screening of mother. *See Section I.C.18.d., Screening).*

For encounters for suspected fetal condition that are inconclusive following testing and evaluation, assign the appropriate code from category 655, 656, 657 or 658.

The observation V code categories:

V29   Observation and evaluation of newborns for suspected condition not found
For the birth encounter, a code from category V30 should be sequenced before the V29 code.

V71   Observation and evaluation for suspected condition not found

V89   Suspected maternal and fetal conditions not found

7) Aftercare

Aftercare visit codes cover situations when the initial treatment of a disease or injury has been performed and the patient requires continued care during the healing or recovery phase, or for the long-term consequences of the disease. The aftercare V code should not be used if treatment is directed at a current, acute disease or injury. The diagnosis code is to be used in these cases. Exceptions to this rule are codes V58.0, Radiotherapy, and codes from subcategory V58.1, Encounter for chemotherapy and immunotherapy for neoplastic conditions. These codes are to be first listed, followed by the diagnosis code when a patient's encounter is solely to receive radiation therapy or chemotherapy for the treatment of a neoplasm. Should a patient receive both chemotherapy and radiation therapy during the same encounter code V58.0 and V58.1 may be used together on a record with either one being sequenced first.

The aftercare codes are generally first listed to explain the specific reason for the encounter. An aftercare code may be used as an additional code when some type of aftercare is provided in addition to the reason for admission and no diagnosis code is applicable. An example of this would be the closure of a colostomy during an encounter for treatment of another condition.

Aftercare codes should be used in conjunction with any other aftercare codes or other diagnosis codes to provide better detail on the specifics of an aftercare encounter visit, unless otherwise directed by the classification. The sequencing of multiple aftercare codes is discretionary.

Certain aftercare V code categories need a secondary diagnosis code to describe the resolving condition or sequelae, for others, the condition is inherent in the code title.

Additional V code aftercare category terms include fitting and adjustment, and attention to artificial openings.

Status V codes may be used with aftercare V codes to indicate the nature of the aftercare. For example code V45.81, Aortocoronary bypass status, may be used with code V58.73, Aftercare following surgery of the circulatory system, NEC, to indicate the surgery for which the aftercare is being performed. Also, a transplant status code may be used following code V58.44, Aftercare following organ transplant, to identify the organ transplanted. A status code should not be used when the aftercare code indicates the type of status, such as using V55.0, Attention to tracheostomy with V44.0, Tracheostomy status.

See Section I. B.16 Admissions/Encounter for Rehabilitation

The aftercare V category/codes:

V51.0	Encounter for breast reconstruction following mastectomy
V52	Fitting and adjustment of prosthetic device and implant
V53	Fitting and adjustment of other device
V54	Other orthopedic aftercare
V55	Attention to artificial openings
V56	Encounter for dialysis and dialysis catheter care
V57	Care involving the use of rehabilitation procedures
V58.0	Radiotherapy
V58.11	Encounter for antineoplastic chemotherapy
V58.12	Encounter for antineoplastic immunotherapy
V58.3x	Attention to dressings and sutures
V58.41	Encounter for planned post-operative wound closure
V58.42	Aftercare, surgery, neoplasm
V58.43	Aftercare, surgery, trauma
V58.44	Aftercare involving organ transplant
V58.49	Other specified aftercare following surgery
V58.7x	Aftercare following surgery
V58.81	Fitting and adjustment of vascular catheter
V58.82	Fitting and adjustment of non-vascular catheter
V58.83	Monitoring therapeutic drug
V58.89	Other specified aftercare

8)   Follow-up

The follow-up codes are used to explain continuing surveillance following completed treatment of a disease, condition, or injury. They imply that the condition has been fully treated and no longer exists. They should not be confused with aftercare codes that explain current treatment for a healing condition or its sequelae. Follow-up codes may be used in conjunction with history codes to provide the full picture of the healed condition and its treatment. The follow-up code is sequenced first, followed by the history code.

A follow-up code may be used to explain repeated visits. Should a condition be found to have recurred on the follow-up visit, then the diagnosis code should be used in place of the follow-up code.

The follow-up V code categories:
V24   Postpartum care and evaluation
V67   Follow-up examination

9) Donor

Category V59 is the donor codes. They are used for living individuals who are donating blood or other body tissue. These codes are only for individuals donating for others, not for self donations. They are not for use to identify cadaveric donations.

10) Counseling

Counseling V codes are used when a patient or family member receives assistance in the aftermath of an illness or injury, or when support is required in coping with family or social problems. They are not necessary for use in conjunction with a diagnosis code when the counseling component of care is considered integral to standard treatment.

The counseling V categories/codes:
V25.0   General counseling and advice for contraceptive management
V26.3   Genetic counseling
V26.4   General counseling and advice for procreative management
V61.X   Other family circumstances
V65.1   Person consulted on behalf of another person
V65.3   Dietary surveillance and counseling
V65.4   Other counseling, not elsewhere classified

11) Obstetrics and related conditions

See Section I.C.11., the Obstetrics guidelines for further instruction on the use of these codes.

V codes for pregnancy are for use in those circumstances when none of the problems or complications included in the codes from the Obstetrics chapter exist (a routine prenatal visit or postpartum care). Codes V22.0, Supervision of normal first pregnancy, and V22.1, Supervision of other normal pregnancy, are always first listed and are not to be used with any other code from the OB chapter.

The outcome of delivery, category V27, should be included on all maternal delivery records. It is always a secondary code.

V codes for family planning (contraceptive) or procreative management and counseling should be included on an obstetric record either during the pregnancy or the postpartum stage, if applicable.

Obstetrics and related conditions V code categories:

V22	Normal pregnancy
V23	Supervision of high-risk pregnancy
	Except: V23.2, Pregnancy with history of abortion. Code 646.3, Recurrent pregnancy loss, from the OB chapter is required to indicate a history of abortion during a pregnancy.
V24	Postpartum care and evaluation
V25	Encounter for contraceptive management
	Except V25.0x
	(See Section I.C.18.d.11, Counseling)
V26	Procreative management
	Except V26.5x, Sterilization status, V26.3 and V26.4
	(See Section I.C.18.d.11., Counseling)
V27	Outcome of delivery
V28	Antenatal screening
	(See Section I.C.18.d.6., Screening)
V91	Multiple gestation placenta status

12) Newborn, infant and child

See Section I.C.15, the Newborn guidelines for further instruction on the use of these codes.

Newborn V code categories:

V20	Health supervision of infant or child
V29	Observation and evaluation of newborns for suspected condition not found

(See Section I.C.18.d.7, Observation)
V30-V39   Liveborn infant according to type of birth

13)   Routine and administrative examinations

The V codes allow for the description of encounters for routine examinations, such as, a general check-up, or examinations for administrative purposes, such as a pre-employment physical. The codes are not to be used if the examination is for diagnosis of a suspected condition or for treatment purposes. In such cases the diagnosis code is used. During a routine exam, should a diagnosis or condition be discovered, it should be coded as an additional code. Pre-existing and chronic conditions and history codes may also be included as additional codes as long as the examination is for administrative purposes and not focused on any particular condition.

Pre-operative examination and pre-procedural laboratory examination V codes are for use only in those situations when a patient is being cleared for a procedure or surgery and no treatment is given.

The V codes categories/code for routine and administrative examinations:

V20.2   Routine infant or child health check
Any injections given should have a corresponding procedure code.
V70   General medical examination
V72   Special investigations and examinations
Codes V72.5 and V72.62 may be used if the reason for the patient encounter is for routine laboratory/radiology testing in the absence of any signs, symptoms, or associated diagnosis. If routine testing is performed during the same encounter as a test to evaluate a sign, symptom, or diagnosis, it is appropriate to assign both the V code and the code describing the reason for the non-routine test.

14)   Miscellaneous V codes

The miscellaneous V codes capture a number of other health care encounters that do not fall into one of the other categories. Certain of these codes identify the reason for the encounter, others are for use as additional codes that provide useful information on circumstances that may affect a patient's care and treatment.

Prophylactic Organ Removal

For encounters specifically for prophylactic removal of breasts, ovaries, or another organ due to a genetic susceptibility to cancer or a family history of cancer, the principal or first listed code should be a code from subcategory V50.4, Prophylactic organ removal, followed by the appropriate genetic susceptibility code and the appropriate family history code.

If the patient has a malignancy of one site and is having prophylactic removal at another site to prevent either a new primary malignancy or metastatic disease, a code for the malignancy should also be assigned in addition to a code from subcategory V50.4. A V50.4 code should not be assigned if the patient is having organ removal for treatment of a malignancy, such as the removal of the testes for the treatment of prostate cancer.

Miscellaneous V code categories/codes:

V07	Need for isolation and other prophylactic or treatment measures
	Except V07.5X, Use of agents affecting estrogen receptors and estrogen levels
V40.31	**Wandering in diseases classified elsewhere**
V50	Elective surgery for purposes other than remedying health states
V58.5	Orthodontics
V60	Housing, household, and economic circumstances
V62	Other psychosocial circumstances
V63	Unavailability of other medical facilities for care
V64	Persons encountering health services for specific procedures, not carried out
V66	Convalescence and Palliative Care
V68	Encounters for administrative purposes
V69	Problems related to lifestyle

15) Nonspecific V codes

Certain V codes are so non-specific, or potentially redundant with other codes in the classification, that there can be little justification for their use in the inpatient setting. Their use in the outpatient setting should be limited to those instances when there is no further documentation to permit more precise coding. Otherwise, any sign or symptom or any other reason for visit that is captured in another code should be used.

Nonspecific V code categories/codes:

V11	Personal history of mental disorder

	A code from the mental disorders chapter, with an in remission fifth-digit, should be used.
V13.4	Personal history of arthritis
V13.6	Personal history of congenital malformations
V15.7	Personal history of contraception
V23.2	Pregnancy with history of abortion
V40	Mental and behavioral problems

Exception:

V40.31 Wandering in diseases classified elsewhere

V41	Problems with special senses and other special functions
V47	Other problems with internal organs
V48	Problems with head, neck, and trunk
V49	Problems with limbs and other problems

Exceptions:

V49.6	Upper limb amputation status
V49.7	Lower limb amputation status
V49.81	Asymptomatic postmenopausal status (age-related) (natural)
V49.82	Dental sealant status
V49.83	Awaiting organ transplant status
V49.86	Do not resuscitate status
V49.87	Physical restraints status

V51.8	Other aftercare involving the use of plastic surgery
V58.2	Blood transfusion, without reported diagnosis
V58.9	Unspecified aftercare

See Section IV.K. and Section IV.L. of the Outpatient guidelines.

e. V Codes That May Only be Principal/First-Listed Diagnosis

The list of V codes/categories below may only be reported as the principal/first-listed diagnosis, except when there are multiple encounters on the same day and the medical records for the encounters are combined or when there is more than one V code that meets the definition of principal diagnosis (e.g., a patient is admitted to home healthcare for both aftercare and rehabilitation and they equally meet the definition of principal diagnosis). These codes should not be reported if they do not meet the definition of principal or first-listed diagnosis.

See Section II and Section IV.A for information on selection of principal and first-listed diagnosis.

See Section II.C for information on two or more diagnoses that equally meet the definition for principal diagnosis.

V20.X	Health supervision of infant or child
V22.0	Supervision of normal first pregnancy
V22.1	Supervision of other normal pregnancy
V24.X	Postpartum care and examination
V26.81	Encounter for assisted reproductive fertility procedure cycle
V26.82	Encounter for fertility preservation procedure
V30.X	Single liveborn
V31.X	Twin, mate liveborn
V32.X	Twin, mate stillborn
V33.X	Twin, unspecified
V34.X	Other multiple, mates all liveborn
V35.X	Other multiple, mates all stillborn
V36.X	Other multiple, mates live- and stillborn
V37.X	Other multiple, unspecified
V39.X	Unspecified
V46.12	Encounter for respirator dependence during power failure
V46.13	Encounter for weaning from respirator [ventilator]
V51.0	Encounter for breast reconstruction following mastectomy
V56.0	Extracorporeal dialysis
V57.X	Care involving use of rehabilitation procedures
V58.0	Radiotherapy
V58.11	Encounter for antineoplastic chemotherapy
V58.12	Encounter for antineoplastic immunotherapy
V59.X	Donors
V66.0	Convalescence and palliative care following surgery
V66.1	Convalescence and palliative care following radiotherapy
V66.2	Convalescence and palliative care following chemotherapy
V66.3	Convalescence and palliative care following psychotherapy and other treatment for mental disorder
V66.4	Convalescence and palliative care following treatment of fracture
V66.5	Convalescence and palliative care following other treatment
V66.6	Convalescence and palliative care following combined treatment
V66.9	Unspecified convalescence
V68.X	Encounters for administrative purposes
V70.0	Routine general medical examination at a health care facility
V70.1	General psychiatric examination, requested by the authority
V70.2	General psychiatric examination, other and unspecified
V70.3	Other medical examination for administrative purposes
V70.4	Examination for medicolegal reasons
V70.5	Health examination of defined subpopulations

V70.6	Health examination in population surveys
V70.8	Other specified general medical examinations
V70.9	Unspecified general medical examination
V71.X	Observation and evaluation for suspected conditions not found

19. Supplemental Classification of External Causes of Injury and Poisoning (E-codes, E800-E999)

Introduction: These guidelines are provided for those who are currently collecting E codes in order that there will be standardization in the process. If your institution plans to begin collecting E codes, these guidelines are to be applied. The use of E codes is supplemental to the application of ICD-9-CM diagnosis codes.

External causes of injury and poisoning codes (categories E000 and E800-E999) are intended to provide data for injury research and evaluation of injury prevention strategies. Activity codes (categories E001-E030) are intended to be used to describe the activity of a person seeking care for injuries as well as other health conditions, when the injury or other health condition resulted from an activity or the activity contributed to a condition. E codes capture how the injury, poisoning, or adverse effect happened (cause), the intent (unintentional or accidental; or intentional, such as suicide or assault), the person's status (e.g. civilian, military), the associated activity and the place where the event occurred.

Some major categories of E codes include:
  transport accidents
  poisoning and adverse effects of drugs, medicinal substances and biologicals
  accidental falls
  accidents caused by fire and flames
  accidents due to natural and environmental factors
  late effects of accidents, assaults or self injury
  assaults or purposely inflicted injury
  suicide or self inflicted injury

These guidelines apply for the coding and collection of E codes from records in hospitals, outpatient clinics, emergency departments, other ambulatory care settings and provider offices, and nonacute care settings, except when other specific guidelines apply.

a. General E Code Coding Guidelines

1) Used with any code in the range of 001-V91

An E code from categories E800-E999 may be used with any code in the range of 001-V91, which indicates an injury, poisoning, or adverse effect due to an external cause.

An activity E code (categories E001-E030) may be used with any code in the range of 001-V91 that indicates an injury, or other health condition that resulted from an activity, or the activity contributed to a condition.

2) **Assign the appropriate E code for all initial treatments**

Assign the appropriate E code for the initial encounter of an injury, poisoning, or adverse effect of drugs, not for subsequent treatment.

External cause of injury codes (E-codes) may be assigned while the acute fracture codes are still applicable. *See Section I.C.17.b.1 for coding of acute fractures.*

3) **Use the full range of E codes**

Use the full range of E codes (E800 – E999) to completely describe the cause, the intent and the place of occurrence, if applicable, for all injuries, poisonings, and adverse effects of drugs.

See a.1.), j.), and k.) in this section for information on the use of status and activity E codes.

4) **Assign as many E codes as necessary**

Assign as many E codes as necessary to fully explain each cause.

5) **The selection of the appropriate E code**

The selection of the appropriate E code is guided by the Index to External Causes, which is located after the alphabetical index to diseases and by Inclusion and Exclusion notes in the Tabular List.

6) **E code can never be a principal diagnosis**

An E code can never be a principal (first listed) diagnosis.

7)   External cause code(s) with systemic inflammatory response syndrome (SIRS)

An external cause code is not appropriate with a code from subcategory 995.9, unless the patient also has another condition for which an E code would be appropriate (such as an injury, poisoning, or adverse effect of drugs.

8)   Multiple Cause E Code Coding Guidelines

More than one E-code is required to fully describe the external cause of an illness, injury or poisoning. The assignment of E-codes should be sequenced in the following priority:

If two or more events cause separate injuries, an E code should be assigned for each cause. The first listed E code will be selected in the following order:

E codes for child and adult abuse take priority over all other E codes.
See Section I.C.19.e., Child and Adult abuse guidelines.

E codes for terrorism events take priority over all other E codes except child and adult abuse.

E codes for cataclysmic events take priority over all other E codes except child and adult abuse and terrorism.

E codes for transport accidents take priority over all other E codes except cataclysmic events, child and adult abuse and terrorism.

Activity and external cause status codes are assigned following all causal (intent) E codes.

The first-listed E code should correspond to the cause of the most serious diagnosis due to an assault, accident, or self-harm, following the order of hierarchy listed above.

9)   If the reporting format limits the number of E codes

If the reporting format limits the number of E codes that can be used in reporting clinical data, report the code for the cause/intent most related to the principal diagnosis. If the format permits capture of additional E codes, the cause/intent, including medical misadventures, of the additional events should be reported rather than the codes for place, activity or external status.

b. Place of Occurrence Guideline

Use an additional code from category E849 to indicate the Place of Occurrence. The Place of Occurrence describes the place where the event occurred and not the patient's activity at the time of the event.

Do not use E849.9 if the place of occurrence is not stated.

c. Adverse Effects of Drugs, Medicinal and Biological Substances Guidelines

1) Do not code directly from the Table of Drugs

Do not code directly from the Table of Drugs and Chemicals. Always refer back to the Tabular List.

2) Use as many codes as necessary to describe

Use as many codes as necessary to describe completely all drugs, medicinal or biological substances.

If the reporting format limits the number of E codes, and there are different fourth digit codes in the same three digit category, use the code for "Other specified" of that category of drugs, medicinal or biological substances. If there is no "Other specified" code in that category, use the appropriate "Unspecified" code in that category.

If the reporting format limits the number of E codes, and the codes are in different three digit categories, assign the appropriate E code for other multiple drugs and medicinal substances.

3) If the same E code would describe the causative agent

If the same E code would describe the causative agent for more than one adverse reaction, assign the code only once.

4) If two or more drugs, medicinal or biological substances

If two or more drugs, medicinal or biological substances are reported, code each individually unless the combination code is listed in the Table of Drugs and Chemicals. In that case, assign the E code for the combination.

5)   When a reaction results from the interaction of a drug(s)

When a reaction results from the interaction of a drug(s) and alcohol, use poisoning codes and E codes for both.

6)   Codes from the E930-E949 series

Codes from the E930-E949 series must be used to identify the causative substance for an adverse effect of drug, medicinal and biological substances, correctly prescribed and properly administered. The effect, such as tachycardia, delirium, gastrointestinal hemorrhaging, vomiting, hypokalemia, hepatitis, renal failure, or respiratory failure, is coded and followed by the appropriate code from the E930-E949 series.

d. Child and Adult Abuse Guideline

1)   Intentional injury

When the cause of an injury or neglect is intentional child or adult abuse, the first listed E code should be assigned from categories E960-E968, Homicide and injury purposely inflicted by other persons, (except category E967). An E code from category E967, Child and adult battering and other maltreatment, should be added as an additional code to identify the perpetrator, if known.

2)   Accidental intent

In cases of neglect when the intent is determined to be accidental E code E904.0, Abandonment or neglect of infant and helpless person, should be the first listed E code.

e. Unknown or Suspected Intent Guideline

1)   If the intent (accident, self-harm, assault) of the cause of an injury or poisoning is unknown

If the intent (accident, self-harm, assault) of the cause of an injury or poisoning is unknown or unspecified, code the intent as undetermined E980-E989.

2)   If the intent (accident, self-harm, assault) of the cause of an injury or poisoning is questionable

If the intent (accident, self-harm, assault) of the cause of an injury or poisoning is questionable, probable or suspected, code the intent as undetermined E980-E989.

f. Undetermined Cause

When the intent of an injury or poisoning is known, but the cause is unknown, use codes: E928.9, Unspecified accident, E958.9, Suicide and self-inflicted injury by unspecified means, and E968.9, Assault by unspecified means.

These E codes should rarely be used, as the documentation in the medical record, in both the inpatient outpatient and other settings, should normally provide sufficient detail to determine the cause of the injury.

g. Late Effects of External Cause Guidelines

1) Late effect E codes

Late effect E codes exist for injuries and poisonings but not for adverse effects of drugs, misadventures and surgical complications.

2) Late effect E codes (E929, E959, E969, E977, E989, or E999.1)

A late effect E code (E929, E959, E969, E977, E989, or E999.1) should be used with any report of a late effect or sequela resulting from a previous injury or poisoning (905-909).

3) Late effect E code with a related current injury

A late effect E code should never be used with a related current nature of injury code.

4) Use of late effect E codes for subsequent visits

Use a late effect E code for subsequent visits when a late effect of the initial injury or poisoning is being treated. There is no late effect E code for adverse effects of drugs.
Do not use a late effect E code for subsequent visits for follow-up care (e.g., to assess healing, to receive rehabilitative therapy) of the injury or poisoning when no late effect of the injury has been documented.

h. Misadventures and Complications of Care Guidelines

1) Code range E870-E876

Assign a code in the range of E870-E876 if misadventures are stated by the provider. When applying the E code guidelines pertaining to sequencing, these E codes are considered causal codes.

2) Code range E878-E879

Assign a code in the range of E878-E879 if the provider attributes an abnormal reaction or later complication to a surgical or medical procedure, but does not mention misadventure at the time of the procedure as the cause of the reaction.

i. Terrorism Guidelines

1) Cause of injury identified by the Federal Government (FBI) as terrorism

When the cause of an injury is identified by the Federal Government (FBI) as terrorism, the first-listed E-code should be a code from category E979, Terrorism. The definition of terrorism employed by the FBI is found at the inclusion note at E979. The terrorism E-code is the only E-code that should be assigned. Additional E codes from the assault categories should not be assigned.

2) Cause of an injury is suspected to be the result of terrorism

When the cause of an injury is suspected to be the result of terrorism a code from category E979 should not be assigned. Assign a code in the range of E codes based circumstances on the documentation of intent and mechanism.

3) Code E979.9, Terrorism, secondary effects

Assign code E979.9, Terrorism, secondary effects, for conditions occurring subsequent to the terrorist event. This code should not be assigned for conditions that are due to the initial terrorist act.

4) Statistical tabulation of terrorism codes

For statistical purposes these codes will be tabulated within the category for assault, expanding the current category from E960-E969 to include E979 and E999.1.

j. Activity Code Guidelines

Assign a code from category E001-E030 to describe the activity that caused or contributed to the injury or other health condition.

Unlike other E codes, activity E codes may be assigned to indicate a health condition (not just injuries) resulted from an activity, or the activity contributed to the condition.

The activity codes are not applicable to poisonings, adverse effects, misadventures or late effects.

Do not assign E030, Unspecified activity, if the activity is not stated.

k. External cause status

A code from category E000, External cause status, should be assigned whenever any other E code is assigned for an encounter, including an Activity E code, except for the events noted below. Assign a code from category E000, External cause status, to indicate the work status of the person at the time the event occurred. The status code indicates whether the event occurred during military activity, whether a non-military person was at work, whether an individual including a student or volunteer was involved in a non-work activity at the time of the causal event.

A code from E000, External cause status, should be assigned, when applicable, with other external cause codes, such as transport accidents and falls. The external cause status codes are not applicable to poisonings, adverse effects, misadventures or late effects.
Do not assign a code from category E000 if no other E codes (cause, activity) are applicable for the encounter.

Do not assign code E000.9, Unspecified external cause status, if the status is not stated.

Section II. Selection of Principal Diagnosis

The circumstances of inpatient admission always govern the selection of principal diagnosis. The principal diagnosis is defined in the Uniform Hospital Discharge Data Set (UHDDS) as "that condition established after study to be chiefly responsible for occasioning the admission of the patient to the hospital for care."

The UHDDS definitions are used by hospitals to report inpatient data elements in a standardized manner. These data elements and their definitions can be found in the July 31, 1985, Federal Register (Vol. 50, No, 147), pp. 31038-40.

Since that time the application of the UHDDS definitions has been expanded to include all non-outpatient settings (acute care, short term, long term care and psychiatric hospitals; home health agencies; rehab facilities; nursing homes, etc).

In determining principal diagnosis the coding conventions in the ICD-9-CM, Volumes I and II take precedence over these official coding guidelines.
(See Section I.A., Conventions for the ICD-9-CM)

The importance of consistent, complete documentation in the medical record cannot be overemphasized. Without such documentation the application of all coding guidelines is a difficult, if not impossible, task.

A. Codes for symptoms, signs, and ill-defined conditions

Codes for symptoms, signs, and ill-defined conditions from Chapter 16 are not to be used as principal diagnosis when a related definitive diagnosis has been established.

B. Two or more interrelated conditions, each potentially meeting the definition for principal diagnosis

When there are two or more interrelated conditions (such as diseases in the same ICD-9-CM chapter or manifestations characteristically associated with a certain disease) potentially meeting the definition of principal diagnosis, either condition may be sequenced first, unless the circumstances of the admission, the therapy provided, the Tabular List, or the Alphabetic Index indicate otherwise.

C. Two or more diagnoses that equally meet the definition for principal diagnosis

In the unusual instance when two or more diagnoses equally meet the criteria for principal diagnosis as determined by the circumstances of admission, diagnostic workup and/or therapy provided, and the Alphabetic Index, Tabular List, or another coding guidelines does not provide sequencing direction, any one of the diagnoses may be sequenced first.

D. Two or more comparative or contrasting conditions.

In those rare instances when two or more contrasting or comparative diagnoses are documented as "either/or" (or similar terminology), they are coded as if the diagnoses were confirmed and the diagnoses are sequenced according to the circumstances of the admission. If no further determination can be made as to which diagnosis should be principal, either diagnosis may be sequenced first.

E. A symptom(s) followed by contrasting/comparative diagnoses

When a symptom(s) is followed by contrasting/comparative diagnoses, the symptom code is sequenced first. All the contrasting/comparative diagnoses should be coded as additional diagnoses.

F. Original treatment plan not carried out

Sequence as the principal diagnosis the condition, which after study occasioned the admission to the hospital, even though treatment may not have been carried out due to unforeseen circumstances.

G. Complications of surgery and other medical care

When the admission is for treatment of a complication resulting from surgery or other medical care, the complication code is sequenced as the principal diagnosis. If the complication is classified to the 996-999 series and the code lacks the necessary specificity in describing the complication, an additional code for the specific complication should be assigned.

H. Uncertain Diagnosis

If the diagnosis documented at the time of discharge is qualified as "probable", "suspected", "likely", "questionable", "possible", or "still to be ruled out", or other similar terms indicating uncertainty, code the condition as if it existed or was established. The bases for these guidelines are the diagnostic workup, arrangements for further workup or observation, and initial therapeutic approach that correspond most closely with the established diagnosis.

Note: This guideline is applicable only to inpatient admissions to short-term, acute, long-term care and psychiatric hospitals.

I. Admission from Observation Unit

1. Admission Following Medical Observation

When a patient is admitted to an observation unit for a medical condition, which either worsens or does not improve, and is subsequently admitted as an inpatient of the same hospital for this same medical condition, the principal diagnosis would be the medical condition which led to the hospital admission.

2. Admission Following Post-Operative Observation

When a patient is admitted to an observation unit to monitor a condition (or complication) that develops following outpatient surgery, and then is subsequently admitted as an inpatient of the same hospital, hospitals should apply the Uniform Hospital Discharge Data Set (UHDDS) definition of principal diagnosis as "that condition established after study to be chiefly responsible for occasioning the admission of the patient to the hospital for care."

J. Admission from Outpatient Surgery

When a patient receives surgery in the hospital's outpatient surgery department and is subsequently admitted for continuing inpatient care at the same hospital, the following guidelines should be followed in selecting the principal diagnosis for the inpatient admission:

- If the reason for the inpatient admission is a complication, assign the complication as the principal diagnosis.
- If no complication, or other condition, is documented as the reason for the inpatient admission, assign the reason for the outpatient surgery as the principal diagnosis.
- If the reason for the inpatient admission is another condition unrelated to the surgery, assign the unrelated condition as the principal diagnosis.

Section III. Reporting Additional Diagnoses

GENERAL RULES FOR OTHER (ADDITIONAL) DIAGNOSES

For reporting purposes the definition for "other diagnoses" is interpreted as additional conditions that affect patient care in terms of requiring:

> clinical evaluation; or
> therapeutic treatment; or
> diagnostic procedures; or
> extended length of hospital stay; or
> increased nursing care and/or monitoring.

The UHDDS item #11-b defines Other Diagnoses as "all conditions that coexist at the time of admission, that develop subsequently, or that affect the treatment received and/or the length of stay. Diagnoses that relate to an earlier episode which have no bearing on the current hospital stay are to be excluded." UHDDS definitions apply to inpatients in acute care, short-term, long term care and psychiatric hospital setting. The UHDDS definitions are used by acute care short-term hospitals to report inpatient data elements in a standardized manner. These data elements and their definitions can be found in the July 31, 1985, Federal Register (Vol. 50, No, 147), pp. 31038-40.

Since that time the application of the UHDDS definitions has been expanded to include all non-outpatient settings (acute care, short term, long term care and psychiatric hospitals; home health agencies; rehab facilities; nursing homes, etc).

The following guidelines are to be applied in designating "other diagnoses" when neither the Alphabetic Index nor the Tabular List in ICD-9-CM provide direction. The listing of the diagnoses in the patient record is the responsibility of the attending provider.

A. Previous conditions

If the provider has included a diagnosis in the final diagnostic statement, such as the discharge summary or the face sheet, it should ordinarily be coded. Some providers include in the diagnostic statement resolved conditions or diagnoses and status-post procedures from previous admission that have no bearing on the current stay. Such conditions are not to be reported and are coded only if required by hospital policy.

However, history codes (V10-V19) may be used as secondary codes if the historical condition or family history has an impact on current care or influences treatment.

B. Abnormal findings

Abnormal findings (laboratory, x-ray, pathologic, and other diagnostic results) are not coded and reported unless the provider indicates their clinical significance. If the findings are outside the normal range and the attending provider has ordered other tests to evaluate the condition or prescribed treatment, it is appropriate to ask the provider whether the abnormal finding should be added.

Please note: This differs from the coding practices in the outpatient setting for coding encounters for diagnostic tests that have been interpreted by a provider.

C. Uncertain Diagnosis

If the diagnosis documented at the time of discharge is qualified as "probable", "suspected", "likely", "questionable", "possible", or "still to be ruled out" or other similar terms indicating uncertainty, code the condition as if it existed or was established. The bases for these guidelines are the diagnostic workup, arrangements for further workup or observation, and initial therapeutic approach that correspond most closely with the established diagnosis.

Note: This guideline is applicable only to inpatient admissions to short-term, acute, long-term care and psychiatric hospitals.

Section IV. Diagnostic Coding and Reporting Guidelines for Outpatient Services

These coding guidelines for outpatient diagnoses have been approved for use by hospitals/providers in coding and reporting hospital-based outpatient services and provider-based office visits.

Information about the use of certain abbreviations, punctuation, symbols, and other conventions used in the ICD-9-CM Tabular List (code numbers and titles), can be found in Section IA of these guidelines, under "Conventions Used in the Tabular List." Information about the correct sequence to use in finding a code is also described in Section I.

The terms encounter and visit are often used interchangeably in describing outpatient service contacts and, therefore, appear together in these guidelines without distinguishing one from the other.

Though the conventions and general guidelines apply to all settings, coding guidelines for outpatient and provider reporting of diagnoses will vary in a number of instances from those for inpatient diagnoses, recognizing that:

The Uniform Hospital Discharge Data Set (UHDDS) definition of principal diagnosis applies only to inpatients in acute, short-term, long-term care and psychiatric hospitals.

Coding guidelines for inconclusive diagnoses (probable, suspected, rule out, etc.) were developed for inpatient reporting and do not apply to outpatients.

A. Selection of first-listed condition

In the outpatient setting, the term first-listed diagnosis is used in lieu of principal diagnosis.

In determining the first-listed diagnosis the coding conventions of ICD-9-CM, as well as the general and disease specific guidelines take precedence over the outpatient guidelines.

Diagnoses often are not established at the time of the initial encounter/visit. It may take two or more visits before the diagnosis is confirmed.

The most critical rule involves beginning the search for the correct code assignment through the Alphabetic Index. Never begin searching initially in the Tabular List as this will lead to coding errors.

1. Outpatient Surgery

When a patient presents for outpatient surgery, code the reason for the surgery as the first-listed diagnosis (reason for the encounter), even if the surgery is not performed due to a contraindication.

2. Observation Stay

When a patient is admitted for observation for a medical condition, assign a code for the medical condition as the first-listed diagnosis.

When a patient presents for outpatient surgery and develops complications requiring admission to observation, code the reason for the surgery as the first reported diagnosis (reason for the encounter), followed by codes for the complications as secondary diagnoses.

B. Codes from 001.0 through V91.99

The appropriate code or codes from 001.0 through V91.99 must be used to identify diagnoses, symptoms, conditions, problems, complaints, or other reason(s) for the encounter/visit.

C. Accurate reporting of ICD-9-CM diagnosis codes

For accurate reporting of ICD-9-CM diagnosis codes, the documentation should describe the patient's condition, using terminology which includes specific diagnoses as well as symptoms, problems, or reasons for the encounter. There are ICD-9-CM codes to describe all of these.

D. Selection of codes 001.0 through 999.9

The selection of codes 001.0 through 999.9 will frequently be used to describe the reason for the encounter. These codes are from the section of ICD-9-CM for the classification of diseases and injuries (e.g. infectious and parasitic diseases; neoplasms; symptoms, signs, and ill-defined conditions, etc.).

E. Codes that describe symptoms and signs

Codes that describe symptoms and signs, as opposed to diagnoses, are acceptable for reporting purposes when a diagnosis has not been established (confirmed) by the provider. Chapter 16 of ICD-9-CM, Symptoms, Signs, and Ill-defined conditions (codes 780.0 - 799.9) contain many, but not all codes for symptoms.

F. Encounters for circumstances other than a disease or injury

ICD-9-CM provides codes to deal with encounters for circumstances other than a disease or injury. The Supplementary Classification of factors Influencing Health Status and Contact with Health Services (V01.0- V91.99) is provided to deal with occasions when circumstances other than a disease or injury are recorded as diagnosis or problems. *See Section I.C. 18 for information on V-codes.*

G. Level of Detail in Coding

1. ICD-9-CM codes with 3, 4, or 5 digits

ICD-9-CM is composed of codes with either 3, 4, or 5 digits. Codes with three digits are included in ICD-9-CM as the heading of a category of codes that may be further subdivided by the use of fourth and/or fifth digits, which provide greater specificity.

2. Use of full number of digits required for a code

A three-digit code is to be used only if it is not further subdivided. Where fourth-digit subcategories and/or fifth-digit subclassifications are provided, they must be assigned. A code is invalid if it has not been coded to the full number of digits required for that code.
See also discussion under Section I.b.3., General Coding Guidelines, Level of Detail in Coding.

H. ICD-9-CM code for the diagnosis, condition, problem, or other reason for encounter/visit

List first the ICD-9-CM code for the diagnosis, condition, problem, or other reason for encounter/visit shown in the medical record to be chiefly responsible for the services provided. List additional codes that describe any coexisting conditions. In some cases the first-listed diagnosis may be a symptom when a diagnosis has not been established (confirmed) by the physician.

I. Uncertain diagnosis

Do not code diagnoses documented as "probable", "suspected," "questionable," "rule out," or "working diagnosis" or other similar terms indicating uncertainty. Rather, code the condition(s) to the highest degree of certainty for that encounter/visit, such as symptoms, signs, abnormal test results, or other reason for the visit.

Please note: This differs from the coding practices used by short-term, acute care, long-term care and psychiatric hospitals.

J. Chronic diseases

Chronic diseases treated on an ongoing basis may be coded and reported as many times as the patient receives treatment and care for the condition(s)

K. Code all documented conditions that coexist

Code all documented conditions that coexist at the time of the encounter/visit, and require or affect patient care treatment or management. Do not code conditions that were previously treated and no longer exist. However, history codes (V10-V19) may be used as secondary codes if the historical condition or family history has an impact on current care or influences treatment.

L. Patients receiving diagnostic services only

For patients receiving diagnostic services only during an encounter/visit, sequence first the diagnosis, condition, problem, or other reason for encounter/visit shown in the medical record to be chiefly responsible for the outpatient services provided during the encounter/visit. Codes for other diagnoses (e.g., chronic conditions) may be sequenced as additional diagnoses.

For encounters for routine laboratory/radiology testing in the absence of any signs, symptoms, or associated diagnosis, assign V72.5 and/or a code from subcategory V72.6. If routine testing is performed during the same encounter as a test to evaluate a sign, symptom, or diagnosis, it is appropriate to assign both the V code and the code describing the reason for the non-routine test.

For outpatient encounters for diagnostic tests that have been interpreted by a physician, and the final report is available at the time of coding, code any confirmed or definitive diagnosis(es) documented in the interpretation. Do not code related signs and symptoms as additional diagnoses.

Please note: This differs from the coding practice in the hospital inpatient setting regarding abnormal findings on test results.

M. Patients receiving therapeutic services only

For patients receiving therapeutic services only during an encounter/visit, sequence first the diagnosis, condition, problem, or other reason for encounter/visit shown in the medical record to be chiefly responsible for the outpatient services provided during the encounter/visit. Codes for other diagnoses (e.g., chronic conditions) may be sequenced as additional diagnoses.

The only exception to this rule is that when the primary reason for the admission/encounter is chemotherapy, radiation therapy, or rehabilitation, the appropriate V code for the service is listed first, and the diagnosis or problem for which the service is being performed listed second.

N. Patients receiving preoperative evaluations only

For patients receiving preoperative evaluations only, sequence first a code from category V72.8, Other specified examinations, to describe the pre-op consultations. Assign a code for the condition to describe the reason for the surgery as an additional diagnosis. Code also any findings related to the pre-op evaluation.

O. Ambulatory surgery

For ambulatory surgery, code the diagnosis for which the surgery was performed. If the postoperative diagnosis is known to be different from the preoperative diagnosis at the time the diagnosis is confirmed, select the postoperative diagnosis for coding, since it is the most definitive.

P. Routine outpatient prenatal visits

For routine outpatient prenatal visits when no complications are present, codes V22.0, Supervision of normal first pregnancy, or V22.1, Supervision of other normal pregnancy, should be used as the principal diagnosis. These codes should not be used in conjunction with chapter 11 codes.

Appendix I
Present on Admission Reporting Guidelines

Introduction

These guidelines are to be used as a supplement to the *ICD-9-CM Official Guidelines for Coding and Reporting* to facilitate the assignment of the Present on Admission (POA) indicator for each diagnosis and external cause of injury code reported on claim forms (UB-04 and 837 Institutional).

These guidelines are not intended to replace any guidelines in the main body of the *ICD-9-CM Official Guidelines for Coding and Reporting*. The POA guidelines are not intended to provide guidance on when a condition should be coded, but rather, how to apply the POA indicator to the final set of diagnosis codes that have been assigned in accordance with Sections I, II, and III of the official coding guidelines. Subsequent to the assignment of the ICD-9-CM codes, the POA indicator should then be assigned to those conditions that have been coded.

As stated in the Introduction to the ICD-9-CM Official Guidelines for Coding and Reporting, a joint effort between the healthcare provider and the coder is essential to achieve complete and accurate documentation, code assignment, and reporting of diagnoses and procedures. The importance of consistent, complete documentation in the medical record cannot be overemphasized. Medical record documentation from any provider involved in the care and treatment of the patient may be used to support the determination of whether a condition was present on admission or not. In the context of the official coding guidelines, the term "provider" means a physician or any qualified healthcare practitioner who is legally accountable for establishing the patient's diagnosis.

These guidelines are not a substitute for the provider's clinical judgment as to the determination of whether a condition was/was not present on admission. The provider should be queried regarding issues related to the linking of signs/symptoms, timing of test results, and the timing of findings.

General Reporting Requirements

All claims involving inpatient admissions to general acute care hospitals or other facilities that are subject to a law or regulation mandating collection of present on admission information.

Present on admission is defined as present at the time the order for inpatient admission occurs -- conditions that develop during an outpatient encounter, including emergency department, observation, or outpatient surgery, are considered as present on admission.

POA indicator is assigned to principal and secondary diagnoses (as defined in Section II of the Official Guidelines for Coding and Reporting) and the external cause of injury codes.

Issues related to inconsistent, missing, conflicting or unclear documentation must still be resolved by the provider.

If a condition would not be coded and reported based on UHDDS definitions and current official coding guidelines, then the POA indicator would not be reported.

Reporting Options
> Y - Yes
> N - No
> U - Unknown
> W – Clinically undetermined
> Unreported/Not used (or "1" for Medicare usage) – (Exempt from POA reporting)

Reporting Definitions
> Y = present at the time of inpatient admission
> N = not present at the time of inpatient admission
> U = documentation is insufficient to determine if condition is present on admission
> W = provider is unable to clinically determine whether condition was present on admission or not

Timeframe for POA Identification and Documentation

There is no required timeframe as to when a provider (per the definition of "provider" used in these guidelines) must identify or document a condition to be present on admission. In some clinical situations, it may not be possible for a provider to make a definitive diagnosis (or a condition may not be recognized or reported by the patient) for a period of time after admission. In some cases it may be several days before the provider arrives at a definitive diagnosis. This does not mean that the condition was not present on admission. Determination of whether the condition was present on admission or not will be based on the applicable POA guideline as identified in this document, or on the provider's best clinical judgment.

If at the time of code assignment the documentation is unclear as to whether a condition was present on admission or not, it is appropriate to query the provider for clarification.

Assigning the POA Indicator

Condition is on the "Exempt from Reporting" list
> Leave the "present on admission" field blank if the condition is on the list of ICD-9-CM codes for which this field is not applicable. This is the only circumstance in which the field may be left blank.

POA Explicitly Documented
> Assign Y for any condition the provider explicitly documents as being present on admission.

Assign N for any condition the provider explicitly documents as not present at the time of admission.

Conditions diagnosed prior to inpatient admission

Assign "Y" for conditions that were diagnosed prior to admission (example: hypertension, diabetes mellitus, asthma)

Conditions diagnosed during the admission but clearly present before admission

Assign "Y" for conditions diagnosed during the admission that were clearly present but not diagnosed until after admission occurred.

Diagnoses subsequently confirmed after admission are considered present on admission if at the time of admission they are documented as suspected, possible, rule out, differential diagnosis, or constitute an underlying cause of a symptom that is present at the time of admission.

Condition develops during outpatient encounter prior to inpatient admission

Assign Y for any condition that develops during an outpatient encounter prior to a written order for inpatient admission.

Documentation does not indicate whether condition was present on admission

Assign "U" when the medical record documentation is unclear as to whether the condition was present on admission. "U" should not be routinely assigned and used only in very limited circumstances. Coders are encouraged to query the providers when the documentation is unclear.

Documentation states that it cannot be determined whether the condition was or was not present on admission

Assign "W" when the medical record documentation indicates that it cannot be clinically determined whether or not the condition was present on admission.

Chronic condition with acute exacerbation during the admission

If the code is a combination code that identifies both the chronic condition and the acute exacerbation, see POA guidelines pertaining to combination codes.

If the combination code only identifies the chronic condition and not the acute exacerbation (e.g., acute exacerbation of chronic leukemia), assign "Y."

Conditions documented as possible, probable, suspected, or rule out at the time of discharge

If the final diagnosis contains a possible, probable, suspected, or rule out diagnosis, and this diagnosis was based on signs, symptoms or clinical findings suspected at the time of inpatient admission, assign "Y."

If the final diagnosis contains a possible, probable, suspected, or rule out diagnosis, and this diagnosis was based on signs, symptoms or clinical findings that were not present on admission, assign "N".

Conditions documented as impending or threatened at the time of discharge

If the final diagnosis contains an impending or threatened diagnosis, and this diagnosis is based on symptoms or clinical findings that were present on admission, assign "Y".

If the final diagnosis contains an impending or threatened diagnosis, and this diagnosis is based on symptoms or clinical findings that were not present on admission, assign "N".

Acute and Chronic Conditions

Assign "Y" for acute conditions that are present at time of admission and N for acute conditions that are not present at time of admission.

Assign "Y" for chronic conditions, even though the condition may not be diagnosed until after admission.

If a single code identifies both an acute and chronic condition, see the POA guidelines for combination codes.

Combination Codes

Assign "N" if any part of the combination code was not present on admission (e.g., obstructive chronic bronchitis with acute exacerbation and the exacerbation was not present on admission; gastric ulcer that does not start bleeding until after admission; asthma patient develops status asthmaticus after admission)

Assign "Y" if all parts of the combination code were present on admission (e.g., patient with diabetic nephropathy is admitted with uncontrolled diabetes)

If the final diagnosis includes comparative or contrasting diagnoses, and both were present, or suspected, at the time of admission, assign "Y".

For infection codes that include the causal organism, assign "Y" if the infection (or signs of the infection) was present on admission, even though the culture results may not be known until after admission (e.g., patient is admitted with pneumonia and the provider documents pseudomonas as the causal organism a few days later).

Same Diagnosis Code for Two or More Conditions

When the same ICD-9-CM diagnosis code applies to two or more conditions during the same encounter (e.g. bilateral condition, or two separate conditions classified to the same ICD-9-CM diagnosis code):

Assign "Y" if all conditions represented by the single ICD-9-CM code were present on admission (e.g. bilateral fracture of the same bone, same site, and both fractures were present on admission)
Assign "N" if any of the conditions represented by the single ICD-9-CM code was not present on admission (e.g. dehydration with hyponatremia is assigned to code 276.1, but only one of these conditions was present on admission).

Obstetrical conditions

Whether or not the patient delivers during the current hospitalization does not affect assignment of the POA indicator. The determining factor for POA assignment is whether the pregnancy complication or obstetrical condition described by the code was present at the time of admission or not.

If the pregnancy complication or obstetrical condition was present on admission (e.g., patient admitted in preterm labor), assign "Y".

If the pregnancy complication or obstetrical condition was not present on admission (e.g., 2nd degree laceration during delivery, postpartum hemorrhage that occurred during current hospitalization, fetal distress develops after admission), assign "N".

If the obstetrical code includes more than one diagnosis and any of the diagnoses identified by the code were not present on admission assign "N".

> (e.g., Code 642.7, Pre-eclampsia or eclampsia superimposed on pre-existing hypertension).

If the obstetrical code includes information that is not a diagnosis, do not consider that information in the POA determination.

> (e.g. Code 652.1x, Breech or other malpresentation successfully converted to cephalic presentation should be reported as present on admission if the fetus was breech on admission but was converted to cephalic presentation after admission (since the conversion to cephalic presentation does not represent a diagnosis, the fact that the conversion occurred after admission has no bearing on the POA determination).

Perinatal conditions

Newborns are not considered to be admitted until after birth. Therefore, any condition present at birth or that developed in utero is considered present at admission and should be assigned "Y". This includes conditions that occur during delivery (e.g., injury during delivery, meconium aspiration, exposure to streptococcus B in the vaginal canal).

Congenital conditions and anomalies

Assign "Y" for congenital conditions and anomalies, **except for categories 740-759, Congenital anomalies, which are on the exempt list.** Congenital conditions are always considered present on admission.

External cause of injury codes

Assign "Y" for any E code representing an external cause of injury or poisoning that occurred prior to inpatient admission (e.g., patient fell out of bed at home, patient fell out of bed in emergency room prior to admission)

Assign "N" for any E code representing an external cause of injury or poisoning that occurred during inpatient hospitalization (e.g., patient fell out of hospital bed during hospital stay, patient experienced an adverse reaction to a medication administered after inpatient admission)